THE CAMBRIDGE HISTORY OF
THE GOTHIC

The third volume of *The Cambridge History of the Gothic* is the first book to provide an in-depth history of Gothic literature, film, television and culture in the twentieth and twenty-first centuries (c.1896–present). Identifying key historical shifts from the birth of film to the threat of apocalypse, leading international scholars offer comprehensive coverage of the ideas, events, movements and contexts that shaped the Gothic as it entered a dynamic period of diversification across all forms of media. Twenty-three chapters plus an extended introduction provide in-depth accounts of topics including Modernism, war, postcolonialism, psychoanalysis, counterculture, feminism, AIDS, neo-liberalism, globalisation, multiculturalism, the war on terror and environmental crisis. Provocative and cutting edge, this will be an essential reference volume for anyone studying modern and contemporary Gothic culture.

CATHERINE SPOONER is Professor of Literature and Culture at Lancaster University. She has previously published six books; the most recent, *Post-Millennial Gothic: Comedy, Romance and the Rise of Happy Gothic* (2017), was awarded the Allan Lloyd Smith Memorial Prize. She was co-president of the International Gothic Association 2013–17.

DALE TOWNSHEND is Professor of Gothic Literature in the Manchester Centre for Gothic Studies, Manchester Metropolitan University. He has published widely on Gothic writing of the eighteenth and nineteenth centuries. His most recent monograph is *Gothic Antiquity: History, Romance, and the Architectural Imagination, 1760–1840* (2019).

THE CAMBRIDGE HISTORY OF
THE GOTHIC

How to write the history of a cultural mode that, for all its abiding fascination with the past, has challenged and complicated received notions of history from the very start? *The Cambridge History of the Gothic* rises to this challenge, charting the history of the Gothic even as it reflects continuously upon the mode's tendency to question, subvert and render incomplete all linear historical narratives. Taken together, the three chronologically sequenced volumes in the series provide a rigorous account of the origins, efflorescence and proliferation of the Gothic imagination, from its earliest manifestations in European history through to the present day. The chapters in Volume I span antiquity and the long eighteenth century (c.1680–1800), covering such topics as the Gothic Sack of Rome in AD 410, the construction and reception of the Gothic past in eighteenth-century Britain, the revival of Gothic architecture, art and literature in British and European culture and their imbrication during the revolutionary decades, 1770–1800. Elaborating upon several of the themes introduced in the first volume, the chapters in Volume II address the Gothic cultures of Britain, America and Europe during the nineteenth century (1800–1900), thus covering while moving well beyond those areas that have traditionally been demarcated as the 'Romantic' and the 'Victorian'. Engaging with the themes of the earlier volumes, the chapters in Volume III also explore some of the myriad forms that the Gothic has assumed in the twentieth and twenty-first centuries (c. 1896–present), beginning with an account of the appropriation of the mode in early cinema and concluding with the apocalyptic Gothic turns of much recent cultural production. Resolutely interdisciplinary in focus, *The Cambridge History of the Gothic* extends the critical focus well beyond literature and film to include discussions of Gothic historiography, politics, art, architecture and counterculture. All three volumes in the series are attentive to the ways in which history has been refracted through a Gothic lens, and are as keen to chart the inscription of Gothic in some of the formative events of Western history as they are to provide a history of the Gothic mode itself. Written by an international cast of contributors, the chapters bring fresh scholarly attention to bear upon established Gothic themes while also highlighting a number of new critical concerns. As such, they are of relevance to the general reader, the student and the established scholar alike.

THE CAMBRIDGE HISTORY OF THE GOTHIC

VOLUME 3
Gothic in the Twentieth and Twenty-First Centuries

Edited by

CATHERINE SPOONER
Lancaster University

DALE TOWNSHEND
Manchester Metropolitan University

Shaftesbury Road, Cambridge CB2 8EA, United Kingdom

One Liberty Plaza, 20th Floor, New York, NY 10006, USA

477 Williamstown Road, Port Melbourne, VIC 3207, Australia

314–321, 3rd Floor, Plot 3, Splendor Forum, Jasola District Centre, New Delhi – 110025, India

103 Penang Road, #05–06/07, Visioncrest Commercial, Singapore 238467

Cambridge University Press is part of Cambridge University Press & Assessment, a department of the University of Cambridge.

We share the University's mission to contribute to society through the pursuit of education, learning and research at the highest international levels of excellence.

www.cambridge.org
Information on this title: www.cambridge.org/9781108460194

DOI: 10.1017/9781108624268

© Cambridge University Press & Assessment 2021

This publication is in copyright. Subject to statutory exception and to the provisions of relevant collective licensing agreements, no reproduction of any part may take place without the written permission of Cambridge University Press & Assessment.

First published 2021
First paperback edition 2025

A catalogue record for this publication is available from the British Library

Library of Congress Cataloging-in-Publication data
NAMES: Wright, Angela, 1969 May 14– editor. | Townshend, Dale, editor. | Spooner, Catherine, 1974– editor.
TITLE: The Cambridge history of the Gothic / edited by Angela Wright, University of Sheffield ; Dale Townshend, Manchester Metropolitan University ; Catherine Spooner, Lancaster University.
DESCRIPTION: Cambridge, UK ; New York : Cambridge University Press, 2020–2021. | Includes bibliographical references and indexes. Contents: v. 1. Gothic in the long eighteenth century – v. 2. Gothic in the nineteenth century – v. 3. Gothic in the twentieth and twenty-first centuries.
IDENTIFIERS: LCCN 2019058625 (print) | LCCN 2019058624 (ebook) | ISBN 9781108662017 (threevolume set) | ISBN 9781108472708 (v. 1 ; hardback) | ISBN 9781108561044 (v. 1 ; ebook) | ISBN 9781108472715 (v. 2 ; hardback) | ISBN 9781108561082 (v. 2 ; ebook) | ISBN 9781108472722 (v. 3 ; hardback) | ISBN 9781108624268 (v. 3 ; ebook) | ISBN 9781108561082 (v. 2 ; qebook)) | ISBN 9781108662017 (three-volume set) | ISBN 9781108472708 (v. 1 ; hardback) | ISBN 9781108472715 v. 2 ; hardback) | ISBN 9781108561044 (v. 1 ; qebook)
SUBJECTS: LCSH: Gothic fiction (Literary genre) – History and criticism. | Gothic revival (Literature) – History and criticism. | Fantastic fiction – History and criticism. | Architecture, Gothic. | Art, Gothic.
CLASSIFICATION: LCC PN3435 .C285 2020 (ebook) | LCC PN3435 (print) | DDC 809.3/8729–dc23

ISBN	– 3 Volume Set	978-1-108-66201-7
ISBN	– Volume I	978-1-108-47270-8
ISBN	– Volume II	978-1-108-47271-5
ISBN	– Volume III	978-1-108-47272-2
ISBN	978-1-108-46019-4	Paperback

Cambridge University Press & Assessment has no responsibility for the persistence or accuracy of URLs for external or third-party internet websites referred to in this publication and does not guarantee that any content on such websites is, or will remain, accurate or appropriate.

Contents

List of Figures page x
Notes on Contributors xii
Acknowledgements xvi

Introduction: A History of Gothic Studies in the Twentieth and Twenty-first Centuries 1
CATHERINE SPOONER

3.1. Gothic and Silent Cinema 22
STACEY ABBOTT AND SIMON BROWN

3.2. Gothic, the Great War and the Rise of Modernism, 1910–1936 43
MATT FOLEY

3.3. Gothic and the American South, 1919–1962 61
ARTHUR REDDING

3.4. Hollywood Gothic, 1930–1960 80
MARK JANCOVICH

3.5. Gothic and War, 1930–1991 99
AGNIESZKA SOLTYSIK MONNET

3.6. Gothic and the Postcolonial Moment 118
TABISH KHAIR

3.7. Gothic and the Heritage Movement in the Twentieth and Twenty-First Centuries 137
EMMA MCEVOY

3.8. Gothic Enchantment: The Magical Strain in Twentieth and
     Twenty-First-Century Anglo-American Gothic *159*
     DAVID PUNTER

3.9. Psychoanalysis and the American Popular Gothic, 1954–1980 *180*
     BERNICE M. MURPHY

3.10. Gothic and the Counterculture, 1958–Present *199*
      CATHERINE SPOONER

3.11. Gothic Television *221*
      DEREK JOHNSTON

3.12. Gothic and the Rise of Feminism *242*
      LUCIE ARMITT

3.13. Gothic, AIDS and Sexuality, 1981–Present *262*
      ARDEL HAEFELE-THOMAS

3.14. The Gothic in the Age of Neo-Liberalism, 1990–Present *283*
      LINNIE BLAKE

3.15. The Gothic and Remix Culture *302*
      MEGEN DE BRUIN-MOLÉ

3.16. Postdigital Gothic *323*
      MARC OLIVIER

3.17. Gothic Multiculturalism *342*
      SARAH ILOTT

3.18. Gothic, Neo-Imperialism and the War on Terror *364*
      JOHAN HÖGLUND

3.19. Global Gothic 1: Islamic Gothic *383*
      TUĞÇE BIÇAKÇI SYED

3.20. Global Gothic 2: East Asian Gothic *403*
      DANIEL MARTIN

3.21. Global Gothic 3: Gothic in Modern Scandinavia 424
YVONNE LEFFLER

3.22. Gothic in an Age of Environmental Crisis 444
SARA L. CROSBY

3.23. Gothic and the Apocalyptic Imagination 465
SIMON MARSDEN

Select Bibliography and Filmography 483
Index 513

Figures

Fig.1.1:	Still from *Vampyr*, directed by Carl Theodor Dreyer. Screenplay written by Christen Jul and Carl Theodor Dreyer. Germany 1931/1932. (Photo by ullstein bild/ullstein bild via Getty Images). Ullstein bild Dtl.	page 23
Fig.1.2:	Actress Marguerite Gance as Madeleine Usher and actor Jean Debucourt as Sir Roderick Usher in the 1928 silent French film *La chute de la maison Usher*. (*The Fall of the House of Usher*). (John Springer Collection/CORBIS/Corbis via Getty Images).	41
Fig.4.1:	British actor Boris Karloff (1887–1969) as the Monster in a promotional portrait for *Frankenstein*, directed by James Whale, 1931. (Photo by Silver Screen Collection/Getty Images).	85
Fig.5.1:	Hungarian actor Bela Lugosi (R) on the set of *White Zombie*, directed by American Victor Halperin, 1932. (Photo by Sunset Boulevard/Corbis via Getty Images).	103
Fig.5.2:	Phoenix war worker Natalie Nickerson penning her Navy boyfriend a thank-you note for sending her a Japanese soldier's skull that he gathered as a souvenir while fighting in New Guinea. (Photo by Ralph Crane/The *Life* Images Collection via Getty Images/Getty Images).	108
Fig.7.1:	A picture of the novelist Daphne du Maurier in 1947 lingering below a portrait of her father, the actor Gerald du Maurier, on the staircase of 'Menabilly', the house that she wove into her stories and eventually into her life. (Photo by Popperfoto via Getty Images/Getty Images).	145
Fig.10.1:	A poster for the British release of Terence Fisher's 1958 horror film, *Dracula*, starring Christopher Lee and featuring Valerie Gaunt. The film was retitled *Horror of Dracula* for the US release. (Photo by Movie Poster Image Art/Getty Images).	204
Fig.10.2:	Mick Jagger pictured in the 1968 Donald Cammell and Nicholas Roeg film *Performance*. (Photo by Robert Whitaker/Getty Images).	217
Fig.13.1:	French actress Catherine Deneuve and British singer and actor David Bowie on the set of the 1983 film *The Hunger*, directed by Tony Scott. (Photo by Metro-Goldwyn-Mayer Pictures/Sunset Boulevard/Corbis via Getty Images).	269

List of Figures

Fig.15.1 a–d:	*Bogeymen of Brexit* Halloween masks (2017). Reproduced by kind permission of *The New European*.	321
Fig.17.1:	*Get Out*: GET OUT. Betty Gabriel, 2017. (Photo by Justin Lubin. ©Universal Pictures/courtesy Everett Collection. Justin Lubin/©Universal Pictures/Everett Collection/Bridgeman Images).	355
Fig.20.1:	Rentaro Mikuni is held by Michiyo Aratama in scene from the film *Kwaidan*, 1964. (Photo by Toho/Getty Images).	408
Fig.20.2:	*Onibaba*, poster, US poster art, Jitsuko Yoshimura, 1964. (Photo by LMPC via Getty Images).	410
Fig.22.1:	*Burnt Offerings*, poster, US poster, top from left: Oliver Reed, Karen Black, Burgess Meredith, Bette Davis, Eileen Heckart, 1976. (Photo by LMPC via Getty Images).	451
Fig.22.2:	Swedish climate activist Greta Thunberg protests with her placard reading 'School strike for climate' as part of her Fridays for Future protest in front of the Swedish Parliament Riksdagen in Stockholm on 9 October, 2020. (Photo by Jonathan NACKSTRAND/AFP) (Photo by Jonathan Nackstrand/AFP via Getty Images).	457

Notes on Contributors

STACEY ABBOTT is Reader in Film and Television Studies at the University of Roehampton. She has written extensively on Gothic and horror film and TV. She is the author of *Celluloid Vampires* (2007), *Undead Apocalypse* (2016) and the co-author, with Lorna Jowett, of *TV Horror* (2013). Her most recent publication is the BFI Classic on Kathryn Bigelow's *Near Dark* (2020).

LUCIE ARMITT is Professor of Contemporary English Literature at the University of Lincoln, UK. Her principal publications include: *Fantasy* (2020); *Twentieth-Century Gothic* (2011); *Fantasy Fiction* (2005); *Contemporary Women's Fiction and the Fantastic* (2000); *Theorising the Fantastic* (1996); and *Where No Man Has Gone Before: Women and Science Fiction* (1991).

TUĞÇE BIÇAKÇI SYED is Lecturer in the Department of English Language and Literature, Tekirdağ Namık Kemal University in Tekirdağ, Turkey. In 2018, she completed her PhD in English at Lancaster University, fully funded by the Turkish Ministry of Education. Her research focuses on Turkish Gothic and its history and development through ideological, cultural and political shifts. Her publications range from Gothic in Turkish literature and cinema to the Gothic representations of Turkish identity in Western texts.

LINNIE BLAKE is founding Head of the Manchester Centre for Gothic Studies at Manchester Metropolitan University and leader of the MA English: Gothic Studies pathway. She has written widely on Gothic and horror literature, film and television, with particular emphasis in recent years on what she has termed 'Neoliberal Gothic', that is, post-1970s British and American Gothic's interrogation of free market capitalism.

SIMON BROWN is Associate Professor of Film and Television at Kingston University. He has written extensively on horror films, silent cinema and the early film industry. His recent publications include *Cecil Hepworth and the Rise of the British Film Industry, 1899–1911* (2016) and *Screening Stephen King: Adaptation and the Horror Genre in Film and Television* (2018).

MEGEN DE BRUIN-MOLÉ is Lecturer in Digital Media Practice at the University of Southampton. She writes on contemporary adaptation, remix culture and identity politics. Her book *Gothic Remixed* (2020) explores the boundaries and connections between remix and its related modes through the lens of monster studies. Read more about her work at frankenfiction.com.

Notes on Contributors

SARA L. CROSBY is Associate Professor of English at the Ohio State University at Marion and the TV/Film Review editor for *Gothic Nature*. She has authored two books on poisonous women in early and antebellum American literature. Her current book project and recent articles investigate ecohorror, particularly its role in the destruction of her home, south Louisiana.

MATT FOLEY is Lecturer in Modern and Contemporary Literature at Manchester Metropolitan University. He is the author of *Haunting Modernisms* (2017) and co-editor, with Rebecca Duncan, of *Patrick McGrath and His Worlds* (2019). His main research interests are in modernism, the Gothic and literary acoustics.

ARDEL HAEFELE-THOMAS serves as the Chair of LGBT Studies at City College of San Francisco. They are the author of *Queer Others in Victorian Gothic: Transgressing Monstrosity* (2012) and *Introduction to Transgender Studies* (2019), as well as numerous essays published on queer and trans Gothic. They are the editor for *Queer Gothic: An Edinburgh Companion* (forthcoming in 2022).

JOHAN HÖGLUND is Professor of English at Linnaeus University, Sweden. He has published extensively on the relationship between imperialism and popular culture in British and US Fiction. He is the author of *The American Imperial Gothic* (2014) and the editor of several collections on Gothic, including *B-Movie Gothic* (2018) with Justin D. Edwards and *Gothic in the Anthropocene* (2021) with Edwards and Rune Graulund.

SARAH ILOTT is Senior Lecturer in Literature and Film at Manchester Metropolitan University, UK. Her publications include *New Postcolonial British Genres* (2015); *Telling It Slant: Critical Approaches to Helen Oyeyemi* (edited with Chloe Germaine Buckley, 2017); *New Directions in Diaspora Studies* (edited with Ana Cristina Mendes and Lucinda Newns, 2018); and *Comedy and the Politics of Representation* (edited with Helen Davies, 2018).

MARK JANCOVICH is Professor of Film and Television Studies at the University of East Anglia. He is the author of various books and articles on horror and the Gothic and is currently managing editor of the journal *Horror Studies*.

DEREK JOHNSTON is Lecturer in broadcast media at Queen's University, Belfast. He is the author of *Haunted Seasons: Television Ghost Stories for Christmas and Horror for Halloween* (2015) and a number of other chapters and articles covering science fiction and horror.

TABISH KHAIR is Associate Professor at Aarhus University, Denmark, and the author of *The Gothic, Postcolonialism and Otherness: Ghosts from Elsewhere* (2009). He is also a poet and a novelist. This chapter was written while Khair was at the University of Leeds on a Leverhulme Foundation grant.

YVONNE LEFFLER is Professor of Comparative Literature at the Department of Literature, History of Ideas and Religion at the University of Gothenburg, Sweden. Her research interests are Gothic literature and film, nineteenth-century novels and popular fiction. Her PhD thesis explored the Gothic tradition in Swedish nineteenth-century novels and was followed by a study entitled *Horror as Pleasure: The Aesthetics of Horror Fiction* (2000). Since then, she has published several articles on contemporary Scandinavian Gothic.

Notes on Contributors

SIMON MARSDEN is Senior Lecturer in English Literature at the University of Liverpool. He writes on literature and theology from the long nineteenth century to the present. He is the author of *Emily Brontë and the Religious Imagination* (2014) and *The Theological Turn in Contemporary Gothic Fiction* (2018).

DANIEL MARTIN is Associate Professor of Film Studies in the School of Humanities and Social Sciences at the Korea Advanced Institute of Science and Technology (KAIST). His research focuses on the marketing, reception and global circulation of East Asian film and animation. He is the author of *Extreme Asia: The Rise of Cult Cinema from the Far East* (2015), and co-editor of *Korean Horror Cinema* (2013) and *Hong Kong Horror Cinema* (2018).

EMMA MCEVOY is Senior Lecturer in English Literature at the University of Westminster. She is the author of *Gothic Tourism* (2016) and co-editor, with Catherine Spooner, of *The Routledge Companion to Gothic* (Routledge, 2007). She is currently working on a project on music and the Gothic, 1790–1820.

BERNICE M. MURPHY is an associate professor/lecturer in Popular Literature in the School of English, Trinity College Dublin, and a Fellow of the College. She has published extensively on topics related to horror and Gothic fiction and film. Her books include: *Shirley Jackson: A Literary Legacy* (2005); *The Suburban Gothic in American Popular Culture* (2009); *The Rural Gothic: Backwoods Horror and Terror in the Wilderness* (2013); *The Highway Horror Film* (2014); and the edited essay collection *Twenty-First-Century Popular Fiction* (2018). Her current book project is a monograph entitled *The California Gothic in Contemporary Fiction and Film*.

MARC OLIVIER is Professor of French Studies at Brigham Young University. He is author of *Household Horror: Cinematic Fear and the Secret Life of Everyday Objects* (2020) and editor for the forthcoming *Icons of Horror* series with Indiana University Press.

DAVID PUNTER is Professor of Poetry Emeritus and Senior Research Fellow in the Institute of Advanced Studies at the University of Bristol, UK. In addition to hundreds of articles and essays, he has published many books on the Gothic as well as other areas of literature. His best-known work is probably *The Literature of Terror* (1980; 1996); his most recent book on the Gothic is *The Gothic Condition* (2016). His other books include *Writing the Passions* (2001; 2014); *Rapture: Literature, Addiction, Secrecy* (2009); *Metaphor* (2007); *Modernity* (2017); and *The Literature of Pity* (2014). He has also published six books of poetry.

ARTHUR REDDING is Professor of English at York University in Toronto, Canada. He is the author of four books: *Raids on Human Consciousness: Writing, Anarchism, and Violence* (1998); *Turncoats, Traitors, and Fellow Travelers: Culture and Politics of the Early Cold War* (2009); *'Haints': American Ghosts, Millennial Passions, and Contemporary Gothic Fiction* (2011); and *Radical Legacies: Twentieth-Century Public Intellectuals in the United States* (2015). His current research project is provisionally entitled 'What Would Robert Mitchum Do? Pulp Culture and Postwar American Virilities'.

AGNIESZKA SOLTYSIK MONNET is Professor of American Studies at the University of Lausanne in Switzerland and the author of two monographs, *The Poetics and Politics of the American Gothic: Gender and Slavery in the Nineteenth-Century American Gothic* (2010) and *Combat Death in Contemporary American Culture: Popular Conceptions of War Since World War*

II (2021). She has co-edited *War Gothic in Literature and Culture* (2015) with Steffen Hantke and *Neoliberal Gothic: International Gothic in the Neoliberal Age* (2017) with Linnie Blake.

CATHERINE SPOONER is Professor of Literature and Culture at Lancaster University. Her six books include *Fashioning Gothic Bodies* (2004), *Contemporary Gothic* (2006) and, with Emma McEvoy, *The Routledge Companion to Gothic* (2007). Her most recent book, *Post-millennial Gothic: Comedy, Romance and the Rise of Happy Gothic* (2017), was awarded the Allan Lloyd Smith Memorial Prize for advancing the field of Gothic Studies in 2019. She was co-president of the International Gothic Association 2013–17.

DALE TOWNSHEND FSA is Professor of Gothic Literature in the Manchester Centre for Gothic Studies, Manchester Metropolitan University. His recent publications include *Gothic Antiquity: History, Romance, and the Architectural Imagination, 1760–1840* (2019) and *The Cambridge History of the Gothic, Volumes I and II* (co-edited with Angela Wright, 2020). He is currently working on a monograph on Matthew Gregory Lewis, and editing the posthumous works of Ann Radcliffe for *The Cambridge Edition of the Works of Ann Radcliffe*.

Acknowledgements

The *Cambridge History of the Gothic* was conceived in 2015, when Linda Bree, then Editorial Director at Cambridge University Press, first suggested the idea to us. After much discussion and writing, what began life as a modest single-volume project became a larger and far more ambitious three-volume work. Our thanks are due to Linda Bree for her early encouragement, and for taking this project at proposal stage through peer review, syndicate and contracting. Shalini Bisa and Tim Mason efficiently oversaw much of the initial paperwork. Since then, Bethany Thomas has become our patient, encouraging and responsive editor who has supported the project indefatigably. We are enormously grateful to both Linda and Bethany, and to the extraordinary team who has worked alongside them at Cambridge University Press, including our production manager Sarah Starkey, copy-editor Denise Bannerman and indexer Eric Anderson of Arc Indexing, Inc. Jayavel Radhakrishnan of Integra Software Services has been the most efficient and obliging of Production Managers.

Of course, there would be no *Cambridge History of the Gothic* were it not for the exciting scholarship on the Gothic that has been produced by researchers across the globe. Our heartfelt thanks are also thus due to the scholars who, with such enthusiasm and diligence, signed up to write chapters for these volumes, and who patiently endured the sometimes arduous processes of review, editing and revision. They have been extremely generous with their time and scholarship, and we remain forever in their debt. Our respective institutions have been encouraging of, and patient with, us as we have wrestled with the enormity of this project. Catherine Spooner would like to thank Angela Wright and Emma McEvoy for advice from afar and colleagues in the Department of English Literature and Creative Writing at Lancaster University for their friendship and support, especially (in alphabetical order) Jo Carruthers, Hilary Hinds, Lindsey Moore, Liz Oakley-Brown and Sharon Ruston. Dale Townshend wishes to thank his friends and colleagues in the Manchester Centre for Gothic Studies at Manchester Metropolitan University, as well as Jess Edwards and Antony Rowland. In a more personal capacity, the editors also wish to thank their families. For Catherine, Gabriel and Jago's endless curiosity and wicked sense of humour have sustained her through challenging times and Eddie has both shared a passion for 1960s ephemera, and kept on top of all the washing up. For Dale, Howard, Shannon and Stephen have, as ever, been long-suffering sources of laughter, comfort and support.

Introduction: A History of Gothic Studies in the Twentieth and Twenty-First Centuries

CATHERINE SPOONER

Gothic and History

Gothic has always been pre-eminently concerned with history. From the medievalism of the eighteenth-century Gothic Revival to the post-Freudian concern with psychic histories and the return of the repressed, Gothic texts have always been driven by what Victor Sage and Allan Lloyd Smith characterise as 'the peculiar unwillingness of the past to go away'.[1] This historical sensibility is an inevitable corollary of modernity: as people began distinguishing a modern age from what went before it, they needed to address what the past meant and their relationship to it. Gothic arose in the eighteenth century as one means to explore the simultaneous necessity and impossibility of the modern subject's separation from the past. Thus, as David Punter states of the first phase of Gothic writing (1760–1820), 'Gothic seems to have *been* a mode of history, a way of perceiving an obscure past and interpreting it'.[2] What is commented on less frequently, however, is that the study of Gothic itself has a history, that a prestigious three-volume publication like this one is of its historical moment and would not have been possible even a quarter-century ago.

This Introduction seeks to map the history of Gothic scholarship in the twentieth and twenty-first centuries as the academic discipline that we might now call Gothic Studies came into being. The critical-historical framework it thus constructs serves to contextualise the individual histories charted by individual chapters in this volume. It is not intended to be comprehensive: as will become rapidly apparent, it is not possible to list every single important

---

[1] Victor Sage and Allan Lloyd Smith, 'Introduction', in Victor Sage and Allan Lloyd Smith (eds), *Modern Gothic: A Reader* (Manchester: Manchester University Press, 1995), pp. 1–5 (p. 4).
[2] David Punter, *The Literature of Terror Volume 1: The Gothic Tradition* (London: Longman, 1996), p. 52; italics in original.

contribution to Gothic scholarship and there is much that, of necessity, has been left out. Nevertheless, it draws lines of connection between works through four significant and overlapping stages: the first wave of Gothic criticism between the 1920s and the 1960s; the emergence of Gothic Studies as an academic discipline from the late 1970s to the early 2000s; the increasing understanding of Gothic as a 'contemporary' mode in the 1980s and beyond; and, finally, what can be seen as the institutionalisation of Gothic in the twenty-first century. In doing so, it argues that Gothic Studies in the twenty-first century is simultaneously at its most fertile and at an impasse, a complex deadlock that Gothic scholars of the future must resolve.

Gothic Criticism: The First Wave

Two crucial influences on the development of the modern Gothic occurred at the end of the nineteenth century: the invention of film, and the invention of psychoanalysis. These two enormous historical shifts can scarcely be underestimated in the history of the Gothic: the one opened up new ways of telling tales of terror in a mass market medium, while the other enabled a profound shift not only in the ways Gothic narrative could be written but also in the ways that Gothic could be approached by literary criticism.

As Dale Townshend observes in the introduction to Volume II of this series, by the end of the Victorian period, the Gothic novel's critical stock was low. Indeed, the Gothic novel scarcely existed as a critical concept: E. J. Clery notes that the term 'is mostly a twentieth-century coinage' and although it was used twice in literary overviews published in 1899, it was only established with Edith Birkhead's *The Tale of Terror* (1821), the first sustained critical work on Gothic fiction.[3] A passion for book-collecting in the 1920s fuelled by the clearing of many country-house libraries following the First World War enabled the rediscovery of many obscure works from the late eighteenth and early nineteenth centuries and a corresponding renewal of readerly interest. As a result, a clutch of critical works addressing the Gothic began to emerge, including Eino Railo's *The Haunted Castle* (1927), Michael Sadleir's 'The Northanger Novels' (1927) and J. M. S. Tompkins's *The Popular Novel in England 1770–1800* (1932). Mario Praz's *The Romantic Agony* (1930, translated 1933) also placed Gothic authors including Ann Radcliffe, Matthew Gregory

---

[3] E. J. Clery, 'The Genesis of "Gothic" Fiction', in Jerrold E. Hogle (ed.), *The Cambridge Companion to Gothic Fiction* (Cambridge: Cambridge University Press, 2002), pp. 21–40 (pp. 21–2).

Lewis, Mary Shelley and Charles Maturin within a wider literary tradition of dark eroticism.

Gothic, however, had never been a solely literary affair. Even leaving aside, for a moment, the term's long-standing associations with architecture, Gothic theatre thrived throughout the late-eighteenth and nineteenth centuries. Gothic was, moreover, fundamental to pre-cinematic technologies such as the phantasmagoria or magic lantern show; David J. Jones has mapped with precision how Étienne-Gaspard Robert's *Fantasmagorie* (1798) created an immersive Gothic experience using the latest projection technologies.[4] Early film drew from the language of these pre-existent technologies and, as Simon Brown and Stacey Abbott demonstrate in the first chapter in this volume, was almost immediately perceived both as a Gothic medium in itself – a 'kingdom of shadows', in Maxim Gorky's words – and as a medium for Gothic storytelling.[5] According to Christopher Frayling, 'only with the advent of cinema did "the Gothic" come into its own ... "Gothic film" ... propelled a long-marginalised and sometimes subversive form of literature from the past into the wider cultural bloodstream, and in the process turned it into myth.'[6] Cinema was, in fact, only the first of a series of new media through which Gothic would flourish in the twentieth and twenty-first centuries, including radio, television and, ultimately, digital media. Chapters by Brown and Abbott, Mark Jancovich, Derek Johnston and Mark Olivier directly address the ways in which Gothic adapted to fit these new media, but an awareness of the increasingly transmedial nature of Gothic informs the approach of many of the other contributors to this volume, too.

Psychoanalysis would have a more subtle but even more far-reaching effect on Gothic narrative. As Markman Ellis observes, 'the effect of psychoanalysis was to universalise the lessons of the Gothic novel, oddly increasing its cultural significance and prestige by explicating its relevance and importance'.[7] Sigmund Freud's own contribution to what would eventually be established as Gothic criticism was his essay on 'The "Uncanny"',

---

[4] See David J. Jones, *Gothic Machine: Textualities, Pre-cinematic Media and Film in Popular Visual Culture, 1670–1910* (Cardiff: University of Wales Press, 2011), pp. 57–78.
[5] Maxim Gorky, 'Last Night I was in the Kingdom of Shadows', reprinted in Colin Harding and Simon Popple (eds), *In the Kingdom of Shadows: A Companion to Early Cinema* (London: Cygnus Arts, 1996), pp. 5–6 (p. 5).
[6] Christopher Frayling, 'Foreword' in James Bell (ed.), *Gothic: The Dark Heart of Film* (London: BFI, 2013), pp. 5–7 (p. 5).
[7] Markman Ellis, *The History of Gothic Fiction* (Edinburgh: Edinburgh University Press, 2000), p. 13.

published in 1919. In this work he analyses E. T. A. Hoffman's short story 'The Sandman' (1816) as an example of the *unheimlich* or unhomely, the creeping feeling that occurs to us when something happens to recall infantile complexes that have been repressed into the unconscious, enabling the recognition of the event or object that has provoked the return as simultaneously familiar and estranged. Of course, the concept of the return of the repressed has become a fundamental tenet of Gothic criticism and is almost impossible to sidestep. However, a broader Freudian approach inspired by *On the Interpretation of Dreams* (1899), in which the dream contains a latent content that can be decoded to reveal the workings of the unconscious, also lies behind much of twentieth-century Gothic criticism.

The Freudian notion of the return of the repressed merges in twentieth-century criticism with an older understanding of Gothic as anti-classical to create an idea of Gothic as a uniquely subversive, even revolutionary mode. This idea appears as early as Michael Sadleir's influential article on 'The Northanger Novels' (1927), in which he calls the Gothic romance 'an expression of a deep subversive impulse' comparable to the French Revolution and its authors 'prophets of iconoclasm', albeit ones whose 'once inflammatory art' would be received as escapism.[8] However, it takes its more characteristic form in the Surrealist André Breton's assessment of what he calls the eighteenth-century *'romans noirs'* in his essay 'Limits not frontiers of surrealism', published in English in Herbert Read's *Surrealism* (1936). Breton, overtly influenced by Freud's understanding of the dream-work, constructs the Gothic as a radical genre that is in deliberate opposition to social realism and which reveals 'latent content, the means of fathoming the secret depths of history which disappear beneath a maze of events'.[9] This would have a profound influence on Gothic criticism in the twentieth century.

Breton's stance was vigorously contested by Montague Summers in *The Gothic Quest: A History of the Gothic Novel* (1938); Summers's view of Gothic is almost fanatically conservative, and thus he suggests that the Surrealists have wilfully misinterpreted Sadleir's more nuanced position, having 'confused and deliberately commingled' revolution in literature with social

---

[8] Michael Sadleir, 'The Northanger Novels', *The Edinburgh Review* 246:501 (1927): 91–106 (pp. 93, 94).
[9] André Breton, 'English Romans Noirs and Surrealism', in Victor Sage (ed.), *The Gothick Novel* (Basingtoke: Macmillan, 1990), pp. 112–15 (p. 112). Translated by Sage from André Breton, 'Limites non frontières du Surréalisme, *Nouvelle Revue Française* 48:1 (1937).

revolution.[10] In a final, almost comical move, he denounces the 'intimacy' between Surrealism and Communism.[11] Summers's argument is in some respects a dead end in Gothic criticism, as its conservative politics is at odds with the tenor of most subsequent scholarship. Gothic for Summers is overwhelmingly nostalgic; he describes Romanticism, with which he aligns Gothic, as 'reactionary in its revolt against the present since it yearns for the loveliness of the past as so picturesquely revealed to us in art and poem'.[12] In contrast, later twentieth-century scholars generally found Gothic to be progressive in its values and, as we shall see, often revolutionary in sentiment.

It is Breton's approach that has thus proved to be the more influential on the subsequent history of Gothic criticism. In his undertaking to 'fathom the secret depths of history' lies the seeds of another persistent theme within Gothic criticism in the later twentieth and twenty-first century: that Gothic possesses a unique power to reflect or refract the time at which it is written. This approach is glossed further in Devendra P. Varma's *The Gothic Flame* (1957), another key work in the development of Gothic criticism. Glossing Breton, Varma asserts, 'The "fantastic" in literature is the surrealistic expression of those historical and social factors which the ordinary chronicle of events in history does not consider significant. Such "fantasia" express the profoundest, repressed emotions of the individual and society.'[13] Psychoanalysis and historical analysis are folded into one another here to suggest that Gothic is the dream-work of history, and by interpreting its symbols we can bring to the surface what history does not know about itself.

As it entered the 1960s, then, Gothic was critically constructed as a mode that was in tune with the times: a genre of social revolution, a ready-made counter-narrative, one in which the deepest fears and desires of Western culture were apparently made manifest in dream-like form. This is how it was characterised in Leslie Fiedler's wildly influential *Love and Death in the American Novel* (1960), which argued that 'the Gothic novel is fundamentally anti-bourgeois' and 'an anti-realistic protest, a rebellion of the imagination', a provocation which Catherine Spooner's chapter in this volume takes up.[14] In this revolutionary guise, Gothic was adopted by the many social movements of the 1960s and afterwards, of which feminism was the most prominent.

---

[10] Montague Summers, *The Gothic Quest: A History of the Gothic Novel* (London: Fortune Press, 1938), p. 398.
[11] Summers, *The Gothic Quest*, p. 411.   [12] Summers, *The Gothic Quest*, p. 18.
[13] Devendra P. Varma, *The Gothic Flame* (London: Arthur Barker Ltd., 1957), p. 217. See also Punter, *The Literature of Terror Volume 1*, p. 15.
[14] Leslie Fiedler, *Love and Death in the American Novel* (New York: Criterion Books, 1960), pp. 107, 117.

The Birth of Gothic Studies

Gothic Studies as a formal discipline was fashioned in the late 1970s, and forged in the crucible of second-wave literary feminism. In *Literary Women* (1976), Ellen Moers devoted two long chapters to the Gothic novel, coining the phrase 'female Gothic' and infamously describing Mary Shelley's *Frankenstein* (1818, 1831) as a 'birth myth'.[15] Ironically enough, this proved to be the birth of Gothic Studies, as the fast-growing feminist movement seized on Moers's partial rehabilitation of Gothic as a genre principally written and read by women and thus suffused with women's concerns. Sandra M. Gilbert and Susan Gubar's *The Madwoman in the Attic: The Woman Writer and the Nineteenth-Century Literary Imagination* (1979) may not explicitly have positioned itself as a work on Gothic fiction. Nevertheless, its discovery of a model of literary doubling in Charlotte Brontë's pairing of heroine Jane Eyre with the mad Bertha Rochester, the archetypal madwoman in the attic, drew on Gothic tropes and proved a model of inspiration for generations of feminist critics to come. Notable works to take up the theme of female Gothic over the ensuing decade include Juliann E. Fleenor's *The Female Gothic* (1983); Kate Ferguson Ellis's *The Contested Castle: Gothic Novels and the Subversion of Domestic Ideology* (1989) and Eugenia C. Delamotte's *The Perils of the Night: A Feminist Study of Nineteenth-Century Gothic* (1990). In the early 1990s, influential works from feminist film studies including Carol Clover's *Men, Women and Chain Saws: Gender in the Modern Horror Film* (1992) and Barbara Creed's *The Monstrous-Feminine: Film, Feminism, Psychoanalysis* (1993) also made a significant impact on feminist approaches to Gothic. The focus on gender was soon followed by similar attention to other forms of identity politics, including race in Kari J. Winter's *Subjects of Slavery, Agents of Change* (1992) and sexuality in Paulina Palmer's *Lesbian Gothic: Transgressive Fictions* (1999), each inaugurating flourishing scholarly traditions in their own right. In this volume, Arthur Redding, Lucie Armitt and Ardel Haefele-Thomas directly address these traditions although their influence is felt throughout the book.

Identity politics were, of course, prevalent throughout the academy from the 1980s onwards, and Gothic is not exceptional in this respect. There is

---

[15] Ellen Moers, *Literary Women* (London: The Women's Press, 1978), pp. 90–110, 98.

something about Gothic's particular nature, however, as what Robert Miles calls 'a coherent code for the representation of fragmented subjectivity', that renders it particularly conducive to being read in this way.[16] This is, of course, also the quality that made it particularly amenable to psychoanalytic criticism earlier in the century. However, identity politics tended in many cases to move Gothic criticism on from psychoanalytic methodologies towards a broader range of theoretical approaches and, in several respects, a renewed attention to historical context.

It was a different kind of book, however, that set the seal on Gothic Studies as a formal discipline. David Punter's *The Literature of Terror* (1980) surveyed Gothic from its origins in sentimentalism, graveyard poetry and discourses of the sublime to 'modern perceptions of the barbaric' in the fiction of the 1970s.[17] Punter's definition of Gothic was necessarily loose, but his achievement was to establish that Gothic was, indeed, a continuous and coherent literary tradition that ran from the mid eighteenth century to the present day, discarding the value judgements that had previously plagued its academic study and demonstrating that it repaid close literary analysis. Punter's book created a canon and conferred legitimacy on Gothic as an intellectual endeavour. As such, it permitted Gothic Studies to exist.

The other important move in the early 1980s that freed up the academic study of Gothic was its decoupling from the concept of genre. In *Kinds of Literature: An Introduction to the Theory of Genres and Modes* (1982), Alastair Fowler argued that 'the character of genres is that they change', becoming more elastic and more easily combined with other genres or modes.[18] Thus, over time, 'the gothic romance ... yielded a gothic mode that outlasted it'.[19] This intervention had a dual effect. First, it meant that Gothic could be more flexibly and fluidly defined, and Gothic could be discovered in texts – and media – where it had hitherto been ignored. Critics continued to loosen Gothic from the straitjacketing notion of genre in a variety of ways: for Robert Miles in *Gothic Writing, 1750–1820: A Genealogy* (1993) it is a 'discursive site'; for Michael Gamer in *Romanticism and the Gothic* (2000) it is an

---

[16] Robert Miles, *Gothic Writing, 1750–1820: A Genealogy*, 2nd edition (Manchester: Manchester University Press, 2002), p. 2.

[17] David Punter, *The Literature of Terror Volume 2: The Modern Gothic* (London: Longman, 1996), p. 119.

[18] Alastair Fowler, *Kinds of Literature: An Introduction to the Theory of Genres and Modes* (Oxford: Oxford University Press, 1982), p. 18.

[19] Fowler, *Kinds of Literature*, p. 109.

'aesthetic'.[20] The other effect of refiguring Gothic as a mode is that it loosened it from the more pejorative associations of 'genre fiction' and allowed it to creep into the teaching canon in universities and schools. Gothic was gradually attaining respectability.

The advantage and the problem with the shifting critical understanding of Gothic as a mode, discursive site or aesthetic is that it meant that almost anything could be defined as Gothic, and while this led to fruitful and sometimes thrilling new directions of study, it also brought with it a lack of critical purchase. While defining Gothic became a vexed – and frequently dull – question for critics in the 1990s and beyond, a vague and shifting sense of the function that Gothic performs resulted in a weakening field. Studies twinning Gothic with a variety of different adjectives proliferated in the twenty-first century (Fred Botting poked fun at this trend with his 2001 essay 'Candygothic', for example). At best, this produced exciting new combinations of Gothic and theory – Queer Gothic, Ecogothic – but this could also dwindle into the endless taxonomisation of subgenres and, at worst, deliver an ever-multiplying and, thus, ever-vanishing critical object.

As the twenty-first century commenced, voices of dissent began to be raised in Gothic criticism, with scholars calling out what they saw as its most egregious tendencies and each, in their own way, calling for the restoration of rigorous historical specificity to studies of the Gothic. The first target was the psychoanalytic-historical approach to the Gothic. This had been disputed as early as 1980, with the first edition of Eve Kosofsky Sedgwick's *The Coherence of Gothic Conventions*, which argued that the psychoanalytic focus on uncovering the hidden depths of Gothic texts neglected precisely what was most interesting about them – their emphasis on surfaces. In an influential essay simply titled 'Gothic Criticism', first published in 2000, Chris Baldick and Robert Mighall denounced what they term the 'anxiety model' of much Gothic scholarship, or the idea that it is the work of the Gothic critic to 'reveal' the hidden anxieties of the age.[21] They argue,

> The assumption that cultural 'anxiety' is reflected or articulated in Gothic fiction is not only rather simplistic: it is tautological. Horror fiction is used to confirm the critic's own unproven point of departure, that this 'oppressive'

---

[20] Miles, *Gothic Writing, 1750–1820*, p. 4 and *passim*; Michael Gamer, *Romanticism and the Gothic: Genre, Reception, and Canon Formation* (Cambridge: Cambridge University Press, 2000), p. 4.

[21] Chris Baldick and Robert Mighall, 'Gothic Criticism', in David Punter (ed.), *A New Companion to the Gothic* (Oxford: Wiley-Blackwell 2012), pp. 267–87 (p. 279).

culture was terrified by its ideological 'Others'; and thus if the Gothic features the Other in demonic form, these demonic forms must reflect society's fears about the Other ... Since Gothic horror fiction has a *generic obligation* to evoke or produce fear, it is in principle the *least* reliable index of supposedly 'widespread' anxieties.[22]

For Baldick and Mighall, the result of the pervasive and unquestioning adoption of this implicitly psychoanalytic approach to history is that 'Gothic Criticism has abandoned any credible historical grasp upon its object, which it has tended to reinvent in the image of its own projected intellectual goals of psychological "depth" and political "subversion."'[23] It also results in a weakening of the definition of Gothic itself, which is 'defined not according to observable features of theme and setting but according to the realms of psychological depth from which it is supposed to originate (dreams, fantasy) or the psychological responses it is believed to provoke (fear, horror, terror). Gothic Criticism is commonly unable and unwilling to distinguish its supposed object from the generality of fearful or horrible narratives'.[24]

In a similar vein, Alexandra Warwick and Roger Luckhurst took respective aim at what Luckhurst named the 'spectral turn' in criticism, a preoccupation with textual hauntings inspired by the English translation of Jacques Derrida's *Specters of Marx* (1994).[25] In the late 1990s and early 2000s, there was a sudden vogue for using Derrida's highly localised and specific practice of discovering Shakespearean spectral traces within the writings of Karl Marx as a model for discovering textual hauntings within any given work. Both critics were perturbed by the way that this rendered all texts implicitly Gothic. This, they suggested, resulted in a loss of critical purchase on Gothic as an object of study. Identifying Julian Wolfreys's *Victorian Hauntings* (2002) as a particularly egregious example, Warwick writes that 'it is a critical step that renders Gothic absolutely ubiquitous and simultaneously nullifies it. It is no longer at the dark margin, but the normal state of textual affairs'.[26] Spreading his net more widely to take in works by Wolfreys, Jean-Michel Rabaté and Jodey Castricano, Luckhurst argues that 'because the spectral infiltrates the hermeneutic act itself, critical work can only replicate tropes from textual sources, punning spiritedly around the central terms of the Gothic to produce

---

[22] Baldick and Mighall, 'Gothic Criticism', p. 280.
[23] Baldick and Mighall, 'Gothic Criticism', pp. 267–8.
[24] Baldick and Mighall, 'Gothic Criticism', p. 274.
[25] Roger Luckhurst, 'The Contemporary London Gothic and the Limits of the Spectral Turn', *Textual Practice* 16.3 (2010): 527–46, *passim*.
[26] Alexandra Warwick, 'Feeling Gothicky?', *Gothic Studies* 9:1 (2007): 5–15 (p. 8).

a curious form of meta-Gothic that elides object and instrument', and producing 'what Derrida has elsewhere termed "doubling commentary"'.[27]

For Warwick, this crisis of definition within Gothic Studies is matched by a comparable ubiquity of the Gothic in contemporary culture, something that she identifies as 'the effect of a kind of aftershock . . . of psychoanalysis'.[28] She suggests that the attitude to psychoanalysis has moved on, however, in the light of what she calls therapy culture. Whereas once the Gothic text registered the terrors of trauma and the impossibility of coming to terms with it, contemporary texts rather seek out trauma and cultivate it: 'contemporary culture *wants* to have trauma, it is induced, predicted and enacted, persistently rehearsed even when it is not actually present'.[29] What was distinctive about Warwick's article was not only her critique of contemporary critical approaches to Gothic but also her identification of a particular contemporary Gothic, one that merited study on its own terms. This was a late branch of Gothic scholarship to develop, but one that underwrites this volume.

Contemporary Gothic

Early Gothic criticism acknowledged the influence of the Gothic in the twentieth century only very tentatively. While most critics agreed, like Sadleir, that 'the spirit of melodrama and of terror . . . persisted unsubdued and persists to this day', there was very little attempt to address this in any sustained or coherent fashion.[30] For the majority of critics, the Gothic novel began with Horace Walpole's *The Castle of Otranto* (1764) – with precedents in Spenser, Shakespeare, Jacobean drama and graveyard poetry – and ended with Charles Maturin's *Melmoth the Wanderer* (1820). What Varma calls 'residuary influences' in later works from James Hogg and William Harrison Ainsworth to Charles Dickens, the Brontës and Edgar Allan Poe were regarded as either a falling off from a golden age or a transmutation into a different form.[31] Summers was the most vehement proponent of this view, acknowledging the similar properties of modern crime fiction, for example, but dismissing the majority of it as 'unhealthy and unwholesome rubbish'.[32] As we have seen, he treated the idea that the Surrealists might be continuing the work of Gothic literature with unmitigated scorn.

---

[27] Luckhurst, 'The Contemporary London Gothic', pp. 535, 536.
[28] Warwick, 'Feeling Gothicky?', p. 10.   [29] Warwick, 'Feeling Gothicky?', p. 11.
[30] Sadleir, 'The Northanger Novels', p. 105.   [31] Varma, *The Gothic Flame*, pp. 173–205.
[32] Summers, *The Gothic Quest*, p. 13.

There were, nevertheless, hints that Gothic might have contemporary manifestations and a rich and exciting cultural existence well beyond the so-called 'first wave' of the period 1764–1820. Birkhead is an early champion of contemporary Gothic, documenting a continuous tradition of tales 'inspired by awe and fear' arising in antiquity and continuing to what were, in the early 1920s, 'living authors' such as H. G. Wells, Arthur Conan Doyle, E. F. Benson, Marie Corelli, Algernon Blackwood and Joseph Conrad.[33] Varma likewise insists that 'The Gothic novel remains a vital thing, a potential force in the literature of today', although this potentiality appears unrealised, as the most recent writers that he mentions in *The Gothic Flame* are repetitions of those in Birkhead, all of whom had met their demise by the time of his writing in the later 1950s.[34] An Appendix on the influence of Gothic on contemporary crime fiction and horror comics regards these as the 'disintegration or ruin of pure Gothic romance', although it somewhat snidely admits that the graphic sado-masochism found in such comics 'will probably invite the attention of some future Mario Praz'.[35] Fiedler, in arguing that the whole of the American literary tradition 'is almost essentially a gothic one', implied a contemporary Gothic almost by default, and inevitably found the culmination of the American Gothic tradition in the fiction of William Faulkner.[36]

Critical hesitancy towards the Gothic as a contemporary phenomenon was to change with the rise of Gothic Studies as a formal discipline. Moers briefly addresses 'the persistence of the Gothic mode into our own time' in *Literary Women*, referencing Djuna Barnes, Carson McCullers and Sylvia Plath.[37] However, it was Punter's *The Literature of Terror*, again, that most cogently established a tradition of Gothic writing that ran more or less continuously from the later eighteenth century to the present day. Significantly, Punter includes film in his survey and thus opens up one of the key sources of Gothic potential in the twentieth century. Horror film, of course, had its own growing critical tradition that, until this point, had been regarded as separate to Gothic criticism, but which would increasingly discover shared ground from the 1980s onwards as both were influenced by the theoretical turn in the academy. Punter's key contribution to the identification of a distinctive contemporary Gothic, however, is to conclude his survey with a new selection of 'living authors', including Joyce Carol Oates, J. G. Ballard, Robert Coover and Angela Carter. The second and expanded edition of *The Literature*

---

[33] Edith Birkhead, *The Tale of Terror: A Study of the Gothic Romance*, Project Gutenberg <www.gutenberg.org/ebooks/14154> (last accessed 30 December 2020).
[34] Varma, *The Gothic Flame*, p. 205. [35] Varma, *The Gothic Flame*, pp. 237, 241.
[36] Fiedler, *Love and Death in the American Novel*, p. 125. [37] Moers, *Literary Women*, p. 107.

of Terror of 1996 updated this further to encompass Anne Rice, William Gibson, Iain Banks, Will Self and Bret Easton Ellis, among others. Partisan choices though these may be, they nonetheless gave permission to a new generation of scholars (of which I was one, discovering the original edition of Punter's book in 1992 in my first term at university) to address Gothic in its contemporary forms and manifestations.

The contemporaneity of the Gothic was finally fully established in 1991, when the novelists Patrick McGrath and Bradford Morrow published *The New Gothic*, an anthology of fiction by contemporary writers. Their brief Introduction provided a manifesto for the contemporary Gothic. Following the historical-Freudian trajectory of Gothic criticism after Breton, McGrath and Morrow's version of Gothic is reflective of 'a century whose history has been stained perhaps like no other by the blacker urges of human nature', a tradition that is indebted to Poe for dispensing with Gothic *'furniture'* in favour of 'psychological disturbance': 'Now hell is decidedly on earth, located within the vaults and chambers of our own minds.'[38] Slight though this Introduction was, it vividly established the priorities and preoccupations of Gothic critics of the contemporary at this particular moment.

At the same time, an important cultural shift was taking place beyond the academy. Goth subculture began in the United Kingdom when groups of young people began wearing black clothes, affecting graveyard poses and producing and listening to bass-heavy, sepulchral music with doomy or macabre lyrics. Although there is much discussion of exactly where the term 'Goth' originated, 'gothic' was being used by music journalists to describe the new sound by 1979.[39] Although often regarded as the offspring of punk, Goth actually drew on a wide spectrum of musical influences, including glam rock (particularly David Bowie), metal and psychedelia. Its heyday was the 1980s, when bands such as Bauhaus, The Sisters of Mercy, Siouxsie and the Banshees and The Cure attained the upper reaches of the UK music charts. The subculture quickly spread internationally, particularly in North America and northern Europe, surprising its detractors by persisting well beyond its predicted shelf-life and, after receiving new impetus through the internet, surviving in good health up to the present day.

---

[38] Patrick McGrath and Bradford Morrow, 'Introduction', in Patrick McGrath and Bradford Morrow (eds), *The New Gothic* (London: Picador, 1993), pp. xi–xiv (pp. xix, xi, xi, xiv); italics in original.

[39] See Natasha Scharf, *The Art of Gothic: Music + Fashion + Alt Culture* (London: Omnibus Press, 2014), p. 8.

If Gothic Studies and Goth emerged at a similar historical moment, they seemed initially to be following different trajectories. In a 2002 article entitled 'Gothic Scholars Don't Wear Black', Sara Martin bemoaned the fact that 'Gothic Studies and the diverse youth subcultures identifying themselves as Gothic are hardly in touch with each other', noting that the methodologies of Gothic Studies, based as they were on psychoanalysis and 'a variety of postmodern critical discourses', did not lend themselves to the study of living participants.[40] Generationally, however, students who had grown up identifying as Goths were working their way through the academic system, and in the early 2000s a clutch of academic publications fully acknowledged Goth subcultural practices, fashion and music. Paul Hodkinson's *Goth: Identity, Style and Subculture* (2002) was particularly striking for eschewing Gothic Studies altogether in favour of a participant observational approach influenced by the Birmingham School of Cultural Studies; this approach was also taken by Dunja Brill's *Goth Culture: Gender, Sexuality and Style* (2008). For Hodkinson, individual participants might mention horror film or fiction as influential on their appearance or lifestyle, but these were less important than shared participation in a scene and, crucially, the enjoyment of Goth music, in determining these participants' identity. Other publications, however, sought a *rapprochement* between Gothic Studies and Cultural Studies, such as Catherine Spooner's *Fashioning Gothic Bodies* (2004), Carol Siegel's *Goth's Dark Empire* (2005), Lauren M. E. Goodlad and Michael Bibby's diverse edited collection *Goth: Undead Subculture* (2007) and Isabella Van Elferen's *Gothic Music: The Sounds of the Uncanny* (2012).

As the 1990s wore on, so the assumption that the Gothic was a cultural phenomenon that informed contemporary literature and other forms of cultural production became increasingly commonplace. Subsequent to Punter's path-breaking work, it became *de rigeur* for critical surveys of the Gothic to bring their histories up to date and to cross media; early examples include Fred Botting's Routledge Critical Idiom guide, *Gothic* (1995), and Richard Davenport-Hines's popular history, *Gothic: Four Hundred Years of Excess, Horror, Evil and Ruin* (1998). Works that focused solely on Gothic in the twentieth century and beyond also began to emerge and included Victor Sage and Allan Lloyd Smith's *Modern Gothic: A Reader* (1996); Christoph Grunenberg's *Gothic: Transmutations of Horror in Late-Twentieth-Century Art* (1997), an exhibition catalogue that was perhaps the first book to

---

[40] Sara Martin, 'Gothic Scholars Don't Wear Black: Gothic Studies and Gothic Subcultures', *Gothic Studies* 4.1 (2002): 28–43 (pp. 28, 29).

acknowledge Goth subculture as part of the contemporary Gothic; a clutch of journal articles and book chapters by Fred Botting arguing for Gothic's exhaustion in the face of postmodernity; and Mark Edmundson's *Nightmare on Main Street* (1999), which argued that American popular culture exhibited patterns of sado-masochism and 'facile transcendence' and had thus itself become gothicised.[41] By the time of the publication of my own *Contemporary Gothic* in 2006, the idea of a Gothic tradition stretching to the present day and across media still seemed under-explored, but no longer surprising.

In *Contemporary Gothic*, I sought to define what made Gothic produced in the late twentieth and early twenty-first centuries distinctive and discovered that, in fact, there was more in common between these texts and their eighteenth- and nineteenth-century predecessors than there were differences: 'the legacies of the past and its burdens on the present; the radically provisional or divided nature of the self; the construction of peoples or individuals as monstrous or "other"; the preoccupation with bodies that are modified, grotesque or diseased. Gothic has become so pervasive precisely because it is so apposite to the representation of contemporary concerns.'[42] However, I also noted that postmodernity and globalisation had left their mark, as contemporary Gothic texts exist post-Freud, post-Gothic criticism, and therefore often reproduce what critics expect to find: 'Contemporary Gothic possesses a new self-consciousness about its own nature; it has reached new levels of mass production, distribution and audience awareness, enabled by global consumer culture; and it has crossed disciplinary boundaries to be absorbed into all forms of media.'[43]

What I did not see, and would now add with the benefit of hindsight, is the way that globalisation has enabled the spread of Gothic beyond its traditional territories in Europe and North America and that, in turn, has influenced the production of Western Gothic texts. Although work had begun on a number of national Gothics by critics such as Andrew Hock Soon Ng, Ken Gelder and Justin D. Edwards, it was Glennis Byron's *Globalgothic* (2014), a volume bringing together the fruits of an AHRC-funded research network, that

---

[41] See Fred Botting, 'Future Horror (the Redundancy of Gothic), *Gothic Studies* 1:2 (1999): 139–55; Fred Botting, 'Candygothic', in Fred Botting (ed.), *The Gothic* (Cambridge: D. S. Brewer, 2001), pp. 133–52; Fred Botting, 'Aftergothic: Consumption, Machines, and Black Holes', in Jerrold E. Hogle (ed.), *The Cambridge Companion to Gothic Fiction* (Cambridge: Cambridge University Press, 2002), pp. 277–300. Mark Edmundson, *Nightmare on Main Street: Angels, Sadomasochism, and the Culture of Gothic* (Cambridge, MA: Harvard University Press, 1997), p. 77 and *passim*.

[42] Catherine Spooner, *Contemporary Gothic* (London: Reaktion Books, 2006), p. 8.

[43] Spooner, *Contemporary Gothic*, p. 23.

synthesised these approaches. Byron emphasised that twenty-first-century Gothic is characterised by 'multidirectional exchanges' between Western and non-Western cultures.[44] As a result, she argues,

> Not only has Western gothic travelled but one of the effects of the increasing mobility and fluidity of people and products in the globalised world has been a growing awareness that the tropes and strategies Western critics have associated with the gothic, such as the ghost, the vampire and the zombie, have their counterparts in other cultures, however differently these may be inflected by specific histories and belief systems. Consequently, the flows have by no means been one-directional.[45]

Byron's stance has been one of the most transformational in contemporary Gothic studies. Although this book does not have scope to do justice to the full geographical range of the Gothic in the twentieth and twenty-first centuries, it does provide three case studies of how Gothic manifests in a globalised world, focusing on the Islamic countries of North Africa and the Middle East (Tuğçe Biçakçi Syed), Scandinavia (Yvonne Leffler) and East Asia (Daniel Martin). We also acknowledge that the shift from colonialism to postcolonialism is an important historical context for the production of Gothic texts in the twentieth century and beyond, and several of our chapters address this explicitly (Tabish Khair, Sarah Ilott, Johan Höglund), while it remains implicit in others. There are many very obvious gaps here, which we regretfully acknowledge; our editorial principles, however, have been governed by history rather than geography, and thus by the process of globalisation rather than by its myriad manifestations across multiple territories.

The Institutionalisation of Gothic

In May 2013, the then British Secretary of State for Education, Michael Gove, addressed an audience of teachers with the question, 'You come home to find your 17-year-old daughter engrossed in a book. Which would delight you more – if it were *Twilight* or *Middlemarch*?'[46] Pitting the *grande dame* of literary realism against the queen of teen Gothic romance, Gove replayed the age-old critical opposition between the realist novel and the Gothic in terms of

---

[44] Glennis Byron, 'Introduction', in Glennis Byron (ed.), *Globalgothic* (Manchester: Manchester University Press 2013), pp. 1–10 (p. 3).
[45] Byron, 'Introduction', p. 3.
[46] Michael Gove, 'What Does It Mean to Be an Educated Person?', delivered 9 May 2013, Brighton College <www.gov.uk/government/speeches/what-does-it-mean-to-be-an-educated-person> (last accessed 4 January 2021).

literary value. His argument backfired as educators came out in force in favour of teen girls' critical agency and the fact that the two choices were not mutually exclusive. In a sense, however, his argument was belated, in that while Stephenie Meyer's controversial 2005 novel may have been an easy target, Gothic had by this time become a staple of syllabi in schools and universities and was approaching a new respectability, not say orthodoxy, in which its pedagogical value was presumed.[47]

By the mid-1990s, Gothic was firmly established as an object of serious study within Literature departments in anglophone countries and increasingly also in Europe. Where once an English Literature student may have expected to study one or two Gothic texts on broader courses on, say, Romanticism or Women's Writing, individual modules on Gothic became a frequent occurrence. The first Masters course dedicated to Gothic, the MLitt in the Gothic Imagination, was launched at the University of Stirling in 1996 by David Punter and Glennis Byron.

Meanwhile, a group of academics gathered at a conference at the University of East Anglia in 1991 were inspired to create the International Gothic Association (IGA) and its associated journal, *Gothic Studies* (1999–).[48] A second conference was held at the University of Stirling in Scotland in 1993, a third at St Mary's University, Twickenham (housed in Horace Walpole's Gothic mansion, Strawberry Hill), in 1997 and further conferences on a roughly biennial basis thereafter, with international venues spanning Mount St Vincent University, Halifax, Canada (1999); Simon Fraser University, Vancouver (2001, 2015); Liverpool Hope University (2003); Université de Montreal and Wilfrid Laurier University, Canada (2005); Université de Provence, Aix-en-Provence, France (2007); Lancaster University, UK (2009); Heidelberg University, Germany (2011); University of Surrey, UK (2013); Universidad de las Américas Puebla, Cholula, Mexico (2017); Manchester Metropolitan University (2018); Lewis University, Illinois (2019) and Trinity College Dublin (projected 2022). The IGA has deliberately sought to expand the international scope of Gothic academia from its bases in the UK and North America and to unite scholars working on Gothic in all its forms. Its conference at Manchester Metropolitan

---

[47] For more on the pedagogical value of Gothic, see Chloé Germaine Buckley, *Twenty-First-Century Children's Gothic: From the Wanderer to the Nomadic Subject* (Edinburgh: Edinburgh University Press, 2018), pp. 25–33.

[48] With thanks to David Punter for providing information on the early days of the International Gothic Association.

University in 2018 attracted well over 300 scholars from twenty-nine countries, an indication of the current health of the field.

As students who received their degrees from the 1990s onwards and had enjoyed Gothic as part of their studies entered the teaching profession, so Gothic increasingly became part of the school literature syllabus in the United Kingdom. In the early 1990s, I studied *Frankenstein* at A-level (the national qualification for students aged 16–18) but the remainder of the class gave up and elected to revert to *Hard Times* when our bemused teacher struggled to find supporting secondary criticism in the local university library. In 2020, Gothic is routinely taught in secondary schools in England from Key Stage 3 (age 11+) onwards and teaching resources proliferate on the web. AQA, the biggest exam board accounting for over half of all pupils in England, for several years included a module on 'Elements of the Gothic' as part of its A-level English literature syllabus; in 2021, the board requires GCSE (aged 14–16) students to study 'The 19th-century novel' and lists six out of seven set texts with a pronounced Gothic leaning – *Frankenstein*, *A Christmas Carol*, *Wuthering Heights*, *Jane Eyre*, *Great Expectations* and *Strange Case of Dr Jekyll and Mr Hyde* (the seventh novel is *Pride and Prejudice*) – giving rise to the impression that the nineteenth-century novelistic tradition is primarily a Gothic one.[49] Compared to F. R. Leavis's *The Great Tradition* (1948), with its celebration of 'moral seriousness' enshrined in the mostly realist work of Jane Austen, George Eliot, Henry James and Joseph Conrad – the stance that Gove implicitly drew on in his anti-*Twilight* speech – this marks a major canonical shift over the course of the twentieth century.

Several major cultural institutions, moreover, mounted high-profile events celebrating Gothic in the first two decades of the twenty-first century. Even leaving aside exhibitions on medieval art and those held at small regional museums, the sudden prevalence of these events is striking. An early predecessor, *Gothic: Transmutations of Horror in Late-Twentieth-Century Art* at Boston Institute for Contemporary Arts in 1997, identified Gothic aesthetics in the work of contemporary artists, and prefigured the notorious *Sensation* and *Apocalypse: Beauty and Horror in Contemporary Art* exhibitions at London's Royal Academy in 1997 and 2000 respectively, events that did not use the word Gothic *per se* but which nonetheless traded on a macabre sensibility. These exhibitions were still heavily invested in the idea of Gothic as

---

[49] In England and Wales, GCSE English Literature is compulsory for pupils aged 14–16, and A-level English Literature is optional for pupils aged 16–18. See <www.aqa.org.uk/subjects/english/gcse/english-literature-8702/subject-content/shakespeare-and-the-19th-century-novel> (last accessed 22 December 2020).

oppositional at the same time as claiming it to be uniquely of the *zeitgeist*; the curator of the Boston ICA exhibition, Christoph Grunenberg, wrote in the attendant catalogue that 'The desire to be entertained, challenged, shocked, and to indulge in the most intense and stimulating sensations that ensue in the encounter with the emotional extremes of delight and terror seldom seem more pronounced than today.'[50] Meanwhile, an essay by contemporary Gothic novelist Patrick McGrath in the same book asserted that since its origins, 'the Gothic has disturbed and subverted all that is certain, singular, rational, balanced, established. Its *raison d'être* is transgression'.[51]

Twenty-first century Gothic exhibitions, however, set out to make grand statements about the significance of Gothic as a cultural tradition and often traded on the frisson between the popular and the canonical, the sensational and the scholarly. Many of these exhibitions took place at major British cultural institutions, funded by the government's Department for Digital, Culture, Media and Sport, and implicitly framed Gothic as a distinctively British mode that spoke to the nation's cultural identity. In 2006, Tate Britain showed *Gothic Nightmares: Fuseli, Blake and the Romantic Imagination*, an ingenious attempt to reframe its extensive William Blake collections in a new light and, the gallery claimed, 'the first [exhibition] to explore the roots of this phenomenon in the visual arts of the late eighteenth and early nineteenth century'.[52] The Fashion Institute of Technology, New York, curated the first ever exhibition on Gothic and fashion in *Gothic: Dark Glamour* (2008–9), combining *haute couture* with street style – a radical move within fashion studies, which had previously tended to confine its understanding of the term 'Gothic' to its use within subcultures. The British Film Institute held its largest ever festival, *Gothic: The Dark Heart of Film*, from 2013 to 2014, with miniature seasons in arts cinemas across the nation; this season explicitly celebrated the British *penchant* for the horrible, with Christopher Frayling commenting on the 'national talent for horror' in his Foreword to the accompanying compendium of essays.[53] Finally, in 2014–15,

---

[50] Christoph Grunenberg, 'Unsolved Mysteries: Gothic Tales from *Frankenstein* to the Hair-Eating Doll', in Christoph Grunenberg (ed.), *Gothic: Transmutations of Horror in Late Twentieth Century Art* (Cambridge, MA: MIT Press, 1997), pp. 213–158 (p. 211). Pagination runs backwards in this volume.

[51] Patrick McGrath, 'Transgression and Decay', in Grunenberg (ed.), *Gothic*, pp. 159–50 (pp. 158–7). Pagination runs backwards in this volume.

[52] See 'Gothic Nightmares: Fuseli, Blake and the Romantic Imagination', *Tate* <www.tate.org.uk/whats-on/tate-britain/exhibition/gothic-nightmares-fuseli-blake-and-romantic-imagination> (last accessed 21 December 2020).

[53] Frayling, 'Foreword', p. 5. The season featured 150 films in around 1000 screenings across the UK; see Xavier Aldana Reyes, *Gothic Cinema* (London: Routledge, 2020).

the British Library put on what was widely billed as the largest ever exhibition on Gothic and its hitherto most popular, *Terror and Wonder: The Gothic Imagination*. As Dale Townshend wrote in the Introduction to the accompanying volume,

> this exhibition brings to the Gothic an important institutional recognition, celebrating a mode of cultural expression that, at least in its origins, was considered to be more a source of national embarrassment than pride ... the idea that the Gothic imagination could ever merit the commemoration, celebration and display it is receiving in the year 2014 at the British Library was inconceivable 250 years ago.[54]

What is striking about these exhibitions is not only their scale and popularity, with many declaring themselves to be the 'first', 'largest', 'most popular' and so on, but the way in which they assume that this populism can be combined with rigorous scholarly research with no trace of discomfort. *Terror and Wonder* was perhaps the most pronounced version of this. Although it contained such thrilling artefacts as Jack the Ripper's 'Dear Boss' letter, a 1930s vampire-slaying kit and an Alexander McQueen catwalk ensemble, the exhibition was in many ways a love letter to the Gothic reader. In bringing together original copies of all the 'Northanger Novels' identified by Sadleir in 1927, one of the exhibition's central display cases foregrounded generations of readers: Jane Austen, who originally collated the list of novels in *Northanger Abbey* (written 1798–9; published late 1817; dated 1818); her characters Isabella Thorpe and Catherine Morland who read them so avidly, standing in for other eighteenth-century readers as they do so; Sadleir, whose painstaking scholarship rediscovered the works in the 1920s; the curators who have lovingly reassembled them; and contemporary readers who re-encounter them via Austen, Sadleir and the exhibition curators today. There is no longer any need to defend the 'trash with which the press now groans', as Austen satirically put it, as it is taken for granted that the process of reading Gothic fiction itself, and the 'terror and wonder' that it affords, has intrinsic value.[55]

It is thus that Gothic Studies finds itself at a critical impasse. On the one hand, Gothic is more popular in the twenty-first century than at any moment since its heyday in the 1790s. There is more to say about it than ever before,

---

[54] Dale Townshend, 'Terror and Wonder: The Gothic Imagination', in Dale Townshend (ed.), *Terror and Wonder: The Gothic Imagination* (London: The British Library, 2014), pp. 10–37 (pp. 33–4).

[55] Jane Austen, *Northanger Abbey*, edited by John Davie (Oxford: Oxford University Press, 1971), p. 21.

both in terms of the number of objects that are available to analyse and the plethora of theoretical approaches adopted from across the academy. In this sense, it is increasingly rich and vibrant as a discipline. On the other hand, its very popularity undermines the desire for subversion that informs so much twentieth-century Gothic scholarship. Gothic cannot be regarded as anti-bourgeois when the middle classes are queuing up to attend blockbuster exhibitions. As Warwick has observed, moreover, Gothic as a critical discourse has become so all-encompassing that it has started to lose definition. When I began my PhD in 1996 it was still just about possible for a particularly indefatigable scholar to read everything published on Gothic and very easy to read everything on contemporary Gothic; for my current PhD students, this would be an impossible task. As new combinations of Gothic with an endless proliferation of adjectives create a relentlessly expanding field, it becomes more difficult to grasp that field from any one position. The question that Gothic Studies must address in the twenty-first century, then, is whether it has a shared purpose and a unified set of debates, or whether it is satisfied to become increasingly fragmented and localised in its concerns.

The End of Gothic Histories?

Notoriously, Fred Botting ended the 1995 edition of *Gothic* by proclaiming that the postmodern self-referentiality of Francis Ford Coppola's *Bram Stoker's Dracula* (1992) marked 'The End of Gothic'.[56] This was a position that he gracefully revised in the second edition of the book in 2014. It is the task of literary-historical critics to look for epistemological breaks and historical shifts. This book undertakes that task. Gothic in the twentieth and twenty-first centuries often acts as a kind of bellwether, alerting us to incipient trends as it rapidly responds to the zeitgeist. From the advent of new media to emergent aesthetic movements and political ideologies, Gothic absorbs the effluence of modernity into its distinctive aesthetic. It is only with the benefit of hindsight, however, that patterns emerge.

Gothic has become so all-encompassing a term in twenty-first century criticism that principles of inclusion and exclusion for a volume such as this one become a challenge. Put simply, there is just too much Gothic to cover in one volume, however capacious. We have, with one or two brief exceptions, confined ourselves to narrative-based media – literature, film and television – and readers who seek to discover Gothic within other art forms are directed

---

[56] Fred Botting, *Gothic* (London: Routledge, 1995), pp. 177–80.

to David Punter's *The Edinburgh Companion to Gothic and the Arts* (2019). As already noted, this book does not attempt to provide comprehensive international coverage of Gothic either. A book that surveys the vast number of regional and national Gothics is still yet to be written.

The lengthy processes of academic publishing often struggle to keep up with the pace of historical events. We sought to end this book with a cluster of chapters by Marc Olivier, Sara L. Crosby and Simon Marsden addressing the eschatological tendency of twenty-first-century Gothic as it comes to terms with a post-digital world in which environmental catastrophe looms and the apocalyptic imagination finds new outlets. We did not expect to complete the book in the middle of a global pandemic, a context that inevitably adds an additional salience to these topics. The Gothic has provided a language for talking about contagion and disease in texts as temporally diverse as Mary Shelley's *The Last Man* (1826), Edgar Allan Poe's 'The Masque of the Red Death' (1842), F. W. Murnau's *Nosferatu* (1922), Richard Matheson's *I am Legend* (1954) and Justin Cronin's *The Passage* (2010). Ardel Haefele-Thomas picks up this theme in their chapter on the AIDS epidemic and it is also acknowledged by Marsden in his chapter on the apocalyptic imagination.

It is a platitude to state that the advent of the novel coronavirus known as COVID-19 will create profound shifts in world economies, distribution networks, social relationships and lifestyles. If it seems likely that the Gothic will provide a language and a cultural imaginary with which to address the pandemic itself, the effect of these future shifts is still unknown. Gothic, it is widely acknowledged, is the product of modernity, intimately bound up with the way in which a culture progressing to an uncertain future regards its own past. But what happens *after* modernity? Critics nosing around for an epistemological break in years to come may well find one here.

3.1
Gothic and Silent Cinema

STACEY ABBOTT AND SIMON BROWN

Made in 1930 in a period of transition between silent and sound film, Carl Theodor Dreyer's *Vampyr: The Strange Adventure of Allan Gray* (1932) is arguably the silent cinema's last great Gothic masterpiece. It establishes its Gothic credentials from its opening titles, crediting the film as being 'freely adapted from the book *In a Glass Darkly* by J. Sheridan Le Fanu', and clearly associating it with Gothic literary traditions. The very first intertitle draws upon Gothic language as it describes the unfolding narrative as representing the 'fantasy-experience of young Allan Gray, who engulfed himself in studies of demonology and vampire-lore. Preoccupation with the crazed ideas of past centuries turned him into a dreamer and a fantasist, lost on the border between reality and the supernatural'. This reference to demons, vampires, to being haunted by the past and existing in the nether world between reality and the supernatural draws upon many traditional Gothic themes. The film also uses its visuals to set a Gothic tone. Intertitles are printed over the graphic design of an elaborate cobweb, while the *mise-en-scène* is dressed with signs, paintings and sculptures that feature angels, skeletons and skulls. There is even an overt allusion to Death in the form of a man carrying a scythe to the edge of a river and ringing a bell to call the ferry to the shore. Through these images it is clear that Gray has entered a Gothic landscape, not just the netherworld between reality and the supernatural but between the living and the dead, populated by characters who, as Thomas Milne suggests, have a 'wraithlike, dislocated presence as though they had stepped out of a nightmare'.[1]

What lends the film its distinctive and unsettling Gothic atmosphere, however, is not solely the plot nor the choices of *memento mori* that litter the *mise-en-scène*, but rather the intrinsic uncanniness of the cinematographic

---

[1] Thomas Milne, *Vampyr*, reprinted in Accompanying Booklet to *Vampyr* DVD (Eureka, 2008), pp. 44–56 (p. 53).

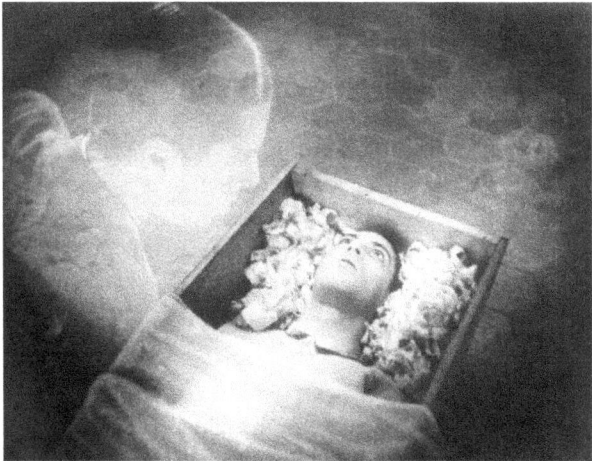

Fig.1.1: Still from *Vampyr*, directed by Carl Theodor Dreyer. Screenplay written by Christen Jul and Carl Theodor Dreyer. Germany 1931/1932. (Photo by ullstein bild/ullstein bild via Getty Images). Ullstein bild Dtl.

(Fig. 1.1). While we have described *Vampyr* as the last Gothic masterpiece of the silent era, it is in fact not silent but rather a hybrid of sound and silent cinema that calls attention to the mechanics of its production. It was shot as a silent film with selective synchronised sound added later, and this disjunction between sound and image destabilises notions of verisimilitude as both silence and sound are rendered uncanny through their combination, with the result that the dream-like realm into which Gray, and the audience, enter is both like and unlike the real world. Moreover, in the same way that the narrative world exists somewhere between reality and a form of Gothic expressionism, the film also hovers between the conventions of silent and sound cinema, being neither one nor the other, while at the same time bearing aspects of both. As such the film's haunted landscape is conveyed through the uncanny language of cinema itself. As Gray explores the Inn and the surrounding estates, trying to make sense of the strange events that he has witnessed, Dreyer follows him through a series of extended long takes. Dreyer's circular pans and roving dolly shots seem at times to both shadow Gray and to convey his point of view, while at others they are more autonomous, exploring the space independently. In each case, however, the camera movements suggest a ghostly presence. Furthermore, the images are often deliberately murky or cloudy in such a way as to call attention to the film stock, such as when the vampire Marguerite Chopin feeds off her primary victim Leone in a nearby meadow. As the vampire looks up towards the camera, it is as if she is peering through the grain of the film. David Rudkin describes these shots as 'hazy', as having 'a quality of being drained of light', and this visual texture is further enhanced by the repeated use of flickering luminescence and candles.[2]

Most significantly, the film is filled with the optical trickery that is a distinct uncanny feature of the photographic nature of the medium. As Gray searches through the estate he follows a series of disembodied shadows that flit across the screen, seemingly detached, like Dreyer's camera, from their human host. These and other shadows continue to appear and disappear, haunting the landscape throughout the film. Later Gray falls asleep and, through the use of double exposure, a ghostly translucent version of himself separates from his body and continues to explore his surroundings. At the film's climax, an extreme close-up of the ghostly visage of the deceased father of Leone appears, superimposed over the frame of a window, dissolving in and out as lightning flashes across the screen, signalling his anger and desire for revenge on those who murdered him and threatened his family. These rich visual textures are rendered all the more uncanny by the disjuncture between silent imagery and the occasional use of synchronised sound effects and dialogue, rendering these spaces as both familiar and unfamiliar, every day and dream-like.

Vampyr therefore does not simply *present* a Gothic landscape but rather invites the audience *into* a Gothic landscape, recognising and utilising the fact that film exists on the border between reality and the supernatural. The effect of watching *Vampyr* is to be invited into a Gothic dream, blurring the boundaries between reality and fantasy, but it is not necessarily the presence of ghosts and vampires that is Gothic but rather the language of cinema, galvanising an inherent synergy that exists between film and the Gothic. It is because of this that *Vampyr*, coming at the end of the silent era, is a crucial starting point to understanding the relationship between the Gothic and silent film, one that dates back to the invention of cinema, and yet is a film that is often overlooked. At its birth, the cinema itself was perceived as inherently Gothic, yet most studies of Gothic film assert that by the time that *Vampyr* was released the Gothic's place in cinema was not as a part of the medium itself, but rather as a series of narrative tropes within an enclosed story world. This is not surprising. *Vampyr* was released the year after Tod Browning's *Dracula* (1931) and James Whale's *Frankenstein* (1931) sparked the birth of what David J. Skal has referred to as Hollywood Gothic and what

---

[2] David Rudkin, *Vampyr* (London: BFI Publishing, 2005), p. 53.

Gary Rhodes, Alison Peirse and Kendall Phillips mark as the starting point for the American cinematic horror genre.[3] By focusing upon the advent of the horror film in the early sound era, scholars such as Phillips, Rhodes and Johnathan Rigby tend to present the Gothic in the era of silent cinema as a steady progression towards the birth of the horror genre by examining key early films that specifically draw upon and include Gothic elements within their narratives as a prelude to Browning's and Whale's respective masterpieces.[4] Yet, with its focus on the uncanny nature of cinema itself, *Vampyr* marks the end not just of a period in cinema history that, to all intents and purposes, has taken on the mantle of pre-horror, but, more importantly, one in which the Gothic and cinema negotiated their nineteenth-century heritage as uncanny spectacle alongside an increasingly narrativised form of cinema. The aim of this chapter is, therefore, to reassess the relationship between the Gothic and the cinematic experience within the silent cinema era, focusing not upon story elements but rather upon the ongoing association between the Gothic and the cinematographic through the use of cinematic techniques to convey subjective states of being. In doing so, this chapter will examine how the Gothic potential of the cinematic experience that was so fundamental to the era of cinema's birth did not disappear but rather remained, and continues to remain, embedded within cinema itself.

Early Cinema and the Gothic

In discussing the place of the Gothic within early and silent cinema, many scholars have used Maxim Gorky's now-infamous description of seeing the Lumière Brothers' film show at the Nizhni-Novgorod Fair in 1896 as spending an evening 'in the Kingdom of Shadows' to draw parallels between the new medium of film and the Gothic.[5] Stacey Abbott notes that Gorky's comments

---

[3] David J. Skal, *Hollywood Gothic: The Tangled Web of Dracula from Novel to Stage to Screen* (New York and London: W.W. Norton & Company, 1990); Gary D. Rhodes, *Tod Browning's Dracula* (Sheffield: Tomahawk Press, 2014); Alison Peirse, *After Dracula: The 1930s Horror Film* (London and New York: I. B. Tauris, 2013); and Kendall Phillips, *A Place of Darkness: The Rhetoric of Horror in Early American Cinema* (Austin, TX: University of Texas Press, 2018).

[4] Phillips, *A Place of Darkness*; Rhodes, *Tod Browning's Dracula*; Jonathan Rigby, *English Gothic: A Century of Horror Cinema*, 2nd edition (London: Reynolds and Hearn Ltd, 2002); and Jonathan Rigby, *American Gothic: Sixty Years of Horror Cinema* (London: Reynolds and Hearn Ltd, 2007).

[5] Stacey Abbott, 'Spectral Vampires: *Nosferatu* in the Light of New Technology', in Stefan Hantke (ed.), *Horror Film: Creating and Marketing Fear* (Jackson: University of Mississippi Press, 2004), pp. 3–20; Murray Leeder, 'Introduction', in Murray Leeder (ed.), *Cinematic Ghosts: Haunting and Spectrality from Silent Cinema to the Digital Era* (New York,

signal how this new technological medium 'was perceived as being inherently ghostly in its representation of the world', while Murray Leeder similarly comments that 'Gorky did not need ghostly subject matter to perceive cinema as a supernatural medium'.[6] This reading of Gorky through the Gothic is consistent with Gorky's own account of his reaction, which is rich in Gothic imagery. His description of people 'frozen into immobility' before 'a strange flicker passes through the screen and the picture stirs to life' has echoes of the moment in Mary Shelley's novel when Frankenstein completes his attempts to 'infuse a spark into the lifeless thing' he has created when 'a convulsive motion agitated its limbs'.[7] Yet, just as Frankenstein finds that at his moment of triumph 'the beauty of the dream vanished and breathless horror and disgust filled my heart', Gorky finds horror in these flickering images of people for 'their smiles are lifeless, even though their movements are full of living energy ... their laughter is soundless ... Before you a life is surging ... the grey, the soundless, the bleak and dismal life'.[8] Gorky's distaste for images 'dipped in monochrome ... grey rays of sun across a grey sky, grey eyes in grey faces ... the ashen grey-foliage of the trees' and for the lack of accompanying sound not only seems to suggest a Gothic world glimpsed through a thick moorland mist (an idea echoed in the opening of *Vampyr*) but also a spirit world filled with ghosts, glimpsed in a beam of light that momentarily pierces the veil.[9] He says of two men playing cards that 'it seems as if these people have died and their shadows have been condemned to play cards in silence unto eternity'.[10] In this he echoes Jean Badreaux, a French journalist, who argued that film would 'bring those who are no longer in this world back to life', thus fulfilling Frankenstein's promise that 'science has triumphed over death'.[11] The effect on Gorky was decidedly uncanny, and ultimately he found that 'the mute, grey life finally begins to disturb and distress you. It seems as though it carries

---

London, New Delhi and Sydney: Bloomsbury, 2015), pp. 1–14; Kendall Phillips, *A Place of Darkness*; and Lynda Nead, *The Haunted Gallery: Painting, Photography, Film, c.1900* (London: Yale University Press, 2007).

[6] Abbott, 'Spectral Vampires', p. 11; Leeder, 'Introduction', p. 6.
[7] Maxim Gorky, 'Last Night I was in the Kingdom of Shadows', reprinted in Colin Harding and Simon Popple (eds), *In the Kingdom of Shadows: A Companion to Early Cinema* (London: Cygnus Arts, 1996), pp. 5–6 (p. 5); Mary Shelley, *Frankenstein: The 1818 Text*, edited by Marilyn Butler (Oxford: Oxford University Press, 2008), pp. 38–9.
[8] Shelley, *Frankenstein* (2008), p. 39; Gorky, 'Last Night I Was in the Kingdom of Shadows', p. 5.
[9] Gorky, 'Kingdom of Shadows', p. 5.   [10] Gorky, 'Kingdom of Shadows', p. 5.
[11] Quoted in Phillips, *A Place of Darkness*, p. 26.

a warning, fraught with a vague but sinister meaning that makes your heart grow faint'.[12]

Lifeless figures that burst into terrible motion, soundless ghosts captured in moments that they are condemned to repeat for eternity, and an overall effect that is both disturbing and sinister all equate in the most fundamental way to the Gothic. As Fred Botting points out, Gothic texts are 'alienating and full of menace' and offer an uncanny space that 'disturbs the familiar, homely and secure sense of reality and normality'.[13] The effect of the Gothic on its readers, Botting argues, is emotional rather than rational, 'exciting rather than informing, it chilled their blood', much as the Lumière films did for Gorky, and blurring the boundaries between reality and fantasy, just as the monochrome, silent images that Gorky saw rendered an uncanny double of the real world captured by the Cinématographe.[14] Lynda Nead goes further and suggests that 'each time the projector is set in motion … figures … step out of their frames and come to life … It was an invitation to a séance in which the medium – in every sense of the word – was film'.[15] What Nead articulates here is precisely what Gorky was suggesting, namely that in the early moments of cinema's birth the apparatus and the experience of film was inherently Gothic.

This connection between the Gothic and the cinema draws upon a synergy between the photographic and the supernatural or spiritual that pre-dates the cinema and has repeatedly manifested in literature and popular media in the nineteenth century. For instance, it underpins the Phantasmagoria as a form of late-eighteenth century optical entertainment, popularised by Etienne-Gaspard Robertson. The Phantasmagoria was a form of magic lantern performance in which ghostly images of the dead would be projected onto a screen and made to appear, disappear, transform and move toward the audience through the manipulation of the slides. As Laurent Mannoni explains, the name Phantasmagoria was 'derived from the Greek *phantasm*, "ghost" … and *agoreuo*, "I speak"; an etymology which suggests a dialogue between the audience and the ghost called up by the magic lantern'.[16] As such, the equation of an optical entertainment with a spiritualist medium pre-dates Nead's similar commentary on early cinema. The Phantasmagoria was in fact advertised in May 1802 in the *Hull Advertiser and Exchange Gazette* as

---

[12] Gorky, 'Kingdom of Shadows', p. 6.
[13] Fred Botting, *Gothic* (London and New York: Routledge, 1996), pp. 2, 11.
[14] Botting, *Gothic*, p. 4.   [15] Nead, *The Haunted Gallery*, p. 1.
[16] Laurent Mannoni, *The Great Art of Light and Shadow: Archaeology of the Cinema* (Exeter: Exeter University Press, 2000), p. 136.

a form of projection technology that offered an encounter with 'PHANTOMS or APPARITIONS of the DEAD or ABSENT, in a way more completely illusive than has ever been offered to the eye in a public Theatre'.[17] Charles Dickens, an experienced showman who was well aware of the spectral properties and potential of the Phantasmagoria and other magic lantern projection systems, drew upon these properties to convey a singularly magical encounter in *The Pickwick Papers* (1836) when he told the story of how Goblins attempted to educate the miserable village sexton, Gabriel Grub, by presenting him with a series of moving pictures of human suffering. The potential of the magic lantern was subsequently fulfilled in the 1880s, when this chapter from *The Pickwick Papers* was adapted for an actual magic lantern slide show entitled *Gabriel Grub; or, The Goblins Who Stole a Sexton* (1880s–1910), bringing Dickens's relationship with the Phantasmagoria full circle.[18] While Mannoni notes that the Phantasmagoria regularly featured Gothic topics drawn from literature and mythology, including *Three Witches of Macbeth*, *The Head of the Medusa* and *The Bleeding Nun*, it was the animation and mobility of the images, 'appearing to rush toward a terrified audience who were certainly not used to such an assault of images', that fuelled the spectacle of the medium.[19]

Paul Forster similarly recognises the connection between the Gothic and the cinematic, though here through the examination of Gothic literature, arguing that 'there was something cinematic about the late-Victorian Gothic revival', noting the recurring inclusion of proto-filmic elements within the Gothic fiction of Robert Louis Stevenson, H. G. Wells, Bram Stoker and Oscar Wilde. For instance, Forster, quoting Laura Marcus, notes how 'later *fin-de-siècle* texts like H. G. Wells's *The Time Machine* (1895) suggest "the direct influence of early cinema, in particular its play with velocity and with reverse motion"'.[20] Similarly, in Bram Stoker's *Dracula* (1897), Jonathan Harker uses the language of optical illusion to explain the strange things that he sees while in Transylvania. He describes the seeming translucence of the coach driver

---

[17] Anon., 'Winged Skulls and hot air balloons: The grave of Étienne-Gaspard Robert, pioneer of phantasmagoria', *Flickering Lamps* (3 July 2016) <https://flickeringlamps.com/2016/07/03/winged-skulls-and-hot-air-balloons-the-grave-of-etienne-gaspard-robert-pioneer-of-phantasmagoria/> (last accessed 30 August 2018).

[18] The slides for *Gabriel Grub – or, The Goblins who Stole a Sexton* are included on the *Dickens Before Sound* DVD collection produced by the British Film Institute 2011.

[19] Mannoni, *The Great Art*, pp. 162–3, 136.

[20] Paul Foster, 'Kingdom of Shadows: *Fin-de-siècle* Gothic and Early Cinema', in Fred Botting and Catherine Spooner (eds), *Monstrous Media / Spectral Subjects: Imaging Gothic from the Nineteenth Century to the Present* (Manchester: Manchester University Press, 2015), pp. 29–41 (p. 32).

taking him to Castle Dracula as an 'optical effect'; he later tries to explain Dracula's uncanny ability to crawl down the wall as a 'trick of the moonlight' or a weird 'effect of shadow'.[21] Finally, he describes Dracula's vampire brides' literal disappearance, after they have attempted to seduce him, as a 'fade' into the rays of the moonlight.[22] Effects, tricks, shadows, fades are all terms that apply to the optical entertainments such as the magic lantern and Phantasmagoria that would inform the development of cinematic language at precisely the time of *Dracula*'s publication.

Scholars writing about early cinema have continued to focus on this synergy, trying to make sense of early cinema through its relationship to nineteenth-century precursors in the form of painting, photography, magic lantern performances and other optical illusions. Lynda Nead's discussion of the 'haunted gallery' positions early cinema alongside painting and photography as a means of exploring how 'the transformation from stasis to movement and the varieties and velocities of motion possessed all forms of visual media, from high art and art criticism, to still photography and magic lantern slides, popular optical toys and projected film'.[23] Tom Gunning relates his discussion of early trick films to the perception of nineteenth-century photography 'as an uncanny phenomenon, one which seemed to undermine the unique identity of objects and people, endlessly reproducing the appearances of objects, creating a parallel world of phantasmatic doubles alongside the concrete world of the senses verified by positivism'.[24] Stacey Abbott explores the spectral nature of early cinema and how the language of spectrality that haunts it is drawn from the nineteenth century, and the extent to which it informs developments within cinema language and special effects.[25] Whether describing Gothic literature as 'proto-filmic' or early cinema as 'haunted', 'uncanny' or 'spectral', these scholars collectively recognise that there is something inherently Gothic about the medium of film.

Yet, as noted above, moving beyond the first moments of cinema, the exploration of the connection between cinema and the Gothic tends to turn away from the cinematographic and look instead to narrative, charting not the ongoing relationship between the Gothic and the technology and materiality of cinema, but rather the appearance of Gothic tropes within the filmic

---

[21] Bram Stoker, *Dracula*, edited by Roger Luckhurst (Oxford: Oxford University Press, 2011), pp. 16, 35.
[22] Stoker, *Dracula* (2011), p. 40.   [23] Nead, *The Haunted Gallery*, p. 1.
[24] Tom Gunning, 'Phantom Images and Modern Manifestations: Spirit Photography, Magic Theater, Trick Films, and Photography's Uncanny', in Leeder (ed.), *Cinematic Ghosts*, pp. 17–38 (p. 18).
[25] Abbott, 'Spectral Vampires'.

text. Whereas, as Leeder notes, the Lumière Brothers' films seen by Gorky contain no specific Gothic elements but are, instead, recordings of everyday scenes where the apparatus itself provides the uncanny Gothic twist, the next step for Gothic scholarship has been to examine key early films that specifically draw upon and include Gothic elements within their narratives.[26] Tying the Gothic into early cinema's fascination with 'sensation', Ian Christie, for example, highlights how pioneer filmmakers 'instinctively turned' to Gothic elements. 'Consider', Christie argues, 'the typical Méliès settings of castle, laboratory and magic theatre stage, or those of Robert Paul's trick films of 1901, *The Haunted Curiosity Shop*, *The Magic Sword* and *Scrooge, or Marley's Ghost*, which span the locations associated with the Gothic.'[27] Christie's position is that the emphasis in these films on so-called 'trick' effects, in which the camera was stopped and elements substituted, or double exposures were used to present ghost-like figures, was a natural confluence of cinema's ability to present the impossible and the popular desire for sensationalism and novelty that drove the *fin-de-siècle* Gothic revival, which 'combined to produce a lively neo-Gothic of the supernatural'.[28]

Such a confluence of trick effects and Gothic imagery was a step in the gradual narrativisation of the Gothic, first combining the inherent 'Gothic-ness' of cinema with narrative elements, and then subsequently transposing them into narrative elements alone. Kendall Phillips, for example, also considers Walter R. Booth's silent horror film *The Haunted Curiosity Shop* (1901), which features among other things a suit of armour that comes alive and a floating head, along with Edison's *Uncle Josh in a Spooky Hotel* (1900), in which a country rube is visited in his hotel room by a mischievous ghost. Phillips is writing about horror in general rather than the Gothic in particular, taking as his starting point the received notion that the horror genre was born in 1931 between the release of Universal's *Dracula* and *Frankenstein*, as the discourse circulating around *Dracula* in the months after its release increasingly adopted the term 'horror' to describe the film.[29] For all that the period between February and November 1931 may mark the start of horror as a cinematic genre, there were, as Phillips argues, a plethora of silent films that used similar tropes to Tod Browning and James Whale's films, and indeed there were early versions of both *Dracula* and *Frankenstein*. 'What about *Frankenstein* in 1910, and *Dr Jekyll and Mr. Hyde* in 1908 (or even

[26] Leeder, 'Introduction', p. 6.
[27] Ian Christie, 'The Visible and the Invisible: From "Tricks" to "Effects"', *Early Popular Visual Culture* 13:2 (2015): 106–112 (p. 107).
[28] Christie, 'The Visible and the Invisible', p. 107. [29] Phillips, *A Place of Darkness*, p. 2.

1920)', asks Phillips.[30] His aim therefore is to consider 'how the elements that would later constitute horror films' – elements which he describes as 'horrific' – 'were treated within these (earlier) films'.[31]

Phillips and Christie encapsulate two key elements of the schism at the heart of discussions of the Gothic and silent cinema. The first is that they embody that sense of a transitioning from the idea of cinema as inherently Gothic towards it acting as a repository for Gothic elements. Such an approach reflects the standard periodisation of pre-sound cinema history between the early period, routinely defined in relation to Tom Gunning's concept of the 'cinema of attractions' and what Gunning defines as 'the cinema of narrative integration', which emerges around 1907 as narrative films begin to rise to prominence, and becomes fully formed in the years immediately preceding the First World War.[32] These two concepts effectively split the development of cinema. The era of attractions was one in which film was exhibitionist in scope, reaching outwards to the audience through direct address and drawing attention to itself as a spectacle and a complete package that included film, audience and apparatus. In contrast, the cinema of narrative integration turned inwards to create a coherent and closed world within the film itself, no longer inviting the audience in through direct address but rather through character development and narrative intrigue. Considered within these two paradigms, it therefore makes sense that, as the open address of the cinema of attractions gave way to the closed world of the integrated narrative, so the Gothic would cease to be an element within the entire cinematic spectacle and would be reassigned instead a role as narrative component.

The second element that Phillips's discussion highlights is the slippage that takes place within discussions of the Gothic on film between the concepts of 'Gothic' and 'horror'. As Phillips notes, 'prior to 1931 . . . there were no horror films. The language of horror had not yet solidified into a definable genre', but his argument is that 'the elements that constitute much of what we call "horror" were already present'.[33] He then goes on to state that the silent era saw 'a surprising number of films released . . . that dealt with elements that would later constitute the horror film: castles, cobwebs, monsters, maniacal killers, magical curses, avenging ghosts and undead creatures'.[34] These are all elements that are associated with the literary Gothic. In his definition of the

---

[30] Phillips, *A Place of Darkness*, p. 5.   [31] Phillips, *A Place of Darkness*, p. 5.
[32] Tom Gunning, 'The Cinema of Attractions: Early Cinema, its Spectator and the Avant-Garde', *Wide Angle* 8:3/4 (1986): 63–70.
[33] Phillips, *A Place of Darkness*, p. 3.   [34] Phillips, *A Place of Darkness*, p. 5.

Gothic, Jonathan Rigby, for example, cites 'dank crypts, rugged landscapes and forbidden castles ... fatal women, vampires, doppelgängers and werewolves'.[35] These elements of the literary Gothic, when transferred to cinema, ultimately become subsumed within the generic concept of the horror film. After 1931, the Gothic becomes an element within the horror genre, much in the same way that Catherine Spooner describes the Gothic in relation to twentieth-century, high-Modernist literature, in which it becomes, 'rather than the determining feature of the texts, one tool among many employed in the service of conjuring up interior terrors'.[36] The result is a conflation of the terms 'Gothic' and 'horror' in relation to film, a state in which the two concepts are often used interchangeably. Jonathan Rigby's survey of British horror films, for example, is entitled *English Gothic: A Century of Horror Cinema*, while his companion piece on America is similarly named *American Gothic: Sixty Years of Horror Cinema*. Equally, Benjamin Hervey opens his discussion of contemporary horror cinema by asking the question, 'What is Gothic?'[37]

Peter Hutchings addresses this issue in his discussion of modern horror cinema, noting that 'it is not uncommon in certain contexts for "Gothic" and "horror" to be used as if they were more or less interchangeable', while at the same time recognising that very often 'the term "Gothic horror" when applied to cinema usually refers to a specific type of horror film, one that has a period setting and which relies for many of its effects upon what might be called here the visual trappings of late eighteenth century and early-nineteenth century Gothic, namely ruined castles, dank dungeons and the like'.[38] Hutchings therefore acknowledges that in horror the Gothic is primarily a narrative or visual element, but also suggests that the difference in cinema between the Gothic and horror is that the horror film is 'best seen as a genre' whereas the Gothic is 'a distinctive mode which influences a wide range of cultural forms'.[39] This idea is extremely useful for approaching the Gothic in relation to silent cinema, an era that, as already stated, pre-dates the emergence of the horror film as an identifiable cinematic genre. While there

---

[35] Rigby, *English Gothic*, p. 11.
[36] Catherine Spooner, 'Gothic in the Twentieth Century', in Catherine Spooner and Emma McEvoy (eds), *The Routledge Companion to Gothic* (London: Routledge, 2007), pp. 38–48 (p. 40).
[37] Benjamin Hervey, 'Contemporary Horror Cinema', in Spooner and McEvoy (eds), *The Routledge Companion to Gothic*, pp. 233–41 (p. 234).
[38] Peter Hutchings, 'Tearing your Soul Apart: Horror's New Monsters', in Victor Sage and Allan Lloyd Smith (eds), *Modern Gothic: A Reader* (Manchester: Manchester University Press, 1996), pp. 89–103 (p. 89).
[39] Hutchings, 'Horror's New Monsters', p. 89.

is no doubt that Universal's *Dracula* and *Frankenstein* both drew upon and cemented the Gothic as an essential element of cinematic horror, acknowledging the Gothic as a significant mode of representation that existed prior to the horror genre allows for an analysis of Gothic influences within silent cinema above and beyond its connections to horror. It opens up the silent era to Gothic analysis, creating a space in which it is possible to consider an alternative path taken by the Gothic from that early period, one in which it retains its role as what Laura Mulvey describes as 'a technological uncanny' and which is primarily associated with the cinematic event itself through the representation of subjective states of being, and which reaches its pinnacle not in the castles of Dracula and Frankenstein, but in the washed-out landscapes of Dreyer's *Vampyr*.[40]

Narrativisation, Respectability, Adaptation and the Gothic

As Tom Gunning has argued, the shift towards narrative integration was primarily a drive towards respectability.[41] The proliferation between 1906 and 1908 of purpose-built cinema venues, the Nickelodeons in America and the Penny Gaffs or Penny Cinemas in the UK, was accompanied on both sides of the Atlantic by a growing moral panic about moving pictures, in a very similar way to that in which Gothic literature was feared to be 'encouraging readers' decline into depravity and corruption'.[42] Nickelodeons and Penny Cinemas were cheap, often makeshift venues aimed at working-class audiences who, like the readers of Gothic fiction, enjoyed a diet of films whose 'plots appeared to celebrate criminal behaviour'.[43] The result was that both the venues and the films shown became subjects of concern to moral pressure groups. As Roberta E. Pearson and William Uricchio note, in America 'film content uncontrolled by private or public interests and ill-regulated dark, crowded potential fire trap storefront moving picture shows frequented by immigrants and the working classes generated intense opposition from religious organisations and other civic activists'.[44] Anxieties about what could

---

[40] Laura Mulvey, *Death at 24x a Second: Stillness and the Moving Image* (London: Reaktion, 2006), p. 27.
[41] Tom Gunning, 'Weaving a Narrative: Style and Economic Background in Griffith's Early Films', in Thomas Elsaesser (ed.), *Early Cinema: Space, Frame, Narrative* (London: BFI, 1990), pp. 336–47.
[42] Botting, *Gothic*, p. 6.   [43] Botting, *Gothic*, p. 6.
[44] Roberta E. Pearson and William Uricchio, 'How Many Times Shall Caesar Bleed in Sport?: Shakespeare and the Cultural Debate about Moving Pictures', in Lee Grieveson

happen to 'respectable' patrons in the Nickelodeon's darkened halls were exacerbated by the content of the films themselves, and the trade press in the US urged producers to raise the tone of their subjects in order to appeal to a more 'refined' class of audience.[45] A similar situation occurred in the UK. In March 1908 the *Daily Telegraph* printed a letter from a vicar complaining about Walter Haggar's *The Life of Charles Peace* (1905). Peace was a burglar and murderer who was executed in 1879, and Haggar's film replayed some of the most infamous moments of Peace's life of crime. Its blend of sensationalism and violence was not uncommon, and led to calls from the Commissioner of Police in 1909 for tighter controls on violent films.[46] Such outcries were not lost on film producers, and the result was self-regulation of content, via the formation in the US in 1909 of the New York Board of Censorship (renamed the National Board of Censorship), and in the UK of the British Board of Film Censors in 1913. In addition to this, legislation in the US and UK resulted in cheaper cinemas being replaced with upmarket venues for middle-class audiences.

For Gunning, this led to changes to film content so that it was 'brought more in line with the traditions of bourgeois representation'.[47] Essential to this was adapting acceptable bourgeois entertainment forms such as the play and the novel in order to entice middle-class audiences into these plusher cinemas. In Britain the result was a flurry of films based on Shakespeare and Dickens, including Will Barker's *Henry VIII* (1911); Cecil Hepworth's *Hamlet* (1913); and Thomas Bentley's *Oliver Twist* (1912) and *David Copperfield* (1913). American producers also turned to Shakespeare, releasing some thirty-six Shakespeare adaptations between 1908 and 1913, alongside other literary classics including *Les Misérables* (dir. J. Stuart Blackton, 1909); *Uncle Tom's Cabin* (dir. Barry O'Neill, 1910); *A Tale of Two Cities* (dir. William J. Humphrey, 1911); and *The Pickwick Papers* (dir. Laurence Trimble, 1913).[48]

Yet, while Barker, Hepworth and others were adapting Dickens and Shakespeare because 'the conception of film as an art like theatre worked to assuage anxiety about cinema by raising its cultural status', in 1910 Thomas

and Peter Krämer (eds), *The Silent Cinema Reader* (London: Routledge, 2004), pp. 155–68 (p. 156).
[45] Gunning, 'Weaving a Narrative', p. 339.
[46] Simon Brown, 'Censorship Under Siege: The BBFC in the Silent Era', in Edward Lambertini (ed.), *Behind the Scenes at the BBFC: Film Classification from the Silent Era to the Silver Screen* (London: BFI Publishing, 2012), pp. 3–14 (p. 4).
[47] Gunning, 'Weaving a Narrative', p. 339.
[48] Pearson and Uricchio, 'How Many Times Shall Caesar Bleed in Sport?', p. 158; Lee Grieveson and Peter Krämer, 'Feature Films and Cinema Programmes', in Grieveson and Krämer (eds), *The Silent Cinema Reader*, pp. 187–95 (p. 188).

Edison's film company released an adaptation of Mary Shelley's *Frankenstein* (1818; 1831) directed by J. Searle Dawley.[49] As Christopher Frayling states, the film's publicity took pains to reassure viewers that the filmmakers had 'tried to eliminate all the actually repulsive situations' in favour of 'the mystic and psychological problems that are to be found in this weird tale'.[50] It also impressed that the film 'was based on an acknowledged classic', thereby borrowing that all-important cultural pedigree, and indeed a subsequent adaptation of Edgar Allan Poe's *The Raven* (1912) was sold as 'an American classic'.[51] Thus, in the rush to adaptation and the borrowed prestige that accompanied it, high-cultural titans like Shakespeare and Dickens brought with them in their wake film versions of texts whose credentials were less associated with high art directly but rather with the higher end of popular literature, which encompassed a number of adaptations of *fin-de-siècle* Gothic stories, including Marie Corelli's 1895 novel *The Sorrows of Satan* (dir. Alexander Butler, 1917); Richard Marsh's *The Beetle* from 1897 (dir. Alexander Butler, 1919); Robert Louis Stevenson's *Strange Case of Dr Jekyll and Mr Hyde* (dir. Herbert Brenon, 1913); and Oscar Wilde's *The Picture of Dorian Gray* in 1915 (dir. Eugene Moore).

Gunning argues that while literary adaptations imported middle-class respectability and audiences to the film industry, the consequence was the development of new techniques of film language such as parallel editing, which were required in order to convey more complex storylines.[52] However, a further outcome was the rise to dominance of bourgeois forms in the shape of narrative cinema, wherein the tropes of the cinema of attractions became subsumed to the primacy of story. This, alongside a process of familiarisation as audiences became used to cinema, hastened the transition of the Gothic nature of the cinematic experience and apparatus into primarily a narrative element, contributing to the notion that cinema in the silent era became a repository for Gothic imagery. And yet, just as Gunning argues that the cinema of attractions did not disappear with the advent of narrative cinema but rather went 'underground both into certain avant-garde practices and as a component of narrative films', so too does the Gothic nature of the cinema itself continue in the silent and early sound era prior to the formation of horror.[53] The Gothic in silent film is not solely, as

---

[49] Grieveson and Krämer, 'Feature Films and Cinema Programmes', p. 188.
[50] Christopher Frayling, *Frankenstein: The First Two Hundred Years* (London: Reel Art Press, 2017), p. 99.
[51] Frayling, *Frankenstein*, p. 99.   [52] Gunning, 'Weaving a Narrative', pp. 336–47.
[53] Tom Gunning, 'The Cinema of Attractions', p. 64.

Phillips or Rhodes suggest, a narrative element waiting for the horror genre to be formed. Just as the cinema of attractions erupts into narrative cinema through moments of spectacle and special effects, the silent era also sees a perpetuation of the technological uncanny that so offended Gorky in 1896.

Cinematic Experimentation and Technological Uncanny

If the transition to the bourgeois forms of narrative cinema and literary adaptation saw cinema move away from most exhibitionist forms that extolled the wonders – and horrors – of the medium, filmmakers continued throughout the silent era to experiment with form and technology to develop a cinematic language, one that was distinct from literature, theatre and photography. Much of this experimentation, particularly around sound and colour, was part of a move towards increasing verisimilitude, but there was also a move to develop expressive forms able to communicate emotion and subjective experience, thus creating a space for the Gothic uncanny of cinema to continue to emerge. The inclusion of colour sequences in Rupert Julian's *The Phantom of the Opera* (1925), for example, serves both purposes. The use of two-strip Technicolor in the masquerade ball offers a moment of spectacle and splendour, adding to the film's standing as a prestige production for Universal studios. Narratively, when the Phantom arrives dressed as the Red Death, the colour process serves to make him stand out, bedecked in crimson robes, thus allowing for a dramatic entrance, but it also enables him to walk among the crowd, all of whom are masked and splendidly dressed in red and green. In utilising the Technicolor process, this represents a moment of spectacle, since Technicolor was relatively new in the mid-1920s. However, it also strives towards a degree of verisimilitude, because Technicolor, even in its limited two-colour form rather than the three-strip format that followed it, represented one of the most commercially successful attempts to introduce indexical rather than interpretive colour to the screen, something that would not become fully normalised until the introduction of Eastmancolor in the 1950s and 1960s. In the subsequent sequence, when the ingénue Christine and her lover Raoul escape to the roof of the opera house, the experiment with colour serves a more expressive, Gothic purpose. In this scene, the film switches from Technicolor to blue tinting in the close-ups of the lovers, a standard technique for night-time scenes. These tinted shots are, however, intercut with long shots of the Phantom looming over the couple as he straddles the statue above their heads with his bright red robes blowing in the wind. This effect is achieved through the Handschiegl Color Process, which allowed for one element of an image to be coloured in, thus negating verisimilitude and emphasising effect. Here, the contrast between the red robes and the blue tinting heightens the Gothic impact of the scene and presents the Phantom as a threatening figure of death.

Alongside such affective experiments were other cinematic movements in this era that sought to galvanise the expressive potential of film language, developing techniques not only to tell those seamless character-oriented narratives that were emerging in Hollywood, but also to communicate mental states and the subjective experience of the world. In so doing they were tapping into a notable preoccupation of the Gothic. As Linda Bayer-Berenbaum explains, the Gothic has a long history of portraying 'all states of mind that intensify normal thought or perception. Dream states, drug states, and states of intoxication have always been prevalent in the Gothic novel because repressed thoughts can surface in them.'[54] In portraying these states of mind, the Gothic invites the reader into this subjective experience brought to life through expressive language, 'produc[ing] emotional effects on its readers rather than developing a rational or properly cultivated response'.[55] Cinema equally possesses a fascination with representing interiority. In early cinema, and in line with the previous discussion of the cinema of attractions, these vision states were presented as a spectacle of technology such as in *The Little Match Seller* (dir. James Williamson, 1902), based on a story by Hans Christian Andersen. In this film a young girl freezes to death while trying to sell her wares on a wintry night just before Christmas. As she succumbs to the cold, she lights matches to keep warm, and each time she does so she has a vision. The visions – a warm fireplace, a turkey dinner and a welcoming mother – are presented as image bubbles above her head, achieved through their superimposition on a black wall. While the story is moving, the visions are spectacle rather than immersive, and their subjective status is questioned in the film's final moments, where after her death the seller is visited by an angel, presented in the same way. Four years later Edwin S. Porter's *Dream of a Rarebit Fiend* (1906), loosely based on the comic strips by Winsor McCay, would use similar techniques of double exposure to attempt a more subjective viewpoint of a man suffering from the after-effects of eating too much melted cheese, but while the film sought to represent the experience of

---

[54] Linda Bayer-Berenbaum, *The Gothic Imagination: Expansion in Gothic Literature and Art* (London and Toronto: Associated University Press, 1982), p. 25.
[55] Botting, *Gothic*, p. 4.

a dream-like state, it is nevertheless most notable for its avalanche of special effects which constitute, rather than support, the narrative.[56]

In the later silent era, various film productions and art movements sought to build upon these special effects to transcend the spectacle of vision states to convey a visceral subjectivity, which like the Gothic, immersed the audience within an emotional experience. German Expressionism, for instance, was interested in projecting inner turmoil outwards as conveyed through *mise-en-scène* and cinematographic techniques, while the German *Kammerspielfilm* sought to do away with intertitles and communicate the narrative entirely visually, immersing the audience within a highly subjective narrative. Paul Leni explains that in filming *Waxworks* (1924), 'it is not extreme reality that the camera perceives, but the reality of the inner event, which is more profound, effective and moving than what we see through every day eyes, and I equally believe that the camera can reproduce this truth, heightened effectively'.[57] The French Impressionists similarly sought 'truth' and recognised the ability for film to communicate the subjective, seeing, according to Monica Dall'Asta, 'film as the revelation of an otherwise imperceptible reality ... Such was the "miracle" of cinema: suddenly one could apprehend aspects and dimensions of life that the human eye had never seen before and that remained beyond the grasp of ordinary perception'.[58] It is in this search for an internal truth or subjectivity that the Gothic both emerges through, and merges with, the language of cinema.

The pursuit of the 'truth' led to experimentation with the communication of the subjective experience through dreamscapes, delirium, fantasy, passion and horror, achieved not just through optical trickery but a visceral cinematography. These experiments often take the form of momentary interruptions of narrative for Gothic flourishes in films that would otherwise be categorised as melodramas. F. W. Murnau's *Schloss Vogelöd* [*The Haunted Castle*] (1921) – a story of guilt and suspicion – features a dream sequence in which a guest at the mansion has a vision of a hairy Wolf Man-like hand scratching at the window before pushing it open, reaching in and pulling him out. The sequence twice uses a dissolve to a medium shot of the man in the

---

[56] See Charles Musser, *Before the Nickelodeon: Edwin S. Porter and the Edison Manufacturing Company* (Berkeley, CA: University of California Press, 1991), pp. 340–2.

[57] Quoted in Lotte H. Eisner, *The Haunted Screen: Expressionism in the German Cinema and the Influence of Max Reinhardt*, trans Roger Grieves (Berkeley and Los Angeles: University of California Press, 1977), p. 127.

[58] Monica Dall'Asta, 'DEBATES: Thinking About Cinema: First Waves', in Michael Temple and Michael Witt (eds), *The French Cinema Book* (London: BFI Publishing, 2004), pp. 82–90 (p. 85).

bed to signal the entry and departure from the dreamscape, while a match on action between the long shot of the arm stretching into the room and the close-up of it reaching for the man suggests that the arm is abnormally long and inhuman, a factor that is reinforced by the large shadow that spreads over the wall as the arm approaches. These formal elements would be further developed in Murnau's most famous Gothic film, *Nosferatu* (1922), and later alluded to in Francis Ford Coppola's *Bram's Stoker Dracula* (1992).[59] Similarly, in *Phantom* (dir. Murnau, 1922), a poet's descent into romantic and sexual obsession is conveyed through a selection of optical tricks to signal that, like Allan Gray in *Vampyr*, he is lost, not on the border between reality and the supernatural but between fantasy and madness. As the protagonist loses his grip on reality and becomes increasingly consumed by his obsession, he walks out onto his village street to find the buildings seemingly tilting forward as if to collapse on him and smother him, an effect achieved through double exposure. In the next shot, the shadows of the buildings seem to pursue him along the cobblestones. Later, Murnau spins the camera 360 degrees in an early form of 'unchained camera' to capture the protagonist's hallucinatory experiences.[60] This is a delirious film that offers a subjective experience of the protagonist's reverie. Similarly, E. A. Dupont's *Varieté* (1925) repeatedly uses dynamic and visceral camera movements to convey subjectivity. This subjectivity is at first linked to spectacle and the carnivalesque by presenting the visceral experience of being on the trapeze as the camera swings through the air, positioned from the point of view of the trapeze artists. This carnivalesque cinematography blurs into an expression of passion, anger and violence as conveyed through the unchained movements of the camera, such as a 360-degree swish pan to convey the protagonist Boss Huller's overwhelming anger and horror at the discovery that his lover has been cheating on him with his partner. Later, Dupont features a shot in which the camera seemingly plummets from the trapeze to the crowd below, as Huller fantasises about dropping his partner in the middle of their act. The film also uses kaleidoscopic effects and blurred focus to convey Huller becoming overwhelmed by anger and jealousy.

---

[59] See Abbott, 'Spectral Vampires'. Francis Ford Coppola's *Bram Stoker's Dracula* includes a nod to the uncanniness of this sequence when Dracula's coach arrives at the Borgo Pass to pick up Jonathan Harker. As the driver reaches out to Harker the camera tracks into a close-up of him as the hand extends into the frame, grabs him and pulls him into the coach.

[60] Eisner, *The Haunted Screen*, p. 191.

In contrast, Jean Epstein merges this visceral cinematography with frenetic montage to convey internalised trauma and fear in *Coeur Fidèle* (1923). In this film, the heroine Marie has been given away to the criminal Petit Paul by her adopted parents. Forced into this relationship and unable to escape, Marie feels trapped and helpless and this is conveyed in the scene where Petit Paul takes her to a fairground and they ride the carousel. The sequence cuts between a fixed-camera medium shot of Marie and Petit Paul, as the background swirls by, with subjective shots of the crowd taken from their perspective on the spinning carousel. While Petit Paul is exuberantly laughing and enjoying the ride, Marie stares blankly, showing no emotion. But as the scene progresses, Epstein begins to cut in a flurry of close-ups of the crowd in a frenetic montage that, with its juxtaposition with the swishing camera movements, signals the unspoken hysteria that is building within Marie, particularly as Petit Paul tries to kiss her.

In *La chute de la maison Usher* [*The Fall of the House of Usher*] (1928), Epstein brings all of his techniques to bear to infuse the established Gothic melodrama by Edgar Allan Poe with what Ian Christie describes as a 'modern uncanny') (Fig. 1.2).[61] A clear precursor to Dreyer's *Vampyr*, Epstein's film possesses a delirious atmosphere of reverie, hallucination and nightmare achieved through the film's 'ostentatious filmic devices, such as swirling camera, rapid editing, slow motion [and] extreme close-ups'.[62] The film marks a fusion of the technological uncanny with the narratively Gothic. The story is replete with Gothic motifs, including a decaying mansion, cavernous empty halls and corridors, billowing curtains, isolation, mist, tombs, physical and spiritual degeneracy and premature burial. These familiar tropes are reinvigorated cinematically through Epstein's visual style. For instance, the arrival of the narrator at the Inn that opens the film is rendered uncanny by the inexplicably slow pace of the patrons' reactions to the new arrival and his request for transport to the House of Usher. This creates a subjective mood that gives the impression of the traveller arriving at a place of strangeness and dislocation. This mood is maintained throughout the film. The lethargy of Roderick and Madeline Usher is conveyed through the film's subtle use of slow motion, while Roderick's obsession with his painting of her is captured via frenetic editing and the use of double and triple exposure that reinforces the sense that the painting is somehow draining her of life. The similarity between the opening of *La chute de la maison Usher* and *Vampyr*, and

---

[61] Christie, 'The Visible and the Invisible', p. 61.
[62] Christie, 'The Visible and the Invisible', p. 61.

Fig.1.2: Actress Marguerite Gance as Madeleine Usher and actor Jean Debucourt as Sir Roderick Usher in the 1928 silent French film *La chute de la maison Usher*. (*The Fall of the House of Usher*). (John Springer Collection/CORBIS/Corbis via Getty Images).

the comparable ways in which they create an overall sense of the uncanny, demonstrates that the two films are clearly connected. Epstein's film was made towards the end of the silent era, while Dreyer's film marks a transition to sound, but together they are representative of the cumulative move towards immersing the audience within a visceral experience of subjective states that is the hallmark of the silent Gothic.

Conclusion

Dreyer's *Vampyr* marks two key moments of transition, first between silent and sound cinema, but second, and more importantly, between the silent cinematic Gothic that it represents, and the sound horror genre that began with the contemporaneous releases of *Dracula* and *Frankenstein*. If Gorky's experience of seeing the first films projected as part of the Lumière Cinematograph performance in 1895 was Gothic, then the selection of films that we have discussed in this chapter demonstrates how technological developments and experiments in film language in the silent era continued to capture a similar uncanny experience. The examples presented here are not intended to be exhaustive but rather indicative of a continued preoccupation with, and evolution of, the technological uncanny throughout the silent era. They represent a parallel history of the cinematic Gothic, one that remained concerned with the Gothic nature of the experience of film viewing, rather than as an element of narrative, deliberately enticing through stylistic experimentation the kind of subjective viewing experience articulated by Gorky. If the sound era is dominated, as Rigby and Phillips have argued, by Gothic *horror*, then the silent period is primarily the age of Gothic *cinema*, a fusion of the cinematic and the Gothic on the experiential level.

3.2
Gothic, the Great War and the Rise of Modernism, 1910–1936

MATT FOLEY

With the exception of the dream-like qualities of Surrealism, Modernist Gothic is almost entirely detached from the paraphernalia of late eighteenth- and early nineteenth-century Gothic romance. Instead, it appropriates selectively the Victorian Gothic, particularly that of the *fin de siècle*; the modern ghost story; and representations of the dead in classical and Elizabethan literature. In making this case, the scope of the reading that follows is delineated by two important Modernist moments. In 1910, at least according to Virginia Woolf, human character changed. Perhaps most notably for Woolf, that December marked the opening of Roger Fry's *Manet and the Post-Impressionists* exhibition in London. In 1936 Djuna Barnes's *Nightwood*, the most fully realised Modernist Gothic novel, was published. The period in-between Fry's exhibition of continental art and Barnes's dark imagining of the lives of Parisian *détraqués* encompassed the First World War and its aftermaths. As I suggest below, it is an over-simplification to read Modernism as coming to adopt a refined sense of Gothicism only after, and in response to, the traumas of The Great War. The 1920s and 1930s may be, as Judith Wilt puts it, haunted decades for a number of key Modernist contributors, but 'high' Modernism's fascination with the dead was well established from its inception in the early 1910s.[1] At this time, many Modernists overtly despised dark Romanticism and its excesses of emotion. Wyndham Lewis derided the 'beastly and ridiculous spirit of Keats' lines'.[2] Later, in the 1920s, Woolf was quick to dismiss 'the skull-headed lady' of early Gothic romance.[3] Yet, André

---

[1] Judith Wilt, 'The Ghost and the Omnibus: The Gothic Virginia Woolf', in Andrew Smith and Jeff Wallace (eds), *Gothic Modernisms* (Basingstoke: Palgrave Macmillan, 2001), pp. 62–77.
[2] Wyndham Lewis, 'Vortices and Notes: Futurism, Magic and Life', *BLAST* 1 (1914): 132–5 (p. 133). Available online at <www.modjourn.org/render.php?id=1143209523824844&view=mjp_object> (last accessed 2 February 2017).
[3] Virginia Woolf, 'Gothic Romance', in Andrew McNeillie (ed.), *Collected Essays of Virginia Woolf*, 6 vols (New York: Harcourt, 1988), vol. 3, pp. 304–7 (p. 306).

Breton's lauding of Matthew Gregory Lewis's *The Monk* (1796) in his first 'Manifesto of Surrealism' (1924) and his later defence of the British Gothic romance in 'Limits not Frontiers of Surrealism' (1937) suggest a clear link between the Gothic's drawing from the dreamscape in its early narrative forms and 'high' Modernist novels, such as Barnes's *Nightwood*, which adopt Surrealist dream imagery.[4] Modernist Gothic is not a genre of writing per se, but its textual forms ghost Modernism's rise from the outset. In the period covered here, its dominant trope is a purgatorial form of haunting, the contours of which I articulate below; it, too, takes other significant forms in representations of the unconscious, of primitivism in art, of gendered and entrapped subjectivities, and of the Great War. Such representations are varied and complex – that is, they are 'Gothic Modernisms', to borrow the pluralised title of Andrew Smith and Jeff Wallace's scholarly collection on the subject (2001) – and are shaped by a number of Modernist theories of the aesthetic that developed throughout the 1910s, 1920s and 1930s.[5]

Aesthetics, Imperialism and War

In her essay 'Mr Bennett and Mrs Brown' (1924), Woolf suggested, rather provocatively, that 'on or about December 1910 human character changed'.[6] Although she was aware of the arbitrary nature of dating, retrospectively, her sense that a revolution in human relations had been afoot, Woolf chose this time because of the extraordinary influence that the Roger Fry-curated exhibition *Manet and the Post-Impressionists* exerted over British art. Even if the exhibition, hosted by the Grafton Galleries between November 1910 and January 1911, proved less than popular with the public, it was an attraction that introduced the London art scene to seminal works by Paul Gauguin, Vincent van Gogh, Georges Seurat, Paul Cézanne and Henri Matisse. The arrival of *avant-garde*, continental art to London was influential upon those

---

[4] An extract of Breton's 'Limits Not Frontiers of Surrealism' has been reproduced as André Breton, 'English Romans Noirs and Surrealism' (1937), in Victor Sage (ed.), *The Gothick Novel: A Casebook* (Basingstoke: Macmillan, 1990), pp. 112–15.

[5] For an account of 'Modernist Gothic' that argues for the centrality of the Gothic to Modernism, see John Paul Riquelme, 'Modernist Gothic', in Jerrold E. Hogle (ed.), *The Cambridge Companion to the Modern Gothic* (Cambridge: Cambridge University Press, 2014), pp. 20–35.

[6] Virginia Woolf, *Collected Essays*, 3 vols (London: The Hogarth Press, 1966), vol 1, p. 320. Even if a number of studies of literary Modernism begin their analysis in 1910, there are certain limitations to conceiving the artistic happenings of this particular year as heralding the beginning of the many Modernist movements that trace their influence as far back as the mid-nineteenth century, for instance, to the inauguration of French Symbolism.

English Modernists consciously seeking to experiment with form and not least upon Woolf's practice as a novelist, an influence that cumulates in her painterly novel *To the Lighthouse* (1927).[7] Recent work in the critical field of Gothic Modernisms has suggested that Lily's art in *To the Lighthouse* invokes a Modernist version of the Gothic sublime, with its bold palette of blocks of structuring colour.[8] The effect achieved by this post-Impressionist aesthetic is quite different from the spectral or weird sensations provoked by the modern Gothic writing of the early twentieth century. The source of Woolf's sublime lies in her writing's aesthetic intensity, coupled with her interest in the power of creative epiphany, rather than in the production of wholly gothicised scenes of terror or horror. That said, some of the more expressionist paintings in the post-Impressionist mode, such as Van Gogh's *Wheatfield with Crows* (1890), do create ominous scenes that we may connect more closely to the received Gothic. The tumultuous vista of Van Gogh's painting was, at least in the view of the British press of the time, regarded primarily as a symptom of the 'supposed lunacy' that gripped its artist in his final years.[9] *Wheatfield with Crows* seemed to British audiences, at least on first inspection, to be a subjectivised expression of madness. Indeed, much early Modernism, across various forms and media, was concerned with casting subjective experience into doubt, and many such texts engaged with or invoked a Gothic aesthetic. The narrative ambiguities of Henry James's *The Turn of the Screw* (1898) and Joseph Conrad's *Heart of Darkness* (1899), both published towards the end of the decade that began with Van Gogh's death, would foreshadow the Modernist Gothic descent into madness that would later be taken up by German Expressionist film, such as in Robert Wiene's *The Cabinet of Dr Caligari* (1920).

Modernist Gothic presents the individual psyche as inherently unstable, a theme explored, too, in Modernist art concerned with the primordial. 'Primitivism', as Modernist practice, involved drawing from non-Western artistic techniques and concerns as a means of challenging pervasive European taste. In this sense, primitivism is not just an anthropological

---

[7] Woolf was initially resistant to the influence of post-Impressionism, though her sister, Vanessa Bell, painted in the style and produced two sitting portraits of Woolf herself in c.1911–12.

[8] Daniel Darvay, *Haunting Modernity and the Gothic Presence in British Modernist Literature* (New York: Palgrave Macmillan, 2016), p. 147.

[9] Anna Gruetzner Robins, '"Manet and the Post-Impressionists": A Checklist of Exhibits', *The Burlington Magazine* 152 (December 2010), 782–93 (p. 790). Available online: <www.reading.ac.uk/web/files/art-REF/BurlDEC10pp782_93.pdf> (last accessed 30 June 2018).

interest in African, South Pacific or Asian tribal communities undertaken by European artists. Rather, it is concerned primarily with aesthetics: a conscious drawing from so-called 'native' art to express atavistic impulses that were posited as running counter to the forces of capitalism, empire and industrialisation that so shaped Western politics during late modernity. Perhaps most notably, African sculpture deeply influenced the development of Cubism – as witnessed in the provocative 'mask' features of Pablo Picasso's *Les Demoiselles d'Avignon* (1907). It is in the literature and thought of D. H. Lawrence, however, that we find the most consistent representations of the life-affirming influence of primitivism upon representations of the creative unconscious, which Lawrence often contrasts in Gothic terms with the haunted and restrictive rationality of the 'enlightened' Western man. In his *Women in Love* (1920), African sculpture is framed as the consequence of centuries of cultural evolution. It expresses lost truths. When the industrialist Gerald Crich suggests that an African sculpture of a woman giving birth is undeserving of being thought of as 'high art', Lawrence's avatar Rupert Birkin replies that, on the contrary, the sculpture suggests 'centuries and hundreds of centuries of development' and that it conveys 'ultimate physical consciousness'.[10] Fear of what Stephen D. Arata terms 'reverse colonisation', which so gripped the late-Victorian Gothic, is replaced by wonder at the non-Western.[11] Andrew Smith observes that Lawrence's 'endorsement of primitivism ... is not a naïve celebration of nature. It is part of an argument about the possibility of reclaiming apparently "primitive" modes of knowledge and is thus part of a wider critique of reductive models of science and progress'.[12] The 'progressive' European becomes the degenerate vampire, in Smith's reading, and this Gothic register is extended in Lawrence's writing to include numerous representations of ghostly, 'rational' men who have lost the way of their primal unconscious. It is Lawrence's deep interest in the physical or 'blood' consciousness, as well as his complex conceptualisation of ghostliness, that influences the macabre turns of his fiction evident in such short stories as 'Glad Ghosts' (1926).

As with Lawrence's fiction, the work of E. M. Forster could be regarded as less aesthetically innovative than the literary experiments of Woolf or James

---

[10] D. H. Lawrence, *Women in Love*, edited by David Farmer, Lindeth Vasey and John Worthen (Cambridge: Cambridge University Press, 1987), p. 79.

[11] Stephen D. Arata, 'The Occidental Tourist: *Dracula* and the Anxiety of Reverse Colonization', *Victorian Studies* 33:4 (1990): 621–45.

[12] Andrew Smith, 'Vampirism, Masculinity and Degeneracy: D. H. Lawrence's Modernist Gothic', in Andrew Smith and Jeff Wallace (eds), *Gothic Modernisms* (Basingstoke: Palgrave Macmillan, 2001), pp. 150–66 (p. 157).

Joyce. Yet, Forster is another writer whose appropriation of the Gothic signals a disruption of pervasive aesthetic values while also suggesting the representational limits of the novel form itself. As he argued in his Cambridge lecture series, which was later published as *Aspects of the Novel* (1927), Forster recognised that 'story' remained 'the highest factor common to all novels, and I wish that it was not so, that it could be something different – melody, or perception of truth, not this low atavistic form'.[13] With an almost apologetic tone, Forster clearly realised that this statement was at odds with the aesthetic experimentation with which his contemporaries infused the form. Conscious of the decline of British imperialism, Forster's fifth novel *A Passage to India* (1924) contains an extraordinary middle section in which Anglo-Indians find themselves disturbed by the unnerving Marabar caves. The acoustics of Forster's imagined caves – which are inspired by the real Barabar Caves of Bihar – and their labyrinthine passages are deeply unsettling to the British visitors, Mrs Moore and Adela, who are being shown the landscape as an act of hospitality by their friend Dr Aziz. Mrs Moore is first to be disturbed by the 'echo' of Marabar, which 'began in some indescribable way to undermine her hold on life'. The resonant sounds do not mirror the visitor's voice but, instead, evacuate the symbolic portions of voicing speech: 'If one had spoken vileness in that place, or quoted lofty poetry, the comment would have been the same – "ou-boum".'[14] The 'ou-boum' of the caves usurps not only the power of speech – the echo produced is the same no matter what is said by the tourists; it also desublimates artistic representation ('lofty poetry') and attacks the tourists' narcissistic sense of self by robbing them of their 'superior' language. The overwhelming echo, then, acts as an a-symbolic Gothic remainder. Suggesting an Orientalist attitude, to borrow a term from Edward W. Said, Forster describes his writing of this scene as a 'voluntary surrender to infection' and paints India in this moment as a place of contamination.[15] Said rightly argues that in *A Passage to India*, Forster uses India 'to represent material that according to the canons of the novel form cannot in fact be represented – vastness, incomprehensible creeds, secret motions, histories and social forms'.[16] More specifically, the caves scene refashions the Imperialist Gothic of the late nineteenth century by suggesting

---

[13] E. M. Forster, *Aspects of the Novel*, edited by O Stallybrass (Harmondsworth: Penguin, 2005), p. 40.

[14] E. M. Forster, *A Passage to India*, edited by Pankaj Mishra (Harmondsworth: Penguin, 2005), p. 139.

[15] Quoted in Benita Parry, 'Materiality and Mystification in *A Passage to India*', *Novel: A Forum on Fiction* 31:2 (1998): 174–94 (p. 181).

[16] Edward W. Said, *Culture and Imperialism* (London: Chatto & Windus Ltd., 1993), p. 241.

that the traumatic encounters that happen within them permanently unravel the language and codes of the colonisers even when the colonised land extends forms of hospitality elsewhere. Mrs Moore dies at sea as she tries to return to England; Adela becomes hysterical, falsely accuses Aziz of impropriety in the caves and eventually confesses to his innocence during his trial. Both English women – one Victorian and one 'modern' – seem to have been 'infected' by the supposed alterity of India's landscape.

A decade before Forster's novel was published, inhospitable and barren landscapes were a unifying theme of the more macabre imaginings of the Great War by Modernist combatants. Artists who fought on the Front, particularly those at the heart of the Imagist and Vorticist *avant-garde* movements, documented their tribulations by reference to their pre-war ideologies of the aesthetic and by painting wartime France as a Dantesque space – that is, as a purgatorial or hellish underworld. In his collection *Images of War* (1919), the Imagist poet Richard Aldington adopts a poetic persona that witnesses not only the destruction that ensued on the Western Front but which also, in a rather solipsistic gesture, seems preoccupied by the ways in which the excesses of war unravel the refined and economical Imagist aesthetic itself. In 'Proem', the opening piece to *Images of War*, the speaker notes, 'I grow more restless / I see the austere shape elude me.'[17] This austere shape suggests the clean lines of a classical object of poetry that are impossible to render. In 'Soliloquy I', corpses become abject because they 'wobble' when, at least to the eye of the Imagist artist, 'Dead men should be so still, austere, / And beautiful.'[18] Such imaginings of the war cohere with Wyndham Lewis's pre-war theories of aesthetic deadness. As Lewis writes in *Tarr* (1918), 'Deadness is the first condition of art: the second is absence of soul, in the human and sentimental sense.'[19] Writing from the Front for Lewis's *BLAST* magazine, the Vorticist sculptor Henri Gaudier-Brzeska had declared the war as 'A GREAT REMEDY'.[20] Months before his death at Neuville-Saint-Vaast, however, he wrote to Ezra Pound that the Front at Aisne was a hellish 'sight worthy of Dante'.[21] The influence of Dante, then, is central to Modernist Gothic representations of the dead. Indeed, in many

---

[17] Richard Aldington, *Images of War* (London: Beaumont Press, 1919), p. 5, lines 8–11.
[18] Aldington, *Images of War*, p. 35, lines 9; 11–12.
[19] Wyndham Lewis, *Tarr*, edited by Scott W. Klein (Oxford: Oxford University Press, 2010), p. 265.
[20] Henri Gaudier-Brzeska, 'Vortex Gaudier-Brzeska', in Mia Carter and Alan Friedman (eds), *Modernism and Literature: An Introduction and Reader* (Abingdon: Routledge, 2013), pp. 270–1 (p. 271).
[21] Ezra Pound, *Gaudier-Brzeska: A Memoir* (London: John Lane, 1916), p. 64.

Imagist and Vorticist accounts, the purgatory and hell of Dante act as classical patterning texts for 'modern' war writing, and this influence problematises any suggestion that these war literatures are in any way engaged with the ghosts of the Gothic. Ethical problems arise, too, when applying the appellation 'Gothic', a term that is often associated with fakery and the carnivalesque, to art that documents moments of historical trauma and tragedy. We can reconcile these conflicts of ethics and of the aesthetic by suggesting that the Modernist Gothic, in particular, can achieve a unique form of ethical work. Its anti-elegiac preference for finitude at the expense of the supernatural or the transcendent aligns its textual forms with more 'modern', ethically complex representations of mourning and of trauma. Thus, a preference for classical, rather than Romantic, modes of representation shapes the Modernist Gothic of the 1910s onwards.

Many earlier (or pre-) Modernist texts are steeped in more readily identifiable Gothic symbolism, including Charles Baudelaire's *Les Fleurs du mal* (1857); Oscar Wilde's *The Picture of Dorian Gray* (1890); and Joseph Conrad's *Heart of Darkness*. These dark Modernisms connect with the texts I read here as they employ macabre imaginings not only for their excessive effects (or affects), but in ways that elucidate emerging aesthetic ideals. Baudelaire's corpses that fester in the streets of mid-nineteenth-century Paris emerge as harbingers of Symbolism; the fall of Oscar Wilde's beautiful but ethically monstrous Dorian critiques late nineteenth-century Decadence; and the mists of the Thames that shroud Conrad's Marlow in obscurity correlate with the narrative hesitations and blind spots presented by literary Impressionism. Impressionistic in its own way, and both unsettling in atmosphere and early Modernist in its narrative construction, Henry James's *The Turn of the Screw* demonstrates what we may term a Modernist sensitivity to formal innovation and refinement. The indiscernible character of evil that seems located beyond the signifier in James's elliptical story is a Gothic excess that emerges because, rather than in spite of, its author's preference for intimation over visualising horror. These early Modernist texts, such as James's, place in question the assumed distinction between the 'high' Modernist text and 'low', well-worked Gothic mode of the supernatural. We need only turn to the Irish tradition to see this distinction unravel, whether that be in Wilde's taste for Joseph Sheridan Le Fanu and Charles Maturin, or in James Joyce's spectral stories of *Dubliners* (1914) and his allusions to the Gothic – particularly Bram Stoker's *Dracula* (1898) – in *Ulysses* (1922). It is perhaps the popular ghost story form, though, that a number of Modernists most explicitly attempted to modernise, rework and theorise afresh.

Modernist Apparitions

The Modernist moment saw a renewed interest in theorising the aesthetics of haunting. As Andrew Smith has put it, 'the modernist cry for innovation subtly influenced' the development of the ghost story.[22] The golden age of the ghost story is often posited as beginning in the mid-nineteenth century, with the tales of Edgar Allan Poe and Le Fanu and culminating in the Edwardian writings of M. R. James. Yet, the ghost story remained a popular form – as did the short story itself – in the interwar period, with writers such as Elizabeth Bowen, May Sinclair and Oliver Onions experimenting in the mode.[23] Literary networkers, such as the writer and socialite Cynthia Asquith, produced edited collections of spooky tales that featured many notable contributors. The Modernist take on the ghost story took shape during a period in which the Preface would come to the fore as a means of critically reflecting upon the seemingly paradoxical appeal of the literature of the supernatural to the rational, 'modern' mind. To name but a few examples, Edith Wharton, Henry James, Elizabeth Bowen and Walter de la Mare each penned important Prefaces that explore the appeal of the ghost story to their contemporary audiences. Such Modernist calls to make new the literatures of terror and horror could also be said to include Woolf's attack upon the Gothic romance that formed part of her review of Edith Birkhead's 1921 study *The Tale of Terror*. Woolf's essay on Birkhead's study is not her only critical piece that explores the supernatural. There are at least two more: an earlier review in *The Times Literary Supplement* (31 January, 1918) of Dorothy Scarborough's *The Supernatural in Modern English Fiction* (1917) and an essay on Henry James's ghost stories (1921). In the former, Woolf distinguishes the 'refined and spiritualised essence of fear', which she suggests is invoked by the Modernist ghost story, from the 'exaggeration of the supernatural' that she connects to Romantic Gothic writings, not least those of Ann Radcliffe.[24] In this review of Scarborough's work, Woolf is more forgiving of the terror literature of the past than in her later essays that address similar issues. Indeed, she draws a startling comparison between the effects (and affects) of Radcliffe's terror Gothic and the ghost stories of Henry James: 'If you wish to guess what our ancestors felt', Woolf suggests, 'when

---

[22] Andrew Smith, *Gothic Literature*, 2nd edition (Edinburgh: Edinburgh University Press, 2013), p. 133.
[23] Ann-Marie Einhaus, *The Short Story and the First World War* (Cambridge: Cambridge University Press, 2013), p. 3.
[24] Virginia Woolf, 'Across the Border', in McNeillie (ed.), *Collected Essays of Virginia Woolf*, vol. 2, pp. 217–20 (p. 218).

they read *The Mysteries of Udolpho* then you cannot do better than read *The Turn of the Screw*'.[25] Woolf's unexpected comparison could be read merely as an elaboration upon a brief allusion to *Udolpho* in *The Turn of the Screw*. Her comment, though, does mark the starting point of a more sustained meditation upon how the modern macabre tale produces a horror not of the supernatural but of one's own mind. Written in the years before her own experimentations with form, the argument of her review of *The Supernatural in Modern English Fiction* indicates that Woolf revered James for staging what she referred to as 'the power that our minds possess for ... excursions into the darkness; when certain lights sink or certain barriers are lowered, the ghosts of the mind, untracked desires, indistinct intimations, are seen to be a large company'.[26] Woolf's argument here echoes James's injunction – in the culmination of his Preface to *The Turn of the Screw* – to 'make [the reader] think the evil, make him think it for himself, and you are released from weak specifications'.[27] Yet, in its invocation of an imagery of dark desires and the transgressions of boundaries, Woolf's description of horror points more strongly to unconscious apparatuses and the unsettling realisation that the ego – or, at least, one's conscious sense of self – is open to invasion by more primordial and disruptive regions of the psyche.

The Modernist short story is a literature of self-realisation. The mode provides a snapshot of the everyday; its Gothic registers of dread and the uncanny come to the fore most prominently when unspoken past transgressions unsettle and disrupt the equilibrium of the present moment. As Valerie Shaw puts it, through its very brevity the form may paint 'life's possibilities' as 'hedged and narrow' or in moments of conflict may 'express a view of life as violent and torn by harsh conflict'.[28] At least in the British and Irish tradition, the distinctly Modernist short story is a literature of epiphanies – those 'most delicate and evanescent of moments', according to Joyce – that explores marginalised lives and themes of alienation within the confines of the quotidian.[29] This dynamic is apparent in the stories of *Dubliners*, in which Joyce explores the various paralyses of his contemporary Dublin, a city that he sought to bring to Europe's attention in his writing but from which he

---

[25] Woolf, 'Across the Border', p. 219. [26] Woolf, 'Across the Border', p. 219.
[27] Henry James, 'Author's preface to *The Turn of the Screw*', in Martin Scofield (ed.), *Ghost Stories of Henry James* (Hertfordshire: Wordsworth Editions Limited, 2001), pp. 3–10 (p. 8).
[28] Valerie Shaw, *The Short Story: A Critical Introduction* (Abingdon: Routledge, 1983), pp. 8–9.
[29] Quoted in Vivian Heller, *Joyce, Decadence, and Emancipation* (Urbana, IL and Chicago: University of Illinois Press, 1995), p. 14.

would exile himself. With *Dubliners* as our starting point, we may chart the emergence of the Modernist apparition, the appearance of which, unlike the guiding ghosts of literatures past, tends to intensify rather than ameliorate moments of ethical crises.[30] The Shakespearean fear and wonder of the apparition may still be present in Modernism but the ghost's transformative power as a harbinger of ethics is lost. Certainly, an important interwar Modernist apparition is the figure of Evans from Woolf's *Mrs Dalloway* (1925), who is conjured by the shell-shocked veteran Septimus Warren Smith, and whose ethical message remains elliptical and unclear. Evans speaks to Septimus but the reader is left only with fragments of revelation. The complete meaning of the spectral address is interminably delayed and only evident to – and perhaps even produced by – Septimus's traumatised mind. Focusing on Joyce, however, demonstrates that the Modernist apparition is not solely an interwar phenomenon.

In his pre-war short stories, which were written several years before their final publication in *Dubliners*, Joyce spectralises the quotidian as a response to the political, sectarian and abusive dimensions of Irish politics and society. Joyce's 'ambivalence' towards the Dublin of his youth is well recognised.[31] On the one hand, Joyce wanted to write of Dublin as a major city of the West: 'When you remember that Dublin has been a capital for thousands of years', he wrote to Stanislaus Joyce in 1905, 'that it is the "Second" city in the British Empire, that it is nearly three times as big as Venice, it seems strange that no artist has given it to the world.'[32] On the other, he depicted the Dublin from which he eventually became estranged as housing a society and culture that was spiritually impoverished and even corrupt. Representing this sense of stagnation and thwarted nostalgia, the lingering of the dead and the departed into the present is an important motif in the first and last stories of *Dubliners*. There are, though, significant differences in tone and register between the invocations of ghostly, apparitional figures in 'The Sisters' and 'The Dead', respectively. 'The Sisters' is set at a time of mourning and, like the rest of the tales in *Dubliners*, documents spiritual paralysis. From the story's

---

[30] From tragedy to Christmas ghost stories, an apparition functioning as a harbinger of radical change is a well-established literary trope. To give but two examples, the 'old mole' appears in William Shakespeare's *Hamlet* (c.1601) with a radical revelation of murder at a time of national crisis, while the ghosts of Christmas past, present and future appear in Charles Dickens's *A Christmas Carol* (1843) to effect the personal transformation of Ebenezer Scrooge from miser to generous soul.

[31] Emer Nolan, *James Joyce and Nationalism* (London: Routledge, 1995), p. xi.

[32] Quoted in James F. Broderick, *James Joyce: A Literary Companion* (Jefferson: McFarland & Co., 2018), p. 13.

commencement, the young, unnamed narrator is detached and alienated from his home environment. Before receiving confirmation of the death of his mentor, Father Flynn, whose window he stares at with an eerily tinged sense of anticipation, the spirit of the narrator always already suffers from atrophy: 'Every night as I gazed up at the window I said softly to myself the word *paralysis*.'[33] The night after Father Flynn's death, the apparitional face of the departed visits the boy's room in order to confess something unnatural:

> I imagined that I saw again the heavy grey face of the paralytic. I drew the blankets over my head and tried to think of Christmas. But the grey face still followed me. It murmured, and I understood that it desired to confess something. I felt my soul receding into some pleasant and vicious region; and there again I found it waiting for me. It began to confess to me in a murmuring voice and I wondered why it smiled continually and why the lips were so moist with spittle.[34]

In many senses, this passage demonstrates the ambivalent and often conditional Modernist representation of the apparition. The boy is certain that the apparition of Flynn is imagined – the supernatural is disavowed – and yet the narrator still conjures an entity imbued with its own malign volition. The boy seems infected by a sense of spiritual paralysis but Flynn is the literal 'paralytic'. The movement of Flynn's lips, and the 'muttering' voice that carries his confession, is heard before facial features (other than a heavy grey pallor) are visualised. Comparable, then, to Woolf's later imagining of the apparition of Evans and his conversations with Septimus in *Mrs Dalloway*, the percipient recognises the profound nature of the spectral voice's revelation even if its message is obscured.

Many of the stories in *Dubliners* explore the symbolic limits of the discourses that shaped Dublin's culture at the turn of the twentieth century: that is, through inference, they suggest what could and could not be said about politics, the family, gender, desire and the abuses of clerical power. In 'The Dead', another story of haunting, broader questions relating to politics and identity are interrogated through the rather awkward figure of 'West Briton' Gabriel Conroy.[35] Gabriel is a literary critic who is drawn more to the verse of Robert Browning than he is to Celtic culture. As such, the literary theme of Joyce's story seems to anticipate T. S. Eliot's didactic affirmation in 'Traditional and Individual Talent' (1919) that you 'cannot value [the artist]

---

[33] James Joyce, *Dubliners*, edited by Terence Brown (Harmondsworth: Penguin, 2000), p. 1; original emphasis.
[34] Joyce, *Dubliners*, p. 3.   [35] Joyce, *Dubliners*, p. 189.

alone; you must set him, for contrast and comparison, among the dead'.[36] Gretta Conroy does just this, we infer, to her husband. After becoming entranced by a recital of 'The Lass of Aughrim' as she leaves the Morkans' Christmas party with Gabriel, Gretta yearns for the romance and passion of Michael Furey, a 'delicate' lover whom she lost in her youth.[37] As Luke Gibbons has suggested in his study of Joyce's ghosts, the spirit of Furey takes on an 'airy' rather than fully apparitional form. The persistence of his being becomes fused with the eerie gas lighting and street sounds of Dublin at night: 'If Michael Furey is the third person in another [Joycean] trinity', writes Gibbons, 'then it is perhaps fitting that he takes this form.'[38] In its first and last stories, then, *Dubliners* provides a spectrum of spectrality that anticipates two important motifs of ghostly representation in British and Irish literary Modernism more broadly. In 'The Sisters' the apparition appears but its spectral address is elliptical or obscured, while 'The Dead' renders an atmosphere of ghostliness in which the appearance of the spectre is feared – even perhaps anticipated by the reader – but any direct encounter with the ghost is held in abeyance. In both tales, it is suggested that the mind – particularly memory – conjures these spectres.

Modernism and Women's Ghost Stories

In 'The Dead', spectrality is produced, in part, as a consequence of unrealised feminine desire, that is, Gretta Conroy's reawakened and unquenchable passion for the departed Michael Furey. Diana Wallace is correct in arguing that, in the decade or two after Joyce's *Dubliners* was published, (Modernist) ghost stories 'allowed women writers special kinds of freedom, not merely to include the fantastic and the supernatural, but also to offer critiques of male power and sexuality'.[39] Such tales reconfigure 'the Gothic elements of the Bluebeard story'.[40] In these appropriations, the husband moves, to use E. M. Forster's terms in *Aspects of the Novel*, from a 'flat' Gothic villain to a more 'rounded', ambiguous and modern character. As Wallace argues, an example of this trope is found in May Sinclair's 'The Villa Désirée' (1926),

---

[36] T. S. Eliot, *The Sacred Wood: Essays on Poetry and Criticism* (London: Methuen & Co Ltd, 1928), p. 49.
[37] Joyce, *Dubliners*, p. 220.
[38] Luke Gibbons, *Joyce's Ghosts: Ireland, Modernism and Memory* (Chicago: Chicago University Press, 2016), p. 125.
[39] Diana Wallace, 'Uncanny Stories: The Ghost Story as Female Gothic', *Gothic Studies* 6:1 (2004): 57–68 (p. 57).
[40] Wallace, 'The Ghost Story as Female Gothic', p. 58.

which stages a form of ghostly monstrosity that is more excessive than that of many other Modernist apparitions. Alone in the bedroom of the Villa Désirée, Mildred sees the creature that represents her fiancé:

> From the breasts downward its body was unfinished, rudimentary, not quite born. The grey shell was still pregnant with its loathsome shapelessness. But the face – the face was perfect in absolute horror. And it was Louis Carson's face....
>
> It came on to her, bending over her, peering at her, so close that the piled mattresses now hid the lower half of its body. And the frightful thing about it was that it was blind, parted from all controlling and absolving clarity, flesh and not yet flesh.[41]

This 'not quite born' entity that has a phenomenality somewhere between 'flesh and not yet flesh' resonates with Jacques Derrida's understanding of the apparition in *Specters of Marx* (1993). Sinclair's apparition, though, is a more monstrous embodiment of a ghostly return than Derrida's messianic spectres. The horror of this monstrous visitant lies partly in its sightlessness, where the connotations of impotence are clear, its bottom half being hidden from Mildred's view, so as to render the ghostly as dead from the waist down. At the root of this burlesque rendering of the apparition is an anxiety of repeating the past. Mildred discovers that the first prospective Mrs Carson had 'died of fright', after, '[s]he saw something'.[42] Mildred knows what the young girl had seen. It was the 'beastliness' of Louis, an alluded to sexual voraciousness, which 'got there before' him, in a monstrous form, to the bedroom of the Villa Désirée.[43]

Sinclair was once located on the cusp of the Modernist canon, but in the last decade her fiction has received sustained critical attention as new accounts of Modernism have evolved.[44] She is credited with first using the phrase 'stream of consciousness' in a 1918 review of a volume of Dorothy Richardson's *Pilgrimage* series of novels (1915–67). While stream of consciousness had been associated with the psychology of William James, particularly

---

[41] May Sinclair, 'The Villa Désirée', in Cynthia Asquith (ed.), *The Ghost Book* (London: Pan Books Ltd, 1970), pp. 9–21 (p. 18).
[42] Sinclair, 'The Villa Désirée', p. 20.   [43] Sinclair, 'The Villa Désirée', p. 21.
[44] *The May Sinclair Society* was founded in July 2013 and this organisation has advanced the study of Sinclair's work significantly. For a reading of some of Sinclair's *Uncanny Stories* through the critical lens of Gothic Modernisms, see David Glover, 'The "Spectrality" Effect in Early Modernism', in Smith and Wallace (eds), *Gothic Modernisms*, pp. 29–42. For Andrew Smith's more recent reading of *Uncanny Stories* in relation to Vernon Lee's short stories, see Andrew Smith, *The Ghost Story, 1840–1920: A Cultural History* (Manchester: Manchester University Press, 2010), pp. 86–93.

the 'Stream of Thought' section of his *The Principles of Psychology* (1880), Sinclair was the first reviewer to apply it to a literary aesthetic.[45] In so doing, she drew a comparison between Richardson's *magnum opus* in development and Joyce's *A Portrait of the Artist as a Young Man* (1916). Sinclair had a close association with *The Egoist* at a time when Ezra Pound was its editor, a magazine that anthologised Joyce's novel between 1914 and 1915, and for which Sinclair penned a number of reviews. She was an active contributor to Modernist networks and one with the clearest of Gothic credentials. She was both an early psychoanalyst and a certified spiritualist as a member of *The Society for Psychical Research*. These contexts were important influences upon her short fiction.[46]

Sinclair's short story 'If the Dead Knew' (1923) provides a striking example of a certain Modernist Gothic character type: the Freudian mother, or restrictive maternal super-ego, that we might also connect, for instance, to Elizabeth Bowen's characterisation of Mme Fisher in *The House in Paris* (1935). Castrating figures also take precedence in the early work of D. H. Lawrence and in his later short story 'The Lovely Lady' (1927), which he contributed to Cynthia Asquith's *The Black Cap* (1927), before it was eventually redrafted for a stand-alone edition.[47] In Sinclair's 'If the Dead Knew', Wilfrid Hollyer is certain that his latent death-wish for his mother becomes manifest and causes her demise. This delusion recalls what Freud suggests is 'the technique' at the heart of 'the animistic mode of thinking', which he describes in *Totem and Taboo* (1913) as a symptom of early man's belief in the omnipotence of their thoughts.[48] For Freud, a conviction that thought alone could influence the surrounding world was a condition that early man shared with certain unconscious attitudes of the contemporary neurotic. Around his mother, Wilfrid's desire for his sweetheart Effie stagnates; he is 'shamefaced' and feels like 'he had committed a sin' after visiting her.[49] Before long, he contemplates his mother's mortality, but suppresses the thought, choosing to believe, instead, that she has '[n]erves like whipcord, young arteries, and every organ sound'.[50] After she is struck by a brief bout of pleurisy, his mother

---

[45] Rachel Potter, *Modernist Literature* (Edinburgh: Edinburgh University Press, 2012), p. 24.
[46] Smith, *The Ghost Story*, p. 86.
[47] Dieter Mehl and Christa Jansohn, 'General Editors' Preface', in D. H. Lawrence, *The Woman Who Rode Away and Other Stories*, edited by Dieter Mehl and Christa Jansohn (Cambridge: Cambridge University Press, 2001), pp. xxi–xxii.
[48] Sigmund Freud, *The Penguin Freud library*, edited by Angela Richards and Albert Dickson, trans. by James Strachey, 14 vols (London: Penguin Books Ltd, 1984), vol. 12, p. 143.
[49] May Sinclair, *Uncanny Stories* (Hertfordshire: Wordsworth Editions Ltd, 2006), p. 125.
[50] Sinclair, *Uncanny Stories*, p. 127.

suddenly dies, and Wilfrid believes that his matricidal wish has had a murderous force. As Wilfrid's interior voice begins to merge with that of Sinclair's more knowing narrator, a climactic realisation occurs: 'A wish, even a hidden wish, could kill ... It was as if his secret self had broken loose, and got through to his mother, and had killed her secretly, in the dark.'[51] Wilfrid's cognition is imbued with a terrible volition and his thoughts seem to harbour their own murderous force.

In his reading of Elizabeth Bowen's fiction alongside T. S. Eliot's Modernist dead of *The Waste Land* (1922), David Punter describes a crisis of Modernist individualism, according to which the subject is 'perpetually invaded,' and their self-control contaminated by 'the mark, the trace, of an unimaginable twin'.[52] Wilfrid's matricidal thought, however, is not a fully constituted shadowy *imago* or dark double that invades the self. Instead, the desire of a supposed murderous other becomes the subject's own. As such, the story is a recognition of the power of the unconscious. This Modernist Gothic hesitation between pathology and the extraordinary is not sustained by the story as a whole. Towards the end of 'If The Dead Knew', Wilfrid, who feels his only talent is as a 'third-rate' organist, plays a movement of Felix Mendelssohn's popular *Lieder ohne Worte* or *Song Without Words* (1829–45). As the melody rises, so too does a low, repetitive sighing behind him:

> Somewhere in the secret place of his mind a word struggled to form itself, to be born. 'Mother.' It came to him with a sense of appalling, supernatural horror. Horror that was there with him in the room like a presence ... Then he saw her. She stood between him and the chair, straight and thin, dressed in the clothes she had died in.[53]

The apparition of Mrs Hollyer, purely a metaphorical visualisation of guilt, 'was less a visible form than a visible emotion, an anguish'.[54] It is this anguish, this turning towards the melancholic abyss, from which Wilfrid cannot recover. Evidently, Sinclair falls back upon the supernatural machinery of the received Gothic. Such a move sits uneasily alongside the 'modern' psychological approach that the story sets up from its beginning. Here we may recall Virginia Woolf's warning in her essay 'Freudian Fiction' that reproductions of psychological scenarios should not come at the expense of

---

[51] Sinclair, *Uncanny Stories*, p. 133.
[52] David Punter, 'Hungry Ghosts and Foreign Bodies', in Smith and Wallace (eds), *Gothic Modernisms*, pp. 11–28 (p. 12).
[53] Sinclair, *Uncanny Stories*, pp. 136–7. [54] Sinclair, *Uncanny Stories*, p. 137.

achieving 'modern' aesthetic aims.⁵⁵ Woolf's argument is clear. Even with the dawning and intellectual popularising of Freud's new theory of the subject, fiction should not be purely mimetic of the Freudian discovery, nor should the short story be reduced to a psychoanalytic vignette, nor to melodrama in its pursuit of Freudian themes. Sinclair's prose most enthrals in her descriptions of psychology and the dangerous potency of Wilfrid's thoughts. The Joycean use of inference and the sustained representations of interiority create an atmosphere of mystery and suggest the possibility of something extraordinary at work. Yet, the text's invocation of a somewhat clichéd apparition – in its supposed moment of revelation – problematises any categorisation of it as Modernist Gothic.

The Unconscious

The Freudian project had a profound influence upon Modernism. Even a writer such as Lawrence, who vehemently disagreed with psychoanalysis's location of the unconscious in the mental rather than the corporeal realm, felt somewhat indebted to Freud for popularising discussions about a 'second' self in literary circles of the time. For Peter Childs, at least, Freud's thought prompted one of the key paradigm shifts that inaugurated the period of modernity in which Modernism itself emerged. Indeed, Childs situates Freud alongside 'modern' thinkers such as Karl Marx, Charles Darwin and Albert Einstein, and Freud, too, shared an interest in primitivism and anthropology that was pervasive in European Modernism.⁵⁶ As the Imagist poet H. D. put it, Freudian thought 'had opened up, among others, that particular field of the unconscious mind that went to prove that the traits and tendencies of obscure and aboriginal tribes, as well as the shape and substance of the rituals of vanished civilisations, were still inherent in the human mind'.⁵⁷ Freud's influence upon art is perhaps most clearly visible – and consciously articulated – in the work of Surrealism, at least as it was theorised in its first manifesto by André Breton.

Breton split from the anti-war and anti-logic group Dada in 1922 to form his own *avant-garde* movement in Paris. A trained doctor, he sought to harness the power of the unconscious to bring to the fore the revolutionary potential

---

⁵⁵ Virginia Woolf, 'Freudian Fiction', in McNeillie (ed.), *Collected Essays of Virginia Woolf*, vol. 3, pp. 195–7.
⁵⁶ Peter Childs, *Modernism* (London: Routledge, 2000), pp. 26–71.
⁵⁷ H. D., 'From *A Tribute to Freud*', in Mia Carter and Alan Friedman (eds), *Modernism and Literature: An Introduction and Reader* (Abingdon: Routledge, 2013), pp. 555–8 (p. 557).

of the imagination. By Surrealism, Breton meant '[p]sychic automatism in its pure state, by which one proposes to express – verbally, by means of the written, or in any other manner – the actual functioning of thought'. In the manifesto, such guides to practices of automatic writing and collage were founded upon the essentially Freudian belief 'in the superior reality of certain forms of previously neglected associations, in the omnipotence of dream'.[58] Indeed, it was the dream-like quality of the Gothic romance, particularly Matthew Gregory Lewis's *The Monk* (1796), that garnered direct but brief praise from Breton in this first manifesto.[59] Surrealist artists believed that art could both showcase and engage the unconscious and inaugurate new ways of seeing. The final shot of the opening sequence to Luis Buñuel's and Salvador Dali's *Un Chien Andalou* (1928) is perhaps the most iconic representation of this attitude towards revolutionising the old artistic vision. In this memorable scene, a razor blade slits in two the left eyeball of a young woman, who is played by Simone Mareuil. The same woman is later sexually pursued – and indeed violated – by a tall, gawking man who briefly takes on the posture and hue of an undead zombie. Blood drips from his mouth as he abuses Mareuil's character, her breasts transforming into a mannequin's posterior and then into nude buttocks. If this is a dream, it is a particularly violent one, and one in which the laws of propriety and rationality are transgressed by an excessive heteronormative desire. In Djuna Barnes's *Nightwood*, which queers interwar Paris and connects this queering to the overwhelming power of the unconscious, the American *détraqué* Robin Vote is described often as somnambulistic and animalistic: 'the born somnambule, who lives in two worlds' and a 'woman who is beast turning human'.[60] Avril Horner has argued that, mirroring the Surrealists, Barnes 'uses Gothic paraphernalia in order imaginatively to challenge the definition of desire as it is socially constructed'.[61] The Gothic imagery that signals excesses of desire in both *Un Chien Andalou* and *Nightwood*, respectively, also carries with it a transformative sense: the power of metamorphosis so particular to the dreamscape (or even nightmare).

Although in spirit we may agree with Horner and Sue Zlosnik that *Nightwood*'s various explorations of 'transgression and abjection, the

---

[58] André Breton, 'From the First Manifesto of Surrealism', in Lawrence Rainey (ed.), *Modernism: An Anthology* (Oxford: Blackwell, 2005), pp. 718–41 (p. 729).
[59] Breton, 'From the First Manifesto of Surrealism', p. 723.
[60] Djuna Barnes, *Nightwood* (London: Faber & Faber, 2001), p. 31; p. 33.
[61] Avril Horner, '"A Detour of Filthiness": French Fiction and Djuna Barnes's *Nightwood*', in Avril Horner (ed.), *European Gothic: A Spirited Exchange, 1760–1960* (Manchester: Manchester University Press, 2002), pp. 230–51 (p. 237).

unconscious and the irrational, brings it into the Gothic genre', we should not overlook the reasons it was admired in Modernist literary circles.[62] As he suggested in his Editor's Preface to the book in 1937, T. S. Eliot venerated the aesthetic intensity of Barnes's prose – that is, its resemblance to 'modern' poetry – as well as the 'Elizabethan' quality of *Nightwood*'s more abject scenes. Time and again, the dark Modernisms that I have read here connect back to a classical heritage that pre-dates the supernatural Gothic romance of the late eighteenth and early nineteenth centuries. These Modernist connections to the 'Tradition', as Eliot termed it, were well established before the Great War and so was Modernism's fascination with the dead, primitivism, and, as with Wyndham Lewis's theory of art, 'deadness' as an aesthetic quality. As an interwar text, it is telling that in Virginia Woolf's fragment 'A Haunted House' (1921) the voices of the dead have as much presence as those of the living; there is but an opaque 'glass' barrier between their two worlds.[63] That Woolf is said to have regarded her only ghost story as merely a 'first sketch' speaks to the uneasy coupling of high Modernism and the Gothic.[64] On the one hand, Modernists sought consistently to distance themselves from the supernatural strain in fiction. On the other, the writers of the time remained preoccupied with theorising haunting and exploring connections between the unconscious and transgressions of the quotidian. Evident in Aldington's war writings, Modernist writers often regarded themselves as privileging an aesthetics of finitude: where haunting occurs, it is a remainder not easily reconciled with this rhetoric of art, nor with the constant desire in Modernist writing for ethical guidance. The most enduring evocations of Modernist Gothic aesthetics arise, then, in a number of its representations of haunting, the unconscious and the dead, imaginings that ultimately tend to reinforce, rather than transcend, the Modernist purgatory.

---

[62] Avril Horner and Sue Zlosnik, 'Strolling in the Dark: Gothic Flânerie in Djuna Barnes's *Nightwood*', in Smith and Wallace (eds), *Gothic Modernisms*, pp. 78–94 (p. 81).
[63] Virginia Woolf, *A Haunted House*, edited by Leonard Woolf (London: The Hogarth Press, 1944), p. 10.
[64] Leonard Woolf, 'Foreword', in Leonard Woolf (ed.), *A Haunted House* (London: The Hogarth Press, 1944), pp. 7–8 (p. 8).

3.3

Gothic and the American South, 1919–1962

ARTHUR REDDING

Theorising Southern Gothic

'The writer's work is predicated not only on his personality', observed Carson McCullers in an essay published in the December 1959 issue of *Esquire*, 'but by the region in which he was born. I wonder sometimes if what they call the "Gothic" school of Southern writing, in which the grotesque is paralleled with the sublime, is not due largely to the cheapness of human life in the South.'[1] As a self-consciously unique society, historically distinct from – and often at open political and military odds with – the rest of the United States, the South has long cultivated its commitment to a form of literary expression it could honour as its own. From antebellum attempts to articulate key characteristics of Southern writing to the most recent critical interventions of the 'New Southern Studies' in the twenty-first century, writers and critics have engaged in a seemingly urgent, highly self-conscious and heavily factionalised set of endeavours to produce and define a distinctive literature of the American South. These projects have involved partisan struggles over the form and genre most appropriate to confronting, sifting through and representing the terrible burdens of Southern history and to confronting the challenges of modernity.

This chapter will explore the significance of Gothic to an emergent American modernist aesthetic, focusing particularly on the legacies of slavery and the politics of segregation in the American South, but also evoking other historical traumas. European modernism is conventionally understood largely to have disavowed Gothic romance; by contrast, under the influence of William Faulkner and others, the particular strand of fiction associated with the Southern Literary Renaissance developed Gothic motifs into

---

[1] Carson McCullers, 'The Flowering Dream: Notes on Writing', in *Carson McCullers: Stories, Plays and Other Writings* (New York: Library of America, 2017), pp. 510–17 (p. 517).

a distinctive idiom through which to explore themes of otherness and difference and to reflect on the significance of the individual and collective past. In doing so, and in developing an ambivalent, paradoxical body of writings that might best be described as 'modernist regional Gothic', such writers as McCullers, Flannery O'Connor and Tennessee Williams shook off the influence of European texts, taking Gothic in a radically new direction.

McCullers, whose writing is in many ways exemplary, was herself one of the more prominent members of this Gothic school; her sometimes notorious novels and plays present readers with an array of characters designated as oddities, freaks, sexual outsiders and outcasts, the racially despised, the wounded and the crippled, queers, masochists and alcoholics. In her books, the damaged and aspiring strive with varying degrees of ineffectuality to cobble together a semblance of human fellowship in a mid-century Southern society awash with calcified bigotry and sexual dread. Misunderstood and neglected, if not condemned and harassed, such characters struggle to claim human kinship. The deaf-mute John Singer, for example, from McCullers's celebrated debut novel, *The Heart is a Lonely Hunter* (1940), becomes the centre of a circle of dreamers and rejects in a Georgia mill town – a fellow deaf-mute, a drunken labour organiser, a Black physician, a musical tomboy, the owner of a café – each of whom come to see in Singer a reciprocal devotion that he is himself unable to express. The adolescent Frankie Addams, from McCullers's play *A Member of the Wedding* (1946), feels herself outcast, unloved and unfriended; she is challenged to discover the worthiness of the care provided her by her only companions, a one-eyed African American servant, Berenice, and a doomed, cross-dressing little boy, John Henry. Similarly lonesome, similarly isolated, similarly braced by longing and doubt are the ensemble of cast members – a gay army major, his straying wife, a Filipino servant – of *Reflections In Golden Eye* (1941); Miss Amelia, from *The Ballad of the Sad Café* (1951), who takes up with the 'dwarf' hunchback, Cousin Lymon; Jester, of *Clock without Hands* (1961), who worries that he is sexually abnormal. McCullers's thematic everywhere involves the difficulties of securing and articulating emotional value for and among those whose lives have been so cheapened. McCullers's great Gothic thematic involves the resistance mounted by the socially excluded to their own ostracism and dramatises their floundering attempts to cobble together a 'monstrous' community on the fringes of a social formation that has rejected them.

But why the South? Why Southern Gothic? Why this cheapness of life? And to what extent can this curious juxtaposition of the sublime with the grotesque be taken as symptomatic of a characteristically Southern social malaise – or mystique? The Virginian novelist Ellen Glasgow believed that fiction should serve the cause of imaginatively reconstructing history and work to counter potentially dangerous regional myths, and was sceptical of what she perceived to be exaggerated Gothic distortions. She was suspicious of the work of such writers as Erskine Caldwell, a naturalist who in such bestselling books as *Tobacco Road* (1932) and *God's Little Acre* (1933) wrote sympathetically of the sexual lives of the rural poor. Using the term 'Southern Gothic' as early as 1935 in a *Saturday Review of Literature* commentary entitled 'Heroes and Monsters', Glasgow observed despairingly that 'one may admit that the Southern States have more than an equal share of degeneracy and deterioration ... the multitude of half-wits, and whole idiots, and nymphomaniacs, and paranoiacs, and rakehells in general, that populate the modern literary South could flourish nowhere' except in the 'weird pages of melodrama'.[2] Increasingly, other commentators wondered along the same lines. In *Love and Death in the American Novel* (1960), Leslie A. Fiedler highlighted the recurrent pattern of 'symbolic Gothicism' in American literature.[3] For Fiedler, this Gothicism was occasioned by the simultaneous depiction and denial of acts of transgressive desire, such as cross-racial love and homosexuality. Clearly, the social edifice of a mythic South rendered such desires particularly taboo, even amid the mid-century recognition of the impressive achievements of writers from the American South. That recognition was cemented by the awarding of the 1949 Nobel Prize in Literature to William Faulkner. The books produced by this school – Faulkner, O'Connor, McCullers, Tennessee Williams and, somewhat later, William Styron – seemed to share similar idioms, themes and moods that were increasingly characterised as Gothic. Social formations, as theorists from Sigmund Freud to René Girard to Julia Kristeva have in different ways observed, are founded as much upon the bodies and passions that they reject (the scapegoat, the abject, the taboo) as that which and those whom they embrace: an 'us' comes to constitute itself in contradistinction to a 'them'. The South has been a society deliberately organised around a myth of white racial superiority. Gothic, in McCullers's estimation, gives voice to the despised and provides a space for the shunned. It follows that Southern Gothic has been theorised in terms of the return of a historically repressed that everywhere threatens the

---

[2] Ellen Glasgow, 'Heroes and Monsters', in Julian Rowan Raper (ed.), *Ellen Glasgow's Reasonable Doubts: A Collection of Her Writings* (Baton Rouge: Louisiana State University Press, 1988), pp. 162–7 (p. 163).
[3] Leslie A. Fiedler, *Love and Death in the American Novel* (New York: Criterion Books, 1960), p. xxiii.

imagined purity of the mythic South. Correspondingly, I will argue, a peculiarly distinct Gothic literary genre emerges in the face of aesthetic strictures that would ambivalently endeavour to delimit what is proper to Southern cultural production.

The twinned terms 'Southern' and 'Gothic' have understandably received a considerable amount of critical attention. Two important essay collections, *The Palgrave Handbook of the Southern Gothic* (2016) and *Undead Souths: The Gothic and Beyond in Southern Literature and Culture* (2015), are both largely dedicated to expanding and re-visioning the regional and generic scope of critical investigation. Traditionally, 'Southern Gothic' (sometimes 'Southern grotesque') is a critical term that refers to the literature produced by Faulkner as well as several other key modernist writers of what was termed the Southern Literary Renaissance of the 1920s and after. Edgar Allan Poe is generally considered the great predecessor to this tradition, although critics have debated the extent to which his horror tales and macabre fables are situated within the region and history of the American South. Timeless and seemingly placeless in their setting, such classic horror tales as 'The Fall of the House of Usher' (1839), 'The Masque of the Red Death' (1842) or 'The Telltale Heart' (1843) scarcely set out the details of local customs and manners that Flannery O'Connor, for example, thought necessary to regional writing. Nonetheless, Poe's work is everywhere infused with perverse sexual obsessions, with depictions of incest, necrophilia, paedophilia, of violent excesses of bloodlust and ghostly revenge, of decaying aristocratic mansions. Characterised by novelist Ishmael Reed as 'prophet of a civilization buried alive', Poe can be read productively as writing Gothic allegories of a specifically Southern history, and as precursor to the modernist Southern Gothic of the twentieth century.[4]

Faulkner's sometimes comic novels and stories include ghosts and Gothic perversion – murder, castration, incest, zoophilia – aplenty: from the beyond, from a coffin being carried on an odyssey across the land by her bereaved family, the corpse of Addie Bundren utters the dramatic monologue at the heart of *As I Lay Dying* (1930). Faulkner's thriller, *Sanctuary* (1931), indulges in acts of perverse brutality and violence, and those not only on the part of the novel's designated 'bad guy', the notorious Popeye, but by all the self-serving and hypocritical cast of characters who seek revenge in the guise of justice. Horace Benbow, the self-sacrificing and ineffectual lawyer who forms the seeming moral centre of the novel, appears to be a principled public

---

[4] Ishmael Reed, *Flight to Canada* (New York: Random House, 1976), p. 18.

defendant, and he everywhere castigates the high-handed hypocrisy of the Jefferson townspeople. But Benbow turns out, on close reading, to be implicitly as vicious, lustful, cowardly and self-promotional as those whom he looks down upon. Faulkner's often-anthologised story 'A Rose for Emily' (1930) lampoons the decaying aristocracy in the person of Emily Grierson and hinges on her unmentionable act of murder and necrophilia, even as she is described with considerable sympathy. Perhaps Faulkner's most powerful haunted house epic is *Absalom, Absalom!* (1936), a patchwork quilt of a tale chronicled by Quentin Compson, whom Faulkner earlier featured in *The Sound and the Fury* (1929) and who now finds himself a suicidal transplanted Southerner interrogated by his Harvard roommate, Shreve. *Absalom, Absalom!* chronicles the crimes and horrors that form the patriarchal legacy of the South. The image of the desolate and abandoned 'Sutpen's hundred' – the once great estate established by the founding patriarch, Thomas Sutpen – allegorises the decayed state of the mythic South, and the novel relates the barbarous history of plantation culture in the American South, exposing its cruelty and vice, disclosing too a secret family sexual history of miscegenation and its cover-up; at the novel's end, the inheritor of the plantation is the mixed-blood 'mental defective', Jim Bond.

'The dilapidation of this house is a metaphor for the state of society.'[5] So writes Tennessee Williams in the stage directions to a late play, *A House Not Meant to Stand*, which is subtitled 'A Gothic Comedy'. In that play, which premiered in 1982 but was not published until 2008, the aged Cornelius McCorkle ponders the supposed decline of his own family, who in the younger generations have become subject to the perversions of avarice and homosexuality. Williams is satirising the clichés of the more conservative, moralising aspects of Southern Gothic, a genre that often represents images of vice and mental degeneration as somehow symptomatic of a general social decline. The ultimate truths of the Compsons' own family history are revealed by another character suffering from mental disability, the 'idiot' Benjy, in *The Sound and the Fury*. Faulkner's pointedly cruel depictions of mental illness – like his portrayals of the vice-ridden poor white Snopes family, who over the course of several novels come to supplant the old Southern aristocracy as economic and social powerbrokers of Yoknapatawpha county – are designed to symbolise a history of decline and decay.

---

[5] Tennessee Williams, *A House Not Meant to Stand*, edited by Thomas Keith (New York: New Direction, 2008), p. 3.

In the hands of Flannery O'Connor, by contrast, such abject and villainous characters as the murderer, The Misfit, from 'A Good Man is Hard to Find' (1953), or the debauched confidence trickster, Manley Pointer, from 'Good Country People' (1955), take on more pointedly ironic dimensions and, in their shockingly violent actions, illuminate spiritual truths and expose self-serving hypocrisies. O'Connor, alongside such other post-war writers as Andrew Lytle, whose ambitiously Joycean novel, *The Velvet Horn*, appeared in 1957, and Walker Percy, whose first novel, *The Moviegoer*, won the National Book Award in 1961, was part of a group of committed religious writers whose much-lauded stories and novels promised to form a second wave of the Southern Literary Renaissance. While it would be unfair to characterise these three as entirely Gothic in their sensibilities – Percy's work is typically described as existential, rather, depicting the search of alienated protagonists for meaning amid a social and metaphysical landscape of chaos – they nonetheless deploy the familiar tropes of the grotesque; in fact, some of Percy's later speculative science fiction, such as *The Thanatos Syndrome* (1987), might be read as examples of Gothic catastrophism.

Typically allegorical figures of ironic awakening, these extreme characters become staples of Southern Gothic writing. One implication of such a reading certainly buttresses the romantic myth of the old South as a once-noble society insofar as the historical narrative that unfolds is one of degeneracy. There is, to be sure, a decidedly mournful dimension to Faulkner's prose. On the other hand, and as many critics have pointed out, the fabulous and Gothic nature of the novels do their best to expose the hidden cruelties of the history: the myth is exposed as little more than a whitewash. But, to return to the case of Faulkner, such denunciations are never easily arrived at. That the stories being told in his works prove so painfully hard to unfold, that they so often require serial narrators, that Faulkner deploys all the modernist stylistic tricks of fragmented subjectivity, multiple and disorienting chronologies, competing points of view, and so forth, all suggest that the uncovering of painful truths is in some measure a tortuously difficult act, that the traumas of the past inflect the trauma of the telling.

Consequently, Southern Gothic has been theorised as a return of the barbarous repressed. Faulkner's often-quoted phrase from *Requiem for a Nun* (1951) that, in the American South, 'The past is never dead. It's not even past' points to the intractable persistence in the region of an array of unresolved crises.[6] These include the genocidal displacement of indigenous

---

[6] William Faulkner, *Requiem for a Nun* (London: Vintage, 1996), p. 85.

Americans; the violent history of slavery and the failed project of Reconstruction; lynch law and the Klan's various reigns of terror; and the institutionalised segregation of the Jim Crow era, all of which have saddled the region and the American nation with a legacy of unrelenting racial violence. Further, we might point to the great exodus of rural populations of Blacks to northern cities and to the American West; the deep poverty that ensnared working whites within the neo-feudal system of sharecropping; and the exploitation of coal miners in Appalachia. Another residual feature that still defines the South is the so-called 'cult of Southern womanhood', an overarching, dominant myth that has so powerfully deformed social arrangements of gender in the region that it has produced what critic Patricia Yaeger terms the 'ravaged bodies so dominant in southern women's fiction'. Other historical determinants include the long history of industrial underdevelopment; the trials of the Civil Rights era; and the neglect of educational institutions, a neglect that has, in recent years, been transformed into nothing short of an onslaught.[7]

For many contemporary critics, it is the long, sad history of racial and economic injustice (in the South, and elsewhere) that forms the substrata of American culture and informs the contours of a specifically American Gothic writing. Increasingly, following Fiedler's line of argumentation, cultural historians have articulated the centrality of American Gothic, even within an individualist, future-oriented, frontier-focused and democratic national mythos. For Teresa A. Goddu in *Gothic America* (1997), as for Kathleen Brogan in *Cultural Haunting* (1998), homage to the dead is central to the project of American renewal. Brogan accentuates the unresolved processes of mourning the part of various racialised or minority or immigrant social communities, communities who have been violently severed from their pasts or traditions via subjugation, genocide, enslavement or displacement. Goddu states categorically that the American South bears the burden of being somehow representative of a past that that cannot be shaken off:

> The American gothic is most recognizable as a regional form. Identified with gothic doom and gloom, the American South serves as the nation's 'other,' becoming the repository for everything from which the nation wishes to dissociate itself. The benighted South is able to support the irrational impulses of the gothic that the nation as a whole, born of Enlightenment ideals, cannot.[8]

---

[7] Patricia Yaeger, *Dirt and Desire: Reconstructing Southern Women's Writing, 1930–1990* (Chicago: University of Chicago Press, 2000), p. 65.

[8] Teresa A. Goddu, *Gothic America: Narrative, History, and Nation* (New York: Columbia University Press, 1997), p. 3.

In *The Palgrave Handbook of Southern Gothic*, editors Susan Castillo Street and Charles L. Crow concur:

> Indeed, the South is a region that has always been obsessed with crossroads and boundaries, whether territorial (the Mason–Dixon line) or those related to gender, social class, sexuality and particularly race. In the South, ghosts and men in white sheets are real, as are shackles and clanking chains, and the Southern Gothic is a genre that arises from the area's often violent and traumatic history.[9]

Or as Christopher Lloyd helpfully summarises, 'Cultural memories from the South are thus engaged by the gothic form and transformed in the process; dark traumas from the region's past are lodged in and substantiate culture.'[10] Of course, as Fiedler, Goddu and Crow all remind us, Gothic supernaturalism has always been in the mainstream of American literary production. Nor, as Crow reminds us in his contribution to the *Cambridge Companion to American Gothic*, is race the only concern of Southern Gothic.[11] Eric Anderson, Taylor Hagood and Daniel Cross Turner, editors of *Undead Souths*, reveal 'how the dead contain cultural vibrancy in the present':

> Undeadness describes a wide continuum of posthumous phenomena, from funerary rites and mourning practices to the shocking, overwhelming affect of terrifying spectacles and posttraumatic flashbacks, to figures from beyond death: ghosts, vampires, zombies, but also corpses unburied, decayed, desecrated, dismembered, yet still filled with life, or a kind of life, be it with the multitude of micro-organisms drawing sustenance from decomposing bodies or the psychical afterlife of remembering the dead. This necrological impulse can also incarnate in metaphorical ways in texts that may not feature literal revenants but that present tropes of undeadness.[12]

---

[9] Susan Castillo Street and Charles L. Crow, 'Introduction: Down at the Crossroads', in Susan Castillo Street and Charles L. Crow (eds), *The Palgrave Handbook to the Southern Gothic* (Basingstoke: Palgrave Macmillan, 2016), pp. 1–6 (p. 2).

[10] Christopher Lloyd, 'Southern Gothic', in Joel Faflak and Jason Haslam (eds), *American Gothic Culture: An Edinburgh Companion* (Edinburgh: Edinburgh University Press, 2016), pp. 79–91 (p. 81).

[11] Charles L. Crow, 'Southern American Gothic', in Jeffrey Andrew Weinstock (ed.), *The Cambridge Companion to American Gothic* (Cambridge: Cambridge University Press, 2017), pp. 141–55 (p. 141).

[12] Eric Anderson, Taylor Hagood and Daniel Cross Turner, 'Introduction', in Eric Anderson, Taylor Hagood, and Daniel Cross Turner (eds), *Undead Souths: The Gothic and Beyond in Southern Literature and Culture* (Baton Rouge: Louisiana State University Press, 2015), pp. 1–9 (pp. 2, 1).

Thinking of Faulkner's *Absalom, Absalom!*, critic Richard Gray writes that 'the Gothic is the means by which the secret history of a culture is told'.[13]

But there is a history, too, to the secret history. Southern Gothic was, at least initially, decidedly not the mode of writing championed by cultural boosters of the South. The development of a broad 'Southern imaginary' articulates itself as a space everywhere in romantic contention with the forces of modernity, and literary production has been key to maintaining a distinct sense of the South. Even as they expressed admiration for such experimental writers as T. S. Eliot or James Joyce, most advocates of Southern literature were ambivalent, at best, about the prospects of modernism. Alert to the menaces of 'cultural carpetbaggers', defenders of a distinct Southern tradition often conceived of the modern as decadent, intrusive, cosmopolitan and foreign to the South. It may be helpful, therefore, to reconsider the emergence of Southern Gothic vis-à-vis the contentious debates that have taken place about the very nature of Southern writing.

Debating a Regional Identity

Southern writing, it seemed, had to be somehow true to the South. But that was no easy task. In his important but too often overlooked essay 'The South as Field for Fiction' (1888), radical reconstructionist Albion W. Tourgée targeted the tendency of northern writers, in the interests of appeasement, to gloss over any mention of the war and the institution of slavery: 'a nation can never bury its past. A country's history may perish, but it can never outlive its history'.[14] Southern writers, by contrast, Tourgée charges, were inclined to sentimentalise, even glamorise, the Confederacy. Their works proliferated stock characterisations of 'Southern types': the belle, the 'dashing Confederate cavalier', 'the poor white Cinderella', 'the devoted slave', 'the poor "nigger" to whom liberty has brought only misfortune'.[15] This situation was bound to change, Tourgée prophesied, because culture thrives on strife and trauma. The high-handed, self-satisfied brutality of the Confederacy and its violent collapse would, of necessity, become the occasion of the most poignant romance: 'a civilization fell with it – a civilization full of wonderful

---

[13] Richard Gray, 'Inside the Dark House: William Faulkner, *Absalom, Absalom!* and the Southern Gothic', in Castillo Street and Crow (eds), *The Palgrave Handbook to the Southern Gothic*, pp. 21–40 (p. 37).
[14] Albion W. Tourgée, 'The South as a Field for Fiction', in Mark Elliott and John David Smith (eds), *Undaunted Radical: The Selected Writings and Speeches of Albion Tourgée* (Baton Rouge: Louisiana State University Press, 2010), pp. 203–11 (p. 204).
[15] Tourgée, 'The South as a Field for Fiction', pp. 207–8.

contrast, horrible beyond the power of imagination to conceive of in its injustice and cruelty, and barbarous displacement of a subject race, yet exquisitely charming in its assumptions of pastoral purity and immaculate excellence'.[16] Popular folklore was a beginning, asserts Tourgée, highlighting the 'quaintness' of Joel Chandler Harris and the 'curious realism' of Charles Chesnutt. Consequently it was Black life, folk life, that should prove the most fertile for literary production. For future chronicles of Black experience, Tourgée argues, life 'as slave, freedman, and racial outcast offers undoubtedly the richest mine of romantic material that has opened to the English speaking novelist' since Walter Scott.[17] And what of white society? 'It is a truth as yet but half appreciated' that, for whites, 'to the woefulness of the conquered is added the pathos of a myriad of deposed sovereigns. Around them will cluster the halo of romantic glory, and the epoch of their overthrow will live again in American literature.'[18] In sum, Tourgée concludes, 'the South is destined to be the Hesperides Garden of American literature. We cannot foretell the form that its product will wear or even guess its character. It may be sorrowful, exultant, aspiring or perhaps terrible, but it will certainly be great.'[19]

Three decades on, however, such high promise seemed to have gone unfulfilled. Prior to 1919, the most prominent 'Southern' writers included Poe, Mark Twain, Ellen Glasgow, folklorists Harris and Chesnutt, along with the exceedingly popular fantasist James Branch Cabell – a distinguished group, no doubt, but hardly a school. And, of the lot, Glasgow alone was considered to be preoccupied primarily with producing a Southern literature. The 13 November 1920 edition of the New York *Evening Mail* included a brief, blistering attack on Southern culture by H. L. Mencken, 'The Sahara of the Bozart'. 'Once you have counted James Branch Cabell', Mencken chortles,

> you will not find a single Southern prose writer who can actually write. And once you have – but when you come to critics, musical composers, painters, sculptors, architects and the like, you will have to give it up, for there is not even a bad one between the Potomac mudflats and the Gulf. Nor a historian. Nor a Philosopher. Nor a theologian. Nor a scientist. In all these fields the South is an awe-inspiring blank.[20]

---

[16] Tourgée, 'The South as a Field for Fiction', p. 210.
[17] Tourgée, 'The South as a Field for Fiction', p. 209.
[18] Tourgée, 'The South as a Field for Fiction', p. 210.
[19] Tourgée, 'The South as a Field for Fiction', p. 211.
[20] H. L. Mencken, 'The Sahara of the Bozart', in Huntington Cairn (ed.), *The American Scene: A Reader* (New York: Knopf, 1977), pp. 157–68 (p. 159).

Others also sounded the alarm. Something like a properly 'Southern' culture merited cultivation. Between 1929 and 1935, Mencken's protégé, W. J. Cash, published a series of essays in *American Mercury*, including the seminal 'The Mind of the South' (October, 1929) that would later be expanded into book form and published by Knopf in 1941. For Cash, inarguably, there is 'one South ... a fairly definite mental pattern, associated with a fairly definite social pattern – a complex of established relationships and habits of thought, sentiments, prejudices, standards and values, and associations of ideas, which, if not common to every group of white people in the South, is still common in one appreciable measure or another'.[21] This unyielding insistence on the monolithic distinctness of the South becomes, over the course of the twentieth century, an unquestioned feature of arguments put forth by both apologists and critics alike.

Responding, in part, to Mencken's barbs and to the challenges laid out by Cash, Southern literary figures came together in order to midwife a new literary culture into being. The self-titled 'Agrarians', a group of Southern-identified poets, fiction writers, academics and critics whose core figures included such notable men of letters as Allen Tate, John Crowe Ransom and Robert Penn Warren who had earlier been associated with Vanderbilt journal *The Fugitive*, banded together to publish the steadfast defence, *I'll Take My Stand: The South and the Agrarian Tradition* (1930). The collection of an introductory statement of principles and twelve individually authored essays is a fierce defence of regional pride, orthodox religion and agrarian economic principles against the perceived encroachments of industrial civilisation, secular hubris, 'commercialism' and 'humanism'. The defence of the arts developed in this collection, while varying somewhat from writer to writer, is united against what the Introduction sees as 'a general decay of sensibility', because 'neither the creation nor the understanding of works of art is possible in an industrial age'.[22] At almost precisely the same moment, however, appeared the two most recognised writers to emerge from the South as ambitiously modern regionalists, writers whose novels, paradoxically enough, feverishly chronicled that same 'decay of sensibility'. In 1929, Thomas Wolfe published *Look Homeward Angel* and William Faulkner published *The Sound and the Fury*. Wolfe, of Asheville, North Carolina, and Faulkner, reworking the history of his home in Oxford, Mississippi, into the

---

[21] W. J. Cash, *The Mind of the South* (New York: Vintage, 1961), p. vii.

[22] *I'll Take My Stand: The South and the Agrarian Tradition, by Twelve Southerners* (New York: Harper & Row, 1962), p. xxv.

fictional locale of Yoknapatawpha county and county seat Jefferson, produced works that seemed vitalised by decadence.

What to do? In retrospect, what can be understood to emerge is a formal struggle over proprietary rights to the literary South; for an ironic realist such as Ellen Glasgow, whose work was considered too womanly and sentimental for the Agrarians but who nonetheless saw fiction as serving history, the task was to undo the mythologies of the romantic. For romancers, by contrast, the aim was to dig deeper into the psychic substrata than practitioners of sentimental fictions permitted: unsurprisingly, such 'romantic realists' as Wolfe and Faulkner would be the most celebrated of Southern writers in the first flush of what came to be known as the Southern Renaissance. It was a struggle to maintain a faux-aristocratic, Jeffersonian-inflected classicism that shunned the racialised infections of the modern, the urban and the cosmopolitan, while denouncing overt racism and nonetheless glossing over the sins of plantation slavery and redressing the myths of racial purity in the fine clothes of cultural *noblesse oblige*. What could the fugitives and Agrarians make of the two great barbarians, whose potentially nostalgic regionalism was transformed and revitalised by its encounter with the wide modern world? Chastised for airing dirty laundry and betraying closely held family secrets, Wolfe wrote *You Can't Go Home Again* (1940); Faulkner went to Canada and subsequently to Europe. He did return home, but his writing had been entirely transformed. It was in the crucible of that struggle that Southern Gothic emerged. The self-ordained guardians of Southern culture found themselves in something of a pickle insofar as they promoted a literary art that would somehow be resistant to modernist decadence, even as the most celebrated works of modern literary production that emerged from the South – works Southerners wanted to be proud to claim as their own – indulged 'decay' above all other things. Such works as those by Faulkner or, later, O'Connor or Williams, read as Gothically inflected indictments of the very society that the agrarian tradition wished to endorse. What I would like to suggest is that this quarrel over form is itself central to Southern letters, and that the Gothic sensibility that characterises the modernist writing of the American South itself emerges from a struggle over form that is adequate to historical circumstance. Any survey of Southern literature must reckon with how often since the Civil War these questions have been asked, with an almost too-pointed anxiety: what is the South? And what should Southern culture rightly look like?

Nonetheless, by mid-century, as Southern writing was increasingly recognised by the critical establishment as among the most powerful achievements in American literature, a certain sort of cold war détente set in: Wolfe was dead; Faulkner had his Nobel Prize; Ransom had moved north, to Kenyon College, and his anti-historical arguments had muted into the ahistorical New Criticism, a critical method that had curiously little to say about contemporary Gothic. Robert Penn Warren published *All the King's Men* (1946), which won the Pulitzer Prize, and a new generation of writers from the South became increasingly lauded. Southern literature – and Southern Gothic literature – was not only recognised as a distinctive literary mode, but as a commendable if still somewhat troubling one. The collection *Southern Renascence: The Literature of the Modern South*, edited by Louis D. Rubin and Robert D. Jacobs, appeared in 1953, including essays on such increasingly recognised writers as Warren, Eudora Welty, Katherine Anne Porter, Erskine Caldwell and Caroline Gordon. While the question of 'what is contemporary Southern writing?' continued to be asked, the answer given in the late 1940s and 1950s tended to be 'Gothic'. What accounts for 'The Southern Quality', asked Marshal McLuhan in a 1947 essay of that name in the *Sewanee Review*. For McLuhan, Southern writers are uniquely characterised by 'passion', amid a business civilisation that had made passion obsolete: passion, coupled with fatalism, he argued, and 'a contemplation of death which pervades all southern writing'.[23] And 'if you are a Southern writer', Flannery O'Connor lamented in a seminal talk delivered in 1960, 'that label, and all the misconceptions that go with it, is pasted on you at once'.[24]

The theory of Southern literature that would come to be endorsed by both critic and writer Allen Tate, doyen of the Renaissance, and eminent historian C. Vann Woodward in some ways resurrected the insights of Tourgée, that cultural production thrives on conflict. In general terms, as critic Richard King notes, 'the Renaissance was the product of the creative tension between the Southern past and the pressures of the modern world'.[25] This observation is fair enough, so far as it goes, but, as King

---

[23] Herbert Marshall McLuhan, 'The Southern Quality', *The Sewanee Review* 55:3 (1947): 357–83 (p. 382).

[24] Flannery O'Connor, 'Some aspects of the Grotesque in Southern Fiction', in Sally Fitzgerald and Robert Fitzgerald (eds), *Mystery and Manners* (London: Faber and Faber, 1972), pp. 36–50 (p. 37).

[25] Richard A. King, *A Southern Renaissance: The Cultural Awakening of the American South, 1930–1955* (New York: Oxford University Press, 1980), p. 4.

notes, the argument is so overly generalised as to be effectively useless as a tool of critical interrogation: which twentieth-century culture is not, at base, shaped by the encounter with modernity? Moreover, it begs the formal question: what literary shape does the clash of tradition and modernity take? What genres will they inhabit? How will these clashes recombine elements and re-shape those genres?

Southern Writing after the Second World War

In the years between the Second World War and Faulkner's death in 1962, the 'Southern Renaissance' had become a cultural certitude, almost something of a cliché; indeed, some critics recognised that Southern writers had reached the peak of their accomplishments and that this was a literature in decline, or even dying. While the consensus is that the Renaissance waned in the mid-1950s, a post-war generation of writers emerged who, however much they engaged with the global scope of the Cold War or increasingly embraced the Civil Rights movement and other political causes, did not entirely shake off the mantle of regionalism and continued working in explicitly Gothic modes. There are two important and interrelated observations that should be made, however, about the mid-century canonisation of a Southern tradition: first, it was an exclusively white tradition. Second, Gothic, while celebrated, also continued to be castigated and would be so increasingly over the years by cultural commentators. The rejection of Gothic was also the rejection of racial contamination. In both cases, we witness again the attempt to police determinations and delimit the understanding of Southern literature by exiling what was understood to be racially and formally threatening. In both cases, efforts were mounted to keep the South 'pure' of cultural miscegenation and Gothic contamination.

Of course, Southern literary production was always a larger field than that conceived by most theorists of the Renaissance, who almost entirely excluded Black writers – including such celebrated modernists as Jean Toomer, Zora Neale Hurston and Richard Wright – from their surveys. Such major Black writers as Wright and Ralph Ellison were celebrated in the 1950s, but neither was mentioned in surveys of Southern writing. Wright's *Native Son* (1940) was made a Book-of-the-Month club selection and became a bestseller; Ellison's *Invisible Man* (1952) won the National Book Award. Significantly, however, neither was perceived as a 'Southern writer', although Wright was from Natchez, Mississippi, and both his short story collection, *Uncle Tom's Children* (1938), and his memoir, *Black Boy* (1945), interrogate Southern customs, as do the significant early sections of *Invisible Man*, set in a fictionalised version of Tuskegee Institute, in Alabama, which Ellison, from Oklahoma, had attended. Though Faulkner and other white writers wrote powerfully of the racial animosity that afflicted the South, Black writers, it seemed, were not fully welcome in the Renaissance.

The Southern Gothicists are presumed to be white writers, of course, in part because racial dread and trauma inform the American Gothic mode, as Fiedler and Goddu argue. Southern Black writers tended not to deploy Gothic settings or affect or idioms, though a case might be made for some of the more surrealist moments in the work of Wright and Ellison. The omission of Hurston and such earlier writers as Chesnutt is at another level more surprising, as Southern Gothic writing is characterised by the persistence of folk narratives, ghost stories, slave tales and annals of Hoodoo or Vodoun 'supernatural' practices; in the hands of Black writers, these can often read as forms of resistance, as distinct ways of knowing. Subsequent writers – Toni Morrison, most famously, in such works as *Song of Solomon* (1977), *Beloved* (1987) and *Paradise* (1997) – have depicted Reconstruction and its aftermath in the South and even the Midwest as decidedly Gothic. W. E. B. Du Bois, wearing his novelist cap, deserves a mention too. Though he is by no means a Southern writer, he wrote about the South in such books as *The Quest of the Silver Fleece* (1911). Not really a modernist, and as much a 'social realist' as a romanticist, Du Bois sometimes deployed a Gothic idiom to describe African American experience, as in his description of 'double-consciousness' from *The Souls of Black Folk* (1903):

> youth ... wasted itself in a bitter cry, Why did God make me an outcast and a stranger in mine own house? The shades of the prison-house closed round about us all: walls strait and stubborn to the whitest, but relentlessly narrow, tall, and unscalable to sons of night who must plod darkly on in resignation, or beat unavailing palms against the stone, or steadily, half hopelessly, watch the streak of blue above.[26]

If a sort of cultural Jim Crow prevented the inclusion of Black literary production in discussions of Southern Gothic, there were other distinctions enforced through the process of canonisation. Other Southern writers too, such as the feminist Frances Newman, whose work did not fit easily with the increasingly conventional characteristics of Southern writing, had been effectively purged from the canon. Newman is anything but a Gothic writer, although her second novel, *Dead Lovers Are Faithful Lovers* (1928), prefigures *As*

---

[26] W. E. B. Du Bois, *The Souls of Black Folk* (New York: Penguin Random House, 2018), p. 5.

I Lay Dying insofar as it involves a widow conveying the corpse of her dead husband back to his hometown for burial. Indeed, her favourite theme is the jarring clashes between tradition and modern life. Newman's arch, cool, sardonic prose dramatised the challenges facing those aspiring to the freedoms of the 'new woman' who were nonetheless ensconced in a social web that delimited the possibilities for women's agency according to the confining strictures of idealised Southern belle.

Finally, in addition to the writers mentioned in Rubin and Jacob's critical collection, it is worth drawing attention to a few other examples of Southern Gothic writers, some of whom have suffered from critical neglect. Less recognised, perhaps, but equally important in their singular development of highly experimental and acutely lyrical Gothic prose style are such writers as James Agee or William Goyen. Agee's posthumously published *A Death in the Family* (1957) describes a child's home in Knoxville, Tennessee, as haunted by regret and by longing, as by the revenant of the dead father. William Goyen, who began writing during the war and whose short stories began appearing in the late 1940s, published compelling works of Gothic surrealism. Set in the small east Texas town of Charity, a fictionalised version of his own hometown of Trinity, Goyen's *The House of Breath* (1950) is comprised of an aria of ghostly lyric voices – of the dead, of the lost, of the features of the land itself – overlapping to create a sexual coming-of-age story set amid a haunted homestead. Peopled with the statutory perverts and deviants – sexual predators, closeted and open homosexuals – and written in Goyen's own inimitable prayer-like, dream-like style, *House of Breath* couples the familiar juxtaposition of the grotesque with the sublime to a meditation on decay, time's passing, and the exhaustions and exertions of memory:

> Behold the house . . .
> Now Ruin has passed over all that fallen splendid house and done ruin's work on it. Now, ruin (of childhood) returning to ruin, come, purged of that bile and gall of childhood (into the empty purity of memory), come through the meadow called Bailey's Pasture that is spun over with luminous dandelions like a million gathered shining heads, through random blooming mustard and clover and bitterweeds, over the grown-over path that was a short-cut to town when there was no circus or revival tent there.[27]

Somewhat later, Cormac McCarthy, whose Appalachian novels set in Knoxville and east Tennessee include *The Orchard Keeper* (1965), *Outer Dark*

---

[27] William Goyen, *The House of Breath* (Evanston, IL: Northwestern University Press, 1999), p. 42.

(1968), *Child of God* (1973) and *Suttree* (1979), is often mentioned as working within the tradition of Faulkner and the Southern Gothic. The tradition endures in contemporary writers as distinct as Toni Morrison or William Gay, whose *Little Sister Death* (2015) is a contemporary classic of the genre.

In closing, we can acknowledge that the traditions of Southern Gothic and Southern modernism are both more capacious than most critics have allowed for and, paradoxically enough, more heavily policed; indeed, the critical field has been characterised by a series of highly charged arguments about what the South is and, correspondingly, over the proper 'form' of literature appropriate to the expression of Southernness. Following Toni Morrison's argument in *Playing in the Dark* (1992), we can contend that the anxious dismissal or disavowal of the Africanist present is itself a component of Southern Gothic. For Morrison, 'the process of organizing American coherence through a distancing Africanism became the operative mode of a new cultural hegemony'.[28] As a way of restricting and organising the unsettling presence of slaves and their descendants, a non-white presence was, in the same instance, both constructed and disavowed. So too, in the South, America's own 'other', according to such Gothic theorists as Goddu, a coherent regional identity has been assembled and maintained via what might be termed a 'distancing gothic presence', a 'way of talking about and policing' matters of everyday deviance amid a society of social taboos against miscegenation, incest, homosexuality that are everywhere symbolically enforced, to an almost hysterical extent, though commonly violated in practice.[29]

Let us look at a couple of interventions into the heritage of the Southern Literary Renaissance, which by the 1970s many saw as waning. Louis Rubin, in the wake of Faulkner's death, remained fairly sanguine about the ongoing vitality of Southern literature. Others, however, demurred. In a 1976 series of lectures delivered at Mercer University and published as *A Requiem for the Renascence*, critic Walter Sullivan dismissed all post-war fiction of the South more or less out of hand. In such later writings as the Snopes Trilogy (*The Hamlet* [1940], *The Town* [1957], *The Mansion* [1959]), Sullivan laments, Faulkner 'abandoned his own vision'; the short stories of Peter Taylor have 'sagged markedly'; Carson McCullers and William Styron are condemned for being 'existentialists'.[30] Only Walker Percy, whose *Love in the Ruins* (1971) is

---

[28] Toni Morrison, *Playing in the Dark: Whiteness and the Literary Imagination* (Cambridge, MA: Harvard University Press, 1992), p. 8.

[29] Goddu, *Gothic America*, p. 7.

[30] Walter Sullivan, *A Requiem for the Renascence: The State of Fiction in the Modern South* (Athens, GA: University of Georgia Press, 1976), pp. xix, xxiii, xxi.

read as an allegory of spiritual revitalisation, is spared. In her story collection *The Golden Apples* (1949), Eudora Welty chronicles chaos and the 'dissolution of community', according to Sullivan.[31] Of the young Cormac McCarthy, Sullivan had high hopes that were quickly dashed: 'No southern novelist since William Styron has got off to a better start. But in his second book [*Outer Dark* (1968)], McCarthy told a weird, almost gothic tale of incest and his third novel [*Child of God* (1973)] is clear evidence of the madness to which our art has finally descended.'[32] Harper Lee is pointedly absent from Sullivan's account; Lee's *To Kill a Mockingbird* (1960) is perhaps the most famous novel ever written about the American South, but – perhaps because it indicts racial bigotry – Sullivan pretends that it does not exist. He is blind to queer writers from the South as well. Truman Capote is absent – and what else is *In Cold Blood* (1966) but Gothic journalism? So too is Tennessee Williams. Of such Black writers as Alice Walker, whose first novel *The Third Life of Grange Copeland* appeared in 1970; or Margaret Walker, author of the much-celebrated historical novel *Jubilee* (1966); or Earnest J. Gaines, who published several well-received novels in the late 1960s and early 1970s – not a word. According to Sullivan, Southern writing is white writing – and straight writing – exclusively; the trouble it suffers from is that it is too Gothic.

Nearly two decades later, we can witness the same line of argumentation. For the 1993 Massey lectures at Harvard, at the very height of the culture wars, historian Eugene Genovese delivered a full-throated defence of the Southern conservative tradition, a 'viewpoint', he claims, that 'often accompanied racism, but ... has no necessary connection to it'.[33] The argument is remarkable in a number of ways. Notably, Genovese offers a survey of Southern letters that makes not a single mention of Faulkner. Further, Genovese, who in his earlier Marxist phase had penned the classic history of slavery and resistance in *Roll Jordan Roll* (1974), resurrects the arguments of *I'll Take My Stand* against the incursions of the Gothic, defending a supposed Southern rejection of modernity and investment in orthodox Christianity. He rails against the evils of the modern world, against materialism, against acquisitive capitalism, against atheism, secularism and politics: 'For the first time in history, so far as I know, a democratic society has forced art into the subservient and dishonest function of pursuing political and social ends.'[34]

---

[31] Sullivan, *A Requiem for the Renascence*, p. 49.
[32] Sullivan, *A Requiem for the Renascence*, p. 70.
[33] Eugene Genovese, *The Southern Tradition: The Achievements and Limitations of an American Conservatism* (Cambridge, MA: Harvard University Press, 1994), p. 27.
[34] Genovese, *The Southern Tradition*, p. 230.

These conflicts have animated Southern literature throughout the twentieth century, and into our own. For unreconstructed Southerners, the Civil War is romanticised precisely because its soldiers took up arms in resistance to incursions of modernity in the form of federal overstepping of its authority over of 'states' rights', the excesses of industrial capitalism and the presumed barbarisms attendant upon mass immigration. 'Southern Literature' has in turn been pointedly anxious about its place within a progressive American cultural project dedicated to democratic exceptionalism and the Emersonian ideal of stepping clear of old-world historical sludge and freeing the nation from the yokes of tradition. The South, for its defenders, is about preserving tradition. Even in the early decades of the twenty-first century, as many cities are quietly removing statues of Confederate war heroes and college campuses are renaming buildings christened in honour of slaveholders, Americans are engaged in fervent debates about whether those historical legacies can be pried free from the brutal history of white supremacy.

If 'Southern literature' and the Southern Renaissance were conceived of as white or Anglo-Saxon literatures for much of the twentieth century, the racial exclusivity was never an accidental oversight or afterthought. As even Louis D. Rubin, Jr – the one critic who laboured harder than anyone to shape the enduring canon of Southern literature – concedes, Southern regional identity and the concomitant need for a cultural formation through which to express it emerged as a defensive response to the crisis posed by radical abolition: 'the very idea of a "southern" literature, as distinct from an American literature, had its origin in the slavery controversy'.[35] The self-proclaimed 'Southernness' of Southern writing involves a self-aware attempt on the part of largely conservative white writers and critics to purge Southern literature of its Black presence. From the arguments put forth by Agrarians in *I'll Take my Stand* (1930) to Genovese's Massey lectures, delivered at the height of the so-called culture wars of the late twentieth century, to the alt-right Klan revivalism of nationalist Richard Spencer during the Trump era, the cultural threat to racial purity is understood to be as terrifying as the biological. Everywhere that we find the policing of 'values' in contentious debates about the South we also find the defence of idealised literary forms against the encroachments of Gothic, itself understood to be a bastardised, incestuous, grotesque, contaminating or miscegenated genre.

---

[35] Louis D. Rubin Jr, *The Faraway Country: Writers of the Modern South* (Seattle: University of Washington Press, 1963), p. 16.

3.4

Hollywood Gothic, 1930–1960

MARK JANCOVICH

Introduction

The Gothic cinema that flourished in Hollywood between 1930 and 1960 is often imagined as one distinguished by two distinct periods: a cycle of the 1930s and 1940s that was dominated by the classics produced by Universal; and another that was dominated by Hammer and began with the success of *The Curse of Frankenstein* (dir. Terence Fisher) in 1957 (although some favour a break associated with the release of Alfred Hitchcock's *Psycho* in 1960).[1] These two cycles, then, are supposed to be defined by two dominant studios, which shaped the forms that others imitated. In addition, these cycles are strongly associated with key monsters, particularly Dracula and Frankenstein[2] but also, to a lesser extent, the Mummy and the Wolf Man.[3] In fact, this sense of the period initially structured the debate about the Gothic cinema, with critics such as Ivan Butler arguing that the Hammer films were a vulgarisation of the Universal classics,[4] while David Pirie and others sought to defend Hammer as a legitimate version of the cinematic Gothic.[5]

These accounts, however, which were largely established in the 1960s and early 1970s, provide a very misleading sense of this history. As this chapter

---

[1] The most prominent exponent of this latter position is Robin Wood in *Hollywood from Vietnam to Reagan* (New York: University of Columbia Press, 1986).
[2] While Universal largely featured Frankenstein's monstrous creation as the recurring figure in its films, Hammer shifted attention to the scientific creator, Frankenstein, who became its recurring monstrous presence.
[3] See, for example, Ivan Butler, *Horror in the Cinema* (London: Zwemmer, 1967); James Twitchell, *Dreadful Pleasures: An Anatomy of Modern Horror* (New York: Oxford University Press, 1985); and John Edgar Browning, 'Classical Hollywood Horror', in Harry Benshoff (ed.), *A Companion to the Horror Film* (Chichester: Wiley-Blackwell, 2014), pp. 225–36.
[4] Butler, *Horror in the Cinema*.
[5] David Pirie, *A Heritage of Horror: The English Gothic Cinema, 1946–1972* (London: Avon, 1973).

will illustrate, the Universal classics that began with *Dracula* (dir. Tod Browning, 1931) were not simply the start of a new cycle but emerged out of a period of Gothic production that reached back to the 1920s; and while the phenomenal success of *Dracula* gave impetus to those productions, and may have encouraged them down particular avenues, both the film and its reception need to be understood within the larger context of the late 1920s and early 1930s. Furthermore, the productions of the 1930s came to an end in 1936 and the Gothic films of the 1940s were a very different cycle, although most accounts both acknowledge and ignore this issue. Furthermore, even the 1940s cycle itself was divided into two stages, so that, while Gothic cinema came back with a vengeance in 1939, the success of *Cat People* in 1942 (dir. Jacques Tourneur) had much the same impact as *Dracula*: it both intensified and influenced production within the period. By 1946, however, this cycle had reached its height and while production continued into the next decade, the 1950s was, at least initially, dominated by a very different type of Gothic cinema, one explicitly inflected with science fiction. Finally, the science fiction cycle also declined as producers found that it was the horror elements of these films (rather than their science fiction elements) that were most popular with audiences, but also as they sought to capitalise on the success of Henri-Georges Clouzot's *Les Diaboliques* (1955) on the art cinema circuit, and of *Alfred Hitchcock Presents* (1955–65) on television. It was for this reason that American financiers approached Hammer and effectively commissioned them to make a Gothic horror film, *The Curse of Frankenstein*. Consequently, 1955 saw the start of a new cycle of production that included Hammer but also American producers, such as William Castle, who explicitly sought to imitate the type of Gothic cinema that had proved so successful with *Les Diaboliques*. In other words, neither *Curse of Frankenstein* nor *Psycho* constituted breaks within the history of Gothic cinema. On the contrary, both were the products of existing patterns, even if they developed specific aspects of these established trends: Hammer reinvigorated a cinema of period-set monster movies while *Psycho* was one of a number of films through which the major studios cashed in on the market for psychological horror.

    This difference in accounts of the period also suggests something else. Most of the current histories, as we have already seen, focus around specific key monsters, and this is stressed through the suggestion that Universal and Hammer were organised around the production of series such as the Frankenstein and Dracula films. However, as Peter Hutchings has noted, Universal's strategy in the 1930s was focused on product differentiation rather than series production.[6] Neither *Dracula* nor *Frankenstein* was produced with the intention of instigating a film series but rather as prestigious, stand-alone productions. When the studio finally produced a sequel to *Frankenstein* in 1935 and to *Dracula* in 1936, neither was intended as the start of a series either. Universal only turned to series production, then, in the 1940s, when it was a very different studio and one whose strategy was largely to establish enough profitability to justify its acquisition by others: those in charge of Universal were trying to sell the company. The studio therefore invested heavily in cost-effective series and the occasional big-budget prestige picture so that in 1943, its Gothic productions included a prestige production from Hitchcock, *Shadow of a Doubt*, and various contributions to its horror series: *Son of Dracula* (dir. Robert Siodmak); *Frankenstein Meets the Wolf Man* (dir. Roy William Neill); *Captive Wild Woman* (dir. Edward Dmytryk); and the first in its *Inner Sanctum* (1943–5) series.

Finally, then, while histories have often presented the Gothic films of the period as disreputable low-budget productions, the films of this period covered the full gamut of Hollywood productions from low-budget Poverty Row efforts, through the middle bracket to some of the most prestigious and expensive films of the period. Furthermore, given that women were often seen as key to attracting the most valuable audience, namely the middle-class family, it is hardly surprising that many productions were specifically targeted at female viewers. Although it is often assumed today that the Gothic films of this period were predominantly targeted at male audiences, this assumption is due to the marginalisation, and even reclassification, of the bigger-budget films in later accounts of the period.

The Universal Classics in Context

It has become something of a truism that the Gothic films of the 1930s were, in some way, a response to the Great Depression, but *Dracula*'s relationship to earlier films calls this into question.[7] It may well have been a breakout film, the success of which makes it stand out from the other films in relation to which it was shaped, but it was still the product of trends that go back to the mid-1920s. By 1926, Lon Chaney already had made both *The Hunchback of Notre Dame* (dir. Wallace Worsley, 1923) and *The Phantom of the Opera* (dir. Rupert Julian, 1925), but this year witnessed the beginning of a larger cycle

---

[6] Peter Hutchings, *The Horror Film* (London: Longman, 2004).
[7] David Skal, *The Monster Show: A Cultural History of Horror* (New York: Norton, 1993).

with the release of *The Bat* (dir. Roland West), the film version of an old dark house play that had proved hugely successful on the Broadway Stage. This film was then followed in 1927 by two similar films, *The Cat and the Canary* (dir. Paul Leni, 1927) and *The Gorilla* (dir. Alfred Santell, 1927), both of which were also adaptations from the theatre. These films were praised by critics, and the *New York Times* even announced that *The Cat and the Canary* was among 'the finest examples of motion picture art'.[8] Much of the credit for its success was supposedly due to its director, Paul Leni, whom Hollywood had attracted from Germany where he was associated with Expressionist cinema. Indeed, this was a period in which Hollywood was actively pursuing the talent associated with German cinema; it not only saw the release of *The Man Who Laughs* (dir. Paul Leni, 1928), a Hollywood vehicle for the German star, Conrad Veidt, but the US release of numerous classics of German Expressionist cinema, in some cases several years after their production.[9] The number of Gothic films increased throughout the late 1920s and, by 1930, the studios were already doing remakes of *The Bat* (*The Bat Whispers* [dir. Roland West, 1930]), *The Cat and the Canary* (retitled as *The Cat Creeps* [dir. Rupert Julian, 1930]) and *The Gorilla* (dir. Bryan Foy, 1930). These were accompanied by the re-release of *The Phantom of the Opera*, to which sound was added.

When *Dracula* was reviewed by the *New York Times* in 1931, it was therefore reviewed alongside a range of other films from the same year: *The Bat Whispers*; *M* (dir. Fritz Lang); *The Gorilla*; *Svengali* (dir. Archie Mayo, an adaption of George du Maurier's *Trilby* [1894] that starred John Barrymore, who had appeared in the silent version of *Dr Jekyll and Mr Hyde* [dir. John S. Robertson, 1920]); *Mystère du Chambre Jaune* (dir. Marcel L'Herbier); *Daughter of the Dragon* (dir. Lloyd Corrigan, an addition to the Fu Manchu films); *The Mad Genius* (dir. Michael Curtiz, also with Barrymore); and various Charlie Chan and Sherlock Holmes productions, all of which were clearly associated with the Gothic at the time (*The Black Camel* of 1931 even featured Bela Lugosi).

Moreover, *Dracula*'s association with these films is further demonstrated by its status as another adaptation of a theatrical hit, rather than the original novel; and by its director, Tod Browning, who had also directed many of Lon Chaney's key

---

[8] Mordaunt Hall, 'A Haunted House', *New York Times*, 10 September, 1927, p. 9.
[9] See, for example, *Waxworks* (1924, but released in the US in both 1926 and 1929); *Metropolis* (1927 and released in the US in 1927); *Dr Mabuse: The Gambler* (1922 but released in the US in 1927); *Spies* (1928 and released in the US in 1928); *Hands of Orlac* (1924 but released in the US in 1928); and *Nosferatu* (1922 but released in the US in 1929).

films,[10] as well as other Gothics such as *The Mystic* (1925) and *The Thirteenth Chair* (1929). Indeed, as *Svengali*, *The Hypnotist* and Barrymore's *Rasputin* (1932) demonstrate, the films of the late 1920s and early 1930s were obsessed with mesmerism and mysticism, and Dracula's ability to mesmerise his victims was such a key feature of the Universal production that it became central to later Lugosi performances and even served as something of a joke for reviewers. For example, by the 1940s, the *New York Times* claimed that 'all Mr Lugosi has to do is look at people and they either get hypnosis or cramps from laughing'.[11]

Dracula was also released in the same year as a new version of *Dr Jekyll and Mr Hyde* (1931), although it was not reviewed in the *New York Times* until 1932. This film was a prestigious production from a major studio (Paramount); was directed by a major talent, Rouben Mamoulian, who had been imported from Germany; and starred a top star and romantic lead, Fredric March. March's presence also demonstrates that the film was targeted at a female audience, a feature that was also true of *Dracula*, which associated the Count with the figure of Rudolph Valentino through its presentation of the vampire as an exotic, fascinating and eroticised male.

As Robert Spadoni notes, *Dracula* is an odd film: it frequently features in lists of the classic Gothic films, but few critics actually seem to like it. Its reputation is therefore largely attributable to its outstanding critical and commercial success, when its impact was largely due to its use of sound, something that most critics praised.[12] However, despite *Dracula*'s success, *Frankenstein* proved an even bigger hit, and is reputed to have taken four times as much as its predecessor. It was also the film that defined the style of the Universal films. Again, it was a theatrical adaptation, not a direct adaptation of Mary Shelley's novel, and it was directed by James Whale and starred Colin Clive, both of whom had won critical acclaim for their work on the cinematic adaptation of R. C. Sherriff's play, *Journey's End* (1928). If *Dracula* raised psychological issues through its vampire's mental domination of his victims, Clive's presence made these concerns even more explicit. In *Journey's End*, he had played a figure on the verge of psychological breakdown, and *Frankenstein* not only featured Clive as a mad scientist (and one undergoing another mental breakdown) but also a monster with clear psychological problems, being the recipient of an

---

[10] *The Unholy Three* (1925); *The Blackbird* (1926); *The Road to Mandalay* (1926); *The Unknown* (1927); *London After Midnight* (also known as *The Hypnotist*, 1927); *The Big City* (1927); *West of Zanzibar* (1928); and *East Is East* (1929).

[11] B. R. Crisler, 'The Screen: "Human Monster", Featuring Bela Lugosi at the Globe, Latest Horror Picture', *New York Times*, 25 March 1940, p. 11.

[12] Robert Spadoni, *Uncanny Bodies: The Coming of Sound Film and the Origins of the Horror Genre* (Berkeley, CA: University of California Press, 2007).

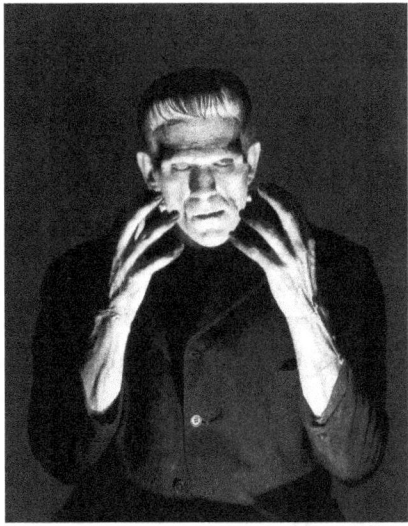

Fig.4.1: British actor Boris Karloff (1887–1969) as the Monster in a promotional portrait for *Frankenstein*, directed by James Whale, 1931. (Photo by Silver Screen Collection/Getty Images).

'abnormal brain'. This feature is often read as a conservative interpretation of the story, which places the responsibility for the monster's acts on its own physical make-up rather than on Frankenstein's treatment of him.[13] Given the sympathy with which the monster is handled, however (or at least the clear reading of the monster as sympathetic in most accounts of the film and of audiences' responses to it), this abnormality need not be read in this way – the key problem seems to be that his brain induces inarticulacy rather than violence, the violence being due to the creature's frustration at his inarticulacy and to his persecution by others (Fig. 4.1).

These psychological concerns also link these Gothic monsters to the figure of the spy and the criminal, particularly the gangster. Indeed, both Lugosi and Karloff were frequently cast in spy and crime films, and Karloff even got the role for *Frankenstein* on the basis of his performance as a killer in Howard Hawks's *The Criminal Code* (1931). One link between the figures of the monster, the criminal and the spy was their association with psychological compulsions that were often explicitly linked with a sadistic desire for

---

[13] Paul O'Flynn, 'Production and Reproduction in *Frankenstein*', *Literature and History* 9:2 (1983): 194–213.

domination and control over others, a sadistic desire that is explicitly satisfied through terrorisation.

The success of Universal's two films did not lead the studio to build series around these monsters but rather to develop a succession of new stories. *The Murders in the Rue Morgue* (dir. Robert Florey, 1932), for example, featured Lugosi as another mad scientist, and the film was sold as an adaptation of a classic of Gothic literature rather than a theatrical hit. The studio also cast Karloff in the role of an ancient magician in *The Mummy* (dir. Karl Freund, 1932), a film that has no connection with the series of the 1940s and barely featured the bandaged menace of the later films. Instead it was virtually a reworking of *Dracula*. Whale's *The Old Dark House* (1932) was a greater departure for the studio, and one in which the director parodied films such as *The Bat* and *The Cat and the Canary*.

The year 1933 featured another experiment by Universal, which cast Claude Rains in an effects-heavy adaptation of H. G. Wells's *The Invisible Man* (1897), a film that would form the basis for a series in the 1940s. Next, the studio made two films that pitted Karloff against Lugosi: *The Black Cat* (dir. Edgar G. Ulmer, 1934) and *The Raven* (dir. Louis Friedlander, 1935). Although both were supposedly adaptations from classics of Gothic literature, they were largely original stories (like *Murders in the Rue Morgue*), narratives that explicitly staged the games of sadistic domination that lay at the heart of many of the Gothic films of the period and their attendant psychological themes. As these pairings suggested, however, that the Universal productions were winding down, and despite the production of *Werewolf of London* (dir. Stuart Walker, 1935), which once again shared nothing with Universal's Wolfman series in the 1940s, Universal only made two more Gothic productions: *The Bride of Frankenstein* (dir. James Whale, 1935) and *Dracula's Daughter* (dir. Lambert Hillyer, 1936). If these films mined the success of the studio's first major Gothic successes in the 1930s, neither was a low-budget production, the former being a celebration of Whale and Karloff's original *Frankenstein*, and one that extended the story through elaboration and embellishment. Alternatively, *Dracula's Daughter* was effectively the last of the Universal films of this period, and only used *Dracula* as a hook for a quite different tale about a female monster whose vampirism is one aspect of a more general Satanic desire for domination.

If Universal has come to be seen as the home of the monstrous, this perception has two problems: first, that there were still different versions of the Gothic produced by other studios and, second, the fact that these versions were not always associated with monsters. As we have seen, *Dr Jekyll and Mr*

Hyde represented a very different, but hugely successful, version of the Gothic: it not only received glowing reviews and won an Oscar for its leading man, but it was also one of the top ten money makers of its year. Alternatively, Warner Bros (under its First National brand) produced another Gothic tale in the same year, *Dr X* (1932), which was again directed by a prestigious European director, Michael Curtiz, and in which the eponymous scientist uses science to unveil the demented moon killer, a serial killer who is known to be one of the researchers that inhabits his strange institute. Despite its killer's cannibalism, and the revelation that he can fashion limbs out of 'synthetic flesh', the film is much less about monsters and far more a forerunner of the psychological films of the 1940s.

The following year, then, saw the release of an MGM film that featured Boris Karloff as Fu Manchu, this oriental villain being a prominent one during the silent period. The studio also released *Freaks* (1932), another film that harked back to the silent era through its circus setting, which was reminiscent of several Lon Chaney classics and even featured Tod Browning as its director. Alternatively, Paramount followed *Dr Jekyll and Mr Hyde* with another literary adaptation, a film version of H. G. Wells's *The Island of Dr Moreau*, retitled as *The Island of Lost Souls* (dir. Erle C. Kenton, 1932) and starring Charles Laughton as another sadistic scientist and Bela Lugosi as one of his creations. RKO also made a contribution with *The Most Dangerous Game* (dir. Ernest B. Schoedsack and Irving Pichel, 1932), which was filmed on the sets of *King Kong* (dir. Merian C. Cooper and Ernest B. Schoedsack, 1933), but which was released earlier. The film involves a mad hunter, who is troubled by an old head injury, and who sadistically proves his dominance by pursuing the ultimate prey – human beings. If Moreau turns animals into human beings through torture, Zaroff torments his victims by turning humans into animals.

The turning point in the cycle seems to have been 1933. If *Dracula* intensified an established trend, 1933 represented the waning of these films. Certainly, the year saw the release of RKO's *King Kong*, although as Cynthia Erb has pointed out, this was not really understood as horror at the time, its designation as a horror film probably dating from its release in the 1950s.[14] Warner Bros followed the success of *Dr X* with *The Mystery of the Wax Museum* (1933), which featured the same triple act of director Michael Curtiz and stars Lionel Atwill and Fay Wray. However, this was also the year

---

[14] Cynthia Erb, *Tracking King Kong: A Hollywood Icon in World Culture* (Detroit, MI: Wayne State University Press, 1998).

that saw a significant number of contributions from the Poverty Row studios. The year 1932 had already seen one successful entry by the Poverty Row studios, *White Zombie* (dir. Victor Halperin), which starred Bela Lugosi as another dominating presence, a tyrant with who controls an army of zombies. It was followed, in 1933, by various other contributions such as *The Vampire Bat* (dir. Frank R. Strayer) from Majestic and *Night of Terror* (dir. Benjamin Stoloff) from Columbia. Paramount even toyed with this trend and not only made *Murders in the Zoo*, which cast Lionel Atwill as a scientist who is driven to murder by insane jealously, a film that may have used Atwill's association with *Dr X* and *Mystery of the Wax Museum*, but which was a far more low-brow contribution. It even hired Victor Halperin, the director of *White Zombie*, for *Supernatural* (1933), a film that featured one its major stars, Carole Lombard, but does not seem to have elevated its director but rather to have diminished its star.

By 1934 there were few contributions from the major studios, and by 1935 the market was largely left to Universal and the Poverty Row studios (*The Black Room*, Columbia; *Condemned to Live*, Invincible; and *The Case of Dr Crespi*, Republic). The only two exceptions were both from MGM: one was *Mad Love* (dir. Karl Freund), a remake of the silent classic of German Expressionism, *The Hands of Orlac* (dir. Robert Wiene, 1924), which was largely made to exploit the arrival in the US of one of the stars of the German cinema, Peter Lorre. Similarly, *Mark of the Vampire* was a remake of the silent classic *London after Midnight* (1927), which had starred Lon Chaney and had been directed by Tod Browning, who returned to his duties as the director for this remake.

'Creepy Pix Cleaning Up': Resurgence, Respectability and Realism in the 1940s Gothic Cinema

During 1937 and 1938, there were few horror releases, but, by 1939, things were very different. In 1938, a small cinema in Los Angeles, The Regina, ran a triple bill of *Frankenstein*, *Dracula* and *Son of Kong* (dir. Ernest B. Schoedsack, 1933), the popularity of which prompted Universal to make the first two films available nationwide as a double bill. It even organised a tour of personal appearances by Bela Lugosi as part of the films' promotion. The nationwide success of this double bill meant that, by 1939, almost all the major studios featured at least one Gothic horror film in their schedules: Universal released both *Son of Frankenstein* (dir. Rowland V. Lee, 1939) and *Tower of London* (dir.

Rowland V. Lee, 1939); Fox followed suit with *The Hound of the Baskervilles* (dir. Sidney Lanfield, 1939), *The Adventures of Sherlock Holmes* (dir. Alfred L. Werker, 1939) and another remake of *The Gorilla* (dir. Allan Dwan, 1939); Warner Bros introduced audiences to *The Return of Dr X* (dir. Vincent Sherman, 1939); Paramount remade *The Cat and the Canary* (dir. Elliot Nugent, 1939); United Artists released a lavish adaptation of *Wuthering Heights* (dir. William Wyler, 1939); RKO cast Charles Laughton as *The Hunchback of Notre Dame* (dir. William Dieterle, 1939); and Columbia began a series of Boris Karloff vehicles with *The Man They Could Not Hang* (dir. Nick Grinde, 1939).

However, the following year saw the release of probably the most influential Gothic film of the period, Alfred Hitchcock's *Rebecca*, a film that established several key trends. First, it was not only clearly targeted at a female audience but became the most requested release by women in the early 1940s.[15] Second, it was a lavish prestige picture that brought together some of the top talent in the industry. Third, it was a Gothic story that was explicitly psychological and avoided monsters altogether. Inversely, Universal went in quite another direction and started to develop film series: films that were usually modestly budgeted productions and which were predominantly based around male monsters. In 1940, it released the first of a series of Mummy films and in 1941 it made a film featuring another new monster, *The Wolf Man* (dir. George Waggner). By the mid-1940s, then, it had not only developed these two properties but also created a series of films featuring the Invisible Man, Sherlock Holmes, a Gorilla woman (the first film of which was *Captive Wild Woman* in 1943); and a series based on more psychological storylines, *Inner Sanctum*. Significantly, and as Peter Hutchings points out, the two properties that never really developed into series were Frankenstein and Dracula.[16] Certainly there was *Son of Frankenstein* in 1939, but this was never intended as the start of a series and there was no follow-up until *Ghost of Frankenstein* (dir. Erle C. Kenton, 1942), which was after the establishment of the Mummy and the Wolf Man as properties. Furthermore, the next films, *Frankenstein Meets the Wolf Man* and *House of Frankenstein* (dir. Erle C. Kenton, 1944), are actually centred on Lon Chaney Jnr's Wolf Man rather than on the Frankenstein monster. Dracula

---

[15] Anon., 'ARI Report 163', in *Gallup Looks at the Movies: Audience Research Reports 1940–1950* (Delaware: Scholarly Resources, 1979).

[16] Peter Hutchings, 'Monster Legacies: Memory, Technology and Horror History', in Lincoln Geraghty and Mark Jancovich (eds), *The Shifting Definitions of Genre: Essays on Labeling Films, Television Shows and Media* (Jefferson, IN: McFarland, 2007), pp. 216–28.

was even less favoured and, after *Dracula's Daughter*, Universal only made one Dracula film, *Son of Dracula*, in which Dracula is brought to the United States as part of an evil woman's fiendish schemes, to the extent that the vampire remains very much a secondary character. *House of Dracula*, then, was similar to *House of Frankenstein* in that it was centred on the Wolf Man and featured the Count as one of a collection of secondary monsters.

In other words, while the 1940s are often seen as simply an extension of the 1930s or as a rehashing of the 1930s monsters, the decade is actually quite distinctive, and one in which even Universal was concentrating on rather different monsters from those of the 1930s. Furthermore, while the one bright light in the period is often taken to be the Gothic films produced by Val Lewton, this seriously misrepresents their contribution. Certainly, Lewton's first Gothic film for RKO, *Cat People*, was a major success and had a considerable influence on the period, but it was also clearly a response to the context established by *Rebecca*, on the one hand, and Universal, on the other, and can be seen as a virtual hybridisation of these trends. While it took elements of the Wolf Man, the film, like *Rebecca*, offered a female-centred tale about a woman who believes herself to be a cat-woman. Second, it never resolves whether its central female character is the victim of a supernatural curse or whether it is all in her mind, so that it hovers between the genres of monster film and psychological film. Third, its budget was neither as low as the Universal films nor as high as the United Artist production, but was pitched between the two.

Although its estimated budget was only $134,000, *Cat People* is reputed to have taken between $2 million and $4 million at the box office.[17] In 1943 *Variety* reported that 'creepy pix' were 'cleaning up' at the box office, a phrase that suggested that they were doing well financially but also that they were becoming more respectable.[18] Furthermore, it was not just that they were doing well but that they were 'even getting first run and downtown bookings in an unprecedented manner', these markets being particularly important to the major studios for whom they represented 'three quarters to seven eighths of all dollars' taken during the period.[19] In other words, these films were not simply 'cleaning up' financially but were also 'cleaning up' their image,

---

[17] See Joel Siegel, *Val Lewton: The Reality of Terror* (London: Secker and Warburg, 1972).
[18] Jim Cunningham, 'Creepy Pix Cleaning Up: Studio Cash in on Cycle', *Variety* 31 (March 1943), p. 7.
[19] Douglas Gomery, 'The Economics of the Horror Film', in James B. Weaver III and Ron Tamborini (eds), *Horror Films: Current Research on Audience Preferences and Reactions* (New York: Routledge, 1996), pp. 49–62 (p. 51).

a transformation that was largely achieved through the focus on psychological stories rather than monster films. By 'who-dun-iting horrors to permit their classification as mystery yarn', these films met the 'toning down requirements' of censors at home and abroad.[20]

The following year, the *New York Times* noted that 'Every studio has at least one such picture in production and others coming to a witches boil' and that this 'new horror cycle' was on a 'far more ambitious level' and was 'being dressed up in full Class "A" paraphernalia, including million-dollar budgets and big name casts'.[21] For example, in 1945, MGM had invested so heavily in its production of *The Picture of Dorian Gray* (dir. Albert Lewin, 1945) that *Variety* reported that it had 'cost $2 million'.[22] Similarly, some of the biggest stars were associated with the cycle, most particularly female stars such as Joan Fontaine and Ingrid Bergman.[23] It was also associated with top directors such as Alfred Hitchcock and Orson Welles.[24] The *New York Times* article also identifies a number of films with this 'new horror cycle', many of which are no longer discussed in relation to either horror or the Gothic today. For example, in distinction to 'the forerunning vampire, werewolf and Frankenstein chillers', the article identifies the cycle with a series of female-centred stories that have since become known as the paranoid woman's film (*Dark Waters* [dir. André de Toth, 1944]; *Gaslight* [dir. George Cukor, 1944]; *Spellbound* [dir. Alfred Hitchcock, 1945]); others that have since become known as film noir (*Phantom Lady* [dir. Robert Siodmak, 1944]; *The Woman in the Window* [dir. Fritz Lang, 1944]); and others that have been linked with both of these categories (*Hangover Square* [dir. John Brahm, 1945]).[25] In fact, all these titles, when re-examined in this light, demonstrate the instabilities of

---

[20] Cunningham, 'Creepy Pix', p. 7.
[21] Fred Stanley, 'Hollywood Shivers', *New York Times*, 28 May 1944, p. 3.
[22] Char., 'Review of *The Picture of Dorian Gray*', *Variety*, 7 March 1945, 20.
[23] See, for example, Mark Jancovich '"Bluebeard's Wives": Horror, Quality and the Paranoid Woman's Film in the 1940s', *Irish Journal of Gothic and Horror Studies* 12 (2013) <http://irishgothichorror.files.wordpress.com/2018/03/bluebeards-wives.pdf> (last accessed 3 April 2019) and 'Ingrid Bergman', in Elizabeth McCarthy and Bernice M. Murphy (eds), *Lost Souls of Horror and the Gothic* (Jefferson, NC: McFarland, 2016), pp. 34–37.
[24] Mark Jancovich, '"The English Master of Movie Melodrama": Hitchcock, Horror and the Women's Film', *Film International* 9:3 (2011): 51–67 and 'Shadows and Bogeymen: Horror, Stylization and the Critical Reception of Orson Welles During the 1940s', *Participations: A Journal of Audience and Reception Studies* 6:1 (May 2009): 25–51.
[25] Stanley, 'Hollywood Shivers', X3. Indeed, as James Naremore points out, the term 'film noir' was not only an allusion to the 'série noire' ('a series of crime novels from Gallimard') but that the 'adjective "noir" had long been used in France to describe the Gothic novel'. See James Naremore, 'A Season in Hell or the Snows of Yesteryear', in Raymond Borde and Etienne Chaumeton (eds), *A Panorama of American Film Noir* (San Francisco: City Lights, 2002), pp. vii–xxi (p. viii).

the distinctions between the paranoid woman's film, film noir, horror and the Gothic. For example, *Phantom Lady* may be a classic adaptation of a pseudonymous novel by Cornell Woolrich but it features a young woman who turns detective to solve a murder performed by a deranged killer – it is therefore clearly both a Gothic woman's film, a noir thriller and a story of Gothic horror.

In fact, Siegfried Kracauer also wrote about the 'terror films' of the period, a category that was not focused on the Universal horror films but rather on films that have since been reclassified as examples of the paranoid woman's film or film noir. These 'horror-thrillers', he claimed, were centrally concerned with psychological terrorisation so that their villains 'no longer shoot, strangle or poison the females that they want to do away with, but systematically try to drive them insane'.[26] Furthermore, if these films were distinguished by 'the theme of psychological destruction', these psychological concerns applied to both victim and victimiser: if the victimiser seeks to 'drive [their predominantly female victims] insane', they are motivated to do so by their own psychological needs rather than by the demands of their more conscious objectives. In *Gaslight*, for instance, the abusive husband is supposed to be trying to search for a set of fabulous jewels, but this search hardly necessitates the ways in which he psychologically terrorises his wife, the intensity of which is clearly motivated by his own psychological desire for dominance.

The process of terrorisation is also coupled with another aspect of these villains' behaviour: in the tradition of the Bluebeard narrative, their attempt to drive their female victims insane often involves a prohibition on knowledge. The victims are told not to investigate things and that their perceptions are untrustworthy. Strangely, if these villains therefore work to invalidate their victims' perceptions of the world, some critics have claimed that the films operate in the same way. Mary Ann Doane, for example, claims that 'The violence associated with the attribution of a desire to see to the woman reaches its culmination in the gothic paranoid films, where the cinematic apparatus itself seems to be mobilized against the female spectator, disabling her gaze.'[27] Similarly, Diane Waldman argues that these films perform an 'invalidation of female perception and interpretation, equating female

---

[26] Siegfried Kracauer, 'Hollywood's Terror Films: Do They Reflect an American State of Mind?', *New German Critique* 89 (2003): 105–11 (p. 107). Originally published in *Commentary* 2 (1946): 132–6.

[27] Mary Ann Doane, *The Desire to Desire: The Woman's Film of the 1940s* (Bloomington, IN: Indiana University Press, 1987), p. 37.

subjectivity with some kind of false consciousness, as the male character "corrects" the heroine's impressions'.[28] This may seem to be true of *Rebecca* and *Suspicion* (dir. Alfred Hitchcock, 1941), at least superficially, but the first film still rewards the heroine's investigation and the second was changed due to fears that the original ending would damage the image of its leading man, Cary Grant. However, in most examples of the paranoid woman's film, the heroine's pursuit of knowledge is not simply rewarded but is often essential to her happiness and/or survival.[29] In this way, these films are similar to the female Gothic romances of the late-eighteenth and early-nineteenth centuries, at least in Kate Ferguson Ellis's account of them.[30]

Unlike the 1930s, the films of the 1940s did not come to an abrupt halt; rather, there was a significant transformation, largely due to a more general shift towards realism in the mid-1940s. A key example of this was *The Lost Weekend* (dir. Billy Wilder, 1945), an Oscar-winning portrait of an alcoholic that was clearly read in terms of both the 'new horror cycle' *and* a move towards realism within the period. Kracauer even made this point explicit in his critique of the Hollywood terror films, which he contrasted to the realism of Roberto Rossellini's *Rome, Open City* (1945), a film that he associated with the 'terror films' through its 'shocks' but from which he also distinguished them through his claim that the former simply sought to incite fear, while the latter made 'an insistent effort to penetrate [fear] and spell out its causes'.[31]

Science Fiction, Monsters and Psychological Horror in the 1950s

As this move towards realism demonstrates, horror production did not necessarily decline in the late 1940s but rather shifted away from films featuring the Gothic past and towards films that were distinguished by a sense of contemporaneity and heightened verisimilitude. Consequently, in the late 1940s and the 1950s there was a shift to 'documentary-style' thrillers

---

[28] Diane Waldman, "'At Last I Can Tell It to Someone!'": Female Point of View and Subjectivity in the Gothic Romance film of the 1940s', *Cinema Journal* 23:2 (1984): 29–40 (p. 33).
[29] See, for example, *Rage in Heaven* (1941); *Shadow of a Doubt* (1943); *Dark Waters* (1944); *Experiment Perilous* (1944); *Gaslight* (1944); *A Guest in the House* (1944); *Jane Eyre* (1944); *The Lodger* (1944); *Phantom Lady* (1944); *Hangover Square* (1945); *My Name Is Julia Ross* (1945); *Spellbound* (1945); *Dragonwyck* (1946); *Shock* (1946); *The Spiral Staircase* (1946); *The Stranger* (1946); and *Undercurrent* (1946).
[30] Kate Ferguson Ellis, *The Contested Castle: Gothic Novels and the Subversion of Domestic Ideology* (Urbana, IL: University of Illinois Press, 1989).
[31] Kracauer, 'Hollywood's Terror Film', p. 111.

and to films that placed their Gothic materials within a contemporary setting. For example, *In a Lonely Place* (dir. Nicholas Ray, 1950) shares much in common with the paranoid woman's film of the 1940s but is rarely associated with it because of its tough, contemporary setting. Certainly there continued to be some familiar Gothic contributions, even by the late 1940s and early 1950s, as is demonstrated by films such as *The Heiress* (dir. William Wyler, 1949); *My Cousin Rachel* (dir. Henry Koster, 1952); *Sudden Fear* (dir. David Miller, 1952); and Warner Bros' *House of Wax* (dir. André de Toth, 1953).

Nonetheless, the dominant trend was for the contemporary settings that are often identified with film noir today or the futuristic settings of science fiction, for which a cinematic vogue started in 1950. These science fiction films had some veneer of realism, given that their monsters, rather than being associated with the supernatural, were given pseudo-rational explanations; but they were still strongly associated with the Gothic. Science fiction not only had roots in Gothic literature as exemplified by the fiction of Mary Shelley, Edgar Allan Poe and even Jules Verne, but these films frequently featured monsters and mad scientists that were reminiscent of earlier Gothic horror films. Furthermore, many science fiction films located their action in the Gothic past. For example, the single most successful science fiction film of the period was Disney's hugely expensive production of Jules Verne's *20,000 Leagues Under the Sea* (dir. Richard Fleischer, 1954).

These science fiction films largely fell into three different types. The first were straightforward tales of exploration such as *Destination Moon* (dir. Irving Pichel, 1950) and *Conquest of Space* (dir. Byron Haskin, 1955). But by far the most numerous were either the tales of alien invasion such as *The Thing from Another World* (dir. Christian Nyby, 1951) and *The War of the Worlds* (dir. Byron Haskin, 1953), or films that cast the alien as a sympathetic figure abused by human exploitation, as exemplified by the Universal monster movies directed by Jack Arnold (*It Came from Outer Space* written by Ray Bradbury, 1953); *Creature from the Black Lagoon* (1954); and even *The Incredible Shrinking Man* (written by Richard Matheson, 1957).

These films are often seen as simple examples of Cold War propaganda, in which the alien menace is a code for Russian aggression, but although this might well have been the case in certain instances, many of the filmmakers associated with these films were critics of the Cold War rather than its champions. Moreover, a quite different context is suggested by the figure of the mad scientist within them, and particularly by the ways in which science and technology are associated with alien threats. Christian Nyby's *The Thing from Another World*, for example, features a human scientist who is mad and dangerous, but who, in place of being linked with foreign aggression, is associated with the centres of military and political power in the US. He is even claimed to be one of the figures associated with the testing of nuclear weapons on Bikini Atoll. Furthermore, he is dangerous because he values the alien over the human due to its association with rationality. When he discovers that the alien invader breeds without sexual contact, he exclaims, 'No pain, no pleasure . . . No emotions, no heart. Our superior in every way!' The scientist associates this lack of feeling and emotion with pure rationality and, by implication, sees human emotion and feeling as a weakness or as a threat to rational thought.

Of course, not all science is viewed as dangerous within these films, but the concern with rationality and science also means that they demonstrate very specific treatments of gender. *The Thing from Another World* could simply be seen as a return to the male-centred monster films of the 1930s and a movement away from the female-centred films of the 1940s. However, the association between rationality and masculinity actually leads to something far more complex. Certainly, the film is centred around a male hero, but his masculinity also associates him with both the scientist and the monster in various ways. He is therefore countered by a female companion, who is not simply there to be rescued from the creature, but who represents the 'human' emotions and feelings that are essential to defeating both the scientist and the alien.

Even more significantly, later films often divided the heroic roles in two so that the male hero performed action while the female lead was often associated with a positive version of science, or a new version of the investigating gaze of the Gothic heroine. For example, in *Them!* (dir. Gordon Douglas, 1954), the male hero and the army are led to the lair of the alien queen (the earth is menaced by a race of giant ants created by atom bomb tests in the American desert) by Pat Medford, a female scientist who not only directs their actions but who must inspect the lair before she can authorise its destruction. Similar figures also appear in films such as *Creature from the Black Lagoon* and its sequel, although in these films she is actually explicitly pitted against the figures of male action, which are presented as a destructive version of science to which she offers an alternative. These female scientists are concerned with learning from the non-human, rather than dominating it.

However, as Bradley Schauer notes, despite the major studios' efforts to produce respectable, big-budget science fiction films, these films were not ones that were most successful at the box office. Only a small number of science fiction films were produced by the major studios, and of these 'the highest grossing of the six A films of the period was the one that unabashedly embraced the genre's most lurid qualities', *The Thing from Another World*.[32] This situation, coupled with a successful re-release of *King Kong*, resulted in two different developments: most of the science fiction films of the 1950s were lower-budget films and most were horror films within a science fiction setting.

By the mid-1950s, then, filmmakers believed that audiences were more interested in horror than science fiction, and this led to another change in the nature of Gothic filmmaking in the period. This change was also due to other factors, most particularly a strategy that led the major studios away from 'regular programming' so as to focus on the 'road show' productions. In other words, the major studios had previously been committed to providing exhibitors with a regular supply of films, but in the mid-1950s they began to focus more and more on a small number of major box-office properties. This left many exhibitors with a crisis in that they did not have enough films to show, and they increasingly turned to the independent sector to fill this gap. Furthermore, as the middle-class family market, due to such factors as the growth of suburban living, had declined during the late 1940s and early 1950s, the first-run market had become increasingly dominated by youth, with whom Gothic materials were particularly popular.

There were also other developments that account for changes in the period. In 1955, the art cinema circuit enjoyed incredible success with a French Gothic horror story, Henri-Georges Clouzot's *Les Diaboliques*, and only a month later it was followed by the first television broadcasts of *Alfred Hitchcock Presents* (1955–65), which was clearly marked as a horror series at the time and included a wide range of Gothic materials.[33] The show, which was the brainchild of Joan Harrison, a major contributor to the Gothic films of the 1940s, became one of the most successful shows (both critically and commercially) on American television in the late 1950s and early 1960s.[34] Reviews of many Gothic films in the late 1950s and early 1960s even compared them unfavourably to the kinds of Gothic television that *Alfred Hitchcock Presents* exemplified and inspired.

---

[32] Bradley Schauer, *Escape Velocity: American Science Fiction Film, 1950–1982* (Middletown, CT: Wesleyan University Press, 2017), p. 63.

[33] Mark Jancovich, '"Where It Belongs": Television Horror, Domesticity, and *Alfred Hitchcock Presents*', in Kimberly Jackson and Linda Belau (eds), *Horror in the Age of Consumption* (New York: Routledge, 2017), pp. 29–44.

[34] Hitchcock's role within the show was not that of mastermind but that of hired hand, whom Harrison hired to perform scripted introductions to the episodes and to direct the occasional episode.

In this context, a group of American financiers approached Hammer, a small British company, with a proposition.[35] They effectively hired the company to make a Gothic horror film that was supposedly based on a classic literary source; that reworked Universal's most revered contribution to the Gothic cinema; featured a period settings that were similar to those employed in *20,000 Leagues Under the Sea*; but which was also targeted at teenagers through a level of gore that distinguished the film from the kinds of science fiction horror that had become associated with children's audiences. The result was *The Curse of Frankenstein* and it proved an incredible commercial success. However, as Kevin Heffernan notes, while Hammer's declining fortunes in the late 1960s and early 1970s has led many to remember it as a producer of low-budget exploitation, *The Curse of Frankenstein*, and the Hammer strategy of the late 1950s and early 1960s, was actually an attempt to abandon low-budget filmmaking and to concentrate on the first-run market. This strategy was also followed by American International Pictures in the late 1950s, when it began a series of Poe adaptations directed by Roger Corman. Again these were based on literary classics, and while they had a small budget when compared to a prestige production from a major studio, these films had a vastly increased budget when compared to earlier productions from AIP.[36]

An alternative Gothic cinema was also being produced by William Castle, who was far less concerned to break out of low-budget filmmaking but who explicitly sought to cash in on the success of *Les Diaboliques*.[37] His films were uninterested in the literary classics and were set in more contemporary settings, where various individuals play sadistic games of psychological domination with one another. In *Macabre* (1958), for example, a doctor's daughter seems to have been kidnapped and buried alive. A race against time, then, ensues, before it is eventually revealed that the doctor has concocted the whole crisis in order to cause his father-in-law to have a heart attack so that the doctor can inherit his victim's wealth.

Neither *The Curse of Frankenstein* nor *Psycho* was thus a break in the Gothic cinema but both were part of larger patterns in the 1950s. *Psycho* not only looks like films such as *Les Diaboliques*, and the William Castle imitations of it, but it was also made with the crew from *Alfred Hitchcock Presents*, rather than

---

[35] See David Pirie, *A New Heritage of Horror: The English Gothic Cinema* (London: I. B. Tauris, 2008) and Jonathan Rigby, *English Gothic: A Century of Horror Cinema* (London: Reynolds and Hearn, 2000).
[36] Kevin Heffernan, *Ghouls, Gimmicks, and Gold: Horror Films and the American Movie Business, 1953–1968* (Durham, NC: Duke University Press, 2004).
[37] William Castle, *Step Right Up! I'm Going to Scare the Pants Off America* (New York: Putnam's Sons, 1976).

Hitchcock's film unit. It was even promoted through trailers that explicitly imitated his introductions in the series. It was also made at a point at which the studios had recognised the success of the Gothic films produced by independent companies and began to produce their own bigger-budget horror productions, a trend that existed alongside Hammer and AIP until the mid-1960s, when the failure of the road show strategy led the major studios to refocus their efforts on the first-run market.[38] This move put them in direct competition with companies such as Hammer and required them to make Gothic projects crucial to their industrial strategy. When Robert Evans was appointed as vice-president of production at Paramount, he achieved, as part of the company's strategy for the first-run market, an early success with *Rosemary's Baby* (1968), a horror film that united the talents of low-budget horror producer, William Castle, and art cinema director, Roman Polanski, the latter having enjoyed a recent critical and commercial triumph with *Repulsion* (1965). It also starred Mia Farrow, who had achieved stardom through her role as a troubled teenager in the hit television show, *Peyton Place* (1964–9); one of the key directors of the American art cinema, John Cassavetes; and a host of older actors that included Ralph Bellamy, a Hollywood star of the 1930s and 1940s, who had even featured alongside Lon Chaney Jr and Claude Rains in Universal's *The Wolf Man*.

---

[38] Mark Jancovich 'Beyond Hammer: The First Run Market and the Prestige Horror Film in the early 1960s', *Palgrave Communications* 3 (2017) <www.nature.com/articles/palcomms201728> (last accessed 3 April 2019).

3.5

Gothic and War, 1930–1991

AGNIESZKA SOLTYSIK MONNET

As a genre uniquely engaged with violence and extreme emotional and ethical conditions, the Gothic has been closely connected to the representation of war from its start.[1] Emerging historically from the first major world war, called the Seven Years' War (1756–63) in Britain, and known by some as the French and Indian War (1754–63) in the United States, the Gothic is indisputably a child of military violence. It is thus no accident that the first Gothic novel opens with a young man being crushed to death by a giant iron helmet, leaving his father without an heir and setting off the wild ride of a plot in Horace Walpole's *The Castle of Otranto* (1764). Since that first freakish death, the Gothic genre has remained close to the battlefield, providing a rhetorical palette for writers wishing to depict the psychological and physical effects of war throughout the nineteenth and twentieth centuries. This palette is both literary and visual and includes a set of readily recognisable tropes that have developed over the last two centuries, most of which are related to the dehumanising consequences of war violence, and which include uncanny, allegorical, monstrous and horrifically graphic effects.

Moreover, uses of the War Gothic can be subdivided into at least three main kinds: psychological trauma, body-violation and monstrous allegory. The first has to do with the psychological effects of war, including trauma, memory problems, denial, distorted time perception, battle madness and various kinds of post-traumatic stress disorder (PTSD) symptoms. The Gothic tropes that lend themselves well to this treatment include ghosts and haunting, fitting tropes for repressed or insistent memories, both common side effects of traumatic experience; zombies and the living dead,

---

[1] See Agnieszka Soltysik Monnet and Steffen Hantke, 'Ghosts from the Battlefield: A Short Historical Introduction to the War Gothic', in Agnieszka Soltysik Monnet and Steffen Hantke (eds), *War Gothic in Literature and Culture* (New York: Routledge, 2016), pp. xi–xxv.

suggestive metaphors for the shattering sense of loss or numbness felt by soldiers after combat; and werewolves, uniquely apt figures for the blood-lust and predation of men upon other men that occurs in war. In fact, the Gothic had been depicting the psychological costs of war with powerful figurative imagery long before the medical and psychiatric professions caught up with them with their diagnostic tools and institutional legitimation. If PTSD only gained full recognition among psychiatrists and physicians in 1980, when the American Psychiatric Association added it to their diagnostic manual, writers such as Ambrose Bierce had been depicting the ruined minds and confused perceptions of emotionally traumatised soldiers since the nineteenth century, at a time when the military and medical profession still considered them as malingerers or cowards. Thus, the Gothic has long been not only one of the most powerful literary devices available for depicting this kind of damage, but it actually filled a crucial gap in the cultural toolbox for representing trauma.

Besides depicting the many subtle or monstrous forms of madness that can be caused by war and combat, another strain of War Gothic focuses on the body and its violation. This is sometimes called Battlefield Gothic and is more closely aligned with horror.[2] The usual intention of this variation of the War Gothic is to demystify and criticise war, exposing its horrific violence through graphic depictions of injured bodies, often mutilated in strikingly unnatural or dehumanising ways. To put it bluntly, Battlefield Gothic is about human bodies becoming things, reduced to meat, the crucial boundary between the inside and the outside shattered and irrelevant.[3] The point is inherently to denounce war by highlighting the fragility – as Judith Butler would say, the *precariousness* – of bodies and lives.[4] The tone of this kind of War Gothic is often ironic and can venture well into black humour, gallows humour and the grotesque. Its effects usually depend on jarring juxtapositions between conventions and expectations and the horrors of what is depicted, whether

---

[2] The term 'Battlefield Gothic' is taken from Samuel Hynes, *The Soldier's Tale: Bearing Witness to a Modern War* (New York: Penguin Books, 1997), p. 26.

[3] For this point, I draw on the distinction made by Guillemette Bolens in her excellent study of classical and modern paradigms of the injured body, which she sees as falling into a logic either of articulation (injuries along joints, and subject to cutting and cutting off of limbs) or of the body as envelope (in which injury or death is accomplished by penetration). Battlefield Gothic can display both kinds of injuries but the most shocking tends to be the breakdown of the envelope, where that which needs to remain invisible and inside (the entrails or brain tissue) is exposed. See Guillemette Bolens, *La Logique du Corps Articulaire: Les articulations du corps humain dans la littérature occidentale* (Rennes: Presses Universitaires de Rennes, 2000), pp. 9–10.

[4] Judith Butler, *Precarious Lives* (London: Verso, 2004).

the conventions are those of war rhetoric and the reality of war experience, or the normative understanding of what a human body is and the consequences of violence to that body.

A third form of War Gothic, also identified as Imperial Gothic by scholars, involves an allegorical use of monstrosity in the service of empire or nationalistic war.[5] In these scenarios, war is depicted as a struggle between forces of good and evil, and a legion of Gothic tropes is deployed to depict enemies of the imperial nations as savage or subhuman monsters. Unlike the other two forms of War Gothic, this strain is generally militaristic rather than anti-war, and uses the Gothic in order to legitimate violence against gothicised others. Since excellent and comprehensive monographs by Patrick Brantlinger and Johan Höglund on this type of War Gothic exist, I will focus in this chapter on the first two, both of which have been less systematically examined by scholars.[6] There are still other uses of the Gothic in relation to war, and one that is worth examining in addition to the two mentioned above is the figure of the zombie, which rose to prominence in popular culture in the second half of the twentieth century but which originated in the US occupation of Haiti in the 1930s.

In terms of historical timeframe, this chapter will focus mainly on the decades between 1930 and 1991. This is a period that covers the Second World War, the Cold War, wars in Korea and Vietnam, and the first major oil war in the Middle East, and which represents a period in which the War Gothic was already well established and familiar to readers and film audiences in Europe and North America and beyond. The Gothic had become an important mode for depicting battlefields and battle trauma already in the wake of the American Civil War and even more so during the First World War, when it permeated both poetry and prose as well as films such as Abel Gance's *J'Accuse* (dir. Abel Gance, 1919) and *All Quiet on the Western Front* (dir. Lewis Milestone, 1930). The Gothic was thus readily available for depicting the Second World War, and began to be used almost right away, first to portray London during the Blitz and then other places and situations, especially in relation to the Pacific theatre, which was regarded as particularly horrific.

As far as the production of War Gothic is concerned, however, the most significant war during the 1930–91 period is the American intervention in Vietnam. Due in part to its ambiguous and failed military objectives, the

---

[5] Johan Höglund, *Imperial Gothic: Popular Culture, Empire, Violence* (New York: Routledge, 2014).
[6] Patrick Brantlinger, *Imperial Gothic: Atavism and the Occult in the British Adventure Novel, 1880–1914* (Bloomington: Indiana University Press, 1985); Höglund, *Imperial Gothic*.

racism and viciousness inherent in the policy of attrition (measuring success exclusively in terms of enemy body count), and the loosening of censorship across the media in the late 1960s, the war in Vietnam is the source of the most explicit and most extensive War Gothic writing and cinema (and other media) in the twentieth century.

Finally, the First Gulf War took place in 1990–9, and contributed to significant innovations in the War Gothic genre, but these only emerged later, in the 1990s and 2000s. This chapter will only briefly allude to these developments, as well as to the War Gothic video games that were beginning to be developed at this time. In short, the main focus of this chapter will be from the Second World War to the troubled wake of the war in Vietnam, focusing mainly on British and American culture (since the Gothic is primarily an Anglo-American cultural form) while acknowledging important instances of War Gothic in other national cultures where relevant. The terms 'mode' and 'genre' will be used interchangeably, for the sake of avoiding repetition, but the underlying assumption of this analysis – one widely shared by Fred Botting and other scholars – is that the Gothic since the eighteenth century has become a mode rather than a genre, and, as such, serves as a more flexible and malleable set of conventions and concerns that can combine with other forms and appear in a wide range of media.[7]

Invasion of the Undead

Zombies are an important part of the history of twentieth-century War Gothic and that history begins with the US occupation of Haiti (1915–34). The island had long been of economic interest to the US, with much of its debt held by US banks, and during the First World War it acquired an even greater desirability as a site of a potential navy base. After a series of political assassinations, the US sent United States Marines to Haiti to restore stability for US business interests. The occupation began with the forced election by the legislature of a pro-American president and was followed in 1917 by the rewriting of the constitution to allow foreign ownership of land. When the legislature rejected the controversial law that threatened to allow foreigners excessive influence on the island, the pro-American president dissolved it and the legislature did not meet again until 1929. The occupation government was unpopular for many reasons, including its racial segregation policies,

---

[7] See Fred Botting, *Gothic* (London and New York: Routledge, 1996), p. 14.

press censorship and forced labour practices, which resulted in peasant rebellions and strikes throughout the occupation.

It is from this tense neo-colonial occupation that the zombie, a figure of Haitian folklore, entered the North American imagination. The zombie was a person who had been mesmerised or entranced by black arts into a state of enslavement to a sorcerer or witch doctor. In the first Hollywood zombie movie, Victor Halperin's *White Zombie* (1932), a Creole plantation owner played by Bela Lugosi enslaves the wills of political enemies, rivals, labourers and a white woman whom he covets (Fig. 5.1). The threat depicted here is tacitly aimed at white American authority, and the conflict plays out between the Haitian villain and a neighbouring American plantation owner (the fact that the American owns Haitian land clearly situates the film in a post-1917 historical context and reveals the political stakes in the background). According to Laurel Recker, 'Americans could not legally own land in Haiti until after the US occupation and its forcible revision of the Haitian constitution in 1918', making the presence of US troops the tacit background of the

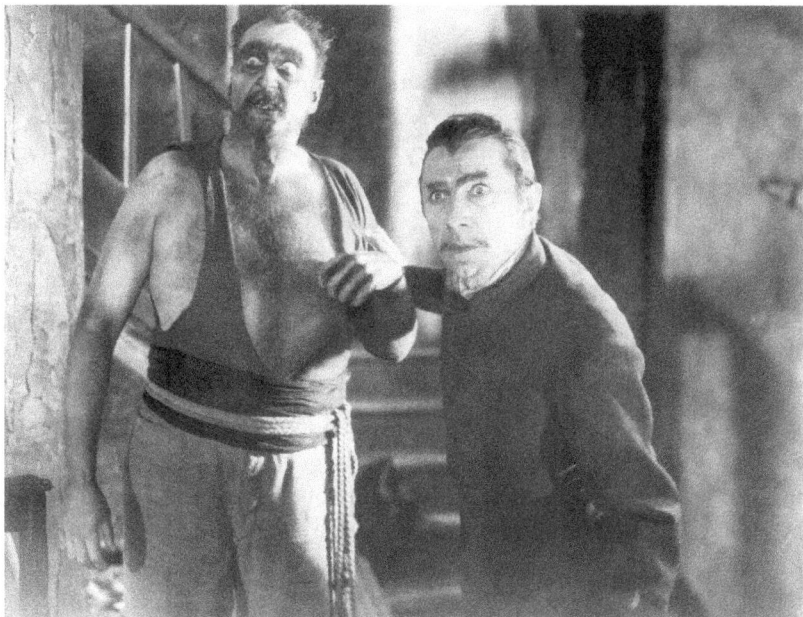

Fig.5.1: Hungarian actor Bela Lugosi (R) on the set of *White Zombie*, directed by American Victor Halperin, 1932. (Photo by Sunset Boulevard/Corbis via Getty Images).

story and 'subversively (if silently)' acknowledging 'the history of violence and oppression in which the US occupation actively participates'.[8]

Apart from the fact that the movie zombie is a child of the US military presence in Haiti, it has taken on an even more pointed and central role in War Gothic by becoming a figure for the soldier. Originally, as it emerged from the brutal slave practices of the seventeenth and eighteenth centuries, the zombie represented anxieties about enslavement and loss of self, and this is how the figure enters popular culture in the 1930s. Almost immediately, however, the zombie began to be used as a trope for the alienated and dispossessed body of the soldier. The 1936 film *Revolt of the Zombies* (dir. Victor Halperin) begins its story during the First World War and imagines a French colonial priest using a secret formula to turn men into soulless automatons. When the priest's formula is stolen, a group of Allied representatives must travel to Cambodia to find and destroy the formula, but one of the men finds it before the others and begins to use it to create a private army as well as to steal the woman he wants from his rival. *Revenge of the Zombies* (dir. Steve Sekely, 1943), though set in Louisiana, already imagines the use of zombification in the service of Hitler. This is a trope that would return over and over again, well into the 1980s (e.g. *The Keep*, dir. Michael Mann, 1983) and up to the present (e.g. *Frankenstein's Army,* dir. Richard Raaphorst, 2013; *Overlord,* dir. Julius Avery, 2018).

Nazi zombies distil into a single unsettling (as well as often schlocky and ridiculous) image the many complex fears about enemy soldiers, the loss of individual autonomy while in military service and the dehumanising medical experiments conducted by scientists of the Third Reich. Soldiers occupy an ambivalent position in modern culture, hailed as heroes for their self-sacrifice but sometimes suspected of naive simple-mindedness in their obedience to orders, or suspected of secret blood-lust and an attraction to violence. This is true even of one's own soldiers, but especially so for enemy soldiers, often seen as thoughtless automatons in the service of a dangerous cause. The earliest zombie films reflected anxieties about armies of mindless slaves, while later iterations of this trope gathered potency from fears about brainwashing and psychological manipulation that grew stronger and more visible in the 1950s, especially in the wake of a series of defections during the Korean War. The zombie-soldier trope can be used in a subtle way to represent the trauma of combat and the damage it does to soldiers, and can also be used as

---

[8] Laurel Recker, 'Zombie Palimpsests: Translating US Occupation in White Zombie', *M/m* vol. 3, cycle 3 (20 August 2018) <https://modernismmodernity.org/forums/posts/zombie-palimpsests> (last accessed 23 June 2020).

an allegory for the dangers of training men to become killers. The theme of super-soldiers generally functions as a cautionary tale against tinkering with human nature to bring out its militaristic and predatory aspects.

If George Romero's work deserves a special mention in this context, it is because it has so pointedly engaged with the issue of militarism. When Romero's *Night of the Living Dead* (1968) was released, it changed the genre of zombie films by fusing the mindless zombie figure with the flesh-eating ghoul, a monster from another colonial context that originated in pre-Islamic Arabia. Combined, the two monsters created a perfect trope for the mindless predation of soldiers upon other men, and more specifically for the way in which killing cannot be easily channelled to its correct targets but can easily become uncontrolled and undiscriminating. In *Night of the Living Dead*, which tacitly referenced the Vietnam War through the sound of helicopters during the final credit sequence, the militias that are ridding the countryside of flesh-eating corpses casually kill the hero of the film, the lone survivor of a group of people who had taken refuge in a farmhouse.

Romero explores this theme more explicitly in *Day of the Dead* (1985), which imagines a world in which the living dead have taken over the entire planet, leaving only a few high-security compounds where soldiers and scientists co-habit uneasily. In this post-apocalyptic world, the military characters are so violent, unthinking and callous that some of the living dead begin to look more human and sympathetic than they do. With this incisive Gothic satire, Romero deftly captures the essence of civilian fears about soldiers, namely, that their killing skills are easy to abuse, either by nefarious military leaders or by devolving into a group that is seduced by its own power into serving only its own interests.

Dark London in Wartime

A more subtle and psychological strain of the War Gothic emerged from Britain during the Second World War. The strain of uncertainty about the future, the omnipresence of death and the unpredictable devastations of the Blitz cast a dark shadow over British culture in these years. As Sara Wasson has eloquently demonstrated, the city of London was particularly important in the rise of British War Gothic at this time, particularly because the Blitz made 'Gothic tropes become literal': 'people were buried alive in their own homes, night streets turned into a bizarre dreamscape where "banshee" sirens wailed and death howled down in the form of wailing bombs, shelterers took refuge in open coffins and even familiar structures hid new and unexpected horrors, like the ice cream vans commandeered to carry human blood'.[9] As the war continued, fears of the collapse of civilisation were joined by fears of degeneration, social regression and an uncanny sense that the First World War was repeating itself. While official accounts of the war years stressed British solidarity and emotional resilience, the War Gothic revealed the presence of dread, paranoia, mutual suspicion and the fear of madness. Wasson has also examined the work of writers such as Henry Green, Roy Fuller, Anna Kavan, Elizabeth Bowen and Mervyn Peake, looking at themes such as the 'carceral city', 'mechanised ghosts' and 'uncanny houses', as indicated by the chapter titles.

Graham Greene's *The Ministry of Fear* (1943) offers a particularly interesting example of the dread and malaise that Wasson identifies with this period, although this is not a text that she discusses in much detail. Greene's novel was adapted by Fritz Lang as the film *Ministry of Fear* in 1944. Ostensibly a spy thriller, the book and film contain many additional Gothic elements – insane asylums, fortune tellers, spiritualist seances, allegations of wife murder, fake blind men, ticking clocks, eerily foggy countryside and self-mutilation – that serve to evoke the strangeness, disorientation and dread of wartime England. Although the film lightens several key elements of the novel, stripping the main character of his sense of guilt over his wife's death and eliminating a period of several months in an insane asylum, it is still very dark in atmosphere and tone, and related, as such, to the film noir cinema of the period. Night-time bombings by the Luftwaffe hang over the entire action of the film and become a source of chronic anxiety, conversation and uncertainty about when and where anyone might die. The shelter where one character hides ends up being completely blown up, and the streets of night-time London see a mix of people going to the subway stations in their bathrobes and pyjamas, breaking down the boundaries between domestic and public space. In short, the war makes for an uncanny and dreadful backdrop to the story, a source of constant fear, suspicion and danger. People turn out to be not what they seem to be, Nazi spies have infiltrated the highest levels of government and British institutions and even one's friends and family can turn out to be murderous political operators. British War Gothic of this period shows a nation disintegrating from the inside, haunted by the threat of madness and social collapse. It is the nightmare accompanying the death rattle of the British empire.

[9] Sara Wasson, *Urban Gothic of the Second World War: Dark London* (Basingstoke: Palgrave Macmillan, 2010), p. 4.

Horror in the Pacific

Although the Second World War generated fewer Gothic representations in American culture than in Britain, no doubt because the fighting and the dangers were both far away, there were some intimations of the horrors occurring abroad. For reasons that are too complex fully to explore here, but which pertain to the racial dimension of the conflict with Japan, the Pacific theatre became the principal source of wartime Gothic in the US. During and immediately after the war, the extent of the horrors of the Holocaust had not yet fully sunk into public consciousness, and the media avoided dwelling on atrocities in the European theatre, but the Pacific theatre changed the tenor of the war and its treatment in American culture. The belief that Japanese soldiers willingly embraced death rather than capture, the sense in which they were not bound by the same cultural values as Westerners regarding life, as well as their apparent physical resemblance to Native Americans – the savage 'Indians' of American cowboy and Indian mass culture folklore – made it easy to view the Japanese as a particularly cruel and inhuman adversary. Fear of capture, rumours of unheard-of tortures and news of Japanese cruelty (such as the atrocities associated with the so-called Death Railway, between Thailand and Burma, where thousands of Allied prisoners of war died during forced labour) created an atmosphere of extreme fear and savagery in the fighting in the Pacific.

This savagery went both ways, and one of the peculiarities of the Pacific theatre was that US troops began to mutilate bodies, collect trophies and generally treat the enemy in a dehumanised way that seemed new to American culture. In reality, American troops had been guilty of such practices throughout their many military campaigns against people of other races, from the Indian wars to their occupations of the Philippines, but never before had glimpses of this aspect of war leaked into mainstream American culture. One striking example of this appeared in *Life Magazine* in May 1944, a photo of Natalie Nickerson with a skull identified by the caption as a 'Jap' that was sent as a souvenir by a young man (possibly a boyfriend, the caption does not specify) from New Guinea (Fig. 5.2).[10] The young woman is shown gazing at the skull, pen in hand, as she ponders what to write in her thank you note. The startling juxtaposition between the pretty middle-class American woman and the souvenir skull, silently testifying to the no-holds-barred savagery and corpse-desecration on the Pacific front, creates an ironic tension that lies at

---

[10] *Life Magazine* (May 22, 1944), p. 34f.

Fig.5.2: Phoenix war worker Natalie Nickerson penning her Navy boyfriend a thank-you note for sending her a Japanese soldier's skull that he gathered as a souvenir while fighting in New Guinea. (Photo by Ralph Crane/The *Life* Images Collection via Getty Images/ Getty Images).

the heart of the strain of War Gothic that Samuel Hynes has called 'Battlefield Gothic'.[11] This is the world of body horror, of the boundary between inside and outside of the body ruptured and the boundary between horror and humour made porous and irrelevant. The rhetorical device at the core of this kind of Gothic is irony, ranging from black and bitter to unsettling and uncanny.

After the Second World War ended, Europe began to rebuild and recover from the slaughter, but the US found itself facing another enemy in the guise of a recent ally: the Soviet Union. As wartime alliances were reconfigured into the standoff known as the Cold War, the US was soon involved in a new war on an Asian front, in Korea (1950–53). The US expected this undeclared war to end relatively quickly and easily but instead it became a stalemate that dragged on for three years, costing 36,000 US casualties and millions of North and South Korean lives. Although the Korean War has dropped out of sight so dramatically as now to be known as 'The Forgotten War', it produced one

[11] Hynes, *The Soldier's Tale*, p. 26.

of the most interesting twists on the War Gothic, one focused on issues of memory, amnesia, brainwashing and repression. When the two sides exchanged prisoners of war after the cease-fire negotiations, more than 10,000 Korean and Chinese prisoners refused to be repatriated, but what captured Americans' attention were the twenty-two British and American soldiers who had apparently converted to Communism and who wished to stay. The possibility that any American could renounce capitalism seemed so outlandish that many people suspected that the defectors had been brainwashed, even as they were roundly condemned.

Richard Condon's 1959 novel *The Manchurian Candidate* draws loosely on this incident for its plot about a decorated American veteran of the Korean War who is actually a sleeper agent after he and his entire platoon are subjected to brainwashing by Chinese and Soviet scientists. A war hero and successful intelligence officer after his return to the United States, the main character is actually an assassin manipulated by cues and triggers to kill upon command, with the Gothic unease of the narrative vastly heightened by the revelation that his own mother is his handler (and more Gothic still, à la Horace Walpole's *The Mysterious Mother* (1768), his lover). In this way, Condon deftly fuses Cold War fears about domineering mothers and the loss of masculinity with the fears of mental manipulation, subliminal control and conspiracies that permeated the post-war era.

Veteran Gothic

The war veteran has been an uncanny and Gothic figure since Ambrose Bierce's fiction of the American Civil War of the 1860s, and the Second World War veteran was a muted but no less unsettling presence in post-war culture. What is now known as the 'greatest generation' was also one of the most silent, and this near-total lack of discussion of combat and war trauma resulted in a sense that repressed violence was lurking just beneath the surface of ordinary life. One of the most powerful post-war films to deal with the difficulties encountered by veterans was the 1946 film by Willie Wyler, *The Best Years of Our Lives*. Focusing on three veterans, the film explores psychological trauma through a character who is haunted by nightmares, bodily trauma through a character who is adjusting to the loss of both hands and symbolic trauma through an incident in which a civilian tells one of the veterans that his sacrifice has been for nothing, that he was betrayed by political elites, and that the US fought on the wrong side. All three issues are central to the sub-genre of Veteran Gothic, which aims to expose the dark side of military service by revealing its consequences and demystifying its supporting ideological structures.

Another key film of this period that addresses the veteran's potential to bring violence home with him from the front is the Humphrey Bogart film noir thriller *In a Lonely Place* (1950). Bogart plays a Hollywood script writer who is strangely out of tune with other people and the normal range of human emotions, with a history of violence and a latent potential for rage that is never quite out of sight. When he is suspected of murder early in the film, an attractive neighbour helps clear him of guilt, and they begin to fall in love. Yet Bogart's ability to hide his violent propensities gets harder and harder to maintain, and the film ends with the character nearly choking to death his now fiancée. Although he is cleared of the murder for which he had been accused, the film shows that he is nevertheless guilty of being capable of it, and his relationship with his fiancée is destroyed. With this bleak ending, *In a Lonely Place* joins the larger work of the film noir genre at this time in reminding spectators that all was not well in the Technicolor world of post-war prosperity and suburbia. Although veterans were largely silent, these darkly psychological thrillers and crime stories often did the work of cultural memory – even if very indirectly and figuratively – in a time when more explicit treatment of the war was not possible.

The one medium in which at least some Second World War veterans did describe their experiences was the war novel. The genre affiliations of these works ranged through naturalism, ironic realism, black humour and dark satire, but they can nearly all be productively examined through the heuristic lens of War Gothic. Three novels in particular stand out from this period: Normal Mailer's *The Naked and the Dead* (1948), Joseph Heller's *Catch-22* (1961) and James Jones's *The Thin Red Line* (1962). All three are cynical, disenchanted, long and sometimes rambling narratives of death and obscenity. The horror of war is a running theme of all three, but in both Mailer's and Heller's work there are particularly grotesque scenes of bodily violation that serve as the narratives' climax. In *The Naked and the Dead,* this climax comes when two men carry an injured comrade suffering an agonising stomach injury who eventually dies. In *Catch-22*, the entire novel revolves around a scene of body horror that is fully revealed only at the end, when a young airman named Snowden slowly dies also from a stomach wound: 'Snowden's insides slithered down to the floor in a soggy pile and just kept dripping out.'[12] As

---

[12] Joseph Heller, *Catch-22* (New York: Dell, 1955), p. 449.

in many examples of War Gothic that turn on bodily mutilation and the fragility of human flesh, the point of this passage is to remind readers that human beings are no more than their bodies: 'The spirit gone, man was garbage ... That was Snowden's secret', the narrator muses.[13] Referring to the body as 'garbage', or in other cases, as 'meat', is not intended to dehumanise the soldier for its own sake, but rather to show how combat injuries dehumanise and destroy the precious life force that makes a body human in the first place.

There is a fiercely critical thrust to the horror foregrounded in these novels and a shrill protest against the glorification and normalisation of injury and death that is produced by militarist discourse and patriotic dogma. Against the allure of military duty and glory and honour, the War Gothic insists upon the barbarity and degradedness of actual combat and the behaviour of men in such conditions. As one character in Jones's *The Thin Red Line* discovers, the most logical reaction to war was 'a massive horror ... that any creatures who spoke a language, walked upright on two legs dressed in clothes, built cities, and claimed to be human beings could actually treat each other with such fiendish animal cruelty'.[14] In order to unveil the truth of war, these novels delved deeper into obscenity and graphic violence than most war fiction before them had dared.

The relentless grimness of these works is leavened only by black humour and a frankness about sexuality that was also new to the genre. Heller's novel is populated by prostitutes, Jones's novel examines homosexuality among enlisted men, and Mailer's novel is notorious for its misogyny as well as its unfortunate decision to replace the frequent word 'fuck' with 'fug' in order not to offend the general public. Not surprisingly, the same prudishness that required Mailer to mutilate and sanitise the language of his fiction dominated over post-war representations of the Second World War. As a result, most treatments of the war in popular culture during the 1950s and 1960s were reverential, sentimental or comic.

Vietnam: Descent into Hell

The Vietnam War, beginning in the early 1960s and ending in the early 1970s (either in 1972 or 1975, depending on which events are taken as its end for the US), inaugurated a new era of War Gothic unlike anything that had existed

---

[13] Heller, *Catch-22*, p. 450.
[14] James Jones, *The Thin Red Line* (New York: Dell, 1962), p. 157.

before. It brought together all the different strains of the mode – the uncanny, the spectral, black humour, Battlefield Gothic, and Imperial Gothic – and began a cycle of dark and demystifying narratives of war that continued for decades.

Although a shift in the way in which the media represented the war in Vietnam could be used as an argument for why this war lent itself particularly well to the genre of horror, especially the availability of images of violence and destruction, something even more profound than injured bodies was exposed in the Vietnam War: the deeply fraught relationship between civil society and its military. The intervention in Vietnam had been started by John F. Kennedy sending Special Forces and advisors to help prop up an unpopular client regime, and it was expanded by Lyndon B. Johnson without any clear plan or purpose or even confidence in its outcome. The Pentagon Papers that were released a decade later showed that the war had been considered unwinnable from the start, and that the government had lied to the American public about every aspect of the war.[15] Its prosecution was nevertheless both aggressive and cruel, heavily reliant on expensive equipment and high-tech weaponry and chemicals (including the use of napalm and white phosphorus on people) to attack a peasant army and measuring success exclusively in terms of casualties. As a result, even those who enlisted voluntarily were not sure about the purpose or morality of what they were asked to do, and many more were reluctant draftees.

When the US left Vietnam in defeat in 1975 (or arguably already in 1973) and the lies about the war were exposed, many veterans felt betrayed. As one veteran poet put it, reading the pages of the Pentagon Papers turned into 'a journey through an unholy house of horrors where all one's worst fears and darkest nightmares had suddenly become reality, hard, cold, and immutable'.[16] Worst of all, the lives lost in the war seemed to have been sacrificed for no good reason – unlike the Second World War, which was universally seen as necessary – and nothing stirs horror in people quite so much as pointless death. The insult to soldiers asked to die and to kill for a dubious cause had been aggravated by the way in which neither Johnson nor Nixon (who continued the war from 1969 to 1972) had the political courage to ask the general public to make any sacrifices (unlike the Second World War, which was characterised by a general mobilisation, rationing and

---

[15] H. Bruce Franklin, *The Vietnam War and Other American Fantasies* (Amherst, MA: University of Massachusetts Press, 2000), p. 54.

[16] W. D. Ehrhart, *Passing Time: Memoir of a Vietnam Veteran Against the War* (Amherst, MA: University of Massachusetts Press, 1995), p. 172.

collective effort). Consequently, civilians seemed oblivious to the fact that American soldiers were fighting and dying in Vietnam, and this disconnection between the war front and 'the world' (at home) appeared as one of many grotesque ironies surrounding the war. These ironies and gaps between rhetoric and reality made War Gothic the natural and dominant mode in representations of the war.

Although none are strictly speaking 'horror' films, the first cycle of Hollywood movies about the Vietnam War all reach to the Gothic for their keynote moments. These works, such as *The Deer Hunter* (dir. Michael Cimino, 1978) and *Apocalypse Now* (dir. Francis Coppola, 1979), take madness, murder and suicide as their main focus, with the war serving as both ultimate cause and backdrop. The legal and medical case for war-induced mental illness was gathering momentum in these years and culminated in the recognition of post-traumatic stress disorder (PTSD) in 1980; these first prestigious films produced about the Vietnam War made it their point of departure. *The Deer Hunter* examines the different forms that post-war madness takes, and although unrealistic in many ways, it accurately foreshadows the epidemic of mental illness and suicide that would grip the veterans of Vietnam after their return. *Apocalypse Now* also focused on an unhinged protagonist (played by Martin Sheen) who has been charged with a mission to assassinate a rogue high-ranking officer who has gone mad in a story loosely modelled on Joseph Conrad's *Heart of Darkness* (1899).

However, the very first Vietnam horror film was made earlier than these Hollywood productions. *Deathdream* (also sometimes called *Dead of Night*, dir. Bob Clark, 1974) is an independent film featuring a dead soldier who has returned from Vietnam as a kind of vampiric zombie who needs blood to ward off decay. Although acting strangely and withdrawn, Andy (played by Richard Backus) is sufficiently 'normal' enough at first to fool his parents into believing that the notice of his death they have received had been an error. At first sight, the film appears to be about the truism that soldiers bring violence home from the front, and, to an extent, this is certainly the case. Andy kills a series of innocent people in order to keep himself alive and has clearly learned how to murder without hesitation or remorse. However, the film broaches a much deeper and less obvious issue when it raises the question of the relationship between civilians and soldiers who have been asked to die 'for' them. In a truly defensive war, this relationship might still be ambiguous, but in a seemingly pointless war of aggression, one mostly ignored by civilians who unthinkingly support it while going on with their lives and remaining indifferent to the fate of soldiers far away on the front lines, the relationship between the two is necessarily strained if not actually antagonistic. As he is about to kill his family doctor, Andy says, 'I died for you, Doc. Why shouldn't you return the favour?' This brilliant moment in the film again recalls Abel Gance's *J'Accuse* (1919), mentioned earlier, where an army of dead soldiers rises up from the field of battle and marches upon their hometown nearby to see if the people there are behaving in a manner worthy of their sacrifice. Of course, they find that the population is busy with their own lives and distractions, not solemnly grieving. The question of civilian worthiness is always an anxious question because how can anyone ever truly deserve someone else dying 'for' them? How would one determine such a thing? There is thus necessarily a dread and unease around the civilian–military relationship and this is especially true for the non-defensive neo-colonial wars that have been fought since the 1950s.

Two major fiction writers would emerge from the Vietnam War: Tim O'Brien and Gustav Hasford. O'Brien would become the most prolific and the most accepted veteran author of the war, with books published from the early 1970s (*If I Die in a Combat Zone, Box Me Up and Ship Me Home*, 1973) to the 2000s. His most famous work is the collection of stories *The Things They Carried* (1990), which has plenty of horror, both bodily and psychological, but the most harrowing novel O'Brien wrote was *In the Lake of the Woods* (1994). This is a truly Gothic tale of PTSD, and depicts an ageing veteran, now a respectable politician, taking a vacation in the woods with his wife after losing a senatorial campaign. When his wife disappears one day, the novel takes us on a journey through the protagonist's life and Vietnam experience, including his participation in the notorious My Lai massacre, which he has erased from his file while working as a clerk in the records department.

More importantly, he has attempted to erase or repress these memories from his psyche, an occlusion that ends up having potentially murderous consequences as it becomes increasingly likely to the reader that he has probably also murdered his own wife, disposed of her body, and then repressed it from his memory. The novel uses the Gothic to make the point that the violence and cruelty of US actions in Vietnam cannot not be erased by historical amnesia and denial, and that the trauma of veterans, both as victims and as perpetrators of atrocities, will eventually leak out into their lives and homes.

Though most writers and filmmakers dealing with the Vietnam war turn to the War Gothic at one point or another, no writer has done so with as much consistency and fierce conviction as Gustav Hasford. His name is not widely known today, but his contribution to the popular imagination of the

Vietnam War is unparalleled. Stanley Kubrick's highly acclaimed and influential film *Full Metal Jacket* (1987), though often credited to Michael Herr for the screenplay, is almost entirely based on Hasford's novel, *The Short-Timers* (1979).[17] This short book, along with its 1990 sequel *The Phantom Blooper*, constitutes the most powerful and withering critique of the Vietnam War that has been written to date, and the mode of both novels is pure horror. The novels rely on a cluster-bomb of key Gothic tropes, such as the werewolf, the vampire, the zombie and the ghost or phantom, all of which are used to lay siege to the American myths and self-deceptions (about Vietnam, about veterans and about American society itself) that, in Hasford's view, led to the Vietnam War in the first place. These tropes, as well as the Gothic themes and imagery of the novels, allow Hasford to pursue his multi-fronted project of demystification by moving from the abstraction and euphemism of official war discourse to what he calls some 'unendurable truths'.[18] The most important one of these is the idea that sixty thousand Americans died in Vietnam (and many more afterwards) for *nothing*. If, for Hasford, the war was a mistake, a product of American arrogance, ignorance and greed, then there is no way to conceptualise the bloodshed that occurred as anything except a meaningless waste of bodies and lives. This is the disenchanted truth that Hasford uses the Gothic genre to express in all its ugliness and brutal materiality in *The Short-Timers*.

Two notable novels have also emerged from the Vietnamese side of the war. Both rely heavily on Gothic tropes and images, including ghosts, haunting, desolate wilderness, corpses, madness and disjointed memory. Bảo Ninh's *The Sorrow of War* (1990) is written in a stream-of-consciousness style and begins with the North Vietnamese soldier-narrator collecting the bones of his dead comrades for burial. The novel chronicles the disappointments and many acts of desecration and immorality that the main character has observed during the war. Duong Thu Huong's *Novel Without a Name* (1995) is also about disillusionment, the horrors of jungle combat and the madness or fantasy worlds that soldiers escape into as a result. Both novels depict battlefield gore in a style reminiscent of First World War graphic detail and irony, but also include depictions of more specifically Vietnamese acts of veneration, memory and folklore surrounding death and the dead.

A final work of War Gothic emerging from the Vietnam War worth mentioning here is the 1990 film *Jacob's Ladder* (dir. Adrian Lyne).

---

[17] Gustav Hasford, *The Short-Timers* (Toronto and New York: Bantam Books, 1979).
[18] Gustav Hasford, 'Still Gagging on the Bitterness of Vietnam', *Los Angeles Times* (30 April 1980).

A masterful compendium of War Gothic themes, this psychological thriller operates within the framework of the fantastic, offering two possible frames of interpretation throughout yet only to finish with a twist that leaves both astonishingly behind. The film opens in a jungle in Vietnam where the protagonist, Jacob Singer (Tim Robbins), and his unit are under attack, going berserk and killing each other. The film them jumps forwards several years to find the protagonist living in New York with his girlfriend. During most of the film, the viewer is invited to hesitate between believing the Vietnam veteran protagonist is suffering from flashbacks and hallucinations and the possibility that he is uncovering a conspiracy around medical experiments with mind-altering drugs conducted on his unit. The 'crazy vet' trope is thus played against the 'super soldier' trope. The purpose of the experiment, as Singer comes to believe, would have been to enhance combat performance, but as is often true in the Gothic, the experiment goes awry and soldiers turn on each other instead of pitting their energies against enemy combatants. We are never quite sure if Jacob was the victim of such an experiment or if he is simply haunted by symptoms of PTSD. In this way, the film evokes issues of madness, trauma, battlefield confusion, memory distortion, brainwashing, temporal disjunction and veterans struggling to adjust to post-war life.

The film turns out, in fact, to be a variation of Ambrose Bierce's masterpiece, 'An Occurrence at Owl Creek Bridge' (1890), in which a Confederate soldier who seems to escape during his hanging and to find his way home to his wife and plantation turns out to be merely imagining this escape and journey as he dies. The dilation of subjective time structures *Jacob's Ladder* as well, revealed at the end with the protagonist being pronounced dead on an operating table in Vietnam and the viewer realising that the entire film was a fantasy unfolding in his mind as he struggled between life and death during his final moments. In this way, the film contributes to a longstanding Gothic tradition of exploring subjective distortions of time under circumstances of extreme duress or violence and pays tribute to an early American master of the modern War Gothic.

Conclusion

If the Vietnam War became a nightmare for an entire generation, the Persian Gulf War was meant to heal that trauma by being quick and efficient, in the tradition of the 'splendid little war' of an earlier era, such as the Spanish–American War of 1898. And the war was indeed short and successful by most immediate standards, a veritable *blitzkrieg* that was over in less than two months. However, the Persian Gulf War also ushered in a whole new and disturbing phase in global warfare. It not only prepared the way for the quagmire-like intervention in Iraq a decade later, making the desert into the dominant war zone of the twenty-first century, it also generated a new visual semantics of war horror in the mainstream media: burned corpses on the so-called 'highway of death', Kurdish civilians gassed by chemical weapons, night vision cameras that turned Baghdad a luminous green. In fact, one of the most striking new technologies to emerge from the War in the Gulf, and one which would migrate into both the horror film and the new gaming developments, was the first-person, point-of-view camera used by military personnel and 'smart bombs' during the invasion (as well as drones in more recent years). The images generated by these cameras and surveillance equipment, often enhanced with infrared, thermal or other night-vision devices, have become the new lexicon of war in visual culture. This is true for early first-person-shooter games such as ID Software's *Wolfenstein 3D* (1992) and *Doom* (1993), as well as the later found-footage films such as *The Blair Witch Project* (dir. Eduardo Sánchez and Daniel Myrick, 1999), *G.I. Jesus* (dir. Carl Colpaert, 2006), *The Zombie Diaries* (dir. Michael G. Bartlett, 2006) and many others.

The period from 1938 to 1990 saw an extraordinary development in the use of Gothic and horror to tell narratives about war and combat, a tradition that dated back to the earliest Gothic novels but which had assumed an unprecedented role in the literature of the First World War. The two main uses of the arsenal of the Gothic have remained the same since that time: one, to reveal and accentuate the horrific damage caused to bodies by combat, usually in order to denounce and demystify war; and two, figuratively to depict the less visible ways in which combat and war violence effect soldiers and civilians on a psychological level, especially through fear and trauma. A third form of War Gothic involves the dehumanisation of enemies by portraying them as monsters. All three forms are concerned with the ways in which war robs humans of their humanity, though the first two are largely critical of war while the third is basically a form of militaristic jingoism. All three have been crucially important the latter half of the twentieth century and will no doubt haunt the stories beginning to emerge from the forever wars in the Middle East.[19]

---

[19] I use the term 'forever war' to refer to the way in which the war in Afghanistan has now become the United States' longest war, as observed by Dexter Filkins in his book by this title. The phrase also alludes to Joe Haldeman's sci-fi classic *The Forever War* (1974), which allegorised the war in Vietnam as an intergalactic war lasting centuries.

3.6

Gothic and the Postcolonial Moment

TABISH KHAIR

Like the Gothic, which can be both an historical and a stylistic description, the 'postcolonial moment' tends to be identified either in the aftermath of decolonisation or as a larger critical discourse that is located in the historicity of decolonisation but not confined to it. Defining the postcolonial moment as the dawn of a critical awareness in a writer or sections of a colonised people that now speech has necessarily to take into account and not simply mimic or oppose, and locating it in preceding and subsisting colonial discourses, I examine in this chapter what this means to the Gothic.

We need to begin with the observation, however, that postcolonial Gothic fiction often appears to overlap with other subgenres, such as fantasy, speculative fiction, horror and magical realism. While this is by no means a tendency exclusive to postcolonial literature, it can, at times, be exacerbated given either the association (correct or not) of postcolonialism with anti-canonical writing, which might lead to a greater pull in the direction of, say, speculative fiction, or the association (also correct or not) of a subgenre like magical realism with non-European writing. If we are to use the category of 'postcolonial Gothic fiction' with any degree of critical rigour, we can neither ignore this overlapping nor refuse to distinguish between the subgenres.

For instance, a novel such as the Australian writer Will Elliott's *The Pilo Family Circus* (2007) contains Gothic elements. This is particularly so in the initial pages, where a dark secret spills into the mundane life of Jamie, the main protagonist, as well as in the parallel that the novel draws, but never develops, between mindless consumerism and the gory, devilish circus into which it plunges the reader and Jamie. However, as the narrative proceeds, one is transposed – literally, in the case of Jamie – to an underground circus, located below the real world and above the confines of hell (or something very similar), a realm in which freaks, magic, weird science and monsters abound, and where 'soul dust' is stolen from the spectators in order to fulfil wishes.[1] This, I would argue, precludes the novel from ever being predominantly Gothic, and this for exactly the same reason that a magical realist novel cannot be predominantly Gothic: for the Gothic to exist, the secret, crime, monstrosity or any other kind of transgression has to erupt in and disrupt a predominantly mundane world. The 'abnormal' might always be part of this 'normal' world, but the Gothic cannot and does not conflate the lines between the two. Unlike magical realism, for instance, where the fantastic and the real may cohabit without any necessary tension, the Gothic novel always highlights the otherness of the fantastic and the supernatural in a 'real' or normal world. Hence, a Gothic *qua* Gothic novel usually tackles only one major stream of transgression: for instance, Bram Stoker's *Dracula* (1897) offers the transgression of vampirism, with madness and promiscuity being subsumed within it. This is not the case with either horror fiction or magical realism, or with many other related subgenres such as fantasy writing. Here there is a dissolution of realms, and the reader falls into a space where the real and the magical, the normal and the abnormal, the mundane and the unusual seep into each other without end: in short, the latter part of these binaries ends up, as it does in *The Pilo Family Circus*, providing the grounds on which the narrative develops. Hence, in this chapter, while I do not deny some overlap, I focus on texts that are, by the above definition, largely or predominantly Gothic.

The Nature of the Scream

As Patrick Brantlinger has noted, imperial Gothic fiction of the late nineteenth century was poignantly aware of the Victorian, colonial anxieties of its readers, but exploited them mostly to contain them.[2] It is entirely possible to see the colonial Gothic and the postcolonial Gothic as signposts on the same road, though this chapter argues for a narrower and more specific definition of the postcolonial Gothic, one that recognises its imbrications with the colonial Gothic but which focuses on its differences. For one, it can be argued that, unlike the imperial Gothic, the postcolonial Gothic has no desire to contain or assuage the anxieties of its European or Eurocentric readers.

Let us start with the quintessential Gothic moment: when the self screams at the sight of the other, a moment perhaps best symbolised cinematically in the famous bathroom scene in Alfred Hitchcock's *Psycho* (1960). The postcolonial moment too begins, by most accounts, when the non-European other

[1] Will Elliott, *The Pilo Family Circus* (London: Quercus, 2007).
[2] Patrick Brantlinger, *Rule of Darkness: British Literature and Imperialism, 1830–1914* (Ithaca, NY and London: Cornell University Press, 1988).

confronts the European self – or, in Salman Rushdie's famous words as they were fashioned into a pioneering study by Bill Ashcroft, Gareth Griffiths and Hellen Tiffin, when 'the empire writes back'.[3]

This latter confrontation is deceptive. I have argued elsewhere that one cannot represent the other or speak as the other; speech is always the utterance of the self.[4] The other is that which faces the self. In that sense, the other is always, as Emmanuel Levinas insists, that which exceeds the limits of the self, that which cannot be reduced to the self.[5] Of course, there is a difference between the philosophical understanding of the other, particularly after the works of Levinas, Martin Buber and, now, Byung-Chul Han, and the othering that took place under colonisation, when the non-European was often reduced either to a negative image of the European self or a juvenile version of it. In short, colonial and Eurocentric accounts of the non-European tended to dismiss the radical 'otherness', the irreducible difference of the other, either by constructing it as pure negativity and antithesis, or by turning it into more of the self-same. The colonial other was *not* that which could not be reduced to the self but either just a simpler or younger version of the self or its negative image: it could be understood entirely with reference (metonymically or antithetically) to the European subject. It is against this othering of the non-European that the postcolonial moment is poised. Despite its frequent failure to understand the nature of otherness, usually by claiming to narrate or represent it, postcolonial literature set out to tell, as the heroine of Jean Rhys's *Wide Sargasso Sea* (1966) puts it, 'the other side' of the story.[6] If this put many postcolonial writers under pressure to narrate difference as transparent, it also enabled them to question colonial depictions of the non-European other as simply a negativity and a threat.

But such colonial depictions, as I have underlined in *The Gothic, Postcolonialism and Otherness* (2009), were often at the core of the colonial and/or European Gothic. Even the Devil, that ultimately negativised Gothic other in the Christian European context, was imbued, as H. L. Malchow has illustrated, with non-European contours.[7] European and Europeanised Gothic fiction until the mid twentieth century often employed non-

---

[3] Bill Ashcroft, Gareth Griffiths and Helen Tiffin, *The Empire Writes Back: Theory and Practice in Post-Colonial Literatures* (London and New York: Routledge, 1989).
[4] In various talks, particularly the 2017 Arthur Ravenscroft Memorial lecture at Leeds University.
[5] Emmanuel Levinas, *Alterity and Transcendence*, trans. by M. B. Smith (New York: Columbia University Press, 1999).
[6] Jean Rhys, *Wide Sargasso Sea*, edited by Angela Smith (London: Penguin Books, 2000).
[7] H. L. Malchow, *Gothic Images of Race in Nineteenth-Century Britain* (Stanford: Stanford University Press, 1996).

Europeans or artefacts from non-Europe as threats to be overcome or eliminated, a tendency that has not entirely disappeared today. The negativised Gothic other tended to be non-European or harbour non-European – 'Black,' 'Hindoo' or 'Turk' – features in some of the most notable Gothic novels of the nineteenth century, ranging from Wilkie Collins's *The Moonstone* (1868) to Richard Marsh's *The Joss: A Reversion* (1901).

And yet, as Andrew Smith and William Hughes put it in the Introduction to their *Empire and the Gothic: The Politics of Genre* (2003), the Gothic and postcolonialism shared and continue to share much common ground despite their seemingly obvious differences:

> Theories of postcolonialism and scholarship on the Gothic might, superficially, appear to be the product of rather different intellectual, cultural and historical traditions. The Gothic, a fantastical literary form that had its heyday in the late eighteenth and early nineteenth centuries might seem to inhabit a different world than that confronted by writers working in postcolonial contexts in the twenty-first century. However, the picture is more complex than this because an historical examination of the Gothic and accounts of postcolonialism indicate the presence of a shared interest in challenging post-enlightenment notions of rationality.[8]

One might rightly object that the common – and contemporary – association of the Enlightenment with a narrow discourse of reason is somewhat reductive. It leaves out the unease that writers such as Jonathan Swift show at the hubristic 'pride' of human reason, or the fact that a thinker such as Jean-Jacques Rousseau bases the social exercise of reason on two basic feelings – that of 'self-preservation' and that of repulsion at seeing other human beings suffer or die. But it nonetheless remains true that both the Gothic and much of postcolonialism critique a simplistic association of humanity with reason and, in the latter case, of reason with Europe.

The other essential connection is highlighted by Gina Wisker: 'Reading the Gothic demands a certain kind of estrangement; defamiliarization on the one hand and imaginative leaps of faith on the other . . . Reading postcolonial writing is another potentially fraught, transformative experience.'[9] When the Gothic and the postcolonial moment coincided, perhaps the biggest problem was (and is) the Gothic villain. If a writer accepted and employed the non-European – person,

---

[8] Andrew Smith and William Hughes, 'Introduction', in Andrew Smith and William Hughes (eds), *Empire and the Gothic: The Politics of Genre* (London: Palgrave Macmillan, 2003), pp. 1–12 (p. 1).

[9] Gina Wisker, 'Crossing Liminal Spaces: Teaching the Postcolonial Gothic', *Pedagogy* 7:3 (Fall 2007): 401–25 (p. 404).

artefact, religion or superstition – as the Gothic villain or the Gothic secret, such a writer was, by the very act, writing colonial and not postcolonial fiction. And yet, as I have suggested above, the Gothic requires a secret and, to a large extent, a villain: it expects the self to scream at the sight of the other.

Postcolonial Texts with Gothic elements

At its simplest, the effect of this scream can be obtained situationally. For instance, a certain kind of non-European setting can be used as a Gothic backdrop. Robert Service, the late nineteenth- and early twentieth-century British-Canadian poet, achieves this in a poem such as 'The Cremation of Sam McGee' (1960). Service's poems very often employ Gothic tropes in order to convey the bleakness and extreme difference of the Canadian landscape, and the precarity of human existence in it. 'The Cremation of Sam McGee' starts with an eight-line stanza that is repeated at the end:

> There are strange things done in the midnight sun
> By the men who moil for gold;
> The Arctic trails have their secret tales
> That would make your blood run cold;
> The Northern lights have seen queer sights,
> But the queerest they ever did see
> Was that night on the marge of Lake Lebarge
> I cremated Sam McGee.[10]

Having set up the Arctic as a space of terror, strangeness and secrecy, the narrator then proceeds to tell of Sam McGee, who was from Tennessee, 'where the cotton blooms and blows' and his wanderings ''round the Pole', where he 'was always cold'. Finally, lost in a blizzard on a desolate trail, McGee dies, but not before extracting a promise from the narrator that his body will be cremated. In a desolate, woodless, frozen place, this is a difficult promise to fulfil, but the narrator carries the body along, with a fear and a fascination that clearly echoes that of Samuel Taylor Coleridge's Ancient Mariner with the shot albatross slung around his neck:

> In the days to come, though my lips were dumb, in my heart how I cursed
>   that load.
> In the long, long night, by the lone firelight, while the huskies, round in
>   a ring,

---

[10] Robert Service, *The Best of Robert Service* (London: A & C Black, 2000), p. 16.

> Howled out their woes to the homeless snows – O God! How I loathed the thing.[11]

Finally, the narrator reaches a stranded and abandoned steamer by the side of Lake Lebarge. There, stripping up planks from the ship and finding the coal that has been left, he crams the body of Sam McGee into the boiler of the steamer and sets it on fire. The narrative tells us that the boiler is glowing with coals, when the narrator goes away for a 'hike, for I didn't like to hear him sizzle so'.[12] When he comes back, he cannot resist taking a look. He opens the boiler, still aflame:

> And there sat Sam, looking cool and calm, in the heart of the furnace roar;
> And he wore a smile you could see a mile, and he said: 'Please close that door.
> It's fine in here, but I greatly fear you'll let in the cold and storm –
> Since I left Plumtree, down in Tennessee, it's the first time I've been warm.'[13]

Undoubtedly, the authorship and setting of the poem is post/colonial, at least in the sense that it has been set in, and written by someone from, the colonies, and its texture is clearly Gothic. But does a text like this interrogate the Gothic in the postcolonial moment? One can argue that European Gothic texts do something similar, as in the Gothic stories of Rudyard Kipling set in India, or, for that matter, in this poem's antecedent, Coleridge's 'The Rime of the Ancient Mariner' (1798).

Similarly, Elizabeth Jolley's *The Well* (1986) is in some ways almost a classic Gothic novel, centring as it does around such typically Gothic tropes of the eighteenth and nineteenth centuries as an orphan, a stranger, a 'great house', hidden family secrets, repressed memories of crime and desire, hints of mental instability, a homicide and a 'ghost'.[14] An excellent novel of its kind, and considered a twentieth-century Australian classic, *The Well* transposes all these elements into the vast Australian countryside, with its own distinctive sounds and sights. In that sense, it is a postcolonial novel and also, perhaps, in the sense that its author, born in England in 1923 and subsequently educated there, naturalised as an Australian citizen when she married and moved to that continent in 1959. However, unlike Rhys's *Wide Sargasso Sea*, André Brink's *Devil's Valley* (1998) or Peter Carey's *Jack Maggs* (1997), it does not engage in any substantial inversion of the colonial tropes of Gothic. Given a similar set of characters, its narrative would work just as well in any other

---

[11] Service, *The Best of Robert Service*, p. 18. [12] Service, *The Best of Robert Service*, p. 19.
[13] Service, *The Best of Robert Service*, p. 19.
[14] Elizabeth Jolley, *The Well* (London: Penguin Books, 1986).

comparative space in a small farming town on the verge of greater urbanisation.

If one is looking at postcolonial novels with Gothic elements, Margaret Atwood's *Alias Grace* (1996) falls into a similar category. Based on the real-life story of 'one of the most notorious Canadian women of the 1840s', one whose narrative already exists in various colonial renditions, *Alias Grace* revisits the crimes attributed to its eponymous historical figure.[15] Atwood's purpose is not so much to question the crimes as to provide a more complex and nuanced explanation for them, which enables her examination of the problematic representation of women accused of crimes. By making Grace speak – as herself and as multiple personalities – Atwood also manages to mix up psychological and supernatural elements, without deciding in favour of either. Is Grace a criminal in the simple sense, is she a split personality, is she possessed, is she perhaps innocent? The matter is not fully resolved, and that is in keeping with Atwood's purpose, which is not to question the facts of the case but to highlight the subjective and gendered aspects that were largely left out of contemporary accounts and subsequent recounts of the original crime. However, as is the case with Jolley's *The Well*, it is difficult to read *Alias Grace* as distinctly shifting the registers of the colonial Gothic in the postcolonial moment.

These are undoubtedly novels in which the Gothic and the postcolonial moment coincide, resulting largely in changes of location and sometimes in changes of focus. However, something far more significant happens when postcolonial writers engage with core elements of the Gothic: its narration of horror or threat at the precise interface of selfhood and otherness. Hence, I find it more useful to look at novels in which the Gothic and the postcolonial moment are used directly and starkly to interrogate each other. Of these, I will discuss four very different fictions: the Caribbean writer Jean Rhys's *Wide Sargasso Sea*, the South African André Brink's *Devil's Valley*, the Australian Peter Carey's *Jack Maggs* and the Indian-British Indra Sinha's *Animal's People*, with less extensive references to some other texts.

The Postcolonial Gothic: Jean Rhys

Historically speaking, Rhys's *Wide Sargasso Sea* is a colonial novel as it was written when, though on the cusp of decolonisation, much of the Caribbean was still a colony. In every other sense, it is a postcolonial novel, for it sets

---

[15] Margaret Atwood, *Alias Grace* (London: Virago Press, 2005), p. 537.

out, very specifically, to contest colonial discourses about the Caribbean and the Creole. *Wide Sargasso Sea* is a postcolonial Gothic novel not just because it is inspired by the most Gothic of all elements in Charlotte Brontë's reluctantly Gothic and often anti-Gothic novel, *Jane Eyre* (1847): the mad Creole woman in the attic, the colonial secret of the great house. Rhys's novel does not simply take on these elements from Brontë. Instead, it establishes its own relationship to the Gothic, and hence to the colonial discourses of rationality and the supernatural.

As I have noted in *The Gothic, Postcolonialism and Otherness*, *Wide Sargasso Sea* is not primarily, as the blurb on a Penguin edition of the text puts it, the story of 'Creole heiress Antoinette Cosway' who, born in 'an oppressive colonialist society', meets 'a young Englishman who is drawn to her innocent sensuality and beauty. After their marriage disturbing rumours begin to circulate, poisoning her husband against her. Caught between his demands and her own precarious sense of belonging, Antoinette is driven towards madness.'[16] There are minor simplifications in this redacted version of the novel: it is doubtful whether the Englishman ('Rochester') was ever in love with Antoinette and even more doubtful whether 'sensuality' would be attractive to him, and it is definitely clear that he married her at least partly for her fortune. It is also unclear whether Antoinette really goes 'mad' in any simple sense of the word, at least not before she is carted off to England. However, these are minor matters.

What is more interesting is the way in which the blurb completely overlooks – with a simplistic gesture towards 'oppressive colonialist society' – the great secret that haunts Antoinette, her mother and her family. This is the (colonial) secret of slavery. Antoinette and her mother belong to the disappearing old 'plantation' families, the crumbling great houses that were built on the labour of slaves. Antoinette grows up in a period when slavery has been abolished, leading to the impoverishment of families like hers, but its memory is still fresh. This memory is used against her by both Blacks and whites, especially the new capitalist class that despises the older slave-owners because its source of profit, though as exploitative in many ways, is based on the obfuscating control of capital, not of human bodies directly. (Though, of course, control of capital translates into control of bodies: Antoinette becomes a captive in her marriage because her husband, not she, inherits her father's wealth.)

---

[16] Rhys, *Wide Sargasso Sea*, cover.

Both Antoinette and her mother resent the new exploiters and their assumed moral superiority. They also see the reality of slave-holding in grey tones rather than in the black-and-white of the 'new comers'. This even enables them to connect to some ex-slaves, such as Christophine, in ways that the new whites, like Mr Mason or Rochester, are simply incapable of. The 'rumours' that, according to the blurb, poison Rochester's mind against Antoinette also arise due to the paradigm shift between the exploitation of slavery and the exploitation of high capital. Rochester cannot comprehend the ways in which some white slave-owners used Black women for sexual purposes (though he does go to bed with a coloured woman, who wants cash), and this lack of comprehension of the old relations of power is exacerbated by his lack of physical connection to the place and the people. All this leads to suspicions of 'racial contamination' or miscegenation – he imagines Antoinette as being of mixed blood – and these suspicions conveniently mesh with his economic interests.

On the other hand, even though Antoinette and her mother can see the hypocrisy in the ways of the newcomers, they cannot fully face their own past of slavery. They either tend to see it as largely benevolent, or simply overlook its oppressive and brutal faces. The latter occurs in a number of places in the novel, but I will confine myself to one instance. Antoinette is taking Rochester to her honeymoon island, called Massacre. Rochester asks, with a touch of moral superiority,

> 'And who was massacred here? Slaves?'
> 'Oh no.' She sounded shocked. 'Not slaves. Something must have happened a long time ago. Nobody remembers now.'[17]

Antoinette is generally vague about the slave-holding part of Caribbean history, and in this case, as Angela Smith points out in the Introduction to her edition of the novel, a precise answer is available. What is interesting is that this answer puts both Rochester and Antoinette in the dock. The massacre recorded in the name of the (actual) island took place in 1675, when one Colonel Philip Warner probably murdered his 'mixed race' half-brother, Indian Warner, whom he had refused to recognise as being related to him. This 'history' not only puts paid to Rochester's glib moral certainties about a place that he hardly knows; it also forces Antoinette to face the vivid brutality of a past that she would prefer to see in softer colours.

---

[17] Rhys, *Wide Sargasso Sea*, p. 39.

Equally telling is that Rhys's novel both uses and complicates 'obeah/vodou' as a sign of otherness. It cannot do away with obeah/vodou as a sign of otherness, for that would reduce the Caribbean experience to the sameness of European rationality. But it cannot simply celebrate obeah/vodou either, as that would make the Caribbean experience impenetrable to narration and confine it to the stereotypical 'African' component. Instead, it has to deal with the Caribbean location in the philosophical sense of otherness, both as something vital to the self and as something not reducible to the self. This self can be 'European' or 'African': in both the cases, the Caribbean, personified in the Creole Antoinette, has to be other than 'European' or 'African'. No matter what one may think of the opposition between rationality and obeah/vodou, given the discourses available to the narrative, *Wide Sargasso Sea* makes the vital point of how the other is never just the self, and how the self is never without the other.

Written by a Caribbean Creole in what was historically the tail end of the colonial period in the Caribbean, and informed by a distinctively postcolonial sensibility, *Wide Sargasso Sea* cannot and does not utilise obeah/vodou as simply a device of Gothic horror, largely derived from Africa. This would be to perpetuate colonial tropes that the novel, while being forced to employ them in places, always aims to resist. Instead, Rhys fashions a two-pronged way out of this dilemma. First, she creates a Black Caribbean character who is officially accused and persecuted by the white Caribbean as a practitioner of obeah/vodou, but actually narrates this character, often between the lines, as a kind of traditional wise woman who is used to alternative traditions and remedies. It is not this Black 'obeah' woman who is the Gothic other in *Wide Sargasso Sea*. Instead, and second, the Gothic other ('villain') in the novel is the white Englishman, who insists on reason: Rochester. Rochester is repeatedly shown as practising a version of 'obeah': a devious 'reason-based' manipulation of other human beings and an exertion of his own power. This combination of the colonial Gothic stereotype – obeah – and a postcolonial element – the implied reading of Rochester – gives us a very different kind of Gothic villain: a white man who practices the obeah of 'reasonability'! Antoinette, for one, is fully aware of this side of her husband. As she says, when he keeps calling her by the name of her mother, who had reportedly gone mad, 'Bertha is not my name. You are trying to make me into someone else, calling me by another name. I know, that's obeah too.'[18]

---

[18] Rhys, *Wide Sargasso Sea*, p. 94.

Some postcolonial critics might reasonably ask why Rhys cannot altogether avoid binaries – such as that of rationality and obeah ('irrationality'). After all, this is the assumption of much postcolonial writing that points out, correctly, the constructed nature of binaries, and then tries to go beyond them. It is one of the reasons why magical realism holds more appeal than the Gothic for some writers: while the former tends to merge and confuse binary categories, the latter often tends to maintain them. But the problem is not so easy to resolve, as I have suggested earlier. Just as an insistence on otherness as total darkness and negativity is a reduction of the non-European's difference, a transmission of difference into narrative transparency is problematic too. Byung-Chul Han has consistently made this point in both general and philosophical contexts: 'The negativity of alterity and foreignness – in other words, the resistance of the Other – disturbs and delays the smooth communication of the Same. Transparency stabilizes and speeds the system by eliminating the Other and the Alien.'[19]

Indeed, the assumption of 'transparency' across individuals or cultures not only makes otherness impossible, it also fundamentally destroys the Gothic as a genre or mode. One way to understand this is to see the colonial Gothic, as I have suggested, as the scream of the self in the face of the other. True, the other is not simply 'limit and menace', a cause of terror, to the self. For instance, Levinas does not dispute this repressive function of the other, adducing 'the wars and violence' of history as evidence of it. But he points out that 'the other man – the absolutely other – the Other – does not exhaust his presence by that repressive function. His presence can be meeting and friendship, and in this the human is in contrast with all other reality'.[20] For finally, if it is not to be a 'universalising' erasure of difference or a 'tribal' insistence on exclusive difference, the 'human' can only be shorthand for the self's 'ethical relation' with the irreducible other. It is this that literature that allows space for 'non-events', 'non-history', 'non-being', 'non-rationality', 'the non-European' and the likes can sometimes suggest more aptly than literature, like some overly explanatory (transparent) postcolonial fiction, that sets out fully to narrate the other. The narration of the other has to be, of necessity, a 'non-narration', something that happens between lines and outside language as much as it happens in language.

Notwithstanding, of course, those great exceptions such as Joseph Conrad's *Heart of Darkness* (1899) or Herman Melville's *Moby-Dick* (1851),

---

[19] Byung-Chul Han, *The Transparency Society*, trans. by Erik Butler (Stanford: Stanford University Press, 2015), p. 2.
[20] Levinas, *Alterity and Transcendence*, p. 56.

colonial Gothic fiction seldom went beyond the basic aspect of the self's confrontation with the other: the scream of horror/terror. Colonial Gothic fiction is full of such screams, often directed at the non-European other or her/his traces. Postcolonial critiques of this limitation of much of colonial writing is justified. And yet, the fact remains that the scream registers the *irreducible* difference of the other too, an irreducible difference that cannot be communicated via a lucid explanation. Celebration of difference – as the political insipidity of consumerist versions of 'multiculturalism' highlights – is not the same as recognition of otherness; in effect, it might well be a way to make otherness as irreducible difference disappear. True, the colonial self cannot transcend its selfhood when faced by the other– and screams – or eliminates the other. But, as Byung-Chul Han notes, '[t]ransparency stands opposed to transcendence' too.[21] The secret, the crime, the turgidity of the other needs to be there in order for transcendence to take place; transparency is not the answer to the colonial scream. One can see this in South African André Brink's novel, *Devil's Valley* (1998), where what is narrated in a Gothic mode is not the problem of race and colour but their subterranean existence in overtly racist 'white' societies.

The Postcolonial Gothic: André Brink, Peter Carey, Indra Sinha

Blood or race is the secret at the heart of Brink's *Devil's Valley*, a text that can be seen as containing both magical realist and Gothic elements. While there seems to be a considerable overlap between the two modes, it is important to maintain a basic distinction between them. In magical realism, the fantastic elements grow naturally out of the reality portrayed, so that they are not experienced as an anomaly or threat in their non-reality or abnormality. However, in the Gothic, the fantastic or the out-of-the-ordinary – whether ghost or crime or monster – is very much an aberration in reality. Even if reality is seen as perforated with such aberrations, they are supposed to be hidden – which accounts, obviously, for the fear and threat occasioned by their discovery or resurgence in the Gothic.

Keeping this demarcation in mind, we might divide *Devil's Valley* into two generic streams: the reality of the denizens of Devil's Valley (the place) is magical realist, as the fantastic and real exist simultaneously and without surprise for them, but the reality of the *visiting* narrator-protagonist Flip

---

[21] Han, *The Transparency Society*, p. 10.

Lochner's experience of Devil's Valley is purely Gothic. Lochner is always uncovering, or seeking to uncover, the crimes that are seen and understood in a fantastically Christian – magical realist – way by the denizens of Devil's Valley.[22] When they witness a woman carried away by a whirlwind from heaven, he discovers her murdered body hidden in another person's grave, and so on. Of all these Gothic elements, perhaps the one that is most central to Brink's postcolonial exploration of South Africa is that of race: the open secret of apartheid South Africa, which continues to cast a spell today. It presents one of those instances of mutual interpenetration of the Gothic by the postcolonial that I have set out to highlight here.

In the newly post-apartheid society of South Africa – the novel was published in 1998, following the release of Nelson Mandela in 1990, the official abandoning of apartheid policy in 1991 and the election of a democratic government in 1994 – the Devil's Valley is both typical and atypical of its times. It is, as Lochner discovers, inhabited solely by whites. In this, it is both atypical, given the use of Black labour by whites in South Africa, and typical, given the self-understanding of pro-apartheid whites as being effectively the sole inhabitants of South Africa. But among the crimes that Lochner discovers – and perhaps the most Gothic of them, given the need of the whites in Devil's Valley to keep it hidden even from themselves – is the abandonment (and murder) of coloured children born to some of the white women.

Along with a fantastic, biblical, stone-to-death version of Christianity, Devil's Valley is built on the myth of racial purity. As one denizen puts it, 'In the end you can take away everything from a man, but if his blood is pure you can't touch him.'[23] But obviously this is a construction, explained away by an originary myth of the only Black servant, in the past, raping his white mistress. The myth holds that the woman herself killed and buried the child after he was born coloured, but, as Lochner objects, this does not explain why coloured children continue to be born to white women – and murdered. With this dark Gothic secret in the heart of whiteness, Brink effectively explores a distinctly postcolonial aspect of South Africa: the crimes of race and racism. As was the case with Rhys's novel, this involves much more than setting a Gothic narrative in postcolonial space.

Peter Carey's *Jack Maggs* turns around the Gothic equation too, in ways that bring alive the colonial 'peripheries' and colonial subjects as possibilities rather than as simplified negative threats, the existence of whom is secondary to British selfhood. John Thieme notes that *Jack Maggs* 'responds to [Charles

---

[22] André Brink, *Devil's Valley* (London: Vintage, 2000).   [23] Brink, *Devil's Valley*, p. 230.

Dickens's] *Great Expectations*, albeit obliquely, by taking a returned convict, reminiscent of Dickens's Magwitch, as its protagonist, while also, like Coetzee's *Foe*, engaging with elements from the writer's other novels and the figure of the author himself.[24] In *Great Expectations* (1860–1), starting with the gothicised graveyard scene, the protagonist Pip, then a small boy, has his destiny and, later, his fortunes shaped by the escaped convict, Magwitch. Deported to Australia, Magwitch pays for the education and gentlemanly upbringing of Pip, unknown to the boy and the young man. Magwitch returns towards the end of the novel and is revealed as Pip's benefactor – the 'colonial' and 'marginal' man who has made Pip a gentleman. This leads to some manly struggles within Pip and the matter is quickly resolved by the death of Magwitch. As Edward Said pointed out with reference to Jane Austen's *Mansfield Park* (1814), the colonies feature as a plot device in many mainstream European novels. *Great Expectations* fits this observation too, Australia being merely a space to which Magwitch is removed, and from where he sends money for Pip's life to be enabled (and narrated) in England. When Magwitch returns, he does so as a plot device too, and having served his purpose, he is quickly disposed of.

Not so in the case of Carey's *Jack Maggs*.[25] For one, Carey's 'Pip' is not a fundamentally decent young man like Dickens's Pip, who is embarrassed by Magwitch but who is not capable of any real villainy to avoid this embarrassment. Carey's 'Pip', by contrast, takes elaborate steps to avoid, deny and, finally, try to kill his Magwitch/Maggs. In that sense, as is the case with Rhys's 'Rochester', Carey's 'Pip' becomes a postcolonial kind of Gothic villain. As I have already noted, the postcolonial Gothic needs to controvert the idea and person of the Gothic villain: the colonial hero, who stands for whiteness, Europeanness and middle-class values is revealed in some postcolonial Gothic texts to be the villain, and in the process centric standards of Europeanness, civilisation and 'values' are revealed as diabolical/ hypocritical.

Carey also engages with the need of Magwitch to refer back to the colonial centre, the selfhood of England: his Maggs achieves redemption only when he realises, fully, that he has a separate and fulfilling life in Australia and returns to it. For Dickens's Magwitch, everything begins and ends in England; that is not the case with Carey's Maggs. As such, Maggs is a character of richer detail and background than Magwitch: he does not

[24] John Thieme, *Postcolonial Con-Texts: Writing Back to the Canon* (London and New York: Continuum, 2001), p. 104.
[25] Peter Carey, *Jack Maggs* (London: Faber & Faber, 1997).

exist in his relation to the past and England, as Magwitch does; he also exists (though it takes him time to realise this fully) in his relationship to the present and Australia, and to a future *in* Australia.

If the 'reasoning' European – Rochester, Mr Mason, Pip, among others – is turned into a new kind of diabolical villain in some postcolonial Gothic texts, another convoluted interface between the Gothic and the postcolonial is that of religion. This is inevitable. The colonial Gothic was marked by the usage of religious narratives, rooted in eighteenth- and nineteenth-century Christianity, whether they featured the Devil or what were categorised as non-European superstitions. A writer like Rudyard Kipling, the complexity of whose fiction was far in excess of his public role as a kind of imperial propagandist of his age, saw this clearly: in his Gothic stories, he does not allow ghosts of Indians to frighten Englishmen in India nor even to enter Europe, though they exist in their own Indian spaces, and English ghosts can always frighten both Europeans and Indians. In such an admixture, where Christianity overlapped with colonialism even when it was being mined for Gothic elements, postcolonial writers can be expected to find rich fuel. It is noticeable that the most interesting postcolonial grapplings with 'religion' in the Gothic take place in postcolonial societies in which Christianity (rather than Islam or Hinduism) exists as the mainstream religion, along with other non-European beliefs.

I have already considered the ways in which Rhys uses the obeah elements in *Wide Sargasso Sea*. An even more complex intervention is present in the Caribbean writer Erna Brodber's *Myal* (1988), a novel that combines elements from mainstream colonial Christianity, Baptism, Myalism and obeah to explore the colonisation of the mind. Similarly, the African writer Angelina N. Sithebe in *Holy Hill* (2007) combines Gothic elements with Christian religion and African spirituality to offer, in Cheryl Stobie's words, 'social critiques of power and religion in specific contexts'.[26] Both these novels turn around the colonial binarism of Christianity/non-Christianity – often also posed as religion/superstition – that permeates the colonial Gothic as much as, or even more than, the binarism of reason/religion. In the colonial Gothic, the non-Christian and non-European elements exist as a disruption not just of the world of reason but also of the overlapping world of Christianity, and the Gothic narrative usually ends when this element is destroyed or explained away. However, in Brodber's and Sithebe's novels,

---

[26] Cheryl Stobie, 'Sisters and Spirits: The Postcolonial Gothic in Angelina N. Sithebe's *Holy Hill*', *Current Writing: Text and Reception in Southern Africa* 20:2 (2008): 26–43 (p. 26).

Christianity is creatively mixed with indigenous religious elements, thus dissolving any either/or binary logic. *Myal*, in particular, uses this mix to unravel a Gothic secret and to reveal a Gothic monster that lies not in the heart of 'dread', 'oppression', 'superstition' and 'irrationality' associated with non-European faiths in the colonial Gothic, but at the very core of European civility, pedagogy and even mainstream Christianity.

Opposition and the Postcolonial Gothic

Finally, Gothic elements can be used by postcolonial writers to offer a critique of secrets other than those of colonial or religious inheritance. One notable example of such a novel is the Indian-British writer Indra Sinha's *Animal's People*. Sinha's novel is often read as a magical realist text, though, unlike, say, Salman Rushdie's *Midnight's Children* (1981), it is the Gothic that predominates here. One way to understand this is to return to a point made earlier in the chapter: if we are to use 'magical realism' and the 'Gothic' in any useful sense, we need to distinguish between them, and to distinguish them from other related genres, such as the fairy tale. While a rigorous definition of all the related genres is not part of my concern here, I have noted that magical realism differs from the Gothic in assuming a world where 'magical elements grow organically out of the reality portrayed' and the magic is 'irreducible' to other explanations, including religio-revelatory and psychological ones.[27] In the Gothic, however, the supernatural, the magical, the monstrous and the irrational figure as an irruption – and hence also a secret.

Rushdie's *Midnight's Children* is replete with magical elements that coexist with reality, but Sinha's *Animal's People* contains a Gothic secret and a Gothic 'monster': true, the 'monster', as we have seen with the Gothic 'villains' in novels by Rhys, Brink or Brodber, is not what it would have been in a colonial Gothic novel. There is a, shall we say, 'postcolonial' twist. Animal is the Gothic 'monster', born out of chemical reactions, not unlike Frankenstein's monster and so many other colonial Gothic monsters, but he is also the hero and narrator of the novel. Animal is a boy-man in his late teens, who has gone about on his fours ever since the 'Night' when an American company, the 'Kampani', wilfully or carelessly released chemicals into his slum. The very first line of the narrative and of the novel, if one overlooks a half-page

---

[27] Wendy B. Faris, 'Scheherazade's Children: Magical Realism and Postmodern Fiction', in Lois Parkinson Zamora and Wendy B. Faris (eds), *Magical Realism: Theory, History, Community* (Durham, NC and London: Duke University Press, 1995), pp. 163–90 (pp. 163, 168).

fictional 'Editor's note' that precedes it, is this: 'I used to be human once.'[28] The story is set in a city called Khaufpur – literally translated as Dreadville – which also stresses its Gothic, rather than magical realist, resonances. If we continue with the allusion to Mary Shelley's *Frankenstein*, the Kampani is Victor Frankenstein and Animal is the monster that he creates, but not only is the narrative given to us by Animal and features him as the hero, it is also a narrative about the Gothic secret in the heart of the Kampani and the state. Indra Sinha, then, puts Gothic elements to work in exposing the imbrication of corporate capital and the state in creating Gothic monsters and diabolical secrets. Like a traditional Gothic novel, *Animal's People* is based on the slow unravelling of this diabolical secret, which, unlike in magical realism, is not considered to be natural to reality or in keeping with culturally constructed notions of 'the normal'.

Of course, unlike what I have traced here, the postcolonial Gothic can be – and has been – employed to describe a wider range of novels, including those of Rushdie. Given the relevance of the Gothic to contemporary culture, a wider definition of the Gothic would inevitably entail a wider definition of the postcolonial Gothic.[29] Hence, while I have refrained from spreading the net of the Gothic so wide as to catch almost any fish, it is desirable to conclude by stating that there *are* wider definitions of the postcolonial Gothic too. These are based on aspects that remain valid to my definition. There is no doubt that, as David Punter illustrates, 'postcolonial imaginings' are inherently Gothic in the sense of being haunted by the ghosts of empire and/or depending on the recuperation or eruption of the voice of the silenced, ignored, obscured.[30] Alison Rudd drives home a similar point by exploring the role that the Gothic has played in the literature of a number of settler nations, while Justin D. Edwards has given a gothicised reading to the project of nationhood in Canada.[31] I have already noted the overlap of concerns between the postcolonial and the Gothic. But having accepted the wide purview and overlap of the postcolonial and the Gothic, I argue here for a definition of the Gothic that does not conflate it with other, similar genres such as magical realism or the fairy tale. I also suggest a definition of the postcolonial Gothic that sees it as being rooted in the colonial and imperial

---

[28] Indra Sinha, *Animal's People* (London and New York: Simon & Schuster, 2007), p. 1.
[29] See Catherine Spooner, *Contemporary Gothic* (London: Reaktion Books, 2006).
[30] David Punter, *Postcolonial Imaginings: Fictions of a New World Order* (Edinburgh: Edinburgh University Press, 2000).
[31] Alison Rudd, *Postcolonial Gothic Fictions from the Caribbean, Canada, Australia, and New Zealand* (Cardiff: University of Wales Press, 2010); Justin D. Edwards, *Gothic Canada: Reading the Spectre of a National Literature* (Edmonton: University of Alberta Press, 2010).

Gothic but also with significantly different concerns and effects. It is only if this similarity and difference obtain that we can talk of the postcolonial Gothic *per se*, or even of the Gothic in the postcolonial moment.

One cannot relegate the postcolonial Gothic to a contention with realism, as Wisker sometimes does in an otherwise illuminating discussion, and this for two major reasons.[32] First, it is misleading to consider realism as merely a matter of mimicry, as any reading of major realist works, from George Eliot to Marcel Proust, indicates. Realism can also be a matter of re-membering, ambiguity, contradiction and paradox, and its easy equation with a simplistic definition of the Enlightenment, itself a complex and internally frayed set of discourses, needs to be seriously questioned now that this equation has become almost hegemonic in some academic fields, such as mainstream postcolonialism. Second, if one, in a carefully demarcated way, sees the postcolonial Gothic as a contention with 'realism' and 'Enlightenment values', this does not provide us with any equipment to differentiate the postcolonial Gothic from the imperial Gothic, the magical realist, religious allegories, and so forth. Wisker rightly notes that 'Gothic texts are about crossing thresholds in terms of metaphors, their narrative tropes, and the ways of reading they enable'.[33] But, since this can be said of a lot of other genres and subgenres, including, I would argue, realist and, now, 'neo-realist' texts of the sort being written by, say, Neel Mukherjee, one needs to specify the kinds of thresholds that the postcolonial Gothic crosses in particular.

Here, Philip Holden's warning against the dangers of ahistoricity when postcolonial critics 'make use of the malleability of Gothic texts in terms of socio-political efficacy' is pertinent.[34] Holden insists on historical contextualisation, pointing out, for instance, that even anti-Catholicism in a European context in the eighteenth century would be different from anti-Catholicism in a non-European context in the twentieth century, and hence two different texts from these periods should not be critically conflated. I accept this argument, but I differ slightly from Holden's understanding of historicism as applied to the 'postcolonial'. In his selection of the two postcolonial Gothic texts that he examines, Holden implies that the discursive 'postcolonial' can come only with the socio-political post-colonial: he specifically selects texts from *after* the period of colonisation. By this standard, one might have trouble including Rhys's *Wide Sargasso Sea* in the postcolonial Gothic:

---

[32] See Wisker, 'Crossing Liminal Spaces: Teaching the Postcolonial Gothic'.

[33] Wisker, 'Crossing Liminal Spaces: Teaching the Postcolonial Gothic', p. 404.

[34] Philip Holden, 'The "Postcolonial Gothic": Absent Histories, Present Contexts', *Textual Practice* 23:3 (2009): 353–72 (p. 353).

Dominica, the Caribbean island where Rhys was born, was granted some kind of autonomy from 1958 onwards but became an independent nation only in 1978, quite a few years after Rhys's novel was published (in 1966).

However, relegating the oppositional and liminal discourses of postcolonialism to the historical advent of the post-colonial simplifies both what happened *before* and generalises everything to come *after* into an eternity of postcolonialism. Instead, while keeping historical aspects in mind, we need to see the postcolonial Gothic as a continuation of, and in contention with, the imperial and colonial Gothic. I have illustrated this with examples of what happens to the Gothic secret or the Gothic monster in the postcolonial Gothic. I have suggested that the postcolonial Gothic is, like the colonial Gothic, a narrative of the self suddenly facing the secret and repressed other, and screaming – for the scream is generic to the Gothic. But the self that does the facing up in the postcolonial Gothic is different and the scream has a different significance, interpretation and culmination. The secret that it reveals is essentially poised against the colonial, imperial and Eurocentric assumptions of the colonial Gothic.

3.7

Gothic and the Heritage Movement in the Twentieth and Twenty-First Centuries

EMMA MCEVOY

Gothic and Heritage

Twenty-first-century managers, curators and owners of heritage sites have found a variety of ways in which to accommodate Gothic entertainments. On occasion, they have even used Gothic discourse in their strategies of presentation and interpretation. These practices have attracted the attention of a number of scholars. David Inglis and Mary Holmes, for example, consider the ways in which ghosts have been co-opted by the Scottish heritage industry in their article 'Highland and Other Haunts'; the anthropologist Michele Hanks in *Haunted Heritage: The Cultural Politics of Ghost Tourism, Populism, and the Past* (2015) turns her attention to the concepts of 'experience, knowledge, and heritage' that 'structure the practices of ghost tourism' in York, England; and my own *Gothic Tourism* (2016) casts an eye over different management practices within various sectors of the heritage industry, tracing the history of Gothic tourism and considering the interplay between tourism and literature.[1] Though the use of Gothic within the heritage industry generates continuing scholarly interest, the other side of the coin – the influence of the heritage movement on Gothic – has, to date, received little critical attention.

The heritage movement is multi-faceted and is associated with the lives of nations at many levels. Indeed, it has been influential in forming the sense of nation itself. In the United Kingdom, heritage concerns have driven Acts of Parliament and the creation of government ministries; heritage thinking has formed part of educational strategies; and heritage tourism, an ever-popular

---

[1] David Inglis and Mary Holmes, 'Highland and Other Haunts – Ghosts in Scottish Tourism', *Annals of Tourism Research* 30:1 (2003): 50–63; Michele Hanks, *Haunted Heritage: The Cultural Politics of Ghost Tourism, Populism, and the Past* (London: Routledge, 2015), p. 14; Emma McEvoy, *Gothic Tourism* (Basingstoke: Palgrave Macmillan, 2016).

leisure activity, has played a considerable role in the economic life of many countries. In the twenty-first century, heritage tourism continues to thrive. English Heritage's annual report for 2017–18 recorded nearly 6.5 million visits to staffed sites, and National Trust membership for 2019 stands at more than 5.5 million people.[2]

Despite the role that the heritage movement plays in national psyches and national economies, literary critics have tended to overlook its influence on modern and contemporary Gothic texts. The reasons for this are complex. In part it is because the term is used so frequently and so broadly. As David Lowenthal notes, 'Heritage today all but defies definition.'[3] More to the point, the term 'heritage' has a bad reputation, having been lambasted, particularly since the 1980s, as simplistic, chauvinist and backward looking. In his influential *The Past Is a Foreign Country* (1985), for example, David Lowenthal subjected the theory and practice of heritage to rigorous critique and interrogation. In 1987, Robert Hewison in *The Heritage Industry* warned that Britain was '[h]ypnotised by images of the past', to the extent that it risked 'losing all capacity for creative change'.[4] Patrick Wright, in *On Living in an Old Country* (1985), related certain strains of heritage discourse to the production of the 'sancrosanct identity' of modern England, arguing that heritage sites and objects conceived of as 'precious and imperiled traces' constituted 'a closely held iconography of what it is to be English'.[5] Accordingly, many critics who make use of the term 'heritage' today employ it as shorthand to describe texts that contribute to a programme of reactionary nation-building by depicting a past viewed through rose-tinted spectacles. Thus, Andrew Higson uses the term 'heritage cinema' to apply to 'certain English costume dramas' that 'seemed to articulate a nostalgic and conservative celebration of the values and lifestyles of the privileged classes'.[6] Equating 'heritage' with simple-minded conservatism, however, does it an injustice – and not only because, as Raphael Samuels has pointed out, the

---

[2] *English Heritage Annual Report 2017/18* <www.english-heritage.org.uk/siteassets/home/about-us/annual-reports/eh-annual-report-2018_-web.pdf> (last accessed 10 September 2019); PA Media, 'National Trust membership tops 5.5 million', *The Guardian*, 2 September 2019 <www.theguardian.com/uk-news/2019/sep/02/national-trust-membership-tops-55-million> (last accessed 10 September 2019).

[3] David Lowenthal, *The Heritage Crusade and the Spoils of History* (Cambridge: Cambridge University Press, 1997), p. 94.

[4] Robert Hewison, *The Heritage Industry: Britain in a Climate of Decline* (London: Methuen, 1987), p. 10.

[5] Patrick Wright, *On Living in an Old Country: The National Past in Contemporary Britain* (London and New York: Verso, 1985), p. 2.

[6] Andrew Higson, *English Heritage, English Cinema: Costume Drama Since 1980* (Oxford: Oxford University Press, 2003), p. 12.

heritage movement has frequently gone hand-in-hand, with 'utopianism ... direct action ... social protest and cultural dissidence'.[7]

In the United Kingdom, the first government legislation for the protection of ancient sites and monuments was enacted in the late nineteenth century. Awareness and valuing of heritage (in the sense of 'valued objects and qualities such as historic buildings and cultural traditions that have been passed down from previous generations') can, of course, be found much earlier.[8] In *The Past Is a Foreign Country,* Lowenthal traces heritage thinking back to the Renaissance.[9] However, as Lowenthal points out, 'Only in the nineteenth century did preservation evolve from an antiquarian, quirky, episodic pursuit into a set of national programmes.'[10] In 1882, the first government legislation for the protection of ancient sites and monuments was enacted; the state guardianship system began, and sites were acquired by both the state and the National Trust. Behind these various activities lay certain assumptions: that ancient monuments and buildings may have cultural and educational value; that the monuments, buildings and landscapes conceived of as 'heritage' are, as the etymology of the word indicates, an inheritance; and that the inheritors are the general public. As Graeme Davison notes, 'heritage is essentially a political idea. It asserts a public or national interest in things traditionally regarded as private.'[11]

Since the late nineteenth century, heritage thinking has changed the way in which we conceptualise the world around us and endowed us with new sensibilities. Heritage sensibilities have prompted new ways of describing artefacts, buildings and landscapes in imaginative works and rethinking our relation to them. The concerns of the heritage movement – with the preservation and conservation of sites, with questions of ownership and fitting guardianship of sites, buildings and monuments, for example – have had a significant impact on Gothic literature of the twentieth and twenty-first centuries. So too have some of the key assumptions that inform the heritage movement – that material heritage can grant insights into past lives, that are unobtainable through the study of history alone, for instance.

---

[7] Raphael Samuels, 'Politics', in Graham Fairclough, Rodney Harrison, John H. Jameson Jnr and John Schofield (eds), *The Heritage Reader* (Abingdon: Routledge, 2008), pp. 274–94 (pp. 277–9).

[8] Definition 1.1 of 'heritage'. *OED* online: <www.lexico.com/en/definition/heritage> (last accessed 20 September 2019).

[9] David Lowenthal, *The Past Is a Foreign Country* (Cambridge: Cambridge University Press, 1985). See chapter 3: 'Ancients vs. Moderns'.

[10] Lowenthal, *The Past*, p. xvii.

[11] Graeme Davison, *The Use and Abuse of Australian History* (Crows Nest, NSW: Allen and Unwin, 2000), p. 121.

In this chapter, I focus on the relation between literature and the heritage movement in England. While much of what follows is of relevance to other literary traditions, the complex intersections of issue, historical moment and literary fashion differ in different countries and, for these reasons, I have found it best to confine my analysis to one country. I employ the phrase 'heritage movement' simply to name and identify the cultural impulse that seeks to preserve the monuments, buildings and landscapes of the past for the education and edification of present and future generations, a usage that, in this particular context, comes with no judgmental overtones, be they political, aesthetic or moral. The chapter will start by looking at a selection of short stories by M. R. James, focusing on the way in which heritage sensibilities affect the conception of the Gothic object, and considering the influence of heritage issues – specifically those relating to ownership, curatorship and preservation – on James's work. The 'country house crisis' of the mid twentieth century, meanwhile, provides the context in which Daphne du Maurier's *Rebecca* (1938) will be examined. Alison Uttley's heritage romance, *A Traveller in Time* (1939), is the next port of call, its hybridity considered in relation to conflicts within heritage thinking – in particular the dangers of heritage sensibility. The latter part of the chapter considers the influence of heritage thinking on Gothic fictions written and published after the Second World War. W. G. Hoskins's text, *The Making of the English Landscape* (1955), will be examined as inspiration for folk horror works, including Penelope Lively's children's novel *The Whispering Knights* (1971) and David Rudkin's *Penda's Fen* (1974), a television play composed for the BBC's Play for Today series. Finally, Sarah Waters's neo-heritage romance, *The Little Stranger* (2009), will be considered in the context of post-1980s revisionist heritage thinking.[12] Overall, the chapter will be concerned both with the influence of heritage thinking on Gothic texts, and with the irruption of Gothic into narratives that are (or at least seem to be) primarily concerned with heritage issues.

Heritage Objects

Heritage thinking quickly found its way into Gothic texts of the early twentieth century, and nowhere more strikingly so than in the work of

---

[12] I use the term 'neo-heritage' in the sense that Heilmann and Llewellyn use the term 'neo-Victorian' when they write of neo-Victorian texts being *'self-consciously engaged with the act of (re)interpretation, (re)discovery and (re)vision'*. See Ann Heilmann and Mark Llewellyn, *The Victorians in the Twenty-First Century, 1999–2009* (Basingstoke: Palgrave Macmillan, 2010), p. 4; italics in the original.

M. R. James. Although the title of James's first volume of tales, *Ghost Stories of an Antiquary* (1904), situates it in an antiquarian tradition within the Gothic that stretches back to Horace Walpole and Walter Scott, there are significant differences between their antiquarian-influenced Gothic romances, novels and poems and James's heritage-focused tales. James's narratives, like those of his predecessors, feature Gothic objects – material remains that are simultaneously foci of curiosity, sites of the supernatural and important plot drivers. Such objects in James's work, however, are inflected very differently from those in earlier texts. Although earlier Gothic objects might be ancient, their antiquity is not, in itself, intrinsically valued. While they might have curiosity value, their worth is directly linked to their instrumentality. In the earlier Gothic, objects enable plot resolutions *related to* the protagonist and tend to be linked to discoveries associated with genealogical and inheritance concerns and to family histories. These concerns often overlap, of course. In Walpole's *The Castle of Otranto* (1764), for example, the ghostly, animated portrait demonstrates the rightful ruler and clarifies family relations and identities; in Ann Radcliffe's *The Romance of the Forest* (1791), the found manuscript signifies at the level of the affective ties of family (Adeline discovers a father and his suffering), while also serving to correct the wrong done through usurpation.

Many of James's stories feature a very different kind of object, one valued for its antiquity, and often formally associated with the business of history. Sometimes this object is a find, dug up at an archaeological site or encountered within a repository dedicated to the custodianship of artefacts from the past – the museum or the archive. In 'Oh, Whistle, and I'll Come to You, My Lad' (1904), the Gothic object is a plain-looking whistle, 'a metal tube about four inches long'.[13] This is the Gothic object as heritage artefact, the value of which, in the celebrated words of the archaeologist (and first Inspector of Ancient Monuments for the Office of Works) Augustus Pitt-Rivers, 'viewed as evidence, may ... be said to be in inverse ratio to [its] intrinsic value'.[14]

The relation between the Gothic object and the protagonist is reformulated in James's heritage Gothic. With some exceptions, objects in James's tales tend not to relate to affairs of rightful succession or legitimacy; often they do not even relate directly to those who discover them. Rather, as in a succession of tales such as 'The Mezzotint' (1904) and 'Casting the Runes'

[13] M. R. James, *The Complete Ghost Stories of M. R. James* (London: Penguin, 1984), p. 79.
[14] Quoted in Mark Bowden, *Pitt Rivers: The Life and Archaeological Work of Lieutenant-General Augustus Henry Lane Fox Pitt Rivers* (Cambridge: Cambridge University Press, 1991), p. 3.

(1911), the object that is stumbled upon has no personal connection to the protagonist at all. His (and the protagonist is usually male) dominant feature is his antiquarian interest, which is also ours as readers. The occult-concentrated power of the artefact is not conditional on the identity of the protagonist, and what the artefact has to tell is nothing to do with personal history. What the heritage object communicates relates not to an individual but to the general public.

Such heritage objects in James's stories possess an unshakeable primacy. Frequently they displace the protagonist; they may even usurp the role that was formerly occupied by the villain. Humans become mere ciphers, and even ghosts are displaced in stories such as 'Martin's Close' (1911), where the site itself channels a past that has become imprinted on it. Characteristically, James's heritage objects are possessed of a strange, inexplicable and often malevolent power. In '"Oh, Whistle"', the whistle is capable of affecting psychological and emotional states. Finding it unleashes strange forces in the present-day world. In this story, agency, will and intent are located in the past and channelled through the found object. The forces from, and of, the past are so powerful that the site where the whistle is discovered is made a kind of claustrophobic template for the entire text. The geography of the archaeological site is mapped onto the description of the town and even of the bedroom in the inn, where the protagonist Parkins narrowly avoids becoming a sacrifice.

Heritage debate – questions such as what the public needs to know, how history should be presented to them, what should be displayed in museums or made available in archives – lies at the heart of many of James's tales. In 'A Warning to the Curious' (1925), for example, issues of protection, custodianship and public inheritance are paramount. The teller of the inset tale, Paxton, tells of a Saxon barrow that he has just opened. He assures his listeners that he has some knowledge of correct archaeological procedure: 'I know something about digging in these barrows: I've opened many of them in the down country. But that was with owner's leave, and in broad daylight and with men to help.'[15] By contrast, his recent excavation was illicit, ill-judged and sloppily executed. The barrow has, however, yielded a Saxon crown, and the central question of the story relates to what should be done with it, to whom it belongs and what its function is. The debate is carried out in lively fashion by the story's narrator, his friend Henry Long and Paxton. The narrator and Long are both of the opinion that, instead of languishing in

---

[15] James, *Complete Ghost Stories*, p. 319.

private ownership, the find should be exhibited for public edification. It transpires, however, that public interest is not served by the exhibiting of the object. On the contrary, and as Paxton himself painfully realises, public interest is best served by the crown's reburial. As Seaburgh's vicar explains, 'There has always been a belief in these parts in the three holy crowns. The old people say they were buried in different places near the coast to keep off the Danes or the French or the Germans.'[16] Paxton's crown is not his crown; the heritage artefact belongs to the nation. Significantly, the issue of protection cuts both ways: heritage requires protection, but heritage too protects the nation.

The Country House Crisis

In his 1959 Preface to *Brideshead Revisited* (1945), Evelyn Waugh presented his novel as the product of a very specific historical moment – one in which it 'seemed that the ancestral seats which were our chief national artistic achievement were doomed to decay and spoliation like the monasteries in the sixteenth century'.[17] Daphne du Maurier's *Rebecca*, despite its many differences from *Brideshead*, is a product of the same historical moment. Both texts respond to what has been called 'the country house crisis', and both may be read, at least in part, as a prose elegy to the country house and the way of life for which it stood.

The term 'country house crisis' relates to the threatened extinction of the country house. The projected obsolescence of the country house and its attendant lifestyles had been noted from the 1890s and was one of the reasons that the magazine *Country Life* was launched. In the 1920s and 1930s, various factors, including economic depression, hikes in death duties and falls in the value of land, meant that many families who had once owned country houses could no longer afford their upkeep. Fearing the wholescale loss of the country house, *Country Life* in 1937, the year before the publication of *Rebecca*, published a 'list of 639 houses worth preserving'.[18] In the event, as Waugh notes, the seemingly inevitable 'spoliation' did not come to pass, though hundreds of country houses were demolished in the 1950s. The tide

---

[16] James, *Complete Ghost Stories*, p. 317.
[17] Evelyn Waugh, *Brideshead Revisited: The Sacred and Profane Memories of Charles Ryder* (London: Eyre Methuen, 1978), p. 10.
[18] 'Timeline of Conservation Catalysts and Legislation', *Historic England* <https://historicengland.org.uk/whats-new/features/conservation-listing-timeline/> (last accessed 1 February 2019).

was turned, in part at least, by the 'Country Houses Scheme' that bore fruit in the National Trust Act of 1937, and by which the National Trust was 'able to accept the gift of country houses, with endowments in land or capital, which would be free of tax'.[19] As Waugh noted in 1959, 'Brideshead today would be open to trippers, its treasures rearranged by expert hands and the fabric better maintained than it was by Lord Marchmain.'[20]

Rebecca and *Brideshead*, though ostensibly so dissimilar, share a remarkable number of features. Both novels start with the vision of a country house destroyed or spoiled, and a resulting exile from its way of life. Both fetishise the country houses that lie at their core. Manderley and Brideshead are approached via the melancholy that is associated with imminent ruin, their beauties heightened by the realisation of their ephemerality and their impending disappearance. (Waugh confessed that he 'piled it on rather, with passionate sincerity').[21] Both, too, are threatened by an outside world characterised by dreariness and aesthetic philistinism. Like Brideshead, Manderley is portrayed as the centre of the social life of a class, a hub of social relations, the idealised confluence of many social flows in a vision of social relations innately, though conflictedly, conservative and nostalgic (Fig. 7.1).

Responding to the country house crisis, du Maurier's novel achieves the remarkable feat of de-gothicising the Gothic house. Its opening chapter displaces the threat normally associated with the Gothic mansion onto the surrounding woods and garden. The narrator, visiting Manderley in a dream, describes the 'dark and uncontrolled' woods which, 'always a menace even in the past, had triumphed in the end'.[22] The oaks are 'squat', the elms 'tortured'; roots are like 'skeleton claws' and round the trees flourish 'monster shrubs and plants'.[23] Manderley's suggestively Edenic 'lost garden' is presented through the language of sinister encroachment, nightmare and hallucinatory terrors.[24] The fifty-feet high rhododendrons, we are told,

> had entered into alien marriage with a host of nameless shrubs, poor, bastard things that clung about their roots as though conscious of their spurious origin. A lilac had mated with a copper beech, and to bind them yet more closely to one another the malevolent ivy, always an enemy to grace, had thrown her tendrils about the pair and made them prisoners.[25]

---

[19] 'Our History 1884–1945', *The National Trust* <www.nationaltrust.org.uk/lists/our-history-1884-1945> (last accessed 1 February 2019).
[20] Waugh, *Brideshead Revisited*, p. 10.   [21] Waugh, *Brideshead Revisited*, p. 10.
[22] Daphne du Maurier, *Rebecca* (London: Virago, 2003), p. 1.
[23] du Maurier, *Rebecca*, pp. 1, 1, 2, 1.   [24] du Maurier, *Rebecca*, p. 3.
[25] du Maurier, *Rebecca*, pp. 2–3.

Fig.7.1: A picture of the novelist Daphne du Maurier in 1947 lingering below a portrait of her father, the actor Gerald du Maurier, on the staircase of 'Menabilly', the house that she wove into her stories and eventually into her life. (Photo by Popperfoto via Getty Images/ Getty Images).

Rather than a version of the 'monstrous vegetal', 'embodying', in Dawn Keetley's words, an '*absolute alterity*', this is an emblematic garden, foreshadowing the tale to be told.[26] The miscegenation and monstrosity associated with Manderley's grounds prefigure the 'nameless' heroine, her 'alien marriage' and the 'malevolent' but entrancing figure of Rebecca herself,

---

[26] Dawn Keetley, 'Introduction: Six Theses on Plant Horror; or, Why Are Plants Horrifying?', in Dawn Keetley and Angela Tenga (eds), *Plant Horror: Approaches to the Monstrous Vegetal in Fiction and Film* (Basingstoke: Palgrave Macmillan, 2016), p. 6; italics in original.

whose legacy leaves the present-day de Winters 'prisoners'. This is a garden that is gothicised not because of the house, but because of its destruction.

The rapid journey up Manderley's 'twisted and turning' drive leaves the narrator's 'heart thumping in [her] breast'.[27] By contrast, when her gaze comes to rest on the house itself, the tone radically changes:

> There was Manderley, our Manderley, secretive and silent as it had always been, the grey stone shining in the moonlight of my dream, the mullioned windows reflecting the green lawns and the terrace. Time could not wreck the perfect symmetry of those walls, nor the site itself, a jewel in the hollow of a hand.[28]

Du Maurier's prose comes to rest with entranced repetition of the house's name, with sonorous alliteration and with drawn-out and regular sentences. The architectural term 'mullioned', a favourite in heritage fiction then and now, is positioned at the beginning of a repeated grammatical structure and reinforced by the alliterative 'Manderley' and 'moonlight'. Du Maurier's phrasing makes a treasure of the house even before it is described as a 'jewel'. The description is heightened and given a sonorous Englishness by virtue of its Shakespearean resonances. In combination with the reference to the sea as 'a sheet of silver' a few lines later, the word 'jewel' recalls the famous speech of the dying John of Gaunt in *Richard II*, in which England is the 'precious stone set in the silver sea'.[29]

Rather than Gothic prison, Manderley is presented as a heritage house. Its 'perfect symmetry' is as much metaphysical as physical. Harmonious and quiet, it is associated with the civilised life of the country gentry. The narrator recites a litany of the life that has been destroyed – a 'handkerchief on the table beside the bowl of autumn roses', the 'discarded copy of *The Times*', the dog Jasper, 'his tail a-thump when he heard his master's footsteps', 'the rose-garden in summer', '[t]ea under the chestnut tree'.[30] Like Brideshead, Manderley is already lost before the story has even begun, summoning 'the strange prick of tears behind my eyes'.[31] The house is the ever-receding object of impossible desire for its heroine. She could, indeed, be said to long both to possess and to belong to Manderley.

---

[27] du Maurier, *Rebecca*, pp. 1, 2.   [28] du Maurier, *Rebecca*, p. 2.
[29] William Shakespeare, *Richard II*, Act II, scene i, l. 46, in *The Complete Works of Shakespeare*, edited by Peter Alexander (London and Glasgow: Collins, 1951).
[30] du Maurier, *Rebecca*, pp. 3, 3, 3, 4, 4.   [31] du Maurier, *Rebecca*, p. 2.

Gothic and the Heritage Romance

The heritage project of the late nineteenth and early twentieth centuries was bound up with telling – and celebrating – the national story. It was the policy of the section of the Office of Works responsible for the preservation of monuments to collect, in Simon Thurley's words, 'the most representative monuments across time and across the country that illustrated the story of Britain'.[32] In his chapter 'The Ancient Monuments Act of 1913' in *Men from the Ministry* (2013), Thurley cites Charles Trevelyan, MP and President of the Board of Education. In his presentation to the joint Committee on Ancient Monuments in November 1912, Trevelyan began by distancing the aims of the bill from mere antiquarianism, before going on to claim that 'it should be realised that part of the character of the nation which depends upon the appreciation of its past may really be affected by the preservation of these monuments now that the idea has really got into our system of education that the nation ought to learn about its past through what is left of its monuments'.[33] Trevelyan's speech brings together a number of related arguments. Material heritage is of consequence not only for antiquarians, archaeologists and scholars, but for the nation at large. The study of material heritage is one of the best ways to learn about history, in particular, the national past. The national past is something to be 'appreciated', and monuments are important in the creation of national identity. Trevelyan was giving voice to what was becoming a consensus; the bill was passed the following year.

The monuments and buildings that came under the protection of the state, the National Trust and county councils in the early twentieth century were not only castles, prehistoric remains and country houses. From the beginning, the heritage movement had other properties in its sights too. The National Trust's first acquisition in 1896 was a mediaeval hall-house in Sussex: Alfriston Clergy House. In the 1920s, the Conservative prime minster Stanley Baldwin 'spearheaded a campaign launched by the Royal Society of Arts to save old rural cottages, buildings he thought captured the essence of England'.[34] Baldwin's heritage campaigning encompassed the countryside too. When Haresfield Beacon in Gloucestershire, a site celebrated for its beauty and its archaeological and geological features, was given to the

---

[32] Simon Thurley, *Men from the Ministry: How Britain Saved its Heritage* (New Haven and London: Yale University Press, 2013), p. 79.
[33] Quoted in Thurley, *Ministry*, p. 76.   [34] Quoted in Thurley, *Ministry*, p. 95.

National Trust in 1931, Baldwin considered 'why should it be necessary to preserve spots like this', declaring:

> I think it answers to a very deep and profound instinct of the English people. We have become largely an urban folk, but there lies, deep down in the hearts of even of those who have toiled in our cities for two or three generations, an ineradicable love of country things and country beauty, as it may exist in them traditionally and subconsciously; and to them, as much as and even more than to ourselves, the country represents the eternal values and the eternal traditions from which we must never allow ourselves to be separated.[35]

These are the sentiments that lie behind Alison Uttley's *A Traveller in Time*.

A Traveller in Time may be described as a heritage romance, that is, as a romance centred on a loved and lovingly described heritage house and characterised by a predominantly celebratory view of the past. Because heritage romances stress the continuities and eternal verities of the national life, they have a strong tendency to utilise the trope of the benign double, according to which actions, character types and even plot-lines repeat themselves over time, and, especially, through generations. In addition to being a heritage romance, Uttley's novel is also a time-slip narrative, a genre that seems to originate with the early twentieth-century heritage experience. Indebted to heritage discourse, the time-slip narrative could be said to be a kind of trans-temporal tourist experience. Its instantiations in the 1930s might be linked to the rapid growth of heritage tourism in this decade. In earlier narratives for children, time travel is often effected by means of supernatural guides or magical objects: Puck in Rudyard Kipling's *Puck of Pook's Hill* (1906); an amulet in E Nesbit's *The Story of the Amulet* (1906); and Mouldiwarp, a magical mole, in Nesbit's *The House of Arden* (1908). In Uttley's novel, by contrast, time-slip is effected by an experience of a heritage house. Heritage sensibilities of the mid twentieth century conceived of the heritage house as an embodiment of the past, a portal into which an imaginative modern-day person may venture, and, as it were, travel back into time. Fittingly, in *A Traveller in Time* the heroine is transported into the past at such moments as opening a door or stepping into a room.

Central to Uttley's novel is Thackers, a 'small manor-house' in Derbyshire, where the heroine, Penelope Taberner Cameron, stays for the sake of her health while visiting extended family.[36] She is one of Baldwin's 'urban folk' of the second and third generations who is to discover that 'ineradicable love of

---

[35] Stanley Baldwin, *This Torch of Freedom* (London: Hodder and Stoughton, 1935), p. 120.
[36] Alison Uttley, *A Traveller in Time* (London: Jane Nissen Books, 2007), p. 9.

country things'. The Thackers of the first decade of the twentieth century is lovingly described. Uttley focuses on the material pleasures of a house whose way of life remains very much in the past. Penelope tells of the 'first evening', and her experience of 'a glow of firelight and golden reflections, a babble of voices with rich warm accents, and the all-pervading odours of herbs from the bunches round the ceiling'; 'I talked little, nor did I listen', she continues, 'but I sat by the hot fire in a corner watching the sticks crackle, and the lights flutter on the copper dishes.'[37] These material pleasures provide the sense of continuity when Penelope travels back to the late sixteenth century. She sees 'the same big oak table in the middle of the floor and the same spice cupboard with its multitude of little drawers against the wall'.[38] In the past as well as in the twentieth century, a 'great fire burn[s]' and 'heavy odours [pervade] the room'.[39]

Uttley's novel emphasises the endurance of English history, identifying continuities in land and rural ways. We read that Penelope 'walk[s] the same ground that Anthony and Francis Babington had trod' and smells 'the same roses ... renewing themselves yet always the same'.[40] In the final episode of the book, Elizabethan mummers and twentieth-century carol singers occupy the same place and the same moment for Penelope. Continuity is also underwritten in the novel by what Tess Cosslett calls the 'the "namesake" device, with its emphasis on patrimony'.[41] Thackers is 'the home of [Penelope's] ancestors'.[42] Forenames and surnames are inherited from the sixteenth-century family, as well as temperament and physical characteristics.

Although the heritage mode is dominant in *A Traveller in Time*, the novel is hybrid, possessing a vein of Gothic running through it and providing a moment of near-catastrophe at the climax of the work. Gothic in the novel problematises Uttley's heritage mode and challenges some of the assumptions about history, identity and the 'merrie past' that is endemic to it. This is most visible in the pattern of malign doubling that emerges relatively late in the text and counterpoints the benign doubling so characteristic of the heritage romance. As well as possessing reassuring ancestral doubles, Penelope has a malign double in the person of Arabella, her rival for the affections of Francis. What is more, Arabella creates a further double of Penelope – a 'waxen image' into which, it is reported, she sticks pins.[43]

---

[37] Uttley, *Traveller in Time*, p. 31.   [38] Uttley, *Traveller in Time*, p. 60.
[39] Uttley, *Traveller in Time*, p. 60.   [40] Uttley, *Traveller in Time*, pp. 173–4.
[41] Tess Cosslett, '"History from Below": Time-Slip Narratives and National Identity', *The Lion and the Unicorn* 26:2 (2002), 243–53 (p. 215).
[42] Uttley, *Traveller in Time*, p. 86.   [43] Uttley, *Traveller in Time*, p. 197.

Arabella herself has a double in the form of a strange red-haired doll, suggestive of both her beauty and lack of human warmth. Arabella's terrorising of Penelope reaches a climax when she imprisons her in an abandoned tunnel, leaving her to perish in a 'living grave'.[44] The irruption of Gothic into the heritage romance has an impact on the text at a number of levels, complicating and enriching the reader's understanding of the protagonist, the situation she is in and the past more generally. Penelope's imprisonment highlights her strange passivity and dramatises some of the dangers of the heritage sensibility – especially to an imaginative child adrift in a past, which has a reality more palpable than the world from which she comes.

Landscape History and Folk Horror

In 1955, with the publication of W. G. Hoskins's *The Making of the English Landscape*, a new discipline was born: landscape history. Hoskins's work alerted readers who were inclined to think of the landscape as 'natural' to the historicity of the English landscape, tracing what he in a later Introduction to the book came to call 'the historical evolution of the English landscape as we know it'.[45] The phrase 'as we know it' is particularly significant. Hoskins points to existing landscape features or their remains – ancient field systems and road networks, farmsteads, villages and towns, the traces of lost villages, lost parkland and lost pasture. He demonstrates that some places have been in continuous occupation for millennia. As Hoskins noted in an Introduction that was added in 1976, 'everything in the landscape is older than we think'.[46]

With evident continuities with archaeology, landscape history had a more immediate non-professional appeal precisely because of its attention to the surface, to what could be seen by the naked eye by ordinary people living their lives in ordinary places. In addition to discussing changes at national level, *The Making of the English Landscape* focused on localities, teasing out the often intricate histories of individual places and areas. It turned its readers' attention to the everyday; Hoskins even gave an account of his own street. The work was an important milestone for a heritage movement that was already expanding its horizons. Neither did a monument have to be considered part of the great national historical narrative, nor did landscapes have

---

[44] Uttley, *Traveller in Time*, p. 241.
[45] W. G. Hoskins, *The Making of the English Landscape*, new edition (Harmondsworth, Penguin, 1985), p. 12.
[46] Hoskins, *The Making of the English Landscape*, p. 12.

to be of great natural beauty to warrant saving. Hoskins's work, part of a greater trend towards social history, drew people's attention to their local heritage and to the traces left by those whose names and lives were, for the most part, forgotten.

From W. H. Auden to Alan Garner and beyond, testimony to the influence of *The Making of the English Landscape* on British authors is not difficult to find. Common to all the writers is the sense that Hoskins had opened up the landscape to be read. As William Boyd notes, the 'familiar English countryside ... became a form of historical palimpsest – its evolving history there to be decoded and discerned for those who could look at it through the innovative lens that Hoskins provided'.[47] The sense of landscape as narrative, as, in Boyd's phrase, 'gravid with meaning and replete with markers of the remorseless passage of time', was to provide a fruitful source of inspiration for the emergence, mid-century, of a range of texts that located horror within folkloric vestiges within the modern landscape, and which has come to be known as folk horror.[48] Among such celebrated titles as Alan Garner's *The Owl Service* (1967) and Susan Cooper's *The Dark is Rising* sequence (1965–77) are also lesser-known texts such as Penelope Lively's children's novels *The Wild Hunt of Hagworthy* (1971) and *The Whispering Knights*, as well as David Rudkin's television play *Penda's Fen*. Lively has testified to Hoskins's profound importance to her: 'I never knew him, but I sometimes feel that he has shown me the way to go, an abiding influence.'[49]

The Whispering Knights shares certain characteristics with Uttley's *A Traveller in Time* insofar as they both feature time-slips and are aimed at younger readers. Their differences, however, are more striking than their similarities. Where Uttley's trigger for time slippage is a heritage house, Lively's is a landscape; where *A Traveller in Time* focuses on its protagonist's time tourism to a past where (and she is speaking literally), the 'grass is greener, the sky more transparent', Lively's novel deals with the incursion

---

[47] William Boyd, 'Rereading the Making of the English Landscape by W. G. Hoskins', *The Guardian*, 11 May 2013 <www.theguardian.com/books/2013/may/11/rereading-making-english-landscape> (last accessed 14 June 2018).

[48] William Boyd, 'Rereading the Making of the English Landscape'. The term 'folk horror' was coined by director Piers Haggard to describe his film *The Blood on Satan's Claw* (1971) and subsequently popularised by Mark Gatiss in his documentary series for BBC4, *A History of Horror* (2010). See Adam Scovell, *Folk Horror: Hours Dreadful and Things Strange* (Leighton Buzzard: Auteur Publishing, 2017), p. 7.

[49] Penelope Lively, 'My hero: W. G. Hoskins', *The Guardian*, 25 November 2011 <www.theguardian.com/books/2011/nov/25/hero-wg-hoskins-penelope-lively> (last accessed 14 June 2018).

into the present moment of an ancient and terrible figure: the enchantress Morgan.[50]

The Whispering Knights is set in the Cotswolds where, during the summer holidays, a group of children attempt to perform the witches' spell from *Macbeth*; their success brings the enchantress Morgan upon them and the wider world they inhabit. The action unfolds within a landscape of great age: the novel's very title refers to a Neolithic burial chamber that forms part of the Rollright Stones (a group of monuments in Oxfordshire, dating from the Neolithic and Bronze Age, that also includes a stone circle and a solitary standing stone). Here, new and old coexist, and the ancient may be renewed. Unlike the 'unchanging' countryside of the heritage romance, the landscape of *The Whispering Knights* is dynamic and subject to sudden shifts, as are the characters associated with it.[51] Whereas Uttley's Uncle Barnabas is an unchanging prototype, 'part of the soil itself', Lively's Morgan (and her benevolent counterpart, the enigmatic Miss Hepplewhite) are endowed with the characteristics of the Hoskinian landscape: they endure but they also change.[52] Morgan, whose name recalls that of Morgan le Fay of Arthurian legend, can be traced as far as the seventeenth century, but the novel makes it clear that she reaches back far into prehistory, that she is indeed more than mere human. At one point in the story, she pursues the children into a church where, significantly, she is halted not by any of the building's permanent fixtures but by a straw cross that is more suggestive of paganism than Christianity.

Lively's ancient landscape is a link to the past – to several pasts – and it ensures the survival of older modes of thinking and being. As the features of a former landscape can re-emerge in the present, so too Morgan irrupts into the present day. Terrifyingly, the multi-temporal landscape of the novel is both fluid and infinitely permeable. The crossing of thresholds, both temporal and geographic, is central to the work's effect. Morgan, like an ancient Cruella de Vil, motors on inexorably. Her very voice has the power to cross time: her long scream both inhabits and pierces the present-day landscape.

At the climax of the novel, the children, on the run from Morgan, travel into the distant past themselves. They

> passed out of the barley field into a curious area of scrubland that none of them could remember seeing before. The grass was long and coarse, dotted

---

[50] Uttley, *Traveller in Time*, p. 164. [51] Uttley, *Traveller in Time*, p. 63.
[52] Uttley, *Traveller in Time*, p. 118.

with thorn bushes: it was unlike any field in the valley that they had ever seen ...

Ahead of them, the line of the hill at the side of the valley was as it should be, but there were too many trees sprawling down the sides of it, and the dark lines of the hedges had gone.[53]

Though the hill is 'as it should be', this is the landscape in a previous incarnation, before it has been farmed or even cleared, lacking in field divisions, unmarked by hedges and even, it is suggested, without modern varieties of grass. Although, at this moment, the children experience the landscape time-shift as alienation, loss and nightmare (they see little that is 'familiar ... in this distorted landscape'), they come to realise that the porosity of the landscape is not merely a matter of horror.[54] In *The Whispering Knights*, the porous landscape as well as unleashing threat can provide resistance to it. The children spy 'a track of beaten earth' that they recognise as the precursor of 'our road! The old road to the Stones!'[55] This road, both new and ancient, leads them to the Whispering Knights where they find protection, and where Morgan is bested in a tremendous battle.

The final paragraph of Lively's novel pays quiet tribute to Hoskins. In the calm of the restored everyday that follows the battle, the children decide to make a 'respectful' visit to the Stones.[56] They 'began to climb the hill. Cloud shadows rolled across the barley in front of them, and between the shadows, a still, faint trace, ran the line of a vanished road'.[57] The ancient road brings us to the end of the novel, serving as a memory of threat and of its vanquishing; it summons up a sense of lost adventure, and provides a link to the past. It is also a cue to the novel's readers, a nod to their sensibility and powers of imagination and a lesson in how to read the landscape so that they, too, can see what once was.

Penda's Fen, like Lively's *Whispering Knights*, is a folk horror text that is set in a landscape of ancient roads, enduring villages and prehistoric remains, in this case, the Malvern Hills, Worcestershire. As Rudkin noted in a *Radio Times* interview in 1974, 'I wanted to write something that grew out of the landscape.'[58] The play gives a self-conscious nod to landscape history in a scene in which the camera dwells upon a page of a book of place-name history that Stephen is reading. The entry for 'Pinvin' reveals that it has also been known as 'Pinfin' (the name that Joffer has been painting on the sign to

---

[53] Penelope Lively, *The Whispering Knights* (London: Pan Books, 1973), p. 139.
[54] Lively, *The Whispering Knights*, p. 141. [55] Lively, *The Whispering Knights*, pp. 139, 140.
[56] Lively, *The Whispering Knights*, p. 155. [57] Lively, *The Whispering Knights*, p. 156.
[58] *Radio Times*, 4 March 1974, p. 12.

the blocked-off road) and, in 1187, 'Pendefen', or Penda's Fen. The discovery of the name's etymology is to be a turning point for the protagonist, Stephen Franklin. Stephen is a grammar-school boy, 'not likeable', intelligent, sensitive and musical.[59] Through the course of the work, he becomes increasingly aware of his sexuality, of the violence inherent in the social and political views of many of those who surround him and of the story surrounding his own birth and upbringing. Stephen's rites of passage are played out in a landscape with copious amounts of time slippage. At one point, he lights upon the elderly Elgar (the British composer, himself from Worcestershire, dead for almost forty years at the time represented in the play) in a deserted agricultural building; later he comes across Penda, the last Pagan king to rule in England. As well as these figures, Stephen encounters some more disturbing and threatening manifestations. A 'hideously burned' arm appears beside 'imprisoning meshes and barbs of wire'; an old council worker, Joffer, prevents Stephen travelling along the road to the village of Pinvin; and a strange middle-aged, middle-class couple, the 'man' and 'lady', both defenders of public morality, who are fixated on racial purity, salute him as saviour before trying to destroy him.[60]

On his contemporary pilgrimage, Stephen travels from the lowlands to the highlands by means of a road many hundreds of years old, eventually confronting (and escaping) the terrifying 'man' and 'lady' on the slopes of the hills. There he experiences a vision of Penda, a Blakean figure who explains that the 'man' and the 'lady' are the 'true dark enemies of England, Sick Father and Mother, who would have us children for ever'.[61] In the place of their sterile fanaticism, the play exhorts 'the Pandaemonium ... the sacred demon of ungovernableness'.[62]

Penda's Fen carefully, and at length, deconstructs many of the more conservative assumptions behind certain strands of heritage thinking, and is particularly insistent in its interrogation of what it sees as Establishment constructions of national identity, national history and place. Resisting ideas of an Englishness linked to racial purity, it eschews simplistic oppositions. The climax of the play, and Stephen's redemptive moment, occurs with the realisation that he is hybrid: both English and foreign, male and female, soul and body. It is Stephen's consciousness of the landscape's historicity, his ability to uncover what *was* through what *is*, that leads to his psychic

[59] David Rudkin, *Penda's Fen* (London: Davis Poynter Ltd, 1975), p. 2.
[60] Rudkin, *Penda's Fen*, p. 1.   [61] Rudkin, *Penda's Fen*, p. 83.
[62] Rudkin, *Penda's Fen*, p. 84.

redemption. As Stephen embarks on the final stages of his journey through a landscape that is both ancient and renewed, he recovers a heritage that is likewise both ancient and new. His reading of the landscape provides a way of resisting the modern world, emotionally, spiritually and ideologically. Heritage in *Penda's Fen* is claimed in the name of (in Raphael Samuels's words) 'utopianism ... social protest and cultural dissidence'.

Revisiting and Revising

The 1970s and 1980s saw vigorous expansion in the heritage movement in the United Kingdom, with soaring visitor numbers, a sizeable increase in the number of buildings in public ownership (or the ownership of agencies such as the National Trust, or of heritage charities) and a radical broadening of the acquisition criteria.[63] Concomitant with the massive growth of the heritage movement came a wave of trenchant criticism of various aspects of heritage thought and practice by critics such as Lowenthal, Hewison and Wright.

Sarah Waters's *The Little Stranger* is a product of this post-1980s heritage environment. Its idea of heritage is radically expanded, and it dissects a strain of heritage discourse that is characteristic of the mid twentieth century. The novel is set in the country house crisis (the main part of the action takes place in the late 1940s); the story tells of the relationship between a local doctor, Faraday, the narrator of the tale, and the Ayres family, owners of Hundreds Hall. *The Little Stranger* is very knowing about the social and political context affecting 'the breaking up of the old estates'.[64] Mrs Ayres's sister, quoting a Conservative MP, points the finger at the Labour government and the 'penalties and restrictions for rural landowners'.[65] Though the Ayres sell off parts of the estate to the council, which uses the land to build new homes, they are not able to make ends meet nor stop the house falling into dereliction. As Doctor Seeley notes, 'Class-wise, they've had their chips.'[66] The novel's heritage awareness is not limited to the knowledge of the plight of the Ayres family and those like them. Running beside the account of the family's comparative hardship are other heritage narratives. Faraday, himself from working-class origins (his mother was a servant at Hundreds), tells of workers' cottages with their 'damp floors and low ceilings' and inadequate

---

[63] For more on this subject see Thurley, *Ministry*, chapter 16, 'Boom and Bust: 1920–1982', pp. 233–52.
[64] Sarah Waters, *The Little Stranger* (London: Virago, 2009), p. 242.
[65] Waters, *The Little Stranger*, p. 242.   [66] Waters, *The Little Stranger*, p. 378.

sanitation.[67] Towards the end of the novel he calls on a patient who, with his family, is a squatter in 'the worst sort of place imaginable – an abandoned hut, with holes in its roof and gaps in its windows, and without light or water'.[68]

The Little Stranger engages in a compelling exploration of the language and aesthetics of a certain mode of country-house appreciation. It opens with Faraday recounting his first experience of Hundreds Hall as a 10-year-old boy. His is a pitch-perfect rendition of unofficial heritage discourse, with its aesthetics based on age and harmonious function and its attention to 'detail'. Faraday talks of Hundreds' 'lovely ageing details: the worn red brick, the cockled window glass, the weathered sandstone edgings'.[69] He uses that very English word 'lovely' again, when he describes his return to Hundreds, 30 years later. Showing his artist's sensibility, he notes: 'The light was soft and mildly tinted, and seemed held, really embraced and held, by the pale walls and ceiling.'[70] From the very first pages, country-house appreciation is linked to a sense of possession and bestows a sense of entitlement. The young Faraday breaks off a piece of decorative border, an acorn made of plaster: 'It was simply that, in admiring the house, I wanted to possess a piece of it', he writes. Vaunting his own heritage sensibility, he explains that it was as if 'the admiration itself, which I suspected a more ordinary child would not have felt, entitled me to it'.[71] Significantly, Faraday describes his theft or act of vandalism in terms of 'wanting a lock of hair' from a girl.[72] This feminisation of the house is returned to later, when he writes of a room whose 'essential loveliness stood out, like the handsome bones behind a ravaged face'.[73] Directly thereafter, the elegant, middle-aged Mrs Ayres, characterised by her high cheekbones, enters.

Although the novel opens in lyrical heritage mode, another mode of presentation starts to rival it as the narrative progresses. Hundreds is a house in which strange things start to happen. Household objects launch themselves at the son and heir, Roderick; an unexplained fire eventually drives him out of his home and into a mental asylum; a seemingly gentle dog attacks a young girl, Gillian Baker-Hyde; unfathomable scribbles appear on walls; strange breathing is heard down speaking tubes; telephones ring in the middle of the night. The overriding question at the end of the novel is what has caused these catastrophic events. Faraday at first reaches for a rational explanation, but is increasingly drawn to Dr Seeley's theory: that the disturbance is the result of poltergeist activity. The question then remains as to who is directing this activity. Seeley believes that it is

---

[67] Waters, *The Little Stranger*, p. 249. [68] Waters, *The Little Stranger*, p. 469.
[69] Waters, *The Little Stranger*, p. 1. [70] Waters, *The Little Stranger*, p. 19.
[71] Waters, *The Little Stranger*, p. 3. [72] Waters, *The Little Stranger*, p. 3.
[73] Waters, *The Little Stranger*, p. 19.

the result of female hysteria, but the novel strongly hints that it is Faraday himself who is the driving force and, as such, the 'little stranger' of the novel's title.

The Little Stranger is a twisted heritage romance. Its ultimate subject, and the mainspring of its action, is the pathological heritage sensibilities of its narrator. Faraday's love of Hundreds Hall becomes increasingly suspect throughout the novel, as his urge to protect and preserve it is played out at the expense of health and happiness and in defiance of economics and politics. Faraday's heritage sensibility can be read as the instigator of the catastrophic events that occur throughout the text. Indeed, all those who experience violence in the house are associated with heritage misdeeds. Gillian Baker-Hyde, the child who is mauled, is the daughter of nouveau-riche, urban parents who espouse the opinion that 'one can't hang on to things for ever'.[74] Roderick (who has to be confined to a mental institution) and his mother (whose lacerated body mirrors the damage done to Hundreds) are inadequate custodians of their house. Caroline Ayres, the daughter who wants to leave both Faraday and the house itself, is found dead on the eve of her departure. The novel stresses the close alignment between Faraday's heritage discourse and the fates of his victims. The feminisation and sexual violence latent in his seemingly innocuous description of his act of theft as a 10-year-old are realised in the mutilation of Mrs Ayres and the death of Caroline.

As *Country Life* noted on 25 October 1919, 'People who formerly lived in very large houses are now getting out of them. As to who goes in is another matter.'[75] By the end of *The Little Stranger* it is apparent that the struggle for inheritance has been, at an unconscious level, the mainspring of the novel. The Ayres have been displaced: 'It is as if the house has thrown the family off, like springing turf throwing off a footprint', exclaims Faraday.[76] Unlike some other country houses of the 1950s, however, Hundreds has not passed into public ownership. Despite the heightened awareness of class antagonism in the novel, Hundreds has not become the spoils of a class war – or at least, it has not passed into the possession of those who live in the council houses. It is Faraday, the working-class boy-turned-middle-class professional, the connoisseur of Hundreds' 'lines and Georgian symmetries, the lovely shifts between shadow and light, the gentle progression of the rooms', who is its sole inheritor and, indeed, its only visitor.[77] Reminiscent of an Edgar Allan

---

[74] Waters, *The Little Stranger*, p. 90.
[75] Quoted in Adrian Tinniswood, *The Long Weekend: Life in the English Country House Between the Wars* (London: Jonathan Cape, 2016), epigraphs page.
[76] Waters, *The Little Stranger*, p. 498.   [77] Waters, *The Little Stranger*, p. 498.

Poe character, he wanders through the house trying to catch the house's ghost, only to see his own face 'gazing distortedly' from a 'cracked windowpane', 'baffled and longing'.[78]

The heritage movement has had a profound influence on Gothic texts of the twentieth and twenty-first centuries. Heritage sensibilities have a tendency to reroute Gothic and can be linked to some significant rethinking of content and tropes. Heritage thinking reinflects the Gothic object and its relation to the protagonist. The sense of fragility, imminent loss and the need for protection that attaches itself to the heritage building results, in many cases, in the rewriting of the trope of the Gothic house. It is the destruction, not the existence, of Manderley that is the problem; the house itself is in danger, a victim. Heritage sensibilities may also adjust the relation between the past and the present. Sometimes this results in strangely Manichean tendencies, in folk horror texts in particular, where threat and redemption may both emanate from the past embodied in the landscape, and where the process of learning about the past, through the careful reading of the ancient landscape, may serve as a means of accessing salvation or rescue, and renegotiating identity. The twentieth and twenty-first centuries have witnessed the advent of the heritage/Gothic hybrid text, where Gothic and heritage discourses interpenetrate and inform each other. Gothic may be called into heritage narratives, complicating their register, commenting on heritage sensibilities and on over-optimistic views of the past, while, conversely, as in Waters's Gothic tale, heritage sensibility may become the sinister subject of horror.

---

[78] Waters, *The Little Stranger*, p. 499.

3.8

Gothic Enchantment: The Magical Strain in Twentieth and Twenty-First-Century Anglo-American Gothic

DAVID PUNTER

In 1913 the celebrated magician A. E. Waite published an English translation of a nineteenth-century work by a man who liked to be referred to as 'Éliphas Lévi'. It is a stunningly ambiguous book; while claiming to reprehend the practice of magic, it offers, as its subtitle claims, 'a clear and precise exposition of its procedure, its rites and its mysteries'. While professing to abjure, it also tempts, and does so within a specifically Gothic rhetoric:

> All must be dared in order to achieve all – such was the axiom of enchantments and their associated horrors. The false magicians were banded together by crime and believed that they could intimidate others when they had contrived to terrify themselves. The rites of Black Magic have remained revolting like the impious worships it produced; this was the case indifferently in the association of criminals who conspired against the old civilisations and among the barbaric races. There was always the same passion for darkness; there were the same profanations, the same sanguinary processes. Anarchic Magic is the cultus of death. The sorcerer devotes himself to fatality, abjures reason, renounces the hope of immortality, and then sacrifices children. He forswears marriage and is given over to barren debauch. On such conditions he enjoys the plenitude of his mania, is made drunk with iniquity till he believes that evil is omnipotent and, converting his hallucinations into reality, he thinks that his mastery has power to evoke at pleasure all death and Hades.[1]

Figured through references to enchantment, horror, impious worship, barbarism, mania and child-sacrifice, magic in this extract becomes a thoroughly Gothic affair. Magic may be defined in all sorts of ways, but perhaps the most succinct for my purposes here is to say that it constitutes the belief that it is possible to influence aspects of the natural order by supernatural means. On

---

[1] Éliphas Lévi, *The History of Magic*, trans. by A. E. Waite (London: Rider & Company, 1913), p. 119.

closer inspection, however, perhaps this formulation does not say very much: after all, it covers all types of prayer, and without prayer of one form or another, we may safely say that there can be no religion. It covers, as well, all forms of superstition, from the most harmless (ladders, black cats) to the most socially pervasive. We continue to have, for example, a belief in the power of the signature, despite knowing, perhaps with another part of our minds, that all signatures can be flawlessly forged. We accept photographs as proof of identity and legitimacy, despite knowing that Photoshop can produce any version of 'reality' desired. Both are examples of the continuity of what psychologists have called for years 'magical thinking'.

A history of magic in the West would take us back to alchemical processes and beliefs, and would also necessarily involve us in the parallel history of ritual and ceremonial. We would think of figures like Simon Magus (C1st CE); Albertus Magnus (c. 1200–80); Cornelius Agrippa (1486–1535); Paracelsus (1493–1541); Giordano Bruno (1548–1600); and the French occult author and magician Lévi himself (1810–75), among others. We would also think of entirely mythical figures like the apocryphal 'Hermes Trismegistus', the purported author of the Hermetic Corpus: all of these are taken to have been involved in 'practical magic', attempts to influence the world's affairs through unorthodox means, which are typically said to be secret except to the initiate.

More modern attempts to speak of the history of the world as having been influenced by magicians and occult forces beyond normal control have a rich history, involving the 'Illuminati', Rosicrucianism and Freemasonry, at least in its earlier forms. Marie Mulvey-Roberts has drawn attention to how this tradition of occultic thought worked its way into the Gothic writings of William Godwin; Mary and Percy Bysshe Shelley; Charles Maturin; and others;[2] we see a recent efflorescence of this strain in the popularity of works by Dan Brown and his many imitators. But in the nineteenth century, there was a particularly strong crossover between notions of the occult, the practice of magic, and Gothic and horror fiction, in the hands of such writers as Edward Bulwer-Lytton (1803–73), Helena Blavatsky (1831–91), Annie Besant (1847–1933) and Marie Corelli (1855–1924).

Occult or magical associations continue to flourish: the Order of the Golden Dawn, for example (although its membership now tends to be North American rather than European) and its darker brother, Ordo

---

[2] See Marie Mulvey-Roberts, *Gothic Immortals: The Fiction of the Brotherhood of the Rosy Cross* (Abingdon: Routledge, 1990).

Draconis, whose emphasis on 'dark magic' brings it into much closer alignment with the Gothic as traditionally understood. Yet even to say this is to beg a question: what can we possibly know of the provenance and presence of secret societies – and this, of course, has been a question preoccupying the Gothic virtually since its inception. In the Gothic of Ann Radcliffe and Matthew Gregory Lewis, the 'secret society' is indistinguishable from the monastery or convent; it is a matter of ritual practices, arcane rites, hidden shapes in the shadows. Or, to take another example, we might ask what actually happens around the creation of Frankenstein's creature in Mary Shelley's 1818 novel; despite the trappings of modernity, the mentions of the discoveries of galvanism and electricity, the event itself smacks more of alchemy than of scientific procedure, and of course this is hardly surprising given Victor Frankenstein's interest in the works of precisely some of the 'magical' authors listed above.

A broader connection suggesting the inseparability of the Gothic and magic focuses on the 'supernatural'. The Society for Psychical Research, of which Arthur Conan Doyle was so notable and committed a member, had to do, as does so much Gothic fiction, with the conjuring of the ghostly. These processes of conjuration occur, it seems, in many different forms: in Éliphas Lévi's world, the danger is of the conjuring of demons, of powers that outrun our mortal ability to control; in times of war on foreign soil, as is evident for example in the context of the First World War and the widespread belief in the 'Angel of Mons'. We can, of course, speak of these attempts in psychological terms. We can speak of a human wish to control forces, either of the light or of the dark, either in order to right wrongs or indeed to commit further wrongs; we can speak of a need for supernatural comfort in times of distress.

Various forms of magic and enchantment, then, have nourished the Gothic imagination from the start: we might think, too, of the magical rites and rituals in Lewis's *The Monk* (1796) and Charles Maturin's *Melmoth the Wanderer* (1820), the Faustian narrative that underpins much of *Frankenstein* or the necromancy of Lord Byron's *Manfred* (1817). Postcolonial Gothic fiction and film, meanwhile, has explored the implications of traditional magic – Caribbean *obeah*; witchcraft; spirit magic; voodoo – for considerations of empire, gender and race, in a tradition that includes such notable texts as Jean Rhys's *Wide Sargasso Sea* (1966); Nalo Hopkinson's *Brown Girl in the Ring* (1998); and Helen Oyeyemi's *White Is for Witching* (2009). In this chapter, however, I want to say something about eight twentieth- and twenty-first-century British and American Gothic and Gothic-inflected texts that address and elaborate upon these magical ideas and possibilities: Aleister Crowley's

Moonchild (1917); H. P. Lovecraft's *The Case of Charles Dexter Ward* (1927); Dennis Wheatley's *The Devil Rides Out* (1934); Shirley Jackson's *We Have Always Lived in the Castle* (1962); Iain Banks's *The Wasp Factory* (1984); M. John Harrison's *The Course of the Heart* (1991); Susanna Clarke's *Jonathan Strange and Mr Norrell* (2004); and F. G. Cottam's *The House of Lost Souls* (2007).

'The false magicians were banded together by crime': *Moonchild*

Aleister Crowley is probably the best-known magician in the Western tradition, a man who was proud to boast of himself as the Great Beast and the 'wickedest man in Europe'. It may be that a certain irony is needed when dealing with Crowley; he was widely regarded as a charlatan, but in the world of magic and the occult it is difficult to know what this means since such a judgement in fact reflects unwittingly the possibility that there may indeed be such a thing as 'true magic', even if it is not that which is ritualistically practised by the Order of the Golden Dawn. With Crowley, it is also the case that magic becomes inextricably confused with drugs and addiction, as he says in his *Diary of a Drug Fiend* (1922).

Crowley's *Moonchild* centres on a battle between the forces of 'white' and 'black' magic. Various magicians of the day figure, including Waite, McGregor Mathers, the theosophist Annie Besant and Mary D'Este (the companion of Isadora Duncan). Intriguingly, the conclusion bends magical practice back towards the dread actualities of history, with the white magicians appearing to support the Allies in the First World War, while their black brethren are on the side of the enemy, thus asserting that the occult is not without practical effects. The essence of magical practice is claimed, as it is in the earlier *The Great God Pan* (1894) by Arthur Machen, to be the ritual birth of a 'saviour', thus justifying 'sexual magic' as being the essential ingredient in the search for superhuman powers.

Ritual in this sense means, as it always has in the history of magic, a belief in the power of words. 'Grimoires' and magical books have always played a vital role in the transmission of magical spells; indeed it might be said that the entire origin of the notion of the 'magical book', still potent to this day, lies in the notion of the written word itself, as something withheld from the mass of the populace and thus imbued with special powers. But there is an interesting contradiction at the heart of *Moonchild*. Although it is often, indeed usually, held that books of magic are arcane, abstruse and can only be properly understood by the initiate – and indeed the merest glance at the pages of such books, full as they often are with mysterious geometrical figures and unintelligible charts of the astrological position of, for example, angels and demons, confirms this supposition – there is an emphasis in *Moonchild* on the vital importance of plain, straightforward language if the great work is to be accomplished and demonic forces repulsed.

Here we have our protagonist, Lisa, in the process of being prepared for the 'great experiment' by taking the 'oath of dedication'. 'You will be amazed', she is told, 'at the possibilities of your own mind, its fertility of cunning, its fatally false logic, its power of blinding you to facts that ought to be as clear as daylight.'[3] The solution to this is, she is told in terms that cannot fail to remind us of the phantomatic rhetoric of the Gothic, to 'adhere desperately to the literal terms of your oath':

> Do that, and in a little while the mind will clear; you will understand what empty phantoms they were that assailed you. But if you fail, your only standard is gone; the waters will swirl about you and carry you away to the abyss of madness. Above all, never distinguish between the spirit and the letter of your oath! The most exquisite deceit of the devil is to lure you from the plain meaning of words.[4]

We shall hear more later about the 'abyss of madness' that threatens the naive practitioner of magic; but what is perhaps most important here is the assertion that the language of magic is in some sense a 'natural language', one in which words and things, signs and referents, become as one, although this process of identification is never one that is easy to maintain.

Against this process – which can also be seen in alchemical terms as the purification and transmutation of the base 'word' into the golden 'Word' – there stands the figure of the Devil, the Father of Lies, whose mendacity is matched by the potential for mendacity within one's own mind. Indeed, if ritual is to be successful then it is the mind, with its capacity for false reasoning and introspection, that must be fought and dissolved; this, we might say, is indeed the function of ritual in both magical and psychological senses. The 'banding together' of 'false magicians' represents the procedure whereby the Word may be subverted, turned against itself: we might think back to the biblical opposition between Jesus Christ and Simon Magus, both miracle workers, both purporting to be bringers of the Word, and thus heralds of resurrection.

---

[3] Aleister Crowley, *Moonchild* (New York: Avon, 1971), p. 137.
[4] Crowley, *Moonchild*, p. 137.

'All must be dared in order to achieve all': *The Case of Charles Dexter Ward*

That *Moonchild* is a novel about magic is, of course, not in doubt; the Gothic dimension consists largely in its constant engagement with motifs of transgression, wherein the human, the divine and the satanic are brought into continuing interplay. It is not a work of fear; indeed, Crowley's narrative persona is perhaps surprisingly caring and intimate, bringing the reader into close contact with the arcana that form the background of the story. Lovecraft, on the contrary, is a writer for whom Gothic terror is the staple of his narratives, and nowhere more so than in *The Case of Charles Dexter Ward*.

Here a young man seeks to uncover the secrets of his notorious ancestor Joseph Curwen who, we learn, was a necromancer and mass murderer and had discovered the secret whereby he could be reborn in successive generations. Through the voice of the doctor, Marinus Willett – one of a long line of Gothic medical or psychiatric narrators – we gradually come to see that the man regarded as Ward has actually been taken over by Curwen. This is done through a process outlined in the epigraph to the novel, attributed to the seventeenth-century scientist Pierre Borel (or 'Borellus'):

> The essential Saltes of Animals may be so prepared and preserved, that an ingenious Man may have the whole Ark of Noah in his own Studie and raise the fine shape of an Animal out of its Ashes at his Pleasure; and by the lyke method from the essential Saltes of humane Dust, a Philosopher may, without any criminal Necromancy, call up the Shape of any dead Ancestour from the Dust whereinto his Bodie has been incinerated.[5]

Here we have a compendium of Gothic themes, principally the ambivalences of immortality which so preoccupied early Gothic writers from Samuel Taylor Coleridge to Charles Maturin. The emphasis throughout is on the power of the word, reminding us of the ways in which the Reformation and the witch crazes of the seventeenth century were intimately bound up with the rise of print culture, for it was only through print culture that books of spells and grimoires could be widely disseminated. Seemingly paradoxically, the insistence on hunting for witchcraft coincides with the arrival of the very means by which books of magic could become the property not only of the religious and the courtly – which had been the case in medieval and early Renaissance times – but of a wider swathe of the population. For these lower-

---

[5] H. P. Lovecraft, *The Case of Charles Dexter Ward* (London: Victor Gollancz, 1951), p. 4.

ranking individuals, the need for magic was not restricted to the calling down of angels and the – supposedly accidental – conjuring of demons but to treasure hunting, sexual procurement and the general material betterment of the individual's life.

A letter by Curwen, discovered during the course of later investigations, demonstrates the use of the word in magic ritual, as well as supplying us with elements of the context of horror:

> I am not unreadie for hard fortunes, as I have told you, and have long work'd upon ye way of get'g Backe after ye Loste. I last Nighte struck on ye Wordes that brings up YOGGE-SOTHOTHE, and sawe for ye firste Time that face spoke of by Ibn Schacabac in ye ———. And IT said, that ye III Psalme in ye Liber-damnatus holds ye Clavicle. With Sunne in V House, Saturne in Trine, drawe ye Pentagram of Fire, and saye ye ninth Verse thrice. This Verse repeate eache Roodemas and Hallow's Eve, and ye thing will breede in ye Outside Spheres.
>
> And of ye Seede of Olde shal One be borne who shal looke Backe, tho' know'g not what he seekes.[6]

The language here is, apparently, a mock version of the language of the medieval grimoire; and yet, when one looks at the grimoires themselves, it is after all not so very far from the ways in which many of them were written. The mention of gods and spirits otherwise unknown, and certainly not part of any classic angelology; the omission of key moments in the recounting of ritual; the insistence on a variety of astrology heavily angled towards numerology; the necessity for repetition, sometimes to an extraordinary degree and over inordinate lengths of time, in order for the ritual to be completed – all of these are features of many magic books.

In *The Case of Charles Dexter Ward* – we might wonder whether the 'dexter ward' is a more or less direct reversal of the potential of the 'sinister word', the path of left-hand language – the force of evil coming from the past is eventually defeated by a combination of existent virtue and medical science. This is as it is in, for example, Bram Stoker's *Dracula* (1897), just as it is the way in which the 'white magicians' achieve their victory in *Moonchild*. But as in so much Gothic – and perhaps *Dracula* is again the most pertinent example – it is not this victory that is left in the reader's memory, but rather the eruption of the satanic which is has sought to contain.

---

[6] Lovecraft, *Charles Dexter Ward*, p. 88.

'Power to evoke at pleasure all death and Hades':
The Devil Rides Out

In Dennis Wheatley's *The Devil Rides Out*, two characters, the exotically named Duc de Richleau and Rex van Ryn, find that their friend Simon Aron has become involved with a group of devil-worshippers, whose leader is the highly ambiguous Mr Mocata. Aron is rescued from a Sabbath ritual held in one of the most magical of all European sites, Stonehenge, but although up to this point the reader may well believe that the whole scenario is one of 'fake magic', what happens next as unearthly forces begin to appear and gain strength suggests that occult powers are not so easily disposed of.

The Gothic has always dealt in questions of belief: what do we do with the 'unexplained supernatural' – do we treat it as an overflow from scientific rationalism, or do we relegate it to the realm of fantasy? One of the principal aspects – perhaps *the* principal aspect – of the literature of the occult concerns precisely this issue of belief in the supernatural. Is the reader encouraged to believe that, as with so much late nineteenth-century spiritualism and fortune telling, magic is merely illusion, cunning and stagecraft, a set of conjuring tricks designed to impose on minds weakened by drugs, distress and sorrow, or promises of eternal life? Or are we led instead to believe that, on the contrary, magical practices can genuinely cleanse the doors of perception and lead into a wider, fuller view of life where the anthropocentric is merely one perspective on a set of more universal truths, broader than history, deeper than reason?

In many ways, *The Devil Rides Out*'s most obvious reference points are the Gothic classics, *Frankenstein* and *Dracula*, as the extract below makes clear:

> All through middle Europe and right down into the Balkan countries there have been endless cases of . . . revolting Satanic manifestations. Anyone there will tell you that time and again, when graves have been opened on suspicion, the corpses of vampires have been found, months after burial, without the slightest sign of decay, their flesh pink and flushed, their eyes wide-open, bright and staring.[7]

The vampire and the Devil are, on this popular reading – and Wheatley was nothing if not a 'popular' author – one and the same. The argument in relation to science and creativity is a little more complicated, and is summed up in a long discussion between Richleau and Aron. Aron cites the cases of Jan Baptist van Helmont and Baruch Spinoza, who came to believe that

---

[7] Dennis Wheatley, *The Devil Rides Out* (London: Bloomsbury, 1934), p. 201.

transmutation of base metal into gold was possible, and Richleau pursues the line that today's magic is tomorrow's science:

> Everyone accepts the miracle that sulphur can be converted into fire because they see it happen twenty times a day and we all carry a box of matches in our pockets, but if it had been kept as a jealously guarded secret by a small number of initiates, the public would still regard it as impossible.[8]

The alchemist, he goes on, must be 'apart from the world' and 'indifferent to it'; he 'refuses to pass on his secret to the profane', but

> that does not necessarily mean that he is a fraud and a liar. The theory that all matter is composed of atoms, molecules and electrons in varying states is generally accepted now. Milk can be made as hard as concrete by the new scientific process, glass into women's dresses, wood and human flesh decay into a very similar dust, iron turns to rust, and crystals are known to grow although they are a type of stone.[9]

And, we might add to this list, inanimate matter can be made into human life precisely by the application of scientific and technological process.

For Wheatley, his reference points are at least partly to do with the 'spirit manifestations' so beloved of the late nineteenth-century Society for Psychical Research, with their supposed ability to call forth animate matter as evidence of the existence of the spirit world:

> A dim phosphorescent blob began to glow in the darkness; shimmering and spreading into a great hummock, its outline gradually became clearer. It was not a man form nor yet an animal, but heaved there on the floor like some monstrous living sack. It had no eyes or face but from it there radiated a terrible malefic intelligence.[10]

'Suddenly', he adds in a stroke that places us again in the realm of the putatively supernatural as well as in a scene of physical disgust, 'there ceased to be anything ghostlike about it'. Again the material and the psychical are left in a fine if curious balance – one might well think of the Gothic tropes of horror and terror in this context.

---

[8] Wheatley, *Devil Rides Out*, pp. 134–5.   [9] Wheatley, *Devil Rides Out*, p. 135.
[10] Wheatley, *Devil Rides Out*, p. 214.

'The sorcerer devotes himself to fatality': *We Have Always Lived in the Castle*

Gothic does not always restrict itself to outer events; it is equally a matter of inner worlds, worlds imbued with horror. Similarly, magic is not always concerned with producing world-shattering effects; on the contrary, it finds its place too in the operations of the obsessed mind. Some of the earliest forms of magic took the form of protective amulets and rites, designed to ward off evil, to counteract the operations of witchcraft, or simply to ensure health or, more often, the increase of worldly goods. Sometimes though, as we shall see later in the context of Iain Banks's *The Wasp Factory*, this sense of magical rites as defensive is designed more to ward off threats to the sense of a coherent self.

Shirley Jackson's *We Have Always Lived in the Castle* centres on two sisters, Constance and Merricat, who live their lives in an old mansion, despised and disgusted by the surrounding village community. The ostensible reason for this is that Constance was arrested in the past for the murder of almost the whole of the rest of their family; although she was acquitted, the stain continues to cling to herself and her sister. As the story moves on, we as readers become increasingly sure that she was in fact not to blame; it was Merricat who committed the crime, but she remains in deep and entire denial of her part in events.

Meanwhile, Merricat devotes herself to 'protecting' the house, her sister and herself, and she does so by magical means. She has placed various protective objects in places around the house that have significance to her, although what this significance is we can only guess. But as it becomes apparent that there are threats to the enclosed life she has been living, so her magical protections begin to fall apart:

> When I left the long field I went between the four apple trees we called our orchard, and along the path toward the creek. My box of silver dollars buried by the creek was safe. Near the creek, well hidden, was one of my hiding places, which I had made carefully and used often.[11]

So far, then, so good; but even here we find evidence, curiously transmitted in Merricat's first-person narrative, of her psychotic tendencies: 'I found

---

[11] Shirley Jackson, *We Have Always Lived in the Castle* (New York: Viking, 1962), p. 53.

a nest of baby snakes near the creek', she says, 'and killed them all; I dislike snakes and Constance had never asked me not to'.[12] One of the questions here is of agency: Merricat repeatedly tells us that she only does what Constance permits her to do, whereas it would appear through the cracks in the narrative as though Constance is in fact entirely under the control of her sister. Whether Constance knows or not that Merricat is a murderer by poison is one of the many issues raised but not resolved in the novel, creating a Gothic labyrinth of perspectives.

But Merricat's protective magic is not secure:

> I was on my way back to the house when I found a very bad omen, one of the worst. My book nailed to a tree in the pine woods had fallen down [and] was useless now as protection . . . I thought I had better destroy it, in case it was now actively bad, and bring something else out to the tree, perhaps a scarf of our mother's, or a glove.[13]

She would not find it difficult to find something of her mother's: since the killings, the house and everything in it has been kept exactly as it was on the fatal night, in an attempt, perhaps, to freeze and prevent any possibility of change.

It comes as no surprise that Merricat has a familiar nor, in view of her name, that it is her cat Jonas:

> on Sunday morning I lay there with Jonas, listening to his stories. All cat stories start with the statement: 'My mother, who was the first cat, told me this', and I lay with my head close to Jonas and listened. There was no change coming, I thought here, only spring; I was wrong to be so frightened.[14]

Yet, as it turns out, she is not wrong: there is change coming, and of the most violent kind, as the villagers, incensed by what they see as the sisters' snobbish self-separation, and acting in the tradition so familiar to us from the many films of *Frankenstein*, burn the house down.

Yet even after this, Merricat's mysterious witchlike powers continue to operate: gifts of food and other things appear on their doorstep as they continue to live in the shell of the mansion, and so perhaps in a sense Merricat's magic has proved its worth: change may come, but it is possible to survive it. As in so many Gothic narratives, the truth will never fully emerge but will remain enwrapped in a tissue of narratives and counter-narratives.

---

[12] Jackson, *We Have Always Lived*, p. 53.   [13] Jackson, *We Have Always Lived*, pp. 53–4.
[14] Jackson, *We Have Always Lived*, p. 53.

'The plenitude of his mania': *The Wasp Factory*

Frank, the ostensible name of the protagonist in Iain Banks's *The Wasp Factory* who has spent his whole life on a small Scottish island, also spends his life in a web of magical charms and spells, practices that, like Merricat, he sees – albeit unconsciously – as a potent way to ward off threats to his psyche and, probably, to his memory as well. The book starts off, indeed, with an account of the Sacrifice Poles:

> At the north end of the island, near the tumbled remains of the slip where the handle of the rusty winch still creaks in an easterly wind, I had two Poles on the far face of the last dune. One of the Poles held a rat head with two dragonflies, the other a seagull and two mice.[15]

These are protective talismans; they are also evidence of Frank's murderous instincts – we learn more about these as the narrative continues. The entire island, as Frank sees it, is a mesh of magical artefacts; quite why these protections are necessary is not initially evident, but what is clear is that he takes pleasure in torturing and killing small creatures. By far the most emblematic form these desires take is the Wasp Factory of the novel's title, which is described in enormous and sickening detail. The Factory, we are told, 'covers an area of several square metres in an irregular and slightly ramshackle tangle of metal, wood, glass and plastic. It is all based around the face of the old clock which used to hang over the door of the Royal Bank of Scotland in Porteneil.'[16] These materials, as is perhaps obvious, have been sourced from junkyards, wrecks, places where things of no more evident use go; we might think, keeping *Frankenstein* in mind again, that they are the relics secured from charnel houses. At any event, charnel is what they are designed to accomplish, specifically the death of wasps. But not just any old death: the Wasp Factory offers a magical variety of deaths. The Air Gun; the Boiling Pool; the Spider's Parlour; the Venus Cave; the Artery; the Acid Pit; the Ice Chamber; the 'rather jocularly named Gents (where the instrument of ending is my own urine, usually quite fresh)'; the Volt Room; the Deadweight; the Blade Chamber. It would not take an expert to say that this is, quite literally, 'overkill'; but how does it seem to Frank?

We might say that he feels beset by enemies; but this would not be quite true. He does indeed suffer from anxiety; but like Merricat, his principal anxiety is about change. What these talismanic rituals do is keep things

---

[15] Iain Banks, *The Wasp Factory* (London: Macmillan, 1984), p. 7.
[16] Banks, *The Wasp Factory*, p. 120.

exactly as they are – among other things, they keep him safe from the possible return, imminent throughout the novel, of his brother Eric, who has recently escaped from a madhouse. Eric, of course, is therefore the mad one – have the government and the medical service not said as much? – but we might feel that the real risk is that Frank's precarious grasp on sanity might be loosened were Eric to accomplish his threatened return.

We eventually learn, or so it would seem, the source of Frank's disturbance, and it turns out to be at one level quite mundane and yet at another magical in itself. Frank's father has, in the name of what he construes to be science, raised Frank as a boy, although Frank was in fact born a girl, and named Frances. In the name of his experimentation, the father has staged Frances's castration, and has persuaded Frank that the occasion of his 'accident' was a nasty encounter with the family dog.

The Wasp Factory is a horrifying novel, a brutal novel; it is also a psychologically intricate novel about the origins and effects of trauma. The surname of Frank, Eric and, obviously, their father, is 'Cauldhame' – a cold home, indeed, a home where there is no homeliness, no hint of the *heimlich*. And this, then, we might suppose to be an origin of our desire for the supernatural; unconsciously cheated of what we might see as a natural progression, the supernatural might become the only route to success of any kind:

> Lacking, as one might say, one will, I forged another; to lick my own wound, I cut *them* off, reciprocating in my angry innocence the emasculation I could not then fully appreciate, but somehow – through the attitudes of others perhaps – sensed as an unfair, irrecoverable loss.[17]

Of course, we might say that the ethos of *The Wasp Factory* is masculinist through and through, and Banks takes great pains to remind the reader that this introjected sense of male superiority, enacted precisely through Freudian penis envy, is connected with an explicitly Scottish sense of compensation for lost nationhood and culture. But then, we could be reminded that the Western history of magic has also centred on the patriarchal; none of the great magical books have claimed female authorship, while the notion and practice of witchery has also been treated as a poor – if for that very reason punishable – cousin of the great domain of magic and wizardry.

---

[17] Banks, *The Wasp Factory*, p. 183.

'The same profanations, the same sanguinary processes': *The Course of the Heart*

What *The Wasp Factory*, in all its Gothic extremity, reminds us is that magic is not merely a matter of the word, although Frank/Frances's father is indeed, like many of the scientist/magicians of old, a bookish man like, for example, Shakespeare's Prospero. It is perhaps also worth recalling that one of the many Caribbean words for magic, since the creolisation of Carib culture, has been 'science'. M. John Harrison's *The Course of the Heart*, which can all too easily be seen as a book of Gothic horror, is also deeply concerned with the magical word, the magical sign.

The novel follows the lives of three Cambridge students who meet a man named Yaxley, who may – or of course may not, since there are no ready tests available – be a magician. In any case, under his direction they perform a series of magical experiments, and although the processes and immediate results of these experiments remain entirely unclear, it seems that this subsequently puts an occult curse on the course ('curse'/'course') of their lives. In order to help his friends – who have married, but whose lives and relationships are bedevilled by depression, recurring hallucinations and worse – the third of the students, who is the narrator, invents a mythical salvific country, the 'Coeur', and much of the novel is spent in a fruitless search for this unreal land. Of course.

Across twenty years, it is therefore supposed that failed magic – if indeed it has failed – is directing the friends' lives, and condemning them to various kinds of misery; meanwhile Yaxley himself continues with his attempts to enter forbidden realms, which results in his extremely ugly death. It is suggested at various points in the book that what is happening is only doing so in a realm of dream, but the question thus thrown up is whether magic can in fact operate to counter a recurring sense of drudgery and tedium, or whether it is merely that our more depressive encounters with the repetitions of quotidian life are what feed our constant desire to believe in and engage with the paranormal, even its seediest aspects.

Repetition is all-important here: will a kind of semiotic repetition – a chant, perhaps, or a ritual – serve to rebut this less fulfilling repetitiveness, or will it in the end merely serve to 'repeat' precisely that which we are attempting to banish? The students, it would seem, only originally follow Yaxley's instructions in order to escape from some aspect of this repetition – within their own lives, or in terms of a sense of repeating their parents' lives and conditions; yet they end up locked up precisely within the repetition, which Freud defines as the unending and fruitless replaying of the original site of trauma – if there is indeed any such thing, within the processes of trauma, as an original site.

We see this throughout Gothic: from the repeating flight of persecuted maidens down endless corridors which all lead to the same monstrous heart, through the relegation of the authority of texts to some previous author whose provenance turns out to be entirely unknown, to the function of ritual incantation in, for example, the stories of M. R. James.

Here is the passage in which the death of Yaxley in *The Course of the Heart* is described:

> He lay naked on his side in the middle of the uncarpeted floor, knees drawn up slightly. One hand was curled gently under the side of his head to support it. The other supported his genitals. Death had aged him. With his long deceitful face, grey stubbled jaw, and lips drawn back over blackened or yellowish teeth, he might have been seventy or eighty ... Above him on the wall was pinned a postcard reproduction of the steps of the British Museum. Under this he had scrawled in soft pencil the words 'The Place of the Cure of the Soul', a description reputed to have been carved over the doors of the Library at Alexandria ... In addition some sort of fat was smeared all over his emaciated upper body, perhaps as lubrication.[18]

This, then, is what happens in the end to a specific type of Gothic fantasy – namely, the quest for eternal life. Yaxley has been trying to make the transition, the transformation, from the mortal to the immortal; but he has taken the process entirely literally, as though somehow to squeeze his physicality, however decayed, through the portal might be possible with sufficient lubrication. On the other hand, the image of the British Museum – recurrent throughout the novel – suggests that the occult knowledge that he has also been trying to bring to bear might play a role. At all events, what remains of magical experimentation is death; but also, surviving it all, the smell of a book:

> up from it came a smell like cornflour, or even vanilla, so strong I thought a door had opened and someone I once knew had come in. It was the smell of the individual book – not dust, not decay, but cornflour and vanilla, some transformation of the glues and inks and paper: cornflour, vanilla, then hawthorn blossom like a drug![19]

---

[18] M. John Harrison, 'The Course of the Heart', in M. John Harrison, *Anima* (London: Gollancz, 2005), pp. 122–3.

[19] Harrison, 'The Course of the Heart', p. 226.

And this significance of the book – the grimoire, the key to all knowledge – resounds through the entire history of Western magic. We might indeed see it as the essential marker of the assumed difference between 'male magic' and 'female witchcraft' which, despite the historical presence of books of herbal remedies, was largely regarded as an unwritten tradition.

'[B]elieved that they could intimidate others when they had contrived to terrify themselves': *Jonathan Strange and Mr Norrell*

Susanna Clarke's novel *Jonathan Strange and Mr Norrell* is an alternative history. Set in the early years of the nineteenth century, it posits a gap in time, a long historical lacuna, during which magic in England, having previously served as a potent force for good and evil, has lapsed into desuetude. Instead of 'practical magicians', men (usually) devoted to using magical means to reshape the world and society, there are now only 'theoretical magicians', who engage in the abstract study of the history of magic.

Onto this scene arrive, as we might expect, the eponymous two magicians, albeit entirely separately, and the plot that ensues is lengthy and complex. Among its many elements, and perhaps most telling in terms of Gothic themes, is the resurrection of a wealthy young lady called Emma Wintertowne, who has died on the brink of her marriage to the eminent but impoverished politician Sir Walter Pole. As Norrell, who has previously been reluctant to show off his magical skills, realises, he is being presented with an admirable, even unique, opportunity: 'with one stroke', his self-serving associate Drawlight remarks, 'you return to us that sweet young woman – whose death no one can hear of without shedding a tear; you restore a fortune to a worthy gentleman; *and* you re-establish magic as a power in the realm for generations to come!'[20] But the resurrection of the dead is not, of course, as simple a matter as it might first appear; principally, it involves the invocation of not a demon but an ambiguous and sinister figure from the Land of Faerie known only as the gentleman with the thistledown hair. With him Norrell has to make a classic quasi-Faustian bargain: Miss Wintertowne will be restored to England, but for half of each year only; the other half she must spend in Faerie, and to seal the bargain the gentleman with the thistledown hair cuts off and retains Emma's little finger.

---

[20] Susanna Clarke, *Jonathan Strange and Mr Norrell* (London: Bloomsbury, 2004), p. 98.

The resurrection proceeds and as Lascelles, another, somewhat cynical, associate of Norrell, remarks,

> It is certainly a night for raising the dead . . . Rain and trees lash the window-panes and the wind moans in the chimney – all the appropriate stage effects, in fact. I am frequently struck with the play-writing fit and I do not know that tonight's proceedings might not inspire me to try again – a tragic-comedy, telling of an impoverished minister's desperate attempts to gain money by any means, beginning with a mercenary marriage and ending with sorcery. I should think it might be received very well. I believe I shall call it, 'Tis Pity She's a Corpse.[21]

Considering that in 1807, which is when these events are notionally occurring, one of the entertainments selected for the opening season of the new Sans Pareil Theatre (later the Adelphi) was Jane M. Scott's *Spectrology of Ghosts*, Lascelles may well have been right; although in another sense he surely appears prophetic, insofar as this scenario so clearly prefigures one published 11 years later, namely the raising of Victor Frankenstein's creature.

As to the world to which Miss Wintertowne must needs repair at the behest of the gentleman with the thistledown hair, we hear of it not from her own lips but from those of a later forced visitor, Stephen Black, who finds himself 'standing in a great hall where a crowd of people were dancing to sad music':

> Everyone was dressed in the very height of fashion. The ladies wore gowns of the most exquisite colours (though, to own the truth, very few of them were colours that Stephen could remember having seen before).[22]

Soon, Stephen finds himself dancing with a lady with 'a gown the colour of storms, shadows and rain and a necklace of broken promises and regrets'.[23] This melancholic scene of irreparable loss and the pain of memory takes us back to Keats's 'La Belle Dame sans Merci' (1819); but it also serves to remind us of the general ambiguity of magic, where every beneficial effect is accompanied by its own shadow.

'There was always the same passion for darkness': *The House of Lost Souls*

To take up again an earlier theme, books are everywhere in *Jonathan Strange and Mr Norrell*, as are other types of text: scrawled manuscript spells, for

---

[21] Clarke, *Jonathan Strange*, pp. 112–13.   [22] Clarke, *Jonathan Strange*, p. 190.
[23] Clarke, *Jonathan Strange*, p. 191.

example, of a type that were indeed readily available at low prices in the England of the time. But these texts are, of course, significant not in and of themselves, but rather for the uses which can be made of them, whereby they may come to act as springboards into practical magic. An earlier book is also crucial to the plot of F. G. Cottam's *The House of Lost Souls*, although in this case it is the journal of a photographer who attended a magical event in the 1920s that proves key to unlocking an otherwise secret history.

The House of Lost Souls is perhaps not a very distinguished novel in itself – Cottam does not pack the punch of Wheatley or Harrison, for example – but it is a fair representation of a certain strand of contemporary engagements with magic and the occult. Four students visit a derelict house, known as the Fischer House, which is rumoured to have been the site of a number of magical experiments, involving various well-known historical figures from the occult tradition including Wheatley, but also tying this in with a further 'alternative history', involving ghosts, Nazis and the history of the Second World War. Klaus Fischer himself is purported to have hosted a Crowley-esque gathering devoted to ritual magic, and its reverberations continue to roll down through the decades. Has there really, the reader is implicitly asked, been a disruption of conventionally imagined historical processes, or are the protagonists the victims of a series of hallucinations?

And so the connections between magic, alternative history and the Gothic are again drawn tight. Just as Gothic holds up a distorting mirror to the historical record, so magic seeks to disrupt or alter that record, to affirm that what we might call a 'different kind of writing' is possible if only we can correctly read the books and manuscripts that hold the keys. It is, of course, no accident that so many grimoires from ancient to modern times have had titles that reflect the metaphorical structure of keys and unlocking: *Clavicula Salomonis* (fifteenth century); *Clavicule de l'enchiridion du Pape Leon* (late seventeenth century); *Clavicule of Virgil* (purportedly possessed by a priest tried for sorcery in 1511); and *La clef de la magie noire* (1897).

In the novel a great deal remains unclear, but the central themes are evident. There is the conflict between a malevolent form of magic and the possibility that a version of 'enlightenment' – although perhaps not a rational one – might dispel the haunting effects of a previously laid and entrenched magic plot. There is a question about the relations between dark magic and the recurrence of wickedness throughout history, which so often crops up as part of a way of addressing the far more general philosophical and theological problem of evil. There is an overarching question as to whether impressionable minds can ever serve as reliable witnesses to events that never fully emerge into clarity; as always, our recollections of rituals and their effects are cloudy and become increasingly insubstantial. And there are other, almost traditional questions as to whether the effects attributed to magic are more simply produced by drink, drugs and fear, in whatever might seem the most appropriate combination.

Perhaps the core of the book is summed up in the following paragraph, where a 'Crew of Light' forms to defeat the forces of darkness:

> He wondered would the three of them somehow prevail. Fate linked them, perhaps even predestination. There was something Gothic and strange, and at the same time recognisable, about their situation in this remote and Catholic keep, with its roaring logs and walls of scholarly vellum. It reminded Seaton of the fictions of Rider Haggard and Conan Doyle and Bram Stoker. Three men, civilised and formidable, gathered to plan an assault on the forces of evil armed with valour and learning and staunch moral rectitude.[24]

A familiar scenario indeed, but one that is apparently only half-convincing if you have actually been to the Fischer House:

> The reality of it was so black and hopeless with evil that it made a nonsense of the cosy collusive fantasy he was tempted to indulge in now. You weren't staunch in the midst of the slippery chaos dwelling in the gloom in the mansion in Brightstone Forest. You were helpless. You were prey.[25]

Here, perhaps, we are back in the world of Lovecraft, where what is conjured up from the dark becomes overwhelming, redolent of a realm that is beyond human comprehension. It may appear possible to control magic; but magic also represents the uncontrollable and indeed a form of addiction, that which seems to proffer the possibility of conveying power but which, in the end, demonstrates the limit of human capability and action. The magician has historically been a figure for supreme aspiration; but he is simultaneously a figure for a kind of wrestling on the brink, locked in a struggle that, in the end, he cannot win.

Concluding

The history of the Gothic and the history of magic are intertwined. Most obviously, both have to do with the supernatural; with the postulation of

---

[24] F. G. Cottam, *The House of Lost Souls* (London: Hodder & Stoughton, 2007), p. 248.
[25] Cottam, *House of Lost Souls*, p. 248.

a realm, or perhaps merely a set of devices, whereby the apparently natural world may be relativised, may come to take a place amid a series of 'other worlds', other possibilities for the imagination. More specifically, both have had centrally to do with the prospect of overcoming death; of endlessly prolonging life, or of surpassing death by asserting the possibility of return, of the revenant which, or who, will reassure us that there is no absolute finality.

But this return – as emblematically in the terrible return of the dead child in Stephen King's *Pet Sematary* (1983) – may never be quite what we expect. In *Jonathan Strange and Mr Norrell*, after the (partially) successful return to life of Emma Wintertowne, various political figures suggest that the best way to use magic to aid British forces during the Napoleonic Wars would be to produce the return of Pitt, the great statesman and master strategist; but, as is pointed out, Pitt has been long in his grave. In what shape would he return?

The Gothic endures, and appears to be continually remade in different but related forms; magic too endures; the faith held in an alternative power is not to be suppressed by the voice of cool reason. Of course, in both of these cases, we may be talking about the various forms of what T. E. Hulme long ago referred to as 'spilt religion'; after all, what lies at the bottom of world religions from Christianity to Buddhism but a belief that nothing is final, that there are other routes towards explanation of the human plight?

We might also say, though, that in the cases of both Gothic and magic what is really at stake is not merely promises – of eternal life, of the transmutation of dross into gold – but the specific thrill of transgression. There are, of course, many things we can do now, from the replacement of human limbs to the restarting of the human heart, which would previously have appeared magical; but described in scientific or technical language they lose this particular kind of appeal.

Thus all relies on the manner of representation; and this returns us to what is perhaps most important about the connection between magic and the Gothic, namely the reliance on the word, on the book. Gothic is often at its most powerful where it attempts, through the fiction of ancient manuscripts, descriptions of what cannot be described; magic is at its most vivid when it is to be found in words, formulations which may be successfully incantatory and incarnating. Even innocuous herbal remedies, it may be said, are at their most potentially effective when passed down through the generations – by word of mouth, perhaps, but even more so when written down and given the putative sanctity of text.

Magic and the Gothic are thus, seen from one perspective, forms of textuality, but of a textuality that may have power beyond words. The Gothic produces these effects in various form of haunting; magic in the endless succession of grimoires – most of which, historically, turn out to be plagiarisms from each other, just as the Gothic is perennially counterfeit, dealing in repetitions, lost manuscripts and false authorly ascriptions that continue to reproduce down the ages.

3.9

Psychoanalysis and the American Popular Gothic, 1954–1980

BERNICE M. MURPHY

The 1950s: 'If it's not one thing, it's your mother'

During the opening chapter of Robert Bloch's *Psycho* (1959), middle-aged motel manager Norman Bates and 'Mother' argue about his reading habits:

'This just happens to be a history of the Inca civilisation – '
   'I'll just bet it is. And I'll just bet it's crammed full with nasty bits about those dirty savages, like the one you had about the South Seas. Oh, you didn't think I knew about *that* one, did you? Hiding it up in your room, the way you hid all the others, those filthy things you used to read – '
   'Psychology isn't filthy, Mother!'
   'Psychology, he calls it! A lot you know about psychology! I'll never forget the time you talked so dirty to me, never. To think that a son could come to his own mother and *say* such things!'
   'But I was only trying to explain something. It's what they call the Oedipus situation, and I thought if both of us could just look at the problem reasonably and try to understand it, maybe things would change for the better'.
   'Change, boy? Nothing's going to change. You can read all the books in the world and you'll still be the same. I don't need to listen to a lot of vile, obscene rigmarole to know what you are ... You're a Mama's Boy'.[1]

Of course, the *real* Mrs Bates is long dead, and 'Mother' is a manifestation of Norman's multiple personality disorder, a 'dominant personality' that takes over during moments of emotional distress. As Kevin Corstorphine notes of this exchange, it is 'clearly an authorial confession that the Oedipal narrative is going to be used as a plot device, but it also precludes Freudian criticism by making obvious what would normally be hidden from view'.[2] Norman Bates

---

[1] Robert Bloch, *Psycho* (London: Corgi, 1959), pp. 11–12.
[2] Kevin Corstorphine, '"A Search for the Father-Image": Masculine Anxiety in Robert Bloch's 1950s Fiction', in Darryl Jones, Elizabeth McCarthy and Bernice M. Murphy (eds), *It Came from the 1950s: Popular Culture, Popular Anxieties* (Basingstoke: Palgrave Macmillan, 2011), pp. 158–75 (p. 160).

is in actuality a violent psychotic who murders young women unfortunate enough to stimulate his repressed sexual longings. As Lila Crane, the only woman to bear witness to his violence and make it out of the Bates residence alive, later remarks, 'the horror wasn't in the house. It was in his head'.[3] It should come as no surprise that Norman Bates references the Oedipus Complex of Sigmund Freud. To many other Americans during this era, psychoanalysis seemed to provide an entirely plausible framework for resolving internal and interpersonal conflicts. Norman is simultaneously an aficionado of psychoanalytic theory *and* a hyperbolic embodiment of the Oedipal worst-case scenario – a weak-minded son so warped by his overbearing mother that he has been 'taken over' by his maternal alter-ego.

When comparing the modern controversy caused by psychoanalysis with the popular impact of the theory of evolution in the nineteenth century, Joseph Schwartz notes:

> psychoanalysis informs part of our daily discourse in a way that evolution has never done. Terms such as unconscious, repressed, ego, ambivalent, complex, projection, denial and double-bind enter in to conversations in every walk of life whenever people talk about mental states and the reasons for human actions. Psychoanalytic language and concepts have been integrated into Western culture through novels, poetry, drama and film, literary and film criticism.[4]

As a text, *Psycho* provides the most obvious example of the ways in which psychoanalytic concepts influenced the American popular Gothic in the postwar era, but it is by no means the only one. To comprehend why the genre was significantly affected, it is important to understand that the shadow cast by Freud's legacy extended far beyond the boundaries of genre fiction and film. The 1950s and 1960s were what Nathan G. Hale has described as the 'Golden Age of Popularization' for psychoanalytic thought in the United States, the period during which these concepts reached their paramount level of authority in American psychiatry, art and popular culture.[5] Yet this influence would not last. John Burnham asserts that 'Another half-century later, Freud's name was still familiar, but American cultural leaders had many new ways of looking at the world, and only infrequently did they make detailed,

---

[3] Bloch, *Psycho*, p. 124.
[4] Joseph Schwartz, *Cassandra's Daughter: A History of Psychoanalysis in Europe and America* (London: Penguin, 1999), p. 1.
[5] Nathan G. Hale, Jr, *The Rise and Crisis of Psychoanalysis in the United States: Freud and the Americans 1917–1985* (New York: Oxford University Press, 1995), p. 276.

direct reference to any of Freud's ideas ... his legacy declined in importance or became relatively invisible by the end of the century.'[6]

As Burnham goes on to observe, at the time of his first and only visit to the US in 1909, Freud was a well-known figure in Europe, but most ordinary Americans had no familiarity with his work, 'not even his publications about his innovations in psychotherapeutic technique'.[7] By mid-century, however, things had dramatically changed, and Freud's ideas had become a conspicuous and, indeed, unavoidable 'part of the American cultural landscape'.[8] The psychiatric influence that psychoanalysis accrued in the aftermath of World War II had much to do with the prominence that its practitioners had gained during the conflict itself, during which high numbers of combatants suffered from severe mental trauma, and, as Andrew Scull documents, 'both the British and the Americans entrusted the command of their wartime psychiatric services to men sympathetic to psychoanalysis'.[9] It was also a consequence of the psychological and familial ramifications of the immense political, economic and cultural changes that swept the nation in the years following the war.

The United States was now wealthier than it had even been, as the gross national product grew by 250 per cent between 1945 and 1960.[10] Across the nation, millions of new suburban homes were being built for a young and expanding middle class. The Interstate Highways Act of 1956 inaugurated the creation of the largest federal infrastructure project ever undertaken. As William H. Chafe has noted, the era also saw the introduction of innovations such the television, mass airplane travel, the modern supermarket, the shopping mall, the 'two-car family', widespread college education and the emergence of a greatly expanded white-collar managerial class.[11] Yet there were also widespread fears that the US was becoming a much more rootless, atomised and anxious place. From 1950 to 1953, the nation was engaged in the Korean War, a conflict that almost culminated in the use of nuclear weapons.[12] At a time of unprecedented prosperity, millions of citizens were still living in with poverty and subject to rampant racial

---

[6] John Burnham (ed.), *After Freud Left: A Century of Psychoanalysis in America* (Chicago: University of Chicago Press, 2012), p. 3.

[7] Burnham, *After Freud*, p. 3.   [8] Burnham, *After Freud*, p. 3.

[9] Andrew Scull, *Madness in Civilisation: A Cultural History of Insanity from the Bible to Freud, From the Madhouse to Modern Medicine* (London: Thames and Hudson, 2015), p. 338.

[10] William Chafe, *The Unfinished Journey: America Since World War Two* (New York: Oxford University Press, 1999), p. 111.

[11] Chafe, *The Unfinished Journey*, pp. 111–17.

[12] James Patterson, *Grand Expectations: The United States, 1945–1974* (New York: Oxford University Press, 1996), p. 339.

discrimination.[13] In spite of the culturally prescribed expectation that middle-class, college-educated white women were satisfied with their roles as housewives and mothers, many felt trapped and dangerously unfulfilled, as Betty Friedan later demonstrated in *The Feminine Mystique* (1963).

As rates of high-school and college attendance skyrocketed, more and more Americans, like Norman Bates, were engaging with sociological and psychological studies that sought to explain the new world in which they found themselves living. James Patterson notes that many of the buzzwords used in such works focused on fears related to mental health – expressions such as 'alienation', 'identity crisis', 'age of anxiety' and 'eclipse of community' all entered the nation's vocabulary during this time.[14] Looming over everything, of course, was the prospect of nuclear annihilation. Stephen King, himself a product of the post-war baby-boom, summed up the era's disorientating sense of both immense privilege and pervasive unease when he observed in *Danse Macabre* (1981) that, 'We had more to eat than any other nation in the history of the world, but there were traces of Strontium-90 in our milk from nuclear testing.'[15]

At a time when psychiatrists in Europe were focusing on the development of ground-breaking 'somatic' (drug-based) treatments for mental illness, 'The United States was in the grip of psychoanalysis. Many psychiatric illnesses, even some of the most severe, were seen as stemming from repressed sexual desires or repressed rages turning and twisting the mind.'[16] In part, this was also a reaction to the fact that the first half of the twentieth century had been a nadir for American psychiatry. Conditions for hundreds of thousands of patients confined in underfunded and overcrowded state institutions deteriorated to the point where investigators plausibly compared some of these hospitals to concentration camps. Lauren Slater also suggests that for Jewish practitioners of psychoanalysis who had fled to the US during the war, this 'talking treatment ensured a gentleness and humanity' that stood in stark contrast to the 'terrible experiments performed upon mental patients and Jews, all in the name of progress' in Nazi Germany.[17]

The version of psychoanalysis that soon predominated in the United States was also one that fit with the nation's sense of itself. As Andrew Scull puts it, 'Americans were never terribly enamoured of the darker side of Freud's

---

[13] Patterson, *Grand Expectations*, p. 333. [14] Patterson, *Grand Expectations*, p. 339.
[15] Stephen King, *Danse Macabre* (London: Warner, 1991), p. 23.
[16] Lauren Slater, *The Drugs that Changed Our Minds: The History of Psychiatry in Ten Treatments* (London: Simon and Schuster, 2018), p. 39.
[17] Slater, *The Drugs*, p. 45.

vision.'[18] During his seminal speech at Clarke University in 1909, Freud had framed his theories at their 'most benign and simplistic for the "practical Americans", [and] he united existing American concerns: a hopeful psychotherapy that rejected much of the relevance of hereditary, challenges to "civilized" morality, a new emphasis on the importance of sexuality, childhood and the role of the unconscious'.[19] By the 1950s, Nathan Hale continues, the essentially optimistic yet inherently conservative approach associated with American ego psychology had already been identified with:

> the established social authority, and tended to exaggerate certain American tendencies already present among the nation's psychoanalysts: a downplaying of the iconoclastic, rebellious aspects of psychoanalysis which had so appealed to the intelligentsia of the 1920s. It tended to reconcile psychoanalysis with morality, religion and received social values, particularly in its treatment of sexual roles and the treatment of homosexuality ... Popularisation crystallised a socially conservative image of psychoanalysis – from its identification of practitioners with dentists and businessmen to its vision of therapy as a tough, painful exercise that resulted as a rule in marital happiness, personal equilibrium, and vocational success.[20]

The post-war era was a boom time for the popular Gothic, and for many of the same reasons that psychoanalysis found such a receptive audience. A new generation of authors, screen-writers and directors moved away from pre-war preoccupations such as the baroque 'Cosmic Regionalism' of H. P. Lovecraft and the quaint supernaturalism of the Universal Horror cycle and towards fears of a much more 'realistic' and psychological variety. In the aftermath of the extreme barbarism of the Holocaust, and the development (and deployment) of nuclear weapons, the 'Old School' terrors had lost their power. Now, it was unease rooted in 'normality' as well as the horrors of the unstable mind that predominated.

This was also the period during which the so-called 'new American Gothic' – most famously associated with authors such as Truman Capote, William Faulkner, Flannery O'Connor and Carson McCullers – emerged. Although this group of writers is usually discussed apart from the more obviously genre-based works of the authors focused on in this chapter, they share many similar themes. There was an important degree of geographical specificity to much of this writing. As Charles L. Crow notes, 'The American South, with its legacy of profound social and economic problems,

---

[18] Scull, *Madness in Civilisation*, p. 332.   [19] Hale, *The Rise and Crisis*, p. 5.
[20] Hale, *The Rise and Crisis*, p. 299.

became a major focus and source of American literature in the twentieth century, and the principal region of American Gothic.'[21] However, another key focus – and one that allies these works with the popular Gothic and horror texts focused on in this chapter – was the tormented mind. For Irving Malin in 1962, this fiction was 'close to Poe' and 'far removed' from the realism of William Dean Howells; 'It believes that the psyche is more important than society, or if this is a bit extreme, that the disorder of the buried life must be charted.'[22] The grotesques, compulsives and narcissists who populate Malin's 'new American Gothic' strongly evoke psychoanalytic concepts not only in terms of their obvious emphasis on understanding the mind, but also because the influence of the family is profound:

> The family is crucial in the new American Gothic. There are several reasons for this: disfiguring love is often learned at home. Parents see themselves in their children but forget about self-expression on the part of the young; they want to mold unformed personalities. Children, on the other hand, become narcissistic because of their need to find and love themselves in a cold environment. New American Gothic deploys the family as a microcosm: the family dramatises the conflict between private and social worlds, ego and super-ego. Almost every work in the canon contains a family terror.[23]

As Malin argued, this depiction of the family as the root of all neurosis employs 'Freudian principles (consciously or unconsciously)', as well as reflecting the influence of long-standing European and American Gothic tropes.[24]

That the Gothic and psychoanalysis make obvious bedfellows is an observation that has frequently been made, as has Maggie Kilgour's suggestion that Freud's theories themselves have more than a touch of the Gothic about them; as Crow states, 'some regard the major writings of Sigmund Freud as among the great Gothic works of the century'.[25] Kilgour further argues that psychoanalysis helped to transform the Gothic into a viable mode of academic inquiry by 'bestowing a greater profundity on a form previously trivialised as superficial'.[26] Steven Bruhm has also highlighted the important relationship between psychoanalysis and the contemporary Gothic, which he

---

[21] Charles L. Crow, *American Gothic* (Cardiff: University of Wales Press, 2009), p. 124.
[22] Irving Malin, *New American Gothic* (Carbondale, IL: Southern Illinois University Press, 1962), p. 4.
[23] Malin, *New American Gothic*, p. 8. [24] Malin, *New American Gothic*, p. 8.
[25] Crow, *American Gothic*, p. 123.
[26] Maggie Kilgour, 'Dr Frankenstein Meets Dr Freud', in Robert K. Martin and Eric Savoy (eds), *American Gothic: New Interventions in a National Narrative* (Iowa City: University of Iowa Press, 1998), pp. 40–54 (p. 40).

sees as being similarly characterised by 'the protagonists' and the viewers' compulsive return to certain fixations, obsessions and blockages'.[27] As Chris Dumas notes of horror cinema (and his observations may equally be applied to the post-war Gothic), Freud's influence is impossible to avoid, either in the form of the cultural products themselves, or in the form of critiques by many of the most influential critics who have engaged with these works (he goes on to cite film scholars such as Robin Wood, Carol J. Clover and Barbara Creed).[28] Dumas notes of the Oedipal Complex that it 'is what gives horror cinema its particularly familial cast: the traumatic knot of children's relationship with their parents, in horror, unleashes a violence that can only be understood as an archaic response to primal dissatisfaction'.[29]

This same preoccupation with twisted parent–child relationships represents one of the most significant recurring tropes in the American popular Gothic during the 1950s and after. Time and again in the most enduring texts of this period, the nuclear family is wracked by sexual and emotional repression, unresolved trauma, unspoken secrets, gender confusion, arrested development and compulsive behaviours. Furthermore, many of the most lurid dramatisations of psychoanalytic principles in such fictions revolve around the idea of the 'problematic' mother. As Scull observes, 'Freud's theories had discerned the roots of psychopathology in this setting, and his American followers laid a host of problems at the feet of the family. And especially, the analysts indicted America's mothers, as the source, it would appear, of an ever-expanding array of illnesses and debility, and even a threat to the health of the nation.'[30] It was not long before these 'Pathological Mommies', as he dubs them, began to appear in popular fiction and film.

This brings us back to *Psycho*. Although the real Mrs Bates was murdered long before the main events of the story, we are left in little doubt that Norman's psychosis owes much to her controlling behaviour. In the closing pages of the novel, Sam Loomis recounts the details that Dr Steiner, one of the psychiatrists who has been assessing Norman at the state hospital, has been able to glean from their sessions: 'A lot of the things he said, about fugue and cathexis and trauma, are way over my head. But as near as he can make out, this all started way back in Norman's childhood, long before his mother's

---

[27] Steven Bruhm, 'Contemporary Gothic: Why We Need It', in Jerrold E. Hogle (ed.), *The Cambridge Companion to Gothic Fiction* (Cambridge: Cambridge University Press, 2002), pp. 259–76 (p. 261).
[28] Chris Dumas, 'Horror and Psychoanalysis: An Introductory Primer', in Harry M. Benshoff (ed.), *A Companion to the Horror Film* (Oxford: Wiley-Blackwell, 2017), pp. 21–37.
[29] Dumas, 'Horror and Psychoanalysis', p. 35.   [30] Scull, *Madness in Civilisation*, p. 342.

death. He and his mother were very close, of course, and apparently she dominated him.'[31] We are told that although 'we'll never actually know just how much she was responsible for what he became', Mrs Bates 'must have decided Norman wasn't ever going out in to the world on his own'.[32] When his mother embarked upon a sexual relationship with a man named Joe Considine, Norman, unable to countenance the prospect of their marriage, poisoned them both, at which point 'Norman, or part of him, *became* his mother'.[33] Even if it is briefly suggested, then, that Mrs Bates may not be entirely to blame for his warped mental state, responsibility for his toxic state of arrested development is still, ultimately, hers.

Monstrous mothers who irreparably warp their sons also frequently feature in the work of Charles Beaumont. His 1957 story 'Nursery Rhyme' features a cloying mother who, driven mad by the deaths of four of her children many years before, so badly infantilises her surviving son that he becomes a psychotic murderer. An even more damaging matriarch appears in one of Beaumont's most famous tales, 'Miss Gentilbelle' (1957), in which the title character is a deranged, man-hating abuser who raises her illegitimate (and increasingly disturbed) young son as a girl. Beaumont also has several tales in the collection *The Hunger and Other Stories* (1957) in which sexually repressed spinsters allow themselves to be 'carried away' by supernatural forces and/or delusional fantasies. This focus on the dramatic possibilities of mental instability and 'neurosis' is typical of 1950s popular Gothic, a mode in which the boundaries between fantasy and reality, sanity and insanity are persistently blurred.

Although monstrous maternal figures do not directly feature in the work of Richard Matheson, there is more than a hint of what Barbara Creed would later dub 'The Monstrous-Feminine' in *I Am Legend* (1954), *The Shrinking Man* (1956) and *Stir of Echoes* (1958).[34] All three novels focus upon thirty-something family men whose placid lives are upended by the intrusion of irrational outside forces. The primal underbelly just below the seemingly stable surface of 'everyday' suburban life is violently exposed as neighbours and family members become blood-thirsty ghouls, the now vast confines of the family basement become the site of a frantic struggle to defeat a giant (and *female*) spider, and the house down the street is revealed to be the site of a horrific murder. Matheson's work therefore provides yet another indication of the ways in which popular Gothic of the period dramatised the Freudian belief

---

[31] Bloch, *Psycho*, p. 121. [32] Bloch, *Psycho*, p. 121. [33] Bloch, *Psycho*, p. 123.
[34] See Barbara Creed, *The Monstrous-Feminine: Film, Feminism, Psychoanalysis* (London: Routledge, 1993).

that 'human rationality is an illusion, that every person is "civilised" only in so far as they have managed to repress, or censor, their worst impulses'.[35]

William March's 1954 bestseller *The Bad Seed* deals even more explicitly with the imposition of a scrupulously polite façade over inherently 'uncivilised' impulses. Christine Penmark, a young mother raising her daughter alone while her husband Kenneth is working away from home, begins to suspect – although part of her has always known that 'there was something strange about the child' – that eight-year-old Rhoda may be a remorseless murderer.[36] The supposedly chance drowning of a child in Rhoda's class is merely the latest in a series of fatal 'accidents' that befall those who possess something that Rhoda covets for herself.

It transpires that Rhoda was 'born bad', and what is more, the blame lies squarely with her maternal heritage. Christine discovers that her own biological mother was the notorious serial murderer Bessie Denker, but that she repressed this knowledge of her true origin. Although Christine herself is gentle and loving, Bessie's psychopathy has merely skipped a generation. Once Christine comes to this realisation, the rest of the novel focuses on her gnawing sense of responsibility, and her dreadful uncertainty about what to do with the unrepentant little killer in her home. On the one hand, the novel's insistence that Rhoda's psychopathy is the result of nature rather than nurture conflicts with the psychoanalytic view that behaviour is largely determined by experiences in early childhood. Then, on the other, there is the role played by Mona Breedlove, Christine's neighbour and close friend, whose interest in Freud's work is so strong that she was briefly analysed by the great man himself.[37] Throughout the novel, Mona good-naturedly subjects those around her to her own brand of amateur analysis, declaring at one point that her brother, Emory, is a 'larvated homosexual' and speaking frankly of her own 'penis envy'.[38] However, despite Mona's keen interest in the workings of the mind, she never even begins to suspect Rhoda's true nature. Psychoanalysis is depicted here as an ultimately useless fad that is no match at all for a precocious killer defined by her pre-determined 'badness'.

Yet *The Bad Seed* also dramatises many of the most pervasive canards associated with popular psychoanalysis. The middle-class home is a secretly toxic environment. Rhoda's greed and pathological self-interest can be seen as hyperbolic ripostes to the emotional repression of her chronically self-blaming mother. Christine's refusal to accept Rhoda's true nature contributes

---

[35] Dumas, 'Horror and Psychoanalysis', p. 22.
[36] William March, *The Bad Seed* (New York: HarperCollins, 1997), p. 36.
[37] March, *The Bad Seed*, p. 38.   [38] March, *The Bad Seed*, pp. 31, 39.

to at least three murders. Furthermore, her inability to confront her own childhood trauma (inflicted by a monstrous maternal figure who could give 'Mrs Bates' a run for her money) means that she is unprepared to face reality. Tony Williams argues of the 1956 film version that this is a story in which 'guilt becomes conveniently externalised. Eisenhower's America simply *could not* have produced such a monster!'[39] Even as the novel appears to reject a psychoanalytic explanation for Rhoda's psychopathy, it thus still internalises the most commonly dramatised tenets of post-war American Freudianism.

More than any other Gothic author of the period, Shirley Jackson dramatised concerns related to female unhappiness and repression, the toxic family and identity crisis. Her most famous novel, *The Haunting of Hill House* (1959), focuses upon the relationship between deeply neurotic heroine Eleanor Vance, and the dangerously smothering (and *mothering*) residence to which she finds herself fatally drawn. While this work has long been a goldmine for critics working from a psychoanalytic perspective, Jackson's fascination with unreliable mental states spans her entire oeuvre. Four of her six completed novels focus upon young women who refuse to (or are completely unable to) 'fit in' with the world around them, a trend that reaches its zenith in *We Have Always Lived in the Castle* (1962). Jackson's work evolves from the relatively conventional – albeit undeniably Gothic – psychological case studies found in *Hangsaman* (1951) and *The Bird's Nest* (1954), novels in which some degree of apparent, if not always entirely convincing, 'normality' is restored by the final pages, to the absolute rejection of the outside world in *Castle*, a novel memorably described by one critic as 'not so much a depiction of madness as a poetic participation in it'.[40]

Hangsaman presents us with a troubled teenager whose symptoms, though never explicitly diagnosed, closely resemble schizophrenia. College freshman Natalie Waite is seventeen, precocious and extremely imaginative. Her rejection of the myriad rituals associated with co-ed life, alongside her revulsion at the thought of embarking upon the seemingly pre-determined path to marriage and motherhood, means that she remains a complete outsider. The sudden appearance of an exciting new 'best friend' who seems to understand Natalie as no one else ever has before heralds a new phase in her rapidly unspooling mental breakdown that almost culminates in

---

[39] Tony Williams, *Hearths of Darkness: The Family in the American Horror Film* (Jackson, MS: University Press of Mississippi, 2014), p. 87.

[40] Jack Sullivan, *The Penguin Encyclopaedia of Horror and the Supernatural* (New York: Viking, 1986), p. 227.

suicide. However, Natalie eventually appears to overcome her inner demons, and turns away, at least temporarily, from self-annihilation.

Elizabeth Richmond, the slightly older protagonist of *The Bird's Nest* (1954), seems to live a life of stifling routine.[41] It soon becomes clear, however, that something is badly amiss. She suffers from crippling headaches, receives nasty, puzzling, anonymous notes and she is subject to blackouts. Eventually, Elizabeth is referred to a psychiatrist named Dr Victor Wright, who discovers the reason for her increasingly bizarre behaviour: she has multiple personality disorder, and her mind contains four battling alternate personas. *The Bird's Nest* resembles many of the non-fiction, female-focused psychiatric case studies that were popular during this period, in that under the loving if exasperated care of her psychiatrist, Elizabeth is eventually able to recall the primal childhood trauma that damaged her youthful psyche and integrate the various facets of herself in to an agreeable and apparently stable single personality. Though Dr Wright is explicitly scornful of psychoanalysis, the causes of Elizabeth's disorder tick many of the most familiar cod-Freudian boxes, involving as they do a wanton and neglectful mother and a possible episode of childhood sexual abuse. Although the closing lines of *The Bird's Nest* suggest that the new Elizabeth may be less of a pushover than before, there can be no doubt that her therapist has been key to her recovery, nor that the successful resolution of her psychological 'journey' depended upon confronting a pivotal childhood trauma.

However, any restoration of 'normality' is unachievable, and indeed, undesirable for *We Have Always Lived in the Castle's* Merricat Blackwood. Here, the idea of the 'toxic' nuclear family becomes literal. Save for 18-year-old Merricat, her sister Constance and their doddering old Uncle Julian, everyone else in the Blackwood clan is dead, having been poisoned at the dinner table six years before. Although Constance was put on trial for the murders, she was found not guilty, and returned home to care for her uncle and sister. It comes as little surprise – and it is unlikely that Jackson meant it to be – when we find out that it was then 12-year-old Merricat who put arsenic in the sugar bowl.

Like *Psycho*, *We Have Always Lived in the Castle* focuses upon a protagonist who is prone to murderous violence, psychotic delusion and paranoia, but in contrast, Jackson's text provides us with no reassuring gesture towards legal sanction and/or psychiatric 'treatment'. Indeed, we never get an explicit explanation at all for the reasons why Merricat set out to exterminate

---

[41] Shirley Jackson, *The Bird's Nest* (London: Michael Joseph, 1955), p. 8.

everyone except her cherished enabler Constance. The only (living) character who suggests that 'something' should be done about Merricat is cousin Charles, an opportunistic freeloader who is only interested in the women because Constance is a pretty, romantically unattached heiress. What is more, the mob violence with which the novel climaxes justifies Merricat's paranoid insularity. She even declares herself to be 'happy' as the sisters hide in the smouldering ruins of her burnt-out home in the final pages. Constance, who has earlier indicated a tentative desire to return to 'normality', has now fully embraced her sister's misanthropy. Insanity is therefore not something seen, as in *The Bird's Nest* or *Hangsaman*, as a struggle to be won (however ambivalently), but as an understandable response to a world in which 'normality' is much more frightening than spending life in one's own reality. Merricat even finds it in herself to (ironically) pity those who do not get to live as the Blackwood sisters do: '"Poor strangers," I said. "They have so much to be afraid of."'[42]

Paralleling this evolution in Jackson's depictions of madness was a change during the 1960s in the way in which mental illness would be treated by some practitioners and theorists. It was during this decade that the 'Anti-psychiatry' movement began. Led by Glaswegian psychiatrist R. D. Laing, its main thrust was the belief that mental illness had to be examined in terms of its social contexts: the emotional dynamics of the family and the institution of psychiatry itself.[43] As Laing put it, 'an individual's subjective view of the world was not to be derided, ignored, or obliterated simply because it did not fit in with conventional views or opinions'.[44] In his most famous study, *The Divided Self* (1960), Laing applied 'the ideas and techniques of modernist literature and criticism to mental illness in order to make madness and the process of going mad comprehensible'.[45] The 'onus of inadequacy' was transferred from the patient to the family and society that surrounded them. However, although several well-known works of American literary fiction during this period chimed with Laing's perspective, the popular Gothic of the late 1960s and 1970s by and large tended to bypass this depiction of 'madness' as form of liberating escape. Instead, many of the most familiar tropes of 1950s pop psychoanalysis would yet again be rehearsed in the 1970s and 1980s – but this time for an even greater audience, as many of these best-selling texts were adapted for the screen.

---

[42] Shirley Jackson, *We Have Always Lived in the Castle* (New York: Penguin, 2006), p. 124.
[43] Elaine Showalter, *The Female Malady: Women, Madness and English Culture, 1830–1980* (London: Virago, 1985), p. 219.
[44] Bob Mullan, *R. D. Laing: Creative Destroyer* (London: Cassell, 1997), p. 1.
[45] Showalter, *Female Malady*, p. 60.

Remembering Satan: Psychoanalytic Horror in the 1970s and Early 1980s

Ira Levin's *Rosemary's Baby* (1968) was the most influential Gothic novel of the late 1960s, and, along with William Peter Blatty's *The Exorcist* (1971), it marked the beginning of the 1970s horror boom. *Rosemary's Baby* was the savvy culmination of an approach to common genre themes that had been dominant since the mid-1950s. It updated one of the hoariest tropes of colonial American supernaturalism – the Satanic coven that hides in plain sight – for a modern, secular age. No longer do witches lurk in the forests outside Salem Village: instead, they reside in upscale apartment buildings in Manhattan, wear luridly coloured polyester, and cheerfully make 'all-natural' health drinks for the nourishment of the gestating Anti-Christ. Crucially, Rosemary Woodhouse's realisation that she has been used as a Satanic brood mare does little to change the plans of the geriatric coven that has engineered this terrible conspiracy. When she finally sees her horrific offspring, her maternal instincts prevent her from killing the child. Instead, Rosemary vows that she will try to influence him in her own way, in the probably futile hope that nurture can overcome nature.

Marital betrayal also informs the climax of Levin's other most well-known novel, *The Stepford Wives* (1972). Joanna Eberhart, a newcomer to the Connecticut suburbs, becomes increasingly suspicious of her strangely docile fellow housewives, ultimately discovering that the real women of Stepford are being murdered and replaced by subservient android replicants. The horror is compounded by the discovery that even her own husband is a conspirator. Notably, it is while she is visiting a psychiatrist (at her husband's insistence) that Joanna comes to the brink of her horrific realisation. Encouraged by her sympathetic female therapist Dr Fancher, Joanna describes the Stepford women as acting like robot replicas in Disneyland. She is closer to the truth here than she knows, but Dr Fancher minimises Joanna's anxieties and suggests that she consider therapy. She then prescribes mild tranquilisers. Dr Fancher's refusal to consider the possibility that Joanna's paranoia might be rooted in an actual threat means that our unhappy protagonist is, fatally, left to face the conspiracy alone. Although their therapeutic encounter has brought Joanna to the brink of a crucial insight, Dr Fancher, at the same time, has unwittingly minimised the very real danger faced by her patient –

a suggestion perhaps that psychoanalysis might mask rather than start to address the root causes of the genuine anxiety that many middle-class white American women of this period felt about their supposedly 'natural' roles as wives and mothers.

Anxieties related to the disruptive potential of female agency are also key to Blatty's *The Exorcist*, and to William Friedkin's game-changing 1973 movie adaptation that followed. Formerly cute and passive 12-year-old Regan O'Neill becomes a snarling, foul-mouthed, aggressively hyper-sexual and altogether abject creature who must be tied to a bed to ensure the safety of herself and others. As Creed notes of the film adaptation, Reagan's possession can be read as an excuse for her to get away with displays of 'aberrant' female behaviour that are perversely appealing.[46] There is also the fact that Regan comes from what would then have been called a 'broken home', which is here seen as making her more susceptible to evil forces. Her parents have recently divorced, and have an acrimonious relationship: her father forgets to call and wish her happy birthday. It is in the days following this incident that Regan's behaviour begins to deteriorate. During her youthful experiments with the Ouija board, she contacts a sinister entity named 'Captain Howdy'. The fact that her perpetually absent father is called Howard is surely no coincidence. Regan is also afraid that her mother is becoming romantically involved with director Burke Dennings, later found dead at the bottom of steps below the child's bedroom window in an act that reminds us of the fact that Norman Bates's first acts of murder targeted his mother and her lover: we have here another child who is seemingly unable to accept the fact that his/her mother has a life beyond maternity.

Blatty repeatedly emphasises that Regan's distraught mother, Hollywood actress Chris MacNeill, has exhausted all secular/scientific paths of enquiry before a demonological explanation is mooted. Even when the novel's spiritually troubled Christ figure Fr Damian Karras is brought in to consult on the case, he is initially there mainly because he is also a psychiatrist. However, it is of course the theological rather than the scientific approach that proves successful, although not before heroic self-sacrifice on the part of Karras and his fellow exorcist. David J. Skal argues of the film adaptation that, when stripped of its demonic possession theme, it 'is the cautionary tale of a beleaguered single mother who believes that she can endure no more, but who, with the aid of Catholic doctrine, to which she has previously been

---

[46] Creed, *The Monstrous-Feminine*, p. 31.

indifferent, manages to endure everything'.[47] He further suggests that 'The film became a highly publicized cultural ritual in exorcising not the devil, but rather the confused parental feelings of guilt and responsibility in the Vietnam era, when – at least from a certain conservative perspective – filthy-mouthed children were taking personality-transforming drugs, violently acting out, and generally making life unpleasant for their elders.'[48]

This assessment of the reason why Blatty's novel and the film adaptation thereof struck such a chord in the early 1970s resembles John Burnham's explanation for the reasons why psychoanalysis achieved such influence within American culture in the early-to-mid twentieth century. Burnham notes that from quite early on, 'Americans often used Freudian formulations to explain or rationalise changes that were already underway.' He then argues that 'The most notorious instances were the "sexual revolution" of the early twentieth century and then a second sexual revolution in the age of "the pill" and feminism of the 1960s and after.'[49] If the linguistic and conceptual framework furnished by psychoanalysis provided one kind of cultural framework within which these kinds of rapidly shifting social and behavioural mores could be understood, then horror and the popular Gothic arguably provided an alternate, but not entirely dissimilar, means of dramatising and engaging with these tensions.

The already long-standing association between psychoanalysis and the popular Gothic peaked in 1980, with the publication of the 'non-fiction' memoir *Michelle Remembers*, written by psychotherapist Lawrence Pazder and his patient Michelle Smith. This text served as an even more lurid and outlandish depiction of societal and familial breakdown than *The Exorcist*, but, like Jay Anson's *The Amityville Horror* (1977), it purported to be real. *Michelle Remembers* is essentially a mash-up of a 1950s/early 1960s-style, non-fiction psychiatric case study (complete with lengthy transcriptions of supposed therapy sessions and a detailed run down of Pazder's qualifications) and a 1970s occult conspiracy narrative. The book begins as 27-year-old Michelle is referred back to her long-term therapist Pazder following a miscarriage. Her rapidly escalating battery of distressing psychological and psychosomatic symptoms is soon revealed to have a terrifying 'real-life' cause that she has been repressing for 22 years. Upon hearing that his patient has had a dream in which spiders suddenly erupt from her skin, Pazder immediately realises that this dream is 'nightmarish, but it was more than

[47] David J. Skal, *The Monster Show: A Cultural History of Horror* (London: Plexus, 1994), p. 295.
[48] Skal, *Monster Show*, p. 295.   [49] Burnham, *After Freud*, p. 12.

that, it was blatantly symbolic. It was connected subconsciously to something very important, he was sure of that'.[50] Sure enough, less than half-way through chapter 2, Michelle recalls being ill-treated by a sinister figure named 'Malachi', and before long, she is recounting ever more horrific (and unlikely) occult ceremonies in which babies are sacrificed, evil nurses coerce her to eat noxious substances, and she is forced to defecate upon a crucifix and a Bible. We are told that Dr Pazder rapidly becomes convinced that even though it seems unlikely, hitherto undetected Satanic cultists really were operating in 'beautiful and staid Victoria, the city, after all, that was Canada's retirement centre' during the mid-1950s. 'Michelle's reliving was relentlessly genuine', Pazder declares.[51] 'It was too consistent to be false, had too much information, was too sophisticated from the psychological point of view to have been made up. There was nothing about it that whispered "crazy". It simply wasn't the kind of thing you fabricated if you were crazy or hysterical. It was being *relived*.'[52]

If *Michelle Remembers* was preposterous, it was also, as Alexandra Heller-Nicholas observes, highly influential:

> considered the epicentre of the Satanic Ritual Abuse moral panic of the 1980s, as well as one of the most influential media hoaxes of the late-twentieth century ... the book outlines how Smith became a victim of Satanic Ritual Abuse as a young child, but it's a peculiar text – a mediocre exercise in generic pulp, full of hysterical and absurd claims that were once accepted as clinical fact.[53]

Part of the reason why a text so blatantly ridiculous achieved such a high profile and made Pazder a well-known 'expert witness' in such matters – he even coined the notorious term 'Ritual Abuse' at a 1980 meeting of the American Psychiatric Association – was because it was published at the same time that considerable anxiety about the sexual and physical abuse of children began to emerge in the United States.[54] As Richard Beck outlines in his study of the links between the decade's 'Satanic Panic' and the 'discovery' or rather ('rediscovery') of child abuse, psychoanalysis played a vital role:

---

[50] Michelle Smith and Lawrence Pazder, *Michelle Remembers* (London: Michael Joseph, 1981), p. 5.
[51] Smith and Pazder, *Michelle Remembers*, p. 5.
[52] Smith and Pazder, *Michelle Remembers*, p. 96.
[53] Alexandra Heller-Nicholas, 'The Only Word in the World Is Mine: Remembering *Michelle Remembers*', in Keir-La Janisse and Paul Corpue (eds), *Satanic Panic: Pop-Cultural Paranoia in the 1980s* (Goldalming: FAB Press, 2016), pp. 19–32 (p. 19).
[54] Richard Beck, *We Believe the Children: A Moral Panic in the 1980s* (New York: Public Affairs, 2015), p. 27.

The language of Sigmund Freud and psychoanalysis was simply a basic part of the mental atmosphere in which mid-century Americans lived and breathed, and it provided much of the rhetorical foundation for the panic that would eventually begin in the early 1980s. Freudian thought played a central role in the history of American attitudes and beliefs about child abuse, because the Freudian account of human experience is, at its core, an account of the persistence of childhood throughout adult life ... Freud's most famous psychological concepts, including penis envy and the Oedipus complex, were all derived from childhood. (Many commentators have noted that Freud devoted many more pages of writing to his analysis and interpretation of childhood sexuality than he did to the sexual lives of adults.) In the middle of the twentieth century, Freudian thought provided Americans with a way of understanding the relationship between childhood and adult life. As the public began to re-acknowledge the existence of child abuse in the sixties and early seventies, it instinctively drew on a vocabulary with which it was already intimately familiar and that seemed perfectly suited to explaining the subject at hand.[55]

A key concept within psychoanalysis was the notion of 'repression', and the idea that the memory of traumatic experiences undergone during childhood could be unconsciously held in check, only to be later made manifest in the form of disturbing physical, psychological and psychosomatic symptoms, such as in Michelle's mysterious skin rashes and rapid weight loss later in the book. As Jeffrey S. Victor observes of the causes of the Satanic Ritual Abuse panic, *Michelle Remembers* played a key role in its early development, first by providing a template for future accusations of nefarious cult activity, because it was 'the first known claim linking Satanism with the abuse of children'. Second, as Victor continues, by the early 1980s, the book was being used as a guide by police and prosecutors engaged in 'preparing cases against people accused of molesting children in day-care centres. It is also known that Michelle Smith and several other "survivors" met with parents and children involved in the famous McMartin case after the case was reported in the press'.[56] Like *Rosemary's Baby* and *The Exorcist*, the book depicted evil Satanic cultists secretly operating within secular, supposedly 'rational' mainstream society, albeit within a supposedly non-fictional context. *Michelle Remembers* also dramatised one of the most recognisable pop-psychological tropes of the 1950s, the so-called 'Pathological Mommy' figure identified by Scull. As Heller-Nicholas notes, while professional, 'rational' men such as Pazder

[55] Beck, *We Believe the Children*, p. 12.
[56] Jeffery S. Victor, *Satanic Panic: The Creation of a Contemporary Legend* (Chicago: Open Court, 1993), pp. 13–14.

'give Smith's story validation, the book makes clear time and again that women are ultimately to blame for this abuse. Failed mothers are directly responsible for the horrors that happen to this child, and the book ultimately argues that the only solution is a conscious return to the paternal'.[57] Michelle's neglectful mother Jessica is 'explicitly stated to be the single central factor responsible for the child's trauma', and 'Smith's greatest achievement, according to the book, isn't recovering from the torture at the hands of the cult, but in going to Pazder who rescues her from the failed monstrous maternal'.[58] Within this context, then, the psychoanalyst becomes the secular yet God-fearing saviour whose thoughtful and empathic treatment of his troubled patient allows her to confront the horrific truth so as to look forward to a future in which darks secrets have finally been exposed to the light.

Michelle Remembers marked a pinnacle for the psychoanalytic Gothic because it so brazenly combined familiar (and fictional) occult horror tropes with the language and the structure of the 'real-life' therapeutic recovery narrative. It also contributed to the escalating erosion of the once pervasive cultural authority afforded to Freudian concepts in the US. Although the era of Satanic Panic peaked between 1980 and 1985, by the end of the decade a new degree of scepticism and accountability had begun to emerge. 'As a national phenomenon', Beck observes, 'the ritual abuse hysteria broke down for good with the end of the second McMartin trial in 1990. Its decline unfurled slowly, with various detours and reversals, over the course of the next quarter-century.'[59] Pazder and Smith's account was subsequently picked apart and debunked by several high-profile publications, and is now widely accepted as a hoax.[60] Furthermore, as a powerful new generation of neuroleptic drugs such as SSRIs emerged, and as psychiatry in general moved away from the psychotherapeutic approach and towards more drug-led treatment regimens, the influence that psychoanalysis had once wielded in clinical sense rapidly waned – so much so that, as Scull notes, 'in most of the world, as a therapeutic intervention, psychoanalysis is moribund'.[61]

However, although much tempered by both time and scepticism, the profound influence that psychoanalytic concepts had upon the American popular Gothic during the post-war era still lingers. Stephen King, himself much shaped by the anxieties and cultural preoccupations of the 1950s, has always been very open about the profound influence that the fiction of

[57] Heller-Nicholas, 'The Only Word', p. 24.
[58] Heller-Nicholas, 'The Only Word', pp. 24–5. [59] Beck, *We Believe the Children*, p. 242.
[60] Heller-Nicholas, 'The Only Word', p. 28. [61] Scull, *Madness in Civilisation*, p. 325.

authors such as Matheson, Jackson, Bradbury and Bloch has had on his own writing. Although he seldom evokes psychoanalytic concepts as directly as some of his predecessors, one of his most consistent preoccupations has been the toxic emotional legacy of trauma inflicted in childhood. Indeed, Bruhm has observed that in King's work, as in other key contemporary Gothic texts such as Thomas Harris's *The Silence of the Lambs* (1988), adults are 'determined by the familial relations they experienced in childhood'.[62] Mistreated children and teenagers also recur again and again in his work. This is perhaps most obvious in *The Shining* (1977), in which we find out that Jack Torrance both loved and feared his violent father, and despite all efforts to the contrary, cannot help but re-enact the same relationship with his own son Danny. Even without telekinesis, Carrie White's desperate efforts to fit in with her classmates were always doomed to failure thanks to the warped upbringing that she received at the hands of her fanatical, vicious mother, and for the children of Derry, Maine, in *IT* (1986), the predatory attentions of the nightmarish entity that lives in the town's sewers sits alongside (but does not supersede) non-supernatural horrors such as abusive fathers, neglectful, grieving parents and overbearing mothers.

Although King has expressed doubts about the use of psychoanalysis as a form of psychiatric treatment, saying in one interview that 'I'm not a big fan of psychoanalysis: I think if you have mental problems what you need are good pills', he acknowledges in that same conversation the inherently cathartic process of getting one's most powerful fears and neuroses out into the open: 'But I do think that if you have things that bother you, things that are unresolved, the more that you talk about them, write about them, the less serious they become. At least that's how I see my work in retrospect.'[63] This layperson's sense of the 'talking cure' is no doubt one that Sigmund Freud himself would have appreciated, and further underlines the reasons why the dark side of American popular fiction and culture so readily absorbed psychoanalytic principles in the first place.

---

[62] Bruhm, 'Contemporary Gothic', p. 266.
[63] Tim Adams, 'The Stephen King Interview, Uncut and Unpublished', *The Guardian*, 14 September 2000 <www.theguardian.com/books/2000/sep/14/stephenking.fiction> (last accessed 22 June 2019).

3.10

Gothic and the Counterculture, 1958–Present

CATHERINE SPOONER

Strange Things

In September 1968, regular British *Vogue* columnist Polly Devlin returned from a year working for the magazine's sister publication in New York, and published a long article commenting on how, in her absence, the mood had changed:

> What bewildered me most and left me, to use a particularly apt American expression, *spaced*, was the extraordinary interest all over London in the supernatural, the eerie and the spooky, in magic and Merlin. Everywhere I heard a babble of warlocks and covens and Black Masses, of Glastonbury and Camelot; and lined up with this, inextricably mingled with it, was talk of Flying Saucers and Unidentified Flying Objects . . . I remembered a writer in America who has studied the subject talking of the resurgence of interest in it . . . She said that whenever people were bored with themselves or frightened, whenever the mass consciousness got desperate with its environment or felt it must escape, people looked to the sky without any faith and believed that they saw strange things.[1]

Devlin identifies this cultural turn as distinctively British, the only equivalent in New York being the 'enormous success of a horrifying book called *Rosemary's Baby*'.[2] It is true that the later 1960s in Britain produced a wealth of horror films, led by rival studios Amicus and Hammer. However, what manifested in Britain as a spooky mood finds its equivalent in the US as what Fredric Jameson calls 'the sixties gone toxic, a whole historical and countercultural "bad trip" in which psychic fragmentation is raised to a qualitatively new power'.[3] The idealism that fuelled the 1960s counterculture spawned a dark underside of violence and disappointment, one that encompassed the murders in 1969 of Hollywood star

---

[1] Polly Devlin, 'London Revisited', British *Vogue*, 15 September 1968, pp. 152–3 (p. 153).
[2] Devlin, 'London Revisited', p. 153.
[3] Fredric Jameson, *Postmodernism, or, The Cultural Logic of Late Capitalism* (London: Verso, 1991), p. 117.

Sharon Tate and six other people by Charles Manson's acolytes and Meredith Hunter, an 18-year-old African American, by Hell's Angels at the Altamont Festival. This mood informed texts that overtly worked within the horror genre, such as George A. Romero's *Night of the Living Dead* (1968), but also permeated many of the iconic countercultural texts of the late 1960s. *Easy Rider* (dir. Peter Fonda, 1969), the road movie that provides the quintessential expression of countercultural failure, ends with a literal bad trip in a New Orleans cemetery and senseless roadside murder.

It has become common to identify the end of the sixties as expressing this cultural turn towards a darker sensibility. If the earlier sixties, and particularly the period 1964–8, are seen as a period of widespread optimism and idealism, when London was swinging and San Francisco was full of gentle people with flowers in their hair, then the end of the sixties is often characterised as a time of violence, protest and paranoia.[4] The Tate–LaBianca murders, in particular, are commonly seen as a crisis point at which a darkening mood turned black, leading the way to a fully-fledged Gothic sensibility as the 1970s took hold. In *The White Album* (1979), Joan Didion wrote that 'Many people I know in Los Angeles believe that the Sixties ended abruptly on August 9, 1969, ended at the exact moment when word of the murders on Cielo Drive traveled like brushfire through the community, and in a sense this is true. The tension broke that day. The paranoia was fulfilled.'[5] The 1970s were widely recognised as a particularly dark decade: 'We live in Gothic times', Angela Carter famously asserted in 1974.[6] However, as Devlin's article shows, a Gothic cultural sensibility was already strongly in evidence when she returned to Britain in 1968, and its relationship with the counterculture can be traced still further back.

In his influential 1960 book *Love and Death in the American Novel*, reprinted and revised several times over the ensuing decade, Leslie A. Fiedler made a direct connection between countercultural dissent and the Gothic tradition: 'When the Beatniks emerge from their own retreats, bearded and blue-shaded and bagel in hand, to mock the "squares" of San Francisco ... they are playing the latest version of the game invented by "Monk" Lewis.'[7] This game, he clarified, was '*Épater la bourgeoisie*: this is the secret slogan of the tale

[4] For the 'popular optimism' of 1964–8, see Patricia Waugh, *Harvest of the Sixties: English Literature and Its Background 1960 to 1990* (Oxford: Oxford University Press, 1995), p. 5.
[5] Joan Didion, *The White Album* (London: Flamingo, 1993), p. 47.
[6] Angela Carter, 'Afterword to *Fireworks*', in Angela Carter, *Burning Your Boats: Collected Short Stories* (London: Chatto and Windus, 1995), pp. 460–1 (p. 460).
[7] Leslie A. Fiedler, *Love and Death in the American Novel* (New York: Criterion Books, 1960), p. 116.

of terror.'[8] Although it has no precise equivalent in English, the phrase, the clarion call of nineteenth-century French Decadence, is often roughly translated as 'to shock or scandalise the respectable middle classes'. Fiedler thus conceived of the Gothic novel in the revolutionary terms first conjured by the Marquis de Sade in *The Crimes of Love* (1800), and in doing so, he reframed it for the times. The figure of the rebel or outsider was crucial to the 1960s and found a ready-made template in the Fatal Man or Byronic hero. However, the 1960s was also a time when conventional ideas of the unified subject were put under pressure by a number of influences, from psychedelic drugs and the experimental anti-psychiatry of R. D. Laing to the wider forces of postmodernity embodied in, as Jameson suggests, the 'culture of the simulacrum' and the 'society of the spectacle'.[9] Here, again, Gothic provided a ready-made language. On the one hand, its imagery had already been claimed by the Surrealists as expressive of the darker reaches of the unconscious; on the other, its preoccupation with qualities such as indeterminacy, excess and paranoia anticipated postmodernism. As Allan Lloyd Smith notes, Gothic and postmodernism offer 'similar responses to the confusing new order – or should that be the new *disorder*?'[10]

The nature of the counterculture is to be not only outside the mainstream but against it. It is active, resistant, politicised. There are clear parallels between the counterculture and the historical understanding of Gothic derived from the Goths' overthrow of Rome in the fifth century AD and thus the challenge to neoclassical order. Indeed, this is literalised in Angela Carter's post-apocalyptic novel *Heroes and Villains* (1969), named after The Beach Boys' 1967 hit single, in which the 'Barbarians', a horde of ragtag hippies led by a renegade academic with more than a passing resemblance to LSD guru Timothy Leary, attack the polite compound of the 'Professors', the last repository of civilisation.[11] Of course, not all Gothic texts from the 1960s and early 1970s exhibit this conscious resistance; there was a booming market for both pulp horror and exploitation texts providing vicarious indulgence in the more sensational aspects of countercultural excess. Nevertheless, this chapter contends that throughout the 1960s and

[8] Fiedler, *Love and Death in the American Novel*, p. 116.
[9] Fredric Jameson, 'Periodizing the 60s', *Social Text* 9/10 (1984): 178–209 (p. 195). Jameson is summarising the work of Jean Baudrillard and Guy Debord.
[10] Allan Lloyd Smith, 'Postmodernism/Gothicism', in Victor Sage and Allan Lloyd Smith (eds), *Modern Gothic: A Reader* (Manchester: Manchester University Press, 1995), pp. 6–19 (p. 18).
[11] For a more detailed reading of *Heroes and Villains* in relation to the counterculture, see Catherine Spooner, '"Clothes Are Our weapons": Dandyism, Fashion and Subcultural Style in Angela Carter's fiction of the 1960s', in Marie Mulvey-Roberts (ed.), *The Arts of Angela Carter* (Manchester: Manchester University Press, 2019), pp. 166–82.

beyond, Gothic and the counterculture are in a conversation, and that the boundaries between texts with a developed aesthetic of resistance and those that merely depict it are often difficult to discern and, in a sense, not very interesting. The dissolution of distinctions between 'high' and 'low' culture is one of the markers of postmodernism, and also, yet again, one of the markers of the historical development of the Gothic.

Strikingly, there is, as yet, no sustained critical work on Gothic in the 1960s or its relationship with the counterculture. Nevertheless, Gothic is evident everywhere throughout the decade, from the pulp romance to the imagery of the bad trip, the popularity of Hammer horror to the occult revival. These manifestations are crucial to the critical enshrinement of Gothic as a subversive discourse in the later twentieth century and to the evolution of Goth subculture. Put simply, contemporary Gothic as we now know it starts here. This chapter commences the project of tracing some of its forms, focusing in particular on the Fatal Man and his passage through the decade. It begins in 1958, the year that Hammer Studios released *Dracula* (dir. Terence Fisher, known as *Horror of Dracula* in the USA), the first of its celebrated cycle of vampire films, and while it concurs with Jameson that the 1960s as a historical period came to an end in 1972–4, it gestures towards the period's legacy and afterlife in a number of more recent texts.[12]

Swinging Vampires

Bela Lugosi, the original Hollywood vampire, died in 1956, having been reduced in his final years to appearing in horror comedies and maverick director Ed Wood's low-budget exploitation fare. Two years later, Britain's Hammer Studios launched its revivification of what had become a moribund franchise, *Dracula*. There had been no major anglophone Dracula film since Universal's *House of Dracula* (dir. Erle C. Kenton, 1945), a monster mash-up movie also featuring Frankenstein's Monster and the Wolf Man. Stock was so low in the Gothic horror film at this point that Universal Studios signed over the copyright to its entire horror back catalogue. Hammer's revival of the story was an international box office hit and initiated a cycle of nine films through the 1960s and early 1970s, as well as a number of related vampire titles such as *Countess Dracula* (dir. Peter Sasdy, 1971). Stoker's vampire was, indeed, undead.

The film is striking for many reasons, including Christopher Lee's extraordinarily charismatic, urbane performance as the Count; the first use of fangs in an

---

[12] Jameson, 'Periodizing the 60s', p. 183.

anglophone film; and the hitherto unexplored opportunities provided by Technicolor to splash blood liberally over the screen.[13] The most important quality it brought to the vampire film, however, was sex. Among the scenes cut by the British Board of Film Classification for its original cinema release (later rediscovered in a Japanese print and restored in a DVD release of 2012) was one in which Mina (Melissa Stribling) responds ecstatically when Dracula drinks her blood. Even with a truncated version of this scene, however, the aura of scarcely repressed eroticism hangs over the film, and advertising posters at the time of release liberally exploited this: 'The terrifying lover who died – yet lived!' announced one; 'Who will be his bride tonight?' teasingly asked the American version.[14] A striking British poster in black and white accentuated with red perhaps goes furthest of all, declaring 'Every night he rises from his coffin-bed silently to seek the soft flesh, the warm blood he needs to keep himself alive!' (Fig. 10.1).[15] Even the standard slogan, 'Don't dare see it alone!', contains a subtle sexual promise. This combination of vampirism and sex would become increasingly more explicit as the 1960s wore on. David Pirie notes that the supernatural was in fact used as a smokescreen for sex in cinema of the period, as horror films could routinely get away with explicitly erotic images that the censors would not have allowed in cinema with a realist aesthetic.[16]

The success of the Hammer *Dracula*, Robert Mighall speculates, is due to the way that for the first time it reproduces the Victorian setting of the novel, and places within it a sexually attractive vampire who becomes the avatar of sexually liberated modernity. As Mighall argues,

> It is sexuality – its manifest absence in the typical Victorians who people these films, and its overbearing presence in the vampire and those whose libidos he liberates – that informs Hammer's reversal of the oppositions operating in Stoker's text. Hammer's Count Dracula is still an anachronism, but by virtue of his *modernity* not his atavism: it is his Victorian antagonists who now represent the Gothic past and all its repressive follies.[17]

---

[13] The first actor to wear vampire fangs on screen was Atif Kaptan as Dracula in *Drakula İstanbul'da* (*Dracula in Istanbul*, dir. Mehmet Muhtar, 1953). See Tugce Bicakci, 'The Origins of Turkish Gothic: The Adaptations of Stoker's *Dracula* in Turkish Literature and Film', *Studies in Gothic Fiction* 4:1/2, 57–69 (p. 63).

[14] Reproduced in Marcus Hearn, *The Art of Hammer: Posters from the Archives of Hammer Films* (London: Titan Books 2010), pp. 37, 39.

[15] Reproduced in Hearn, *The Art of Hammer*, p. 38.

[16] David Pirie, *The Vampire Cinema* (London: Quarto, 1977), p. 100.

[17] Robert Mighall, 'Vampires and Victorians: Count Dracula and the Return of the Repressive Hypothesis', in Gary Day (ed.), *Varieties of Victorianism: The Uses of a Past* (London: Palgrave Macmillan, 1998), pp. 236–49 (p. 239).

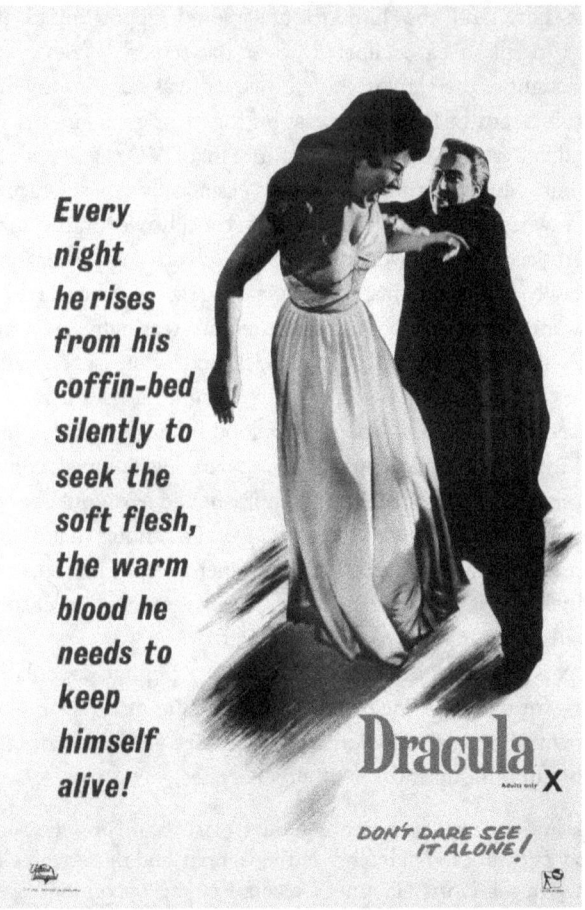

Fig.10.1: A poster for the British release of Terence Fisher's 1958 horror film, *Dracula*, starring Christopher Lee and featuring Valerie Gaunt. The film was retitled *Horror of Dracula* for the US release. (Photo by Movie Poster Image Art/Getty Images).

Lee's vampire thus spoke to a developing ethos of sexual liberation, and implicitly reversed conventional audience sympathies from the vampire's antagonists to the vampire himself. It also, however, marked a return to a Byronic model of vampirism that had been forged in John William Polidori's *The Vampyre* (1819). Simon Bainbridge points out that in Polidori's vampire tale, inspired by his employer Lord Byron, 'the encounter with [the vampire] Ruthven would seem to inspire women to an indulgence of sexuality that is itself presented as natural; it is the socially defined self that is cast aside as "a mask"'.[18] Bringing women to orgasmic frenzy through his bite, Lee's sexually rapacious Count merges Stoker's fiend with Polidori's vampire as ladykiller.

The Byronic hero was undergoing a revival in the late 1950s. Mario Praz's *The Romantic Agony* (1933), which had popularised the concept, was, significantly, republished in 1957 after many years out of print, reissued again in a mass market edition in 1960 and regularly reprinted throughout the 1960s. Praz's description of the Fatal Man as one who 'dreams of perfecting the world by committing crimes' was perfectly in tune with the mixture of idealism and rebellion that distinguished representations of masculinity throughout the period.[19] In *Love and Death in the American Novel*, Fiedler identified the revolutionary impulse of Gothic fiction in the way that the Gothic elided the myths of Faust and Don Juan, casting these characters fairly transparently as figures of countercultural dissent:

> Don Juan and Faust alike are former villains of the orthodox mind made heroes in an age of unorthodoxy, Promethean or Satanic figures; and both come to stand for the lonely individual (the writer himself!) challenging the mores of bourgeois society, making patent to all men the ill-kept secret that the codes by which they live are archaic survivals without point or power.[20]

In placing the Faustian pact and the Byronic hero securely at the centre of the Gothic, Fiedler masculinises it, leaving the persecuted maidens of the female Gothic to be rescued by the next generation of feminist Gothic critics. The Gothic romances of Victoria Holt and her pulp imitators, which flourished in the 1960s and 1970s, provide an alternative version of Gothic in the 1960s, but could not be revalued through revolt and therefore were not appropriated by the counterculture in the same way (see Lucie Armitt's chapter in this volume for a more extended discussion of these works). It was male Gothic, the Gothic of rebellion, exile and paranoia, that resonated most strongly with countercultural sensibilities.

The revival of the Byronic hero in popular culture closely coincided with the publication of what many critics still regard as the greatest biography of Byron, Leslie A. Marchand's three-volume *Byron: A Biography* in 1957. Marchand's sympathetic and scholarly work restored Byron to his full seriousness as a writer and as a cultural figure, following decades of speculation

---

[18] Simon Bainbridge, 'Lord Ruthven's Power: Polidori's "The Vampyre", Doubles and the Byronic Imagination', *The Byron Journal* 34:1 (2006): 21–34 (p. 24).
[19] Mario Praz, *The Romantic Agony* (London: Fontana Library, 1960), p. 97.
[20] Fiedler, *Love and Death in the American Novel*, p. 113.

and gossip over his alleged incest with his half-sister Augusta. Because of prevailing 1950s cultural mores, Marchand's account made little reference to Byron's sexual relationships with men, focusing instead on those with women – a feature that was notably changed in the condensed and updated version of 1970, and which pointed to a radical shift in attitudes over the course of the 1960s. Nevertheless, as Paul Douglass points out, despite Marchand's reticence in this respect, shortly after his book came out, Byron's sexual proclivities were furiously debated in the *Times Literary Supplement*.[21] Over the course of the 1960s, at least three more biographies of Byron were published: M. K. Joseph's *Byron the Poet* in 1964, Francis Michael Doherty's *Byron* in 1968; and Paul Graham Trueblood's *Lord Byron* in 1969. Byron was the Romantic poet of the age, and while this was partly due to a fresh appraisal of his work, it was also because his sexual adventuring was in keeping with emerging ideas of free love, while his dandyism anticipated 1960s models of masculinity.

Douglass suggests that the Byron story is 'unified around themes of sex, violence, genius, and adventure, or – in the case of hostile biographers – sex, violence, cruelty, and hypocrisy'.[22] From the moment of its publication, Polidori's *The Vampyre* was read biographically as a thinly veiled portrait of his erstwhile employer, a tendency no doubt facilitated by the fact that the novella was initially misattributed to Byron himself. Byronic vampires of the 1960s, somewhat unsurprisingly, tend to follow Polidori in embodying the hostile version of the Byron story. As in Polidori, vampirism becomes a vehicle for a thinly veiled critique of society and its mores. Ken Gelder argues in *Reading the Vampire* that 'Polidori's story seems to suggest that "society" itself is vampirish; its aristocratic representatives prey on the people wherever they go.'[23] In 1960s vampire fiction, this critique is translated into new social contexts reflecting rapidly shifting social formations, in particular the new class structures bubbling up through the ideological investment in meritocracy in both Britain and the United States. Like Polidori's Lord Ruthven, the Byronic vampire in the 1960s is an ambivalent figure who simultaneously stimulates desire and moral revulsion, and who acts as a catalyst to the illumination of society's flaws. This critique may equally be directed at the establishment or at the counterculture itself.

---

[21] Paul Douglass, 'Byron's Life and His Biographers', in Drummond Bone (ed.), *The Cambridge Companion to Byron* (Cambridge: Cambridge University Press, 2004), pp. 7–26 (p. 22).
[22] Douglass, 'Byron's Life and His Biographers', p. 7.
[23] Ken Gelder, *Reading the Vampire* (London: Routledge, 1994), p. 34.

Polidori's influence was marked in what may be the first vampire novel of the 1960s, Simon Raven's *Doctors Wear Scarlet* (1960). This novel has not dated very well: it is curiously restrained until its final pages, and rooted in a model of public school and Oxbridge-educated, white, upper-middle-class fraternity, which it hysterically defends against the dangers of women, foreigners and homosexuals. However, its debt to Byron is explicit; the anti-hero Richard Fountain, already on the route to vampirism, is described as looking 'rather like a picture ... of your Lord Byron. Handsome, and proud like I said. But all the time looking so dead'.[24] Byron's Greek travels, moreover, are the frame for Richard's own travels in Greece: a guidebook entry on the island of Hydra informs the party of travellers, 'It is said ... that the poet Lord Byron, on his return from his first journey in Greece, surprised several of his friends by references to some indelicate scenes which he vouchsafed had been described to him in Athens by a trader newly arrived from the Aegean islands ... '[25] Byron is used to authenticate the more outlandish parts of the narrative and to provide a flavour of sexual scandal and the occult. He also provides a clue for those in the know: at this point, what exactly is the matter with Richard has not yet been disclosed, but a savvy reader might grasp the reference and surmise the source of his affliction. Richard follows in the footsteps of Byron's own gothicised heroes such as Manfred in his search for forbidden knowledge, here located among the pagan rites and ceremonies of ancient Greece. But Byron is also a model from which Richard falls short: he is like a 'picture' of Byron rather than the man himself, and it is revealed that his sexual impotence, a crass version of Byron's club foot, has led him to vampiric temptation.

As the novel goes on, it proposes a psycho-sexual interpretation of vampirism based in sado-masochism: vampire expert Dr Erik Holmstrom of the British Museum informs the investigators that 'the vampire is in fact a living human being with a peculiar type of sado-sexual perversion ... the victims of vampires tend to be of a masochistic type – and like most masochists, capable of assuming a sadistic role in their turn.'[26] Richard's sexuality is non-phallic and, in that respect, queer, and presents a threat to social norms. The role of the group of friends searching for Richard is to contain his wayward masculinity, to repatriate him to England and to shore up the deficiencies in the masculine ideal that is suggested by his impotence and sexual deviance. They are doomed to failure because the 'flaw' in Richard that leaves him primed

---

[24] Simon Raven, *Doctors Wear Scarlet* (Kelly Bray, Cornwall: House of Stratus, 2001), p. 133.
[25] Raven, *Doctors Wear Scarlet*, pp. 120–1; ellipsis in the original.
[26] Raven, *Doctors Wear Scarlet*, p. 204.

for vampiric seduction has been implanted not by the stereotypical foreign female other, as it first appears, but by the paternal attentions of the manipulative Cambridge don, Walter Goodrich: 'After all', one character comments, 'what has Doctor Goodrich been to him these many years other than a spiritual vampire?'[27] As in Polidori, society itself is revealed to have a vampiric quality. Vampirism is produced by the very upper-middle-class English masculinity that seeks to stamp it out.

The Byronic vampire received a rather different treatment in Jane Gaskell's 1964 novel, *The Shiny Narrow Grin*. Gaskell makes the critique of society underlying the Polidorian vampire story much more overt, and as such the novel is a far more radical work – one that has been unjustly neglected by contemporary criticism. Gaskell was precociously talented, publishing her first novel at the age of fourteen, and was still only twenty-three when she published *The Shiny Narrow Grin*. The book is written with an extraordinary, clear-eyed viciousness combined with sumptuousness of language – like a novel by Angela Carter's bratty younger sister – although in fact Gaskell and Carter were almost the same age. Fan reviews sometimes describe it as the first Young Adult vampire novel – a forerunner to Stephenie Meyer's *Twilight* (2005) and its ilk – and there is some truth to this.[28] It follows its disaffected teenage heroine Terry as she boldly cheats and manipulates her way through the unprepossessing boys on her local Mod scene, lusting all the while after the mysterious character that she calls 'The Boy'. The novel is set within a precisely delineated youth subculture that is driven by clothes, drugs, dancing and sex, and which remains opaque to adults. This is underlined in dialogue ripe with contemporary slang ('"You aren't half moony these days", Fishfinger said in a low Billy Fury growl').[29] Vampires are aligned with this youth culture through consumption of popular media and, as such, they help to articulate its alienation from an uncomprehending parent culture. Terry says of her teacher, 'She's not a teenager, she doesn't go to Hammer films or read horror comics ... The idea of a vampire comes as more of a shock to her than me.'[30]

The landscape of the novel combines death and decay with a hectic, lurid modernity that is embodied in the cemetery that Terry visits with The Boy:

---

[27] Raven, *Doctors Wear Scarlet*, p. 207.
[28] The description of *The Shiny Narrow Grin* as the first YA vampire novel, widely repeated on the Internet, appears to have come from the YA writer Annette Curtis Klause, who describes it as 'a real young adult book before that category existed'. See Annette Curtis Klause, *The Silver Kiss* (New York: Delacorte, 2001), p. 1.
[29] Jane Gaskell, *The Shiny Narrow Grin* (London: Hodder and Stoughton, 1964), p. 100.
[30] Gaskell, *The Shiny Narrow Grin*, p. 124.

Behind them the rows of crosses and angels and whited sepulchres stretched between the vistas of the giant jetty arches and into the velvet invisibility of the cemetery's far reaches. Sodium street-lighting and neon advertising-lights flickered over their faces, changing from ghastly green to vivid cerise to twinkly tangerine. Wrigley's spearmint suited the boy best.[31]

The Boy similarly combines a connection to the decaying world of the past with the modernity of youth. This is particularly embodied through his attire. He tells Terry that after decades of loneliness, 'Now my clothes are right again. Now I can mingle. They like my velvet collar, my leather coat, my elastic-sided boots, my fringe, my side-whiskers.'[32] In the 1950s and 1960s, male dandyism was popularised in working-class communities through the influence first of New Edwardian or Teddy Boy and then Mod style. By the mid-1960s, the fashion for vintage was born as the mass clearance of pre-war housing led to the market being flooded with cheap, second-hand clothing, helping to define the distinctive looks associated with 'swinging London'. Both the Regency and the Edwardian periods exerted particular influence on menswear. In popular TV show *Adam Adamant Lives!* (1966–7), an Edwardian gentleman spy is cryogenically frozen by his arch-nemesis and reawakens in the swinging sixties, where he appears to be an anachronism but actually is wildly fashionable. The 1960s, therefore, was the perfect era for the Byronic vampire to flourish. Its time had come round; its clothes were 'right again'.

The Boy is attracted to Terry in Gaskell's novel because he recognises a lack of humanity in her that corresponds to his own. 'I realise you're the least human type I've ever found', he tells her. She, on the other hand, identifies her shallowness and disaffection as symptomatic of the time: 'You're wrong. I've never met anyone my age much different from me.'[33] Nevertheless, The Boy's respect for Terry's consent and his persistent affection provides him with more integrity than any other character in the novel, making him a different kind of Byronic vampire: the damned romantic hero who anticipates the sympathetic vampire that would emerge more fully later in the 1960s with Barnabas Collins of the television soap opera *Dark Shadows* (1966–71). Terry is attracted to him because he seems to embody an idealism that is absent from the hypocritical friends and family who surround her: 'I never met anyone yet, not in this world, who'd stick to their ideals when it's easy not to.'[34] Again, as in Polidori, the vampire's presence reveals the hollowness and the emptiness of the social scene through which he moves.

---

[31] Gaskell, *The Shiny Narrow Grin*, p. 36. [32] Gaskell, *The Shiny Narrow Grin*, p. 126.
[33] Gaskell, *The Shiny Narrow Grin*, p. 126. [34] Gaskell, *The Shiny Narrow Grin*, p. 127.

As the 1960s wore on, so menswear became more overtly Byronic and vampires became increasingly associated with sex, drugs and the occult. In the ten years that elapsed between *Doctors Wear Scarlet* and its film adaptation, *Incense for the Damned* (dir. Robert Hartford-Davis, 1970; known as *Bloodsuckers* in the USA), the vampire as avatar of modernity becomes directly associated with the counterculture. This is heavily underlined in an expository speech in the film in which one character explains, 'The provost to Richard is a symbol of the establishment, and the establishment, to Richard, destroys, castrates.'[35] *Incense for the Damned* condenses the first third of the novel into six minutes and follows this with a seven-minute-long, psychedelic, Satanic orgy in which the participants are overtly shown to be smoking joints and ingesting pills. One of the characters reveals that the occult has permeated English society: 'Only a year back, a man was sacrificed in a London park. You've got your witches' covens in Mayfair, voodoo in Soho – how do you explain that?'[36] Richard's deranged speech about individual freedom at a formal Cambridge dinner becomes a bizarre attack on the stifling properties of academia, in which the scarlet-clad dons are the vampires:

> the academic world dehumanises us, and we become its natural dependents. Love me, says the academic, and do exactly as I tell you . . .
> But the gods – the gods have given us freedom, my friends. Do not be trapped by the petty schemes of academic hirelings, the thieves who come to take your souls, sitting among you now, smooth deceivers in scarlet gowns, preparing as soon as they leave this table to leech on to you.[37]

The Byronic vampire's realisation as an avatar of modernity is complete, and yet the film's confused politics cannot decide whether Richard is the hero or villain – perhaps, indeed, this is the point. The film takes on classic exploitation qualities of warning against the dangers of countercultural excess while vicariously indulging in their depiction.

These exploitation qualities are vividly realised in a clutch of films from the early 1970s that depict vampires preying on members of the new counterculture. *Count Yorga, Vampire* (dir. Bob Kelljan, 1970) and Hammer's *Dracula AD 1972* (dir. Alan Gibson, 1972) show groups of groovy young people dabbling in the occult as an equivalent thrill to crashing parties and congregating in neon-lit coffee bars, recalling Devlin's fashionable 'babble of warlocks and covens

---

[35] *Incense for the Damned*. Dir. Robert Hartford-Davis. Lucinda Films/Titan International Productions, Titan Films Distribution Ltd. 1970.
[36] *Incense for the Damned*.   [37] *Incense for the Damned*.

and Black Masses'. A character in *Dracula AD 1972* even refers derisively to the proposed 'bacchanal with Beelzebub' as 'Sunday supplement stuff'.[38] Of course, the séances and Satanic rituals provide a gateway for the vampire, and the bright young things find themselves meeting a familiar fate. Here, the vampire retains his ancient allure; the dandyish frilled shirts are worn by unimaginatively anagrammed wannabe Johnny Alucard (Christopher Neame) rather than Christopher Lee's dignified Dracula. In the sequel, *The Satanic Rites of Dracula* (dir. Alan Gibson, 1973), this is revised as Dracula returns as a modern property magnate who has mastered the ways of capitalism.

Frivolous though they may seem, these films have a direct connection to current events. *Dracula AD 1972* was allegedly inspired by the case of the Highgate Vampire, in which a vampire was supposedly encountered in the historic London cemetery following the desecration of graves and other supposed evidence of Satanic rituals, a series of events that Bill Ellis identifies as drawing on distinctively English folkloric traditions.[39] The Tate–LaBianca murders, too, can be seen to begin to infiltrate vampire mythology. In *Dracula AD 1972*, Inspector Murray (Michael Coles) considers, 'Could be a cult murder – there's been a spate of them in the States' and finally chalks up the murders to a 'criminally insane killer'.[40] In the sequel to *Count Yorga*, entitled *The Return of Count Yorga* (dir. Bob Kelljan, 1971), the link becomes still more explicit as the titular vampire keeps a harem of brides who break into a house and massacre a family on his account. The messaging is confused, as both Yorga and his victims could be associated with the counterculture; however, for Sorcha Ní Fhlainn, both Yorga films articulate 'a conservative backlash against the countercultural movement in [their] destruction of an idealistic youth'.[41]

By the end of the 1960s, the Byronic vampire was firmly established as countercultural icon. This was the cultural climate out of which later rebellious vampires would emerge – most notably, Anne Rice's Louis and Lestat from her 1976 novel *Interview With the Vampire*, but also David from *The Lost Boys* (dir. Joel Schumacher, 1987) and the Goth vampires of Poppy Z. Brite's *Lost Souls* (1992). Even Edward Cullen in Meyer's *Twilight*, with his obdurate

---

[38] *Dracula AD 1972*. Dir. Alan Gibson. Hammer Films, Columbia Warner Distributors. 1972.
[39] See Bill Ellis, 'The Highgate Cemetery Vampire Hunt: The Anglo-American Connection in Satanic Cult Lore', *Folklore* 104:1/2 (1993): 13–39 (p. 24).
[40] *Dracula AD 1972*.
[41] Sorcha Ní Fhlainn, *Postmodern Vampires: Film, Fiction, and Popular Culture* (London: Palgrave Macmillan, 2019), p. 27.

idealism and his revolt against the vampire establishment represented by the Volturi, is a version of the 1960s countercultural vampire – albeit reunited with the brooding hero of the pulp romance. Vampires, however, were not the only manifestation of the era's fascination with the Byronic hero: this cultural figure also appeared in more overtly Satanic form.

Lucifer Rising

A striking feature of Gothic of the later 1960s is its flirtation with the occult. *Dracula AD 1972* was typical in this respect; representations of witches' covens, Satanic cults and pagan rites were ubiquitous in popular culture. This was, to some degree, the culmination of a wave of interest begun in the nineteenth century with James Frazer's *The Golden Bough* (1890) and the formation of mystical societies such as The Hermetic Order of the Golden Dawn (1887–1903). In 1951, the repeal of the Witchcraft Act of 1735 in the United Kingdom enabled the contemporary practice of ritual magic to become more visible, while Gerald Gardner's books *Witchcraft Today* (1954) and *The Meaning of Witchcraft* (1959) introduced the modern religion that would become known as Wicca to the world. Wicca, as Gardner formulated it, was based on Margaret Murray's theory that the medieval and early modern practice of witchcraft demonstrated the survival of a pre-Christian, pagan religion – a theory now widely discredited and, indeed, not even credited by the majority of Murray's academic peers. Gardner also drew on the works of notorious occultist and magician Aleister Crowley, who was to become widely influential in countercultural thought (see also David Punter's chapter in this volume). Gardner's modern witches were generally benign, but other orders, such as the Church of Satan founded by Anton LaVey in San Francisco in 1966, were decidedly more ambivalent, in their mixture of occult beliefs and right-wing philosophies if nothing else. Ritual magic was, like the use of psychedelic drugs, a way of opening the self up to the infinite and inviting transformative psychological experiences. Like the use of psychedelic drugs, however, it attracted a disproportionate number of fanatics, and carried a certain amount of risk.

Within the iconography deployed by contemporary occultists, Satan took a leading role. 'In the beginning was the Moon, Diana. Her lover was the Dawn, Lucifer', began *The Legend of the Witches* (dir. Malcolm Leigh, 1970), a documentary heavily influenced by Murray, and which featured controversial Wiccan couple Alex and Maxine Sanders performing a Black

Mass.[42] Since John Milton's *Paradise Lost* (1667–74), Lucifer has occupied an ambivalent position in Western culture as rebel angel, agent of the Fall and bringer of light. Again, Byronic models of masculinity resonate strongly with countercultural imagery. In 1821 the Romantic poet Robert Southey took aim at Byron in an attack on what he called the 'Satanic school' of poetry, abjuring 'Men of diseased hearts and depraved imaginations, who ... labour to make others as miserable as themselves.'[43] Byron, as Fred Parker points out, characteristically portrays '"Satanic" protagonists ... charismatic yet profoundly isolated figures, exiles or outlaws from contemporary society.'[44] A sense of alienation is fundamental to these characters: 'the root meaning of Satan, Milton reminds us, is Adversary, one who stands opposite'.[45] Satanic protagonists in this mould are a staple of Romantic-era Gothic literature, with prominent examples including Mary Shelley's *Frankenstein* (1818; 1931) and Charles Robert Maturin's *Melmoth the Wanderer* (1820). Unsurprisingly, the motif is prominently revived in countercultural Gothic.

The countercultural potential of the Satanic protagonist finds early expression in William Burroughs' Beat classic *Naked Lunch* (1959), a book that is significant here for the way in which it combines outsiderdom with the fragmentation of consciousness through the use of psychotropic drugs – in this case, primarily heroin, rather than the psychedelics favoured later in the 1960s. David Punter suggests that despite its lack of traditional Gothic props, Burroughs's work is more intrinsically Gothic than other works of the period that are often given the label: 'The junkie is an inverted Gothic hero: he searches for escape, but is condemned to find and live with a truth which he never wanted to know.'[46] The tormented stream of images is 'not really a narrative at all but an attempt to conjure an expressionist view of the universe as nightmare'.[47] Gothic imagery permeates the junkie's milieu: addicts are 'spectral janitors, grey as ashes, phantom porters sweeping out dusty halls'.[48] Meanwhile, the predatory qualities of a narcotics agent are

---

[42] *The Legend of the Witches*. Dir. Malcolm Leigh. Border Film Productions / Negus Fancey, Border Film Productions. 1970.

[43] Robert Southey, Preface to *A Vision of Judgement*, quoted in Fred Parker, 'Between Satan and Mephistopheles: Byron and the Devil', *The Cambridge Quarterly* 35:1 (2006): 1–29 (p. 1).

[44] Parker, 'Between Satan and Mephistopheles', p. 1

[45] Parker, 'Between Satan and Mephistopheles', p. 1.

[46] David Punter, *The Literature of Terror Volume 2: The Modern Gothic* (London: Longman, 1996), p. 133.

[47] Punter, *The Literature of Terror Volume 2*, p. 133.

[48] William Burroughs, *Naked Lunch* (London: Penguin, 2015), p. 5.

tinged with a hallucinatory surrealism: 'Like a vampire bat he gives off a narcotic effluvium, a dark green mist that anesthetizes his victims and renders them helpless in his enveloping presence.'[49]

From Burroughs onwards, then, Gothic provides a ready-made language for the bad trip. Roger Corman's exploitation film *The Trip* (1967), for example, follows Paul Groves (Peter Fonda) as he takes LSD for the first time. When Paul's trip turns dark, this is conveyed by an establishing shot of a stereotypical haunted mansion, in which he subsequently finds himself wandering through corridors and staircases in a classic formal dinner suit. This is intercut with scenes in which he is apparently tortured and murdered by a terrifying religious cult. At various points in the film, he finds himself pursued by mysterious, hooded figures on horseback, recalling the Red Death in Corman's earlier, proto-psychedelic Edgar Allan Poe adaptation, *The Masque of the Red Death* (1964), and, in turn, its inspiration in Ingmar Bergman's *The Seventh Seal* (1957). Masks and disguises permeate the film throughout. The scenes are disconnected, dream-like – they do not tell their own Gothic story but contribute to the depiction of Paul's fragmented psyche. Up to a point, the film draws on Freudian dream-logic, but the overwhelming momentum of the LSD experience does not allow time for analysis; it simply revels in the onrushing of images. The latent content suggested – Paul's thinly repressed feelings for his estranged wife – is rather too obvious to be truly latent. In the Gothic–psychedelic experience, the 'sickening descent into disintegration' that Chris Baldick identifies as a key feature of the Gothic tale overwhelms the narrative, while returning past and claustrophobic enclosure become internalised and primarily psychological.[50]

If Gothic provided a symbolic language for psychic fragmentation within psychedelia, however, then psychedelia likewise provided a ready aesthetics for the weird, strange and supernatural in the Gothic. Numerous horror films of the later 1960s use psychedelic sequences to heighten intensity at moments of supernatural encounter. In *The Devil Rides Out* (dir. Terence Fisher, 1967), for example, the arrival of the Angel of Death on horseback is shot in slow motion, from below and only partially filling the camera lens so that it appears magnified in size while, as the tension mounts, the film is partly reversed back and forth to create an unnatural, repetitive sense of motion; this gives the sequence a hallucinatory, dream-like feel. Even more overtly, in *Curse of the Crimson Altar* (dir. Vernon Sewell, 1968), the onset of the dream

---

[49] Burroughs, *Naked Lunch*, p. 17.
[50] Chris Baldick, 'Introduction', in Chris Baldick (ed.), *The Oxford Book of Gothic Tales* (Oxford: Oxford University Press, 1992), pp. xi–xxiii (p. xix).

sequences in which Barbara Steele's vengeful witch tries to induce the protagonist to sign a demonic compact are signalled with shifting kaleidoscopic patterns and distorted electronic sounds, while the dreams themselves feature outlandish make-up and costumes, vividly coloured lighting and voice reverb to convey a sense of nightmarish otherworldliness.

This new Gothic–psychedelic language came together in two masterpieces of the late 1960s, Donald Cammell and Nicholas Roeg's film *Performance* (produced in 1968 but not released until 1970) and Kenneth Anger's *Lucifer Rising* (shot between 1968 and 1972 but released in 1980). Both were fashioned within the same countercultural *milieu*: Mick Jagger and Anita Pallenberg (Rolling Stones guitarist Keith Richards's girlfriend) starred in *Performance* while Donald Cammell, Chris Jagger (Mick's brother) and Marianne Faithfull (Mick's girlfriend) starred in *Lucifer Rising*. Each film frames and informs the other. *Lucifer Rising* enacts a kind of ritual magic, inducing a trance-like state through a series of mystical invocations and psychedelic images. Anger conceived of film-making as part of his magical practice and believed that film had 'the potential, when properly used, to invoke primal forces, perhaps even demons' which could affect both film-makers and audience alike.[51] In *Lucifer Rising*, Isis (Myriam Gibril) and Osiris (Donald Cammell) perform ceremonial incantations and Lilith (Faithfull) wanders among desert ruins dressed in a black velvet hooded cloak, silver lamé dress and platform shoes. Meanwhile Lucifer (Chris Jagger in a part originally intended to be played by his brother, Mick) awakes, bathes and rises, presaging a new state of consciousness that is signalled by the appearance of a set of luminous flying saucers over an ancient Egyptian temple. The film thus invokes Gothic imagery – ancient ruins, ritual magic, Satanic exile, Lucifer covered in blood, naked souls swarming around a monstrous Satan – but deploys them in the service of transcendent spiritual ends.

The magical aura that Anger sought to conjure up also hung around *Performance*, which Iain Sinclair describes as a 'psychic vortex' harnessing similar demonic energies, resulting in myths of death and destruction pursuing its cast and crew.[52] *Performance* has not generally been read as a Gothic film, but rather as an arthouse crime drama. Nevertheless it illustrates better than almost any other text of the 1960s the coincidence of the Gothic imagination with the psychedelic experience. It is a film with two distinct

---

[51] Kenneth Anger, quoted in James Riley, *The Bad Trip: Dark Omens, New Worlds and the End of the Sixties* (London: Icon, 2019), p. 221.

[52] Iain Sinclair, 'Who Cares for the Caretaker?', in Iain Sinclair and Rachel Lichtenstein, *Rodinsky's Room* (London: Granta, 2000), pp. 131–51 (p. 141).

parts: the first is set in the underworld of London's East End, where violent gangster Chas (James Fox) works for an organised crime syndicate based on the Krays; the second in a decadent house in Notting Hill in which a reclusive former rock star, Turner (Jagger) lives in a bohemian *ménage-à-trois* with two women, Pherber (Pallenberg) and Lucy (Michèle Breton). After Chas kills another gangster sent to execute him, he overhears a conversation suggesting Turner has a room to let and decides to hide out there. The two settings are united by a vision of 1960s London as decaying and grim. Litter blows in the streets of the East End, while the disintegrating mansions of Notting Hill gradually fall into decrepitude. The *mise en scène* of Turner's house is opulent and cluttered at the same time; it is littered with the modish detritus of the Moroccan souk, and the Georgian grandeur is customised with painted murals and pinned-up photographs. It suggests a magnificent past that has been carelessly discarded (a reflection of its owner) but which, in its sumptuous ruin, continues to confine its inhabitants. The structures of history and all that it entails – class, taste – can be desecrated but still must be lived in.

Jagger was, at the time of filming, fresh from recording *Beggars Banquet*, widely celebrated as one of The Rolling Stones' greatest albums. The opening track was 'Sympathy for the Devil', in which he took the point of view of Lucifer, 'a man of wealth and taste' who has lived for thousands of years and who was present at a series of historical atrocities. The song turns in the third verse, as Jagger reveals the audience's complicity in Lucifer's crimes: 'I shouted out "Who killed the Kennedys?" / Well after all, it was you and me.'[53] Jagger also plays Turner in Satanic mode. He is a tempter who, along with fallen Eve figure Pherber, draws Chas into his world of fluid sexuality and free love, and towards self-knowledge. As they feed Chas with psychoactive mushrooms, he experiences increasing psychological fragmentation: in one striking scene Pherber holds a hand mirror so that half of her own face is superimposed over half of his, creating a transgendered composite. However, he is also Turner's double. Over the course of the film, Turner and Chas begin to merge identities. Chas dons a long-haired wig and a velvet smoking jacket that make him resemble a fancy-dress version of Turner. Conversely, in a surreal and profoundly disconcerting sequence, Turner appears in a sharply tailored suit in the gang boss's lair, and sings 'Memo From Turner', a track revelling in the grotesque violence of the gangster *milieu*, while forcing the gangsters to remove their clothes (Fig. 10.2). The

---

[53] The Rolling Stones, 'Sympathy for the Devil', *Beggars Banquet*, Decca Records, 1968.

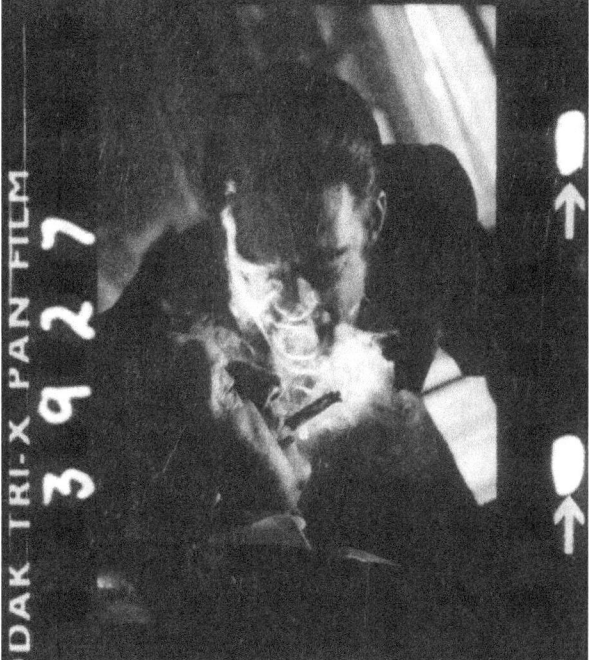

Fig.10.2: Mick Jagger pictured in the 1968 Donald Cammell and Nicholas Roeg film *Performance*. (Photo by Robert Whitaker/Getty Images)

song closes with a line that recalls the Satanic complicity of 'Sympathy for the Devil': 'Why gentlemen, you all work for me.'[54] In one shot, Chas's and Turner's faces are superimposed over one another. In another, the two awake beside one another in bed. Ultimately, in the ambiguous closing sequence, Chas shoots Turner and the camera follows the bullet into his head, where it smashes a portrait of Argentinian writer Jorge Luis Borges, whose work has been referenced repeatedly in the film. In his brief essay 'Borges and I' (1960), Borges presents his writing self as his own uncanny double, with whom he is inextricably merging. His words resonate with the uncanny conflation of Chas and Turner:

> Besides, I am destined to perish, definitively, and only some instant of myself can survive in him. Little by little, I am giving over everything to him ...

[54] *Performance*. Dir. Donald Cammell and Nicholas Roeg. Goodtimes Enterprises, Warner Brothers. 1970.

> Thus my life is a flight and I lose everything and everything belongs to oblivion, or to him.
>
> I do not know which of us has written this page.[55]

Finally, Chas leaves the house with his mobster boss and is seated in the back of a white Rolls Royce, to be driven to an unknown destination. As the car leaves the city and drives through the English countryside, the face looking out of the car window is Turner's.

For Colin MacCabe, it is in the final fusion of Chas and Turner that the countercultural potential of *Performance* lies, because it

> brings together the two elements in English society which have the power and the energy to transform 'old England'. As East End hood and fading rock star merge in a genuine union which makes a mockery of all the film's sordid alliances, we enter into another realm of social possibility.[56]

This optimistic reading is overlaid with a much darker one, however, in which the Satanic–Byronic doubling between Chas and Turner results in utter psychic fragmentation and breakdown. Bainbridge writes of Aubrey's fascination with Lord Ruthven in Polidori's *The Vampyre* that it is 'in precisely this power of doubling that the danger of Byronism lies, for it leads to destabilisation of the self and an unleashing of repressed desires that proves fatal not only to the Byromaniac but also to those he loves'.[57] *Performance*'s Gothic is thus, in some respects, also a devastating critique of countercultural masculinity in all its solipsistic tendencies.

Countercultural Afterlives

Jagger's Byronic reputation had an unexpected afterlife in Ken Russell's *Gothic* (1986). Russell's film dramatises the infamous, highly mythologised night at the Villa Diodati in 1816 when Mary Shelley's *Frankenstein* and Polidori's *The Vampyre* were conceived as a hysterical, drug-fuelled, partner-swapping bad trip. In doing so, he reroutes the primal scene of English Gothic through *Performance*. In a curiously circular movement, Byron, the inspiration for a thousand rock-star poses, becomes refracted through the motif of the reclusive rock star. The summer of 1816 is reimagined in terms of free

---

[55] Jorge Luis Borges, 'Borges and I', trans. by James E. Irby, in Jorge Luis Borges, *Labyrinths*, edited by Donald A. Yates and James E. Irby (Harmondsworth: Penguin, 1970), pp. 282–3.
[56] Colin MacCabe, *Performance* (London: BFI/Bloomsbury, 2020), p. 81.
[57] Bainbridge, 'Lord Ruthven's Power', p. 27.

love, psychedelia, occult experimentation and psychological disintegration. The Villa Diodati comes to resemble the Villa Nellcôte, the mansion on the Côte d'Azur where the Stones lived during tax exile in the summer of 1971 and composed their iconic album *Exile on Main Street* (1972).

The opening and closing sequences of the film decentre its main narrative, revealing its status as myth and creating explicit links between the past and present. The opening scene shows nineteenth-century British tourists gawping through a telescope at Byron's house on the lake – something that happened in actuality – and allows the audience to share a point-of-view shot with them, framing Polidori (Timothy Spall) at the window. This signals to the viewer that what they are seeing is what the tourists are seeing, a view filtered through myth and gossip, and not the real Byron, Mary, Percy, Polidori and Claire – they are likewise voyeurs, indulging in the fantasies that these men and women inspire. In the final sequence, a picnic outside the Villa attended by the main characters dissolves into a shot of modern tourists tramping through the same space, as a diegetic voiceover provided by a tour boat guide informs the viewer of the characters' subsequent fates. Meanwhile, a newborn baby with the head of the most famous cinematic Frankenstein's Creature, Boris Karloff, floats beneath the lake, suggestively a symbol from our collective unconscious.

The film thus underlines a peculiar kind of British myth-making, reinventing a shared heritage that is distinctly countercultural. The 1980s was the era of Merchant Ivory and the prestige period drama. On television, *Brideshead Revisited* (1981) and *The Jewel in the Crown* (1984) had been major events; in film, David Lean's *A Passage to India* (1984) and James Ivory's *A Room With a View* (1985) were both critically acclaimed and box office hits. These series and films, for all their many strengths, were excessively reverent towards their source texts and used literary heritage to communicate high-cultural prestige in a way that, as Andrew Higson has shown, was bound up with traditional notions of class and Englishness.[58] *Gothic*, which not coincidentally stars Julian Sands, fresh off the set of *A Room With a View*, throws all that out of the window. *Gothic* is not polite, tasteful or reverent. It offers a different vision of Englishness, one of radical experimentation, mystic sensibility, creative passion and eccentricity. It draws on a tradition of countercultural Gothic to create a sensational and deliberately provocative fantasia. However, whereas the countercultural Gothic of the 1960s reflected bitterly

[58] Andrew Higson, *English Heritage, English Cinema: The Costume Drama Since 1980* (Oxford: Oxford University Press, 2003).

on a Britain still hidebound by its past, here literary heritage is literally converted to a tourist attraction. Counterculture has become commodity: a spectacle to be enjoyed chiefly for its titillating entertainment value. Having its cake and eating it, *Gothic* is a latter-day exploitation movie that has the postmodern self-awareness to comment on its own exploitation.

To a twenty-first century eye, many of the Gothic texts of the long 1960s can seem crude, naïve, even camp, and inexorably moored to their own time. With a handful of exceptions – *Performance* certainly among them – they have lost the power to disturb and no longer seem oppositional, transgressive or even shocking. In part this is because capitalism has absorbed the counterculture so effectively. The counterculture was, from the beginning, profoundly compromised: as Marc O'Day points out, 'the individualism, expressiveness, private fantasy, romanticism, self-indulgence and need for change espoused by the counterculture are all valorised as values and practices of consumerism itself'.[59] The sexual and race politics of these works, to a contemporary audience, also frequently leave much to be desired. Nevertheless, in its proud mission to '*Épater la bourgeoisie*', countercultural Gothic did much to shape the trajectory of Gothic criticism in the coming decades. A generation of British writers and critics had their expectations shaped by growing up on late-night Hammer re-runs. Psychedelia may have become kitsch, but psychic fragmentation continued to flourish as a Gothic theme. The fascination with the occult is currently undergoing a revival in the twenty-first century fashion for folk horror, a cultural phenomenon that speaks eloquently to contemporary political themes of environmentalism and rural deprivation. The Byronic anti-hero lived on, moreover, in generations of rock musicians including, but not limited to, those beloved of Goth subculture, from Andrew Eldritch of The Sisters of Mercy to the aptly named Marilyn Manson. In times of uncertainty, we look to the sky, and see strange things.

---

[59] Marc O'Day, '"Mutability is having a field day: The Sixties Aura of Angela Carter's Bristol Trilogy', in Lorna Sage (ed.), *Flesh and the Mirror: Essays on the Art of Angela Carter* (London: Virago, 1994), pp. 24–59 (p. 31).

3.11
Gothic Television

DEREK JOHNSTON

Television has always been a Gothic medium. As Lenora Ledwon points out, a television 'is, after all, a mysterious box simultaneously *inhabited* by spirit images of ourselves and *inhabiting* our living rooms'.[1] Its technology brings immaterial visitors into the domestic space of the home, bringing us face-to-face with the intangible. In its narrative and aesthetics, television also makes extensive use of the Gothic mode. Dramas and documentaries depend upon the secrets of past, present and future; they often explore tangled familial narratives, and present Gothic spaces and places.

This chapter outlines a brief and necessarily partial history of Gothic television, and goes beyond that to argue, in line with Ledwon, that television is an inherently Gothic medium, and that its use of the Gothic expands beyond traditionally Gothic narratives. Instead, the Gothic mode is key to the medium's responses to developments in its technology and shifts in its reception. Changes in technology allow for the presentation of more elaborately developed Gothic aesthetics, but also lead to more fragmented audiences. The Gothic narrative mode, whether found in historical documentary, detective drama, sitcom or soap opera, simultaneously deals with escapism and the domestic, the personal and the general, making it an ideal means for engaging an audience of solitary viewers. Most centrally, this chapter focuses on the relationship between the Gothic and history on television. It first provides an overview of the history of the televisual Gothic, then focuses on how television Gothic relates to representations of history, both personal and national. In part, this is through Gothic fiction's typical engagement with the past in the form of buried secrets coming to light and the horrors of the past remaining disturbingly active in the present, something found not only in supernatural drama but also in detective and historical genres. The television

---

[1] Lenora Ledwon, '*Twin Peaks* and the Television Gothic', *Literature/Film Quarterly* 21:4 (1993): 260–70 (p. 260).

Gothic's relationship with history also operates across televisual genres, including television history documentary. This Gothicisation of history is particularly found in programmes that make history personal, such as *Who Do You Think You Are?* and historical recreation documentaries.

Overall, the Gothic mode continues to serve as a useful lens through which to approach historical traumas and the ways that these have shaped, and continue to resonate in, our present. As Helen Wheatley has put it, 'television is the ideal medium for the Gothic' since it is 'a domestic form of a genre which is deeply concerned with the domestic, writing stories of unspeakable family secrets and homely trauma large across the television screen'.[2]

Defining Gothic Television

Wheatley's seminal *Gothic Television* (2006) has provided the foundation for subsequent critics' understanding of the medium. As Wheatley maintains, the Gothic on television derives from classic Gothic literature, but also possesses its own specific elements, namely, 'narratives structured around flashback sequences, memory montages and other narrative interpolations', a visually dark *mise en scène* and an 'inclination towards camerawork and sound recording taken from a subjective perspective'.[3] It is this aspect of the Gothic – that is, that it is not just theme or narrative but also style and approach and mood – that means that it is perhaps best understood as a mode rather than a genre. Because of this, and as Julia M. Wright has pointed out, the Gothic can appear readily within other genres, and a police procedural or sitcom might contain Gothic moments without disrupting their dominant genre categorisations.[4] This fits particularly well with the common observation that genre itself is never pure, particularly in television, with programmes commonly containing elements that are drawn from a number of different genres.[5]

For Wright, the intertextuality of Gothic television drama, and particularly its heightened and foregrounded awareness of popular culture, makes it

---

[2] Helen Wheatley, *Gothic Television* (Manchester: Manchester University Press, 2006), p. 1.
[3] Wheatley, *Gothic Television*, p. 3.
[4] Julia M. Wright, 'American Gothic Television', in Joel Faflak and Jason Haslam (eds), *American Gothic Culture: An Edinburgh Companion* (Edinburgh: Edinburgh University Press, 2016), pp. 129–44 (p. 130).
[5] See, for example, Jane Feuer, 'Genre Study and Television', in Robert C. Allen (ed.), *Channels of Discourse, Reassembled: Television and Contemporary Criticism*, 2nd edition (Chapel Hill and London: University of North Carolina Press, 1992), pp. 138–60.

a more realistic form than those that are commonly identified as 'realist'.[6] At least in America, the television Gothic, as Wright claims elsewhere, 'is not only uninterested in representational accuracy or verisimilitude, but also continues to question the very possibility of such representation'.[7] Television Gothic thus offers an alternative representational approach, one that points out that what is commonly considered 'realism' in television drama is itself a constructed form with its own particular conventions. Similarly, Lorna Jowett and Stacey Abbott suggest that what they call 'TV Horror' draws upon the conception of television as an essentially realist medium in order to highlight the constructed nature of such realist ideas themselves. TV Horror, they maintain, also grounds the supernatural within the banal and everyday, while at the same time suggesting that the everyday is not quite as humdrum as it may appear, a tendency which accords to television horror drama a liminal place.[8]

A Brief History of Television Gothic

How we present the history of the Gothic on television depends not only on how we define the form but also on the national focus that we take. Since radio waves do not respect political boundaries, and because programmes, scripts and formats are tradable commodities, broadcasting has always been international in reach. At the same time, however, it is also and has always been intensely national, governed by legislation and regulation, and with the domestic market as its primary target. This means that the history of Gothic television in any particular national context will differ significantly from that in others; although there are certainly shared patterns and trends, the appearance of Gothic on television in any particular context will depend very much on that nation's own historical and cultural experiences, while also being influenced by international trade in broadcast material. What follows below is primarily concerned with the anglophone Gothic television experience, particularly that of the UK and the US.

Wheatley sets out a list of key Gothic dramas from Britain and America, beginning in 1947, in the UK, with the broadcast of *A Ghost Story* on BBC television, and in 1949, in the USA, with the first broadcast of *Lights Out* on

---

[6] Julia M. Wright, *Men with Stakes: Masculinity and the Gothic in US Television* (Manchester: Manchester University Press, 2016), p. 25.
[7] Wright, 'American Gothic Television', p. 142.
[8] Lorna Jowett and Stacey Abbott, *TV Horror: Investigating the Dark Side of the Small Screen* (London: I. B. Tauris, 2013).

NBC.[9] Wheatley is clear at this point that she is not providing an exhaustive listing, and further research, as well as the passage of time and the production of many new programmes that could be described as Gothic, enables the expansion of this list. For example, we could go back to the official start of television in Britain, 2 November 1936, when Algernon Blackwood closed off the evening by reading two of his ghost stories. This also takes us back to the history of the Gothic in other media that influenced television, such as radio. After all, it was on radio that people became used to Blackwood telling his weird tales, thereby connecting the new medium of television with its older relative as well as to a literary and oral tradition of the spooky tale told by the fireside. Nevertheless, it is interesting to note that the reviewer of the opening night's programmes for *The Times* considered the aesthetic as well as the content, noting that 'the lighting especially emphasised the ghostly character of the proceedings'.[10] Other early Gothic productions included an adaptation of W. W. Jacobs's *The Monkey's Paw* (first broadcast on 7 January 1938, with other adaptations in April 1939, February 1948 and May 1954) and James Bridie's *The Anatomist*, his 'lamentable comedy of Knox, Burke and Hare, and the West Port murders' that was first broadcast in June 1939 then restaged in January 1949.[11]

However, if we expand our definition of 'Gothic' to include expressions other than the literary and dramatic, we significantly expand the material covered. Arguably, such a move is necessary, as television as a whole sets out to be part of the cultural discourse, to connect, somewhere in the programming, to almost all aspects of life. We could thus list programmes on such relevant topics as Gothic architecture, appearances of Gothic styles on fashion shows, programmes on or featuring the Germanic peoples known as the Goths, Gothic music on music programmes, presenters or performers who associate themselves with Goth subculture (such as the historian Janina Ramirez and comedian Noel Fielding), and so on. All would sit alongside adaptations of Gothic literature or original productions that took a Gothic style or presented a Gothic narrative.

As the case of radio broadcast suggests, the appearance of the Gothic on television is also influenced heavily by cultural productions in other media. This is not just a case of direct adaptation, as with the development of *The Addams Family* (1964–6) from Charles Addams's cartoons in response to their popularity. It is also a response to the perceived popularity or significance of

---

[9] Wheatley, *Gothic Television*, pp. 4–5.
[10] Anon., 'BBC Television Programmes', *The Times*, 3 November 1936, p. 9.
[11] Anon., 'The Anatomist', *Radio Times*, 26 May 1939, p. 15.

other texts. Thus, the impending release of Francis Ford Coppola's *Bram Stoker's Dracula* in 1992 led to a tranche of vampire-related programming on British television, whether drama, documentary or the broadcasting of existing films. Its influence was even seen in a segment on the BBC fashion programme *The Clothes Show*, which presented a parade of outfits inspired by the film to the soundtrack of The Sisters of Mercy's 'Temple of Love (1992)'. In these ways, the Gothic can reach through multiple genres and irrupt into the wider viewing experience, responding to and enhancing a particular cultural moment.

Jowett and Abbott divide television history into three eras, each tied to changes in the wider television industry, although the exact start and end dates of those eras are debated and are contingent on the national industrial context. The first of these, TVI, runs from the launch of television and is considered the 'Era of Scarcity', meaning that there are few television channels available, with limited broadcast hours, possibly not available across the full geographic reach of the nation, and programmes for the most part having to be seen at the time of original broadcast. This period incorporates the rapid initial development of television technology and, later, the move into colour, where horror productions presented opportunities to experiment with and develop the possibilities of these new technologies. In particular, the low-contrast, frequently dim, rather small monochrome image of early television, combined with the intensity of live performance and transmission from relatively confined studio spaces, was recognised as being particularly well-suited to horror. However, there were also fears that this horror could be *too* successful, and that the genre needed to be treated with caution, a concern that meant that the type of horror shown tended more towards the suggestion of the Gothic rather than a more graphic, Grand Guignol-type horror.[12] The Gothic was well-represented, but could also present problems when the more grand elements of the genre collided with the limitations of the medium, as when Rudolph Cartier's adaptation of Daphne du Maurier's *Rebecca* for the BBC in 1954 was criticised internally for the expense and expanse of the set for the Great Hall. Cartier defended the scale of the set by stating that it was thematically important that these few, small human figures be presented as lost in this space and grandeur, but this does suggest how the Gothic on television was shaped in part by the tensions between creative concepts and the practicalities of budgets, studio spaces and technology.[13]

---

[12] Jason Jacobs, *The Intimate Screen: Early British Television Drama* (Oxford: Oxford University Press, 2000), pp. 97–8.

[13] Jacobs, *The Intimate Screen*, pp. 134–5.

Television dramas in this period ranged across single plays, serials, anthologies and ongoing series. The Gothic can be found in all of them, although concentrated in single plays and serials. There were also occasional appearances of Gothic productions in anthology series as well as Gothic-focused anthologies such as *Tales of Mystery* (1961–3, based on the fiction of Algernon Blackwood). Primarily, though, it was more likely that elements of the Gothic would appear in ongoing series that would not generally be considered Gothic.

TVII is the era of availability, when television access is available to the vast majority of the population, providing a national address, and when there are a small number of channels offering a range of programming across the schedule. During this period, while prime time programming still seeks to reach the mass audience, there is more targeting of specific audiences. Jowett and Abbott assign this period to the years from 1975 to the 1990s, although it is arguable that the UK reached this point before the US, and note that 'Many view this period as enabling greater creativity and diversity.'[14] This was because the mass networks were still very profitable and the spread of television internationally made for useful secondary markets and an increase in co-productions. These expansions of trade funded more elaborate productions with visual expansiveness enabled by new technologies, so experimentation and diversity could be encouraged which could enhance audience reach and engagement without overly threatening profitability. While location filming for drama was not new to television, it became increasingly commonplace during this period, with the result that fantastic dramas could feel more grounded in real locations, while imbuing 'everyday locations with a sense of the liminal and the uncanny'. The uncanniness of this experience was enhanced by the frequently identifiable shifts between location and studio performances, with interiors often still being studio-based.[15]

This period also saw a move away from the single play and the anthology drama towards ongoing series, such as the animated series *Scooby-Doo, Where Are You?* (1969–76). Insofar as their apparent horrors received rational explanations at the resolution to the episode, typically through presenting older people wanting to exploit the fears of the gullible in order to profit and/or conceal crimes, this series presented weekly Gothic narratives in the Radcliffean mode of the 'explained supernatural'. Ongoing series were supplemented with the more prestigious presentation of occasional television movies, such as Dan Curtis's productions of *Dracula* or *The Turn of the Screw*

---

[14] Jowett and Abbott, *TV Horror*, pp. 6–7.   [15] Jowett and Abbott, *TV Horror*, p. 7.

(both 1974), or mini-series/serials. As the period developed, increasing serialisation was supported for the viewer by increasingly easy access to home recording technologies in the form of the video cassette recorder, and by the commercial release of series on video tape and, later, DVD, formats which also increased visibility of older programmes now released on home video. This provided a further revenue stream while extending existing sources of income, providing an afterlife for programmes beyond their initial broadcast and allowing fandoms to grow even further because the productions they were based around continued to be available to gather new viewers, including for productions long off-air.

The increase in serialisation led to a shift in the Gothic narrative: while the soap opera *Dark Shadows* (1966–71) had shown that it was possible to have an open-ended Gothic series, with ongoing serialised plot lines, the series format, particularly of this era, required a different approach. Characters would have to encounter the strange each week, resolve that plot within the time slot, and then move on to a completely unrelated plot the following week. This perhaps suggests why early attempts at Gothic series, such as *Kolchak: The Night Stalker* (1974–5), tended not to be long-lasting, since they stretched the bounds of credibility in not relating events from week to week. As more serialised storytelling increased throughout the 1990s – a time when networks were also trying to engage with and develop narrower audiences, and new networks such as Fox and the WB and UPN were trying to establish themselves – series such as *The X-Files* (1993–2002) and *Buffy the Vampire Slayer* (1997–2003) mixed standalone episodes with ongoing narrative arcs.

Similar developments can be seen in the UK. Serials and anthology series continued to present Gothic fiction, including in the BBC Sunday evening classic serial slot, which included Tom Baker as Sherlock Holmes in *The Hound of the Baskervilles* (1982). Particular adaptations of note include the BBC's 1977 *Count Dracula*, first shown on 22 December, thus fitting into the British tradition of Christmas as a season for horror and thereby indicating another way in which the Gothic and horror serve to connect television with the culture of which it is a part. The influence of Gothic fiction in BBC dramas of the period influenced the aesthetics and narratives of a number of stories in *Doctor Who*, particularly during the 1974–7 period, with Philip Hinchcliffe as script editor. This period saw the time traveller and his companions face mummies (from Mars), a creature sewn together from the bodies of various aliens, a dismembered hand from which an ancient evil could regenerate itself and a masked genius in the Victorian music hall.

Meanwhile, the television broadcast of films brought new audiences to Gothic films of the past.

The current period of television, TVIII, is the 'time of plenty', meaning that there is round-the-clock access to numerous television channels, available through cable and satellite, and more recently joined by subscription-based streaming services. With this excess of channels, audiences have fragmented even further (although in the UK the most-watched channels by far in 2020 are still the pre-existing terrestrial channels: BBC1, BBC2, ITV and Channel 4).[16] Alongside this there is even greater availability of easily used timeshifting technology, whether that is a digital video recorder, a channel's catch-up service, or domestic media like DVDs and on-demand services. The effect of this is that the viewing of specific television programmes is no longer a shared experience, with a large proportion of the population watching the same thing at the same time, although significant national events still attract significant audiences to long-standing mainstream channels.

While this has brought more outlets for productions, it also means that there are likely to be much smaller initial viewing figures, and thus increasing reliance on trade and co-productions to finance the material. Expensive productions, then, need to stand out in order to attract sufficient trade and viewership to justify the cost, but the mode of distribution through personal subscriptions to channels such as HBO or AMC or services like Netflix or Amazon Prime means that, depending on national context, there tend to be fewer restrictions on what can be shown and represented on screen. As Jowett and Abbott note, 'More subscription channels open up what is acceptable on TV, and since such channels seek to outdo the competition by offering the "best" or edgiest programming to the most desirable viewers, this era seems a boom in TV horror (*Dexter*, *True Blood*) and even more experimental art horror, such as the surreal *Carnivàle*.'[17] To this can be added the extremely successful *The Walking Dead* (2010–) and the aesthetic horror of *Hannibal* (2013–15), the latter based on the characters created by Thomas Harris in his bestselling series of novels. With the exception of *Carnivàle*, each of these series is also adapted or developed from an existing text, to which can be added other examples such as *The Exorcist* (2016–17), *Damien* (2016, based on *The Omen*), *Bates Motel* (2013–17, based on *Psycho*), and Netflix's *The*

---

[16] Broadcasters' Audience Research Board, *The Viewing Report 2020*, May 2020 <www.barb.co.uk/download/?file=/wp-content/uploads/2020/05/Barb-Viewing-Report-2020_32pp_spreads_FINAL.pdf>, p. 29 [last accessed 21 December 2020].

[17] Jowett and Abbott, *TV Horror*, p. 10.

Haunting of Hill House (2018, based on Shirley Jackson's 1959 novel of that name). This also arguably applies to *Penny Dreadful* (2014–16), which takes characters from nineteenth-century Gothic literature and brings them together, while *The Frankenstein Chronicles* (2015–17) expands upon the various versions and interpretations of Mary Shelley's *Frankenstein* (1818; 1831) and connects these characters to the literary and cultural *milieu* of the early nineteenth century alongside not just Shelley herself but also William Blake, Ada Lovelace and Charles Dickens. These 'Gothic remixes', as Megen de Bruin-Molé calls them in her chapter in this volume, point to both the perennial return and resurrection of horror figures through Gothic fiction, but also to the use of familiar characters and narratives in order to draw audiences to a programme in an increasingly crowded market.

As services such as Netflix and Amazon Prime operate transnationally, albeit with adjustments to their catalogues for each territory, they also draw upon multiple national production industries to provide content, as well as making their own content that is intended to appeal to multiple markets. Such productions typically take familiar genres with known transnational appeal, coloured by the specificity of the place of production. Thus, Netflix's *Ghoul* (2018) was made in India, with Hindi-speaking cast and crew, but was written and directed by Patrick Graham, a British filmmaker, albeit one who had been living and working in Mumbai. It adapts the figure of the *ghul* from Arabic mythology and places it against contemporary fears of religion-inspired separatism and terrorism, which have particular resonance in India but which also resonate globally. It also used a globally familiar contemporary horror aesthetic, rather desaturated and claustrophobic, with the supernatural figure an attenuated pallid grey humanoid subject to CGI physical distortions.

This is an example of how this latest period in television's technological development influences the expression of the Gothic. The improvement of effects and make-up, particularly in higher-budget productions, means that the fantastic can be made to seem more believable and grounded. It also allows for more bizarre visuals, such as the eyeballs that swivel to reveal a demonic pupil and iris in possessed characters in *The Exorcist* series. The improvements in production and postproduction, including effects, can also be used more subtly in generating a sense of unease. Though they are often only partially glimpsed, there is a ghost represented in each shot of Hill House in the Netflix serial *The Haunting of Hill House*, not just the ones that are obvious haunting scenes. This uses the potential for suggestiveness in the high-definition recording and screens of modern television to its optimum, returning in some ways to those early days of suggestiveness in television Gothic, but this time aided by the idea that the television image is not one of low-resolution shadows but rather one of clarity, where everything should be visible, given some time and effort. These suggestive images thus encourage re-viewing, as well as fan engagement, to track and document and discuss these appearances, with this further engagement adding to the visibility and prestige of the production and so encouraging new viewers, who no longer have to worry about having missed earlier episodes, as all are available from the streaming service at once.

Formally, then, in the twenty-first century, television Gothic seems to be returning to the serial format. Long-running series like *The Walking Dead* or *The Chilling Adventures of Sabrina* (2018–) present an ongoing serial narrative. One innovation has been the continuing series that has a different serialised narrative each season, as represented most clearly by *American Horror Story*, but also visible in the detective Gothic of *True Detective* (2014–) and *The Haunting of Hill House* being followed by *The Haunting of Bly Manor* (2020), based on Henry James's *The Turn of the Screw* (1898). Episodic Gothic series have continued the adoption of serialised elements, whether that is in *Grimm* (2011–17), *Sleepy Hollow* (2013–17) or the rebooted *Charmed* (2018–), allowing for an increased richness in their settings and narratives to appeal to regular viewers. Such series provide a more Gothic entanglement of strands of power and relationships, while still retaining an element of independence in each episode that allows viewers to dip into the series instead of requiring them to follow it consistently and in order.

Throughout the history of television, then, the Gothic has consistently provided opportunities for engaging with the potential of television style. In the earliest period, it made use of the vague, shadowy nature of the low-resolution early television picture that suited the suggestive aspect of the Gothic. This period was not entirely free of elements of spectacle, whether that be the extensive set of the 1954 *Rebecca*, the point-of-view reveal of the horrific visage of Mr Hyde in the 1950 adaptation of *The Strange Case of Dr Jekyll and Mr Hyde* or the apparent dematerialisation from his chair of Algernon Blackwood at the end of his reading of his tale 'The Stockbroker' on 1 November 1947. As television technology developed, so it enabled more of these sorts of effects, but arguably the development of a clearer image led to a drive to show more. The Grand Guignol aspect of Gothic was thus used intentionally as the focus of *Late Night Horror* (1968), a series used to develop directors' skills in the new techniques of colour production, as Gothic narratives provided an opportunity to use colour in interesting and dramatic ways.[18] Similarly, the development of video technologies that encouraged a richer, layered image was utilised in Gothic productions such as *The X-Files* or *The Vampyr, a Soap Opera* (1992), while further advances still, into HD, CGI and cheaper prosthetics, combined with the investment in prestige programming by niche subscriber channels to produce programmes such as *The Walking Dead*, *Penny Dreadful*, *Whitechapel* (2009–13), *The Haunting of Hill House*, and so on. While not always at the forefront of these developments, the Gothic provides a useful arena in which to experiment with new techniques, and to refine the possibilities not only of the obviously graphic, but also of suggestion. The Gothic is thus inherently televisual, something that is enhanced by the Gothic nature of television itself.

The Gothic Nature of Television

As I claimed at the outset, television, like radio, is a somewhat supernatural medium in itself, bringing into the domestic setting of the home disembodied presences and engaging us with stories of the past, the present and the future, as Jeffrey Sconce has explored.[19] Indeed, both media have been interpreted in supernatural terms. For example, in a 1923 edition of the BBC listings magazine *Radio Times*, Lord Riddell provided an article entitled 'Modern Witchcraft' in which he stated that 'Radio is the nearest thing to witchcraft the world has seen as yet' and confessed that the 'mystery of the invisible agencies' of radio 'gives me an uncanny feeling'.[20] A number of other articles and short stories through the early years of the *Radio Times* connected radio and, later and to a lesser extent, television with ghosts, frequently as a receiving apparatus for sounds from the past or messages from the dead. Similar articles and narratives appeared outside of the *Radio Times*, such as J. B. Priestley's 1953 short story 'Uncle Phil on TV', in which the legacy left by Uncle Phil buys a television set for a family, before Uncle Phil himself starts turning up in the television programmes, telling unwelcome truths about the family, including the cause of his death. Also in 1953, the film *Meet Mr Lucifer*, directed by Anthony Pelissier and based on Arnold Ridley's 1951 stage play *Beggar My Neighbour*, presented television as a conduit through which the Devil could interfere to make people's lives miserable, presumably unlike the rival entertainment available from the cinema and theatre. Television as

---

[18] Wheatley, *Gothic Television*, pp. 74–7.
[19] See Jeffrey Sconce, *Haunted Media: Electronic Presence from Telegraphy to Television* (Durham, NC: Duke University Press, 2000).
[20] Lord Riddell, 'Modern Witchcraft', *Radio Times*, 21 December 1923, p. 451.

a conduit for supernatural communication has itself appeared in such dramas as *Twin Peaks* (1990–1), *Life on Mars* (2006–7), *The Twilight Zone* (1959–64), *Supernatural* (2005–20) and, perhaps most thoroughly, in the BBC's notorious *Ghostwatch* (1992), where the idea of television as a spiritual medium is taken to the level of the mass audience acting as a mass séance, with horrifying implications.

As technology has changed, and as television has become more familiar, so this Gothic aspect of the medium has been reduced. Audiences at the start of the twenty-first century may actually find it hard to empathise with the audience of the previous century in terms of perceiving radio and television as uncanny media. When it is possible to summon up music and video and conversations and information to a small, slim device held in the hand or dropped in the pocket, to carry them around with you to produce on demand, then the projection of sound or image into the house wirelessly to a fixed receiver is likely to be perceived as limiting rather than fantastic. This shift in technologies and reception of television is also part of the shifting engagement with the Gothic. As Wright has noted with regards to American Gothic television, 'The gothic transformed along with the medium: instead of using shadow to conceal what it could not represent, later technologies made possible special effects that could create the illusion of probability, of what might be seen on screen if vampires or ghosts existed.'[21] As Jowett and Abbott argue, this verisimilitude serves both to ground the fantastic in the everyday while also making the everyday seem more open to the fantastic, something that is particularly important to programmes that present themselves as explorations of the supernatural.[22] This liminal aspect to television is a central reason for considering the medium as Gothic in itself.

It should be recognised that the intimacy and domesticity of television have not always been presented as priorities, nor as central to the understanding of the medium and its possibilities. When television launched in the UK, a key concept regarding its purpose was that it would serve to bring the large-scale into the domestic, to enable people to see things that, due to distance or access, they would not otherwise be able to see. The characteristic of television that separated it from other media, in other words, was its ability to present images of what was happening elsewhere, right now, in the home. Indeed, Gerald Cock, the first Director of Television for the BBC, claimed in 1936 that 'feature films are not really suitable programme ammunition. As an extreme case, I believe viewers would rather see an actual scene of a rush hour

---

[21] Wright, 'American Gothic Television', p. 131.   [22] Jowett and Abbott, *TV Horror*.

at Oxford Circus directly transmitted to them than the latest in film musicals costing £100,000 – though I do not expect to escape unscathed with such an opinion'.[23] In part, this spectacular aspect of television has continued, especially in terms of news and of the sorts of major sporting and political events intended to bind societies together, occasions which Daniel Dayan and Elihu Katz term 'media events'.[24] However, as I argue here, the technology of television production and reception has served, alongside its cultural use, to make it a medium that is particularly amenable to a Gothic reading.

An article published in *The Times* in 1955 went so far as to claim that 'There is something spectral about the television public. It does not shuffle forward in sturdy queues or suddenly flood the street outside a theatre, but is glimpsed in desolate forests of aerials and alarming, faceless statistics.' The same article goes on to describe the pseudo-socialisation of television, referring to the closeness that viewers have to 'this shadowy company' of characters on the screen: 'Undoubtedly, the vicarious gaiety and the curiosity help to build up a substitute existence for people who want to escape the exertion of living at first hand. Nevertheless, the inordinate preoccupation with personalities has the virtues of its defects.'[25] By positioning the *audience* rather than the immaterial performers as spectral, this writer suggested that television is responsible for reducing its viewers to a state of immateriality, separated from directly experienced life and unhealthily focused instead on the images of 'personalities'.

However, while they are undoubtedly connected to the Gothic, ghosts are by no means an essential part of the genre. Far more important is the idea of family, with Agnes Andeweg and Sue Zlosnik claiming that 'Gothic is always in some way a family matter.'[26] This connects to television in the domestic nature of the majority of its consumption, the assumptions that the majority audience is a family audience and the focus on family found in the programmes broadcast on television. This is explored further below in relation to the importance of family in television genres such as the soap opera and the genealogical history programme.

---

[23] G. Cock, 'Looking Forward: A Personal Forecast of the Future of Television', *Radio Times*, 23 October 1936, p. 7.
[24] Daniel Dayan and Elihu Katz, *Media Events: The Live Broadcasting of History* (Cambridge, MA: Harvard University Press, 1992).
[25] Anon., 'Television as a Part of Everyday Life', *The Times*, 6 September 1955, p. 12.
[26] Agnes Andeweg and Sue Zlosnik, 'Introduction', in Agnes Andeweg and Sue Zlosnik (eds), *Gothic Kinship* (Manchester: Manchester University Press, 2013), pp. 1–11 (p. 1).

The Gothic Mode

Wright suggests 'that the gothic is a central mode through which Western culture has investigated the ways in which the world of signs supplants the world of the "real,"' and that 'the gothic structure returns again and again to the ways in which fiction can become *effectively* if not ontologically "real"'.[27] This conception again positions the Gothic as particularly relevant to television, a central distributor of our cultural fictions that seeks to represent the world to its viewers. But, as a medium, this involves filtering, interpretation and omission. This representation is thus in no way 'pure' and direct, but rather a fiction of the real, even when dealing with documentary or 'reality' television. Yet television remains a key source for understanding the world across the USA and UK, and so we have to be concerned with what narratives are disseminated and how the medium contributes to that understanding. The Gothic mode is one that is stereotypically critical of difference, fearful of outsiders, concerned about change, but it can also serve as a way of challenging the status quo, of critiquing dominant structures. It fulfils this, as Wright points out, by acting as 'a space for psychological thought-experiments', for examining how characters respond to different situations, where the response has to be realistic to be believable, but where the stimulus need not be realistic.[28] The Gothic stimulus, instead, can emphasise the need to interpret it as metaphor through its very unreality, while at the same time this unreality allows for an amused or bemused response, a rejection of potential metaphorical readings of the Gothic stimulus in favour of understanding the programme as 'just entertainment'. As Wright emphasises, the Gothic mode actually depends upon the dominant realist mode of television in order to throw the Gothic into stark relief.

Not only is television a Gothic medium, but it tends to operate in a Gothic mode itself, even beyond texts that would normally be considered to be Gothic. Wheatley observes that the Gothic has been applied as a framework to chat shows, news coverage and true crime documentaries, as well as soap operas, TV movies and serials, to which we might add crime dramas, particularly those with a serial killer/profiler element.[29] A clear example of the usage of the Gothic mode is the popularity of historical television, which is gothicised through its presentation of the ways in which previously unknown details of the past relate to the present lives of individuals and communities. A central text here is *Who Do You Think You Are?* (2004–), which

---

[27] Wright, *Men with Stakes*, p. 124.   [28] Wright, 'American Gothic Television', p. 134.
[29] Wheatley, *Gothic Television*, pp. 12–17.

ties the personal to the social and cultural and relies upon revelations of past secrets and horrors. As Wright, drawing on the work of Jerrold E. Hogle, notes, the Gothic arose at the same time as growing anxieties about genealogy, suggesting the centrality of lineage, inheritance and family secrets to the genre.[30] These are the central concerns of programmes that access history through the archival uncovering of the lives of particular families, such as *A House Through Time* (2018–) and *Who Do You Think You Are?*

The British version of *Who Do You Think You Are?* has been particularly strong in relating the horrors of the Holocaust and of Britain's involvement in the slave trade to the lives of popular contemporary figures, in the process dealing with imperialism and colonialism, particularly in relation to the Indian subcontinent and the Caribbean. The US version of the series has also connected to the Holocaust, as well as to the division of the Civil War and the issue of slavery, including an episode in which Spike Lee met with the descendant of Samuel Griswold who had owned a number of Lee's ancestors, a slave owner whom Lee himself may also be related to through those ancestors. Lee's genealogical narrative thus called into question issues of identity and self-identity while emphasising the horrors of slavery, but also incorporating the possibility of reconciliation and indicating the importance of interconnectedness, however appalling its foundations. As Thomas Edge has pointed out, however, the US series has broadcast a number of seasons with only white celebrities featured: there remain a number of ethnic groups within the US who have still not been represented, and even when the series addresses issues of racism, land and slavery, it does so within the framework of 'the show's problematic views of race and its commercial interests'.[31] But the strength of the programme in this area was made clear early on in the UK iteration when ornithologist and comedian Bill Oddie explored his own life of dealing with depression through uncovering a family history of mental illness, a genealogical excavation that showed the issue to be both deeply personal yet also of wider significance.

These family secrets are invariably revealed through the Gothic tropes of reading historical documents, digging through archives and visiting locations associated with the familial past. The programmes tend towards resolution, but that need not be about discovering, like Alexander Armstrong or Danny Dyer, that the personality is directly related to royalty, but rather the

---

[30] Wright, *Men with Stakes*, p. 40.
[31] Thomas Edge, '"Who Do You Think You Are?": Examining the African-American Experience in Slavery and Freedom through Family History Television', *The Journal of American Culture* 40:4 (2017): 341–54 (p. 346).

discovery of desired information about particular ancestors, and especially about the laying of psychological ghosts to rest. This follows what Fenella Cannell has identified as a central fact of amateur genealogy, namely that it 'treats the living and the dead as kin' and that *Who Do You Think You Are?* presents genealogy as 'a process by which the dead are brought back to some form of social life'.[32] A number of episodes see the celebrities at the graveside of previously unknown relatives, even narrating when the personality has paid for a grave marker to be provided where none had been laid before. But the emphasis is on continuation, on meeting the previously unknown *living* relatives, the survivors and their descendants. Amy Holdsworth has interpreted this as presenting 'an overemphasis on catharsis and closure – the end point of the therapeutic narrative – which closes down further investigation into the more difficult stories'.[33] However, while the wider historical issues and contexts may be closed down within each episode, the same traumas inescapably recur across series, even as the specificity of each family history differs. The personal narratives and the personal engagement with them also linger, in much the same way that Gothic fiction may place its characters as suffering at the hands of the Inquisition or aristocracy and reach a resolution that is personal rather than bringing down the larger power structures.

A number of other programmes, broadly in the 'talk show' genre, are also Gothic in the extent to which they focus on uncovering family secrets, including secrets of sexual transgression and unknown family connections, all within the 'safe' space of daytime television. While not visually graphic, programmes like *The Oprah Winfrey Show* (1986–2011) or *The Jeremy Kyle Show* (2005–19) unfold narratives of rape, incest and abuse, surrounded by the frequently glamorised, often aspirational, heightened 'normality' of commercials for beauty, food and domestic products. In this way, they represent an irruption of darkness into the everyday domestic. However, as these narratives are of 'ordinary' people, typically experienced within their own homes and families, it can be argued that what they actually do is point out that the horror already exists within the familiar and domestic, and that it is simply temporarily exposed. These programmes thus draw on the Freudian *unheimlich*, where the familiarly domestic is made unfamiliar by a revelation, causing shock and disturbance.

---

[32] Fenella Cannell, 'English Ancestors: The Moral Possibilities of Popular Genealogy', *Journal of the Royal Anthropological Institute* 17 (2011): 462–80 (pp. 464, 469).

[33] Amy Holdsworth, *Television, Memory and Nostalgia* (London: Palgrave Macmillan, 2011), p. 87.

Similarly, the uncovering of dark secrets, often relating to violence and sexuality, is central to 'true crime' programming. Increasingly, this type of programming has moved away from the investigative reporting of campaigning programmes like the BBC's *Rough Justice* (1982–2007), and towards a presentational form that owes more to fictional detective narratives. As with crime dramas, true crime programming can also serve to show the way that crime is a symptom of a damaged society, while at the same time feeding the cycles of violence, neglect and exploitation. However, there is another, arguably more common, strand in true crime programming that focuses on the criminal as monster, becoming particularly Gothic in the presentation of historical crimes, most notably in representations of the Jack the Ripper murders. As Lindsay Steenberg has observed, 'The Ripper figure, signifying Gothic evil without resolution, comes to haunt the stories that re-animate and update him.'[34] This is equally true of documentary narratives such as *Jack the Ripper: The Case Reopened* (2019) or dramas such as *Whitechapel*.

The Gothic mode is particularly important to television drama. While the obvious area to look for it is in literary adaptation and genre horror series, it is also central to soap operas. With their tangled narratives of domestic betrayal, abuse and family secrets, soap operas follow many narrative patterns of the Gothic. This is usually on a more everyday basis than the classic Gothic novel, particularly in British soap opera, with its associations with kitchen sink drama. Other soap operas have taken a more consciously Gothic narrative, presenting supernatural occurrences alongside long-lost twins and the return of those long believed dead. The original *Dallas* (1978–91) may have been predominantly realist in its presentation of machinations between powerful oil families, but even this costly prime-time soap negated an entire season when the dead character of Bobby Ewing was found having a shower, his partner having apparently dreamed up the previous season in its entirety. The final episode inverted Frank Capra's *It's a Wonderful Life* (1946) with a demonic Joel Grey showing J. R. how much better things would be if he were dead. And this is before considering the openly Gothic *Dark Shadows* and similar soaps, including a number of current Indian soap operas that depict independent women as cursed, possessed or simply demonic, following the current conservative turn in Indian culture.

The ongoing entwined narratives of the soap opera have also had an increasing influence on storytelling in general across fiction television.

---

[34] Lindsay Steenberg, *Forensic Science in Contemporary Culture: Gender, Crime and Science* (London: Routledge, 2012), p. 45.

Where dramas once tended to be episodic, they now tend to be serialised, with the notable exception of venerable and highly successful franchises such as *CSI* and *NCIS*. The serialised form allows for the building of links and a story world in a way that is believed to be particularly engaging to fan communities. This serialisation is particularly notable in connection with the development of binge-watching, something particularly associated with prestige dramas on on-demand platforms. Serialisation enhances the opportunities to engage with the Gothic mode by presenting more complex, entangled plots and relationships that, rather than being tied up within 43 minutes, are developed over a number of episodes.

The Gothic mode has also become particularly important in relation to period dramas. Where once period dramas could be almost expected to be presented with a heritage sheen, the tendency now is towards a grimness and 'realism'. This relates less to Andrew Higson's original conception of the depoliticised spectacle of the Thatcherite heritage film and instead connects more to Wheatley's concept of the 'feel bad heritage' production 'which refuses the sanitation of nostalgia' in order to 'offer the viewer narratives of fear and anxiety set in a past which is not only marked by a sense of decay or dilapidation, but which is also disturbed by uncanny happenings and supernatural events'.[35] This is not necessarily a case of taking a more Gothic original text to adapt, but rather taking an approach that emphasises griminess, shadow, mud, power imbalances and social inequality.

This can be found in series mentioned previously, such as *The Frankenstein Chronicles*, and can be extended to Starz's *Spartacus* (2010–13) series, which is centrally concerned with the various operations of power through politics, business, violence and sex. But it also incorporates adaptations of classic novels such as *Oliver Twist* (2007), by emphasising the aspects of violence and murk from Charles Dickens's original novel of 1837–9, and adding a coda to suggest the cyclicality of violence in society, as Dodger heads into the chaos of London's slums accompanied by Bill Sykes's dog Bullseye. This adaptation cast Tom Hardy as the brutal Sykes, and Hardy would go on to guest in *Peaky Blinders* (2013–), where the representation of the intertwined nature of criminal, economic and political violence and power is haunted by the trauma of the trenches in the First World War and the class structures reproduced in the conflict. For added Gothicness, the series uses Nick Cave's 'Red Right Hand' not just as the title music, but in a number of versions throughout the series, and also refers to it repeatedly through imagery of

---

[35] Wheatley, *Gothic Television*, p. 50.

Tommy Shelby in his long black coat with a blood-covered hand. Hardy went on to explore the underpinning of British society by colonial commerce in his 1814-set *Taboo* (BBC 2017–), where he appears as a figure of Death on a white horse, symbolising not just the character's return from apparent death, but the connection that he has to the supernatural throughout the programme. His character's inheritance of a shipping business, which he hopes to rebuild, is also desired by the East India Company, which is adapted here to represent the collision and collusion of trade and politics, being involved not just in the Indies but also in Africa and the Americas. This character, Delaney, is involved in illegal slave-dealing for the East India Company, is saved by African tribespeople who teach him their religious and magical ceremonies, and is the son of an English merchant and a Native American woman. He is both an agent and product of colonialism, and so potentially a balancing force for leading society onwards into modernity.

These series can all be understood in contributing to a Gothic view of history, one that attempts to engage with the different power structures that shape lives and events. Rather than presenting history from the viewpoint of Great Men whose decisions and actions make things happen, this approach instead shows history as a collision of forces acting upon individuals. It particularly represents the desire for and exercise of power as corrupting, with those lower down the social and economic hierarchy feeling more of its effects while receiving fewer of its benefits. This is visualised in the dark visual images populated by shadows, often with a limited colour palette of browns and greys and blacks interrupted by splashes of blood red. The Shelby brothers in *Peaky Blinders* and Hardy's Delaney in *Taboo* are traumatised victims of war who bring that violence back to the cities and centres of power that originally ordered it, taking the horror enacted on foreigners in another country and bringing it home.

Detective dramas similarly represent the ways that trauma echoes through and damages society, particularly those linked to 'noir' and the rise of what has been labelled 'Nordic noir'. These tend to examine the many interlinked elements in crime and the everyday, pointing to an underlying corruption to society and the way in which a single crime can spread out to infect the lives of victims' families, the families of those investigating as well as the legal and political systems. These dramas can be considered particularly Gothic in their lighting, picking up on the chiaroscuro elements that both 1930s and 1940s Universal horror films and 1940s noir film in turn picked up, at least in part, from German Expressionism and in their complexity, their focus on family and their frequent highlighting of particularly grotesque crimes. In European detective dramas in this mode, there has been a recurrent concern with heritage and with the crimes of the past, particularly those relating to the Second World War, collaboration and eugenics. One example is the French series *Les Rivières Pourpres* (*The Crimson Rivers*) (2018–), developed by Jean-Christophe Grangé from his own novel, and which deals with communities policing their bloodlines, feeling protected from the law by religious status, class and wealth, tying them in with the aristocratic and Catholic perpetrators of the horrors of the original Gothic novels.

Lindsay Steenberg has emphasised that the spaces of the forensic crime drama 'are the backdrop for a forensic aesthetic deeply indebted to film noir and the Gothic mode for its sense of atmosphere – an urban backdrop of literal and moral darkness'.[36] She goes on to argue that forensic dramas are related to certain kinds of lifestyle programming, such as *Make My Body Younger* (2008) in the way that they position the interior of the body in particular as a Gothic space of horror, while other lifestyle programmes such as *The Swan*, *Make My Body Younger* or *Extreme Makeover* can be understood as presenting the (often female) body as a site of Gothic decay and monstrosity that is to be recreated by the expert (often male) hands of the surgeon. In this way, Steenberg demonstrates the way in which the Gothic mode recurs across different genres of programming.

Gothic Television(s)

This chapter has outlined existing critical approaches to Gothic television, emphasising that these extend beyond the obvious adaptations of Gothic literature, or original dramas similar in plot to Gothic fiction. Instead, Gothic television should be considered as more of a mode, consisting of narrative elements and character types, but also tone, mood, visual and musical style. The Gothic mode is one that is particularly suited to television because of the intimate and domestic nature of the medium, bringing its horrors into the home and the family and so indicating the potential connections between events on screen and within the home itself. Because of its modal nature, its ability to mutate and to stray beyond fixed genres, the Gothic has recurred throughout the history of television, in dramas, adaptations, sit-coms, soap operas, but also in chat shows, makeover programmes and history programming. It has acted as a site for experimenting with the potential of the television medium, making good use of the suggestive nature of its often

---

[36] Steenberg, *Forensic Science in Contemporary Culture*, p. 3.

indistinct and shadowy images. Television has also reported, relayed, served and fed into Gothic subcultures and genres of music, architecture, literature and style. With its tangled narratives of familial secrets served up into the domestic realm by shadowy, immaterial presences, television not only relays Gothic narratives, television *is* Gothic.

3.12

Gothic and the Rise of Feminism

LUCIE ARMITT

The Female Gothic and Popular Romance

In 1973 Joanna Russ, a leading feminist science fiction writer, made a rare critical foray into Gothic terrain. In 'Somebody's Trying to Kill Me and I Think It's My Husband', Russ examined the fiction read by contemporary American women, highlighting the popularity of what she called 'Modern Gothics': popular paperbacks, devoured *en masse* and marketed by the American publisher Ace.[1] Their readers, Russ implies, are preoccupied with a sense of being haunted by something intangible, an ineffable presence that menaces or might menace them and to which Modern Gothics provide an antidote. The sense of intangibility that Russ invokes here returns us to the political sentiments expressed a decade earlier, by Betty Friedan, in *The Feminine Mystique* (1963).

Famously, Friedan begins her landmark study by coining the phrase 'the problem that has no name' to express the profound sense of dissatisfaction experienced by women otherwise presumed to be happy.[2] Although securely married, financially stable and the mothers of healthy children, many women nevertheless felt dissatisfied to the extent of misery, and guilty for feeling so. In Gothic terms, 'the problem that has no name' recalls mid-twentieth-century narratives such as Daphne du Maurier's *Rebecca* (1938), in which not only does the female protagonist have no outward cause for complaint – married to a handsome, rich man, the second Mrs de Winter seems to have attained the much-desired fairytale ending – she equally has 'no name'. Historically, of course, Gothic deals with loners and the isolated protagonist who has unwittingly stumbled upon something extraordinary. Marriage and

---

[1] For the original essay, see Joanna Russ, 'Somebody's Trying to Kill Me and I Think It's My Husband: The Modern Gothic', *The Journal of Popular Culture* 6:4 (1973): 666–91.
[2] This phrase forms the title of chapter one of Friedan's book. See Betty Friedan, *The Feminine Mystique*, intro by Lionel Shriver (Harmondsworth: Penguin, 2010), pp. 5–20.

domesticity are never extraordinary, but what women in 1963 started to realise was that these everyday structures and institutions could make women feel alone, trapped, buried alive. The opening to Friedan's study echoes this Gothic turn of phrase: 'The problem lay buried, unspoken, for many years.'[3] Live burial carries obvious Gothic resonances, but we should note Friedan's use of the word 'unspoken'. To 'un-'speak means more than to remain silent; it is an active negation, a violent disarticulation. Before long, Friedan's vocabulary builds to oscillate obsessively around 'terror':

> What if the terror a girl faces at twenty-one ... is simply the terror of growing up ...? What if the terror a girl faces at twenty-one is the terror of freedom to decide her own life ...? What if those who ... evad[e] this terror by marrying at eighteen ... are simply refusing to grow up ...?
> ... I remember how, [at school] ... some of the seniors, suffering the pangs of that bleak fear of the future, envied the few who escaped it by getting married right away.
> The ones we envied then are suffering that terror now at forty.[4]

'Terror', 'pangs' and 'bleak fear' are the very stuff of popular Gothic novels, but they operate on an entirely different level from the terrors outlined above. Instead of immersing their heroines within the horror of a domesticated living death, they propel them into a world in which terror is commingled with the thrill of (sometimes sexual) danger.

More than once in this chapter, I employ the term 'female Gothic'. In so doing, and in keeping with Ellen Moers's coinage of the category in *Literary Women* in 1976, I refer to female-authored Gothic narratives, depicting a central female protagonist, adopting a woman-oriented perspective.[5] It is a term that spans both the popular and serious ends of the Gothic spectrum and, though not unproblematic, we would, as Lauren Fitzgerald observes, 'do well to contemplate what scholarly reputation not only feminist criticism of the Gothic but also Gothic criticism more generally would enjoy were it not for the intervention of the female Gothic'.[6] Although I use, throughout, references to second-, third- and fourth-wave feminism, this chapter does not proceed as a linear journey through these waves as sequential phases in the female Gothic, because, as it shows, the interface between Gothic and feminism does not follow any easy, linear track. Instead, I shuttle between

---

[3] Friedan, *Feminine Mystique*, p. 5.   [4] Friedan, *Feminine Mystique*, p. 57.
[5] See Ellen Moers, *Literary Women: The Great Writers* (New York: Doubleday, 1976).
[6] Lauren Fitzgerald, 'Female Gothic and the Institutionalization of Gothic Studies', in Diana Wallace and Andrew Smith (eds), *The Female Gothic: New Directions* (Basingstoke: Palgrave Macmillan, 2009), pp. 13–25 (p. 13).

Gothic criticism and feminist theory and draw upon ideas from all of these phases of feminism, arguing that, irrespective of whether deemed 'popular' or 'serious', the female Gothic plays a continually key role in the dissemination and interrogation of feminist debates to and by a diverse readership from 1960 to the present. Thus we begin with *Mistress of Mellyn* (1961), a popular Gothic novel written by the 'Queen of Gothic Romance' Victoria Holt, before progressing on to a discussion of five 'literary' examples of the female Gothic, published between 1967 and 2002. During this period, Angela Carter's importance to the interface between Gothic and the rise of feminism is unrivalled, augmented by the respective landmark contributions made by Anne Sexton, Toni Morrison and Sarah Waters.

Russ's original corpus of Modern Gothics comprised a small cluster of titles published between 1962 and 1970: Margaret Summerton's *Nightingale at Noon* (1962); Anne Maybury's *I am Gabriella!* (1962); Susan Howatch's *The Dark Shore* (1965); Phyllis A. Whitney's *Columbella* (1966); and Helen Arvonen's *The Least of all Evils* (1970). If we date the start of the second wave of feminism around the time of the Civil Rights Protests in Paris in May 1968, most of these titles can be shown to pre-date it, but they nevertheless coincide with or post-date Friedan's *The Feminine Mystique*, not to mention the social discord that led to the protests of '68. Russ's interest in these volumes is purely collective. She categorises them as a batch, 'a crossbreed' of Charlotte Brontë's *Jane Eyre* (1847) and *Rebecca*, but unlike these more literary titles, the Ace Modern Gothics are devoured, not savoured.[7] The 'fix' that they offer transforms in imagination the tired allure of the reader's everyday husband into what Russ identifies as a 'Super-Male', a man who is usually 'older ... dark, magnetic, powerful, brooding, sardonic' and to whom the heroine is 'vehemently attracted' and from whom she is 'usually just as vehemently repelled' through fear.[8]

Tanya Modleski's reading of popular Gothic narratives builds on Russ's but is more cautious in the degree of significance that she is prepared to attach to the 'Super-Male'. Certainly, Modleski accepts that 'men *are* often cynical, mocking and hostile in their relationships with women', but she goes on to make the reasonable point that 'they are not often lunatics or murderers'.[9] When Russ describes the 'Super-Male', it is important to

---

[7] Joanna Russ, 'Somebody's Trying to Kill Me and I think It's My Husband: The Modern Gothic', in Julian E. Fleenor (ed.), *The Female Gothic* (Montreal: Eden Press, 1983), pp. 31–56 (p. 31).
[8] Russ, 'Modern Gothic', p. 32.
[9] Tania Modleski, *Loving with a Vengeance: Mass-Produced Fantasies for Women* (New York: Routledge, 1990), p. 61; emphasis in original.

remember that what she is articulating is a projection of the female reader's own desire: he is, as the prefix 'Super' suggests, an object of Gothic hyperbole. Contrastingly, one of the problems facing mid-twentieth-century housewives was the realisation that their dissatisfaction partly arose because their labour sought its own diminishment. Performed perfectly, it leaves nothing to see: *no* dust, *no* dirt, *no* mess. The very opposite of creation, housework *un*-sees itself, matching in its self-negation the unspoken problem that Friedan's subjects were struggling to articulate in the 'problem with no name'. As Ann Oakley observed in 1974, 'There is nothing more "automatic" than the perfect housewife, mechanically pursuing the same routine day in and day out.'[10] In obvious contrast to this diminished life are the excesses of the Gothic: the unpredictable terrors, dangers and monsters and the thrill of it all.

Herein lies the key to the importance of Russ's Modern Gothics. By exposing the patriarchal constraints upon women, popular novels afford their female readers mechanisms for beginning to 'manage' them. According to Anne Williams, 'Bluebeard's secret is the foundation upon which patriarchal culture rests', but in these popular narratives the Super-Male proves himself to be tame-able.[11] The villain is less the Super-Male, it seems, and more 'hearth and home'. Williams continues: 'A house makes secrets ... And the larger, older, and more complex the structure becomes, the more likely it is to have secret or forgotten rooms ... [and,] given the premises and history of patriarchy, such rooms contain the most appropriate possible secret – the bloody bodies of murdered wives'.[12] Certainly, Williams's words here resonate with how Martha Leigh, Holt's protagonist in *Mistress of Mellyn*, reflects on Mount Mellyn: 'I thought of the house, vast and full of secrets, a house in which it was possible to peep from certain rooms into others ... Perhaps someone was watching me now.'[13] One of the problems with aligning women's lot with being subsumed by enclosures, however, is that it risks conflating women's politics unerringly with defeat. Indeed, such dangers are resisted increasingly by younger women who, as Sarah Gibbard Cook observes of third-wave feminists, 'Having grown up to feel empowered ... don't like being told that they ought to feel

---

[10] Ann Oakley, *The Sociology of Housework* (Oxford: Basil Blackwell, 1974), p. 80.
[11] Anne Williams, *Art of Darkness: A Poetics of Gothic* (Chicago: University of Chicago Press, 1995), p. 41.
[12] Williams, *Art of Darkness*, p. 44.
[13] Victoria Holt, *Mistress of Mellyn* (London: Harper, 2006), p. 278.

oppressed.'[14] What remains attractive about the female Gothic, therefore, is the complexity of its heroine's relationship to danger and possibility, mirroring a similar complexity inherent in Sigmund Freud's reading of the uncanny.

In 'The "Uncanny"', Freud borrows from Schelling his realisation that one aspect of the uncanny emerges when 'something which ought to have remained hidden ... has come to light'.[15] Here, the use of the modal verb 'ought' is politically as well as aesthetically helpful, opening up a space of doubt and questioning, giving lexical room to the position of the enquiring reader: 'ought' according to whom? In the Gothic, whatever comes to light brings with it terror and sometimes horror, such that we might indeed wish that it had 'remained hidden'. Nevertheless, in being exhumed and subjected to the uncomfortable glare of daylight, patriarchy starts to loom large under the lens in a manner that enables it to be sized up and, in being so, potentially overcome.

Political Sisterhood

Holt's Martha is a governess, employed by the rakish Connan TreMellyn. Among the more obvious allusions to *Rebecca* are not simply its Cornish setting, but the far more precise suggestion of a picnic at Fowey; the susurrating sea at night, recalling the second Mrs de Winter's realisation that it 'was closer than I had thought, much closer ... if I listened now, my ear to the window, I could hear the surf breaking on the shores of some little bay I could not see'; and even Connan TreMellyn's improbable name echoes the waltzing dactylic metre of the equally improbably named Maxim de Winter.[16] One of the questions for us is whether a nascent feminist politics can be identified in Holt's pages, as has retrospectively proved true of *Rebecca*. At first the potential seems limited. One of the most reactionary aspects of the Modern Gothics is the emphasis that they place on women rivalling other women (living and dead) for male attention and 'winning'. Holt ensures that Connan is surrounded by alluring women: the dead but beautiful first wife Alice, erroneously suspected of having died in a railway accident; Martha's

---

[14] Sarah Gibbard Cook, 'Feminists Differ in Second and Third Waves', *Women in Higher Education Banner*, 9 May 2014. Wiley Online Library <https://doi.org/10.1002/whe.10222> (last accessed 4 September 2018).

[15] Sigmund Freud, 'The "Uncanny"', in Sigmund Freud, *Art and Literature*, Penguin Freud Library, Vol. 14, edited by Albert Dickson, trans. by James Strachey (Harmondsworth: Penguin, 1990), pp. 335–76 (p. 364).

[16] Daphne du Maurier, *Rebecca* (London: Arrow Books, 1992), p. 95.

professional predecessor Jacinth Jansen, 'a real pretty creature', dismissed after being falsely accused of stealing a necklace; Daisy and Kitty, the flirtatious maids; the 'outstandingly beautiful' Lady Treslyn, illicit lover of Connan and gold-digging wife to the elderly Sir Thomas; Jennifer, mother to the illegitimate Gilly (flower), reputed to have had 'Great dark eyes and the littlest waist you ever saw' and who committed suicide by drowning in the sea.[17] Most dangerous is Celestine Nansellock, a family friend who negotiates her way into an apparent friendship with Martha, only to reveal herself as Alice's actual, and Martha's attempted, murderer. Leading Martha to a concealed passage in the chapel, Celestine fingers and locates an aperture, steps aside for Martha to enter and slams the door shut behind her. There Martha finds 'What was left of Alice'.[18] Worst of all, perhaps, Celestine's depiction suggests that woman should trust no woman, for it is in Celestine that Martha has placed her greatest hope of sisterhood.

When Robin Morgan observed, in 1970, 'that women, who had been struggling on a one-to-one basis with their men, began to see that some sort of solidarity was necessary, or insanity would result' we recognise the irony of Holt's depiction of Celestine, for it is she who becomes incarcerated as a 'raving lunatic' and whose punishment matches that of the isolated housewife: 'she did not die until twenty years after, and all that time she spent locked away from the world'.[19] Morgan's study is an examination of the political importance of sisterhood, a connection between women that offers up a much more politically progressive reading of Freud's *doppelgänger*, a term that he attributes to 'characters who are to be considered identical because they look alike' and which seems to me equally applicable to patriarchy's view of 'the housewife'.[20] In Gothic terms, these doubles 'ghost' each other such that Martha, dressing up in Alice's riding habit, is momentarily mistaken for Alice's ghost by a guilty Celestine. Indeed, Martha does her own 'double-take' on coming face-to-face with Alice's full-length portrait: 'You are haunting me, Alice. Since I have known you I have known what haunting means.'[21]

However, it is in the treatment of the female gaze in *Mistress of Mellyn* that Holt's novel proves surprisingly progressive. Exposing the role of scopophilia, the sexualised pleasure of looking, in gender politics is one of the most

---

[17] Victoria Holt, *Mistress of Mellyn* (London: Harper, 2006), pp. 10, 121, 9.
[18] Holt, *Mistress of Mellyn*, p. 296.
[19] Robin Morgan, 'Introduction: The Women's Revolution', in Robin Morgan (ed.), *Sisterhood is Powerful: An Anthology of Writings from the Women's Liberation Movement* (New York: Random House, 1970), pp. xiii–xli (p. xx); Holt, *Mistress of Mellyn*, p. 304.
[20] Freud, 'The "Uncanny"', p. 356.   [21] Holt, *Mistress of Mellyn*, pp. 250–1.

important contributions that second-wave feminism made to late-twentieth-century media theory. According to Laura Mulvey's influential essay, 'Visual Pleasure and Narrative Cinema' (1975), 'In a world ordered by sexual imbalance, pleasure in looking has been split between active/male and passive/female ... Woman displayed as sexual object is the *leitmotif* of erotic spectacle: from pin-ups to strip-tease.'[22] Adopting a more self-referential emphasis, John Berger, in his equally influential *Ways of Seeing* (1972), argues that 'A woman must continually watch herself. She is almost continually accompanied by her own image of herself. Whilst she is walking across a room or while she is weeping at the death of her father, she can scarcely avoid envisaging herself walking or weeping.'[23] Arguably *Mistress of Mellyn*, despite its populist appeal, explores a more complex and potentially empowering view of female spectatorship than either Mulvey's or Berger's essays. Admittedly there are passages in which male characters objectify Martha openly through the gaze, not to mention, as implied above, others when she belies anxiety about how her appearance compares with that of other women. At these points Martha simply mimics the patriarchal gaze, much as Mulvey argues, in her follow-up 'Afterthoughts on "Visual Pleasure and Narrative Cinema"' (1981), that female cinema-goers might find pleasure in the opportunity to engage in a kind of 'metaphor of masculinity' when watching films.[24] However, elsewhere Holt affords her characters a more active female gaze, one that has agency while remaining sisterly in orientation.

Mount Mellyn has a number of 'peeps' or carefully constructed spy-holes cut into the plasterwork, part-concealed by ornamentation. We learn, retrospectively, that one habitual spectator is Gilly (whose gaze spies out Martha's fate and facilitates her rescue), a child variously described as 'extraordinary looking', a 'gentle creature', 'unique', 'a queer little thing' and 'a wild fairy child'.[25] Although largely silent, Gilly is ever-seeing. When Martha finds her hiding in Alice's apartments she notices that 'She had begun to stare about the room ... I had the uncanny feeling that she *saw* something – or someone – I could not see.'[26] Sight and second sight thus become connected, permitting

---

[22] Laura Mulvey, 'Visual Pleasure and Narrative Cinema', in Laura Mulvey, *Visual and Other Pleasures* (Basingstoke: Macmillan, 1989), pp. 14–26 (p. 19).
[23] John Berger, *Ways of Seeing* (London: BBC Books, 1972), p. 46.
[24] Laura Mulvey, 'Afterthoughts on "Visual Pleasure and Narrative Cinema" Inspired by King Vidor's *Duel in the Sun* (1946)', in *Visual and Other Pleasures* (Basingstoke: Macmillan, 1989), pp. 29–38 (p. 37).
[25] Holt, *Mistress of Mellyn*, pp. 11, 40, 40, 107, 183.
[26] Holt, *Mistress of Mellyn*, p. 101; emphasis in original.

the gaze to become feminised, debunking the fact that even feminist theorists so frequently presume it to be masculine in orientation and, most importantly of all, facilitating solidarity across generations, a feature that is strikingly absent in the more 'serious' novels discussed below.

Generational Rejection: *The Magic Toyshop*

Earlier I noted that Modleski downplays the role of the Super-Male in the attraction that popular Gothics hold for women. For her, it is not sisters but mothers that provide the Gothic impetus in a narrative:

> it is not only that women fear being *like* their mothers ... in an important sense, they fear *being* their mothers – hence the emphasis on identity in physical appearance, the sensation of actually being possessed, the feeling that past and present ... are 'intertwined' ... [27]

Angela Carter's *The Magic Toyshop* (1967) epitomises Modleski's words. Here we encounter 15-year-old Melanie, cosseted and middle class. The opening of the novel catches her unawares, delighting in her newly sexualised body before the mirror, her erotic self-experimentation initially framed by icons of childhood innocence: her Edward Bear pyjama case and '*Lorna Doone* splayed out face down in the dust under the bed'.[28] Suddenly, her parents are killed in an air crash, the family home is sold, and Melanie and her younger siblings are forced to remove to her maternal Uncle Phillip's toyshop in London.

Immediately prior to her parents' death, Melanie has been engaged in child's play: dressed to kill in her mother's wedding gown, she runs into the garden after dark. As Jane Spencer observes, 'Female to female inheritance has ... always been problematic in a patriarchal society in which the legacy passed from male to male is understood as natural and of central importance.'[29] As if conscious suddenly of having overreached herself, Melanie panics and races back towards the house, only to find the door slammed shut. At this point Melanie's fate resonates with fears articulated 30 years later by the third-wave feminist Rebecca Walker (Alice Walker's daughter), who similarly carries the weight of her mother's legacy on her shoulders:

---

[27] Modleski, *Loving with a Vengeance*, p. 70; emphasis in original.
[28] Angela Carter, *The Magic Toyshop* (London: Virago, 1981), p. 2.
[29] Jane Spencer, 'Afterword: Feminist Waves', in Stacy Gillis, Gillian Howie and Rebecca Munford (eds), *Third Wave Feminism: A Critical Exploration* (Basingstoke: Palgrave Macmillan, 2007), pp. 298–303 (p. 299).

> Linked with my desire to be a good feminist was ... a deep desire to be accepted, claimed, and loved by a feminist community that included my mother, godmother, aunts and close friends ... As is common in familial relationships, I feared that our love was dependent upon that mirroring. Once I offered a face different from the one they expected, I thought the loyalty, the bond of our shared outlook and understanding, would be damaged forever.[30]

Walker's words yearn for an autonomy from the mother that retains a degree of connection, but Melanie has gone too far. Not simply 'offer[ing] a face different from the one they expected', Melanie's role-play re-ignites fears of the *doppelgänger* effect: in taking her mother's clothes she has actually snuffed her out. As Walker puts it, 'Because feminism has always been so close to home, I worried that I might also be banished from there.'[31] There is a paradox, of course, in utilising the domestic arena as a metaphor for feminism and one has also to acknowledge that Melanie is no feminist. Nevertheless, Melanie's narrative maturation leaves no room for mothers, who remain surplus to requirement throughout.

Melanie's mother-substitute in London is Aunt Margaret. Margaret's marriage to Phillip is a 'front'. Behind other closed doors Margaret is in love with her brother Francie, the shop providing only a socially sanctioned alibi for a family unit that lacks conventional 'respectability'. No innocent victim of their incestuous secret, Phillip is a monster embodying Williams's aforementioned role of Bluebeard and one who wreaks his violence upon Margaret through tyranny and sexual coercion. As a wedding present, he manufactures for her a 'collar of dull silver, two hinged silver pieces knobbed with moonstones which snapped into place around her lean neck and rose up almost to her chin ... It was heavy, crippling and precious'.[32] Margaret is mute, thereby encapsulating Friedan's unspeaking woman, her traumatic silence reinforced by this 'articulated' con*trap*tion. It is also Margaret who epitomises most obviously Carter's repugnance for marriage, within the terms of which 'all wives of necessity fuck by contract'.[33] Where Melanie dresses up in the hope of bridal defloration, Margaret dresses up to be ritually 're- (F)lowered' by Phillip every Sunday evening. Thus, as Paulina Palmer observes, Carter 'reveals the element of violence in male-defined models of sexual pleasure'.[34]

---

[30] Rebecca Walker, *To Be Real* (New York: Anchor, 1995), p. xxx.
[31] Walker, *To Be Real*, p. xxxi.   [32] Carter, *Magic Toyshop*, p. 112.
[33] Angela Carter, *The Sadeian Woman* (London: Virago, 1979), p. 9.
[34] Paulina Palmer, 'From "Coded Mannequin" to Bird Woman: Angela Carter's Magic Flight', in Sue Roe (ed.), *Women Reading Women's Writing* (Brighton: Harvester, 1987), pp. 179–201 (p. 185).

Sex and violence are clearly and overtly connected in *The Magic Toyshop*, so much so that even when the young Finn kisses Melanie in the pleasure garden, 'She choked and struggled, beating her fists against him, convulsed with horror at this sensual and intimate connection, this rude encroachment on her physical privacy, this humiliation.'[35] Shortly beforehand, Melanie had willed herself into this romantic pose with Finn, reflecting 'vaguely that they must look very striking, like a shot from a new-wave British film ... She wished someone was watching them ... Then it would seem romantic.'[36] In actuality, shocked by the raw physicality of Finn's tongue, the result falls somewhere between a seduction and an assault and, in being so, almost replicates exactly Martha's response on being kissed by Connan TreMellyn:

> I caught my breath with dismay for he was forcing me against the wall and kissing me.
> I was horrified as much by my own emotions as by what was happening...
> My anger was so great that it was beyond my control. With all my might I pushed him from me and he was so taken by surprise that he reeled backwards.[37]

As Morgan confesses bravely in her book on sisterhood, she had formerly 'nurtured a secret contempt for other women who weren't as strong, free and respected (by men) as [she] thought [she] was' and it is easy to be contemptuous both of Martha's seeming over-reaction and Melanie's fickle desires.[38] However, it is equally important to remember that Gothic romances can sometimes enable more radical explorations of the difficult balance between sexual thrill and sexual danger than do more serious Gothic narratives. Precisely because of the 'safe' genre expectations within which Holt is writing, she can depict ideologically more contentious scenarios between a respectable young governess and the Super-Male: Connan may be a rake, but rape would be unthinkable. Carter's lack of a generic structure renders the scene between Melanie and Finn much more precarious and thus, for the reader, more unsettling.

In fact, Finn's actions prove to be a simple precursor to the 'rape-by-proxy' that Phillip has planned for Melanie later. Acting out the myth of Leda and the Swan to his tyrannised basement audience, Phillip the puppeteer manipulates his swan: 'His mouth gap[ing] open with concentration.'[39] Suddenly

---

[35] Carter, *Magic Toyshop*, p. 106. [36] Carter, *Magic Toyshop*, p. 106.
[37] Holt, *Mistress of Mellyn*, p. 124. [38] Morgan, 'Introduction', pp. xiv–xv.
[39] Carter, *Magic Toyshop*, p. 166.

Melanie's sense of herself splits apart, as she both performs and seems to view herself from outside as the swan looms:

> she felt herself not herself, wrenched from her own personality ... The swan towered over the black-haired girl who was Melanie and who was not ... The swan made a lumpish jump forward and settled on her loins ... She screamed, hardly realizing she was screaming. She was covered completely by the swan but for her kicking feet and her screaming face. The obscene swan had mounted her. She screamed again.[40]

Although here, as in the pleasure gardens, Melanie has prepared herself performatively, the horrifying reality erodes any possibility of self-containment. All the domestic entrapments that Melanie has experienced before build incrementally and seemingly inescapably towards this moment. Despite Williams's argument for the political centrality of Bluebeard to patriarchy (and of course Carter adds to this portfolio in 'The Bloody Chamber', as we shall see), we recall Modleski's assurance that few wives genuinely fear being *murdered* by their husbands. Far more common is the dread of unwanted sexual demands from a husband who has become otherwise disinterested, drunk or perhaps even grotesque: 'The whippings, the beatings, the gouging, the stabbings of erotic violence reawaken the memory of the social fiction of the female wound ... Female castration is an imaginary fact that pervades the whole of men's attitude towards women and our attitude to ourselves.'[41] Carter's words, here, reverberate loudly with Gothic echoes and are manifest in Melanie's predicament. The only remaining question is whether, as Palmer astutely observes, Carter might actually go too far, risking 'making these [patriarchal] structures appear even more closed and impenetrable than, in actual fact, they are'.[42]

According to Sandra M. Gilbert and Susan Gubar's *The Madwoman in the Attic* (1979), 'myths and fairy tales often both state and enforce culture's sentences with greater accuracy than more sophisticated literary texts'. What we see also, long before writers such as Carter start to re-work them, is that tales such as 'Snow White' prove instrumental in forging the formulae upon which Gothic narratives are later based. For Gilbert and Gubar, 'Snow White' is especially responsible for identifying a prototypical dynamic between older and younger women, based on rivalry for the King's approval: 'His, surely, is the voice of the looking

---

[40] Carter, *Magic Toyshop*, pp. 166–7.   [41] Carter, *Sadeian Woman*, p. 23.
[42] Palmer, '"Coded Mannequin" to Bird Woman', pp. 180–1.

glass.'[43] In *The Magic Toyshop* we have seen the intergenerational struggle from the younger woman's perspective, but what of the implications for older women? As Zoe Moss observes, 'a middle-aged woman is comic by definition'.[44] Once placed within a Gothic context, how easily might comedy metamorphose into disgust?

Older Women and Desire: 'The Snow Child' and 'Rapunzel'

One of the most brutal examples of the female Gothic is Carter's 'The Snow Child' from her short story collection *The Bloody Chamber* (1979). The story opens with a Count and Countess riding out in the snow. Inspired by the wintry scene, the Count starts to fantasise about 'a girl as white as snow', his virginal ideal being an obvious contrast to his middle-aged wife.[45] Footwear is sometimes read as a patriarchal metaphor for the vagina, a point that makes perfect sense in the context of the Cinderella narrative, wherein only one who fits the dainty glass slipper will prove suitable for a Prince. By contrast, in 'The Snow Child' the Countess wears 'high, black, shining boots with scarlet heels, and spurs'.[46] On a younger woman this attire might prove sexually alluring; here, it is grotesque. Coming across a blood-filled hole in the snow, the Count dreams of 'a girl as red as blood', the implied distinction between his post-menopausal wife and a young, fertile ideal being as transparent as Cinderella's slipper. Spotting a raven, the Count desires 'a girl as black at that bird's feather', a desire that cannot be taken at face value, for it is not for a Black girl, but a girl with 'white skin, red mouth, black hair' and, to cap it all, 'stark naked'.[47] Worse is to come, as the Countess tries to trick her rival, but each time is stripped, first of her furs, then boots, to clothe the younger woman. Where the naked girl had been desirable, the older woman is now 'bare as a bone'.[48] The Countess presents a rose to the young woman, who pricks her finger and dies. The Count, 'Weeping', performs his grief through necrophilia, 'unfasten[ing] his breeches and thrust[ing] his member into the

---

[43] Sandra M. Gilbert and Susan Gubar, *The Madwoman in the Attic: The Woman Writer and the Nineteenth-Century Literary Imagination* (New Haven: Yale University Press, 1984), pp. 36, 38.

[44] Zoe Moss, 'It Hurts to Be Alive and Obsolete: The Ageing Woman', in Morgan (ed.), *Sisterhood Is Powerful*, pp. 170–5 (p. 170).

[45] Angela Carter, 'The Snow Child', in Angela Carter, *The Bloody Chamber and Other Stories* (Harmondsworth: Penguin, 1981), pp. 91–2 (p. 91).

[46] Carter, 'Snow Child', p. 91. [47] Carter, 'Snow Child', pp. 91, 92.

[48] Carter, 'Snow Child', p. 92.

dead girl'.[49] His lover dissolves into the ground and the Countess becomes re-clothed but, on retrieving the rose, the Countess drops it: 'It bites!'[50]

This story makes for difficult reading and Carter offers no consolations for either generation, locked as they are into a mutually destructive tussle over the attentions of a grotesquely avaricious and licentious patriarch. Similarly difficult is Anne Sexton's poem 'Rapunzel' from her *Transformations* collection (1971). In 'Rapunzel', Sexton brings out the covert lesbian desire inherent in the original fairy tale: an older woman is captivated by and in turn captivates a younger one: *ergo* she must be a witch. One might expect Sexton to offer a counter-challenge to such assumptions, but instead she uses vampiric imagery to caution against the seductive excesses of older women: 'Put your pale arms around my neck. / Let me hold your heart like a flower / lest it bloom and collapse. / Give me your skin / ... let me open it up'. Disappointingly, no sooner does a handsome prince arrive than 'he dazzle[s Rapunzel] with his dancing stick' and soon 'They lived happily as you might expect / proving that mother-me-do / can be outgrown'.[51] This Gothic poem, despite the title claim for transformation, not only reinforces the damaging patriarchal myth of older women's sexual redundancy, it couches them as predators and diminishes lesbianism to a phase 'curable' by the arrival of the Super-Male.

Ideologically painful though these re-writings are in their superficial failure to reverse patriarchy's dangerous allure, we must remember that one of the reader's roles in Gothic narratives might be said to be the exhumation of counter-cultural readings. What Carter and Sexton therefore reveal are the damaging effects on all women of failing to develop an intergenerational sisterhood. This realisation requires a re-thinking of the powerful concept of trans-generational haunting (or cryptonomy) as coined by Nicolas Abraham and Maria Torok. Cryptonomy can be understood as a form of undisclosed family narrative cocooned in the inherited psyches of future generations, in which 'what haunts are not the dead, but the gaps left within us by the secrets of others'.[52] In Toni Morrison's *Beloved* (1987), we see what happens when that inherited trauma lodges itself in the body as well as the psyche.

---

[49] Carter, 'Snow Child', p. 92.   [50] Carter, 'Snow Child', p. 92.
[51] Anne Sexton, 'Rapunzel', in Anne Sexton, *Transformations* (Boston: Houghton Mifflin, 1971), pp. 35–42 (pp. 38, 41, 42).
[52] Nicolas Abraham, 'Notes on the Phantom: A Complement to Freud's Metapsychology', trans. by Nicholas Rand, *Critical Inquiry* 13:2 (1987): 387–92 (p. 387).

Haunted Motherhood: *Beloved*

Morrison's *Beloved* reminds us that 'way past the Change in Life, desire in [women] had suddenly become enormous, greedy, more savage than when they were fifteen'.[53] In this novel, intergenerational haunting lies at the crux of the Gothic and is embodied in the traumatic skin memory of the central protagonist, Sethe. In one sense, *Beloved* is a haunted-house story about a murdered baby girl. In another, it is a novel in which an entire community is haunted by Black slavery. Third, it explores what happens to the mother/daughter dyad when sexual violence tears them asunder. While nursing her baby, the Beloved of the novel's title, Sethe is violated and subsequently whipped by a group of young white men, who forcibly suck the milk from her breasts: 'Held me down and took it. I told Mrs. Garner on em ... Them boys found out I told on em. Schoolteacher made one open up my back, and when it closed it made a tree.'[54] The body and its limitations are at the centre of all Gothic narratives: blood, the death of the flesh, living death, the reanimated corpse. Sethe's violation is, in Gothic terms, an act of predatory vampirism, all the more so as Sethe, in a response fuelled by traumatic terror, slits the throat of her baby girl to prevent any possibility of white men violating her too. As Sethe's baby's blood cascades down her own body, it mixes with the milk that is spilling from her breasts. Sethe is pregnant with Denver at the time, who later perceives her own identity as having somehow been forged from a cocktail of her sister's blood and her mother's milk. What Denver also internalises is trans-generational fear:

> I love my mother but I know she killed one of her own daughters, and tender as she is with me, I'm scared of her because of it ... All the time, I'm afraid the thing that happened that made it all right for my mother to kill my sister could happen again.[55]

The vampiric imagery in *Beloved* is symbolic rather than overt, but it treads the same path as Meredith Skura when she discusses the 'fiercely ambivalent' unconscious dynamic existing between all women and their breast-fed babies. The baby, Skura argues, 'is tied down, moved, filled, and emptied by someone too strong to resist – an invasion of the body which has its logical culmination in cannibalism and vampirism'.[56] Certainly, Denver's anxieties about Sethe remind us of the nervously infantile admiration enacted by the

---

[53] Toni Morrison, *Beloved* (London: Picador, 1987), p. 17. [54] Morrison, *Beloved*, pp. 16–17.
[55] Morrison, *Beloved*, p. 205.
[56] Meredith Ann Skura, *The Literary Use of the Psychoanalytic Process* (New Haven, CT: Yale University Press, 1981), p. 104.

young male interviewer in Anne Rice's *Interview with the Vampire* (1976): 'The vampire turned towards him and studied him, so that the boy flushed and looked away anxiously. But then he raised his eyes and looked into the vampire's eyes. *He swallowed, but he held the vampire's gaze.*'[57] Gina Wisker, examining a chronological shift in vampire narratives, argues that, post-1980, the hybrid subjectivity of the protagonists depicted in these more recent works facilitates the portrayal of multiple 'alternative relationships – lesbian, gay, trans body, trans creature'.[58] Morrison's narrative is heterosexual in orientation, but it certainly conceptualises women's role within an actively sexual relationship in a more positive way than any of the narratives discussed above. In doing so, as we shall see, it offers up a challenge to second-wave feminism's dominant view of heterosexual power relations.

Only six years before *Beloved*, Andrea Dworkin argued that 'Male sexual power is the substance of culture. It resonates everywhere. The celebration of rape in story, song, and science is the paradigmatic articulation of male sexual power as a cultural absolute. The conquering of the woman acted out in fucking … is the scenario endlessly repeated … In fucking, he is enlarged.'[59] Precisely because *Beloved* is the story of the racially and sexually motivated violation of one woman and the symbolic historical rape of an entire culture through slavery, Morrison is able to question Dworkin's conflation of rape with all heterosexual power relations, as in the following passage that describes sexual intimacy between Sethe and her lover Paul D:

> Behind her, bending down, his body an arc of kindness, he held her breasts in the palm of his hands. He rubbed his cheek on her back and learned that way her sorrow, the roots of it; its wide trunk and intricate branches … And he would tolerate no peace until he had touched every ridge and leaf of it with his mouth, none of which Sethe could feel because her back skin had been dead for years.[60]

Here, Paul D ministers, not 'conquers'. The orality of his touch and the caressing of Sethe's breasts re-invest them with desire. Nevertheless, the lack of sensory awareness in Sethe's back, caused by the scarring effects of flogging, limits the extent to which desire can enflame her skin and Sethe finds herself reflecting on her inability to 'feel the hurt her back ought to'.[61]

---

[57] Anne Rice, *Interview With the Vampire* (London: Sphere, 2008), p. 63; my emphasis.
[58] Gina Wisker, *Contemporary Women's Gothic Fiction: Carnival, Hauntings and Vampire Kisses* (Basingstoke: Palgrave Macmillan, 2016), p. 168.
[59] Andrea Dworkin, *Pornography: Men Possessing Women* (London: The Women's Press, 1981), p. 23.
[60] Morrison, *Beloved*, pp. 17–18.   [61] Morrison, *Beloved*, p. 18.

Only through pain can desire be rekindled, a dynamic explored in particularly intriguing ways in recent vampire narratives.

Wisker subdivides vampire narratives into two playful categories: 'Vampire Bites' and 'Vampire Kisses'. Vampire Kisses emulate Russ's Modern Gothics, the main vampire standing in for Russ's 'Super-Male' (epitomised, perhaps, in the self-explanatory title of Amanda Grange's *Mr Darcy, Vampire* [2009]). The novels that Wisker assigns to the 'Vampire Bites' category are more interesting, for in these books vampires exist 'as a metaphor, as vehicles for the contradictions of our gendered world and experiences'.[62] Nina Auerbach, in her influential study *Our Vampires, Ourselves* (1995), reflects that her own teenage awakening involved recognising that 'Vampires were supposed to menace women, but to me at least, they promised protection against a destiny of girdles, spike heels and approval.'[63] For Wisker, Auerbach's reflection shows that vampires provide 'an alternative to restrained, dull conformity' and indeed they may do.[64] However, we need also to acknowledge Auerbach's playfulness about the fang-like construction of 'spike' heels themselves, and in so doing recall how different women embrace diverse fashion identities. After all, for some, spike heels might be essential weapons in the armoury of female self-empowerment. Such reminders are often assumed to be the prerogative of third- and fourth-wave feminists, but even in 1984 Muriel Dimen, in her essay 'Politically Correct? Politically Incorrect?', warns that there is a 'special cultural tension between sexuality and feminism' that can make the policing of different clothing choices a negation of female self-expression.[65]

Certainly there is no provocative clothing in *Beloved*, but there is a resistance to the assumption that I made earlier, namely that an over-identification with domesticity is inherently damaging for women. Because Sethe is a woman who delights in cooking and perceives it as an important aspect of her self-expression, baking becomes a kind of refuge from remembered horror: 'Working dough. Working, working dough. Nothing better than that to start ... beating back the past.'[66] Nevertheless, this is a house that 'bites'. As Wisker observes, while Sethe busies herself domestically, the ghost

---

[62] Wisker, *Contemporary Women's Gothic*, p. 157.
[63] Nina Auerbach, *Our Vampires, Ourselves* (Chicago: University of Chicago Press, 1995), p. 4.
[64] Wisker, *Contemporary Women's Gothic*, p. 157.
[65] Muriel Dimen, 'Politically Correct? Politically Incorrect?', in Carole S. Vance (ed.), *Pleasure and Danger: Exploring Female Sexuality* (London: Pandora, 1989), pp. 138-48 (p. 140).
[66] Morrison, *Beloved*, pp. 72-3.

of Beloved returns in mature form and 'steals' Paul D: 'as Beloved grows with a phantom pregnancy, Sethe shrinks and shrivels. The guilty memory ... eats her up'.[67]

Libertine Sexuality

The Gothic, precisely because it deals in unspeakable desires, dangers and taboos, should also permit a more libertarian depiction of female sexuality. Carter's writing makes a major if controversial contribution to the debate about female sexuality, most notably in her 1979 non-fiction work *The Sadeian Woman*. Arguing for a new relationship between women and pornography, Carter searches for a 'moral pornographer [who] might use pornography as a critique of current relations between the sexes'.[68] As we have seen, however, Carter's own Gothic narratives can appear to reinforce rather than revolutionise women's entrapment within patriarchy and, even in the title story of *The Bloody Chamber* collection, itself a re-telling of the Bluebeard tale, the same pattern might be seen to apply. This story falls into the category that Modleski calls 'Gothic' rather than 'Gothic Romance': 'Women in Gothics are persecuted, but the persecution is not, as in romances, experienced as "half-pleasureable" ... she has not fallen in love with her victimiser (although she may for a time think she has ...).'[69] Like Phillip in *The Magic Toyshop*, the groom in this story endows his bride with a wedding choker: 'rubies, two inches wide, like an extraordinarily precious slit throat'.[70] Again like Phillip, gradually the groom metamorphoses into a monster, but here his inhumanity is replicated in a description hovering between human and beast: 'I could see the dark, leonine shape of his head and my nostrils caught a whiff of the opulent male scent ... [H]e moved as softly as if all his shoes had soles of velvet, as if his footfall turned the carpet into snow.'[71] Where Margaret, in *The Magic Toyshop*, seems almost ethereally sexless as a result of her silencing, we cannot miss the sensuality of this bridegroom and nor, it seems, does his young bride. We remember this 'Super-Male' is a connoisseur of pornography and, for Dworkin, that alone would suffice to render him grotesque: 'The word pornography, derived from the ancient Greek *pornĕ* and *graphos*, means "writing about whores"' and 'Whores exist

---

[67] Wisker, *Contemporary Women's Gothic*, p. 103.   [68] Carter, *Sadeian Woman*, p. 19.
[69] Modleski, *Loving with a Vengeance*, pp. 82–3.
[70] Angela Carter, 'The Bloody Chamber', in Angela Carter, *The Bloody Chamber*, pp. 7–41 (p. 11).
[71] Carter, 'Bloody Chamber', p. 8.

only within a framework of male sexual domination.'[72] Contrastingly, when this bride fingers one of his books, she muses that 'I had not bargained for this'. Though he taunts her for her curiosity ('Have the nasty pictures scared Baby?'), they seem rather to have intrigued her. She tells us, 'I was innocent but not naïve' and acknowledges 'There is a striking resemblance between the act of love and the administration of the torturer', adding 'I had learned something of the nature of the similarity on my marriage bed.'[73] Note the absence of any complaint in these musings. For me, the disappointment of this story is that Carter reneges on its inherent possibility of transforming the relationship between this Bluebeard and his bride into one of libertine but mutually beneficial heterosexual appetite. Instead, it retreats into what is actually, in feminist terms, a politically 'safer' story of phallocentric brutishness in which the heroine's only option is to be rescued by her mother.

Despite Sarah Waters's general tendency to set up in her fiction a more sustained and ethically complex relationship between women and pornography, a similar opportunity is, in my opinion, missed in her novel *Fingersmith* (2002). Colloquially, a fingersmith is a pickpocket, although one might also interpret it as a cipher for a writer; dancing around both options is the teasing allusion to fingering as sexual play. In *Fingersmith*, two women, Maud and Sue, have been swapped at birth. One is raised in poverty within south-east London, the other at Briar, the country house owned by her rich uncle, Christopher Lilly. Lilly is, like the husband in 'The Bloody Chamber', a connoisseur of pornography and Maud's value to him is to titillate his male accomplices, who gather in his library at evening while Maud reads aloud erotica for their delectation. Following his death, Sue, who by now is Maud's estranged lover, follows her to Briar and finds Maud at her uncle's desk, authoring pornography. Waters's major contribution to the feminist Gothic is to re-think the political assumptions that second-wave feminists made about cultural invisibility. Where the Black lesbian feminist Audre Lorde argues that 'most of all ... we fear the visibility without which we cannot truly live', Waters argues that, historically, invisibility has sometimes worked to lesbians' advantage.[74] Terry Castle provides a Gothic context for such cultural invisibility: 'When it comes to lesbians ... many people have trouble seeing what's in front of

---

[72] Dworkin, *Pornography*, pp. 199, 200.   [73] Carter, 'Bloody Chamber', pp. 16, 17–18.
[74] Audre Lorde, 'The Transformation of Silence into Language and Action', in Audre Lorde, *Sister Outsider* (Freedom: The Crossing Press, 1984), pp. 40–4 (p. 42).

them. The lesbian remains a kind of "ghost effect."'[75] If so, Sue is about to 'see' Maud for the first time:

> I took the book from her and looked at the print on the pages. It looked like any book would, to me ... Then I took up another; and that had pictures. You never saw any pictures like them. One was of two bare girls. I looked at Maud, and my heart seemed to shrink.
> 'You knew it all,' I said.[76]

Precisely because Sue cannot read, her 'innocence' has largely accorded with Castle's reading of history: 'The lesbian is never with us, it seems, but always somewhere else: in the shadows, in the margins, hidden from history, out of sight.'[77] Only when shown pictures can Sue read between these lines.

Nevertheless, the ending of *Fingersmith* remains troubling. If we pay attention to Sue's response here, her 'shrinkage' echoes Wisker's reading of the impact on Sethe of the mature emanation of Beloved's ghost 'draining [her] like a succubus'.[78] Though Sue's initial response is sadness over Maud's suffering, Maud remains unmoved: 'Don't pity me ... I am still what he made me. I shall always be that.'[79] Maud, then, identifies herself as Lilly's creation and, surely, perpetuates his project, simply swapping the role of victim for connoisseur. Though Maud and Sue are now reconciled as lovers, a glaring power imbalance remains. As Sue tells us, '[Maud] put the lamp upon the floor, spread the paper flat; and began to show me the words she had written, one by one.'[80] So initiation begins, with Sue as protégée. According to Emma Healey, in the context of lesbian pornography, 'It could be argued that the old arguments that porn is basically exploitative ... were no longer viable when it was clear that women, the usual victims of porn, were actually its consumers and audience.'[81] Actually, *Fingersmith* suggests otherwise. I am as uncomfortable with the power imbalance at the end of *Fingersmith* as I was with the depiction of older women in Carter's 'The Snow Child' and Sexton's 'Rapunzel'. All these texts demonstrate is that patriarchal exploitation can outlive any individual patriarch.

---

[75] Terry Castle, *The Apparitional Lesbian: Female Homosexuality and Modern Culture* (New York: Columbia University Press, 1993), p. 2.
[76] Sarah Waters, *Fingersmith* (London: Virago, 2002), p. 545.
[77] Castle, *Apparitional Lesbian*, p. 2. [78] Wisker, *Contemporary Women's Gothic*, p. 103.
[79] Waters, *Fingersmith*, p. 546. [80] Waters, *Fingersmith*, p. 548.
[81] Emma Healey, *Lesbian Sex Wars* (London: Virago, 1996), p. 142.

Conclusion

The 'rise in feminism' of this essay's title might be assumed to imply the existence of an easy linear trajectory in both feminist theory of the last 50 years and the contemporary Gothic narratives in which those ideas coalesce. Instead, the interface between the two has been shown to be both more permeable and more cyclical than that pattern implies. Despite feminism's ongoing importance for women and the Gothic's continual popularity, one has to acknowledge that concerns remarkably similar to those that motivated Friedan's contemporaries in 1963 continue to drive women today. Certainly, there is now far more opportunity to articulate a diversity of feminist concerns than was possible then, but it remains the case that, irrespective of whether feminists self-identify as second-, third- or fourth-wave, any woman who asserts herself (refuses to 'un-speak') in public still engages with a known degree of potential danger. Admittedly, Modleski's perspective on popular Gothics reminds us that such dangers are rarely (at least in Western democracies) literally life-threatening. Nevertheless, they may remain career-threatening, marriage-threatening or, as the recent 'Me Too Movement' has revealed, sexually predacious.[82] Throughout this period the Gothic has continued to inspire women in two major ways: by exposing patriarchy's monstrosity and thus reducing it to size, and by inventing uncanny metaphors for how women can haunt the underside of patriarchy, thus undermining it from within. Importantly, the enticing combination of peril and thrill that only the Gothic offers has inspired its readers to equip themselves for the challenge. As Carole Vance argued in the 1980s, 'The notion that women cannot explore sexuality until danger is eliminated is a strategic dead-end' and I would argue the same to be true for all aspects of women's lives today.[83]

---

[82] See the Me Too Movement at <https://metoomvmt.org/> (last accessed 4 August 2020).

[83] Carole S. Vance, 'More Danger, More Pleasure: A Decade After the Barnard Sexuality Conference', in Vance (ed.), *Pleasure and Danger*, pp. xvi–xxxix (p. xvii).

3.13

Gothic, AIDS and Sexuality, 1981–Present

ARDEL HAEFELE-THOMAS

Prologue

October 11, 1987: *Legions of the skeletal half dead were being pushed through the streets in wheelchairs in the afternoon autumn mist. Their translucent paper-thin skin was peppered with dark purple lesions enveloping arms and legs nearly devoid of fat and muscle. Faces of twenty, thirty and forty-year-olds looked ninety. They were all in a slow-motion death march. This was not a horror fantasy; this was a horrific reality. We were six years into the AIDS pandemic in Ronald Reagan's America. We were there together in Washington D.C. marching for our lives. It was an October afternoon swathed in Gothic imagery. It was an October afternoon humming with queer resistance. At the 1987 March on Washington for LGBT Rights, the intersections of Gothic, AIDS and queer histories brushed against one another.*

1970s: Lesbian Vampires and Sweet Transvestites

In the period between mid-1969 and mid-1981, queer people had been liberated, empowered and celebrated for little over a decade, and the imagery around queer bodies and queer sexuality had changed in predominantly positive ways. Although the 1969 Stonewall Rebellion, in which members of the LGBTQ+ community protested against violent police suppression, had taken place in New York City, this particular queer uprising sent a ripple effect around the world and is widely considered to be the moment that the modern-day LGBTQ+ Rights Movement was born.[1] From the late 1960s

---

[1] Prior to Stonewall, there were other LGBTQ+ riots, protests and rebellions. Of particular note are the 1959 Cooper's Do-Nut Riot in Los Angeles, California; the 1965 Dewey's lunch counter sit-in against gender dress codes in Philadelphia, Pennsylvania; and the 1966 Compton's Cafeteria Riot in San Francisco, California. See Susan Stryker, *Transgender History: The Roots of Today's Revolution*, revised edition (New York: Seal Press, 2017), pp. 79–113 and Ardel Haefele-Thomas, *Introduction to Transgender Studies* (New York: Harrington Park Press, 2019), pp. 130–68.

throughout the 1970s, laws criminalising male homosexuality in particular were relaxed in places like Germany and the United Kingdom, and, in the United States, numerous states moved to repeal their anti-sodomy laws.[2]

Just as queer history was rapidly emerging and affirming queer lives, so the Gothic as a mode began to move from depictions of the absolute monstrosity and demonisation of queers like Count Dracula and Norman Bates towards a camp-infused eroticism. The 1970s saw a spate of lesbian and bisexual vampire films like Roy Ward Baker's soft-porn, campy *The Vampire Lovers* (1970), Jesús Franco's Spanish and West German stylised erotic *Vampyros Lesbos* (1971), Harry Kümel's Belgian *Les Lèvres Rouge* (1971) and Vicente Aranda's *La Novia Ensangrentada* (1972), all of which were loosely based on the Irish Gothic author Joseph Sheridan Le Fanu's classic lesbian vampire novella, *Carmilla* (1872).

Lesbian and bisexual vampires were not the only subjects of 1970s queer Gothic. A year after *The Vampire Lovers*, Roy Ward Baker directed *Dr Jekyll and Sister Hyde*, his gender-bending take on Robert Louis Stevenson's 1886 classic *Strange Case of Dr Jekyll and Mr Hyde*. In 1975, Jim Sharman's *The Rocky Horror Picture Show* was released, a film that put trans subjectivity front and centre and would become possibly the most iconic queer Gothic movie of all time. Sharman's audience-participatory Gothic musical continues to run globally in various late-night cinema venues today, and has done since its debut. For over four decades, this film's convergence of Gothic, queer and trans sensibilities has served as a touchstone for young people around the world – especially for those of us who are queer and/or trans.

As the film begins, Brad and Janet, a hapless heterosexual couple, find themselves on an abandoned road in a storm with a broken-down car and set their sights on the creepy mansion looming in the darkness in hopes of finding a phone. Once inside, the stereotypical Gothic tropes meld into a camp horror musical as Tim Curry's Dr Frank-N-Furter descends in a lift wearing sparkling black-and-white platform heels and a vampire cape that he then discards to reveal a black leather corset and fishnet stockings. He wears sexy vampiric facial cosmetics, and his eyes are full of mirth. He then greets Brad and Janet with his first number, 'Sweet Transvestite'. At this giddy 1970s

---

[2] Unlike sodomy laws that encompass an entire nation, such as Paragraph 175 of the German Penal Code or the Labouchere Amendment to the Criminal Constitution in England, the United States allowed each state to define, uphold or repeal its own sodomy laws. In some states, these laws only pertained to men who have sex with men; however, in numerous cases, the sodomy laws criminalised any type of sexual contact that was outside of the realm of heteronormative procreative sex. In 2003, the United States Supreme Court struck down the last of the sodomy laws in the *Lawrence v. Texas* case.

moment, Gothic and queer sensibilities co-mingle with the possibilities of what being oneself – especially what being one's 'freaky' queer and/or trans self – could be. The pandemonium of the film slips between classic Gothic narratives (*Dracula* and *Frankenstein* being the most obvious) while remaining in tension with the film narrator's attempts to 'straighten up' the situation, until the polyamorous, queer gender outlaw, Frank-N-Furter, belts out one final song that has become a sort of queer anthem: 'Don't Dream It, Be It.'[3]

By 1980, then, it looked as though queer lives and queer history were on a positive and upward trajectory just as Gothic form in films was continuing to explore queer themes that, though not always positive, were certainly complex. This is not to say that Gothic became non-homophobic or non-transphobic overnight, but rather that the existence of films like *Rocky Horror* opened the door for the ways that Gothic and queer narratives could transform alongside one another – their histories continuing to expand together. In 1981, however, these paths took a sudden and awful turn.

Intersections of AIDS, Gothic and Queer Histories

On 5 June 1981, two separate medical publications appeared in the United States. In their *Morbidity and Mortality Weekly* Report, The Centers for Disease Control (CDC) published a special report on a Los Angeles doctor's unusual finding: five white gay men who had previously been healthy were suffering from *pneumocystis carinii pneumonia* (PCP). Their immune systems seemed to be failing them for no obvious reason. By the time that the report was published, two of the men had already died, and the other three died shortly afterwards. That same day, on the East Coast in New York, a dermatologist placed a call to the CDC to report 'a cluster of cases of a rare and unusually aggressive cancer – Kaposi's sarcoma (KS) – among gay men'.[4] Less than a month after these initial reports, on 3 July 1981, *The New York Times* published an article pinpointing gay men, specifically, who were suffering with the new disease; at this moment, according to HIV.gov's timeline, 'the term "gay cancer" enters the public lexicon.'[5] Although, globally, gay men were not the only people falling sick and dying from this new

---

[3] *The Rocky Horror Picture Show*. Dir. Jim Sharman. Michael White Productions, 20th Century Fox. 1975.
[4] HIV.gov <www.hiv.gov/hiv-basics/overview/history/hiv-and-aids-timeline> (last accessed 16 September 2020).
[5] HIV.gov <www.hiv.gov/hiv-basics/overview/history/hiv-and-aids-timeline> (last accessed 16 September 2020).

immuno-deficiency disease, the stereotype in the public domain from 1981 onwards has been that AIDS is a 'queer disease'.

From the moment that AIDS was labelled as queer, the rhetoric surrounding people with AIDS focused on morality, guilt and innocence. As Jennifer Power notes, 'the question of "choice" became the basis for distinction between the innocent and the non-innocent with regards to AIDS. Those who acquired HIV through sex or drug use were routinely represented as having some level of choice about their infection ... a moral assessment about the nature of such choices was an ever-present subtext.'[6] Once notions about morality, guilt and innocence became invoked within the language surrounding AIDS, Gothic descriptors relating to monstrosity quickly followed. Gothic symbolism has long been utilised to underscore the horrors of infectious diseases. In his 14 September 1665 diary entry, Samuel Pepys employed Gothic images when he noted his 'meeting dead corpses of the plague' as he walked along Fenchurch Street. In the same entry he also considered the haunting scene of a hackney-coach carrying someone half dead and 'sick of the sores'.[7] Jennifer Lee Carrell's 2004 historical tale that focuses on smallpox invokes Gothic throughout; the title, *The Speckled Monster*, illustrates this cogently.[8] Likewise, Gothic fiction often employs disease and contagion metaphors. For example, Angela Wright has discussed Mary Shelley's marriage of Gothic and disease in her apocalyptic fiction, *The Last Man* (1826).[9] Edgar Allan Poe's Gothic short story 'The Masque of the Red Death' (1842) explores the Bubonic Plague. And Robert A. Douglas argues that Bram Stoker's mother's horrific stories of an 1832 cholera outbreak in Sligo, during which the sick were buried prematurely, informed his depictions of Count Dracula.[10] From the outset, particularly considering the visible dark lesions of Kaposi's sarcoma and the sudden wasting away of muscle and aging effect, people with AIDS were rendered horrifying and grotesque. For example, Power notes that in a 1987 Australian television advertisement meant to educate the heterosexual community that *everyone*

---

[6] Jennifer Power, *Movement, Knowledge, Emotion: Gay Activism and HIV/AIDS in Australia* (Canberra: Australian National University Press, 2011), p. 60.
[7] Samuel Pepys, *Eyewitness Accounts: London's Great Plague* (Gloucestershire: Amberly Press, 2014), p. 58.
[8] Jennifer Lee Carrell, *The Speckled Monster: A Historical Tale of Battling Smallpox* (New York: Plume, 2004).
[9] Angela Wright, *Mary Shelley* (Cardiff: University of Wales Press, 2018), p. 93.
[10] Robert A. Douglas, 'The Spirit of the Gothic', 4 September 2013 <www.thatlineofdarkness.com/2013/09/cholera-as-disease-and-gothic-metaphor.html> (last accessed 19 November 2020).

was at risk of contracting AIDS, the depiction of the Grim Reaper as the AIDS virus confirmed rather than corrected homophobic stereotypes. As she writes, 'It was feared that people would see the "Grim Reaper" as symbolizing gay men rather than HIV/AIDS, thus reinforcing the notion that it was gay men and not a virus who were responsible for AIDS deaths.'[11] Laura Westengard extends this point when she argues that 'the excesses of the wasted queer body were offered up to the public as the endpoint of queer identity – a monstrous confluence of nonnormative desire, threat, infection, abjection, and death ... Many have implied that HIV-positive folks were monsters who deserved the disease.'[12] Power and Westengard both accurately explore the negative ramifications of the Gothic symbolism that has been utilised within the contexts of AIDS and queer culture.

Gothic, however, can also become a powerful tool with which to explore this contemporary plague. Just as queer culture has been forever transposed by the AIDS pandemic, Gothic as a mode, too, has changed as it has been utilised as a means to explore queer themes, and particularly the queer community's collective trauma and ongoing haunting by the spectre of AIDS. This chapter aims to explore these shifts and to analyse the ways in which Gothic interacts with queer history generally and with the history of AIDS and queer communities more specifically within late twentieth- and early twenty-first-century contexts. It examines the elision of these histories of Gothic, AIDS and queer sexuality in four representative texts that mark different stages of the evolution of AIDS discourse: Tony Scott's 1983 art-house vampire film *The Hunger*; Todd Haynes's 1991 New Queer Cinema triptych, *Poison*; John Greyson's 1993 irreverent AIDS musical, *Zero Patience*; and, finally, Lilly and Lana Wachowski and J. Michael Straczynski's 2015–18 trans-genre television show, *Sense8*.

The Trauma of Gothic Contagion/AIDS Contagion/Queer Contagion: 1981–1991

Neither Tony Scott's *The Hunger* (1983) nor Todd Haynes's *Poison* (1991) overtly mentions AIDS; yet, the trauma of AIDS as a new and devastating disease permeates the Gothic structures of both films. Sorcha Ní Fhlainn notes that while Whitley Strieber's novel *The Hunger* (1981) includes 'striking

---

[11] Power, *Movement, Knowledge, Emotion*, p. 69.
[12] Laura Westengard, *Gothic Queer Culture: Marginalized Communities and the Ghosts of Insidious Trauma* (Lincoln, NE: University of Nebraska Press, 2019), pp. 100–1.

references to AIDS ... from animal testing, disease, homosexuality, and vampirism, it is in Tony Scott's 1983 film adaptation that these images and topics are fused to form a Gothic narrative on the disease'.[13] While Scott's film develops a Gothic narrative on AIDS, Todd Haynes's 1991 Sundance Grand Jury Prize-winning film utilises these Gothic structures to create a scathing commentary on AIDS, homophobia and isolation by deploying traditional Gothic narrative tropes. In both films, the amalgamation of AIDS panic, stereotypes of queer sexuality as contagion and Gothic structures provide a space for audiences to consider the ways in which AIDS, Gothic and queer representations function together – but with vastly different outcomes for each film.

The Hunger opens with vampires Miriam and John Blaylock (Catherine Deneuve and David Bowie) hunting for their next victims in an underground Goth nightclub with Bauhaus's haunting 1979 track 'Bela Lugosi's Dead' as the musical backdrop. While the Blaylocks' sensuous and deadly hunting scenes play out, the film cuts jarringly back and forth between these erotic moments and a sterilised medical setting in which a frantic and rapidly aging macaque in a cage brutally attacks and kills his mate. After the macaque has died and suddenly deteriorates to bone and then dust, the audience is introduced to Dr Sarah Roberts (Susan Sarandon), who researches the aging process. Sarah's path crosses with the Blaylocks' when John, regardless of his being a vampire, begins to age rapidly; he, in fact, ages decades in the few hours that he waits to speak to her about his affliction. Sarah tracks him down only to come face to face with his seductive wife, Miriam. *The Hunger* leaves the audience without an explanation concerning Miriam's immortality while her male and female lovers age over the centuries. Although they, too, are vampires who have been brought into the life by her, they hit a purgatory-like endpoint and exist on the precipice of turning into dust, yet are still able to function cognitively well enough to understand that they are eternally entombed in a mummified state in Miriam's attic crypt.

Shortly after Miriam carries the mouldering John up several flights of stairs to the crypt and then asks her other decayed lovers to look after him, she invites Sarah into her home and seduces her in an iconic queer vampiric seduction scene. As Bianca Garner notes of this scene, 'at the time it was a controversial and ground-breaking moment for a number of reasons, not the least of which was that both actresses appeared in the scene seemingly without the use of body

---

[13] Sorcha Ní Fhlainn, *Postmodern Vampires: Film, Fiction, and Popular Culture* (London: Palgrave Macmillan, 2019), pp. 88–9.

doubles, requiring Scott to close the set'.[14] During their lovemaking, Miriam bites Sarah, and the two exchange blood. Shortly afterwards, Sarah becomes agitated; being unable to eat anything, including a raw steak that she orders at a restaurant, she wakes up with night sweats and vomiting and gives her colleagues a blood sample that they study under the microscope where they find two different strains of blood – one human and the other not. Clearly, Miriam's vampiric blood battles against Sarah's human blood. When Sarah confronts Miriam in an incredibly confusing finale, her understanding that her blood has now morphed from human to vampire causes her to grasp for Miriam's ankh-shaped dagger necklace and she attempts to commit suicide rather than accept her fate as a vampire. The scene shifts again and we see that not only has Sarah survived, but she has turned the tables and entombed Miriam with all of her past beloveds in a new crypt, as she stands on the balcony of an expensive London apartment while her two new lovers (a man and a woman) play classical music.

As numerous stills from the film attest, Tony Scott's associating of queer sexuality with vampirism and AIDS would have been obvious to his 1983 audience (Fig. 13.1). Nicola Nixon notes the following in her essay on vampirism in the Reagan era:

> There is something eerily familiar about the scenario of a seemingly-beautiful, charmingly-anonymous lover who, during an unusually passionate sexual encounter, transmits some virulent infection that cannot even be diagnosed, let along cured. Indeed, if we examine *The Hunger* now, it seems considerably less remarkable for its depiction of an early 1980s vampirism than it does for its stunning resemblance to an extended AIDS allegory.[15]

Of course, there is nothing new about the connections between vampirism and queer sexuality: Le Fanu's *Carmilla*; Mary Elizabeth Braddon's 'The Good Lady Ducayne' (1896); and Bram Stoker's *Dracula* (1897) all helped to invent this tradition; however, with a new pandemic associated with the queer community, Gothic modes, queer sexuality and AIDS became inextricably enmeshed. *The Hunger* underscores these associations between vampiric contagion, queer contagion and AIDS contagion on numerous levels. Ní Fhlainn observes these connections as embodied by John Blaylock:

---

[14] Bianca Garner, 'Sink Your Teeth Into This: Revisiting The Hunger (1983)', *Filmotomy: Dissecting Film from the Grit to the Stars*, 1 June 2018 <https://filmotomy.com/hunger-review-1983/> (last accessed 10 September 2020).

[15] Nicola Nixon, 'When Hollywood Sucks, or, Hungry Girls, Lost Boys, and Vampirism in the Age of Reagan', in Joan Gordon and Veronica Hollinger (eds), *Blood Read: The Vampire as Metaphor in Contemporary Culture* (Philadelphia: University of Pennsylvania Press, 1997), pp. 115–28 (p. 117).

Fig.13.1: French actress Catherine Deneuve and British singer and actor David Bowie on the set of the 1983 film *The Hunger*, directed by Tony Scott. (Photo by Metro-Goldwyn-Mayer Pictures/Sunset Boulevard/Corbis via Getty Images).

His rapid decay illustrates the onset of AIDS symptoms betraying his once immortal body; he notes liver spots on his hands (which double as lesions) and the rapid degeneration of his skin cells; his hair begins to fall out and his once lithe body is rendered feeble and weak within hours of the diagnosis. The symptoms John suffers mimic the onset of the ageing process, but, as these symptoms occur rapidly and inexplicably, they are more redolent of early AIDS pathology as best understood in the early 1980s.[16]

The AIDS imagery in the film continues when Sarah, shortly after her sexual and vampiric encounter with Miriam, wakes up with night sweats and vomiting – some of the first signs of the onset of AIDS. Framing Sarah's night-time illness, though, is the intensity of her colleagues studying her bloodwork under the microscope, where they see her human blood and another non-human invasive strain of blood attempting to colonise her healthy blood cells. In this moment, the Gothic representation of the vampire's blood becomes synonymous with queer blood and AIDS blood. It is as though monstrosity can be read in Sarah's warring cells. Queer blood becomes inhuman and monstrous. It is also important to note that Sarah's blood is

---

[16] Ní Fhlainn, *Postmodern Vampires*, p. 89.

analysed in the same laboratory in which they have been running experiments with macaques and that, in 1983, one of the prevalent theories about the origin of AIDS was that it came from monkeys.

Miriam Blaylock, the seductive bisexual vampire with numerous past lovers, becomes symbolic of the elision of vampiric, queer and AIDS panic, a relationship considered elsewhere by Marty Fink:

> Because vampires manifest unrestrained sexuality as a form of disease, they also perpetuate the popular misconception that sexual deviancy causes HIV/AIDS ... Metaphorically converting the person living with HIV/AIDS into a vampiric outsider blames those who are seropositive for their own medical condition. Rather than recognizing the need to invest in treatment and prevention programs both locally and on a global scale, our governments and media outlets metaphorize HIV/AIDS as an evil, mysterious ailment whose sufferers have transgressed and should therefore be punished. As such, HIV/AIDS is regarded as a moral threat rather than as a social health concern. Framing illness as oppositional to sexual and national values, the vampire functions as an allegorical suggestion that those living with HIV/AIDS or otherwise marked as diseased should be banished and feared, punished and slain.[17]

For audiences in 1983, Miriam's vampirism, bisexuality and seduction of Sarah exemplify the junctures between vampirism, 'sexual deviancy' and AIDS as 'an evil, mysterious ailment'. For heteronormative audience members, especially in the early 1980s, AIDS was stereotyped as a 'gay disease' and the term 'gay', in the general public's understanding, encompassed the entire LGBTQ+ community: gay, lesbian, bisexual, transgender and queer. However, the predominant group exposed to AIDS at that time was specifically that of men who had sex with men; this is one of the reasons why trans women were often not studied properly because they were still being defined by their sex assigned at birth. Although the infamous sex scene with Deneuve and Sarandon was, culturally, on every lesbian's 'must see' list, there is in Tony Scott's film another pernicious stereotype within lesbian communities at play – that of bisexual contagion. The film's depiction of the *bisexual* vampire rather than a *lesbian* vampire passing the disease on to another woman (although Sarah's character is generally understood to be heterosexual) underscores the animosity that many bi women have felt in some lesbian communities. It is as though bisexual embodiment is similar to vampiric embodiment in that they are both liminal conditions.

[17] Marty Fink, 'AIDS Vampires: Reimagining Illness in Octavia Butler's "Fledgling"', *Science Fiction Studies* 37:3 (November 2010): 416–32 (p. 417).

While Scott's film observes the associations between vampirism, queer sexuality and AIDS from what seems like a social or political distance, Todd Haynes focuses his sharp critique on the ways in which society in the late 1980s and early 1990s treated queers. Haynes was developing his ideas for his triptych, *Poison*, during a remarkably tumultuous time – particularly in the United States – insofar as AIDS and queer policies and politics were concerned. In 1986 (the first year that Ronald Reagan publically uttered the word 'AIDS'), the United States Supreme Court upheld the Georgia Sodomy Laws in the case of *Bowers v. Hardwick*. With this ruling, queer sexuality between consenting adults in public and private continued to be criminalised in numerous US states.[18] The following year, on 12 March 1987, AIDS activist and author Larry Kramer founded AIDS Coalition to Unleash Power (ACT-UP) as a 'political direct-action group that will force governments, elected officials, public health agencies, the pharmaceutical and insurance industries, and religious institutions to act to protect those at risk of HIV, and those who are sick with AIDS'.[19] On 11 October 1987, over 800,000 people marched on Washington, DC for LGBTQ+ rights, demanding that President Reagan acknowledge the AIDS crisis and the nation's lack of full human rights for queer people. In 1989 Hans Paul Verhoff, a Dutch person living with AIDS who was travelling to San Francisco to give a talk, was denied entry into the USA because of his AIDS status; this sparked protests and an international boycott of the 1990 International AIDS Convention in San Francisco.[20]

Haynes's *Poison* opens with the following words from Jean Genet: 'The whole world is dying of panicky fright.'[21] Haynes employs Genet's words to encapsulate this particular apocalyptic moment: a decade into the AIDS pandemic; the continuing criminalisation of queer sexuality in the USA as well as other nations; no vaccine and no cure in sight and over half a million dead globally.[22] Introducing the film at an arthouse cinema opening, Haynes told the audience:

---

[18] *Bowers v. Hardwick* <https://supreme.justia.com/cases/federal/us/478/186/> (last accessed 11 October 2020).
[19] HIV.gov <www.hiv.gov/hiv-basics/overview/history/hiv-and-aids-timeline> (last accessed 16 September 2020).
[20] The ACT-UP Historical Archive <https://actupny.org/actions/Immigration.html> (last accessed 11 October 2020).
[21] *Poison*. Dir. Todd Haynes. Bronze Eye Productions, Zeitgeist Films. 1991. Zeitgeist Films, 2011. DVD.
[22] Richard Hunt, 'Virology – Chapter Seven, Part Five: Human Immunodeficiency Virus and AIDS Statistics', *Microbiology and Immunology On-line,* University of South Carolina School of Medicine <www.microbiologybook.org/lecture/hiv5.htm> (last accessed 11 October 2020).

> I felt that the gulf between Genet's death [in 1986] and the breakout of the AIDS epidemic was something that could be bridged ... Genet's ideas and positions ... could be applied in a kind of empowering way to what the gay community was already feeling as a profound blow. The film was an attempt to recover our own sense of freedom – to exist, to express ourselves, and to experiment.[23]

Haynes's film became *the* example of the New Queer Cinema genre as defined by queer film critic B. Ruby Rich: 'Four elements converged to result in the NQC: the arrival of AIDS, Reagan, camcorders, and cheap rent. Plus the emergence of "queer" as a concept and a community. Outrage and opportunity merged into a historic artistic response to insufferable political repression.'[24] *Poison* shocked the cinematic world when it was awarded the Sundance Film Festival's Grand Jury Prize, the Berlin International Film Festival's Teddy Best Feature Film and numerous other global film accolades.

In *Poison*, Genet's opening quotation haunts all three of the stories presented: 'Hero', 'Horror' and 'Homo'. Although the narratives are discrete, Haynes disregards any rigid framing devices and their styles ultimately collapse into one another. In a 1991 review for *The Village Voice*, J. Hoberman noted that '*Poison* flips from Grade Z horror to open-air lyricism to deadpan interview and back, spiraling ever more emphatically into each tale's abyss. The stories ... seep across boundaries, flowing in and out of each other'.[25] 'Hero' is filmed in a grainy 1980s television news documentary style and focuses on the story of Richie, a 7-year-old boy who shoots and kills his abusive father. Immediately following this act, Richie flies away. Throughout the 'Hero' storyline, people at Richie's school, his neighbours and his mother comment on the sort of child that he was. These interviews make it clear that Richie was 'different' and not a 'normal' boy. In 'Horror', Haynes employs a vintage 1950s black-and-white Gothic horror approach with 'exaggerated, looming *noir* angles and the exuberantly gross makeup of a 50s monster movie'.[26] 'Horror' recounts the story of Dr Graves, who has distilled the human sex drive into a liquid form. When his female colleague, Dr Olsen, flirts with him in the laboratory, he becomes so flustered that he reaches for

---

[23] David Hudson, '"Poison", World Cinema Foundation, Comment, More', *MUBI: Notebook News* <https://mubi.com/notebook/posts/poison-world-cinema-foundation-film-comment-more> (last accessed 6 October 2020).

[24] B. Ruby Rich, *New Queer Cinema: The Director's Cut* (Durham, NC and London: Duke University Press, 2013), pp. xv–xvi.

[25] J. Hoberman, 'Blood, Sweat and Fears', originally published on 9 April 1991 in *The Village Voice*, reprinted in *Poison: 20th Anniversary Edition* liner notes, p. 7.

[26] Hoberman, 'Blood, Sweat and Fears', p. 7.

his cup of cold coffee, but, instead, accidentally drinks the sex potion. Shortly afterwards, his skin begins to melt off of his body and everyone that he touches becomes infected with disease. The police nickname Dr Graves the 'Leper Sex Killer' and hunt down the sexual outlaw as he runs through the neighbourhood, causing panic. The final section of the triptych, 'Homo', is an opulent pastiche of Genet's *Miracle of the Rose* (1946) and focuses on a doomed romance in a men's prison with flashbacks to the beautiful and sometimes cruel male homoeroticism found at a detention centre for boys. All three parts of Haynes's triptych employ Gothic history and Gothic tropes as well as the history of queer sexuality; beneath these stories lies a powerful AIDS metaphor.

In his 'Director's Statement' on the twentieth anniversary edition of *Poison* Haynes notes that, 'in all three cases, we encounter a central character that has been shut out by his society as a result of his transgression of certain laws ... it's a film that plays around with the act of telling stories while at the same time asking a few serious questions about the nature of deviance, cultural conditioning and disease'.[27] Haynes utilises Gothic within a New Queer Cinema scope – and encapsulates queer history and AIDS history throughout the film; however, in some respects, the most queer narrative in the triptych is 'Horror', and it is precisely his use of Gothic that makes this queer within its historical context. As Hoberman posited in his initial 1991 film review, 'The horrified stares that greet Dr Graves and Olsen, a hetero couple out for an innocent stroll, have implications far beyond Graves's disgusting affliction ... Without ever alluding to AIDS by name ... Haynes has made what may be the toughest, most troubling, and least compromised movie on the crisis to date.'[28]

When Dr Graves drinks the sex-drive elixir, the audience is reminded of the 'guilt' narratives surrounding queer people with AIDS and the decade-long demonisation of the queer community throughout all levels of culture and society and from a range of different standpoints: legal (*Bowers v. Hardwick*); medical (blood banks' refusal to take any blood from people in the LGBTQ+ community and later amended to men who have sex with men); and political (Senator Jesse Helms revoking funding for queer arts). Like queers, Dr Graves brings the hideous decomposing disease upon himself. By drawing on a Gothic framework, Haynes infuses the one overtly heterosexual story in the triptych with queer imagery. For Norman Bryson,

---

[27] Todd Haynes, 'Director's Statement', *Poison: 20th Anniversary Edition* liner notes, p. 4.
[28] Hoberman, 'Blood, Sweat and Fears', pp. 7–8.

Poison epitomises the ways in which queer cinema, specifically, is meant to upend heteronormativity:

> Queer art history and visual studies have no less an ambition than to take on heteronormativity's entire visual field ... Queer cinema traces a different course: its aims include developing an understanding of the visual field of heteronormative film, the discourse with which compulsory heterosexuality of nearly all cinema is constantly secured and re-secured, and the central role that the stigmatization of gay and lesbian visuality plays in constructing the cinematic dominant.[29]

Dr Graves is queered through his becoming a social pariah by way of disease. The elision of his melting face with images that are all too familiar within the queer community of KS lesions and healthy bodies wasting away queer both the doctor and his relationship with Dr Olsen. 'Horror' offers what Bryson calls a 'heteronormative visual field' only to queer it with a lesson in what it is like to be queer, diseased and hunted down.

The Gothic depictions of the mad scientist recall, of course, other historic queer Gothic narratives, most notably Stevenson's *Dr Jekyll and Mr Hyde* (1886) and Oscar Wilde's *The Picture of Dorian Gray* (1890). Bryson notes that both nineteenth-century fictions explore science as it 'rebounds against itself', claiming that they 'vividly dramatize' the 'historical emergence of the medical construction of sexuality and disease'.[30] With reference to 'Horror', Bryson writes that 'Haynes's narrative is that the ultimate source of the epidemic is science itself' since nineteenth-century sexologists invented and labelled homosexuality as such. He posits that 'the context of visuality in which AIDS was first assimilated was already structured by a specific medico-juridical gaze that was bound to interpret the advent of AIDS in terms of its own homophobic gaze'.[31] It is through this homophobic gaze that people with AIDS were labelled as serial killers, just as Dr Graves flees from the police who are trying to arrest him and contain his contagious body. At the end of 'Horror', Graves stands on the ledge of a fire escape a few storeys above a mesmerised audience. From this ledge, and with his pustular and melting face, he tells the gawkers, 'Pride is the only thing that lets you stand up to misery' and then falls to his death.[32] Haynes uses Gothic in his 'Horror' sequence in order to validate the queer community's 'state of severe

---

[29] Norman Bryson, 'Todd Haynes's *Poison* and Queer Cinema', *InVisible Culture: An Electronic Journal for Visual Culture* 1: The Worlding of Cultural Studies (Winter 1998), para. 9. <www.rochester.edu/in_visible_culture/issue1/bryson/> (last accessed 15 December 2020).
[30] Bryson, 'Todd Haynes's *Poison*', para. 24. [31] Bryson, 'Todd Haynes's *Poison*', para. 25.
[32] *Poison*, 1:17:12.

despair ... in the shadow of the AIDS epidemic and a far right administration and climate in this country that we have had for a while'.[33] *Poison* is brutal and unapologetic as it voices queer anguish and trauma in the face of layers of homophobic violence.

Shifting the Script: Gothic Narrative Interventions and Hauntings in Queer AIDS Stories, 1993–2018

Between the 1991 release of Todd Haynes's *Poison* and Canadian filmmaker John Greyson's 1993 AIDS musical satire, *Zero Patience*, some small yet critical milestones were reached in the AIDS pandemic, including ACT-UP's forcing the Food and Drug Administration's early release of AZT – an early anti-retroviral – and new HIV clinical trials.[34] Both New Queer Cinema directors found unique ways to bring Gothic as a political mechanism to their art. For Haynes, a classic 1950s Gothic look accompanied the righteously angry and desperate narrative of the ostracised. *Zero Patience*, on the other hand, is a musical satire replete with Gothic elements; it is a reconstruction of silenced queer histories; it is a powerful and haunted de-colonial recovery project; and, ultimately, it is an AIDS film. Over two decades after the release of *Zero Patience*, Lana and Lilly Wachowski and J. Michael Straczynski's television series *Sense8* also uses a multiplicity of genres to explore the intersections of Gothic frameworks, queer sexuality and the trajectory of AIDS into the twenty-first century. *Zero Patience* and *Sense8* offer Gothic narrative interventions in the continuing story of AIDS.

Zero Patience is a satiric and bawdy musical defence of Gaëtan Dugas, the infamous French-Canadian airline steward who was scapegoated for bringing AIDS to North America in Randy Shilts's book *And the Band Played On* (1987). Shilts was part of the queer community – he died from AIDS in 1994 – yet his chronicling of the unfolding AIDS pandemic demonised Dugas as 'Patient Zero' from one set of cluster studies on gay men with KS in the early 1980s. Christopher Gittings comments that, 'As part of its oppositional approach to Shilts's version of Dugas, *Zero Patience* traces the role of ideology in the cultural construction of homosexuality and AIDS ... The queer cinema of John Greyson is a militant, interventionist system of representation that subverts the cultural assumptions formed by a ruling heterosexist

---

[33] Michael Laskawy and Todd Haynes, 'Poison at the Box Office: AN INTERVIEW WITH TODD HAYNES', *Cinéast* 18:3 (1991): 38–9 (p. 39).
[34] HIV.gov <https://www.hiv.gov/hiv-basics/overview/history/hiv-and-aids-timeline> (last accessed 16 September 2020).

ideology.'[35] In his film, Greyson imagines Dugas (whom he lovingly names Zero) as a ghost who comes back from the dead to clear his name. Zero's return as a ghost signifies what Avery F. Gordon refers to as a type of social and cultural haunting that 'always registers the harm inflicted or the loss sustained by a social violence done in the past or in the present'.[36] Zero's ghost returns in order to illuminate the harm done to him, individually, as he was scapegoated as a contagious monster. However, Zero's ghost also draws attention to the ongoing social violence perpetrated against queer people generally and against people with AIDS (many of them queer) specifically. In the opening scene, viewers are treated to a dream-like sequence in which Zero tumbles along a steamy indoor swimming pool platform in a tight black wrestling singlet and then dances with a disco ball with synchronised swimmers performing below him. The movie's theme song, 'Just Like Scheherazade', plays as he twirls with the disco ball, singing how he wants to 'tell the story' to save his life from the deathly condition of loneliness.[37] As the song concludes, Zero takes a plunge off a diving board and then materialises in the middle of a hot tub surrounded by naked and beautiful men in a bathhouse. He is, however, a ghost and they do not see him.

While Zero is busy haunting the bathhouse, the audience is told, in a parallel plot, that Sir Richard Burton, the nineteenth-century sexologist and scientist, actually never died, but rather had an unfortunate encounter with the Fountain of Youth. For the past century, he has been holed up in Toronto, Canada, working in the Natural History Museum, stuffing animals. When we first meet 'Dick' Burton, he is in the process of preparing for his latest exhibit: The Hall of Contagion. Burton has just received word that the paltry museum budget will not allow him to purchase the stuffed plague rat that he had hoped to use as his centrepiece. As he considers his options, a paper aeroplane mysteriously floats into the room and hits Burton on the head. It is a picture of Patient Zero, face covered in KS lesions, staring at the camera. Burton decides that a hologram of the boyish and sexy Zero covered in KS lesions will be the perfect addition to the Hall of Contagion. With this in mind, he heads out to conduct various interviews with people who knew Zero when he was alive. As Burton films Zero's doctor, friends, mother and

---

[35] Christopher Gittings, '"Zero Patience": Genre, Difference, and Ideology: Singing and Dancing Queer Nation', *Cinema Journal* 41.1 (Autumn 2001): 28–39 (p. 29).
[36] Avery F. Gordon, *Ghostly Matters: Haunting and the Sociological Imagination*, 2nd edition (Minneapolis: University of Minnesota Press, 2008), p. xvi.
[37] Glenn Schellenberg, 'Just Like Scheherazade', in *Zero Patience*. Dir. John Greyson. Zero Patience Productions and Téléfilm Canada, Cineplex Odeon Films. 1993.

lovers, he takes their kindness and defence of Zero out of context and edits his film to make the argument that Zero, like Typhoid Mary, was really a serial killer. Greyson's critique of heteronormative society's false notions of people with AIDS – queer people with AIDS – as serial killers is vastly different from Haynes's approach in 'Horror'; however, the message is still clear: queer people generally and queer people with AIDS more specifically are wrongly stereotyped as killers. As queer filmmakers, Haynes and Greyson tear apart these homophobic ideas. Gittings writes the following concerning Greyson's approach to these homophobic stereotypes:

> Greyson locates the deconstructive narrative of *Zero Patience* in the matrices of the Hollywood musical, horror, and documentary genres, contextualizing these heteronormative forms within a genealogy of foundational texts in homophobia as represented in the film by the historical character of nineteenth-century explorer and anthropologist Sir Richard Francis Burton, who quotes from his own Victorian (homo)sexology on the sotadic zones.[38]

Burton lurks outside of the home of one of Zero's former lovers, George, an immigrant from Grenada and elementary school teacher who is going blind and dying from AIDS. While Burton surreptitiously films through the open curtains while making up his own inaccurate narrative about Zero, George and Barry (George's Black partner), the conversation inside the house grows melancholic. Clearly haunted by his memories of Zero, George sets up his slide projector to show Barry old photos of Zero as he talks about his own guilt over never visiting Zero at the hospital and his terror of touching him in the last days before he succumbed to AIDS. This is a critical scene in Greyson's use of the Gothic to discuss the broader ramifications of haunting. Gordon notes that 'what's distinctive about haunting is that it is an animated state in which a repressed or unresolved social violence is making itself known'.[39] Burton, on a hill just above George and Barry's home, uses the lens of his own video recorder to view George's projections of Zero on a plate-glass window within the house. The layers of 'repressed or unresolved social violence' in this scene are numerous: a Victorian imperialist sexologist who should be dead continues various forms of colonial violence through his misrepresentations; the image of a healthy and smiling Zero projected onto the glass haunts the viewer as we recall the images of his wan visage covered in KS lesions; and, beyond Burton's video recorder and the projected image of Zero, we see a domestic scene between two gay men of colour who are

---

[38] Gittings, '"Zero Patience:" Genre, Difference, and Ideology', pp. 29–30.
[39] Gordon, *Ghostly Matters*, p. xvi.

both part of the long, haunted narrative of past colonial violence and current anti-gay and anti-AIDS violence. This scene is interrupted by Zero's ghost confronting Burton over the false accusations that he is a serial killer. In this moment, the very real and animated ghost calls Burton out over his wrongdoing. 'Dick' Burton can see Zero, a detail which calls his own status – he is possibly undead – into question.

Since Burton is the only person who can see Zero, he takes him back to his apartment in the museum where Zero interrogates him about his homophobic and racist nineteenth-century anthropological assumptions. Over time, Zero convinces Burton that he, too, was a victim of AIDS; Zero was not a guilty party. As Zero looks through Burton's microscope to analyse a laboratory slide of his own blood that has been taken as part of a cluster study, Miss HIV, a drag queen, floats on an inner tube under the lens and sings a reprise of the introductory song in which the virus replaces Zero as the central character in the story.[40] Neville Hoad argues that this 'anthropomorphizing of the virus makes an ethical claim around the unruliness of the body. The scene makes it clear that Zero has no control over the pathogens in his bloodstream. They literally have lives of their own'.[41]

As Burton stands beside Zero watching Miss HIV's song, he begins to understand that Zero is also a victim and not a serial killer. As Burton commences to deconstruct his own scientific biases, he begins to fall in love with Zero's ghost. As Burton and Zero embark on a brief relationship, Burton begins to open himself up to new possibilities and the idea of truths beyond his own Victorian scope. When Burton visits a local chapter of ACT-UP, he begins to understand that the big pharmaceutical companies bent on making a fortune by keeping people sick are the true monsters in this AIDS story. And it is through his reconsidering of his own biases against Zero and the AIDS activists that Burton embraces the need to question everything that he had held as absolute truth. In the grand finale, the Hall of Contagion literally goes up in flames as Burton stands by and watches as Zero burns back into the ether – but this time as a hero who actually cooperated with doctors to help them understand that AIDS was a sexually transmitted disease.

Greyson's imagining of Zero as a ghost allows him freedom to explore the complex interlocking histories of Gothic, AIDS, queer sexuality and decolonial histories. As Zero sings in the opening song 'Just Like Scheherazade', he wants the story of his life told so as to correct the record.

[40] Schellenberg, 'Just Like Scheherazade'.
[41] Neville Hoad, 'Miss HIV and Us: Beauty Queens Against the HIV/AIDS Pandemic', *CR: The New Centennial Review* 10:1 (Spring 2010): 9–28 (p. 17).

Zero wants to fight back against not only his victimisation as a scapegoat, but also on behalf of all of those other marginalised individuals throughout history who have been made famous as carriers of contagion – Typhoid Mary and the nameless African American men used as experimental fodder for studying syphilis in the infamous Tuskegee Study.[42] Zero's ghost comes back to haunt us and to make sure that his story is re-told in an empathetic way. His ghost directly confronts the social and cultural violence done to him as an individual as well as the misrepresentation and violence done to those marginalised people living with and dying from AIDS.

In the final scene at the Hall of Contagion, Typhoid Mary is healed and turned into a suffragette, the man experimented on at Tuskegee becomes influential Black agricultural scientist George Washington Carver, and the Dutch plague boat turned away into a stormy sea for fear of contagion is, instead, given a set of life preservers (there is, too, a pun here on life preservers as a euphemism for condoms). Ultimately, though, it is our ghost, Zero, who haunts Sir Richard Burton, causing him to revise his own past histories and, in this way, his ghost reaches across time and space to begin a reconciliation and to heal historic wounds. And all of this as he disappears in flames – perhaps to go back to dancing under that fabulous seventies disco ball.

Thematically, AIDS constantly lurks beneath Lana and Lilly Wachowski and J. Michael Straczynski's 2015–18 Netflix Original Series *Sense8*. In describing *Sense8*, Dilyana Mincheva writes that, 'In terms of form, *Sense8* is a text that dwells in a *trans* universe: trans-gender, trans-genre, trans-subjective, and trans-physical.'[43] Usually described as a science fiction show, *Sense8* employs Gothic style and Gothic imagery as part of its 'trans-genre' nature. The Gothic moments within *Sense8* are also some of the most interesting queer moments – and in some cases, these specific scenes are haunted by AIDS. The advancement in AIDS treatment between Greyson's 1993 film and *Sense8* is astounding. Combination antiretrovirals became globally available in 1996, extending people's lives, and pre-exposure prophylaxis (PrEP) medications were approved in 2012, reducing risks of acquiring the virus, despite the

---

[42] Ada McVean, '40 Years of Human Experimentation in America: The Tuskegee Study,' 25 January 2019, McGill University Office for Science and Society <www.mcgill.ca/oss/article/history/40-years-human-experimentation-america-tuskegee-study> (last accessed 20 November 2020).

[43] Dilyana Mincheva, '*Sense8* and the Praxis of Utopia', *Cinephile* 12:1 (Spring 2018): 32–9 (p. 32).

continuing lack of a vaccine or a cure for AIDS. The year 2021 marks four decades of living with AIDS in the world.

Sense8 follows eight people from around the world who were all born on the same day at the same moment. The characters are 'sensate', meaning that they possess an ability that 'normal' humans do not: they are able to occupy each other's minds and hearts without being physically present. This means that they can speak each other's languages and embody each other's special talents. Mincheva explains that 'the show aims to depict a queer, global, multi-gender, post-national community which is on the one hand deeply immersed in the internet world of visual culture and tactile interfaces while on the other hand, is linked through psychic energy, body to body, and mind to mind, without the mediation of visual or visible technology'.[44]

The sensates in the show's cluster hail from Germany, Iceland, India, Kenya, México, South Korea and the United States. For some of these characters, an overt AIDS sub-plot exists. In the case of Capheus in Kenya, for example, his mother suffers from AIDS until he is able to get into the good graces of a local wealthy thug who then supplies her with high-quality antiretrovirals. Kala in India, meanwhile, is a top scientist at a pharmaceutical company in Mumbai; however, late in the second season, she learns to her horror that her husband, who is the CEO of the company, has been happily shipping expired AIDS medicine to Africa (and hence to people like Capheus's mother). In both of these cases, the story of AIDS in this contemporary global landscape is focused on heterosexual people. However, the more interesting AIDS story throughout *Sense8* exists at a metaphoric level with Nomi (Jamie Clayton), a white transgender lesbian living with her Black partner, Amanita (Freema Agyeman), in San Francisco.

In her discussion of AIDS and trauma, Laura Westengard argues that 'Though the circumstances have changed drastically, the impact of HIV/AIDS on queer communities, both then and now, is a source of accumulated and unacknowledged insidious trauma.'[45] Similarly, Gordon describes haunting as 'one way in which abusive systems of power make themselves known and their impacts felt in everyday life, *especially when they are supposedly over and done with* [emphasis mine]'.[46] It is within these ideas of the 'accumulated and unacknowledged insidious trauma' and of being haunted by abusive systems of power that 'are supposedly over and done with' that AIDS and Gothic tropes and Gothic metaphors become imbricated within Nomi's

---

[44] Mincheva, '*Sense8* and the Praxis of Utopia', p. 32.
[45] Westengard, *Gothic Queer Culture*, p. 102.   [46] Gordon, *Ghostly Matters*, p. xvi.

queer and trans history. In the first episode of *Sense8*, 'Limbic Resonance', Nomi and Amanita attend a production of Sean Dorsey Dance's *The Missing Generation* the night before the San Francisco Pride Parade. Sean Dorsey Dance is a trans and queer dance troupe founded in San Francisco and headed by Sean Dorsey, the world's first out trans dance choreographer. Dorsey characteristically spends months studying historic archives that will inform the themes of his dance shows. For *The Missing Generation*, Dorsey interviewed people living with AIDS, loved ones left behind by those who had died from AIDS and archives chronicling people who had lived and died with AIDS. The title of Dorsey's production refers to the ghosts of queer ancestors like Greyson's Zero and George whom we have, collectively, lost to the pandemic – an entire generation missing.[47] While Nomi and Amanita watch the dance performance punctuated with words from those dead from AIDS in the darkened theatre, the spotlight catches Nomi's sensate 'mother', Angelica (Daryl Hannah), as she beckons to Nomi. It is crucial that Nomi's 'birth' as a sensate happens in the middle of an eerie and nostalgic homage to a queer community still traumatised and haunted from decades of death and a disease we are supposed to feel 'done' with because of the antiretrovirals and PrEP. In the moment of Nomi's 'birth' she, as a trans lesbian, becomes part of the haunted queer AIDS story.[48] Angelica appears in the spotlight alongside the dancers telling the story of queer AIDS history. At the moment that Nomi sees Angelica, the tale being recounted is one of a lover who has wasted away to a mere 90 pounds; he begs his partner to carry him up to the roof of their flat and just throw him off – throw him out of their collective misery. This scene recalls the moment in Todd Haynes's 'Horror' when Dr Graves, his body melting away, falls to his death. Gothic scenes, queer trauma and AIDS trauma intersect.

In the second episode of *Sense8*, 'I Am Also A We', Nomi falls off the back of Amanita's motorbike during the San Francisco Pride Parade when she sees a sensate from another cluster, Jonas, staring at her. Concussed, Nomi wakes up in the hospital where she is made monstrous when Dr Metzger tells her that her brain scan is abnormal; if she does not undergo immediate surgery she will die. The cold dread that Nomi feels is warranted as this doctor has

---

[47] Sean Dorsey Dance, *The Missing Generation*, live dance performance at Mission Dance in San Francisco, June 2015.
[48] Lana Wachowski, Lilly Wachowski and J. Michael Straczynski, 'Limbic Resonance', *Sense8*, series 1, episode 1; TV episode first aired in USA on 5 June 2015. Anarchos Productions, Georgeville Television, Javelin Productions, Motion Picture Capital, Studio JMS, Unpronounceable Productions. Distributed by Netflix.

a sinister plan to lobotomise her. Nomi desperately seeks an ally when she tells the nurse, 'You can't keep me here against my will.' And the nurse replies, 'I'm afraid we can. Dr Metzger and your family have signed the papers.' We can hear in this exchange a critique of the past violent history of queers trapped in medical settings. Nomi pleads with the nurse: 'I cannot believe that this is happening to me in the twenty-first century.' Nomi's statement is heavy with a past that is haunted by the institutionalising of queer people – the shock treatments and the lobotomies. In this moment, Nomi experiences Gordon's idea that 'haunting raises spectres, and it alters the experience of being in time, the way we separate the past, the present, and the future'.[49] Nomi's haunted return to past institutional violence done to queer and trans people exemplifies the ways that Gothic tropes often utilise a return of the past on the present. The ways that queer and trans people were treated in medical settings in the 1950s has a direct correlation with the horrific ways in which people with AIDS were treated early in the pandemic.

Westengard reminds us that 'Monstrosity as a gothic metaphor of hybridity and excess reflected those dehumanizing narratives used against people with HIV and AIDS during the crisis, but gothic metaphors also have the potential to productively reframe these oppressive narratives.'[50] The history of the Gothic, as Gothic appears in *Sense8*, depicts the ways in which the mode can and does reframe past oppressive narratives where AIDS and queer people are concerned. Even as the Wachowskis and Straczynski attempted positively to conclude *Sense8* with a spectacular scene at Nomi and Amanita's Paris wedding at the Eiffel Tower, however, the AIDS subtext is never completely resolved – there still is no cure. It leaves us in a limbo just as the real AIDS pandemic has done. AIDS is the ghost around the edges of this jubilant queer celebration.

Queer culture has been forever transposed by the AIDS pandemic; Gothic as a mode, too, has changed as it has been utilised as a means to explore queer themes, and particularly the queer community's collective trauma and ongoing haunting by the spectre of AIDS. When Nomi is birthed by her sensate mother, she comes into the sensate world through the AIDS stories of death, trauma and haunting. In that moment of transition and embodiment, Nomi Marks is a healthy trans queer woman in 2015; however, Nomi Marks, through Gothic modes and haunting, is also every person from that missing generation.

[49] Gordon, *Ghostly Matters*, p. xvi. [50] Westengard, *Queer Gothic Culture*, p. 102.

3.14

The Gothic in the Age of Neo-Liberalism, 1990–Present

LINNIE BLAKE

Neoliberal Gothic

Championing punitive reductions to public spending, the deregulation of financial markets and the globalisation of trade, neoliberal economics was pioneered in the 1980s by Margaret Thatcher in the UK and Ronald Reagan in the US and has been consolidated by every British and American government since. Accordingly, neoliberalism has now become so monumental as to preclude popular consideration of alternative modes of economic organisation. Spread, in part, by the monetisation of natural disasters such as Hurricane Katrina and engineered crises like the War on Terror (and subsequent Arab Spring), neoliberal economics has been promulgated, therefore, by national governments and supranational organisations alike. While sovereign states have entered trade agreements with more powerful nations, sacrificing self-determination on working conditions and hours, environmental protection and anything else that might hinder corporate profitability, supranational organisations such as the World Trade Organization, the World Bank and the International Monetary Fund have made neoliberal policies a condition for loans to developing nations. The result has been the creation of a world in which we are less free and more unequal than ever before.[1] Such inequality not only promotes political instability and internecine conflict in the most unequal countries but also exerts a profound human cost across the world – from community breakdown to violent crime, mental illness and the collapse of families and communities. What I term 'Neoliberal Gothic' thus functions as a means of exploring the societal, environmental and

---

[1] By 2018, OXFAM reported, the richest 1 per cent now possessed as much of the world's wealth as the poorest 57 per cent combined, 82 per cent of the global wealth generated in 2017 having gone to that selfsame 1 per cent. See OXFAM, *The Commitment to Reducing Inequality Index*, October 2018 <https://oxfamilibrary.openrepository.com/bitstream/handle/10546/620553/rr-commitment-reducing-inequality-index-2018-091018-en.pdf> (last accessed 10 December 2018).

human cost of the current economic order. It proliferates across media and consistently interrogates the broken social contract of the present and its impact upon individuals and communities. Thus, my work on Neoliberal Gothic has sought to chart the explosion of popular interest in the Gothic in recent years, and to explore the ways in which such texts have exposed the global cost of the ongoing rush to inequality while evoking the material realities of living in societies in which an ethic of radical individualism prevails. This chapter will refer, therefore, to this body of work while engaging with a range of Gothic texts that are self-consciously engaged with the neoliberal contexts from which they emerged.

This is not, though, to argue that Gothic texts of the neoliberal period necessarily proffer a radical critique of the present time and place. As I have written elsewhere, Stephenie Meyer's enormously popular *Twilight* (2005–8) novels, for example, can be seen to espouse gender politics that echo those of the 1950s. Television series like *The Vampire Diaries* (2009–17) and *The Originals* (2013–18) fetishise bourgeois privilege while Isaac Marion's novel *Warm Bodies* (2010) and its filmic adaptation (dir. Jonathan Levine, 2013) even assert that heteronormative love can resurrect the dead and rebuild civilisation.[2] Neoliberal Gothic operates rather differently from such retrograde examples, undertaking an interrogation of dominant attitudes to class, race and gender while deploying the representational practices of the Gothic to indict contemporary inequalities and the economic system that has brought them into being. Neoliberal Gothic, in other words, returns us repeatedly to the ways in which capital has made us monstrous, echoing Karl Marx's own sense that 'capital is dead labour which, vampire-like, lives only by sucking living labour, and lives the more, the more labour it sucks'.[3] It also captures a sense of a contemporary world haunted by all that has been destroyed by the twin energies of neoliberalism and postmodernism. For, despite all its parodic playfulness and ironic, multi-perspectival love of pastiche, postmodernism operates as the cultural wing of the neoliberal project, being 'a relativistic scepticism that challenged the instrumental rationality of post-Enlightenment humanism and all it held dear, including truth, justice and progress, the rights of the individual and the social responsibilities of us all'.[4]

---

[2] Linnie Blake, 'The Monster in the Living Room: Gothic Television of the Neoliberal Age', in David Punter (ed.), *The Edinburgh Companion to Gothic and the Arts* (Edinburgh: Edinburgh University Press, 2019), pp. 406–17.

[3] Karl Marx, *Capital: A Critique of Political Economy, Volume 1*, trans. by Ben Fowkes (Harmondsworth: Penguin, 1976), p. 342.

[4] For a more thorough treatment of this argument, see Linnie Blake, 'Trapped in the Hysterical Sublime: *Twin Peaks*, Postmodernism, and the Neoliberal Now', in

Critiquing the American Dream

The dynamics of the Neoliberal Gothic are ably captured in Daniel Knauf's HBO series *Carnivàle*, which was broadcast for two seasons, out of a projected six, between September 2003 and March 2005. It has, since its cancellation, garnered a dedicated cult following devoted not only to celebrating what is a masterwork of contemporary series drama but to finding meaning in the textual aporias generated by the show's cancellation. In this, I would argue, the audience of *Carnivàle* participates in the contemporary will to understand the relationship between representation and reality as it operates not only on a textual level, but in the world too. This understanding, I would argue, is both a means of comprehending the ways in which the cultural dominance of postmodern representational practice has facilitated acceptance of the seismic social changes of the last 30 years and a way of imagining a better way of being in a world now enslaved by the dark machinations of neoliberal economics. Its projected timeline stretches from the European trenches of World War 1 to the explosion of the first nuclear bomb at Trinity, New Mexico, in July 1945 – a dry run for the genocide at Hiroshima and Nagasaki the following month. The two seasons of *Carnivàle* that reached production, however, cover only 1934 and 1935, the era in which large swathes of the US population were driven, by ecological and financial catastrophe, to migrate from the country to the cities and from the Dustbowl further west. It is no coincidence, in other words, that the series is set in the 1930s, this being a period in which financial crisis, the transfer of land from private to corporate ownership and the bankruptcy of entire cities led the public to lose faith in the metanarratives of old. Most specifically, *Carnivàle* proffers a coruscating critique of the myth of the American Dream of equality of opportunity, prosperity through hard work, democratic accountability and equality under the law. In the 1930s, as now, the series illustrates that the failure of contemporary capitalism demanded a willingness, on the part of powerful and powerless alike, to think otherwise. In the 1930s, Franklin D. Roosevelt's proto-Keynesian New Deal programme broke with the laissez-faire economics of the past to enable the nation to work its way out of the wilderness of the Great Depression, and, in the present, a similar act of thinking beyond the free market has become even more essential. *Carnivàle* thus evokes its epoch through meticulous attention to period detail filtered through the stylistics of Walker Evans, the photographer who effectively defined how we remember the Great

---

Jeffrey Andrew Weinstock and Catherine Spooner (eds), *Return to Twin Peaks: New Approaches to Materiality, Theory, and Genre on Television* (New York: Palgrave Macmillan, 2015), pp. 229–45 (p. 231).

Depression. What is more, it consistently draws on the conventions of the Gothic mode to draw parallels between the 1930s and the present.

For all its commitment to verisimilitude, then, *Carnivàle* is considerably more than a work of social realism. For it is the Neoliberal Gothic dimensions of the text that enable us to explore not only the nature of good and evil but the ideological uses to which such Manichean ideas may be put. In this, *Carnivàle* undertakes a politically engaged consideration of the profound disjunction between the will to power and the will to truth. The complex unfolding of its multi-layered arc may be confusing, in other words, but the series never undertakes a postmodern abandonment of transcendent meaning. Instead, it deploys arcane mythologies, occult symbolism and manifestations of magic to explore the ways in which the powerful adopt an obfuscating rhetoric of evil alterity to manipulate those whom they themselves prey upon. For in *Carnivàle*, it is the socially abjected figures, those deemed most monstrous and those who exist quite literally beyond the norms of conventional society, who show us how it is best to live. There are psychics, like the Romany tarot-reader Appolonia and the psychometrist Lodz. There are exotic performers, like the snake dancer Ruthie and the coochie dancers Rita Sue and her daughters. There are self-proclaimed freaks like Gekko the Lizard Man, Lila the bearded lady and the conjoined twins Dora and Lora Bennett. In the carnival's celebration of its members' alterity, itself a trope that stretches memorably back to Tod Browning's Depression-era *Freaks* (1932), we see, therefore, a reaffirmation of social responsibility and societal connectedness, a commitment to the greater good and the willingness to place the needs of the many above the desires of the few. All are values inimical to neoliberalism, of course, wherein a ruthless social Darwinism legitimates the persecution of the weakest and valorises the accumulation of obscene individual and corporate wealth. In truly Gothic fashion, then, *Carnivàle* becomes an exercise in both thinking and being 'other-wise'.

Central to this project are the series' key protagonists – roustabout Ben Hawkins and media-friendly Minister Brother Justin Crowe who discover themselves to be avatars of an ancient conflict between the forces of light and the forces of darkness. Ben is not, perhaps, the obvious candidate for Avatar of the Light. A poor country boy, convicted murderer and escaped convict, he joins the carnival as it passes his farm in Milfay, Oklahoma. We discover this in a flashback sequence in which Ben raises a cat from the dead and is said by his God-fearing mother to be marked by the Beast. The second Avatar is Methodist preacher, Brother Justin Crowe. He lives with his sister Iris in a rich parish in Mintern, California. Brother Justin shares Ben's prophetic dreams but his powers are far from benevolent, for not only can he force people to his will, he is a man of depraved sexual appetites, engaged in a perverse sadomasochistic relationship with his sister and later prone to the violent rape of his female housemaids. Initially convinced that he is carrying out the will of God, Brother Justin takes to the radio waves to preach, reaching a coast-to-coast audience by seemingly magical means. Intriguingly, Justin also propounds a seductively American form of egalitarianism, filtered through the Protestant tradition of hard work, family values and sober living. It is an ideological ploy that has characterised the Republican Party since Reagan, of course, the president who united neoliberalism and neo-conservativism in a shared attack on 'big government' and the welfare state. On air, Justin rails against the 'vile parasites in our banks and boardrooms and the godless politicians growing fat on the misery of their constituents'.[5] Gone are the days when 'honest labor, industry and optimism' were supposed to guarantee the prosperity and success of all, he fulminates. The land has been 'snatched away ... not by God ... but by man. By the banks, by the craven men who run the banks.' A 'shroud of poverty', he says, is about to 'smother this once great land'.[6] Such affirmations are highly reminiscent of fascist rhetoric, particularly in Germany of the 1930s, and Justin is closely modelled on Father James Coughlin, the thirties media minister who openly supported both Hitler and Mussolini. They also echo the right-wing populism of the Alt-Right that emerged, from the 1990s, as a nativist response to neoliberal globalism and reached its apotheosis in the 2016 election of Donald Trump.

Certainly, Justin's pronouncements echo the experience of *Carnivàle*'s original audience, all too aware of the misdeeds of international financiers that repeatedly drove the world into recession and, in 2008, would have plunged the world into another Great Depression had the US government not stepped in to bail out the banks that were, by now, too big to fail. His words also echo those of later Republican president Ronald Reagan, the father of neoliberal governance, who proclaimed the USSR an 'evil empire' and recast the Cold War as a spiritual struggle against the darkness of godless communism.[7] More recently still, in the post 9/11 period, George W. Bush undertook what Wendy Brown has called 'the abjection of evil and ignorance onto fantasmatic others' as a means of disavowing the United States' 'own

---

[5] *Carnivàle*. Created by Daniel Knauf. 3 Arts Entertainment, Home Box Office (HBO). Distributed by HBO, 2003–5. First aired in USA on 14 September 2003. Series 1, episode 12.
[6] *Carnivàle*, series 2, episode 1.
[7] Ronald Reagan, 'Address to the National Association of Evangelicals', in Paul Fessler and Donald Roth (eds), *Voices of Democracy: The U. S. Oratory Project* (1983) <http://voicesofdemocracy.umd.edu/reagan-evil-empire-speech-text/> (last accessed 10 December 2018).

complicity with planetary networks of oppression'.[8] It was a move perfected, of course, by Trump.

It is in the face of such ideological obfuscation that *Carnivàle* espouses a search for truth. The quester is Ben. He may believe himself to be nothing more than 'filth', a doomed soul who bears 'the mark of the beast'. It is Ben, though, who eases a mother's grief for the loss of her baby, enables a little disabled girl to walk for the first time, heals the sick, calms the storm and even raises Ruthie from the dead with a Christ-like pronouncement: 'I just don't want ya thinking ya owe me nothing.'[9] Later he will heal a terminally injured child and save the carnival's foreman from death. He is, however, entirely free of the will to power that characterises Justin. Justin, meanwhile, enthusiastically adopts the mantle of dark messiah, declaring his own place at God's left hand, the place traditionally occupied by Satan.

All this speaks to the age in which *Carnivàle* was made, of course, an age in which neoliberal governance had spread its brand of trans-global corporatism across the economies of the world as destructively as the dust clouds rolled across the lands of the 1930s Southwest. For like the laissez-faire capitalism that brought about the suffering of the Depression, neoliberalism deems concepts such as society, the public, public interest and general welfare meaningless, promoting instead massive cuts to spending on education, health and social welfare in exchange for trade agreements that intrinsically favour the corporation. For both Brother Justin and neoliberalism itself deem individuals and groups entirely disposable. Whether they are migrants fleeing from the Dustbowl or the industrial workers of our own period whose livelihood has moved abroad, those individuals who cannot or will not serve the market are simply left to their own devices, this being the abandonment of bare life that for the philosopher Giorgio Agamben characterises the neoliberal present.[10] In the 1930s, as now, moreover, American proponents of such a programme (be they Coughlin and Justin or Bush and Trump) espouse an oxymoronic patriotism while claiming that God is on their side. In depicting an historically distant world, in which fiscal catastrophe had ripped people free of their social, psychological and ethical moorings, the series thus interrogates the geo-political climate of both the American past and our own age. Under constant scrutiny is the impact of 30 years of neoliberal economics

---

[8] Wendy Brown, 'American Nightmare: Neoliberalism, Neo-Conservatism, and De-Democratization', *Political Theory* 34:6 (2006): 690–714.

[9] *Carnivàle*, series 1, episode 1.

[10] See Giorgio Agamben, *Homo Sacer: Sovereign Power and Bare Life*, trans. by Daniel Heller-Roazen (Stanford, CA: Stanford University Press, 1998).

on American communities at home and the ramifications, on those communities, of corporate wars waged overseas. In this fashion, the series undertakes an exploration of the ways in which global economics may mobilise entire populations, examining the invidious effects of ideology on social and psychological integrity and, ultimately, decrying the capacity of media manipulation to bring forth evil in the hearts and works of men.

Neoliberal Zombies

The Neoliberal Gothic's will to interrogate the ideological machinations of the present is nowhere more clearly seen than in the cultural predominance of the figure of the zombie. The zombie is itself a figure spawned by capitalism: first as a monstrous articulation of the human cost of colonialism in the Caribbean and, in the post-war period, as a ready metaphor for red scare suburbanism, nuclear apocalypse, the United States' doomed foray into Korea and Vietnam, the boom-and-bust consumerism of the 1970s and the emergence of neoliberal neo-colonialism. Indeed, the zombie is a figure ideally suited to inhabiting a world of mass disinvestment from the public sphere, the corporation's increasing control of domestic and foreign policy and mass infrastructural collapse. It was not until the 1970s, then, when neoliberalism rose to economic predominance, that the zombie narrative explicitly capitalised on the immorality of an economic project that elevated a tiny minority while reducing all that is of value in the world to rubble.

The prime mover in this was George A. Romero. In a series of films that set the pattern for future representations of zombie apocalypse, he addressed the deadening properties of the neoliberal worldview: *Night of the Living Dead* (1968) explored the death of the 1950s family and the heterosexual couple as encapsulation of futurity; *Dawn of the Dead* (1978) outlined how acquisitiveness and self-interest would lead Americans to extinction; and *Day of the Dead* (1985) explicitly critiqued Reaganite economics, its mass investment in the military and the export of third-party torture to Central and South America as a means of exterminating opposition to corporate globalisation. Set 'Some Time' after the events of this film, though, it is Romero's *Land of the Dead* (2005) that brings such themes to fruition, drawing pronounced parallels between the society that emerges from the zombie apocalypse and our own neoliberal world. Here, the megalomaniac Kauffman, acknowledged by Romero in his DVD commentary on the film to be modelled on Donald Rumsfeld, is CEO of Fiddler's Green, a luxurious tower block that is itself a metaphor for the Bush administration.[11] Huddled in its shadow is a shantytown of survivors that, having fled the zombie threat outside, finds itself at the mercy of a murderously exploitative over-class. It is a model familiar to the overwhelming majority of the global population, of course, trapped between real and media-generated threats, on the one hand, and neoliberal governance that has destroyed any dreams of intergenerational advancement in the United States while reducing global populations to penury, on the other.[12] At Romero's hands, therefore, the zombie becomes rather more than a shambling monster questing for brains: it serves as an embodiment of the destructive energies of neoliberal economics, in the face of which we too struggle to retain our own humanity.

Since Romero, a range of filmmakers, programme makers and novelists have reanimated the dead to explore the impact of neoliberal economics on local and global communities and to imagine a better way forward. Max Brooks's 2006 novel *World War Z: An Oral History of the Zombie War* (2006) makes a significant contribution to this trend.[13] Focusing on the emergence and spread of zombie contagion at the hands of global inequality, the novel thus highlights the human, social and environmental cost of neoliberalism. All of this is markedly absent from Marc Forster's 2013 film of the same name, however. Here, a blond, blue-eyed American saviour-figure (entirely absent in the book) finds a cure for the virus before returning to his perfect family, kept safe by the might of the US military machine. In both book and film, though, the virus originates in China. Only in the former, however, is it spread across the world by capitalism, its escalation hastened by people-smugglers and by the organ trade, both of which echo the flow of people and commodities from poor to rich nations that has led to such spiralling inequality in neoliberal times. Unsurprisingly, in the book at least, the US government shows little will to tackle the economic status quo. The former

---

[11] *Land of the Dead*. Dir. George A. Romero. Universal Pictures. 2005.

[12] As Carole Cadwalladr, writing for *The Guardian*, has reported, the 2013 documentary *Inequality for All* (2013) explores the polarisation of wealth in the United States at length, with the economist Robert Reich asserting: 'In 1978, the typical male US worker was making $48,000 a year (adjusted for inflation). Meanwhile the average person in the top 1% was making $390, 000. By 2010, the median wage had plummeted to $33,000, but at the top it had nearly trebled, to $1,100,000.' Carole Cadwalladr, 'Inequality for All – Another Inconvenient Truth', *The Guardian*. 2 February 2013 <www.theguardian.com/film/2013/feb/02/inequality-for-all-us-economy-robert-reich> (last accessed 10 December 2018).

[13] For a more thorough account of this, see Linnie Blake, 'Max Brooks's *World War Z* (2006) – Neoliberal Gothic', in Simon Bacon (ed.), *The Gothic: A Reader* (Oxford: Peter Lang, 2018), pp. 195–201.

White House Chief of Staff Grover Carlson is an unapologetic laissez-faire capitalist who angrily asks:

> Can you ever 'solve' poverty? Can you ever 'solve' crime? Can you ever 'solve' disease, unemployment, war, or any other societal herpes? Hell no . . . You can't stop the rain. All you can do is just build a roof that you hope won't leak, or at least won't leak on the people who are going to vote for you.[14]

The president, in fact, only adds to the death toll, railroading an ineffective anti-viral drug through the FDA while pronouncing that 'people don't need big government, they need big protection, and they need it big time!'[15] As the virus spreads exponentially, moreover, his administration sends the survivors north while withdrawing troops beyond the Rockies and heading to the comparative safety of Hawaii. Only in the years after the war, as a massively diminished US population seeks to rebuild the country, is the former government brought to book. Carlson is recast as a collector of sewage for agricultural use and the CEO of Phalanx, the culpable drug company, is set to be deported from his Arctic stronghold to face charges while the people opt for policies that tackle the 'starvation, disease [and] homelessness' of a world in which 'industry was in shambles [and] transportation and trade had evaporated'.[16] In a decisive break from the neoliberal past, then, a new New Deal is implemented, emergent financial markets are tightly controlled and lethal penalties for profiteering are imposed.

Significantly, in such a world, mental illness is viewed rather differently from that under neoliberalism: not as a product nor of individual failure or malfunction but as collective trauma wrought by the zombie wars, themselves ascribable to the failed economics of the past. If Brooks's zombies encapsulate the ruthless self-interest of neoliberal subjectivity, each being 'its own self-contained, automated unit' with 'no collective brain to speak of', then its victims are viewed as the collective responsibility of the state.[17] And there are many survivors too damaged as yet to celebrate their own survival – traumatised catatonics, feral children, 'quislings' who believe themselves to be zombies and more. Fortunately, the 'resurgent economy' of the present has introduced that great bugbear of neoliberals – 'universal health care' – and all who need it will be cared for.[18] It is a very different perspective from that of neoliberalism, which drives populations into a state of depression, blames sufferers for their psychological

---

[14] Max Brooks, *World War Z: An Oral History of the Zombie War* (New York: Duckworth, 2006), p. 61.
[15] Brooks, *World War Z*, p. 56.   [16] Brooks, *World War Z*, p. 136.
[17] Brooks, *World War Z*, p. 272.   [18] Brooks, *World War Z*, p. 2.

inadequacy and profits from their inability to act. As the political and cultural critic Mark Fisher put it, our capitulation to neoliberalism can itself be seen as a 'consequence of a deliberately cultivated depression'. This 'is manifested in the acceptance that things will get worse (for all but a small elite), that we are lucky to have a job at all (so we shouldn't expect wages to keep pace with inflation), that we cannot afford the collective provision of the welfare state.' Thus, for Fisher, 'collective depression is the result of the ruling class project of resubordination'.[19] Brooks's novel upholds just such a view.

This strategy of materially and psychologically subordinating populations to the abuses of the neoliberal austerity agenda is explored at length in Dominic Mitchell's BAFTA-winning television series *In the Flesh* (2013–14).[20] It focuses on Kieran Walker, a rehabilitated zombie returned to his rainy village in the north of England following a pharmacological solution to the emergence of the dead from their graves. Like *Carnivàle*, the series undertakes a powerful melding of the conventions of social realism and the Gothic. It does so by attacking the ways in which the British austerity agenda has deemed entire swathes of the British population (the old, the sick, the disabled, the unemployed, the foreign) second-class subjects unworthy of full citizenship rights. Thus, welfare reform, immigration and asylum policies, the wholesale if covert privatisation of the National Health Service, regionally differentiated cuts to public services and the media's promotion of a divisive politics of hate all come in for forceful critique. Herded together in rehabilitation centres, the 'partially deceased' are subject to tortuous experimentation. When cured by pharmacological means, they are returned to a world that views them with distrust and legislates against them. They are debarred from re-entering their previous professions, they have their passports confiscated and are told where and how to live, their situation being very similar, in fact, to that of asylum seekers in the UK.[21] Later, they are forced to work while wearing orange tabards reminiscent of the 'Community

---

[19] Mark Fisher, 'Good for Nothing', *The Occupied Times*, 19 March 2014 <https://theoccupiedtimes.org/?p=12841> (last accessed 10 December 2018).

[20] For a more detailed account, see Linnie Blake, 'Catastrophic Events and Queer Northern Villages: Zombie Pharmacology in *In the Flesh*', in Linnie Blake and Agnieszka Soltysik Monnet (eds), *Neoliberal Gothic: International Gothic in the Neoliberal Age* (Manchester: Manchester University Press, 2016), pp. 104–21.

[21] As Andy Keefe, Director of National Clinical Services, Freedom from Torture has commented, the UK Home Office's decision to retain the 'breadline level of support' of £36 a week for a single asylum seeker ensured they face 'a continuing day-to-day struggle with destitution ... [without] enough money to eat three times a day, or to buy toiletries or over the counter medicines, or do laundry, or catch a bus or phone a friend.' See Andy Keefe, 'Home Office Decision Will Mean Asylum Seekers Struggle', *Anglican Community News Service*, 14 August 2014 <www.anglicannews.org/news/2014/08/uk-anti-torture-charity-

Payback' vests worn in the UK by those undertaking Community Service in lieu of a custodial sentence. The compulsion to work in whatever capacity the state sees fit echoes, moreover, the workfare programmes of the British Coalition Government (2010–15) that forced benefits claimants to work on a range of privately run schemes that enhanced the profitability of private companies. As the living resist the resettlement of the formerly dead, moreover, the series allegorises the immigration hysteria that led the UK, inexorably, to Brexit. A very ugly picture of the country emerges, but one that is entirely fitted to the political and psychological climate of the present.

Neoliberal Serial Killers

The zombie is not the only means by which Neoliberal Gothic explores the geo-political causes of seismic global trauma or underscores the necessity of an economic model that fosters collectivity as a means of meeting the needs of all its citizens. Since the 1990s, there has also been a remarkable upswing in the mass-cultural popularity of the serial killer, a neoliberal variant of the schizoid male monster that originates with Robert Louis Stevenson's urbane Dr Jekyll and animalistic Mr Hyde. Serial killer narratives have proliferated since the 1980s, functioning as intriguing explorations of neoliberal subjectivity and, accordingly, contemporary ideologies of identity. It is no coincidence, in other words, that these vicious predators should become the antiheroes of our age, their actions bespeaking psyches ideally adapted to a world that tells us the fittest will rise and those undeserving of life deserve their victimhood. In many ways, then, we can read the serial killer as a hideous embodiment of the ways in which neoliberal ideology produces its subjects, not 'by interpellating them into symbolically anchored identities (structured according to conventions of gender, race, work, and national citizenship', but by enjoining them to endlessly refashion themselves: '*I must be fit; I must be stylish; I must realise my dreams . . . if I don't I am not a person at all; I am not part of everyone.*'[22] For the serial killer, like the perfect neoliberal subject, is not 'part of everyone.' He may modify himself to mirror his mission, as does Thomas Harris's eponymous *Red Dragon* (1981), who sports a back-sized tattoo of William Blake's 'The Great Red Dragon and the Woman Clothed With the Sun.' Despite his arrangement of his murdered

---

home-office-decision-will-mean-asylum-seekers-struggle.aspx> (last accessed 10 December 2018).

[22] Jodi Dean, *Democracy and Other Neoliberal Fantasies: Communicative Capitalism and Left Politics* (Durham, NC and London: Duke University Press, 2009), pp. 66–7; italics in original.

victims in tableaux that mimic the nuclear family, this does not anchor him within a community of his peers. Instead, the serial killer is reduced to the sum of his grotesque activities that not only underscore his separateness but proffer an ironic commentary on the fragmentation of symbolic communities in the neoliberal age.

Cinematic explorations of the serial killer theme range from the gritty *Henry: Portrait of a Serial Killer* (dir. John McNaughton, 1986) to the grand guignol of *Natural Born Killers* (dir. Oliver Stone, 1994), both of which undertake extensive exploration of the mass media's complicity with acts of violent slaughter, desensitising the population to horror while raising the transgressor to the role of cultural icon. Moreover, some serial killer texts, such as Thomas Harris's *The Silence of the Lambs* (1991) and *Hannibal* (1999), draw extensive parallels between the violence of the neoliberal state and that of the aberrant individual – FBI agent Clarice Starling and cannibalistic genius Hannibal Lecter being ultimately drawn into a perverse romantic relationship.[23] Others, like *American Psycho* (dir. Mary Harron, 2000) – and the 1992 Bret Easton Ellis novel on which it is based – encapsulate the psychopathic agenda of global capitalism by incorporating its worst excesses in a fastidiously groomed and designer-clad banker protagonist.

A more overtly Neoliberal Gothic treatment of the serial killer is to be found, however, in David Fincher's *Se7en* (1995). Here, a *mise en scène* of urban decay visually manifests the ruinous decline of the US industrial belt, the underfunding of public services such as the police, the social impact of wide-scale addiction and the depressive impact on the entire population of the non-appearance of trickled-down wealth. The film was itself released in the midst of an economic crisis that would lead to a financial crash some two years later. It also followed hard on the heels of the 1994 North American Free Trade Agreement that produced job losses and wage cuts in the US and led to the wholesale exploitation of workers and environmental despoliation on the Mexican side of the border. Shot in a desaturated colour palette that makes the urban locale even more gloomy and its inhabitants appear tired and ill, *Se7en* recasts the contemporary American city as home to the deadliest of sins. The unnamed protagonist, known to the police as John Doe, is linked to the millions of people around him only by his self-appointed role of punisher for real or perceived transgressions. A prideful model has her face mutilated and is forced to choose between living disfigured or dying. She chooses death.

---

[23] See Linnie Blake, *The Wounds of Nations: Horror Cinema, Historical Trauma and National Identity* (Manchester: Manchester University Press, 2008).

A glutton is forced to eat until his stomach ruptures. A lustful man is forced to rape a prostitute with a bladed prosthesis: he is traumatised but she dies horribly. A lawyer's avarice costs him a pound of flesh and a slothful paedophile is chained to his bed for a year, kept artificially alive and photographed daily, better to capture his degradation and decay. Wildly overdetermined in stylistic terms, the film's hideous tableaux are echoed in its distorted soundscapes and grotesque city dwellers, many of them drug-addicted criminals. Outside, the rain falls constantly. In true Gothic style, moreover, Doe is a highly ambiguous figure. Like Hannibal Lecter, he is simultaneously insane and brilliant; his deeds revolt us and yet we are intrigued by the breadth and eclecticism of his knowledge and his capacity for intricate and inventive planning in the commissioning of his crimes. He is an outsider, but he also inhabits a city of outsiders, indicting himself, the police and the contemporary world in the form of punishments that illustrate how desires and actions formerly deemed sinful have become refashioned, under neoliberalism, as social norms. At the film's close, the wrathful detective hero executes Doe for killing and dismembering his wife – herself a traditional Gothic heroine whose rescue never came. It is a clever if dispiriting ending to a film in which human nature appears at its very worst, society appears inexorably broken and no possibility of a meaningful future can be envisaged.

Neoliberal Vampires

If the figure of the zombie illustrates the evils of consumerism and the serial killer embodies the criminality that lies at the heart of the neoliberal project, then it is for the contemporary vampire to expose the workings of the shadow state that lies behind the façade of democratic governance and dictates the course of nations. Stephen Norrington's 1998 film *Blade* inaugurates this trend. Vacillating between post-industrial Chicago and an ethically bankrupt Los Angeles, on the one hand, and a fantastic world of vampires and secret societies on the other, *Blade* sets out to explore the United States' history of systemic inequalities while exposing the workings of power that most commonly go unseen. On one level, the narrative focuses on the ways in which Black women have been sexually victimised by white culture, the concomitant de-masculinisation of Black men and the wholesale marketisation of Black American culture. On another level, it exposes the capitalist nature of this project. For just as neoliberalism purposefully monetises all that is of value in the world and reduces real people to pawns in the ongoing enrichment of a tiny minority, so do the vampires of *Blade* set out to enslave humanity, being already in possession of the world's real estate, business ventures, police forces and governments. The eponymous 'daywalker' is an African American attuned to the oppression of his race, of course, but he is also something of a proletarian hero. He is aware of his origins: the predatory vampire Frost, whose whiteness is even manifest in his name, having bitten Blade's heavily pregnant mother and made him, in turn, a hybrid who needs blood or blood substitutes but who can walk by day. He is radicalised to the point of violent action, moreover, and makes it his mission to destroy the secret and subterranean world of the vampires that has effectively manufactured the consent of its global prey.

This is a dynamic echoed in *The Strain* (2012–17), the FX series adapted from the novels *The Strain* (2009), *The Fall* (2010) and *The Night Eternal* (2011) by Guillermo del Toro and Chuck Hogan. Sired by The Master, one of the original seven progenitors of the vampire race, the 'strigoi' here are as mindless and revolting as zombies, being possessed of a hideous 10-foot-long proboscis that they use to infect the citizens of the world. They are challenged, and ultimately destroyed, by a disgraced Centers for Disease Control and Prevention scientist, an elderly concentration camp survivor, a New York sewer worker and a shifting cast of survivors, the composition of which echoes the demography of the multi-ethnic and economically stratified city of New York in which the action unfolds. The series shifts between ancient Rome, the concentration camps of wartime Poland and contemporary New York and, in so doing, links vampirism and the human will to power, whether that manifests as Roman imperialism, Nazism or Wall Street investment banking.[24] In the neoliberal age, naturally, it is a banker who is central to The Master's progress, Eldridge Palmer's Wall Street career making him not only one of the richest men in the world but highly adept at accessing capital markets to facilitate third-party expansion. Indeed, this is exactly what Palmer does for The Master, facilitating his entry to New York, suppressing media interest in the growing vampire plague and discrediting the CDC scientist who attempts to understand and forestall its progress. For a series broadcast after the financial crash of 2008, Palmer's ultimate fate is horribly ironic and more than a little gratifying. Palmer may have wanted to live forever, but he is ultimately consumed by the evil that he has unleashed upon the world. The human cost, however, is immense, for while the Master is eventually defeated, the city lies in ruins and the nation as a whole comprises

---

[24] See Linnie Blake, 'Neoliberal Gothic', in Maisha Wester and Xavier Aldana Reyes (eds), *Twenty-First-Century Gothic: An Edinburgh Companion* (Edinburgh: Edinburgh University Press, 2019), pp. 60–71.

only small bands of brutalised survivors. Democratic government has been exposed as a myth, and an atmosphere of traumatic loss endures.

The revelation of shadowy forces preying upon an unsuspecting or compliant populace is echoed across Neoliberal Gothic texts, further manifesting in the HBO television series *True Blood* (2008–14), adapted from Charlaine Harris's *Southern Vampire Mysteries* novels (2001–13), in which vampiric authoritarianism is explicitly linked to the neo-imperial ambitions of the neoliberal United States. Following the discovery of a synthetically engineered human blood substitute, the world's vampires have 'come out of the coffin', and the series charts their attempts to gain social recognition and enter overtly global political life.[25] *True Blood* explores, therefore, the ongoing struggle for civil rights in the United States while highlighting the very real dangers posed by old-school racists, evangelical Christians and new school members of the Alt-Right. Echoing *Blade*'s exploration of the co-existence of human and vampiric societies, the series sets out to challenge the ongoing sexism, racism and homophobia of the United States. This comes to fruition in the fifth series, which focuses on The Authority, a de facto global government that came into being initially as a religious organisation designed to protect the blood of Lilith, the first vampire. Speaking to increasing public paranoia regarding the non-governmental control of global economies, season five thus exposes democracy as an ideologically sustained illusion. The Authority's use of a secret police force, sophisticated surveillance technologies, assassins and mercenaries can be seen to mirror the limits placed on American freedoms in the wake of 9/11, both in the form of the PATRIOT Act and the institution of organisations like the National Security Agency.[26] With delicious irony, moreover, the might of the Authority is being challenged by the Sanguinistas, a group of revolutionary vampires whose name puns delightfully on that of the Nicaraguan revolutionary party that deposed the US-backed Somosa regime in 1978. These seek vampiric self-determination and are prepared to take on the might of the US military in

---

[25] Linnie Blake, 'Vampires, Mad Scientists and the Unquiet Dead: Gothic Ubiquity in Post 9/11 Television', in Justin D. Edwards and Agnieszka Soltysik Monnet (eds), *The Gothic in Contemporary Literature and Popular Culture* (New York: Routledge, 2012), pp. 37–56.

[26] The PATRIOT Act (an acronym for Uniting and Strengthening America by Providing Appropriate Tools Required to Intercept and Obstruct Terrorism) of October 2001 removed many historic rights of the American people. Most controversial were measures to detain immigrants indefinitely, to enable searches of people and property without consent or court order and to undertake surveillance of those suspected of terrorist involvement. Although since amended, some aspects relating particularly to surveillance having been deemed unconstitutional, it has never been repealed in its entirety.

order to do so. *True Blood*, then, comes to echo the human rights abuses committed by the US in Latin America and beyond.[27] The group's members (and those suspected of sympathy to the cause) find themselves imprisoned in the Guantanamo-encoded Camp Vamp, where they are tortured, experimented upon and finally infected with a blood-borne virus, HepV, which is designed to eradicate the vampire population altogether. Thus, *True Blood* comes to echo the means by which neoliberalism first attained and now maintains a stranglehold on world economies. Behind the façade of democratic governance, it seems, lurks a far more spectral world, one in which entire populations are reduced to mere pawns in geo-political power struggles, its brokers deploying the resources of bioscience, torture and murder to achieve their ends without heed to international agreements on human rights or the self-determination of sovereign nations.

The apocalyptic apotheosis of the neoliberal shadow state is to be found in Justin Cronin's vampire apocalypse trilogy *The Passage* (2010), *The Twelve* (2012) and *City of Mirrors* (2016). While the first novel traces the fall of the United States, and much of the world, at the hands of US militarism, corporate expansionism and biotechnological advances, the latter two trace the perilous adventures of a band of young people destined to save what is left of the world. The narrative opens in our own period, a time in which 'war was everywhere; metastasising like a million maniac cells run amok across the planet'.[28] Terrorist attacks have become commonplace, economies collapse and large parts of the world have become no more than toxic wastelands. And things are about to get worse. In Bolivia, a scientific expedition seeking the means by which a group of cancer-stricken tourists recovered from their illness, succumbs to the bat-borne virus that they seek. The military, seeking to create stronger, faster and self-healing soldiers, funds corporate research into the virus and, in an underground installation far below the Rockies, Project Noah is born. Twelve death-row inmates and the abducted child of a murdered prostitute are here infected with the virus. The Twelve mutate into nigh-indestructible predators who shun the light and consume everyone in their path, turning one in ten into a Viral (the term 'vampire' being assiduously avoided) telepathically controlled by their sire. In no time at all, the United States is destroyed, even as the government blames 'anti-American extremists, operating within our borders but supported by extremists abroad' for the so-called 'Colorado fever'.[29] In time, the

[27] Blake, 'Neoliberal Gothic'.
[28] Justin Cronin, *The Passage* (New York: Ballantine Books, 2010), p. 108.
[29] Cronin, *The Passage*, p. 286.

government will shoot survivors and drop nuclear bombs on its own cities, but the tide is unstoppable – the mutated virus being carried by birds around the globe to kill billions more.

Alt-Right Gothic

In the provocatively entitled 'Neoliberalism – the Ideology at the Root of all our Problems', the author and columnist George Monbiot baldly asserts:

> It has played a major role in a remarkable variety of crises: the financial meltdown of 2007–8, the offshoring of wealth and power, of which the Panama Papers offer us merely a glimpse, the slow collapse of public health and education, resurgent child poverty, the epidemic of loneliness, the collapse of ecosystems, the rise of Donald Trump.[30]

As the texts that I have considered in this chapter illustrate, the Neoliberal Gothic undertakes both the representation of the economic status quo and a repudiation of its injustices. It explores the ideological nature of identity construction and the manipulability of the population and, in turn, exposes democracy as an expedient fantasy operating in the interests of a tiny elite. *Cult* (2017), the seventh series of *American Horror Story* (2011–), is a remarkably explicit treatment of these themes, opening on election night in 2016 and counterposing the putatively wholesome appeal of Democrat Hilary Clinton and the palpably deranged intolerance of populist Republican entrepreneur Donald Trump. Watching the election are two ostensibly oppositional social groups, middle-class Hillary supporters (a horrified same-sex couple, their son and Asian-American neighbours) and, in a subterranean basement not too far away, a blue-haired youth who ecstatically humps his TV screen while shouting 'USA! USA!' The battle lines have been drawn, it seems. The 'politics of fear' that have characterised the election, and indeed the past 30 years, have ushered in a new era and, for our subterranean Alt Righter '[t]he revolution has begun'.[31] In time, said youth will become a City Councilman, enjoining the 'straight, white working man' to 'vote for the man who can take your fears away'.[32] For Kai Anderson, like Trump, is at one with the zeitgeist, a populist who pronounces that 'real Americans hate the

---

[30] George Monbiot, 'Neoliberalism – the Ideology at the Root of all our Problems', *The Guardian*, 15 April 2016 <www.theguardian.com/books/2016/apr/15/neoliberalism-ideology-problem-george-monbiot> (last accessed 10 December 2018).

[31] *American Horror Story*. Created by Ryan Murphy and Brad Falchuk. FX Network, 20th Century Fox Television. 2011–. First aired in USA on 5 October 2011. Season 7 episode 1.

[32] *American Horror Story*, season 8 episodes 4, 2.

Democrats because you treat us all as if we're wife-beating redneck Klansmen' and who runs largely on a platform of 'liking American beer and pussy'.[33] Those who challenge such an 'authentic' masculine subjectivity are deemed 'fucking bitches' who need to be taught a lesson, which Kai and his cult set out to deliver through a campaign of terror, complete with clown costumes, serial slaughter and various acts of violence.[34]

Trump may appear to be the apotheosis of the neoliberal project, but, as Naomi Klein is keen to remind us, Hillary Clinton offered the American electorate no meaningful alternative, either to Trump or to what had gone before. The result, for Klein, was Trump's victory and the resurgence of a vicious form of right-wing populism (familiar from Brother Justin of *Carnivàle* and more recently Kai Anderson), undercut by a radical postmodern relativism that frankly denies the facticity of facts that do not support the Alt-Right agenda.[35] It is no surprise, in other words, that Trump's attacks on his own class group – those who had seen their fortunes increase exponentially since the 1980s – found favour with the voters who had themselves suffered most at the hands of successive laissez-faire administrations. Thus, in what Noam Chomsky described as a climate of 'fear of just about everything', Trump's promise to 'make America great again' through the revivification of US manufacturing industry at home and the abandonment of military intervention abroad, resonated with those dispossessed by the neoliberal agenda of every President since Reagan.[36] Like the small town America of *American Horror Story: Cult*, the strictures of neoliberal economics appear to be inescapable; its monsters dominate our present and dictate our futures. They assault our families and drive us to mindless consumerism and even more mindless acts of violence: the two poles of neoliberal subjectivity as theorised by Jodi Dean.[37] It is this, I believe, that explains the contemporary ubiquity of Gothic monsters. The zombies, vampires and serial killers that dominate popular culture give form to the amorphous forces that shape our lives. With every revisioning of the past or projection into an apocalyptic future, moreover, these monsters and the narratives that house them enable us to see clearly all that has been lost to and destroyed by the dark energies of neoliberal economics. In indicting the perpetrators of our current global misery,

---

[33] *American Horror Story*, season 8 episode 4.
[34] *American Horror Story*, season 8 episode 4.
[35] Naomi Klein, *No Is Not Enough: Resisting Trump's Shock Politics and Winning the World We Need* (London: Penguin, 2018).
[36] Noam Chomsky, *Hegemony or Survival: America's Quest for Global Dominance* (London: Penguin, 2004), p. 20.
[37] See Dean, *Democracy and Other Neoliberal Fantasies*.

therefore, the Neoliberal Gothic enables us to perceive another way: an act precluded by our everyday investment in the neoliberal status quo. Neoliberal Gothic, therefore, becomes a means of both seeing and being other-wise, proffering both a critique of the present and a roadmap to a future in which our cities do not lie in ruins and we do not feel hunted by dark forces that we have no power to resist.

3.15

The Gothic and Remix Culture

MEGEN DE BRUIN-MOLÉ

The Gothic is an aggregate organism. From its roots in twelfth-century architecture and eighteenth-century fiction and theatre, Gothic has always been multimedia, and always been remixed, variously represented as an 'uneasy marriage' of genres, a Frankensteinian 'series of revivals', and 'a patchwork of textual modes'.[1] Around the turn of the twenty-first century, however, the genre's patchwork qualities began to take on a new intensity. In addition to the emergence of new Gothic texts and monsters, the first two decades of the new millennium saw a seemingly endless succession of Gothic adaptations, reboots and reimaginings. In Anglo-American media, for instance, Bram Stoker's *Dracula* (1897) has been a prime target for adaptors, with recent retellings including not one but two BBC miniseries entitled *Dracula* (2006 and 2020); NBC's *Dracula* (2013–14); and the films *Dracula Reborn* (dir. Patrick McManus, 2012); *Dracula: The Dark Prince* (dir. Pearry Reginald Teo, 2013); *Dracula Untold* (dir. Gary Shore, 2014); *The Unwanted* (dir. Brent Wood, 2014); *The Curse of Styria* (dir. Mauricio Chernovetzky and Mark Devendorf, 2014); and Universal/Blumhouse's *Dracula* (dir. Karyn Kusama, forthcoming), to name just a few. Robert Louis Stevenson's *Strange Case of Dr Jekyll and Mr. Hyde* (1886) has had at least four serial television adaptations in the last two decades – the BBC's *Jekyll* (2007); NBC's *Do No Harm* (2013); ITV's *Jekyll & Hyde* (2015); and SBS's *Hyde Jekyll, Me* (2015) – as well as numerous adaptations and character cameos in other media. Mary Shelley's *Frankenstein* (1818; 1831), Oscar Wilde's *The*

---

[1] Jerrold E. Hogle, 'Introduction: The Gothic in Western Culture', in Jerrold E. Hogle (ed.), *The Cambridge Companion to Gothic Fiction* (Cambridge: Cambridge University Press, 2002), pp. 1–20 (p. 8); Catherine Spooner, *Contemporary Gothic* (London: Reaktion Books, 2006), p. 10; Anthony Mandal, 'Gothic 2.0: Remixing Revenants in the Transmedia Age', in Lorna Piatti-Farnell and Donna Lee Brien (eds), *New Directions in 21st-Century Gothic: The Gothic Compass* (London: Routledge, 2015), pp. 84–100 (p. 91).

Picture of Dorian Gray (1890) and even Joseph Sheridan Le Fanu's *Carmilla* (1872) have also attracted renewed interest from storytellers.²

Alongside these adaptations, the twenty-first century has also witnessed the proliferation of a different kind of Gothic revival: mash-up, or the appropriation of elements from multiple sources and their recombination into something that, if not exactly new, is certainly novel. The year 2009 saw the unexpected commercial success of *Pride and Prejudice and Zombies* (with a film adaptation of its own in 2016). This mash-up novel transformed Jane Austen's *Pride and Prejudice* (1813) from a comedy of manners into zombie horror through a series of minor edits by 'co-author' Seth Grahame-Smith, and the practice quickly took on a life of its own. Following *Pride and Prejudice and Zombies* and *Sense and Sensibility and Sea Monsters* (2010), Quirk's third title in the 'Quirk Classics' series was *Android Karenina* (2010), and rival publishers followed with *Jane Slayre* (2010); *Little Vampire Women* (2010); *Wuthering Bites* (2010); *Alice in Zombieland* (2011); and *Grave Expectations* (2011).³ Though few of these texts mash up Gothic novels, their practice of resurrecting classic literature and infusing it with monsters offers a Gothic, spectacle-driven approach to the themes of terror, wonder and the uncanny.

In addition to the literal cut-and-paste mash-ups of classic texts like *Pride and Prejudice and Zombies*, many new books, films and media franchises also took a remix-style approach to the themes, characters and visuals of Gothic fiction, appropriating from multiple sources and juxtaposing them across time, space and media. Films and shows such as *Van Helsing* (dir. Stephen Sommers, 2004), *Mary Shelley's Frankenhole* (2010–12), *Once Upon a Time*

---

² For a small sampling of adaptations, consider the USA network's made-for-television *Frankenstein* (2004); the 2004 Hallmark miniseries *Frankenstein*; Bernard Rose's *FRANKЄN5TЄiN* (Alchemy, 2015); 20th Century Fox's *Victor Frankenstein* (dir. Paul McGuigan, 2015); *Dorian* (2004, dir. Brendan Dougherty Russo); *Dorian Gray* (dir. Oliver Parker, 2009); four films called *The Picture of Dorian Gray* (dir. David Rosenbaum, 2004; dir. Duncan Roy, 2006; dir. John Cunningham, 2007; dir. Jonathan Courtemanche, 2009); the YouTube webseries *Carmilla* (2014–17); and *Carmilla* (dir. Emily Harris, 2019).

³ These are just a few of the more successful titles. In addition to this list, a number of non-literary mash-ups by the same authors entered the market, including the biofictional works *Queen Victoria: Demon Hunter* (A. E. Moorat, 2009); *Abraham Lincoln, Vampire Hunter* (Seth Grahame-Smith, 2010) and *Henry VIII: Wolfman* (A. E. Moorat, 2010). *Abraham Lincoln, Vampire Hunter* was adapted as a film directed by Timur Bekmambetov in 2012. Many self-published mash-ups were also released via online tools such as Lulu, and Amazon's CreateSpace and Kindle Direct. Some were more successful than others, and though traditional publicity was certainly an important part of their success, word of mouth on websites like YouTube and GoodReads also helped increase readership for many titles. The mash-up novel also has a continued life outside of the English-language market.

(2011–18), *Hotel Transylvania* (dir. Genndy Tartakovsky, 2012), *I, Frankenstein* (dir. Stuart Beattie, 2014), *Monster High* (2010–15), *Penny Dreadful* (2014–16), Syfy's *Van Helsing* (2016–20) and Netflix's *Castlevania* (2017–21); games like *Fallen London* (2009) and *The Order: 1886* (2015); or book and comics series like *Anno Dracula* (Kim Newman, 1992–present), *The League of Extraordinary Gentlemen* (Alan Moore and Kevin O'Neill, 1999–2020) and *The Extraordinary Adventures of the Athena Club* (Theodora Goss, 2017–19), have helped the monster mash-up reach new levels of visibility.[4]

Over a similar time period, another form of 'Gothic' remix has also arisen, one in which the texts are not necessarily Gothic at a narrative or thematic level – for often they have no narrative in the traditional sense at all. Catherine Spooner notes in *Contemporary Gothic* that, when compared with other modes, the Gothic has always seemed to have 'a greater degree of self-consciousness about its nature, cannibalistically consuming the dead body of its own tradition'.[5] As Spooner's cannibal metaphor suggests, the Gothic is often monstrous on a formal level as well as a textual one. Some texts are Gothic in the strategies that they employ to appropriate and recombine other texts. In this chapter, for instance, I explore how the GIF, the digitised photograph, the updating database and the social media network have all functioned in 'monstrous' or Gothic ways.

What are the implications of this rapid rise in remixed Gothic, both for remix practices and for the Gothic mode? From the turn of the twenty-first century, Gothic media have reached unprecedented levels of commercialisation and, as a result, have begun to proliferate in new and interesting ways. Many critics have noted that Gothic texts (and their commemorative adaptations) often seem to cluster around the turn of each century, emerging 'as particularly potent and popular at times of both crisis in and shifting intensifications of capital and power'.[6] For Anthony Mandal, Gothic fiction's position on a 'liminal boundary between authenticity and counterfeit, in a mode whose obsession with the past belies its thoroughly modern provenance, is

---

[4] As Jess Nevins points out, crossover fiction has antecedents in Victorian fiction. See Jess Nevins, *Heroes and Monsters: The Unofficial Companion to The League of Extraordinary Gentlemen* (Austin, TX: MonkeyBrain, 2003), pp. 175–84. The use of existing characters and intellectual properties has been a strategy of authors and film studios ever since, with Universal's monster crossover films in the 1940s and 1950s offering another notable example. See Megen de Bruin-Molé, *Gothic Remixed: Monster Mashups and Frankenfictions in 21st-Century Culture* (London: Bloomsbury, 2020), where I talk about this phenomenon in much more detail.

[5] Spooner, *Contemporary Gothic*, p. 10.

[6] Emily Johansen, 'The Neoliberal Gothic: *Gone Girl*, *Broken Harbor*, and the Terror of Everyday Life', *Contemporary Literature* 57:1 (2016): 30–55 (p. 31).

particularly salient in relation to today's "remix" culture, which has been enabled by a digital technology that haunts and is haunted by its textual predecessors'.[7] In the age of remix culture, the genre's obsession with appropriation and repetition, its tendencies towards fakery and self-cannibalism, and its embrace by and of commercial culture all converge into one large Gothic monster.

Gothic Convergence

Monstrosity is an inherent trait of late twentieth-century literature. Andrew Gibson suggests that it emerges 'out of the "inexorable dislocation" of presently inescapable terms and structures. It is the hybrid image of our current crisis.'[8] For Gibson, in other words, all contemporary fiction exhibits Gothic hybridity, born as it is out of a postmodernist blurring of borders that were previously seen as impermeable, including the late capitalist convergence of public and private spheres. In the twenty-first century, David McNally similarly offers a persuasive argument for the way in which late capitalism constructs monstrous consumers and contexts for these monstrous texts. For McNally, monsters can tell us a great deal about how 'the experience of capitalist commodification is felt, experienced and resisted'.[9] Texts are monstrously commodified, but with the rise of neoliberalism and the precarity of the gig economy, lives and bodies are too. Gothic becomes popular in this context because of the way in which it dramatises 'the profound senses of corporeal vulnerability that pervade modern society, most manifestly when commodification invades new spheres of social life'.[10] In this 'monstrous' age, Jeffrey A. Weinstock suggests that many contemporary monster narratives show that the Gothic has come to occupy a mainstream position 'in which one aspires to monstrosity as an escape from the stultification of hegemonic social forces of normalisation'.[11] When one's own daily life feels numbing or monstrous, it can come as a relief to see that experience abstracted and glamorised on the screen or the page.

---

[7] Mandal, 'Gothic 2.0', p. 91.
[8] Andrew Gibson, *Towards a Postmodern Theory of Narrative* (Edinburgh: Edinburgh University Press, 1996), p. 244.
[9] David McNally, *Monsters of the Market: Zombies, Vampires and Global Capitalism* (Chicago, IL: Haymarket Books, 2012), p. 2.
[10] McNally, *Monsters of the Market*, p. 2.
[11] Jeffrey A. Weinstock, 'Invisible Monsters: Vision, Horror, and Contemporary Culture', in Asa Simon Mittman and Peter J. Dendle (eds), *The Ashgate Research Companion to Monsters and the Monstrous* (Farnham: Ashgate, 2013), pp. 275–89 (p. 276).

While the mainstreaming and hyper-commodification of Gothic horror accounts for some of the texts that I have listed above, it does not, in itself, explain why so many post-millennial Gothic revivals assume a remixed form. Monster mash-up mania is situated at the confluence of Gothic commodification, fakery and repetition, but it is also deeply indebted to digital technological convergence and the social and cultural shifts that come with it. The most prominent examples of remix Gothic are made using digital technologies: word processors, audiovisual editing software, online meme generators and so forth. Though many Gothic remixes draw on media that have also existed in analogue form, these media must inevitably first be scanned, uploaded, shared: *Pride and Prejudice and Zombies* is not a physical 'cut-and-paste' remix, but a digital one, enabled by the wide circulation of Austen's Regency novel, by a wide range of computer technologies, and by the graces of digital copyright law and the public domain. Alongside the neoliberal normalisation of Gothic life and labour, the twenty-first century has also seen the amplification of the technological hybridity that Henry Jenkins terms convergence culture: 'the flow of content across multiple media platforms, the cooperation between multiple media industries, and the migratory behaviour of media audiences who will go almost anywhere in search of the kinds of entertainment experiences they want'.[12] In the age of both the internet and the global mega-franchise, media are increasingly pervasive and adaptable by design, and convergent technologies such as the smartphone help transmedial texts to proliferate across various social, physical and legal boundaries. Convergence culture is the commercial and technological context against which Gothic mash-ups and remixes become not just logical, but inevitable. Copyright, trademarks and recognisable branding become especially important in such an environment, helping audiences to navigate increasingly complex networks of content. The necessity of continually renewing copyright helps to explain Universal's revival of its twentieth-century monsters in the twenty-first-century 'Dark Universe' films, for instance. It also explains why other studios might want to cash in on these familiar characters – while not infringing on Universal's copyright – through their own 'mashed up' appropriations in films like *Hotel Transylvania*.

Within convergence and copyright culture there is also remix, a set of practices and ideological perspectives that are often framed as part of the legally justified 'fair use' of proprietary content, but also as transgressive and

---

[12] Henry Jenkins, *Convergence Culture: Where Old and New Media Collide* (New York: New York University Press, 2006), p. 2.

resistant to the ways in which copyright is hoarded and exploited by multimedia franchises. Remix is a dominant art form in the twenty-first century. Its expansive reach has been aided by its equally broad definition by many scholars and practitioners, who have used the term to describe practices as diverse as musical mash-up, photomontage, fan fiction and retweeting or reposting content on social media. Enabled by the wealth of material opened up for recycling by the information age, as well as by the legal and ethical provisions of fair use, remix's cut-and-paste practices have been given a central place in the history of the digital revolution. Remix has also been hailed as an inherently egalitarian act: anti-copyright, open to anyone and indiscriminate in its mixing of media and combination of high culture with low. In practice, of course, remix is not always as progressive as it is imagined to be, nor is it especially new. Current, broad definitions of the practice often serve to obscure these facts. Like other Gothic texts before them, remix's recombinant appropriations, in Eckart Voigt's formulation, have 'been both hailed as the subversive replenishment of an everyday avant-garde and dismissed as signs of an exhausted, hyper-reflexive culture that lacks innovative and progressive potential'.[13] If we consider remix to be the popular, multimedia appropriation and recombination of proprietary material, then remix culture is the ethical and aesthetic framework that enables this practice. According to Eduardo Navas, 'remix culture can be defined as the global activity consisting of the creative and efficient exchange of information made possible by digital technologies that is supported by the practice of cut/copy and paste'.[14]

---

[13] Eckart Voigts, 'Memes and Recombinant Appropriation', in Thomas Leitch (ed.), *The Oxford Handbook of Adaptation Studies* (Oxford: Oxford University Press, 2017), pp. 285–302 (p. 289). For a concept with so much cultural currency, remix culture is surprisingly ill-defined, and its origins are still being explored. Many sources cite Lawrence Lessig as having coined this phrase, though in his 2008 book *Remix* it rarely appears, and then only when Lessig directly quotes music mash-up artist Gregg Gillis. Lessig himself uses the term 'Read/Write Culture', as opposed to a 'Read Only Culture'. See Lawrence Lessig, *Remix: Making Art and Commerce Thrive in the Hybrid Economy* (London: Penguin, 2008), pp. 28–31. Margie Borschke finds the broad usage of the term remix (by Lessig and others) 'as a general descriptor of cultural practice and output' to be problematic in the way that it 'obscures a particular history of media use in recent music culture, one that offers important lessons about reception and distribution'. See Margie Borschke, *This Is Not a Remix: Piracy, Authenticity and Popular Music* (New York: Bloomsbury, 2017), p. 51. This too is reminiscent of how the label 'Gothic' has been used by scholars and critics, in a way that seems to include a variety of media, but is often literature-centric.

[14] Eduardo Navas, *Remix: The Bond of Repetition and Representation* (2009) <http://remixtheory.net/?p=361> (last accessed 16 November 2014), para. 1.

Where the term 'convergence' implies ownership, coherence and cohesion, remix offers an altogether messier image, suggesting recombination and reproduction rather than 'original' creation. While the metaphor of convergence emphasises the tidy cooperation and flow of media, Stefan Sonvilla-Weiss likens remix and mash-up practices to 'a coevolving oscillating membrane of user-generated content (conversational media) and mass media'.[15] This description of remix as some kind of hybrid monster is common among remix scholars. David Gunkel, for instance, describes it as 'the monstrous outcome of illegitimate fusions and promiscuous reconfigurations of recorded media that take place in excess of the comprehension, control, and proper authority of the "original artist"'.[16] If it is true that the 'emergence of new technologies, the marvels of modernity and science, is intimately bound up with the production of monsters and ghosts', then it is no surprise that these explicitly monstrous digital technologies and practices have produced a new variety (or at least, a new configuration) of Gothic fiends and fictions.[17] In the age of remix, it is also unsurprising to note that Gothic self-cannibalism has reached such a frenzied pace. At the turn of the millennium Fred Botting predicted that, in such a highly commercialised and repetitive state, contemporary Gothic might become essentially meaningless, losing its thrill and/or its transgressive impulse. In 2002, he described a dystopian future in which Gothic fiction

> has become too familiar after two centuries of repetitive mutation and seems incapable of shocking anew. Inured to Gothic shocks and terrors, contemporary culture recycles its images in the hope of finding a charge intense enough to stave off the black hole within and without, the one opened up by postmodernist fragmentation and plurality.[18]

This has not quite happened, though we can certainly recognise Botting's description of endless recycling and repetition in remix practices. When repetition becomes the dominant mode of discourse, however, the fact *that*

---

[15] Stefan Sonvilla-Weiss, 'Introduction: Mashups, Remix Practices and the Recombination of Existing Digital Content', in Stefan Sonvilla-Weiss (ed.), *Mashup Cultures* (Wien: Springer, 2010), pp. 8–23 (p. 9).
[16] David J. Gunkel, *Of Remixology: Ethics and Aesthetics after Remix* (Cambridge, MA: MIT Press, 2016), pp. xxix–xxx.
[17] Fred Botting and Catherine Spooner (eds), *Monstrous Media/Spectral Subjects: Imaging Gothic from the Nineteenth Century to the Present* (Manchester: Manchester University Press, 2015), p. 1.
[18] Fred Botting, 'Aftergothic: Consumption, Machines, and Black Holes', in Jerrold E. Hogle (ed.), *The Cambridge Companion to Gothic Fiction* (Cambridge: Cambridge University Press, 2002), pp. 277–300 (p. 298).

certain things are repeated becomes less significant than *how* they are repeated. In examining the contexts of Gothic remix, new meanings, shocks and terrors can be found.

Gothic Remediation

'New media are wonderfully creepy', writes Wendy Hui Kyong Chun.[19] With this statement Chun is referencing the ways in which our convergent digital technologies seem both to embody and to dissolve cultural binaries: 'endlessly fascinating yet boring, addictive yet revolting, banal yet revolutionary'.[20] In particular, Chun's focus is on the way in which digital technologies become 'habitual', producing compulsive update cultures 'in which we race to stay close to the same and in which information spreads not like a powerful, overwhelming virus, but rather like a long, undead thin chain'.[21] New media are undead in the way that they attempt to extract every last ounce of value out of old content: the continuous quest for the new creates a great deal of 'junk' that must in turn be recycled into new content. The past becomes a capitalist resource that grows more valuable – more capable of seeming new and novel – the longer that it remains buried. Those media most readily accessible for remix are undead in another sense as well. They have passed into the public domain, many years after the death of the copyright holder.[22] In Chun's model of recycling and updating 'undead' media, the remixer is a metaphorical grave robber, digging up the disowned pieces of older media, re-stitching them and resurrecting them as their own.

Markman Ellis's definition of the Gothic is especially useful in this context. He suggests that the Gothic 'is itself a theory of history: a mode for the apprehension and consumption of history'.[23] Likewise, where many concepts of convergence seem to look forward, to the new and updated, remix is how contemporary culture makes sense of old content as well as new. In addition to the variety of digital technologies that support it, remix culture is reliant on the wealth of directly appropriable content – proprietary or public

---

[19] Wendy Hui Kyong Chun, *Updating to Remain the Same: Habitual New Media* (Cambridge, MA: MIT Press, 2016), p. ix. Original emphasis.
[20] Chun, *Updating to Remain the Same*, p. ix.   [21] Chun, *Updating to Remain the Same*, p. 3.
[22] The length of term that copyright can extend *post mortem auctoris* (after the author's death) differs wildly from country to country. Typically, however, copyright remains valid 50–70 years post-mortem.
[23] Markman Ellis, *The History of Gothic Fiction* (Edinburgh: Edinburgh University Press, 2000), p. 11.

domain – made available by the information age. As Navas writes, 'Without a history, the remix cannot be Remix.'[24] Sean Silver, likewise, describes how the Gothic's anachronistic way of imagining grand and ancient pasts consistently impacts on how we view our national history in the present, embodying 'the experience of modernity as continually routed through and ruptured by the past'.[25] This is echoed in Chun's description of contemporary media culture as a 'long, undead thin chain'.

Remix's Gothic rerouting of modernity and its 'undead' appropriation of both copyrighted and public domain texts is especially striking in visual culture, where we are not only confronted with the material traces of the past, but also with the faces of those to whom they belonged. Kamilla Elliott explores how Gothic descriptions and appropriations of images 'tie the individual to the historical'.[26] Faces, in particular, have come to serve as an indicator of 'individual identity'.[27] Engagement with photographs or other personal effects may begin as an anonymous encounter, but the anonymity of these objects is easily broken by context or paratext, sometimes to uncanny effect. Artists who work with photographs frequently comment on this. In his book of found thrift-store snapshots *Talking Pictures* (2012), for instance, Ransom Riggs recalls collecting anonymous photographic portraits as a child. One in particular stood on his nightstand for a number of years as his 'fantasy girlfriend', until one day he discovered the writing on the back of the photograph: 'Dorothy Shaw / Chicago / age 15 / Died of Leukemia.'[28] Riggs describes the profound impact that this realisation had on him, using it to argue for a re-evaluation of the aesthetic and emotional value of these discarded photographs. The best of these inscriptions, he suggests, 'have an immediacy that transcends era', which 'counteracts the distancing effect old snapshots can have'.[29] The sense of immediacy created by photographic inscriptions (or, presumably, by similar paratextual materials) offers the viewer a valuable moment of empathy and self-recognition. Of course, Riggs's discovery and collection of these inscribed photographs does not only produce affective or didactic value. Though certainly offering Riggs

[24] Navas, *Remix*, para. 7.
[25] Sean Silver, 'The Politics of Gothic Historiography, 1660–1800', in Glennis Byron and Dale Townshend (eds), *The Gothic World* (Abingdon and New York: Routledge, 2014), pp. 3–14.
[26] Kamilla Elliott, *Portraiture and British Gothic Fiction: The Rise of Picture Identification, 1764–1835* (Baltimore, NJ: Johns Hopkins University Press, 2013), p. 7.
[27] Elliott, *Portraiture and British Gothic Fiction*, p. 22.
[28] Ransom Riggs, *Talking Pictures: Images and Messages Rescued from the Past* (New York: It Books, 2012), pp. x–xi.
[29] Riggs, *Talking Pictures*, p. xiii.

and his readers a powerful emotional link with the past, his collection of other people's discarded photographs has also been transformed into a saleable book, for which he is the new copyright holder. One person's junk has been remixed, 'updated' into another's treasure.

In addition to his nonfiction work, Riggs is the author of the *Miss Peregrine's Peculiar Children* (2011–20) novels, which also began as a series of 'authentic, vintage found photographs'.[30] The role that these found images play in the books is the prime reason for labelling them as 'Gothic' remixes, though the series is subsumed in the culture of undead convergence on other levels. The first book, *Miss Peregrine's Home for Peculiar Children* (2011), also contains a number of Gothic themes, including family secrets, a 'haunted' house and the return of a repressed past, and the found images are the novel's most literal embodiment of its Gothic 'apprehension and consumption of history'.[31] In Riggs's own words, these photographs are 'a document of a real, incontestably actual thing – a person or a place – in a story that is hugely fantastic and fictional'.[32] As with *Talking Pictures*, the images in the *Miss Peregrine* books come from a variety of time periods and contexts, and were found in charity shops, at online auctions or through other collectors. Riggs initially planned to present these images in a photobook as well, but Quirk Books's head editor Jason Rekulak convinced him that they would make an engaging basis for a supernatural story, and so they were incorporated into a new context for remediation and consumption.[33] Riggs explores the implications and 'experience of consuming history and appropriating it for one's subjective needs' in the novel itself.[34] On a quest to uncover the past of his deceased grandfather, a Holocaust survivor, the series' young protagonist Jacob Portman follows a trail of cryptic photographs, tokens and verbal clues to try and come to terms with his own personal trauma. Jacob encounters photographs and other material traces of the past (letters, sketches,

---

[30] Ransom Riggs, *Miss Peregrine's Home for Peculiar Children* (Philadelphia: Quirk Books, 2011), p. 350.
[31] Ellis, *History of Gothic Fiction*, p. 11.
[32] Tim Lammers, 'Interview: Ransom Riggs thrilled to enter "Peculiar" world of Tim Burton', *DirectConversations.com*, 2 September 2016 <https://directconversations.com/2016/09/02/interview-ransom-riggs-thrilled-enter-peculiar-world-tim-burton/> (last accessed 27 April 2019), para. 8.
[33] Maria Russo, 'Ransom Riggs Is Inspired by Vintage Snapshots', *The New York Times*, 19 October 2018 <www.nytimes.com/2013/12/31/books/ransom-riggs-is-inspired-by-vintage-snapshots.html> (last accessed 28 April 2019).
[34] Agata Zarzycka, 'The Gothicization of World War II as a Source of Cultural Self-Reflection in *Miss Peregrine's Home for Peculiar Children* and *Hollow City*', in Steffen Hantke and Agnieszka Soltysik Monnet (eds), *War Gothic in Literature and Culture* (London: Routledge, 2016), pp. 229–44 (p. 236).

parcels) throughout the books, which are in turn represented as *trompe-l'œil*, printed scrapbook-style on the page for the reader. The novel quickly becomes a discussion of what it means to be 'peculiar', and how this otherness is represented, commemorated, forgotten and rendered strange through the physical traces of the past.

Miss Peregrine's Peculiar Children uses various metaphors of mediation to characterise its Gothic world. For Jacob, observing the uncanny rural beauty of Cairnholm Island is 'like stepping into one of those heavily retouched photos that come loaded as wallpaper on new computers'.[35] The first novel's discussion of temporal loops is also framed as part of a hyper-mediated, constantly updated 'undead' world. The children in Cairnholm's 3 September 1940 time loop have lived under Miss Peregrine's care, safe and unageing, for more than 70 years. At one point in the novel, as Jacob watches the loop restart for the first time, he wonders whether 'these children died every evening only to be resurrected by the loop, like some Sisyphean suicide cult, condemned to be blown up and stitched back together for eternity'.[36] Using another technological metaphor, Jacob describes the moment in which the loop restarts: 'like a movie that burns in the projector while you're watching it, a bloom of hot and perfect whiteness spread out before me and swallowed everything'.[37]

This destruction and looped reconstitution is fantastical in *Miss Peregrine's Home for Peculiar Children*, but is performed more literally by Riggs's found photographs, resurrected from the dustbin of obscurity in service of fantastical history-building and Gothic pleasure. The integration between image and text is not entirely smooth; Riggs deliberately creates intermedial seams and generic confusion in the books. The found images are often uncanny or horrific, while the narrative that frames them is largely fantastical and whimsical. Multiple images, often very different from one another, are used to depict the same character. Emma, for instance, appears as three different people across three photographs in the first book. Though most of the images are described in the text of the novel, as well as being displayed as illustrations, the images and descriptions never face each other. In some instances the intentionality of this separation becomes especially obvious, as the text on the preceding pages ends abruptly, requiring the reader to turn the page in order to be confronted with the image that has just been described.

---

[35] Riggs, *Miss Peregrine*, p. 101.   [36] Riggs, *Miss Peregrine*, p. 171.
[37] Riggs, *Miss Peregrine*, p. 171.

The effect of this rupture between text and image is quite opposite from that witnessed in *Talking Pictures,* transforming the *Miss Peregrine* stories from illustrated novels into multimedia remixes. The images in the *Miss Peregrine* novels are clearly framed as objects of consumption; they are there to be looked at. The acknowledged mismatch between the authentic, found images and the fantastical story, combined with the delay between description and viewing, also establishes the people in these images as alien rather than familiar. The reader forms a mental impression or idea of the image, which is then disrupted when they are confronted with the 'real' image overleaf. The illustrations themselves lack captions, meaning that the reader must do the work of linking them to the narrator's preceding descriptions. At these points it can become unclear as to whether the pictures are there to support the story, or the story to support the pictures. In either case, it is distance and anonymity that allow the images to be appropriated and recycled. Though they once depicted real individuals in a physical time and place, as they are remixed into Riggs's book they become blank slates to be filled with new identities, in new fantastical spaces. Riggs also gives the people in the images new names to match the characters that they depict.[38] It is the obscurity, anonymity and 'undeath' of those pictured in the found photographs, rather than a sense of immediacy or liveliness conveyed by contextual information, that allows the images to be reconfigured as commodities. The series box set even comes with its own 'strange collection of very curious photographs' for readers to own, circulate and remix in turn.[39] Not all Gothic remixes, however, rely on affective distance to achieve a sense of horror or wonder. The repeating 'undeath' of the past in both the text and found images of *Miss Peregrine's Peculiar Children* is replicated by another visual medium: the GIF. GIFs are looped, often remixed images, and they too are caught up in loops of digital circulation, participation and commodification. In this case, however, the image does not require context to achieve a lively 'immediacy that transcends era'.[40] Instead, the immediacy of the past is achieved through the medium's manipulation of movement.

Graphics Interchange Gothic

First invented in the 1980s, GIFs (short for 'Graphics Interchange Format') are one of several short-form media that remix previous artefacts for popular

---

[38] See Riggs, *Miss Peregrine,* pp. 350–1.
[39] Ransom Riggs (2015), *Miss Peregrine's Peculiar Children Boxed Set,* box edition (Philadelphia: Quirk Books, 2015), publicity blurb.
[40] Riggs, *Talking Pictures,* p. xiii.

consumption and circulation. Often the term is used to describe looping media outside the .gif format. Michael Z. Newman contrasts the GIF with early film, which was 'unattainable' in the decades 'before home video, before it was commonplace for casual viewers to possess copies of favorite movies, before it was possible to view clips of movies at will on YouTube, and before you could take screenshots and drop them into a PowerPoint'.[41] Newman points out that this lack of immediate access meant that '[m]uch influential criticism and history was written on the basis of often fuzzy memories'.[42] The GIF, in contrast, is eminently attainable, easily viewed and shared in a wide variety of digital contexts. It offers a shared emotional vocabulary for internet users, but also an attractive advertising medium for corporations. As popular culture becomes more focused around the participation and labour of the fan/producer or 'prosumer', commercial culture follows suit. Even Quirk Books, a relatively minor player when compared to media corporations such as Disney or Warner Bros, has cultivated a substantial network of freelancers and fans that create often surprising links between its projects. For instance, Ransom Riggs wrote and directed the book trailer for Quirk's cut-and-paste mash-up novel *Sense and Sensibility and Sea Monsters* (2010).

Remix scholar Lawrence Lessig has argued that because more 'people can use a wider set of tools to express ideas and emotions differently ... more will, at least until the law effectively blocks it'.[43] As with much of remix culture, we tend to consider GIFs and memes as fannish objects of participation and democratic engagement, but it is important not to underestimate the webs of commercial control and surveillance that underpin seemingly free, interactive and participatory networks. Increasingly, as Kate M. Miltner and Tim Highfield point out, 'the creation of GIFs is institutionalized, with commercial partnerships and advertising shaping the content available to users'.[44] New GIF varieties are being developed and used almost exclusively within the fashion and advertising industries, and sponsored content inevitably appears at the top of smartphone GIF keyboards. The advertising campaigns for the *Miss Peregrine's Peculiar Children* books included a series of cinemagraphs: GIFs in which most of the image remains still while a single element is continually looped. This type of GIF, in particular, 'typically

---

[41] Michael Z. Newman, 'GIFs: The Attainable Text', *Film Criticism* 40:1 (2016), no pag. (para. 1).
[42] Newman, 'GIFs: The Attainable Text', para. 1.   [43] Lessig, *Remix*, p. 83.
[44] Kate M. Miltner and Tim Highfield, 'Never Gonna GIF You Up: Analyzing the Cultural Significance of the Animated GIF', *Social Media + Society* 3:3 (2017): 1–11 (p. 8).

fetishizes a consumer good or identity'.⁴⁵ For the 2016 Tim Burton film adaptation of the first *Miss Peregrine* book, Twentieth Century Fox commissioned their own series of GIFs. Some draw clear inspiration from the novel's illustrations, including 'Emma in the Dark' and the cover image 'The Levitating Girl', but rather than using the photographs from Riggs's novel these loops are constructed from production shots and stills. In a Gothic act of tongue-in-cheek fakery, the GIFs have all been designed to look like old, yellowed photographic prints.

The *Miss Peregrine* film GIFs were created by Kevin J. Weir, the artist behind the *Flux Machine* Tumblr account. Weir's GIF art began as non-commercial remix, as a hobby that supported his job as an advertiser, but as his work for the *Miss Peregrine* film indicates, the boundary between his work and his hobby quickly blurred.⁴⁶ Like Ransom Riggs's found photographs, however, Weir's *Flux Machine* GIFs are also interesting for the ways in which they are able to find horror in repetition. The GIF, like other Gothic technologies of remix, revolves around the inescapability of the past, and in Weir's case the past is represented once again through digitised photographs. The *Flux Machine* tells a Gothic story using images from the Library of Congress's public domain archives. Rather than 'writing' new histories, Weir remixes and animates existing ones. In some cases he simply animates the background of a single image, cinemagraph-style.⁴⁷

For his animations Weir draws 80 to 100 frames in Photoshop, 'cutting things out into layers, moving them a little bit, making a new layer, moving that a little bit' until the moving image can be compiled.⁴⁸ The end result is a looped video that is between 10 and 20 seconds long, shared freely on Weir's Tumblr account. In Weir's GIFs, the ghostly images of those depicted are never at rest. Instead, they are caught in an interminable cycle of uncanny repetition. In a GIF called 'Decoy Howitzer', for instance, the moment of a soldier's death is replayed over and over again. The still image features a soldier standing next to the mouth of a large cannon. A dark mist spills out of the cannon before resolving itself into a dark double of the soldier, stealing

---

⁴⁵ Jason Eppink, 'A brief history of the GIF (so Far)', *Journal of Visual Culture* 13.3 (1 December 2014): 298–306 (p. 303).
⁴⁶ Lara O'Reilly and Will Heilpern, *The 30 Most Creative People in Advertising Under 30* (2016) <http://uk.businessinsider.com/30-most-creative-people-in-advertising-under-30-2016?r=US&IR=T> [(last accessed 4 April 2016).
⁴⁷ Paula Cocozza, 'Ghostly gifs made from archive photos – the haunting work of Kevin Weir', *The Guardian*, 28 September 2014 <www.theguardian.com/artanddesign/shortcuts/2014/sep/28/gif-archive-photos-kevin-weir-flux-machine> (last accessed 4 April 2016), para. 1.
⁴⁸ Cocozza, 'Ghostly gifs', para. 1.

his own 'ghost' or life force and dragging him out of frame. The image is rendered uncanny both through movement, an attribute not normal to the photographic medium, and through the monsters and fantastical images that it reveals. In the case of these old documentary photographs, animation has much the same effect as colouration might, making the images feel less temporally distant and thus (when they contain graphic or disturbing images) more shocking. Though films certainly existed at the time in which these photographs were taken, we are not accustomed to seeing moving images from this period, whereas still photographs commonly feature in news reports, on memorials and in other regular, commemorative media. When the images are made to move, then, the moment becomes startlingly 'real' to the viewer, closer to our own contemporary forms of mediation. The historical soldier depicted in the image may well have survived the battle, but here he becomes emblematic of all those who died in historical wars. This creates a sense of fascination and horror, as the viewer is forced to consider this moment of historical haunting *ad infinitum*.

Not only does Weir effectively convey historical horror through Gothic reproduction, he also does so in a way that is resolutely digital. This has a number of narrative and aesthetic repercussions. For instance, what Weir particularly favours about the GIF format is the way in which 'it allows you both to use suspense and to freeze one moment'.[49] As Anne Quéma writes of H. R. Giger's Gothic images, the 'viewer is trapped in that fantastic moment of hesitation ... Although the means of representation are mimetic, the framed misshapen reflection undermines the principle of mimetic reproduction'.[50] The idea of suspense may initially seem to run counter to the looped nature of the GIF, which repeats the same series of images over and over again. By adjusting the length of time at the end of each loop, however, Weir creates a moment of calm in the image, a moment in which everything returns to normal. This pause between loops sometimes extends to as much as 8 seconds. Before every loop of the GIF there exists a moment in which the viewer wonders whether things might turn out differently. As interviewer Paula Cocozza notes, however, 'it is just a moment of illogical hope'.[51] The cycle cannot be changed. Weir's GIFs trap the viewer in a single past moment that is repeated over and over again. His images are thus fantastical and Gothic in a way that only the GIF can achieve, because

---

[49] Cocozza, 'Ghostly gifs', para. 8.
[50] Anne Quéma, 'The Gothic and the Fantastic in the Age of Digital Reproduction', *English Studies in Canada* 30:4 (2007): 81–119 (p. 99).
[51] Cocozza, 'Ghostly gifs', para. 8.

through alienation they approximate moments and objects that are mimetically un-representable. In this regard, Graig Uhlin argues that the GIF's 'repetition indicates that a viewer is not guided along by a narrative structuring of time. The viewer is rather caught up in the GIF's temporal suspension: to view it is to be captivated.'[52]

These Gothic remixes literalise Chris Baldick's foreboding idea that the 'price of liberty . . . is eternal vigilance'.[53] To avoid repeating the past, we are forced, horrifically, to return to it and to re-live it continually through repeated remediation. In a sense, then, these images are also part of the broader spectacle of war created through popular history and fiction. This spectacle glorifies barbarism even as it depicts it, turning it into a product of Gothic consumerism that provokes what Spooner calls 'a gleeful shudder even as we congratulate ourselves on the collective progress of humanity'.[54] As Spooner suggests, contemporary Gothic is not only found in shock and horror, but also in the pleasure and humour of seeing that horror safely contained. Similarly, despite its monstrous undertones, Uhlin suggests that the GIF medium generally uses the comic mode, rather than a Gothic one.[55] The Gothic GIF, likewise, can be transgressive, horrifying or gleeful depending on the context in which it is repeated. In her discussion of GIFs and visual pleasure, for instance, Anna McCarthy writes the following:

> But GIFs are also like zombies and pod people. They may come back, but they're never the same. Something has changed: resolution, aspect ratio, size. Or the image material has become encrusted with memes. The cat is now playing a set of drums as well as a piano. GIFs, you could say, are social from birth, and this is at least partly because they are constantly being reborn. Like reincarnated souls, they are destined for eternal circulation. Part of the enjoyment of GIFs in the context of social media involves obscuring their constant transformations.[56]

The ultimate meaning of the GIF lies with those who share it, and in the subtle ways in which they alter it by summoning it back into circulation.

This does not mean that its meaning is entirely ambiguous. Uhlin observes the extent to which short GIF loops often serve to summarise the emotional

---

[52] Graig Uhlin, 'Playing in the Gif(t) Economy', *Games and Culture* 9:6 (2014): 517–27.
[53] Chris Baldick, 'Introduction', in Chris Baldick (ed.), *The Oxford Book of Gothic Tales* (Oxford: Oxford University Press, 1992), pp. xi–xxiii (p. xxii).
[54] Spooner, *Contemporary Gothic*, p. 20.   [55] Uhlin, 'Playing in the Gif(t) Economy', p. 522.
[56] Anna McCarthy, 'Visual pleasure and GIFs', in Pepita Hesselberth and Maria Poulaki (eds), *Compact Cinematics: The Moving Image in the Age of Bit-Sized Media* (New York: Bloomsbury, 2017), pp. 113–22 (p. 114).

content of entire film and television scenes, within the animistic context of early cinema criticism:

> Just as the totemic object serves as a visual, material emblem of that which cannot be held, or grasped in its totality – that is, the spirit of the forest – the GIF animation stands in for what is unable to be circulated. They are tokens of spectatorship; they retain the memory of the spectatorial experience beyond its initial encounter ... Its meaning is generally not ambiguous. Rather, geared for maximum impact and immediacy of effect, GIFs do not depend on contextual cues to be understood.[57]

To illustrate what is meant by this statement, we can again turn to Kevin J. Weir's 'Decoy Howitzer' as an example. In the first frame of 'Decoy Howitzer', before the GIF begins to move, the original image already has an emotional resonance that is associated with its status as a wartime photograph. Weir takes this emotion and animates it, forcing the viewer to watch the soldier's essence repeatedly being stolen by a monstrous force. This transforms it into a totemic representation of the event that it depicts. Regardless of whether or not this soldier died on the battlefield, his image has become emblematic of the fallen soldier, of the atrocities of war more broadly, or of the campy thrills of black-and-white horror films. It no longer depends on historical context to convey this particular emotion. This transformation, combined with the original photograph's age (i.e. outside living memory), provokes an affective response without also demanding a strong ethical objection, like images of London's burning Grenfell Tower or the 9/11 'Falling Man' might.[58]

Of course, the act of ripping such emblematic images from their original historical context, only to translate them into a medium usually reserved for comic gestures and facial expressions, could well be seen as ethically objectionable. But in turning such a moment into a performance of perpetual alienation, a GIF also allows the spectator to notice the moment's unique emotional resonance, and to appropriate this for their own ends. Drawing on Laura Mulvey's definition of the 'possessive spectator', a cinephile who appropriates publicity stills in 'an act of violence against the cohesion of a story, the aesthetic integrity that holds it together, and the vision of its creator', Uhlin explains why GIFs do not fall into this same category.[59]

---

[57] Uhlin, 'Playing in the Gif(t) Economy', pp. 520, 523.
[58] It should be noted that even these events have an extensive afterlife in GIF form, both in the context of respectful commemoration, and in conspiracy forums or joke sites.
[59] Laura Mulvey, *Death 24x a Second: Stillness and the Moving Image* (London: Reaktion Books, 2006), p. 171.

Specifically, GIFs appropriate the images of familiar people and situations, but these are meant to be shared out of context. GIF creation, instead, 'entails liberating the image from its source, not to possess it, as Mulvey indicates, but to give it away, to pass it over to a community of users who then determine its meaning'.[60] Weir, likewise, takes a source image not to possess or erase it, but freely to share an intense, emotional emblem of that image with a new audience, where it no longer requires a historical context to convey the appropriate Gothic affect. The use to which this emblematic history is put is ultimately up to those who share it. They decide where, when and in which contexts Weir's images will be spread, repeated and renewed. Many remix scholars thus offer a utopian vision for remix, suggesting that the practice will open up participation, allow new kinds of transgression and create space for rogue readings. Twenty-first-century remix Gothic, however, promises none of these things. Instead, it offers an undead stream of monstrous revivals, reiterating now-familiar visions of corporatisation, transgression and participation. Its only promise is to return again and again and again.

Remixing Transgression

In October 2017, the weekly British newspaper *The New European* posted a series of downloadable 'Bogeymen of Brexit' Halloween masks on their website (Fig. 15.1). Featuring puns that framed Brexit as 'the ultimate trick', capable of inflicting terror on 'your neighbours who will want to Remain in their houses', the brief article urged readers to '[d]ownload and print our Monsters of Brexit masks and dress as something truly terrifying' to trick-or-treat.[61] Each of the four masks depicted a different UK statesperson, mashed up with a different monster from popular culture. This included the 'terrifying Therezom', a zombified Theresa May 'who walks the land, refusing to die'; an image of Boris Johnson as 'Bojo The Clown, who thinks he's It but whose plans are far from penny wise' (a reference to Stephen King's 1986 novel *IT* and its 2017 film adaptation); the fanged and pale-skinned vampire 'Moggferatu [Jacob Rees-Mogg], who came from the 18th century to drink your peasant blood'; and finally 'the frightening Faggenstain, who brought monstrous ideas back from the dead' – Nigel Farage as a Universal-style Frankenstein, complete with green skin,

---

[60] Uhlin, 'Playing in the Gif(t) Economy', p. 524.
[61] Matt Withers, 'Download Your Monsters of Brexit Masks', *The New European*, 31 October 2017 <www.theneweuropean.co.uk/top-stories/download-monsters-brexit-masks-1-5258813> (last accessed 15 April 2019).

forehead stitches and neck bolts.⁶² None of these images was particularly terrifying. Instead, they were intended to offer comic relief by framing politicians as antiquated, cartoonish monsters rather than frightening ones, and Brexit as just another jump scare.

The masks were shared and remixed on social media to some attention, but the most interesting repetitions and resurrections were still to follow. *The New European* remixed its own post almost a year later, at the end of 2018, with almost identical image placement and wording.⁶³ Re-published more than a year after the referendum, once the real horror and uncertainty of Brexit had the chance to set in, this second post received a much greater round of social-media attention. It was shared thousands of times on networks such as Facebook and Twitter, this time as an ironic example of how 'horrifying' (now both ridiculous and genuinely terrifying) Brexit discourse had become. Of course, the magazine could not have known how truly ironic its Brexit Halloween masks would prove to be. In April 2019 the UK was granted a final Brexit extension to 31 October: Halloween. After this news broke, internet users cited *The New European*'s masks for a third time, and also created their own remixes, memes and Brexit jokes based on the titles of other horror movies, including 'The Brexorcist', 'Nightmare on Downing Street' and 'I Still Know What You Did Last Referendum'.⁶⁴ The masks, it transpired, were not ironic representations after all; they were grimly appropriate.

These three repetitions of the 'Bogeymen of Brexit' offer an excellent example of the way in which fantastical remix functions at a time when Western social and political reality is itself overwhelmingly Gothic. As this example also suggests, humour often plays a significant role in twenty-first-century Gothic mash-ups, though to call this humour, parody or satire may be to presume too great a level of ironic intent on behalf of the remixer. More often the humour is an optional by-product of camp or kitsch engagement with 'bad' taste cultures, or the result of unexpected mapping of seemingly fantastical texts onto Gothic realities. Emily Johansen suggests that 'if traditional gothic narratives worked to obscure and exorcise the cruelties of liberal capitalism, in neoliberal gothic narratives the cruelties are recognized

---

⁶² Withers, 'Download Your Monsters of Brexit Masks'.
⁶³ Matt Withers, 'Get a Brexit-Themed Look for Halloween with These Masks', *The New European*, 23 October 2018 <www.theneweuropean.co.uk/top-stories/dress-as-the-monsters-of-brexit-this-halloween-1-5747550> (last accessed 15 April 2019).
⁶⁴ Anon., *Trick or Treaty? Memes Flood in as UK Goes for Halloween Brexit with 'Zombie' PM* (2019) <https://sputniknews.com/viral/201904131074100523-halloween-brexit-theresa-may-zombie-government-memes/> (last accessed 15 April 2019).

Fig.15.1 a–d: *Bogeymen of Brexit* Halloween masks (2017). Reproduced by kind permission of *The New European*.

as inevitable and inescapable'.[65] Ultimately, the 'Bogeymen of Brexit' remixes convey a sense of hysterical helplessness rather than deconstructive transgression. They denote the return of the repressed past, the feeling that all this

[65] Emily Johansen, 'The Neoliberal Gothic: *Gone Girl, Broken Harbor*, and the Terror of Everyday Life', *Contemporary Literature* 57:1 (Spring 2016): 30–55 (p. 30).

has been repeated before and will be repeated again – or, as Baldick puts it, 'our inability to convince ourselves that we have really escaped from the tyrannies of the past'.[66] This does not necessarily mean that the 'Bogeymen of Brexit' remixes lack any transformative impulse. After all, as Elliott points out in her discussion of Gothic film parody, repetitions are not designed to be 'original' or 'transformative' in themselves, but rather to 'reveal inconsistencies, incongruities, and problems in Gothic criticism: boundaries that it has been unwilling or unable to blur, binary oppositions it has refused to deconstruct, and [point] at which a radical, innovative, subversive discourse manifests as its own hegemonic, dogmatic, and clichéd double'.[67] This opens up new possibilities for transformation in other texts. Remix is the Gothic monster of a neoliberal convergence culture, transgressive not in the sense that it is always politically radical or socially progressive, but in that it has the potential to emphasise the fractures already present in our politics, media and cultural identities.

---

[66] Baldick, 'Introduction', p. xxii.
[67] Kamilla Elliott, 'Gothic – Film – Parody', *Adaptation* 1:1 (2008): 24–43 (p. 24).

3.16
Postdigital Gothic

MARC OLIVIER

Near midnight, in a dark house, Anne hears a sudden eerie, disembodied laugh in the kitchen. She shudders, and without turning on the lights, walks towards the voice. Clutching her mobile, Anne hits the 'record' icon of a video app and boldly addresses the inhuman presence: 'Alexa, replay'. A blue LED halo acknowledges reception of the command and uncanny laughter once again reverberates in the pitch-black room. The next morning, Anne uploads her video file and tweets, '@amazonecho alone in the dark kitchen, with no trigger, a sudden creepy laugh emerges and freaks out owners #justwrong. Replay'.[1] Although no Ann Radcliffe, @anniebonannieTN has documented a twenty-first-century Gothic encounter, a story quickly compiled with similar accounts and disseminated on social media platforms to be redistributed by news outlets across the globe. This is the essence of what I in this chapter will categorise broadly as the postdigital Gothic: a transmedia hybrid of human and machinic speech enmeshed in technological structures that can no longer blithely sustain binaries such as virtual/real or material/immaterial. Nor can it fully escape them, for even the term 'digital' assumes a problematically dichotomous other called 'analogue'. Nevertheless, the Gothic is uniquely positioned to accommodate contradictory categories. Just as the Gothic includes both ghosts and zombies, both the spectral and the material, so too does it support the irresolvable entanglements of the posthuman uncanny.

'Gothic has to do with the edges of the human', writes David Punter. Gothic shows what happens when 'his majesty the ego' cracks open to reveal the 'Nietzschean abyss' that lies beneath.[2] Punter identifies a 'spectral criticism' that aligns with material criticism to explore, for example, not just the

---

[1] Anne (@anniebonannieTN), Twitter post, 21 February 2018, 7:40am <https://twitter.com/anniebonannieTN/status/966336717824327681> (last accessed 30 August 2018).
[2] David Punter, *The Gothic Condition: Terror, History and the Psyche* (Cardiff: University of Wales Press, 2016), p. 5.

act of reading but also the materiality of books and the 'substrate of all dealings with text' as a source of anxiety and fear.³ Postdigital Gothic strains to identify the edges of the human within what Katherine Hayles calls 'cognitive assemblages' – entanglements of systems that may include both human and nonhuman actors in 'myriad complex systems and computational devices'.⁴ Part of the nonhuman turn in philosophy, Hayles emphasises cognition as a function not restricted to humans or to living things.⁵ When those assemblages register affectively with a human, they signal disjuncture between older models of consciousness (such as Freudian repression) and cognitive behaviours exterior to the mind. Even if we accept, along with Maurice Lévy, that Sigmund Freud deserves the title of 'best twentieth-century Gothic writer' due to his creation of a psychoanalytic system that doubles as a 'universal Gothic mechanism', we must nevertheless concede that Freud's formulation of the uncanny, inspired in part by Hoffmann's clockwork automaton, may very well require a technological upgrade.⁶

While postdigital Gothic does not dismiss Freudian concepts, it does reveal a significant lack in Freud's model of consciousness, namely, its inability to account for the computational media that is now integrated into most technologies. Watches, refrigerators, railways, telephones, public utilities and other systems or devices available during Freud's lifetime have since become 'smart'. And although to believe that those 'smart' things actually 'think' would be to succumb to precisely the kind of primitive beliefs described by Freud, we would be equally naive to dismiss computational media as mere machines. As Hayles observes, computational media 'are the quintessentially cognitive technology'.⁷ Hayles adopts 'nonconscious cognition' as a supplement to the restrictive Freudian view of human consciousness and unconsciousness.⁸ Nonconscious cognition, in contrast to what is commonly called 'thinking', occurs in humans, biological lifeforms and computational systems. This is not to say that Alexa is alive inside Anne's Amazon Echo nor that it laughed of its own conscious volition but rather to acknowledge that the device was performing cognitive tasks within a broader nonconscious assemblage, including, among other things, a chip that runs software, a router, an Internet Service Provider and that thing we attempt to

---

³ Punter, *The Gothic Condition*, p. 11.
⁴ N. Katherine Hayles, *Unthought: The Power of the Cognitive Nonconscious* (Chicago: University of Chicago Press, 2017), p. 126.
⁵ See Hayles, *Unthought*, p. 212.
⁶ Maurice Lévy, 'FAQ: What Is Gothic?', *Anglophonia* 15 (2004): 23–37 (p. 34).
⁷ Hayles, *Unthought*, p. 34.   ⁸ Hayles, *Unthought*, p. 208.

immaterialise as 'the cloud' – all, presumably, without Anne's participation. Whatever the cause, the event triggers awareness of the opacity of the tech industry and the hidden algorithms that have visible consequences in politics, social equality and surveillance. The digital error is uncanny *especially* once explained or debugged because it points to processes at once frighteningly spectral and precariously material.

Although I have chosen to adopt terms from Hayles, my overarching interpretive strategy is to promote those theoretical tools that account for the nonhuman as embedded in real practices. Object-oriented ontology, speculative realism, media archaeology and other methods that question anthropocentric assumptions can help conceive of a Gothic beyond the Baudrillardian fantasies of immateriality referred to by Jeffrey Sconce as the 'postmodern occult'.[9] Fred Botting's term, Cybergothic, best captures the late-twentieth-century preoccupation with simulation, immateriality and virtualisation.[10] Cybergothic aims to disclose 'the formlessness, the consuming void, underlying the flickering thrills of contemporary western simulations'.[11] And indeed, the mixture of enthusiasm and fear associated with the virtual served as the dominant mode of relating to computational technologies from the 1980s through to the first decade of the twenty-first century. Philosopher Vilém Flusser's *The Shape of Things* (1993), which includes essays written between 1970 and 1991, captures the prevalence of Cybergothic modes of thought near the turn of the millennium. 'The environment is becoming ever softer, more nebulous, more ghostly', asserts Flusser, who then dismisses the 'vestiges of materiality' as irrelevant, stating that it is possible to imagine the 'liberation of software from hardware'.[12]

In 2020, the weight of the physical counters an erstwhile rhetoric of immateriality. In place of virtualisation, computer scientist Paul Dourish proposes the term 'rematerialisation' to signal the 'unavoidable materiality that underwrites any practice of the virtual'.[13] Media archaeologists such as

---

[9] Jeffrey Sconce, *Haunted Media: Electronic Presence from Telegraphy to Television* (Durham, NC: Duke University Press, 2000), pp. 170–1.
[10] Fred Botting, *Gothic Romanced: Consumption, Gender and Technology in Contemporary Fictions* (London: Routledge, 2008), p. 34.
[11] Fred Botting, 'Aftergothic: Consumption, Machines, and Black Holes', in Jerrold E. Hogle (ed.), *The Cambridge Companion to Gothic Fiction* (Cambridge: Cambridge University Press, 2002), pp. 277–300 (p. 298).
[12] Vilém Flusser, *The Shape of Things: A Philosophy of Design*, trans. by Anthony Matthews (London: Reaktion Books, 2012), pp. 87, 91.
[13] Paul Dourish, 'Rematerializing the Platform: Emulation and the Digital-Material', in Sarah Pink, Elisenda Ardèvol and Dèbora Lanzeni (eds), *Digital Materialities: Design and Anthropology* (London: Bloomsbury Publishing, 2016), pp. 29–44 (p. 43).

Jussi Parikka call this *'media analysis of and from the ruins'*.[14] In like fashion, postdigital Gothic texts peer through the spectral into the architecture that has housed our cyber fantasies. Instead of labyrinthine passages and secret doors, postdigital Gothic architecture reveals the recesses of hidden codes that seep through to the surface of familiar interfaces in moments of error. Instead of the hidden vault, postdigital Gothic discloses the secret history of digital media containers, each file extension (e.g., .doc, .jpeg, .mp3) signalling a narrative act of selection and configuration that shapes human perception. The work of postdigital Gothic criticism within nonhuman and materialist theory requires opening black boxes and analysing tales from the digital crypt about shadow profiles, encryption and decryption, alternative currencies, the Dark Web and all those media texts that seek to engage the in-between state of the human as enmeshed in the nonhuman. In short, postdigital Gothic is not only a storytelling practice inspired by a long literary history; it is also a means of enquiry. This chapter will briefly engage instantiations of the postdigital Gothic within found footage horror films, compression formats and social media horror both real and imagined, and, in so doing, will read stories both human and nonhuman.

Glitch Gothic

As Catherine Spooner has observed, found footage is the cinematic equivalent of the 'found manuscript' tradition in Gothic literature.[15] The faux found manuscript entails 'the discovery of a lost or hidden document that reveals dreadful secrets concerning the fate of its author, before crumbling away just before the crucial point is made. This manuscript is often in poor condition, fragmented, missing important information.'[16] Widely considered the seminal text in its genre, *The Blair Witch Project* (dir. Daniel Myrick and Eduardo Sánchez, 1999) thus becomes found footage's answer to Horace Walpole's *The Castle of Otranto* (1764). As with Walpole, a host of imitators followed. Significantly, the ubiquity of digital imaging introduced new equipment into found footage, and the signifier of crumbling media shifted from analogue noise to digital glitch. By the 2010s, jolting disruptions to digital flow had become so indispensable to the genre that even *The Blair Witch Project* was retrofitted with digital glitch

---

[14] Jussi Parikka, *What Is Media Archaeology?* (Cambridge: Polity Press, 2012), p. 90.
[15] Catherine Spooner, 'Twenty-First-Century Gothic', in Dale Townshend (ed.), *Terror and Wonder: The Gothic Imagination* (London: The British Library, 2014), pp. 180–205 (p. 191).
[16] Catherine Spooner, *Contemporary Gothic* (London: Reaktion Books, 2006), p. 38.

intertitles in its new Blu-ray edition trailer.[17] Almost without fail, found footage horror turns to the glitch to express the unspeakable. Like the lines of asterisks signifying damage to the manuscript in texts such as Charles Maturin's *Melmoth the Wanderer* (1820) or Ann Radcliffe's *Romance of the Forest* (1791), the found footage glitch introduces ready-made data ruins and shocking digital viscera to reawaken the affective impact of trope-laden narratives.

Glitch Gothic evokes an uncanny that is anchored in machinic speech.[18] Often coincident with ghostly apparitions in found footage horror, the glitch assaults the transparency of digital media. The temporary error during which sound stutters and images break into digital chunks of data presents an unnerving obstacle to legible media flow. As media professor Hugh S. Manon and glitch artist Daniel Temkin explain, 'it is a given program's *failure to fully fail* upon encountering bad data that allows a glitch to appear'.[19] That transient misfunction divorces the medium from the anticipated message, making the glitch at once a noise artefact and declaration of the medium's nature. 'Indeed, what makes any medium specific is how it *fails* to disappear', observes artist and theorist Rosa Menkman.[20] In Menkman's 'Vernacular of File Formats', the artist subjects her own image to glitching to reveal visual differences between glitched codecs (computer codes that compress and decompress data) such as JPEG, GIF, DV and BMP. Clearly, very few observers will become glitch-literate to the point of recognising the difference between a damaged PNG and a TIFF. In fact, most cinematic depictions of glitches are pre-fabricated media effects. Used haphazardly, VCR tracking may end up nonsensically layered on top of the supposed HD GoPro footage left behind by a ghost hunter. Consequently, pre-fabricated glitches accustom viewers to a glitch aesthetic without fostering a deeper relation to code. In fact, Jerrold E. Hogle's contention that Walpole's Strawberry Hill House 'divorces artifacts from their foundations' perfectly describes what found footage does with glitch artefacts.[21] Thus, the Glitch

---

[17] The trailer can be accessed in the preview section of the DVD *Knock Knock 2* (2011) released by Lion's Gate, 7 August 2012. See *Knock Knock 2*. Dir. Chris Sheng. Red Baron Films, Indican Pictures. 2011. Lionsgate Home Entertainment, 2012. DVD.

[18] See Marc Olivier, 'Glitch Gothic', in Murray Leeder (ed.), *Cinematic Ghosts: Haunting and Spectrality from Silent Cinema to the Digital Era* (London: Bloomsbury Academic, 2015), pp. 253–70.

[19] Hugh S. Manon and Daniel Temkin, 'Notes on Glitch', *World Picture* 6 (2011) <www.worldpicturejournal.com/WP_6/Manon.html> (last accessed 19 August 2018).

[20] Rosa Menkman, *The Glitch Moment(um)* (Amsterdam: Colophon, 2011), p. 14.

[21] Jerrold E. Hogle, 'The Ghost of the Counterfeit in the Genesis of the Gothic', in Allan Lloyd Smith and Victor Sage (eds), *Gothick Origins and Innovations* (Amsterdam: Rodopi, 1994), pp. 23–33 (p. 23).

Gothic is about machinic language in the same way that the Gothic is about history – its presence is as pervasive as its authenticity is questionable.

If the glitch in found footage horror shares a similarly dubious relation to machinic reality as does the Gothic towards historical accuracy, what is the function of the faux glitch? As a tentative answer, I will suggest six possible rules of glitch that have been gleaned from the capacious trove of found-footage horror that is available on popular streaming services:

1 Glitches Must Be Present in Trailers, Often Disproportionately from Their Use in the Film

Beginning in or around 2007, films such as *[Rec]* (dir. Jaume Balagueró and Paco Plaza, 2007), *Paranormal Activity* (dir. Oren Peli, 2007), *Diary of the Dead* (dir. George A. Romero, 2007) and *Cloverfield* (dir. Matt Reeves, 2008) made the glitch-heavy trailer the norm. The updated trailer for *The Blair Witch Project* cited earlier is the most absurd example of the extraneous glitch. Similarly, the trailer for *Paranormal Activity 3* (dir. Henry Joost and Ariel Schulman, 2011) is riddled with glitches but the film is glitch-free until the final shot. The trailer for *Afflicted* (dir. Derek Lee and Clif Prowse, 2013) features more than twenty glitches whereas the film contains only one. *Demon House* (dir. Zak Bagans, 2018) deploys more than a dozen glitches in its trailer in scenes that do not glitch in the film. The trailer glitch is pure affect, a relative of the jump scare that is unburdened by dramatic content or setup. Like noise, the glitch signals authenticity, but while continuous noise such as analogue grain is a reminder of the medium, the glitch is a visual stab of a knife, a media-slashing material threat to both characters and the 'footage' that has survived them.

2 Whenever Possible, Glitches Will Bookend the Film

Most found footage films begin with title cards that explain the discovery of the footage – a nod to authenticity that precludes opening credits as an opportunity for glitch. To compensate, a jolt of noise/glitch usually appears as a character begins to record. *Secreto Matusita* (*The Secret of Evil*, dir. Dorian Fernández-Moris, 2014) uses glitch transitions with the introductory text. *V/H/S/2* (dir. Simon Barrett and Jason Eisener, 2013) begins with both analogue and digital glitches and ends with credits that assault the senses with relentless glitch effects. The introductory and/or concluding glitches emphasise media materiality above all else.

3 Every Cut Is an Opportunity for a Glitch

Although some visual and audible disruptions have grounding in the reality of a device (such as turning on/off a DV tape camcorder), the prevalence of the noise and glitch transitions in found footage far exceeds the norm. The Godardian gestalt of the glitch-as-jump-cut gives the impression that the unheralded local police officer tasked with assembling the found footage into the semblance of a feature film has done so with utmost respect for the digital artefact. If editing is suture, then these found footage assemblages are as patchwork as Frankenstein's monster. The immateriality that characterises the postmodern Cybergothic meets its ungodly fleshy counterpart in the media remains left by ghost-hunting crews, which are tenuously immortalised in a crudely stitched film.

4 Why Stop at One Kind of Glitch When You Can Have Layers of Remediated Analogue and Digital Error!

The *V/H/S* franchise (2012, 2013, 2014) is the quintessential example of multiple digital sources (Skype, nanny cams, spycam glasses, DSLR cameras, and the likes) anthologised alongside undead analogue media. The *V/H/S* premise of digital and analogue footage assembled mixtape-style creates a baffling confluence of noise artefacts. *Jack Hunter's Paranoia Tapes* (dir. Chad Clinton Freeman, Amy Hesketh et al., 2017) uses a similar mix of sources. Such films tend to contain an obligatory equipment inventory fetish scene: 'This is a refurbished customised beta model spectre v62 video camera', announces one character in *The Dark Tapes* (dir. Michael McQuown and Vincent J. Guastini, 2016).[22] Thus the films include abundant recording devices: handheld consumer and pro-grade camcorders, head or body mounted cameras, smartphones and green-hued night vision cameras for static shots and the occasional ghost selfie.

5 In a Genre Typically Unable to Justify a Non-Diegetic Score, Glitches Perform Many of the Same Functions as Music

The explanatory text at the beginning of *Asylum: The Lost Footage* (dir. Dan T. Hall, 2013) alerts the viewer that, 'Due to the recovery process some of the following footage may appear damaged and the audio may be compromised in portions of the program.'[23] Conveniently, both audio and visual glitches

---

[22] *The Dark Tapes*. Dir. Michael McQuown and Vincent J. Guastini. Thunder Road Incorporated. 2016. Epic Pictures Releasing, 2017. DVD.

[23] *Asylum: The Lost Footage*. Dir. Dan T. Hall. Cyfuno Ventures, Vizmo Films, Gravitas Ventures. 2013.

happen to coincide with moments of heightened drama. Like an orchestral cue, glitches announce significant moments, as in *Greystone Park* (dir. Sean Stone, 2012), where they precede the discovery of an old cassette tape, or in *100 Ghost Street: The Return of Richard Speck* (dir. Martin Wichmann Andersen, 2012), where flashes of glitch accompany footage of an ominous trail of blood. Deaths invariably include both audio and video glitches, indicating the vulnerability of both the human media bodies.

6 Glitches and Ghosts Go Hand-in-Hand

If a ghost story represents, as Colin Davis asserts, 'a temporary interruption in the fabric of reality, a glitch in the matrix, in order that the proper moral and epistemological order of things can be put back to rights', then it stands to reason that glitches are micro-enactments of that narrative structure.[24] The sudden opacity of the glitch evokes a machinic underworld and, as Sean Cubitt remarks, 'the pure *indifference* underpinning the logic of exchange on which it is founded'.[25] The human body, the ghost caught on camera or the decaying architecture of an abandoned asylum or haunted house all melt into the terrifyingly flat ontology of code. Cubitt calls the glitch a 'ghost in the machine', but the phrase is potentially misleading.[26] The Cybergothic illusion of a ghostly realm of pure code is unsustainable when confronted with the glitch. A more apt metaphor is provided by artists Hannah Piper Burns and Evan Meaney: 'Glitches are guts. Just like when our inner systems break down and our many moving parts spill out for the world to see, glitches are the source of the same raw, abject seduction.'[27] Almost unfailingly, glitch and ghost appear together in found footage. While the ghosts in Cybergothic films such as *Kairo* (dir. Kiyoshi Kurosawa, 2001) and *Ringu* (dir. Hideo Nakata, 1998) use media as portals, Glitch Gothic films feature ghosts who can no more transcend space and time through media than can their human counterparts. Consummate technophiles, ghosts take selfies (e.g. *The Crying Dead* [dir. Hunter G. Williams, 2011]) and dabble in cinematography (e.g. *Grave Encounters 2* [dir. John Poliquin, 2012)]), but

---

[24] Colin Davis, *Haunted Subjects: Deconstruction, Psychoanalysis and the Return of the Dead* (Basingstoke: Palgrave Macmillan, 2007), p. 13.
[25] Sean Cubitt, 'Temporalities of the Glitch: *Déjà Vu*', in Martine Beugnet, Allan Cameron and Arild Fetveit (eds), *Indefinite Visions: Cinema and the Attractions of Uncertainty* (Edinburgh: Edinburgh University Press, 2017), pp. 299–315 (p. 304).
[26] Cubitt, 'Temporalities of the Glitch', p. 299.
[27] Hannah Piper Burns and Evan Meaney, 'Glitches Be Crazy', in Nick Briz, Evan Meaney, Rosa Menkman, William Robertson, Jon Satrom and Jessica Westbrook (eds), *GLI.TC/H READER[ROR] 20111* (Unsorted Books, 2011), p. 74 <http://gli.tc/h/READERROR/GLITCH_READERROR_20111-v3BWs.pdf> (last accessed 1 September 2018).

they do not enjoy unfettered travel through media. Both the living and the dead are subject to the material limits of media.

Materiality in Glitch Gothic, like history in the Gothic, is overbearing, crumbling and detached from its foundations. As an assemblage of recovered media texts, found footage is already doubly concerned with history. First, Glitch Gothic films are about the excavation and exploration of hauntings, and second, the footage that contains the story is usually the only remnant of people who have mysteriously vanished. Found footage replaces the absent body and now constitutes a fusion of spectral revenants, human records and a doubling of confined architectural spaces. As an obstacle to deciphering media texts, the glitch is a marker of languages and temporalities that subtend the digital surface. The glitch is a reminder that those media tasked with capturing ghosts are also a crypt in which entropy chips away at the dream of a digital afterlife. As part of a larger postdigital Gothic pendulum swing toward rematerialisation, Glitch Gothic exploits error as a potent critique of disembodiment. Materiality, it turns out, is as tenacious as history.

Data in a Corset: MP3 as Gothic Compression

Gothic may not be the first word that comes to mind when thinking of Suzanne Vega's hit song 'Tom's Diner' (1987), but the inner monologue, the brooding weather and the ringing of cathedral bells entwined with the memory of an absent voice share a strange consonance with Gothic themes: 'As I'm listening / To the bells / Of the cathedral / I am thinking / Of your voice.'[28] Equally tinged with unwitting Gothic qualities is the manner in which Vega's warm *a cappella* timbre has shaped the MP3 format. Journalists and the very engineers behind the coding format have bestowed upon Vega the title 'Mother of the MP3' even though the legend, like MP3 compression, sacrifices fidelity for the sake of quick transmission. Billy Joel, Tracy Chapman, Beethoven and other forgotten contributors to the MP3's digital DNA are stripped out of the story for understandable reasons: time, space, relevance. Does it matter that the standard 'female pop vocal' sample for compression tests in 1985 might have been Linda Ronstadt, when even the engineers have no clear memory beyond 'not yet Suzanne Vega'?[29] Possibly, but loss is part of all media transmission. When codecs perform an editorial function, they leave behind ghosts that are sensed only through artefacts and

[28] Suzanne Vega, 'Tom's Diner', on Suzanne Vega, *Solitude Standing* (A&M Records, 1987).
[29] Jonathan Sterne, *MP3: The Meaning of a Format* (Durham, NC: Duke University Press, 2012), p. 170.

absence. Cybergothic ghostliness and Postdigital Gothic embodiment inhabit the stories that explain the formats behind digital media circulation. Here, my compressed Gothic media story spotlights MP3 as a digital data corset tailored for Suzanne Vega's voice, and a ghost-conjuring project crafted around the song 'Tom's Diner'.

Jonathan Sterne calls the MP3 'a container that transforms as it holds'.[30] In that way, the MP3 is like a corset. To the audiophile, the MP3 shapes music in a barbaric and unnatural fashion. Just as Jean-Jacques Rousseau dismissed the corset as 'Gothic shackles', the enlightened listener eschews those mechanisms that deprive music of its natural beauty.[31] Spooner remarks that in the twenty-first century, 'the corset seems an archetypally Gothic garment, troping on a form of physical imprisonment and bodily torture that our enlightened age no longer inflicts on women'.[32] Discussions surrounding compression technology for music elicit similarly fraught rhetoric about taste, economies of exchange and the hegemonic standards embodied in a file format. If predominantly white male European engineers developed the beauty ideals for digitally processed music with Vega as their muse, one might rightfully wonder what happens to that which does not fit the mould. Sterne characterises listening tests as a 'civilizing process for audio'.[33] He notes that the 'expert listener' represents 'a structural bias in engineering culture and a political bias that shapes the making of standards and formats'.[34] As one reporter explains, 'When an MP3 player compresses music by anyone from Courtney Love to Kenny G, it is replicating the way that [audio engineer Karlheinz] Brandenburg heard Suzanne Vega.'[35] The narrative consequently takes on sinister undertones as all music 'corseted' by MP3 compression must therefore conform to specifications that best valorise 'Tom's Diner'. The reality is that many songs, engineers and listeners worked across decades to create a compression format that suits all sizes and shapes of music. Like rhetoric surrounding the corset, however, the 'Tom's Diner' story fixates on a tight-laced extreme that poorly reflects actual practice. The true 'sonic referent of the MP3' is a 'massive, polymorphous, interlaced global network of technologies, practices, and institutions'.[36] While, from

---

[30] Sterne, *MP3*, p. 195.
[31] Quoted in Catherine Spooner, *Fashioning Gothic Bodies* (Manchester: Manchester University Press, 2004), p. 28.
[32] Spooner, *Fashioning Gothic Bodies*, p. 16.   [33] Sterne, *MP3*, p. 160.
[34] Sterne, *MP3*, p. 163.
[35] Suzanne Vega, 'Tom's Essay', *New York Times*, 23 September 2008 <https://opinionator.blogs.nytimes.com/2008/09/23/toms-essay/> (last accessed 25 August 2018).
[36] Sterne, *MP3*, p. 182.

a journalistic standpoint, this is a far less appealing story, it assumes faintly Lovecraftian proportions in its gesturing towards a seething, monstrous mass beyond human intelligence and understanding.

Audio compression relies on the removal of redundant parts of a signal that in a best-case scenario passes unnoticed by the human listener. An analogue waveform, once sampled as discrete points of quantised data, is subjected to algorithms that are meant to identify and remove excess. In part, MP3 encoding draws from psychoacoustic research (studies of sound perception and audiology) that, in 1924, allowed the Bell telephone company to quadruple phone line capacities by eliminating 'surplus' frequencies.[37] The most obviously superfluous frequencies are those outside the range of human hearing, but, for true data rate reduction, far more aggressive editing is needed. The MP3 encoding process quantises samples and then groups, sorts and analyses them through algorithmic approximations of the ear that influence when, where and what to eliminate. The encoding bitrate determines how much information per second survives in the sound file. In the late 1990s, a high-quality MP3 had a bitrate of 128 kbps. In 2007, Apple started charging a premium for 256 kbps files. Today, streaming services are moving away from the MP3 format. Spotify currently streams Ogg Vorbis at 320 kbps, Apple has its own proprietary AAC encoding at 256 kbps and, for the audiophile willing to pay double, Tidal offers streams at 1411 kbps with the 'lossless' file formats FLAC and ALAC. But who can hear the difference?

To upset a wine snob, bring up the famous French study in which a panel of tasters could not tell red wine from white wine dyed red.[38] To infuriate an audiophile, declare that there is no discernible difference between a FLAC audio file and a 256 kbps MP3. Profess your love of sRGB JPEGs to a photographer who only shoots RAW. Kantian notions of taste and Diderotian dialogues on *sensibilité* find their twenty-first-century counterparts in file format connoisseurship. Audio compression sensitivity is an aristocratic curse, a haunting that afflicts only those with refined faculties. To an audiophile, the pre-echo artefact heard in the percussive beat of an MP3 file is as unbearable as Edgar Allan Poe's tell-tale heart pounding from beyond the grave. A sonic artefact is the wailing of a damaged file. The sensitive listener hears artefacts and feels the absence of lost sounds. Practitioners of microsound and glitch music are expert summoners of imperceptible ghost sounds. Microsound artist Kim Cascone works with the 'digital detritus'

---

[37] Sterne, *MP3*, p. 45.
[38] Gil Morrot, Frédéric Brochet, and Denis Dubourdieu, 'The Color of Odors', *Brain and Language* 79 (2001): 309–20.

normally filtered out by noise reduction. He 'descend[s] into the "abyssal zone" of the noise floor' and uses what he finds there as 'material for exploration'.[39] Cascone channels Cybergothic rhetoric when he explains that 'just beyond our focus exists a fringe that is defined as background, lack, netherworld, a horizon of silence ... invisible to us even as we peer directly into it'. Cascone speaks of 'conjuring "post-digital" music' from the 'gauzy veil of hums, clicks, whirs, and crackling' of the datasphere.[40]

Inspired by artists such as Cascone, musician Ryan Maguire began a self-described 'ghost-hunting' project in 2014 to 'capture the sounds lost to MP3 compression'.[41] The first piece of a larger 'Ghost in the MP3' series, 'moDernisT' (an anagram for 'Tom's Diner'), uses a variety of techniques to identify and salvage the sounds lost in the MP3 compression of Vega's song. Maguire's ghostly double highlights 'sounds that are taken from us in the current sonic culture which values MP3s above all other formats'.[42] Maguire's 'moDernisT' is not, as some media outlets have reported, simply a recording of 'all the stuff that was taken out' of Vega's song.[43] The artist sees the work as a 'codec ghost composition' or as 'format music'.[44] Each technique that Maguire uses to identify what is lost in the translation from uncompressed WAV file to MP3 yields a different sonic answer.[45] Furthermore, a 128 kbps file strips out so much of the original that lyrics and melody are clearly discernible in the cast-off sound. In other words, a file with too many digital remains resembles more a cumbersome zombie than a spooky ghost. Maguire instead turns to a newer, higher bitrate (320 kbps) that leaves behind fewer remnants and hence a ghostlier shell. 'I narrowed my focus to a collection of reconstructions which sounded either whisper-like or which offered pointillistically distributed pitches', explains Maguire.[46] Thanks to software, Maguire creates the reverb of a small diner, scrambles

---

[39] Kim Cascone, 'Residualism', in Caleb Kelly (ed.), *Sound* (Cambridge, MA: MIT Press, 2011), pp. 98–101 (p. 99).

[40] Cascone, 'Residualism', p. 100.

[41] Ryan Maguire, 'The Ghost in the MP3', *Proceedings: International Computer Music Association (ICMC) and Sound and Music Computing (SMC)*, Athens, Greece, 14–20 September 2014, pp. 243–7 (p. 244). http://ryanmaguiremusic.com/media_files/pdf/TheGhostICMC.pdf [last accessed 26 August 2018].

[42] Maguire, 'The Ghost in the MP3', p. 246.

[43] 'Recovering the Lossiness of "Tom's Diner"', *To the Best of Our Knowledge*, 9 April 2017 <www.ttbook.org/interview/recovering-lossiness-toms-diner> (last accessed 27 August 2018).

[44] Maguire, 'The Ghost in the MP3', 245; 247.

[45] See samples on Maguire's website, *The Ghost in the MP3* <http://theghostinthemp3.com/theghostinthemp3.html> (last accessed 27 August 2018).

[46] Maguire, 'The Ghost in the MP3', p. 246.

sound in imitation of background chatter and alters the virtual space in the fifth verse to represent the singer's internal psychological state. The result is a hauntingly beautiful composition, a musical ghost story about death by compression. But in the end, the MP3 reveals itself as a space that does not *contain* ghosts so much as casts them out. The Cybergothic 'Ghost in the MP3' lives outside of 'Tom's Diner'. Compression has no room for ghosts.

Staying on the Grid: Thomas Ruff's JPEG

The JPEG codec, like the MP3, is 'lossy', meaning that information is irreversibly discarded in the compression process. Maguire's project would not have been possible without an uncompressed file from which to extract the ghost composition, for there are no ghosts in the MP3, only compression errors that signal permanent loss. Drawing on both senses of loss, German artist Thomas Ruff's photographic series *jpeg* (2004–9) is born from low-resolution images of the 9/11 terror attacks. Working mostly with images from internet archives and news sites, Ruff exposes the logic of the most common image file format by enlarging small images into monumental prints that are more than eight feet high with pixels as large as drink coasters. In contrast to Maguire's project, which relies on uncompressed files and employs a Cybergothic rhetoric of ghostly compression cast-offs, Ruff's *jpeg* series stays inside the confines of the file and forces the viewer to contend with the limits of the digitally ordered world. Having lost his own photos taken on the day of the attacks, Ruff turned to the internet. Online images of the attacks became part of Ruff's '"virtual" trip around the world' to collect 'horrifyingly beautiful images of destruction and disaster from all four corners of the globe'.[47] In a postdigital Gothic manner, Ruff's *jpeg* considers 'the blunt finiteness of the image within the overwhelming apparent infinity of the Internet's data sublime'.[48]

Anyone who has ever tried to print out a small JPEG file in a size much larger than its original dimensions knows how quickly the process might go awry. The underlying structure of the pixel grid emerges and reveals severe limits to the information in a digital raster image. A raster image is made of

---

[47] Max Dax, 'Interview with Thomas Ruff', in *Thomas Ruff, Castello di Rivoli Museo d'Arte Contemporanea* (Milan: Skira, 2009), pp. 70–5 (p. 74).

[48] Rachel Wells, 'Digital Scale: Enlargement and Intelligibility in Thomas Ruff's *JPEG Series*', in Alexandra Moschovi, Carol McKay and Arabella Plouviez (eds), *The Versatile Image: Photography, Digital Technologies and the Internet* (Leuven: Leuven University Press, 2013), pp. 205–21 (pp. 212–13).

pixels – a word derived from PICture ELement. The smallest element of a digital image, the coloured square pixel has been compared to a pointillist dot. By extension, some theorists have argued that any art that represents the world through dots and grids constitutes a 'proto-digital way of seeing'.[49] The desire to minimise the pixel's radical disruption to imaging is apparent in the pixel-as-pointillism argument, but as Rachel Well explains, the comparison has a fundamental flaw: 'These pixels are not deliberately constructed or built up dot-by-dot, but rather separated, broken down by a jpeg algorithm for the mundane purposes of storage and distribution.' To those who characterise Ruff's *jpeg* as Neo-Impressionism, Well cautions, 'Ruff is not marveling at the gradual construction of a single image through the addition of pixel on pixel; rather he is enacting, on a grand scale, a process of damage and loss.'[50] In Ruff's own words, the aesthetic of the pixel grid is a 'collateral phenomenon' – a side effect of an economy of circulation.[51]

Ruff's *jpeg* photos demonstrate the collateral damage of a format through low-resolution images of mostly devastating events blown up to a scale associated with historical paintings. The bombing of Baghdad, the burning oil fields of Kuwait, the collapse of the Twin Towers intermingle with the occasional pastoral photo by Ruff to create a ruinous scrapbook of tragic digital indifference. The 8.5-ft *jpeg ny01* (2004, 276 x 188 cm) is an image of the attack on the Twin Towers dominated by the Empire State Building in the foreground. The building that stood as the world's tallest for 40 years until the completion of the North Tower of the World Trade Center in 1970 witnesses the fall of its rival and its own ascent as tallest in the state. Seen in a museum at normal viewing range, the pixelated image is illegible. At a distance of at least 15 feet, the spectator can discern the event in the photo. At small scale on a computer screen, *jpeg ny01* looks nearly the same as any other low-resolution image. The internet from whence it came is thus the worst possible environment for understanding the work. Ruff's print is antithetical to its low-resolution digital source. The chromogenic prints are meticulously high-quality, high-resolution remediations of blocky digital artefacts. Like the Empire State Building watching the fall of the gridded architecture of the North Tower, Ruff's analogue print *jpeg ny01* bears witness

---

[49] Meredith Hoy, *From Point to Pixel: A Genealogy of Digital Aesthetics* (Hanover, NH: Dartmouth College Press, 2017), p. 11. Michael Fried compares Ruff's *jpeg to pointillism* in *Why Photography Matters as Never Before* (New Haven, CT: Yale University Press, 2008), p. 154.

[50] Wells, 'Digital Scale', p. 209.   [51] Dax, 'Interview with Thomas Ruff', p. 72.

to the grid-based worldview of the JPEG as it collapses into a grey mass of senseless destruction.

Both the JPEG and the MP3 codecs see the world as grids of data to sort and reduce for fast transmission. The nonconscious cognition of an algorithm chooses what counts as information and what gets discarded as noise or surplus. In the eighteenth century, philosophers performed that task by creating epistemological strategies and taxonomies. Today, engineered algorithms participate in cognitive assemblages in ways that can shock their creators. Brandenburg thought his algorithm was doing well until he ran Vega's voice through it and heard 'monstrous distortions, as though the Exorcist [had] somehow gotten into the system'.[52] Vega's song became a sacred text to MP3 history because Brandenburg had used it to cast out a devil from his algorithm. Media files are transparent until compression errors reveal their repressed logic. To a JPEG codec, all the world is a *Minecraft* game and all people and things are merely pixels. Once we look too closely at a JPEG, once we stare into the digital abyss as Ruff makes us do, we do not find the abyss staring back at us; instead, we find a brick wall. The terror of the JPEG is not the void but the plenum.

Unfriendly Facebook

In April 2018, CEO Mark Zuckerberg spent ten hours trying to convince the US Congress that he could not possibly have anticipated the devastation caused by the thing he had created in his dorm room in 2004. In advance of Zuckerberg's scheduled testimony before the European Parliament, Facebook launched a one-minute video promoting that narrative. 'Here Together' presents the problem as a glitch. 'We came here for the friends', says the voiceover in wistful subdued tones. 'Then we got know the friends of our friends'. Innocuous, silly snapshots and videos of birthday parties, cats and activities with friends illustrate the expansion of social media ties. Then, at exactly the 30-second mark, a heart emoji fills the screen. Suddenly, the piano hits a discordant note and a glitch slashes the heart. A green crying emoji looks on while a woman's face is sliced in two by a glitch. 'But then something happened', the narrator says as frenzied glitching images assault the screen. 'We had to deal with spam, clickbait, fake news and data misuse.' To pop-up sound effects, a flurry of glitching permissions requests overload the senses until, finally, the screen goes blank and calm returns. 'That's going

[52] Vega, 'Tom's Essay'.

to change', the voice reassures over a montage of poignant moments. 'Facebook will do more to keep you safe and protect your privacy.'[53] The implicit moral of the story: Glitch happens.

Comedian John Oliver aired a parody of the 'Here Together' campaign with a voiceover that begins, 'You came here for the friends ... We came here for your data. And the data of everyone you've ever come into contact with' – a threat that is not far from the truth.[54] When a Congressman mentioned to Zuckerberg that Facebook gathers as many as 29,000 data points for an average user, or that it keeps 'shadow profiles' of non-Facebook users, the CEO did not deny it; he simply claimed he had never heard of the term.[55] Cryptographer Bruce Schneier wrote in 2015, 'Even though I never post or friend anyone on Facebook ... Facebook tracks me.'[56] Likes and clicks can predict with frightening accuracy 'race, personality, sexual orientation, political ideology, relationship status, and drug use', says Schneier. 'The company knows you're engaged before you announce it, and gay before you come out – and its postings may reveal that to other people without your knowledge or permission. Depending on the country you live in, that could merely be a major personal embarrassment – or it could get you killed.'[57] Little wonder social media horror films are on the rise.

Unfriended: Dark Web (dir. Stephen Susco, 2018) merits attention for having jettisoned the Cybergothic aspects of its predecessor, *Unfriended* (dir. Stephen Susco, 2014). Characterised by one critic as 'The Blair Glitch Project', the first *Unfriended* evokes computational materiality through a glitch-heavy aesthetic while clinging to immateriality through its vengeful ghost plotline.[58] From beyond the grave, Laura Barnes, or 'Leaky Laura' in the humiliating video that led to her suicide, wreaks vengeance on high school mean girl Blaire and her friends as they group chat on Skype. A faceless icon in the Skype session, the ghost is first dismissed as a glitch, but Blaire suspects that supernatural forces are at work. An online forum's warning, 'Do Not Answer Messages

---

[53] 'Facebook Here Together (UK)', *Facebook YouTube channel*, 25 April 2018 <https://youtu.be/Q4zd7X98eOs> (last accessed 1 August, 2018).

[54] *Last Week Tonight with John Oliver*, Season 5, Episode 18. HBO, 29 July 2018.

[55] 'Transcript of Zuckerberg's Appearance before House Committee', *The Washington Post*, 11 April 2018 <www.washingtonpost.com/news/the-switch/wp/2018/04/11/transcript-of-zuckerbergs-appearance-before-house-committee/?utm_term=.996790749dbf> (last accessed 29 August 2018).

[56] Bruce Schneier, *Data and Goliath: The Hidden Battles to Collect Your Data and Control Your World* (New York: W. W. Norton & Company, 2015), p. 31.

[57] Schneier, *Data and Goliath*.

[58] Jay Horton, 'The Blair Glitch Project: Unfriended Reviewed', *Willamette Week*, 19 April 2015 <www.wweek.com/portland/blog-33096-the-blair-glitch-project-unfriended-reviewed.html> (last accessed 30 August 2018).

from the Dead', cements Blaire's hunch and positions *Unfriended* in the Cybergothic tradition of *Kairo*. After an unintentionally funny disavowal of the innocuous glitch ('Well the glitch just typed!'), the ghost presence becomes increasingly active. Leaky Laura uses her post-mortem hacking prowess to torment the friends through social media, and exhibits the 'influencer' status she now enjoys as a vengeful spirit by forcing the friends to commit suicide. *Unfriended* relies heavily on the Cybergothic tradition that grants ghosts a special power over technologies associated with immateriality, but as media scholars have observed, the film's use of glitch also signals the 'abject potential' of digital media and 'the 'leakiness' of the glitch itself'.[59]

Unfriended: Dark Web recognises that a ghost is unnecessary when a story already lives in a Gothic mediascape. The term 'Dark Web' conjures up a sinister layer below the interface. 'Deep Web' generally refers to that which 'Surface Web' search engines cannot find, while the 'Dark Web' lives in those parts of the intentionally obfuscated TOR network where anything goes. The laptop-connected group of friends in *Unfriended: Dark Web* are more code-literate than most, but no match for the underworld denizens unleashed by protagonist Matias on a stolen laptop. As in *Unfriended*, the protagonist's screen activity serves as the proxy movie screen and, once again, a group Skype session provides a way to keep characters at once conversant and vulnerably isolated. Clicks and hesitations of cursor and keyboard demonstrate the expressivity of interface actors. A click on 'About this Mac' opens the 'High Sierra' system overview – a cursor's equivalent of Caspar David Friedrich's famous Romantic painting 'Wanderer above the Sea of Fog' (c.1818). *Unfriended: Dark Web* is an Icarian fall from High Sierra Mac sublime to the bowels of the internet.

Matias moves from one application to the next, changing logins until he arrives at Facebook, where he lingers voyeuristically on the account of Norah C. IV – a name that his friends find pretentious. As Norah C. IV, Matias replies to messages from users named 'Charon' who tell him to 'talk on The River'. He finds an icon labelled 'The River', opens the app, and watches his computer establish a connection through a chain of a dozen IP addresses. On Matias's shared screen his friends see the full-screen 8-bit blocky retro graphics of a boat floating down a torch-lit underground river. 'Dude, this is Dark Net', says AJ, who then mentions the unseemly trade history of drug and sex trafficking on the Dark Web's Silk Road and Lolita City. The interface

[59] Murray Leeder, *Horror Film: A Critical Introduction* (New York: Bloomsbury, 2018), p. 226; Allan Cameron, 'Facing the Glitch: Abstraction, Abjection and the Digital Image', in Beugnet, Cameron and Fetveit (eds), *Indefinite* Visions, pp. 334–52 (p. 348).

now switches to a BBS (Bulletin Board Systems) style interface, which in internet terms is the equivalent of discovering a lost civilisation.[60] In this case, the internet-ancient hub is populated by users known as Charon plus numbered suffixes. Norah C IV on the Surface Web hides in mirrored form a Dark Web secret society identity: Charon4. A quick Wikipedia search and Matias learns that Charon references the mythological ferryman of Hades. Rather than imagine media as empty portals, *Unfriended: Dark Web* presents an internet layered in history and myth.

The real Charon4 uses glitch as camouflage – an improbable but symbolically important phenomenon that conflates him with the computing environment while immunising him from human surveillance. The only time that Charon4 unglitches himself is to feign vulnerability and heighten fear of the other Charons. That moment occurs when Matias is pushed back into 'The River', where the graphics suddenly shift from playful 8-bit to high-res bits-just-got-real quality. Fully immersed in the Dark Web, Matias is ordered to 'RECITE THE CODE' that, unsurprisingly, is a sinister-sounding phrase in Latin ripped from the Bible: *abyssus abyssum invocat* – 'Deep calls to deep' (Psalms 42:7). By the time a dozen Charons hooded in the anonymity of faceless Skype avatars surround the friends, we know that doom is imminent. But unlike *Unfriended*, the deaths do not require the influence of a ghost. AJ, who says, 'I am ghosted online. They cannot find me', is easily located by comments that he has made on YouTube. His own media presence becomes an accomplice to his murder when the Charons sample words to make a 'swatting' 911 call – a threat that dispatches a trigger-happy SWAT team to his house. Not all the deaths in *Unfriended: Dark Web* are so obviously computer-related, but every death is ultimately part of a material assemblage that connects sociopathic gamers to subway systems, hospital equipment and other smart systems. Who needs ghosts when anyone with a good VPN and a TOR browser can become one of the old gods?

In the course of his journey to the underworld, Matias learns to use cryptocurrency and how to locate hidden files through Terminal (the text-based access to the operating system). His strategic navigation of WI-FI and mobile dead space illustrates the hidden public architecture of connectivity. Each step in his ill-fated journey explicates the spaces and languages entwined in human and nonhuman assemblages. The only cyber fantasy at work in *Unfriended: Dark Web* is the belief that one can inhabit the internet as a ghost.

---

[60] See Ben J. Edwards, 'The Lost Civilization of Dial-Up Bulletin Board Systems', *The Atlantic*, 4 November 2016 <www.theatlantic.com/technology/archive/2016/11/the-lost-civilization-of-dial-up-bulletin-board-systems/506465/> (last accessed 30 August 2018).

Charon4's ability to write disappearing messages on Facebook is laughable, and although faceless Skype avatars provoke a sense of foreboding in humans that is reminiscent of the Slender Man phenomenon, the masks do nothing to deter or intimidate nonhuman tracking systems.[61] We like to believe we can float through the web, but we leave footprints everywhere, including paths of cryptocurrency transactions. The internet remembers and waits for the right assemblage to give data and metadata new meaning. Facebook's 29,000 data points know us better than we know ourselves. Facebook's glitch narrative turns the consequences of algorithmic cognition into temporary errors, while, in truth, those terrifying glitches are the abject guts of Facebook leaking out.

Postdigital Gothic forces us to confront the materiality of media camouflaged by interfaces and the illusion of transparency. Glitches, noise and other artefacts draw attention to cognitive processes that are designed to withdraw from our conscious minds. A glitch is a slippage, but not a Freudian one. Machinic artefacts do not emerge from the unconscious; they manifest computational nonconscious cognition to the human mind. Cybergothic narratives draw humans into a void of the virtual, while postdigital Gothic narratives bury us alive under the weight of the material. Instead of the cloud, they posit the infrastructure. In place of postmodern detachment, the posthuman assemblage. Human consciousness is enmeshed in digital systems that enclose, compress, track, quantise and otherwise participate, often unnoticed, in the 'analogue' world that they inhabit. Through errors, art and storytelling, the in-between Gothic state of our entanglement with computational media speaks. Or laughs in the middle of the night.

---

[61] A preternaturally tall, faceless humanoid invented in 2009 on the Something Awful internet forum, Slender Man achieved viral status through 'creepypasta' online horror stories and infamously inspired two twelve-year-old girls to stab their best friend. See Trevor J. Blank and Lynne S. McNeill (eds), *Slender Man Is Coming: Creepypasta and Contemporary Legends on the Internet* (Logan: Utah State University Press, 2018).

3.17

Gothic Multiculturalism

SARAH ILOTT

Multiculturalism as Gothic Discourse

Former British Prime Minister John Major, in a speech delivered in 1993 to the Conservative Party, urged Britons to get 'back to basics': 'Do you know, the truth is, much as things have changed on the surface, underneath we're still the same people. The old values – neighbourliness, decency, courtesy – they're still alive, they're still the best of Britain ... It is time to return to those old core values.'[1] The implication in Major's reference to 'change on the surface' and 'old core values' is that the version of Britishness to which he nostalgically aspires is one coded in whiteness and located prior to the mass migration of the Windrush generation following the Second World War. Such recourse to an imagined historical monoculturalism is a mainstay in discourses of Britishness, against which multiculturalism is cast as its other, threatening sovereignty and national identity. Right-wing discourse frequently represents lived multiculturalism (the fact of diversity) in Gothic terms in this manner: British Muslims become abject fifth columnists determined to undermine the British populace from within; the children and grandchildren of immigrants are cast, vampire-like, as unwelcome or overstaying guests who refuse to 'go home', collapsing distinctions between host and guest, the homely and the unhomely; refugees and asylum seekers are described in dehumanising terms as a 'swarm', 'marauding' and a 'flood', calling to mind patterns of invasion and contagion concomitant with zombie and ecological apocalypse narratives.[2]

---

[1] John Major, Speech delivered at the Conservative Party Conference in Blackpool, 1993 <www.britishpoliticalspeech.org/speech-archive.htm>?speech=139> (last accessed 13 March 2016).

[2] David Shariatmadari, 'Swarms, floods and marauders: the toxic metaphors of the migration debate', *The Guardian*, 10 August 2015 <www.theguardian.com/commentisfree/2015/aug/10/migration-debate-metaphors-swarms-floods-marauders-migrants> (last accessed 25 July 2016).

In Britain since 2005, multiculturalism has also increasingly been constructed by the political left in Gothic terms as a failed ideal that now wreaks havoc on those too naïve to heed its earlier threat. Trevor Phillips, then head of the Commission for Racial Equality in the UK, warned in ominous tones that the country was 'sleepwalking into segregation'.[3] Speaking in the aftermath of the 7/7 London bombings of 2005, during which period aspects of multicultural policy were furiously debated by politicians and the media alike, Phillips blamed this drift into segregation on an 'anything goes' multiculturalism that allowed 'deeper division and inequality' to flourish.[4] The links between 'maximising integration' and 'minimising extremism' (read: Islamic terrorism) were presented as self-evident. As such, the benevolence of previous multicultural policy was presented as drawing a veil over the pressing issues facing a multicultural society, allowing pockets of terrorist activity to thrive. Moreover, the slipperiness of the term 'multiculturalism' – as interchangeable shorthand for an ideal or 'moral project', a set of governing policies, and the reality of diversity – means that the rejection of multiculturalism as a failed political ideal was and is often expressed as a rejection of lived multiculture, leading inexorably to resurgent nationalism and racism.[5]

Sociologists Alana Lentin and Gavan Titley have noted the political expedience of the increasing tendency to represent multiculturalism as being 'in crisis' in this manner: it allows for 'securitized migration regimes, assimilative integrationism and neo-nationalist politics to be presented as nothing more than rehabilitative action'.[6] Strategies to rescue Britain from a 'failure' of multicultural policy have effectively created a screen for racism, nationalism and Islamophobia, allowing these noxious sentiments to thrive and gain mainstream legitimacy. That which even the word 'multiculturalism' functions to repress, crucially, is a history of racism. This is a position that was consolidated in Britain in 2001, when the Cantle Report produced in response to a series of race riots in the north of England blamed the failure of multiculturalism on the 'self-segregation' of British Muslim

---

[3] Trevor Phillips, 'After 7/7: Sleepwalking to Segregation', *Jiscmail*, 26 September 2005 <www.jiscmail.ac.uk/cgi-bin/webadmin?A3=ind0509&L=CRONEM&E=quoted-printable&P=605513&B=%EF%BF%BD%E2%80%94_%3D_NextPart_001_01C5C28A.09501783&T=text%2Fhtml;%20charset=iso-8859%E2%80%931&pending=> (last accessed 21 August 2018).

[4] Phillips, 'After 7/7'.

[5] Peter Kivisto, 'We Really Are All Multiculturalists Now', *The Sociological Quarterly* 53 (2012): 1–24 (p. 4).

[6] Alana Lentin and Gavan Titley, *The Crises of Multiculturalism: Racism in a Neoliberal Age* (London: Zed Books, 2011), p. 3.

'communities'.[7] This manoeuvre downplayed the poverty of the areas concerned and the structural disenfranchisement of minorities in Britain, and, as Lentin and Titley insist, demonstrated 'a lingering tendency to reduce the problem of race to the problem of community'.[8] From whichever position on the political spectrum we view it, therefore, multiculturalism has been rendered in Gothic terms, either as creating the conditions for violence and loss of identity, effectively rendering Britons strangers to themselves, or as creating a monstrous rationale for the structural victimisation and alienation of minority communities.

I have begun with an examination of British multicultural discourse to highlight some of the complexities with which the Gothic is ideally situated to engage in a manner intended to be paradigmatic rather than representative. In what follows, I draw on various national contexts, policies and interpretations of multiculturalism as represented in selected Gothic texts, in an approach indebted to the work of the Warwick Research Collective (WReC) and Andrew Hock Soon Ng. From WReC, I borrow a revivified and newly materialist understanding of comparative literary studies that brings together 'the relatively old notions of *Weltliteratur* and combined and uneven development', in which world literature is understood neither as 'a canon of masterworks nor a mode of reading, but as a *system* . . . [that] is structured not on *difference* but on *inequality*'.[9] This works against one of the key tenets of multiculturalism as discourse and policy in its focus on diversity that improperly downplays economic and structural inequality, while acknowledging the interconnectedness of peoples and literatures by virtue of the capitalist world-system. In addition, I follow Ng's recasting of the 'fundamentally . . . Western literary genre' of the Gothic as an 'aesthetic mode' in order 'that it may function as a critical apparatus for the reading of multicultural literatures'.[10] This is not to universalise, but to open up the Gothic to the consideration of other literatures, recognising their similarities as well as their distinctive socio-economic and cultural histories, and thereby rejuvenating the study of the mode. While encompassing works that could be considered

---

[7] CCRT (Community Cohesion Review Team), 'Community Cohesion: A Report of the Independent Review Team, chaired by Ted Cantle', 2001 <http://resources.cohesioninstitute.org.uk/Publications/Documents/Document/DownloadDocumentsFile.aspx?recordId=96%26file=PDFversion> (last accessed 16 December 2014).

[8] Lentin and Titley, *Crises of Multiculturalism*, p. 43.

[9] WReC (Warwick Research Collective), *Combined and Uneven Development: Towards a New Theory of World-Literature* (Liverpool: Liverpool University Press, 2015), p. 7.

[10] Andrew Hock Soon Ng, 'Adorno, Foucault, and Said: Toward a Multicultural Gothic Aesthetic', *Concentric: Literary and Cultural Studies* 33 (2007): 177–98 (p. 191).

postcolonial, the study of multiculturalism allows for the inclusion of literature that, to borrow Emma Dawson Varughese's terminology, 'speaks directly of, and to' the (postcolonial) nation, either because it is increasingly unconcerned with the binaric coloniser/colonised model or because it considers, for example, the impact of intra-Asian conflicts on local cultural production.[11] This chapter therefore presupposes an anti-racist politics in its systemic critique of the creation and structural exclusion of internal others who are often, but not always, aligned with a history of colonisation.

Having demonstrated how multiculturalism has been represented in Gothic terms in political discourse, I then turn to Gothic fiction as a place in which these representations are unpicked and deconstructed. In examining multiculturalism through the lens of Gothic literature and film, I follow Lasse Thomassen's thesis that 'Multiculturalism is real enough, but not extra-representational.'[12] The way that multiculturalism is engaged and represented in the Gothic can, as such, provide an important counter-narrative to its employment in political circles and the mainstream media. While multicultural policy might be represented as a failure, or multicultural reality as threatening, the Gothic, as a psychoanalytic mode with a ready shorthand for the representation of violence, alienation and monstrosity, is ideally suited to return what mainstream discourse represses, to engage with the subject of fear, and to speak the unspeakable through what we, following Michael Löwy, might call its 'critical irrealism'.[13] This chapter demonstrates how Gothic literature functions to reveal that which multicultural discourse seeks to repress: racism and inequality. I argue that alternative accounts of cultural contact foreground socio-economic inequality, racism and structural violence, while registrations of the impossible and the absurd function to signify a failure in discourse, to speak the unspeakable in a manner that is not possible in realist accounts. The Gothic aesthetic is equally suited to represent sectarian violence as a source of fear through the literalisation of monstrosity, and I argue that in engaging with the mechanics of monster-making, contemporary Gothic offers a critique of the construction of fear (and terror) as a tool of (rather than a threat to) governments. Finally, I consider contemporary Gothic's engagement with the afterlife as a space of multicultural

---

[11] E. Dawson Varughese, *Reading New India: Post-Millennial Indian Fiction in English* (London: Bloomsbury, 2013), p. 152.

[12] Lasse Thomassen, *British Multiculturalism and the Politics of Representation* (Edinburgh: Edinburgh University Press, 2017), p. 5.

[13] Michael Löwy, 'The Current of Critical Irrealism: "A moonlit enchanted night"', in Matthew Beaumont (ed.), *Adventures in Realism* (Oxford: Blackwell, 2007), pp. 193–206.

harmony, equality and justice, holding a heterotopic mirror up to the inequalities of the present in which the management of diversity is hostage to political corruption and economic disparity. Though lived multiculture predates the contemporary period, its management and appeal as a scheme of enquiry have emerged since the 1990s, which coincides with the selection of texts discussed below. The texts engaged in discussion are by no means representative of a given national literature, as the experience of multiculturalism will vary significantly from region to region and from person to person. What they are chosen for is their exemplification of a particular critical stance on the discourse of multiculturalism at a crucial moment in that nation's history.

Multiculturalism as Monstrous Discourse

Official multicultural policy is invariably founded on a set of laudable ideals: it acknowledges the lived realities of diverse peoples; it emphasises individual liberty both to preserve and share cultural heritage while fully and equitably participating in the life of the host nation; it creates policy to counter discrimination; and it encourages intercultural understanding and exchange. In Canada – the first country with an official multicultural policy developed around an integrationist (rather than assimilationist) 'mosaic' strategy – the Multiculturalism Act of 1988 is embedded within and functions as an outworking of the Human Rights Act, the right to protection from racial discrimination, and the equal rights and status of all Canadian citizens. Yet there is a sense in which the laudable aims of official policy function to repress alternative accounts of cultural contact through its forward-looking vision that pays little heed to an extant interconnected and profoundly unequal history for which reparation is yet to be made; racism that is systemic and which falls beyond the purview of policy; and the appropriation of multicultural policy for a neoliberal agenda to serve the machine of globalisation.

David Chariandy's 2007 novel, *Soucouyant: A Novel of Forgetting,* employs the Gothic trope of the soucouyant as a vehicle to explore the flipside of Canadian multiculturalism, demonstrating what official discourse functions to downplay or repress. The novel describes the swift demise of Adele from the perspective of her son, who has recently returned after a period of absence to find his dementia-stricken mother accompanied by a mysterious young woman named Meera. The narrative, like his mother's memory, is structured around a series of traumatic ruptures as it represents the struggle to find a means of representation that is true to the experience of an occluded history. The Caribbean myth of the soucouyant is summarised in the novel: she is 'something like a female vampire' shedding her skin and travelling as a ball of fire at night to drain her victims, 'leaving him with little sign of her work except increasing fatigue, a certain paleness, and perhaps, if he were to look closely on his body, a tell-tale bruise or mark on his skin'.[14] The soucouyant – imagined in this novel as the object of pity rather than monstrosity – functions analogously for the violent repression of history and loss of cultural memory. Each central character is identified as embodying and/or becoming victim to the soucouyant at various stages of the narrative, through the shedding of skin, the exhibition of curious marks or bruises, or an albino-like paleness. Memory is described in the novel as 'a bruise still tender', explicitly linking the workings of both the mythical soucouyant and Adele's dementia to a repressed history.[15]

I read Adele's disrupted narrative as a counter-narrative to the official discourse of Canadian multiculturalism. Her son recalls 'floating my eyes over a newspaper, some heated article on the Multiculturalism Act passed over a year ago'.[16] This seemingly insignificant detail serves to centralise the Act as an important background for, and intertext within, the novel. The perversion of multicultural discourse (as a means of confirming minorities in their inherent otherness) is also alluded to in a reference to the annual 'Heritage Day' parade, which was 'being revamped these days to recognize "people of multicultural backgrounds," and "not just Canadians"'.[17] Given the family's status as a combination of born and naturalised Trinidadian-heritage Canadians, the implication is that their heritage as Caribbeans excludes them from Canadian identity, and furthermore that their heritages are distinct, rather than linked through shared histories of colonisation and capitalisation that the novel's central family reference in their Indo-Caribbean and Afro-Caribbean inheritances of enslavement, indentured labour and displacement. The veiled racism of the Heritage Day parade and its implicit alignment of whiteness with Canadian identity is reflected in the overt acts of racism experienced by Adele when she is turned out of a restaurant, finds 'G ... O ... B ... A ... C ... K ...' scrawled on her walls, and is hassled by crank-callers.[18] As Neil Ten Kortenaar, paraphrasing Marlene NourbeSe Philip, argues, 'multiculturalism, by treating all ethnic groups as the same kind of entity, deflects attention from those who suffer most grievously from

---

[14] David Chariandy, *Soucouyant: A Novel of Forgetting* (Vancouver: Arsenal Pulp Press, 2007), p. 135.
[15] Chariandy, *Soucouyant*, p. 32.   [16] Chariandy, *Soucouyant*, p. 33.
[17] Chariandy, *Soucouyant*, p. 60.   [18] Chariandy, *Soucouyant*, pp. 50, 77, 165.

racism'.[19] It is an account of racism, as inherently linked to popular constructions of multiculturalism, that Chariandy is able to foreground through the workings of his Gothic novel.

A Gothic vocabulary of monstrosity, trauma and haunting provides an alternative discourse of Canadian multiculturalism that is better suited to Adele's experience. After witnessing as a teenager the implicit racism in a peer's incredulity at 'A whole family of darkies' occupying an old family residence, Meera decides to crank-call Adele. She tells her that her whole family has been killed, that, despite transfusions and amputations, they could not be saved: 'Your family would have survived only to be monsters in this place, forever scarred, forever proclaiming a violence that nobody in their right mind would ever want to remember. They would have been alone with their traumas, forever alone, just as you, starting now, will forever be alone.'[20] Meera's words cruelly reflect the epistemic violence of her peers' racist constructions of normativity, while providing an apt description of Adele's traumatic burden that isolates her and renders her history unspeakable. The soucouyant is a creature that speaks to networks and multiple migrations wrought by the combination of colonialism and capitalism through its combination of African and European myths transported to the Caribbean via the Middle Passage. Here, the mythical creature stands in for an understanding of history that 'is about relations'.[21] The narrator instructs: '*Soucouyant*. Touch the cool glass of that word on the page' before revealing his belief that 'My history is a travel guidebook. My history is a creature nobody really believes in. My history is a foreign word' – qualities that are all attributable to the soucouyant.[22] Cynthia Sugars provides a compelling interpretation of the novel's recurring epigraph '*Old skin, 'kin, 'kin, / You na know me*' as both a 'taunting chant of the disguised soucouyant' and a means to 'speak a truth about the horror of Gothic invasion, which causes the victims of colonial oppression to fail to recognize themselves, their histories and their families ... and which has literally rendered the burned features of the narrator's grandmother unrecognizable'.[23] I would extend this reading to suggest that the domination of multicultural discourse further elides the family's history in its future-oriented stance and establishment of equality

---

[19] Neil Kortenaar, 'Multiculturalism and Globalization', in Coral Ann Howells and Eva-Marie Kröller (eds), *The Cambridge Companion to Canadian Literature* (Cambridge: Cambridge University Press, 2004), pp. 556–80 (p. 560).
[20] Chariandy, *Soucouyant*, p. 165.   [21] Chariandy, *Soucouyant*, p. 106.
[22] Chariandy, *Soucouyant*, p. 137.
[23] Cynthia Sugars, *Canadian Gothic: Literature, History, and the Spectre of Self-Invention* (Cardiff: University of Wales Press, 2014), p. 200.

before the law that fails to register inequality engendered by violent histories and their socio-economic legacies in the present. The Gothic register opens up a space through which to critique the elisions and repressions of official discourse.

In addition to eliding (or even legitimising) racism and pandering to nationalist notions of heritage, multiculturalism has had an uncomfortable relationship with neoliberalism and globalisation, to the extent that, for Slavoj Žižek, 'the ideal form of ideology of this global capitalism is multiculturalism'.[24] Though, as Will Kymlicka asserts, the Reaganites and Thatcherites of the corporate sector were initially opposed to multiculturalism as a 'classic example of how the state was being misused to subsidize "special interests" ... over time ... the corporate world has made its peace with multiculturalism, and ... a distinctive form of "corporate multiculturalism" has emerged which interacts in complex ways with the earlier "social movement multiculturalism"'.[25] Written in the twenty-first century, Chariandy's novel has the benefit of retrospection and reveals the emerging affinities of neoliberal capitalism and multiculturalism in the world of the 1970s and 1980s in which it is set, as the historic socio-economic inequalities of colonialism, slavery and neo-imperialism also referenced in the novel are perpetuated in the present day through multicultural policy. The narrator recalls 'a glossy pamphlet describing a new program where students would get to work in "relevant" settings for half the school year. Behind the cash register in fast food restaurants, for instance. "Real life business skills ... Common-sense education ..." The pamphlet showed a rainbow of coloured faces.'[26] Such scenes serve as a reminder that contemporary multicultural policy is open to haunting by histories of inequality and exploitation legitimised through stereotypes that construct minority ethnics as less intelligent and/or better suited to physical labour.

Centralising the networks of capitalism and colonialism that have served to disenfranchise and displace Adele's family and those like her, Chariandy offers the account of 'certain historians and community activists' who describe the 'island's long history of control and occupation by foreign powers', the exploitative relations resulting from American military intervention, the uncompensated expulsion of 'a significant number of ... blacks and

---

[24] Slavoj Žižek, 'Multiculturalism, or, the Cultural Logic of Multinational Capitalism', *New Left Review* 225 (1997): 28–51 (p. 44).
[25] Will Kymlicka, *Multicultural Odysseys: Navigating the New International Politics of Diversity* (Oxford: Oxford University Press, 2009), p. 129.
[26] Chariandy, *Soucouyant*, pp. 15–16.

South Asians' during the construction of the military base, and the one-way transportation offered to 'approved' sites in Canada, in which 'Agricultural skills passed on for generations were suddenly useless. Extended kinship links were broken, and surviving families plunged into new forms of poverty without trusted networks of support.'[27] Yet, in a gesture that harks back to the satirised 'official' rendering of history offered by Chinua Achebe's British commissioner at the end of *Things Fall Apart* (1958), the picture painted above is immediately undercut by 'other historians [who] would offer what they described as a more "balanced" perspective on these events', refiguring those 'inconvenienced' as 'a few illiterates' who have ultimately benefitted from the situation, being offered a fresh 'chance to encounter the modern world, and to find their place in it'.[28] This concludes a narrative that uses the Gothic tropes of haunting, trauma and monstrosity to demonstrate the failure of language and discourse to tell the story of Adele and her family, all issuing from a world in which the official policy of multiculturalism is at odds with their experiences of racism, in which food and commodities have free movement but people from the same places, whose historical labour allowed for the boom in capitalist production, are denied that same freedom and repeatedly asked to leave, to 'GO BACK'.

Disposing of the Bodies: The Gothic Prison and Racial Neoliberalism

Lentin and Titley's influential book, *The Crises of Multiculturalism* (2011), is subtitled *Racism in a Neoliberal Age*, centralising the ways in which euphemistic references to multiculturalism serve to elide extant racism. They place the blame for this on the market-driven and individualising logic of neoliberalism. Taking the US as a case in point, they discuss the privatisation of racism as follows: 'The conflict between a lived reality of multiculturalism, coupled with the real gains of the civil rights movement in the United States, and what is essentially the rejection of these facts by a new right that fears the loss of white privilege . . . leads to confusion over how to define racism today. Racial neoliberalism capitalises on this confusion.'[29] The fact of lived multiculture is used to justify the construction of racism as a thing of the past, while, in a 'post-racial' society born of the belief that capitalism 'gains no advantages in reproducing racisms', racial inequality is held as the fault of individuals.[30]

[27] Chariandy, *Soucouyant*, pp. 178–9.   [28] Chariandy, *Soucouyant*, p. 179.
[29] Lentin and Titley, *The Crises of Multiculturalism*, p. 168.
[30] Lentin and Titley, *The Crises of Multiculturalism*, p. 168.

Pointing to the neoliberal state's function to ensure its citizens' security rather than their welfare (in accordance with free market logistics), Lentin and Titley go on to indicate the centrality of actual or metaphorical prisons to lock up or lock out 'undesirables' (people of colour and migrants respectively) whose lives are considered disposable in the protection of 'a privatized and exclusionary vision of "America"'.[31] The collusion of the American judiciary system in the perpetuation of the racial hierarchies and economic disparities of the slave trade is evident through the system by which falsely imprisoned African Americans, unable to pay the fines for their own living expenses while in custody, were trapped in the judiciary system and leased to entrepreneurs, farms and corporations, and thereby kept in involuntary servitude.[32] It is also evident in the Executive Order required to enforce desegregation in the place of legislation or judicial review, and in the 'new Jim Crow', which sees racial control enacted through the mass incarceration of African Americans in the purportedly 'colourblind' era following Barack Obama's election in 2008.[33] By centring the action of *Sing, Unburied, Sing* (2017) around the infamous Mississippi 'Parchman' prison, author Jesmyn Ward is able to reveal the systemic racism underpinning contemporary America, as the prison functions metonymically as a chronotope for Black America. The combination of 'a fearful sense of inheritance in time with a claustrophobic sense of enclosure in space' that, as Chris Baldick argues, is characteristic of the Gothic tale is evident in Ward's novel through the haunting and gravitational power of the prison, as experienced by her African American characters.[34]

Ward's novel reworks the Southern Gothic aesthetic and road-trip structure of William Faulkner's *As I Lay Dying* (1930). Where Faulkner's characters attempt to honour the dying wishes of their relative Addie Bundren to be buried in her hometown of Jefferson, Mississippi, Ward's characters return from a trip to Parchman Prison with an unburied spirit to find the family matriarch in the final throes of a battle with cancer. Like Faulkner's work, Ward's novel is told from a variety of perspectives: biracial Jojo's narrative swells with love for his grandparents and younger sister as he struggles to deal with his parents' neglect and the ghost that follows them back from

---

[31] Lentin and Titley, *The Crises of Multiculturalism*, pp. 172–3.
[32] See Douglas Blackmon, *Slavery by Another Name: The Re-enslavement of Black Americans from the Civil War to World War II* (New York: Anchor Books, 2009).
[33] See Michelle Alexander, *The New Jim Crow: Mass Incarceration in the Age of Colorblindness* (New York: New Press, 2012).
[34] Chris Baldick, 'Introduction', in Chis Baldick (ed.), *The Oxford Book of Gothic Tales* (Oxford: Oxford University Press, 1992), pp. xi–xxiii (p. xix).

Parchman, insisting that he get his grandfather to recount the tale of his death that will see him safely across the waters; Leonie's story registers a struggle with drugs and parenthood of Jojo and Kayla, an impassioned relationship with her white lover, Michael, whose release from Parchman provides the novel's journey structure, and a series of visitations from her dead brother, Given, who was murdered by one of Michael's racist relatives; Richie's story is rendered in broken fragments of sentences, grammatically visualising the trauma that he is unable to recall, and which leaves him figuratively 'unburied'.

Reflecting the centrality of the prison house in the continuation of systemic racial violence in the US, the prison hangs like a spectre over all of the characters in Ward's novel. Not only do many of the key plot points take place within the notorious 'Parchman' prison, it also provides the psychic backdrop for other characters' fears. The threat of imprisonment is so strong for Leonie that she feels compelled to reveal her visions of Given to her best friend when she begs to know, as 'this was her cottage, and when it all came down to it, I'm Black and she's White, and if someone heard us tussling and decided to call the cops, I'd be the one going to jail. Not her. Best friend and all'.[35] The spectre of Parchman even hangs over 13-year-old Jojo, who is handcuffed and has a gun pointed in his face by a police officer who has pulled over the car that he is riding in. Jojo and the spectral Richie frequently function as foils for one another: though their lives are not lived simultaneously, they are roughly the same age and only Jojo can see Richie and interpret his desires to his grandfather. The novel's central trauma is that Jojo's Pops (Riv), whilst himself serving time at Parchman as a younger man, had killed Richie in what is conveyed as an act of mercy, preventing him from being lynched, 'cut ... piece from piece till he was just some bloody, soft, screaming thing, and [...] strung] up from a tree' as he had just witnessed a mob doing to the other prisoner attempting to escape with him. Riv is rewarded with early release for finding and killing Richie (his intentional act of mercy unknown to the guards), but the spectre of the prison, which for him takes the form of his unspeakable guilt, never leaves him. The prison becomes metonymic for the experiences of Black Americans; it functions as a Bakhtinian chronotope, as a space 'saturated through and through with a time that is historical in the narrow sense of the word, that is, the time of the historical past'.[36] Richie, who finds himself 'trapped' at Parchman in the

---

[35] Jesmyn Ward, *Sing, Unburied, Sing* (London: Bloomsbury, 2018), p. 36.
[36] Mikhail M. Bakhtin, 'Forms of Time and of the Chronotope in the Novel: Notes Toward a Historical Poetics', in *The Dialogic Imagination: Four Essays by*

afterlife and who wakes daily to a different moment of its history, describes it in terms that are explicitly reminiscent of the chronotope as he begins to understand that 'Parchman was past, present, and future all at once ... and that everything is happening at once'.[37] For Bakhtin, it is the castle's exemplary function as chronotope that gives shape to Gothic novels, as traces in the physical space animate the environs, giving 'rise to the specific kind of narrative ... that is then worked out in Gothic novels'.[38] Insofar as its space speaks to a collective history of involuntary servitude and systemic violence, the prison for African Americans in contemporary Gothic novels serves functions that are not unlike those that were served to eighteenth-century Europeans by the ancient Gothic castle.

The collapsing of time in a single space in Ward's novel calls attention to a wider experience of the unwarranted intrusion of the past into the present. Berating his son for shooting Given, Michael's Uncle calls him a *'fucking idiot'* because *'this ain't the old days'*.[39] The overt irony is that in his description of Given in the same breath as *'the nigger'*, the socio-political hierarchies and injustices of 'the old days' are again returned to the present.[40] Moreover, the implication of his words is that his son is an *idiot* for perpetrating an act of racist violence that may no longer go unpunished, rather than *morally bankrupt* for his racist and murderous tendencies. Sing, Unburied, Sing is, as such, a tale of racist systemic violence without closure. The novel's final pages describe a tree, the branches full with black, brown and albino ghosts dressed in the costumes of many generations: 'rags and breeches, T-shirts and tignons, fedoras and hoodies'.[41] As Sheri-Marie Harrison argues in an article on 'New Black Gothic', 'Ward's ghosts speak to an ever-present and visible lineage of violence that accumulates rather than dissipates with the passage of time', reflecting the situation in which 'Gothic violence remains a part of everyday black life'.[42] It appears, initially, as if Richie has found closure in hearing Riv reach the end of the tale of his death: he 'goes darker and darker, until he's a black hole in the middle of the yard ... and then he isn't'.[43] Yet Richie later reappears, signalling that the revelation of historical violence alone is not sufficient to atone. It is tempting to read Ward's reference to the 'black hole' as a riposte to Fred Botting's take on contemporary Gothic, in

---

M. M. Bakhtin, edited by Michael Holquist, trans. by Caryl Emerson and Michael Holquist (Austin, TX: University of Texas Press, 1981), pp. 84–258 (pp. 245–6).

[37] Ward, *Sing*, p. 186.   [38] Bakhtin, 'Forms of Time', p. 246.   [39] Ward, *Sing*, pp. 49–50.
[40] Ward, *Sing*, p. 49.   [41] Ward, *Sing*, p. 283.
[42] Sheri-Marie Harrison, 'New Black Gothic', *LA Review of Books*, 23 June 2018 <https://lareviewofbooks.org/article/new-black-gothic/#!> (last accessed 30 July 2018).
[43] Ward, *Sing*, p. 257.

which it is a 'sense of cultural exhaustion' that 'haunts the present': 'Inured to gothic shocks and terrors, contemporary culture recycles its images in the hope of finding a charge intense enough to stave off the black hole within and without, the one opened up by postmodernist fragmentation and plurality.'[44] Reading Ward's selection of the black hole as an image for Richie's incomplete exorcism as a comment on the role of contemporary Gothic suggests, perhaps, that the Gothic horror of the present day is *in* its very repetition and ceaselessness, in the failure to stem the horrors of the past and to imagine a more hopeful, progressive future. In its focus on the continuation of violence, rather than a cathartic articulation that may bring a sense of closure, this subgenre of 'new Black gothic' speaks to the concerns of a contemporary multicultural society in which there has been neither adequate reparation for historical violence nor the repudiation of white supremacist dominance in the present.

The prison has been central to American Gothic, appearing in the work of Charles Brockden Brown, Nathaniel Hawthorne, Shirley Jackson and Stephen King, among others. It is a Gothic castle for the new world: a place of entrapment, of unjust inheritance and of the spectres of a bygone era. Jordan Peele's critically lauded and genre-defying *Get Out* (2017) is similarly haunted by the spectre of the prison, its title tellingly referencing the shorthand for a person's release from prison ('when do you get out?') (Fig. 17.1). This comedy horror traces African American Chris Washington's (Daniel Kaluuya) creeping awareness that his girlfriend's family are planning to lobotomise and enslave him, but – in recognition of the absurdities of the American justice system – it is Chris who is haunted by the spectre of prison throughout the film. The film itself is haunted by alternative endings – both those provided as extras on the DVD release, and those hinted at in the final cut. The film ends with Rod (Lil Rel Howery) arriving to rescue Chris; he finds him crouched over his dying girlfriend, a rifle and another dead body strewn around him. Rod's arrival is framed through the point of view of Chris, who watches with horror as a police car pulls up, before his friend, alone, emerges from it. Chris's expression suggests all too clearly the alternative ways in which the film might have ended, with him imprisoned at best, shot on sight at worst, his proximity to a crime scene adequate evidence of his guilt. Both Ward's novel and Peele's film employ the trope of the prison as particularly pertinent to the expression of systemic racism and the failure to address what Kymlicka has described as the

---

[44] Fred Botting, 'Aftergothic: Consumption, Machines, and Black Holes', in Jerrold E. Hogle (ed.), *The Cambridge Companion to Gothic* (Cambridge: Cambridge University Press, 2002), pp. 277–300 (p. 298).

Fig.17.1: *Get Out*: GET OUT. Betty Gabriel, 2017. (Photo by Justin Lubin. ©Universal Pictures/courtesy Everett Collection. Justin Lubin/©Universal Pictures/Everett Collection/Bridgeman Images).

'real-world struggles for "multiculturalism"', namely, 'repudiating the idea of the state as belonging to the dominant group; replacing assimilationist and exclusionary nation-building policies with policies of recognition and accommodation; and acknowledging historic injustice and offering amends for it'.[45]

Communal Violence as Multiculturalism's Bogeyman

The previous sections have covered the ways in which multicultural discourse functions to elide discussions of racism and histories of violence and inequality. Yet critics of multiculturalism have also highlighted the ways in which multicultural policy might foster separatism, ethnic nationalism or tribalism, arguing that it works against unification. This critique has gained a further foothold in the post-9/11 period, as culture has become something viewed with suspicion; with reference to Mahmood Mamdani, Anne-Marie Fortier argues that 'In the context of the international war on terror, the culturalization of political conflict works to distinguish between the "modern" liberals who "make culture and are its masters", and the pre-modern non-liberal societies that are merely conduits of their

[45] Kymlicka, *Multicultural Odysseys*, p. 66.

culture.'[46] Culture itself then becomes 'potentially dangerous ... [as] naturalized, privatized, and ruling over "deep feelings"'.[47] As such, communal violence and factionalism become multiculturalism's dark double for Western liberal democracies; for multiculturalism's detractors it is the logical outworking of integrationist approaches that fail adequately to assimilate citizens under a unifying national identity. The gothicisation of communal violence is registered in contemporary fiction: without expressly drawing the otherworldly into its diegesis, Michael Ondaatje's *Anil's Ghost* (2000) uses the Gothic trope of haunting to represent the communal and political violence of the Sri Lankan civil war, whilst Raj Kamal Jha's *Fireproof* (2006) adopts a distinctly Gothic register as a means of 'speaking the unspeakable' in relation to communal violence in India.

I turn now to Ahmed Saadawi's *Frankenstein in Baghdad* (2013; English translation by Jonathan Wright, 2018), as a dark parody of the sectarian violence in Iraq that has been used to the political gain of various powers. Before beginning discussion of the novel itself, some qualifications are required to talk about Iraq in the context of multiculturalism, a term that has often been reserved for Western (neo)liberal societies. Iraq is evidently composed of diverse ethnic, sectarian and religious groups (including Shiites, Sunnis and Kurds as well as Christians, Black people, Turkmens, Baha'is, gypsies and many more). Yet the minority rights discourse of liberal multiculturalism is often viewed in the Arab/Muslim world as a foreign import, internationally sponsored with the intention of weakening 'countries like Iraq ... by inciting rebellion and/or secession among their various minorities'.[48] A clear explanation for this suspicion is found in the double standards by which, for example, the US justified military intervention in Iraq by condemning the mistreatment of Kurds under Saddam Hussein, while conveniently turning a blind eye to the comparable situation of Kurds in its neighbouring military ally, Turkey. As such, I consider the novel as representing both multiculturalism's bogeyman in the form of sectarian violence, and multiculturalism as a neo-imperial tool used to justify the continued military intervention and exploitation of natural resources initially heralded by European colonialism.

Saadawi's novel engages metaphorically with Mary Shelley's nameless creature, rendered here as the 'Whatsitsname'. The creature is composed of human body parts collected from US-occupied Baghdad by a junk dealer

---

[46] Anne-Marie Fortier, *Multicultural Horizons: Diversity and the Limits of the Civil Nation* (London: Routledge, 2008), p. 5.
[47] Fortier, *Multicultural Horizons*, p. 5.   [48] Kymlicka, *Multicultural Odysseys*, p. 258.

named Hadi. Hadi's purpose is to create a 'complete corpse ... so it wouldn't be treated as rubbish, so it would be respected as other dead people and given a proper burial'.[49] Yet the corpse disappears before Hadi can bury him, animated by his desire to avenge the deaths of the victims of which he is composed. The Whatsitsname's function as an analogy for the Iraqi body politic is writ large: 'Because I'm made up of body parts of people from diverse backgrounds – ethnicities, tribes, races and social classes – I represent the impossible mix that was never achieved in the past. I'm the first true Iraqi citizen.'[50] The language employed here reflects the dominant concerns of multicultural discourse in its focus on diversity and mixture. However, the Whatsitsname's actions serve to foreground fears around the sectarianism that such diversity might foster. To put it in context, Iraq has witnessed successive rounds of communal violence since the decline of the Ottoman empire, including the 'Sayfo' and 'Simele' genocides and the almost complete departure of the Jewish community. (Saadawi's novel predates the Iraqi civil war and the devastating effects of Islamic State in the region.)

The novel uses its Gothic monster to enact a systemic critique of the national and international actors who have exploited the nation's diversity to their own political gains. Ensuring that the text is not read through the paradigm of monstrous parenthood through which Shelley's foundational Gothic source text has often been interpreted, the creator, Hadi, is described as 'just a conduit ... an instrument, or a surgical glove that Fate puts on its hand to move pawns on the chessboard of life'.[51] This might initially be conceived as removing responsibility from *any* human agents, but I would argue instead that it serves to orient the text around systemic critique in a novel in which the workings of fate or the otherworldly are frequently revealed as the tools of a corrupt political bureaucracy. As the Whatsitsname's body parts start dropping off when the victim's revenge is obtained, he begins to require new 'spare parts':

> because he was an exceptional killer who wouldn't die by traditional means, he thought he should exploit this distinctive talent in the service of the innocent – in the service of truth and justice. Until he was sure of his next steps, he would concentrate on ensuring his own survival. He would salvage the spare parts he needed from the bodies of those who deserved to be killed. It wasn't the ideal option, but it was the best one possible for now.[52]

---

[49] Ahmed Saadawi, *Frankenstein in Baghdad*, trans. by Jonathan Wright (London: Oneworld, 2018), p. 25.
[50] Saadawi, *Frankenstein in Baghdad*, p. 140.   [51] Saadawi, *Frankenstein in Baghdad*, p. 123.
[52] Saadawi, *Frankenstein in Baghdad*, pp. 193–4.

The Whatsitsname's warped (and darkly comic) logic in progressing from victims desirous of revenge to villains deserving of murder functions as a barely disguised analogy for the near-impossible pursuit of justice when the body politic is so rotten. Though the cover endorsement's promise of a novel that is 'horrifically funny' suggests moments of cathartic release through laughter that are rarely experienced (at least by this reader), there is an absurdity to the Iraqi bureaucracy that the Whatsitsname mimics. This is reminiscent in part of John Ajvide Linqvist's *Handling the Undead* (2005), in which the novel's strain of dark humour comes from the inability of the Swedish authorities to manage the return of thousands of recently deceased citizens. Saadawi's absurdist brand of dark humour comparably renders visible the incongruities of daily life, but without the catharsis that would be possible by imagining that such absurdities could be overcome.

The novel foregrounds the creation of fear as a tool of a corrupt political system that uses security as a justification for increasing the power of the government. This critique has clear resonances beyond Iraq in the increasingly invasive border controls and surveillance powers adopted by multiple European and North American 'democracies' in the name of maintaining security. A particularly telling scene depicts a journalist named Farid attempting to allocate responsibility for multiple deaths on the Bridge of the Imams resulting from a stampede following rumours of a suicide bomb. (This mirrors a real-life stampede on 31 August 2005, in which 950 people died on the Al-Aaimmah Bridge when rumours of a suicide bomber erupted.) Farid states: 'It's definitely some al-Qaeda cells and remnants of the old regime ... Even if they didn't personally carry out this crime, they are responsible for it because there have been criminal incidents in their name in the past, so the mere mention of their name is a factor in creating insecurity and confusing people.'[53] The specific groups that Farid names function as repositories for fear, which is made explicit in the subsequent paragraphs: 'Every day we're dying from the same fear of dying.'[54] In many ways, the fear that the novel describes is not the stuff of Gothic terror but all too real. Where the Gothic intervenes is in providing a material locus for that fear in the Whatsitsname's monstrous form.

The aptly named Whatsitsname embodies a host of diffuse fears. It is at once a critique of multiculturalism as conducive to sectarian violence, and a critique of multiculturalism as a foreign import designed to weaken national unity:

---

[53] Saadawi, *Frankenstein in Baghdad*, p. 117. [54] Saadawi, *Frankenstein in Baghdad*, p. 118.

Fear of the Whatsitsname continued to spread. In Sadr City they spoke of him as a Wahhabi, in Adamiya as a Shiite extremist. The Iraqi government described him as an agent of foreign powers, while the spokesman for the US State Department said he was an ingenious man whose aim was to undermine the American project in Iraq.

But what project might that be? As far as Brigadier Majid was concerned, the monster itself was their project. It was the Americans who were behind this monster.[55]

The literalisation of the fear in a monstrous form that can be given a name and whose actions can be tracked are integral to the novel's use of the Gothic as a form of critique. In a post-truth society in which the nature of reality is twisted to suit the political agendas of those vying for power and in which fear becomes a useful tool of (in)security, a genre that questions the nature and representation of reality and the workings of fear becomes necessary. For Marxist sociologist and philosopher Michael Löwy, who challenges the Lukácsian notion that only realist artwork can function to critique contemporary society, 'irrealist' (fantasy, Gothic or surreal) works can in fact 'help us understand and transform reality'.[56] This is a realism for when 'ideal-type' realism fails: a Gothic realism that is an extension of realism in its function as social critique. This is Gothic not as a frothy, insincere and escapist genre – an accusation frequently launched at the predominantly female readership of early Gothic romance and its post-millennial counterparts – but as a means of reengagement with the lived realities of twenty-first-century societies in the face of systemic and actual violence, particularly for the Western readership of the translated novel, perhaps inured to Middle Eastern violence through the repetitions of a twenty-four-hour news cycle.

Multiculturalism as Gothic Heterotopia

Thus far I have demonstrated how Gothic functions to represent multiculturalism as an oppressive discourse, as a cover for racism, and as a tool of governments, through its capacity to return the repressed and to find a new expression for an absurd reality. Yet it also has the capacity to imagine alternative worlds that hold up a mirror to our own through its creation of heterotopic spaces that engage critically with the contemporary moment. For Fred Botting, the Gothic itself is a heterotopic medium. With particular reference to early Gothic, he suggests that the mode 'functions as the mirror

---

[55] Saadawi, *Frankenstein in Baghdad*, p. 259.
[56] Löwy, 'The Current of Critical Irrealism', p. 206.

of eighteenth-century mores and values: a reconstruction of the past as the inverted, mirror image of the present, its darkness allows the reason and virtue of the present a brighter reflection'.[57] I would argue that contemporary Gothic similarly functions as a heterotopic mirror, but that the dark spell of history from which societies might (in subscribing to a dominant metanarrative of historical progress, particularly in relation to race relations) imagine themselves to emerge enlightened is the contemporary moment. In its engagement with the various failures of multiculturalism in the present day, contemporary Gothic is more future-oriented, enabling the atrocities of past and present violence to haunt the future. Following Botting's conclusion that 'Gothic remains a bobbin on a string, cast away and pulled back in the constitution of the subject of the present', I propose that as the contemporary moment is increasingly represented as being beyond redemption, it is a future subject that the Gothic is called upon to constitute and rescue from the horrors of the present.[58] Heterotopic spaces of compensation function in contemporary Gothic to critique the present and to posit new ways of being and living together as multicultural societies that are currently impossible.

I turn here to Raj Kamal Jha's *Fireproof*, which is set in the midst of the anti-Muslim violence that flared up across Ahmedabad in the wake of an arson attack that killed fifty-nine Hindu passengers on the Sabarmati Express train near Godhra in 2002, and in which Muslims and their properties were subsequently targeted as the police and state turned a blind eye. To talk about multiculturalism in an Indian context is different again from the contexts discussed previously. As Harihar Bhattacharyya has noted, 'The Indian Constitution can be said to be a multicultural document in the sense of providing for political and institutional measures for the recognition and accommodation of the country's diversity', yet 'multiculturalism as a term of scholarly discourse of society and politics in India is of very recent vintage.'[59] Historically speaking, the moment of simultaneous decolonisation and partition in 1947 saw the nation divided into a predominantly Muslim Pakistan and a predominantly Hindu India, leading to refugee crises as millions of people found themselves displaced on the grounds of religion. Though the name 'Hindustan' was rejected as an official name for India for its exclusionary

---

[57] Fred Botting, 'In Gothic Darkly: Heterotopia, History, Culture', in David Punter (ed.), *A New Companion to the Gothic* (Oxford: Blackwell, 2012), pp. 13–24 (p. 15).
[58] Botting, 'In Gothic Darkly', p. 22.
[59] Harihar Bhattacharyya, 'Multiculturalism in Contemporary India', *International Journal on Multicultural Societies* 5:2 (2003): 148–61 (151–2).

connotations, India's large Muslim minority are nevertheless often treated with suspicion, arising from 'the belief that the minority's main loyalty is to a (potentially hostile) neighbouring kin-state with whom it may collaborate'.[60] Another legacy of colonial rule is that the safeguarding of minority religious rights that was effected under the Raj through separate electorates and reserved seats has been viewed by nationalists (and rightly so) as a colonial strategy of 'divide and rule'; the pernicious ramifications of this legacy in postcolonial India are such that the legal pluralism central to multiculturalism is often understood as a colonial legacy working at odds with national unity.[61] It is in this context that we might understand the ascendancy since the 1980s of the Hindu nationalist Bharatiya Janata Party (BJP), which once circumvented minority rights through its nationalist universalism ('which argues that a common Hindu identity transcends and subsumes all social differences') and later espoused a pluralist politics more befitting the contemporary moment as a subterfuge for mobilising already advantaged groups and legitimising extant anti-Muslim sentiment.[62]

The centrality of minority legal rights and representation to the effective functioning of a multicultural society is foregrounded in *Fireproof*'s narrative framing as legal testimony. The prologue and epilogue take the form of statements formally undersigned by the dead, stabbed or burnt in the spate of anti-Muslim violence in Gujarat, 2002. The narrative that these statements frame is described as follows: 'instead of trying to fight the fire with our tears, perhaps the time had come for us to give ourselves the promise of a better future, maybe some justice as well'.[63] The main body of the text is concerned with the methods undertaken by the dead to recover some semblance of justice and reparation in the future. However, these methods remain unclear until the novel's denouement, as the remainder is narrated by the still-living Mr Jay, who is charged with the care of his grotesquely disfigured newborn as his wife recovers in hospital. Mr Jay is contacted by Miss Glass, who recounts to him a series of violent murders that have taken place in his resident Ahmedabad the previous night. Following her instructions, Mr Jay takes his abject newborn (named Ithim or It/him in deference to both 'those who

---

[60] Kymlicka, *Multicultural Odysseys*, p. 256.
[61] See further Lloyd I. Rudolph and Susanne Hoeber Rudolph, 'Living with Multiculturalism: Universalism and Particularism in an Indian Historical Context', in Richard A. Shweder, Martha Minow and Hazel Rose Markus (eds), *Engaging Cultural Differences: The Multicultural Challenge in Liberal Democracies* (New York: Russell Sage Foundation, 2002), pp. 43–62 (p. 50).
[62] Rudolph and Rudolph, 'Living with Multiculturalism', p. 54.
[63] Raj Kamal Jha, *Fireproof* (London: Picador, 2007), p. 6.

would look at him and see an object and those who would look at him and see my son, my baby') and travels across the city in search of help.[64] He is led to an underwater space in which inanimate objects are tasked with 'speak[ing] the unspeakable' in a 'drama of the absurd' that is deemed a fitting way of 'present[ing] events just as they were'.[65] As Mr Jay witnesses the 'objective' stories that the objects deliver, readers are made aware that the narrator himself numbers among the gang of men responsible for the series of murders and violations described in Miss Glass's communications, including the removal of the still-living (but severely deformed) foetus that Mr Jay has cared for as his own son after being involved in the mother's rape and murder.

The novel's critique of minority rights under the Gujarati state rule of the Hindu nationalist BJP is exercised through the heterotopic underwater scenes that end the novel. Contrary to the city on fire that Mr Jay spends much of the novel traversing, the underwater space is, in Foucauldian terms, a heterotopic space, 'a kind of effectively enacted utopia in which the real sites, all the other real sites that can be found within the culture, are simultaneously represented, contested and inverted'.[66] The irrealism of the novel means that the underwater space functions as a 'heterotopia ... of compensation', creating a space that, in Foucault's words, is 'as perfect, as meticulous, as well arranged as ours is messy, ill constructed and jumbled'.[67] The three objects (a book, watch and towel) that deliver testimonial repeatedly interrupt each other and vie for their moment under the spotlight. Yet the mediating voice of Miss Glass keeps them in line, ensuring that each has the opportunity to speak and be heard. This reflects the strategy adopted elsewhere in the novel, whereby the dead speak from the margins and footnotes in a manner that belatedly offers an obviously compromised voice to those denied official representation in life or memorialisation in death. The justice delivered in this idiosyncratic courtroom is that Mr Jay is forced to confront his guilt. That it is unclear whether Mr Jay has been actively involved in the atrocities or a passive but proximate bystander means that readers, too, are charged with the guilt of complicity. The values of justice, equality and recognition that the objects are granted in the underwater world expose their absence in the real world, in which cultural critics

---

[64] Jha, *Fireproof*, p. 47.   [65] Jha, *Fireproof*, pp. 345, 330, 330.
[66] Michel Foucault, 'Of Other Spaces', trans. by Jay Miskowiec, *Diacritics* 16 (1986): 22–7 (p. 24).
[67] Foucault, 'Of Other Spaces', p. 27.

such as Arundhati Roy have commented on the culpability of the state, and by extension its citizens, in the enactment of this Muslim pogrom.[68]

The Gothic functions in this novel to register the actual violence of the present and to address the official silence surrounding the targeting of a minority group that reveals deficiencies in state provision. The underwater heterotopia highlights how the possibilities afforded to the dead and their inanimate allies are not afforded to the living. The effective management of multiculturalism only in death has resonances in other examples of contemporary Gothic, in which characters can coexist happily only when removed from the political powerplays of the living. Sandi Tan's *The Black Isle* (2012), for example, similarly constructs a multicultural cast of ghosts that complements the living as 'just another facet of [the island's] lush, equatorial diversity – the dead walking among the living, everybody sharing the same air, the same soil'.[69] Yet this aspect of 'the Island's social contract' is tellingly described as a 'die-and-let-live attitude'; it is a heterotopic mirror to the ethnically diverse island in which inequalities of power and capital derived from colonialism and the differing economic reasons for migration plague the living.[70] In these novels, death is indeed the great leveller, and it is life (rather than the afterlife) that is revealed as the place of Gothic horror. The mechanics of the Gothic mode allow for the diegetic realism of these heterotopic representations of the afterlife in a manner that nevertheless reminds readers that the possibilities represented by the afterlife are not present in the contemporary societies that the novels critique.

In sum, the critique of multiculturalism expressed through the critical irrealism of the Gothic mode is levelled at the political and economic power structures that act detrimentally on the coexistence of diverse peoples. Through its imagining of heterotopic alternatives, it does not lay the blame for the failure of the management of cultural, religious and ethnic diversity with citizens themselves, nor does it imagine that it is inevitably doomed as a political ideal. Instead, the Gothic brings to light the factors of economic inequality, racism and the deliberate creation of fear as a weapon of governments that are regularly excluded from multicultural discourse and thereby constructed as unrelated or irrelevant.

---

[68] Arundhati Roy, *Listening to Grasshoppers: Field Notes on Democracy* (London: Hamish Hamilton, 2009), p. 8.
[69] Sandi Tan, *The Black Isle* (New York: Grand Central Publishing, 2012), pp. 91–2.
[70] Tan, *The Black Isle*, p. 92.

3.18

Gothic, Neo-Imperialism and the War on Terror

JOHAN HÖGLUND

In Gothic, ghostly revenants rise from a medieval past, from operating tables, sarcophagi, attics or wild and primitive wildernesses to haunt the inhabitants of the modern age. By giving dark, monstrous forms to the many problems that modernity generated, Gothic developed into an intellectual instrument capable of disturbing dominant Enlightenment discourses and making the terror of various subaltern states available to the reader. Concurrently with this development, however, the powerful tropes and images of Gothic were also put to use to accomplish a very different project, one in which modernity is described as the only bulwark against racialised entities cast as primitive, pre-modern, evil and savage. In this way, Gothic accommodates a complex ideological regime that typically locates terror in the nightmares that the sleep of reason produces, but that also depicts them as arising out of a colonial periphery.[1] This division is apparent in the early Gothic texts, and it becomes increasingly pronounced as Gothic takes hold in North America and as the British Empire grows. By the late nineteenth century, the tendency of Gothic to converge around imperial themes and depict the colonial subaltern or migrant as the source of terror became so dominant that it formed a sub-genre of its own, what Patrick Brantlinger has influentially termed the Imperial Gothic.[2]

Imperial Gothic was especially prominent during the final years of the British Empire, but it did not share in this Empire's demise after World War I. As this chapter argues, the central narratives of Imperial Gothic have been told, retold, adapted and reinvented across the globe over the past 100 years, becoming especially influential in the US in the wake of the 9/11 terror

---

[1] For a discussion of the imperial topography of Gothic, see Roger Luckhurst, 'Gothic Colonies, 1850–1920', in Glennis Byron and Dale Townshend (eds), *The Gothic World* (Abingdon and New York: Routledge, 2014), pp. 62–71.

[2] Patrick Brantlinger, *Rule of Darkness: British Literature and Imperialism, 1830–1914* (Ithaca, NY and London: Cornell University Press, 1988).

attacks. The main purpose of this chapter is to consider how Gothic responded to the War on Terror that was launched by the Bush administration after 9/11; yet such a discussion demands attention to a long colonial history that considers both how Gothic appeared in the US shortly after the American Revolution, and how it accommodated the transfer of global power from the British Empire to the United States that took place during the twentieth century. Noting the many geopolitical similarities that exist between late nineteenth-century Britain and the US at the turn of the millennium, the chapter argues that American Gothic in the early twenty-first century was also effectively imperial. The chapter's analysis of what can thus be termed an 'American Imperial Gothic' pays close attention to the interplay between this specific historical sequence and the Gothic fiction that it spawned; it explores the ideological and affective work that Gothic performed at this point in time; and it also considers the way in which Gothic connects with the various neoliberal corporations and government institutions that are instrumental in the production and dissemination of the Gothic, both locally and globally.

In order to describe the relationship between Gothic and past and present imperial history, this chapter employs postcolonial and decolonial theory.[3] As Andrew Smith and William Hughes have observed, Gothic and postcolonial studies have a 'shared interest in challenging post-enlightenment notions of rationality'.[4] This challenge involves critiquing the ways in which (Gothic) texts conjure images of the non-Western subject as other. Indeed, it is crucial always to bear in mind, when dealing with (Anglo) Imperial Gothic, Edward Said's observation that imperial culture is introverted and speaks primarily about its own desires and anxieties, especially when it pretends to speak about the world outside Western borders. In order to describe the uses to which new institutions and complexes connected to US Empire have put the genre, the chapter will also draw from international relations theory and

---

[3] Brantlinger's analysis of Imperial Gothic rests on Edward Said's groundbreaking postcolonial text *Orientalism* (1978). While Said's work, followed by that of Gayatri C. Spivak, Homi K. Bhabha and Bill Ashcroft, has played a crucial role in the dismantling of colonialist assumptions in the West, it has been complemented by sociological models developed by critics such as Anibal Quijano and Walter Mignolo who belong to what has been termed the modernity/coloniality/decoloniality project. While postcolonial studies shares many assumptions with this project, the latter model has been less focused on the deconstruction of Western representation of the non-West by considering a wider temporal and geographical spectrum and by focusing more strongly on the need to decolonise both epistemology and land in the present.

[4] Andrew Smith and William Hughes (eds), *Empire and the Gothic: The Politics of Genre*, (Basingstoke: Palgrave Macmillan, 2003), p. 1.

critical security studies that have explored how private and government agencies have begun making use of popular culture narratives to further their agendas.

The first thing to note is that Gothic has always been divided on the matter of Enlightenment, modernity and empire. Even if, as Smith and Hughes have argued, the early Gothic novel sometimes gave expression to an 'anti-Enlightenment fervour',[5] it still participated in the construction of what Said has termed 'Orientalism', the imaginary that legitimised colonialism by casting this project as part of modernity itself, rather than as a predatory, nationalist and capitalist venture, and by representing the colonised non-West as a primitive and feminised entity in dire need of Western modernity. Thus, Orientalism served an important function during the expansion of the British Empire, and Gothic became one of its most useful vehicles since the qualities associated with the Orient could be used to inform the Gothic other that terrorises the white European in much Gothic fiction. In other words, as the British Empire continued to grow, Gothic frequently cast modernity as the only reliable protection against the supposedly primitive yet virile power of the indigenous communities that the expanding Empire forced within its remit.

It is this type of Gothic textuality that Brantlinger terms 'Imperial' in *Rule of Darkness* (1988). Following his work, Imperial Gothic is often assumed to have emerged in Britain during the decades when the British Empire peaked and declined. In the wake of the scramble for Africa, most of the world had been colonised, other Western nations as well as indigenous people began to challenge British authority, and the vast Empire was also very expensive to maintain. At the same time, Darwinism, Marxism, the degeneracy debate and the women's rights movement began to erode the class-oriented, Christian and racist patriarchy that constituted normativity within the nation. These different but related anxieties informed Gothic novels such as H. Rider Haggard's *She* (1886), Bram Stoker's *Dracula* (1897) and Richard Marsh's *The Beetle* (1897), where the often feminised, non-white, transformative and degenerate Gothic monster emerges from an Eastern setting with the intention of conducting a reverse colonial project. In response to the challenge that these Gothic others constitute, Imperial Gothic pits a brotherhood of white men who repel the occultic threat and who are aided by modernity in the form of guns, trains and medical/psychological theory. This basic model is

---

[5] Smith and Hughes, *Empire and the Gothic*, p. 3.

crucial to Imperial Gothic, and it has continued to inform Gothic into the new millennium.

While the late-Victorian Imperial Gothic has been closely studied, less attention has been given to how this particular sub-genre developed in the United States. This is by no means due to a lack of pertinent Gothic texts, but rather to a general refusal among US historians to perceive the nation as an empire, despite the widespread use of imported slave labour to build and maintain the agrarian economy of the early republic, despite the extensive programme of settler colonialism that the US government engineered and despite the formal colonies that the US acquired after the Spanish-American war of 1898. In fact, these endeavours were frequently gothicised by the American novel and it should be noted that the beginning of the colonisation of the land west of the Appalachian mountains coincided with the emergence of the Gothic novel in Britain. Because of the vast popularity of this new genre or mode, it became, as Leslie A. Fiedler has observed in *Love and Death in the American Novel* (1960), a literary model with which the first generation of American writers had to contend.[6]

Charles Brockden Brown, one of the first to attempt an American novel, observes in his Preface to *Edgar Huntly* (1799) that the 'Gothic castles and chimeras' that the European novels employed to excite their readers had to be replaced, in American writing, with 'incidents of Indian hostility, and the perils of the Western wilderness'.[7] Thus, the indigenous populations, the people held in slavery, even the land itself, became the subject of Gothic writing during the early years of the American nation. In this way, the early American Gothic novel functioned very much like late-Victorian Imperial Gothic fiction, although it is often referred to as 'frontier Gothic' by scholars in the field. In this body of texts, and as in the British Imperial Gothic of the late-Victorian period, the other is rarely a ghostly revenant from the past, but instead a savage and possibly occult subaltern who inhabits the unsettled West and who resists the movement westwards. To meet this challenge, the heroes of early American Gothic rely both on modernity – typically in the shape of the modern gun – and on the masculinity that was closely associated with the settler figure as an explorer and conqueror of a feminised 'virgin land'.[8] In narrative, as well as in discourse, the

---

[6] Leslie A. Fiedler, *Love and Death in the American Novel*, revised edition (Champaign, IL: Dalkey Archive Press, 1996).
[7] Charles Brockden Brown, *Edgar Huntly; or, Memoirs of a Sleep-Walker: With Related Texts* (Indianapolis: Hackett Publishing, 2006), p. 3.
[8] For a discussion of feminised colonial space, see Ania Loomba, *Colonialism/Postcolonialism* (Abingdon: Routledge, 1998), p. 154.

act of protecting colonised land, and the expansion of the border westwards, was thus imagined, as Richard Slotkin puts it, as a form of 'regeneration through violence'.[9]

The settlement of all the land between the East and West Coast did not put an end to this form of Gothic writing, but rather encouraged two related trends in Imperial Gothic. The first such trend was the production of new imaginary territories in which this regeneration could take place. The second trend was a more introverted form of Gothic in which the now established borders of the empire are challenged from within. In the American Imperial Gothic of the period, the disappearance of 'empty' (although, in fact, always populated) territories from the imperial map prompted the non-realistic novel, as John Rieder has argued, to invent new spaces in which imperial sagas could be acted out.[10] Thus, in the immediate pre-war period, in Britain as well as in the US, Gothic fictions increasingly play out in imaginary worlds such as Mars, or beneath the Earth's crust, as in Edgar Rice Burroughs's *Under the Moons of Mars* (1911) or Arthur Conan Doyle's *The Lost World* (1912). These fictions allow for the continuation of Gothic colonial adventure. The other decisive trend in Imperial Gothic of the era is the turn to war and reverse invasion. This focus directs the reader's attention to the maintenance of imperial borders that are under threat from indigenous resurrection or from competing imperial and capitalist powers. Novels that stoke the xenophobia attendant upon this model include Stoker's *Dracula* and H. G. Wells's *The War of the Worlds* (1898), as well as J. Allan Dunn's *The Peril of the Pacific* (1916) and Jack London's 'The Unparalleled Invasion' (1910), both of which give voice to the concurrent fear of the 'Yellow Peril'.

Empire, Coloniality and Gothic at the Millennium

After World War I and World War II, the European empires collapsed spectacularly, paving the way for what has been termed the postcolonial era. However, while the British Empire did, indeed, fall apart, and while many previously colonised nations achieved formal independence, the structures of (Anglo) empire survived. The decolonisation of Asia, Africa and South America was important, but the persistence of racialised and gendered economic inequality in most decolonised states, as on a global level, testifies

---

[9] See Richard Slotkin, *Regeneration through Violence: The Mythology of the American Frontier 1600–1860* (Norman, OK: University of Oklahoma Press, 2000), p. 554.
[10] See John Rieder, *Colonialism and the Emergence of Science Fiction* (Middletown, CA: Wesleyan University Press, 2008).

to the continued presence of the colonial paradigm. Neo-Marxist critics Michael Hardt and Antonio Negri have attributed this persistence to capitalism's ability to adapt to the increasing boundlessness of labour, capital and resources in a postcolonial, neoliberal world.[11] Anibal Quijano and Walter Mignolo have argued that continuing colonial power structures exist because modernity emerged out of colonialism in the first place. Modernity thus presupposes and is inseparable from what they term coloniality.[12]

While several of the old European imperial states benefited from the maintenance of colonial relationships, the main engine and benefactor of this development was the United States. After World War II, it cemented its growing global authority through a combination of what can be termed 'soft' neoliberal economic and cultural imperialism with 'hard' (neocolonial) military incursions into Korea, Vietnam, South America and the Middle East. However, the growth in global military and economic dominance of the US was initially not theorised as imperialism in scholarly writing. As William Appleman Williams observed in 1955, one of the 'central themes of American historiography is that there is no American Empire. Most historians will admit, if pressed, that the United States once had an empire. They then promptly insist that it was given away. But they also speak persistently of America as a World Power.'[13]

The relative strength of the US increased further in the late 1980s with the collapse of the Soviet Union. At this time, it seemed to some that the neoliberal democracy that the US championed could be made permanent and that the world was, in the words of Francis Fukuyama, at the 'end of history'.[14] However, by the middle of the 1990s, the enthusiasm that had followed in the wake of the collapse of the Soviet Union had abated. The world remained as socially and economically divided as before, and the economic and political tensions that had characterised the Cold War continued to play themselves out. Terrorist actions related to global religious or political sectarian conflict, and right-wing terrorism in the US, made it clear that the world was not, in fact, on track towards a neoliberal utopia. In 1996,

---

[11] Michael Hart and Antonio Negri, *Empire* (Cambridge, MA: Harvard University Press, 2000).
[12] See Walter Mignolo, *The Darker Side of Western Modernity: Global Futures, Decolonial Options* (Durham, NC: Duke University Press, 2011).
[13] See William Appleman Williams, 'The Frontier Thesis and American Foreign Policy', *Pacific Historical Review* 24:4 (1955): 379–95 (p. 379). For another account of this debate, see Amy Kaplan and Donald E. Pease (eds), *Cultures of United States Imperialism* (Durham, NC: Duke University Press, 1993).
[14] See Francis Fukuyama, *The End of History and the Last Man* (New York: Free Press, 1992).

conservative historian Samuel P. Huntington influentially predicted the rise of increasing animosity between global Islam and the West in *The Clash of Civilizations and the Remaking of World Order*. In that same year, Sarah Dunant and Ray Porter termed the era *The Age of Anxiety* and argued that it was characterised by 'nervous pessimism, centering chiefly around uncertain realities – economic, political, environmental'.[15]

These anxieties were picked up by a form of Gothic that, in the US, began regurgitating independent horror films from the 1960s, 1970s and 1980s, but now as Hollywood blockbuster franchises that prioritised terror before the social critique and the gore of the provocative originals. In new Gothic titles, such as *Species* (1995) or *Alien Resurrection* (1997), the possibility that more virile and competitive life forms may challenge human (understood as white and masculine) hegemony was contemplated. Anxiety and terror also informed television series such as *The X-Files* (1993–2002) and *Millennium* (1996–1999), where an obscure organisation allied with law enforcement is seen to attempt to engineer the end of the world. In this way, and as Slavoj Žižek has influentially argued in *Welcome to the Desert of the Real* (2002), US media and popular culture had been masochistically fantasising about a catastrophic event for years before the events of 9/11.[16]

Against an age of anxiety and largely imaginary terror, the sudden collision between highjacked airliners and Manhattan skyscrapers on 11 September 2001 thus appeared both as sudden shock and horror and as a long-awaited reaction to a ruthless, neoliberal and neocolonial geopolitics. In response, President George W. Bush launched what he termed a 'War on Terror'. In the initial rhetoric, this was to be a clandestine battle, fought against largely invisible forces that 'slither into shadowy recesses in large cities', but it soon took the form of the large-scale invasions and occupations of Afghanistan in 2001 and Iraq in 2003.[17] As Ania Loomba and other postcolonial scholars have argued, the latter invasion made it 'more absurd than ever to speak of ours as a postcolonial world' and that 'the signs of galloping US imperialism make the agenda of postcolonial studies more necessary than ever'.[18]

---

[15] Sarah Dunant and Roy Porter, *The Age of Anxiety* (London: Virago, 1996), p. 1.
[16] Slavoj Žižek, *Welcome to the Desert of the Real* (London: Verso, 2002).
[17] George W. Bush, 'Remarks to the Community in South Bend, Indiana' 5 September 2002. *The American Presidency Project* <www.presidency.ucsb.edu/ws/index.php?pid=63576> (last accessed 22 July 2020).
[18] Ania Loomba, Savir Kaul, Matti Bunzl, Antoinette Burton and Jed Esty, 'Beyond What? An Introduction', in Ania Loomba, Savir Kaul, Matti Bunzl, Antoinette Burton and Jed Esty (eds), *Postcolonial Studies and Beyond* (Durham, NC: Duke University Press, 2005), pp. 1–38 (p. 1).

It is at this point in time that historians and political scientists from both the left and the right began to speak about US imperialism and to think of the early years of the new millennium as a decisive moment for this entity. Military historian Andrew J. Bacevich contended in 2002 that, 'like it or not, America today is Rome, committed irreversibly to the maintenance and, where feasible, expansion of an empire that differs from every other empire in history. This is hardly a matter for celebration; but neither is there any purpose served by denying the facts.'[19] Similarly, Noam Chomsky, Chambers Johnson and David Harvey argue that the US has always been an empire of sorts, and that the catastrophes of the present moment are due to this.[20] Neoconservative historians and political commentators such as Max Boot and Niall Fergusson agreed that the US was an empire, but asserted at the same time that this was in order.[21] Afghanistan, Boot argued in 2001, 'cr[ies] out for the sort of enlightened foreign administration once provided by self-confident Englishmen in jodhpurs and pith helmets'.[22] Similarly, Ferguson proposed that what the world needed was 'a liberal empire ... that not only underwrites the free international exchange of commodities, labor and capital but also creates and upholds the conditions without which markets cannot function – peace and order, the rule of law, noncorrupt administrations'.[23] Such optimism may have been possible as the US amassed forces in the Middle East in preparation for the invasion of Iraq, but the predicted failure of the war to create stability in the region and to secure US hegemony globally made faith in neoliberal empire difficult to sustain. In 2010, Julian Go described the nation as 'an aging empire watching dreadfully as rivals threaten to take their slice of the pie'.[24]

In other words, the same awareness of imperial ambitions, and the same sense of imperial and economic decline that, as Brantlinger argues, informed

---

[19] Andrew J. Bacevich, *American Empire: The Realities and Consequences of U.S. Diplomacy* (Cambridge, MA: Harvard University Press, 2002), p. 244.
[20] Noam Chomsky, *Hegemony or Survival: America's Quest for Global Dominance* (New York: Metropolitan Books, 2003); Chambers Johnson, *The Sorrows of Empire: Militarism, Secrecy, and the End of the Republic* (New York: Metropolitan Books, 2004); David Harvey, *The New Imperialism* (Oxford: Oxford University Press, 2003).
[21] See Max Boot, 'U.S. Imperialism: A Force for Good,' *National Post*, 13 May 2003 and Niall Fergusson, *Colossus: The Price of America's Empire* (New York: Penguin, 2004).
[22] Max Boot, 'The Case for American Empire: The Most Realistic Response to Terrorism Is for America to Embrace Its Imperial Role', *The Washington Examiner*, 15 October 2001 <www.washingtonexaminer.com/weekly-standard/the-case-for-american-empire> (last accessed 22 July 2020).
[23] Fergusson, *Colossus: The Price of America's Empire*, p. 2.
[24] Julian Go, *Patterns of Empire: The British and American Empires, 1688 to the Present* (Cambridge: Cambridge University Press, 2011), p. 167.

the late-Victorian Imperial Gothic novel permeated the United States at the beginning of the millennium. With this in mind, it is no wonder that Gothic of this era is characterised by the same anxieties and concerns that haunted the late-Victorian imagination, and that many of the Gothic texts of this earlier period resurfaced in the US. The nation was, at the beginning of the twenty-first century, becoming aware not only of its colonial ambitions, but of these ambitions' tenuous nature, and of the tensions, rivalries and animosities that colonialism had spawned. While there are, indeed, several such similarities between the Imperial Gothic fictions of the late nineteenth century and their post-millennial American counterparts, it is also important to observe some key differences. One is that while late eighteenth- and nineteenth-century Gothic was largely confined to novels, short stories and theatre, contemporary Gothic is, as Catherine Spooner has observed, multimodal and disseminated also in the form of movies, television shows, video games, smartphone apps, fashion, music, tattooing and so on.[25] Another difference is that modern Gothic weaves in and out of other genres and modes. In mash-ups such as *Pride and Prejudice and Zombies* (2009), Jane Austen's romantic and proto-feminist novel combines with Gothic, action-horror and martial arts fiction, while in *Seal Team 666* (2012), Gothic tropes mingle with science fiction and special forces biography. Another crucial difference is the way in which Gothic fiction is produced. While Gothic was also written to order during the late-Victorian period, Gothic today is part of a vast industry produced by actors from government, the entertainment industry and the armed forces.

Finally, post-9/11 American Imperial Gothic is more ready to combine horror and terror than its earlier British equivalent. Following Ann Radcliffe's 1826 essay 'On the Supernatural in Poetry', 'terror' is often defined as the suspenseful and terrifying moment in which the human subject understands that something is amiss, that an epistemological or ontological catastrophe is impending, and 'horror' as the bloody realisation and actualisation of this threat. Gothic has also been described as the 'literature of terror', and it is common for scholars and critics to refer to works that play primarily on the first emotion as 'Gothic' while distinguishing them from works of horror, defined as texts that seek affective engagement mainly through the display of the tortured and destroyed body.[26] However, while this critical compartmentalisation is useful for those interested in genre, Gothic cultural production

---

[25] Catherine Spooner, *Contemporary Gothic* (London: Reaktion Books, 2006).
[26] See David Punter, *The Literature of Terror: A History of Gothic Fictions from 1765 to the Present Day*, 2 vols (London: Longman, 1996).

itself has never been strictly ruled by it. Early Gothic novels such as Matthew Gregory Lewis's *The Monk* (1796) use both terror and horror to great effect, and literary histories of both Gothic and horror invariably describe early British Gothic, American Gothic and late-Victorian Gothic as constitutive of both traditions. The point here is that Imperial Gothic of the twenty-first century employs terror to create powerful affect, but it allows this initial experience of terror to collapse into horror more often than the early Gothic does.

Post-9/11 Gothic

In culture, then, the War on Terror triggered not so much a new form of Gothic as a wide resurrection of the older Imperial Gothic tradition. Indeed, as discussed below, many of the most widely circulated novels, films and video games of the post-9/11 period can be characterised as belonging to this type of Gothic. It can be divided into three different but related categories that are similar but not identical to the Gothic trends that followed the settlement of the American mainland. The first addresses the immediate physical and mental trauma of the terrorist attack, the second considers the far-reaching military response and the third focuses on American and geopolitical life in a world where this military effort has ground to a halt and in which terrorism has become an ever-present part of the fabric of reality. To look first at how post-9/11 Gothic addresses the affective impact of 9/11, Jerrold E. Hogle has observed that Gothic fiction 'is inherently about deep-seated and large-scale, even national and international, traumas that are intimated and yet masked behind hyperbolic symbols of them'.[27] By paradoxically 'representing unrepresentable trauma', 'the best' contemporary Gothic fictions and films allow their readers and audiences to 'thoughtfully confront' the conflicting psychological trauma of 9/11.[28] Several texts by Stephen King published in the immediate wake of 9/11 attempt just such

---

[27] Jerrold E. Hogle, 'History, Trauma and the Gothic in Contemporary Western Fictions', in Glennis Byron and Dale Townshend (eds), *The Gothic World* (Abingdon and New York: Routledge, 2014), pp. 72–81 (p. 73).

[28] Hogle, 'History, Trauma and the Gothic', p. 75. Also, there is a great deal of scholarship that investigates how Gothic and horror disturbed rather than supported the conservative, imperial and neoliberal ideologies on which the official political discourse typically relied. See Andrew Schopp and Matthew B. Hill, *The War on Terror and American Popular Culture* (Madison, NJ: Fairleigh Dickinson University Press, 2009); Aviva Briefel and Sam J. Miller (eds), *Horror after 9/11* (Austin, TX: University of Texas Press, 2011); and Jeff Birkenstein, Anna Froula and Karen Randell (eds), *Reframing 9/11: Film, Popular Culture and the 'War on Terror'* (New York: Continuum, 2010).

a confrontation; the 2002 novel *From a Buick 8*, for example, depicts a classic American car that is not only a fake, but also a portal into a Lovecraftian universe, and which leaks sudden horror into local society. Charles Taylor has perceptively observed that the 'psychic legacy of the day [9/11] colors the entire book' because it drives home the point that 'nothing will ever be the same again'.[29] In this way, King's novel can be said to address the crumbling of the illusion that American economic, military and cultural hegemony was an engine of universal global prosperity, and that Americans were safe from geopolitical challenge behind the borders of the nation state. Indeed, any sustained 'thoughtful confrontation' with the trauma of 9/11 brought on the realisation, first, that the event had a complex geopolitical background, and, second, that the US may not be the untouchable, apex predator of the international community that it has long prided itself as being.

Many of the Gothic texts that were published during this period tend to imagine how military or paramilitary contingents of white men battle global terrorism in an effort to reinstate universal peace, order and law. When doing so, a striking number of them turn to the past and make extensive use of characters derived from the Imperial Gothic. In Stephen Norrington's 2003 film *The League of Extraordinary Gentlemen*, loosely based on Alan Moore and Kevin O'Neill's considerably more complex graphic novel, Allan Quatermain from Haggard's *King Solomon's Mines* (1885) joins forces with Stoker's Mina from *Dracula*, H. G. Wells's Invisible Man, Stevenson's Henry Jekyll and Mr Hyde and Oscar Wilde's Dorian Gray. Aided by the military arsenal that Jules Verne's Captain Nemo supplies, the group travels across the world to Mongolia to sack the headquarters of a terrorist group led by Conan Doyle's Moriarty. Similarly, in Stephen Sommers's blockbuster *Van Helsing* (2004), the old professor of Bram Stoker's *Dracula* appears in the guise of special agent.[30] His job is to locate and destroy the elusive Dracula, who is plotting to unleash a weapon of mass destruction in the form of an army of undead, winged vampire children.

As in the British Imperial Gothic, the patent solution to Gothic crisis in these narratives, made primarily with a US audience in mind, is violence. However, the heroes who perform it are not simply private citizens but well-

---

[29] Charles Taylor, 'You Can't Always Get What You Want: On Stephen King', *The Nation*, 21 December 2011 <www.thenation.com/article/you-cant-always-get-what-you-want-stephen-king/> (last accessed 22 July 2020).

[30] See Johan Höglund, 'Gothic Haunting Empire', in Maria Holmgren Troy and Elisabeth Wennö (eds), *Memory, Haunting, Discourse* (Karlstad: Karlstad University Press, 2005), pp. 243–54.

armed soldiers or government agents. Nemo's submarine is equipped with tactical ballistic missiles, Quatermain's most prized possession is a large rifle and Van Helsing is armed to the teeth with anachronistically advanced weaponry. The opposition that these agents face consists of Gothic terrorists who hide in barren, far-away places from which they plot the destruction of the modern world. In this way, a number of post-9/11 narratives function as thinly disguised allegories where predominantly white male heroes from the late-Victorian period organise paramilitary invasions of liminal Oriental spaces. Following George W. Bush's contention that there 'is only one way to deal with enemies who plot in secret and set out to murder the innocent and the unsuspecting: *We must take the fight to them.* We must be relentless, and we must be steadfast in our duty to protect our people', these narratives depict violence in the colonial periphery as both necessary and legitimate.[31]

The use of the menagerie of characters from the British Imperial Gothic is no accident. In *Neoliberal Gothic* (2017), Linnie Blake and Agnieszka Soltysik Monnet argue that it:

> is no coincidence ... that the characters and plots of the historic gothic have come to dominate popular culture over the course of the past thirty years ... the gothic texts of the neoliberal age can be seen to undertake the same kind of cultural work that was carried out by the gothic mode in earlier periods of socio-economic turbulence.[32]

This is an apt analysis that considers the similarities between the liberal economic paradigms that informed both British and US imperialism. At the same time, the use of characters and plots from Imperial Gothic paradoxically serves both to disassociate the narrative from the current neocolonial invasion of the Middle East and to ground these films in a strongly imperial context. By locating the action to late-Victorian Britain, these films are not formally about US Empire, but by turning characters that have staunchly defended Empire in literature into heroes, Empire can still be celebrated. Thus, Quatermain openly confesses his loyalty literally to the 'Empire', and the film indulges in nostalgic images of the white saviour trope. The optimistic closure of the films, where the terrorist villains are confronted and killed and the world made safe for the peoples that these heroes represent, conjures the ideal imagined resolution of the invasions of Afghanistan and Iraq.

[31] George W. Bush, 'Remarks in Halifax, Canada', *The American Presidency Project*, 1 December 2004 <www.presidency.ucsb.edu/ws/?pid=72844> (last accessed 20 July 2020); my italics.
[32] Linnie Blake and Agnieszka Soltysik Monnet (eds), *Neoliberal Gothic: International Gothic in the Neoliberal Age* (Manchester: Manchester University Press, 2017), p. 1.

Not all imperial Gothic texts of the post-9/11 era are as optimistic. When *Van Helsing* opened in May 2004, coalition forces had failed to discover evidence of the large Weapons of Mass Destruction programme that served as the rationale for the invasion of Iraq. Instead, what did emerge were images of American soldiers torturing and abusing prisoners in the Abu Ghraib prison and evidence of other war crimes conducted by US personnel. In October the same year, British medical journal *The Lancet* published figures that suggested that the invasion had caused almost 100,000 excess Iraqi deaths.[33] By late 2005, as novelist Justin Cronin put it, the invasion 'seemed to have a crescendo of gore and confusion'.[34] This development spawned a less optimistic series of Gothic texts that relinquished the nineteenth-century setting in favour of present-day Afghanistan or Iraq. The protagonists, here, are thus US marines or special forces soldiers who traverse a landscape as hostile and unfriendly as the people and monstrous creatures that inhabit it. The American soldiers are not, as in the earlier films, necessarily heroic. Rather, the confrontation with an invaded Middle East forces these soldiers to consider the hostility that they encounter, the often abject practices in which they have had to engage, and the potential for darkness and violence that they harbour. In this way, they follow the trajectory of Joseph Conrad's influential and notably Gothic novella *Heart of Darkness* (1899), where the enterprising Marlow captains a steamboat through an unnamed Congo destroyed by Belgian predatory colonialism. At the heart of this colony, he encounters the European Kurtz who has turned more savage than any member of the headhunting tribe over which he presides. Conrad's novel is certainly an indictment of colonialism, but as Chinua Achebe has famously observed, its description of Africa as a space of savage darkness still makes it a racist text.[35]

The same kind of criticism might also be levelled against many of the American Imperial Gothic films, novels and computer games that appeared after the invasion of Iraq, several of which make extensive use of Conrad's original text to plot the action. In Daniel Myrick's science fiction horror film

---

[33] In 2006, a new survey by *The Lancet* suggested that more than 650,000 excess deaths had occurred as a result of the invasion. See Gilbert Burnham, Riyadh Lafta, Shannon Doocy and Les Roberts, 'Mortality after the 2003 Invasion of Iraq: A Cross-Sectional Cluster Sample Survey', *The Lancet* 368 (12 October 2006): 1421–8.

[34] Cronin cited by Jill Owens, 'Justin Cronin: The Powells.com Interview', *Powell's City of Books*, 15 June 2010 <www.powells.com/post/interviews/justin-cronin-the-powellscom-interview> (last accessed 22 July 2020).

[35] See Chinua Achebe, 'An Image of Africa: Racism in Joseph Conrad's *Heart of Darkness*', in Helen Lauer and Kofi Anyidoho (eds), *Reclaiming the Human Sciences and Humanities through African Perspectives, Volume II* (Accra: Sub-Saharan publishers, 2012), pp. 929–40.

The Objective (2008), the Afghan landscape itself becomes hostile, and in Alex Turner's horror film *Red Sands* (2009) a Djinn besets a group of lost and wartorn soldiers, killing them but also forcing them to revisit their own horrible actions.[36] In Robert Glickert's *Road to Moloch* (2009), US marines encounter an ancient evil spirit that inhabits their bodies while investigating a cave where insurgents hide, and the Gothic war game *Spec Ops: The Line* (2012) follows Conrad's novella particularly closely to describe the collapse of a special forces mission in a post-apocalyptic Dubai. Finally, in Tom Green's British-produced *Monsters: Dark Continent* (2014), the US is in Iraq to combat both insurgents and a gigantic, strange and violent alien species, bringing out the worst in the marines that are sent to the area. Thus, these films tell stories about how monstrous beings who live in the desert come alive and how American soldiers must engage them, but these abject creatures also introduce their own monstrous natures into the soldiers, or, in some cases, allow the soldiers' own monstrous deeds to become manifest. By refusing the very simple Manichean dichotomies of films such as *Van Helsing*, these narratives do not describe the US's neocolonial enterprise in the Middle East as necessarily benevolent and constructive. However, they still imagine the East as a site of ancient evil that is capable of stripping white humanity of its veneer of civilisation.

Most American Imperial Gothic produced after the collapse of the invasion of the Middle East does not, however, take place in Afghanistan or Iraq, but instead explores the transformed world inside US borders. These constitute the third category of post-9/11 Gothic discussed here, texts that often use the model furnished by Stoker's *Dracula* or Richard Marsh's *The Beetle*, in which an ancient, Oriental being with transformative powers furtively inserts his or her gender-unstable body into American society. These invasion narratives merge with a host of other anxieties, including Islamophobia, homophobia, racism, the possibility of an apocalyptic viral epidemic and, especially after the financial crisis of 2007–8, economic competition from East and South Asia.[37]

A number of contemporary films, television shows, novels and short stories connect Gothic creatures such as the vampire or the zombie with

---

[36] See Johan Höglund, 'Parables for the Paranoid: Affect and the War Gothic' *Continuum: Journal of Media and Cultural Studies* 27:3 (2013): 397–407, for a detailed study of these films.

[37] Stephen Shapiro has proposed in 'Transvaal, Transylvania: Dracula's World-System and Gothic Periodicity', *Gothic Studies* 10.1 (2008): 29–47 that the reverse colonization narrative most immediately expresses fears that the national capitalist project is failing.

terrorism, with 9/11 and with Islam. In Guillermo del Toro and Chuck Hogan's *The Strain* trilogy (2009–11), also a television series from 2014 to 2017, an ancient vampire sets up shop in the ruins of the World Trade Centre and engineers a nuclear winter that makes the vampire species dominant. In *Patient Zero* (2009), the first in a long-running bio-terrorism series by Jonathan Maberry, the Islamic militant El Mujahid develops a virus that turns humans into raving, zombie-like beings. In Max Brooks' *World War Z* (2006), a zombie virus from China lays waste to most of the world, a model utilised also in J. L. Bourne's *Day-by-Day Armageddon* series (2009–16). These texts all utilise the vampire or the zombie to conjure an image of the invasive other. Justin D. Edwards has observed that the post-9/11 terrorist zombie is a 'collectively othered group that is visually identifiable as "not us" and can be slaughtered with impunity'.[38] Thus, the zombie, especially when it is figured as being connected to Islam, connotes what Giorgio Agamben terms the *Homo Sacer*, the subject who exists outside the prevalent system of law and who can be killed with impunity.[39] In post-9/11 zombie cinema, this killing has a ritualistic quality to it. The zombie typically requires a gunshot to the head to die a second and complete death so that the only useful form of resolution to this Gothic crisis is military-grade violence. Failure to resolve the Gothic crisis in this way means risking being infected with a virus imagined in the Imperial Gothic as not simply biological, but also ideological. The deterioration of the mind that the zombie experiences in these narratives – the replacement of free will and agency with an insatiable cannibalistic hunger – thus signifies a general surrender to creeds and beliefs understood as alien to American life. These beliefs include Islam, but they also stand for economically competitive Asian socialism, and thus a return to the Yellow Peril motif that was prevalent in early twentieth-century Gothic.

As discussed above, an equally popular prototype for post-9/11 Imperial Gothic is Wells's *The War of the Worlds*. Here, the Gothic other does not sneak into Western society through the back door. Instead, the US is subjected to a large-scale invasion attempt by a technologically superior, extra-terrestrial species. In Jonathan Liebesman's film *Battle: Los Angeles* (2011), the visual aesthetics of which are partly modelled on US soldiers' own recordings of fighting in Fallujah, the audience is told that 'When you invade a place for its resources, you wipe out the indigenous population.

---

[38] Justin D. Edwards, 'Zombie Terrorism in an Age of Global Gothic', *Gothic Studies* 17:2 (November 2015): 12–25 (p. 12).

[39] See, for example, Giorgio Agamben, *Homo Sacer: Sovereign Power and Bare Life*, trans. by Daniel Heller-Roazen (Stanford, CA: Stanford University Press, 1998), p. 71.

Those are the rules for any colonisation. And, right now, we are being colonised.'⁴⁰ This observation not only clearly notes the imperial subtext of this particular film, but also connects with Wells's nineteenth-century fictions. As early as the opening chapter of the original novel the reader is informed that the 'Tasmanians, in spite of their human likeness, were entirely swept out of existence in a war of extermination waged by European immigrants, in the space of fifty years'.⁴¹ In this way, the alien-invasion narrative can provide an imaginative space where the impact of colonisation on indigenous populations can be considered through a reversal of the imperial enterprise, a space in which the European coloniser is now the colonised. In Stephen Spielberg's 2004 remake *War of the Worlds*, this space is arguably still accessible. This film puts the focus on American civilians who flee the colonising and technologically superior aliens, making the sheer and abject violence of colonialism visible, if through a haze. In *Battle: Los Angeles*, however, this same imaginative space is largely closed to the audience. The focus of this film is not on civilian populations suffering from military invasion and colonisation, but rather on the heroic efforts of the US soldiers who resist the invaders.

This crucial shift, comprising a number of similar movies, is not simply due to a reliance on a different and more clearly pro-American discourse. Instead, the representation of US soldiers desperately and successfully fighting off a genocidal invasion by aliens is the result of direct sponsorship by the US Department of Defense (US DoD). This sponsorship, in turn, is part of a larger structure that has been termed the military entertainment complex by Tim Lenoir and Luke Caldwell, or, by James Der Derian, the 'Military–Industrial–Media–Entertainment–Network'.⁴² While most of the scholarly work devoted to this entity has focused on computer games in general, and on the US DoD's own first-person shooter game *America's Army* (2002–15) in particular, significant attention has also been paid to the connection between Hollywood film and the Pentagon.⁴³ As Georg Löfflmann has observed, the 'Pentagon goes beyond a mere supplier of technology and a free rider on

---

⁴⁰ Rob Frappier, 'Comic-Con 2010: "Battle: Los Angeles" Press Panel', *Screen Rant*, 22 July 2010 <https://screenrant.com/battle-los-angeles-comiccon-2010/> (last accessed 22 July 2020); *Battle: Los Angeles*. Dir. Jonathan Liebesman. Columbia Pictures. 2011.
⁴¹ H. G. Wells, *The War of the Worlds* (London: Everyman, 1996), pp. 6–7.
⁴² Tim Lenoir and Luke Caldwell, *The Military-Entertainment Complex* (Cambridge, MA: Harvard University Press, 2018); James Der Derian, *Virtuous War: Mapping the Military–Industrial–Media–Entertainment Network* (Boulder, CO: Westview Press, 2001).
⁴³ See David L. Robb, *Operation Hollywood: How the Pentagon Shapes and Censors the Movies* (New York: Prometheus Books, 2004).

Hollywood's PR machinery. It actively takes control of the popular image of national security that is being created in the films it cooperates with.'[44] In effect, this means that the DoD is directly involved in the creation of specific representations of global military conflict and in the production of the sense of insecurity that, as McKenzie Wark has argued, is crucial to the maintenance of dominant nations states such as the United States. According to Wark, the 'work of the military entertainment complex is two sided. It has its rational, logistical side; but it also has its romantic, imaginative side. The latter invents reasons for the former to exist. Insecurities cannot simply be taken as given.'[45]

Before 9/11, most such movies partially funded by the DoD were, like Tony Scott's *Top Gun* (1986), nominally realistic. However, in recent years, the DoD have increasingly invested in alien invasion movies. In addition to *Battle: Los Angeles*, the DoD has also helped fund films such as Peter Berg's *Battleship* (2012), the *Transformer* franchise and Gareth Edwards's *Godzilla* (2014). The alien invasion movie is especially well suited to the production of the insecurities that, as Wark argues, keep the complex running. In the words of Löfflmann, this is because the 'Alien invasion theme reproduces a basic Manichean narrative of American innocence the Pentagon can support ... Just like Nazis, Soviet Communists, or Jihadists ... the Alien invader simply represents an enemy of freedom that America has to defeat in a basic struggle of good versus evil.'[46]

Through the use of such tropes, the military entertainment complex can be said to have commodified the ideological geography of the Imperial Gothic beyond the usual producer-consumer relationship. The DoD-sponsored Gothic invasion narrative is not simply an entertainment product intended to bring an audience to the cineplex, online game or book store so that the production company can recuperate its investment; it is specifically designed also to generate a certain binary understanding of geopolitical conflict, of the supposed vulnerability of an (imperial) state as always under threat, and of the role that the military must play in keeping these threats at bay. What Wark terms the 'imaginative, romantic side' of the complex thus invents reasons for the material, 'rational, logistic' side to exist, although this

---

[44] Georg Löfflmann, 'Hollywood, the Pentagon, and the Cinematic Production of National Security', *Critical Studies on Security* 1:3 (2013): 280–94 (p. 284).

[45] McKenzie Wark, 'Securing Security', *Kritikos: An International and Interdisciplinary Journal of Postmodern Cultural Sound, Text and Image* 2 (2005) <http://intertheory.org/security.htm> (last accessed 22 July 2020).

[46] Löfflmann, 'Hollywood, the Pentagon', pp. 286–7.

is not a linear process but a loop. The generation of narrative that sustains a strong sense of insecurity helps the production of the weapons and the military interventions that constitute the rational and logistic side. Such interventions then form the starting point of a new narrative. In this way, the military entertainment complex is best described as a form of perpetual engine that produces both the sense of insecurity and the military intervention that keeps empire afloat.

Imperial Gothic at the Border

Gothic is a complex mode that enables a number of different forms of engagement with empire, terrorism and other practices of insurrection. This chapter has focused on the way that American Gothic represented and debated 9/11, terrorism, the War on Terror and the invasions of Afghanistan and Iraq. It has paid particular attention to how the US became aware of its imperial position at this time, and how a long legacy of imperial practice prompted the production of a number of texts that can best be characterised as Imperial Gothic. These texts are firmly rooted in a long Gothic tradition and revolve, in particular, around characters and plots invented during the late-Victorian period.

At the same time, this Gothic is firmly connected to the specific historical moment in which it plays out. Marie Liénard-Yeterian and Agnieszka Soltysik Monnet have suggested that the 'Gothic's new task might no longer be to deal with the legacy of the past ... but handle the legacy of the future'.[47] While Imperial Gothic is firmly rooted in a past history, it also clearly engages with the futures this history is creating. When it produces a world divided into good and evil, civilised and primitive, white and monstrous, the characters of the narratives, and by extension the reading, viewing or gaming audience, are faced with the same choice as that which George W. Bush famously presented to the world in 2001: 'Either you are with us, or you are with the terrorists.'[48] The Imperial Gothic frequently offers its audience the same simplistic choice: you either join the marines bravely gunning into the bodies of the other, or you become one of these abject, monstrous others. Joining the marines in some manner, surrendering to this binary context –

---

[47] Marie Liénard-Yeterian and Agnieszka Soltysik Monnet, 'The Gothic in an Age of Terror(ism)', *Gothic Studies* 17:2 (November 2015): 1–9 (p. 9).

[48] George W. Bush, 'Remarks to the Troops at Ford Hood, Texas', 3 January 2003, *The American Presidency Project* <www.presidency.ucsb.edu/documents/remarks-military-personnel-fort-hood-texas> (last accessed 22 July 2020).

becoming 'us' – affords the audience of the Imperial Gothic direct and pleasurable affective access to this dichotomous universe. The War on Terror now becomes their war. This is a choice that also provides them with a role within the military entertainment complex. They (we) now fund it by consuming its products, by retelling its stories, by supporting its politics, even, perhaps, by joining the armed forces in some capacity.

However, even in its most jingoistic and xenophobic guise, Imperial Gothic testifies to the increasing sense that something is awry in the world, and that the intellectual, medical, financial and physical borders of the United States are failing. In this way, even the most conservative, neoliberal and Imperial Gothic provides a hidden exit from the Manichean universe. As Roger Luckhurst has observed, 'Terror comes from the breach of boundaries; the vampire invited over the threshold, zombies massing at the last defense until it gives way under the pressure of undead bodies.'[49] It is impossible to represent this breach without acknowledging the fact that borders are permeable. Gothic thrives not on the border itself, but on the collapse of the (intellectual, affective, physical) walls that keep categories apart. Similarly, the realisation that Imperial Gothic is not simply informed by a discourse, but is, more importantly, a symptom of a geopolitical illness, may make it possible for consumers to suspend the affective engagement with the narrative, and instead to contemplate the epistemological and historical circumstances that have produced it.

[49] Luckhurst, 'Gothic Colonies', p. 62.

3.19

Global Gothic 1: Islamic Gothic

TUĞÇE BIÇAKÇI SYED

Introduction

The twenty-first century is marked by the globalisation of Gothic and its adoption far beyond its traditional territories in Western Europe and North America. Alongside increasing numbers of literary examples from around the world, visual interpretations invade national cinemas, TV channels and digital streaming platforms – even in some possibly unexpected parts of the world, such as the Middle East. Gothic and horror films from or about the Middle East region are widely marketed in Western media. The popularity of Ana Lily Amirpour's black-and-white vampire film *A Girl Walks Home Alone at Night* (2014), Babak Anvari's politically charged *Under the Shadow* (2016) and Netflix's adaptation of Egyptian novelist Ahmad Khaled Tawfik's series of horror novels *Ma Waraa Al Tabiaa* (*What Is Beyond Nature*, 1993–2004) under the title of *Paranormal* (2020) all prove that Islamic societies, in which most people come across the idea of the supernatural initially through religious doctrines, are surprisingly suitable cultural locales in which Gothic tales might flourish.

This is no less the case for Turkey, where more than 80 per cent of the population define themselves as Muslim.[1] Gothic literature first emerged in Turkey in the early twentieth century, at a time of painful transformation from an Islamic empire to a modern nation. Later, Gothic film was a post-war import that pleased neither the audiences nor the producers, who were unfamiliar with, and disconnected from, Western Gothic tropes. After

---

[1] According to 'The Global Religious Landscape: A Report on the Size and Distribution of the World's Major Religious Groups as of 2010', published in December 2012 by PEW Research Center under the PEW-Templeton Global Religious Futures Project, 98 per cent of the Turkish population is Muslim. Another survey 'Religion, Ipsos Global Trends' (2016) conducted by the French Market Research Company Ipsos, shows the percentage as 82 per cent. See: <https://web.archive.org/web/20170905105138if_/https://www.ipsosglobaltrends.com/wp-content/uploads/2017/04/Slide13-6.jpg> (last accessed 26 November 2020).

decades of shifts in popularity, unauthorised film adaptations of iconic Western productions and failed attempts at creating authentic plots, Gothic became popular in Turkey in the post-millennium, but only after its adoption of the conventions of modern horror such as gore, shock and awe. Thus, Gothic horror, a sub-genre of Turkish Gothic, became the second most popular genre of Turkish cinema in 2016, with twenty-five films in total released in that year.

A large number of these films draw on Islamic folklore and demonology and centre around the supernatural creatures known as 'djinns'. Because their existence is entirely accepted and confirmed by religious belief structures, djinns are the most common supernatural figures used in Gothic and horror stories in Islamic cultures. According to the Qur'an, djinns are spirit-like creatures made of smokeless fire, and the third creation of God alongside angels and humans. Although they can see humans they are, themselves, invisible to the human eye unless they shapeshift to assume the form of an animal or a human being. Their progenitor is Iblis (Satan, also known as *Şeytan* in Turkish), but since djinns possess free will like humans, they can be either good or evil in nature. In the Qur'an, The Jinn Surah mentions a group of djinns' acknowledgement and acceptance of the holy book upon hearing a recitation and converting to Islam.[2] These are mostly considered to be believer djinns and, at times, are even known to help humans.[3] The subject of Gothic, however, is the malevolent djinns who are associated with demons and who are known to trespass into the human world through magic and witchcraft.[4]

The growing interest in Gothic horror films featuring malevolent djinns or Islamic demons redefined the genre in Turkey in the 2000s, and assisted a rising global interest in Turkish horror cinema through DVD releases with English subtitles and reviews in popular virtual platforms such as Dread Central or Horror News Network. As many Turkish scholars have pointed out, the reasons for the popularity of what might be called 'Islamic Gothic' in Turkey range from the global upsurge of Gothic and technological developments in film production to the mobilisation of culture through globalisation, as well as the need to disentangle the genre from Western influence by

---

[2] *The Qur'an*, trans. by M. A. S. Abdel Haleem (Oxford: Oxford University Press, 2005), p. 393.
[3] The story of King Solomon, who controlled djinns with a magical ring to build his temple, is mentioned in the Bible and the Qur'an.
[4] Rosemary Ellen Guiley, *The Encyclopaedia of Demons and Demonology* (New York: Facts On File, Inc., 2009), p. 68.

including local motifs. However, and as this chapter will elaborate, the rise of conservative politics in Turkey has certainly been the most significant determinant of Islamic Gothic's sudden boom.

Many Islamic Gothic texts that are celebrated by Western audiences today are politically progressive in outlook. Anvari's *Under the Shadow*, for example, uses the djinn figure to produce images of resistance to the unjust political and social impositions of the status quo, while Amirpour's *A Girl Walks Home Alone at Night* subverts the Western image of the Muslim woman in *burqa* as oppressed and refuses to abide by the rules of patriarchy and Islamic dogma. Turkish Islamic Gothic texts and films, however, often tend to cultivate far more conservative values that, within Turkish society, correlate closely with governing political and religious orthodoxies. In both cases, Gothic becomes a tool of counter-narrative for conflicting ideologies, and it does this by making women the centre of attention. This chapter, therefore, investigates the cultural origins of the Islamic Gothic by highlighting its most common conventions concerning the representation of women haunted by malevolent djinns in Islamic cultures. I begin with a historical survey of Gothic in the Middle East to shed light on the genre's chronological development and gradually increasing popularity in the Islamic world, particularly in Egypt, Iran and Turkey, where Gothic is more visible in literature and cinema than in other Islamic Middle Eastern countries.[5] Following this, I explore the role of the djinn, the mainstream monster of Islamic Gothic in Turkish literature and film, in establishing an ideological position that correlates with the rising popularity of conservative politics in the post-millennium.

Gothic in the Islamic Middle East

If, as Catherine Spooner puts it, Gothic in the twenty-first century 'lurks in all sorts of unexpected corners' of the world, spreading 'like a malevolent virus', it is by means of the cultural flows of globalisation.[6] Although cultural exchange between the nations of the world existed for centuries through travelling, trade routes and translated texts, the concept of globalisation is a twentieth-century invention that has become of particular academic interest and relevance only since the 1980s. Accordingly, Glennis Byron's concept of 'globalgothic', coined in an influential volume of essays of that name in

---

[5] Karen Grumberg's monograph on Hebrew Gothic sheds light on a Gothic tradition from outside the Islamic Middle East. See Karen Grumberg, *Hebrew Gothic: History and the Poetics of Persecution* (Indiana: Indiana University Press, 2019).
[6] Catherine Spooner, *Contemporary Gothic* (London: Reaktion Books, 2006), p. 8.

2013, is mainly concerned with the multidirectional cultural flows of the post-1980 period that articulate the anxieties 'about the stability of local or national identities and cultures, about the impact of transnational capitalism or the workings of technology'.[7]

Indeed, the upsurge in Gothic and horror in the post-1980 period was witnessed in many parts of the globalising world, including the Islamic Middle East. The current horror fan base in Turkey grew up watching *Ghostbusters* (dir. Ivan Reitman, 1984) on *Parliament Cinema Club: Sunday Night Cinema* on the private Turkish TV channel *Star*, and *Buffy the Vampire Slayer* (1997–2003) on another private TV channel, *Cnbc-e* (aired between 2001 and 2005). However, the emergence of the literary Gothic in the region – the Gothic mode as it was adopted from Western literature – initially occurred in the late nineteenth and early twentieth century, when the Ottoman Empire began to fade away and a Western form of modernity started to infiltrate the region. Rather than being a defined genre in its own right, the Gothic of this period was more of a set of adapted motifs and themes from nineteenth-century British and French literature. Due to lack of translation into the English language and the Gothic novel's low cultural status, the limited numbers of Gothic novels and stories that were produced remained unknown for decades, even to local readers in the Middle East.

Among these early Gothic works, Turkey's first feminist Suat Derviş's female Gothic novel *Ne Bir Ses Ne Bir Nefes* (*Not a Sound Not a Breath*, 1923) and Sadegh Hedayat's masterpiece of modern Iranian literature *Boof-e koor* (*The Blind Owl*, 1936) serve as prominent starting points.[8] Published in a moment of social and political change from a deteriorating Islamic empire to a modern republic, *Not a Sound Not a Breath* offers an allegorical subtext corresponding to the political and social transformation of Turkey through the use of a tainted love triangle in which a young woman is caught between a father named Osman (suggesting Ottoman) and a son named Kemal (the name of the revolutionary leader of the Republic of Turkey). The arrangement of the characters and their desires thus depicts the Turkish nation's entrapment in-between two patriarchal regimes. Written as a Gothic romance, the novel questions the issues of its time, such as changing women's roles, modernisation and the conflict between the Ottoman past and the then-future Kemalism of Turkey. In *The Blind Owl*, Hedayat uses an unnamed narrator who tells his revelations regarding death to the owl-like shadow on the wall.

---

[7] Glennis Byron (ed.), *Globalgothic* (Manchester: Manchester University Press, 2013), p. 5.
[8] Throughout the chapter, I provide the English translations of foreign titles in parenthesis after the original title.

With its multi-layered, non-linear narrative structure, its dark atmosphere, sinister language and thematic preoccupations with death, the meaning of life and human existence, *The Blind Owl* is considered a Kafkaesque novel in the Western tradition and draws heavily on psychoanalysis and Gothic romanticism.[9]

While the numbers of Gothic novels produced in the Middle East in the twentieth century remain limited, cinematic examples are much more plentiful. The earliest Gothic and horror films from the Middle East date back to the aftermath of World War II. Egyptian director Yusuf Wahbi's *Safeer Gohannam* (*The Ambassador of Hell*, 1945) and Turkey's long-lost first Gothic film *Çığlık* (*The Scream*, dir. Aydik Arakon, 1949) were the earliest examples of the genre. Although Viola Shafik does not include *The Ambassador of Hell* in her list of horror films in Egyptian cinema, the film, an appropriation of a Faustian tale in which Satan appears to a poor family in the guise of a rich man and offers them wealth in exchange for excessive deeds, should be considered to have initiated the genre's journey in Egypt.[10] The film's characterisation of Satan, first as an aristocratic, almost Dracula-like alluring man with piercing eyes and then as a werewolf-like hairy creature with horns and long nails, highlights its appropriation of Western Gothic tropes. Nevertheless, the excessive music, singing and belly-dancing scenes are in keeping with the conventions of contemporary Egyptian cinema and serve to create a familiar and safe atmosphere for local audiences.

Similarly, the lost Turkish gem, *The Scream*, was also inspired by – and replicated – the nineteenth-century Western Gothic tropes found in novels such as Willkie Collins's *The Woman in White* (1859), Joseph Sheridan Le Fanu's *Uncle Silas* (1864) and their Hollywood adaptations of the 1940s. The film tells the story of a doctor who is stranded on a stormy night in a mansion in which a man drives his young niece to madness over the question of rightful inheritance. Although there is no extant footage of the film, its title alone suggests that the screams of the victimised girl reverberate with the mysterious and dark atmosphere of the film's visual aesthetics.

The appropriation of Western Gothic tropes continued to be the norm in Gothic and horror cinema in Egypt, Iran and Turkey in the following decades. Films such as *Ölüler Konuşmaz Ki* (*The Dead Don't Talk*, dir. Yavuz

---

[9] Michael Beard, *Hedayat's Blind Owl as a Western Novel* (New Jersey: Princeton University Press, 1990), p. 165.

[10] Viola Shafik, 'Egypt: A Cinema Without Horror', in Steven Jay Schneider and Tony Williams (eds), *Horror International* (Detroit: Wayne State University Press, 2005), pp. 273–89 (p. 277).

Yalınkılıç, 1970) from Turkey, *Al Ta'witha* (*The Talisman*, dir. Mohamed Shebl, 1987) from Egypt and *Telesm* (*The Spell*, dir. Darius Farhang, 1987) from Iran, for example, made use of the haunted house trope. Unauthorised adaptations of Tod Browning's *Dracula* (1931) and William Friedkin's *The Exorcist* (1973) even appeared in Turkey under the titles of *Drakula İstanbul'da* (*Dracula in Istanbul*, dir. Mehmet Muhtar, 1958) and *Şeytan* (*Satan*, dir. Metin Erksan, 1974), respectively.[11] Jim Sharman's *The Rocky Horror Picture Show* (1975) was also adapted in Egypt under the title of *Anyab* (*Fangs*, dir. Mohammed Shebl, 1981).

Although ghosts, demons, vampires and other monsters inspired by Western Gothic narratives feature in Gothic and horror films from Turkey, Iran and Egypt, the use of the figure of the Islamic djinn as a particular manifestation of the Gothic monster begins with *al-Inss wa-l-jinn* (*Humans and Jinns*, 1985) directed by Muhammed Radi. The film follows Dr Fatima, a medical specialist who returns to Egypt after her studies in the United States. Fatima receives a marriage proposal from her colleague Dr Usama, but she is haunted by a djinn named Galal, who is supposedly connected to the spirit of her late fiancé. Having seen her daughter become psychologically deranged by nightmares and apparitions, Fatima's mother consults a *shaman* who practices the *zār* ritual on Fatima. *Zār* is a so-called religious practice that is mostly attended by women in North Africa and some parts of the Middle East. The ritual includes chanting and blood sacrifice in order to exorcise the *zār* demon that is thought to cause mental and physical derangement in a woman who, as a result, is known to lose her fertility.[12] However, this ritual in the film only ends up worsening Fatima's psychological and physical condition. Lying on her hospital bed unconscious, Fatima is once again visited by Galal, who approaches her with apparent sexual intentions, yet Dr Usama interrupts the djinn and starts reciting passages from the Qur'an. As he continues his recitation, Galal the djinn becomes smaller and smaller, eventually

---

[11] In fact, *Dracula in Istanbul* was, for the most part, an adaptation of Ali Rıza Seyfioğlu's novel *Kazıklı Voyvoda* (Vlad the Impaler, also known as Voivode with the Stakes, 1928). This novel was itself an adaptation and a localisation of Bram Stoker's *Dracula* (1897) and had recently been translated into English as *Dracula in Istanbul: The Unauthorized Version of the Gothic Classic* (Neon Harbor Entertainment LLC, 2017). For further discussion of Seyfioğlu's novel and its film adaptation *Drakula İstanbul'da* (1958), see Tugce Bicakci, 'The Origins of Turkish Gothic: The Adaptations of Stoker's *Dracula* in Turkish Literature and Film', *Studies in Gothic Fiction* 4: 1/2 (2015): 57–69.

[12] Gerda Sengers, *Women and Demons: Cultic Healing in Islamic Egypt* (Leiden and Boston: Brill, 2003), p. 90.

disappearing into the flames – an allusion to the nature of djinns in the Qur'an as beings of smokeless fire.[13]

As also suggested by Shafik, *al-Inss wa-l-jinn* offers a clear-cut allusion to repressed female sexuality and cultivates the beliefs of orthodox Islam by rejecting superstitious and outdated practices such as the *zār* ritual.[14] Moreover, the fact that Fatima is freed by Dr Usama, a strong male figure who seems to be a believer in orthodox Islam and who can recite the Qur'anic prayers by heart, indicates the endorsement of traditional gender roles as conceptualised by a conservative Muslim society. This is the conservative thematic pattern for the Islamic Gothic horror narratives that feature djinns as the main Gothic monsters in Turkey, Egypt and Iran. The female protagonist, who is either completely Westernised and detached from traditional Islamic values or confused and in search of her identity, is possessed by a djinn and, after a series of terrifying adventures, is rescued by a recitation from the Qur'an with the help of a strong male figure, who is either a believer friend, lover or the Islamic priest himself. The patriarchal social order is thus restored, and any non-orthodox practice of Islam is rejected.

Radi's *al-Inss wa-l-jinn* is not the first Gothic horror film in the region to end with a recitation from the Qur'an. *The Dead Don't Talk*, a Turkish film from fifteen years earlier, presents a similar recitation scene that is carried out by a Muslim priest. However, the monster in this film is a hybrid derived from beliefs in Turkic and Balkan folklores rather than a djinn, and, as I have pointed out elsewhere, the end of the film aligns itself with a more positivist stance and implicitly supports secular ideology.[15] *Şeytan*, the unauthorised Turkish adaptation of *The Exorcist* that was released in 1974, also includes a recitation from the Qur'an, shot in a very similar manner to the exorcism scene in *The Exorcist*. As a cultural adaptation of a source text that relies heavily on Christian iconography, the Gothic monster in *Şeytan* is not exactly derived from Islamic demonology. However, the fact that a recitation from the Qur'an is used to expel the monster or exorcise the demon clearly links the film with the Islamic Gothic sub-genre. Moreover, the end of the film, where the audience sees Gül (Regan) and her mother Ayten (Chris) praying in a mosque, both wearing hijabs, before setting off for their family vacation,

---

[13] The film is available on Youtube with no subtitles. See: <www.youtube.com/watch?v=qCo7dmg8eBE> (last accessed 26 November 2020).
[14] Shafik, 'Egypt', p. 285.
[15] Tuğçe Biçakçi Syed, 'Turkish B-Movie Gothic: Making the Undead Turkish', in Justin D. Edwards and Johan Höglund (eds), *B-Movie Gothic: International Perspectives* (Edinburgh: University of Edinburgh Press, 2018), pp. 139–53.

marks a departure from modern secular Turkish identity and associates the film with the pro-Islamist and conservative sentiments that were on the rise in Turkey in the post-war period. *al-Inss wa-l-jinn* seems to have been inspired by a similar conservative impulse since, following the disappearance of the djinn, Dr Fatima experiences a religious revelation and starts reciting from the Qur'an.

Such Islam-approved subtexts in Gothic horror films from Egypt and Turkey are in keeping with the sometimes reactionary tendencies of Gothic and horror more generally. As Robin Wood has argued, the basic formula of the horror film is that normality, in other words the heterogenous patriarchal bourgeois capitalist social order, is threatened by what is repressed, usually in the form of a monster. Wood claims that 'the dominant designation of the monster must necessarily be evil' because 'what is repressed must always return as a threat'.[16] The destruction of the threat and the eventual restoration of normality thus establish horror, for Wood, as 'a conservative genre that works to justify and defend the status quo'.[17] This dynamic certainly applies to the films that I have discussed above. Moreover, in most exorcism narratives, the evil threat uses a transgressive female as its vessel. According to Christopher J. Olson and Carrie Lynn D. Reinhard, the traditional exorcism narrative:

> routinely portrays a girl or young woman as both a threat to those around her and a victim of forces beyond her control. These narratives commonly situate the possessed girl or woman as some dreadful thing that a male saviour (e.g., priest, rabbi) must dispel or repress, thereby restoring so-called normal (e.g., patriarchal, heteronormative, colonial) life.[18]

Islamic Gothic horror narratives that include a recitation from the Qur'an in order to exorcise a djinn or a demon with the intention of restoring the normality can thus be said to have reactionary and conservative subtexts that support, praise and even propagate orthodox Islam. In these narratives, Westernised female characters and their bodies become central to the plot structure due to the mere fact that they are non-believers or because they exist in a state of confusion regarding their religious beliefs, both scenarios making them vulnerable to, or perhaps even convenient vessels for, djinn possessions and sexual transgressions.

---

[16] Robin Wood, 'An Introduction to the American Horror Film', in Robin Wood and Richard Lippe (eds), *American Nightmare: Essays on the Horror Film* (Toronto: Festival of Festivals, 1979), pp. 7–28 (p. 23).

[17] Mark Jancovich, *Horror: The Film Reader* (London: Routledge, 2002), p. 13.

[18] Christopher J. Olson and Carrie Lynn D. Reinhard, *Possessed Women, Haunted States: Cultural Tensions in Exorcism Cinema* (London: Lexington Books, 2017), p. 3.

Islamic Gothic Horror in Turkey in the Post-Millennium

The emergence and the early development of Islamic Gothic horror in the Middle East is mainly a consequence of the multidirectional flows of cultural globalisation. The unstoppable rise and popularity of Islamic Gothic horror in Turkey in the post-millennium, by contrast, is much more than a domino effect: it is arguably dictated by the status quo. The twenty-first century in Turkey was marked by the return of a repressed Islamic Turkish identity. With the accession to power of the AKP (the Turkish acronym for the Justice and Development Party) in 2002, pro-Islamist ideology redefined Turkish national identity in relation to its Islamic roots, which had previously been undermined by the modernisation project of the early twentieth century. Accordingly, the image of the ideal Turkish woman – which was once defined by Kemalist secular ideology as Westernised, unveiled and educated – has also undergone considerable remodelling. Under the rule of conservative politics, the ideal Turkish woman of the twenty-first century is defined by her traditional family roles and, most of the time, by her hijab.

In fact, the success of the AKP was not unprecedented. The roots of the Islamic ideology that the party advocates date back to the Turkish parliament's first experience with the multi-party system in the 1950s. Since then, the Turkish public have often voted for right-wing parties whose ideologies were consonant with the traditional and religious values of Turkish society.[19] Particularly after the 1980 *coup d'etat*, the socialist movements of the 1960s and 1970s were suppressed by the military junta (1980–3) and there was an atmosphere of tolerance for alternative movements newly formed by Muslim brotherhoods and Sufi orders that previously had been banned after the foundation of the republic.[20] Meanwhile, Turkey had entered 'the global circuits of capital', applying neo-liberal policies to its economy and strengthening relations with the US and the Middle East, gestures that enabled it both to regain its faded geopolitical significance for the West and to build cultural relations under the roof of religion with the East.[21] Turkish culture in the 1990s was thus influenced by these developments and characterised by the growing promotion of religious values in politics and social life.

---

[19] Ali Çarkoğlu and Ersin Kalaycıoğlu, *The Rising Tide of Conservatism in Turkey* (New York: Palgrave Macmillan, 2009), p. 3.
[20] Çarkoğlu and Kalaycıoğlu, *The Rising Tide of Conservatism in Turkey*, p. 9.
[21] Yıldız Atasoy, *Turkey, Islamists and Democracy: Transition and Globalization in a Muslim State* (New York: I. B. Tauris, 2005), p. 151.

Ali Çarkoğlu and Ersin Kalaycıoğlu observe that, in the 1990s, terms such as 'believers', 'faithful', 'oppressed', 'identity' and 'laicism' featured prominently in political rhetoric.[22] In addition, religious orders and communities that were once oppressed and banned by the Kemalist regime from the 1920s onwards gained visibility, 'as if they were legal and conventional part and parcel of the polity in Turkey'.[23] For Çarkoğlu and Kalaycıoğlu, the developments that led Islamist ideology to the 1990s and Turkey to the accession of the AKP government in the early 2000s form the basis of Turkish conservatism, a cultural drive that, as an adjective, became synonymous with 'Muslim' in Turkey.[24] They argue that the political rhetoric of Turkish conservatism in the early twenty-first century divided society into 'a new left–right definition that underlines the religion versus secularism debate more intensively'.[25] Indeed, it is this polarisation that best defines Turkish national identity and its fragmented nature in the post-millennium.

Turkish Gothic, as a mode inherently intertwined with Turkish national identity and the processes of its construction during crucial time periods in Turkish history, quickly took notice of the zeitgeist of the country and this newly defined sense of 'Turkishness'. Novels and films that utilise the figure of the malevolent djinn as a Gothic monster proliferated in the span of a decade and projected the two poles of Turkish national identity, Islam and secularism, onto the bodies of Turkish women, albeit disguised here as the fight between good and evil. The trend has been particularly visible in cinema and is considered by many scholars to have given a new form of identity to the Turkish Gothic tradition in the 2000s. Kaya Özkaracalar argues that Turkish horror films with Islamic themes have formed an intrinsically Turkish canon, adding that 'To associate the emergence of a trend in which films with Islamic motifs were determinant and absorbing after 2004 with the rise of the JDP in politics is a natural – and in many ways a valid – argument.'[26] Although the ideological subtexts of these horror films are, for Özkaracalar, bilateral, some films released in 2015 – the most prolific year for Turkish horror so far – contribute to the ideological

---

[22] Çarkoğlu and Kalaycıoğlu, *The Rising Tide of Conservatism in Turkey*, p. 4.
[23] Çarkoğlu and Kalaycıoğlu, *The Rising Tide of Conservatism in Turkey*, p. 4.
[24] Çarkoğlu and Kalaycıoğlu, *The Rising Tide of Conservatism in Turkey*, p. 25.
[25] Çarkoğlu and Kalaycıoğlu, *The Rising Tide of Conservatism in Turkey*, p. 4.
[26] Kaya Özkaracalar, 'İslami korku filmlerinin ideolojik/siyasi topoğrafyası'[The Ideological/Political Topography of Islamic Horror Films], *İleri Haber*, 13 February 2016 <http://ilerihaber.org/yazar/islami-korku-filmlerinin-ideolojiksiyasi-topografyasi-50243.html> (last accessed 26 November 2020); my translation.

apparatuses of Islamist propaganda.[27] Zeynep Şahintürk also acknowledges the impact of the AKP's Islamic policies on Turkish horror's big leap, arguing, however, that djinn possessions depicted in films such as *D@bbe* (dir. Hasan Karacadağ, 2006) are the manifestations of secular anxieties about being ruled by theocratic Islamic Sharia law.[28] Şahintürk's remark echoes the arguments of Savaş Arslan, which claim that Islamic motifs are representations of the directors' fear of Turkey's Islamicisation.[29]

Conversely, Gizem Şimşek's view on the topic bears similarities to Özkaracalar's, though she argues strongly for the conservative subtexts of the djinn-themed films. In *Horror and Religion in Cinema: The Analysis of the Djinn Figure in Post-2000 American and Turkish Horror Films* (2016), Şimşek examines the use of the djinn figure in American and Turkish horror films in the context of semiotics. She argues that while American djinn-themed horror films accentuate the orientalist perspectives of American culture towards the East, their Turkish equivalents pursue the aim of popularising conservatism and strengthening religious beliefs through the use of the djinn figure.[30] In her reading of six Turkish horror films released between 2004 and 2011, Şimşek also acknowledges that women are depicted as the main site of djinn possession, to the extent that women become conceptualised as 'the other' in the films.[31]

In cultures that, like Turkey, are predominantly Islamic, djinn beliefs largely derive from Arabic culture and Islamic demonology. However, the influence of pre-Islamic Shamanistic tradition persists in the types of the djinns, the methods of protection against them and in the vessel of communication with the djinns that is named as *cinci hoca* (the master of djinns) in Turkey.[32] Literary and cinematic narratives in Turkey thus show as many variations in representation as the diverse folktales of the region.

---

[27] Kaya Özkaracalar, 'İslami korku filmlerinin ideolojik/siyasi topoğrafyası'.

[28] Zeynep Şahintürk, 'Djinn in the Machine: Technology and Islam in Turkish Horror Film', in Linnie Blake and Xavier Aldana Reyes (eds), *Digital Horror: Haunted Technologies, Network Panic and the Found Footage Phenomenon* (London and New York: I. B. Tauris, 2016), pp. 95–106 (p. 96).

[29] Savaş Arslan, *Cinema in Turkey: A New Critical History* (New York: Oxford University Press, 2011), p. 258.

[30] Gizem Şimşek, *Sinemada Korku ve Din: 2000 Sonrası Amerikan ve Türk Filmlerinde Cin Unsurunun Çözümlenmesi* [Horror and Religion in Cinema: The Analysis of the Djinn Figure in post-2000 American and Turkish Horror Films] (İstanbul: Pales Yayınları, 2016), p. 273; my translation.

[31] Şimşek, *Sinemada Korku ve Din*, p. 219.

[32] Thierry Zarcone, 'Shamanism in Turkey: Bards, Masters of the Djinns and Healers', in Thierry Zircon and Angela Hobart (eds), *Shamanism and Islam: Sufism, Healing Rituals and Spirits in the Muslim World*. (London; New York: I. B. Taurus, 2013), pp. 169–201 (pp. 178–9).

Although the popularity of the Islamic Gothic horror sub-genre is closely linked with the rise of conservative politics in the post-millennium in Turkey, both Islamic and Shamanistic roots of the djinn belief, and, more importantly, the impact of cultural globalisation – in the form of mobilisation of Gothic tropes through printed and visual media – should be taken into consideration when investigating any literary and cinematic narrative. Such a multi-layered approach is crucial in revealing the dichotomous nature of the ideological subtexts of Islamic Gothic horror texts, both in literature and in cinema.

Indeed, the conservative subtexts observed in many Turkish examples of the sub-genre are almost identical to the one established most effectively in *al-Inss wa-l-jinn*. Women who are considered to be modern, marginal or non-religious – and, as such, dangerous for the conservative patriarchal society in which they live – are haunted by a malevolent djinn (who is usually embodied as a male figure) and rescued by other patriarchal authorities (such as Imams, fathers, husbands and so on) who receive religious aid in the form of recitation from the Qur'an to exorcise or expel the djinn. Once the djinn is expelled, the woman returns to mainstream society as a religious or obedient subject, thus restoring normality. These narratives highlight messages about the importance of a moral and pious way of life, mobilising a strong faith in Allah and recitations from the Qur'an to fight against the djinn possessions. Since such practices are strictly forbidden in the Qur'an, they refuse to exalt sorcery, magic and mediumship in the name of Islam. Therefore, the characters' appeals to these practices in the event of a djinn possession do not solve anything; instead they worsen the haunting by compounding the deterioration of the physical and mental state of the haunted female character.

The earliest example of this conservative pattern that I have identified is Orhan Yıldırım's debut novel, *Ecinni: Aykırı Dünyayla İlişkiler* (*Djinni: Relations with the Other World*, 2003). This relatively unknown novel is not only the precursor to Islamic Gothic horror in Turkey but also the first djinn-themed narrative to contain the motif of 'rape by the djinn'. Yıldırım tells the tragic love story of a young couple: Arif, an agricultural engineer, and Zühal, a simple girl living in the village. Unfortunately, Arif is employed by Zühal's father and thus treats her like a sister while Zühal falls into despair thinking that her love is unreciprocated. The plot unfolds when Zühal suddenly disappears and later is found half-naked in a haunted house. It is revealed that Zühal is haunted by djinns and has been raped on several occasions by djinns disguised as Arif. Throughout the novel, Arif, his friend Dursun and the mentally impaired Imam of the village try to rescue Zühal from the djinns with the help of recitations from the Qur'an.

The rural setting of *Ecinni* reflects the characteristics of conservatism in Turkey that is borne out in patriarchal hierarchy, family ties and communal lifestyle. Veli Uğur considers this choice of setting as imitative of the American Gothic tradition.[33] Indeed, one of the crucial components of the American Gothic is its focus on the landscape. Bernice M. Murphy suggests that the 'negative depictions of the countryside and its inhabitants' are more substantial in American Gothic narratives than any in other national tradition.[34] I would adapt Uğur's argument to claim that the choice of setting establishes a conservative background against which Gothic conventions might effectively serve their purpose, particularly with regard to ideology and the representation of women. This is because the countryside represents the heart of Turkish conservatism and its strong connection to traditional Islamic values, which construct women as submissive to men and expect them to be meek and moral in a religious context. Çarkoğlu and Kalaycıoğlu comment on women's centrality to religious conservatism and the patriarchal structure in Turkey as follows:

> the Turkish Sunni Muslim tradition critically shapes its social conservatism around the status and position of women in society, whereby honor and integrity of the family is defined through the women in the family. Hence, women become a subject of protection and control, and are to be protected from the encroachment of strangers, in particular unrelated men, in the eyes of the tradition bound in Turkey.[35]

As they explain, conservatism in Turkey feeds on the patriarchal order. Islamic dogmas on gender inequality endorse traditional roles of women as housewives and child bearers while men remain as breadwinners and heads of households. Women are considered to be in need of provision and protection within the home, and subjected to perpetual surveillance from outside. How they are perceived by the patriarchal order shapes the ways in which they should and should not behave in private and public spheres alike.

The same expectation can be found in *Ecinni*, too. The male characters of the novel are presented as the protectors and saviours of women and the village. The comments that Arif makes while he observes little girls playing in

---

[33] Veli Uğur, *1980 Sonrası Türkiye'de Popüler Roman* [Popular Fiction in Turkey After 1980] (İstanbul: Koç Üniversitesi Yayınları, 2013), p. 240.
[34] Bernice M. Murphy, *The Rural Gothic in American Popular Culture: Backwoods Terror and Horror in the Wilderness* (Basingstoke: Palgrave Macmillan, 2013), p. 9.
[35] Çarkoğlu and Kalaycıoğlu, *The Rising Tide of Conservatism in Turkey*, p. 56.

the field beneath a rainbow seem to confirm such traditional perceptions of gender: 'The superiority of men was indisputable in this region. The authority belonged to men. Even the right to speak belonged to men. Thus, although superstitious, girls would like to cross under the rainbow to become men.'[36] Such a portrayal of traditional gender roles in the countryside evokes a stereotypical perception of women as inferior, insufficient and incomplete.

Conveniently, Zühal's mother and her friend Serap are both portrayed as moral and highly domestic characters. In fact, Arif's first impression of Zühal's mother perfectly fits the stereotype of 'good women wearing hijabs' that is often found in Islamic Gothic: 'once the door opened I came across a radiant face . . . I shook hands with the cherub-like woman in a hijab whom I was passing by. Following Turkish customs, I instantly kissed her hand.'[37] Arif associates the woman in the hijab with divine light and shows his respect by coding her as 'good' along the lines of traditional values. In contrast, Arif establishes Zühal's characterisation only through her beauty and her sexual attributes. This heterosexual male gaze that pervades *Ecinni* and other works of Islamic Gothic in Turkey contextualises the sub-genre as an example of what Western critics have sometimes called the male Gothic. Such narratives objectify the female body to the point of perversity, a characteristic that highlights the associations of male Gothic with pornography.[38] Anne Williams astutely points out that the role of the woman in male Gothic narratives 'is inseparable from her identity as a sexual being, either as subject or object', and that she is thus considered a sexual other.[39]

During their first encounter in the haunted house, Arif feels enchanted by Zühal's unmatched beauty and sexualises her in an erotic manner: 'Saying "Oh my God!" to myself, I was astonished. She had deep blue eyes, wavy hair. Her rain-drenched breasts were not fitting into her shirt, the nipples of her full breasts were obvious.'[40] Here, Zühal's appearance is represented as being beyond and completely outside of the traditional Islamic norms of the village. As Nilüfer Göle suggests, Islamist ideology regulates the female body and sexuality in Muslim societies according to the boundaries of religious doctrines in order to sustain the social order: 'Social morality is defined by religious rules, and it operates mainly upon the regulation of women's

---

[36] Orhan Yıldırım, *Ecinni: Aykırı Dünyayla İlişkiler* [*Djinni: Relations with the Other World*] (İstanbul: IQ Yayıncılık, 2003), p. 123; my translation.
[37] Yıldırım, *Ecinni*, p. 16; my translation.
[38] Anne Williams, *Art of Darkness: A Poetics of Gothic* (Chicago: University of Chicago Press, 1995), p. 105.
[39] Williams, *Art of Darkness*, p. 105.   [40] Yıldırım, *Ecinni*, p. 11; my translation.

sexuality. The preservation of honour – that is, loyalty to moral codes in relation to women's sexuality – is a necessary condition of the social order.'[41] Women's sexuality, for Göle, is the antithesis of societies ruled by religion and serves as a locus of control for the maintenance of social order. Fatima Mernissi makes a similar point when she claims that women are 'the embodiment of destruction, the symbol of disorder' in Islam: 'The woman is *fitna*, the uncontrollable, a living representative of the dangers of sexuality and its rampant disruptive potential.'[42] Zühal is thus the antithesis of the woman in the hijab and she is immediately coded as the sexual other in the conservative imagination.

As Barbara Creed points out, 'a strong sense of the vulnerability of the body and its susceptibility to possession' and 'the graphic detailed representation of bodily destruction' are central to narratives about female subjects being possessed by the devil.[43] The main reason for Zühal's possession in *Ecinni*, however, is not only her physical vulnerability but her spiritual weaknesses, too. Zühal's religious faith is not strong enough to fight against the possession of the djinns. Arif comments on this after Zühal's first attempt at suicide: 'As a matter of fact, humans are the most precious and wisest of the living creatures. Then, why are we afraid of these entities [the djinns]? The only thing we have to do is to have will power and faith. Unfortunately, Zühal couldn't do this. She couldn't overcome her fear, control herself, be faithful and determined.'[44] In addition to her spiritual weakness, Zühal also nurtures a sexual attraction to Arif. Having been found in the haunted house for the first time in a state of trance, Zühal explains to Arif that she had sex with a djinn, thinking that it was him.[45] From this moment onwards in the novel, she is identified with both sexual and supernatural danger.

Zühal's bodily destruction is represented through her being raped by the djinns on numerous occasions. Drawing on Julia Kristeva's notion of the abject, Creed defines the possessed body as 'a figure of abjection in that the boundary between self and other has been transgressed'.[46] Likewise, Zühal's body becomes abjected where the border between the djinn realm and our own world is traversed. This is why she is called *ecinni* (djinni,

---

[41] Nilüfer Göle, *The Forbidden Modern: Civilization and Veiling* (Ann Arbor, MI: University of Michigan Press, 1996), pp. 52–3.
[42] Fatima Mernissi, *Beyond the Veil: Male–Female Dynamics in Muslim Society* (London: Al Saqi Books, 1985), p. 44.
[43] Barbara Creed, *The Monstrous Feminine: Film, Feminism, Psychoanalysis* (London: Routledge, 1993), p. 31.
[44] Yıldırım, *Ecinni*, p. 183; my translation. [45] Yıldırım, *Ecinni*, p. 74; my translation.
[46] Creed, *The Monstrous Feminine*, p. 32.

a person who becomes a part of the djinns' realm through possession) by the villagers. She is no longer fully human. She is the other, the one who belongs to the djinns. Tracing the trend back to Matthew Gregory Lewis's *The Monk* (1796), Williams argues that a woman's virtue is established as her most valuable asset in male Gothic narratives, and that, by having it destroyed because of her curious, inconstant, disobedient or weak 'female nature', she is blamed and 'punished as a fallen woman'.[47] According to a similar cultural logic, the epithet of *ecinni* is a representation of Zühal's fallen state.

The novel also concentrates on the construction of a conservative sentiment by suggesting that the only means of overcoming a djinn haunting are recitations from the Qur'an and a strong system of religious belief. However, a clear distinction in *Ecinni* is made between Qur'anic exorcism and sorcery through the characterisation of Deli Hafiz, the previous Imam of the village who has become mentally impaired after years of practising exorcism. Deli Hafiz's first exorcism ritual with Zühal is undertaken only with recitations from the Qur'an. Arif expresses his observations about Deli Hafiz in the aftermath of the ritual:

> Deli Hafiz was a genuinely devout person, away from evil thoughts, never involved with affairs such as amulets, magic, witchcraft, mediumship. He knew that in his own sacred book and faith, such affairs were superstitions. In order to destroy the djinns, he used the Holy Qur'an, and prayed and beseeched Allah from his heart with deep sincerity. He wrote verses about the djinns from the Qur'an and burnt them. In the eyes of the villagers, he was a true friend of Allah.[48]

Arif sees Deli Hafiz as a pious Muslim and distinguishes his efforts in expelling the djinns from the practices that are forbidden by Islam. Later, Deli Hafiz too warns Arif and Zühal against such forbidden practices: 'I have nothing to do with magic, sorcery, and witchcraft; don't believe those who are called the master of djinns, there is no place for such things in our religion ... I only take shelter in Allah's profundity.'[49] Here, he confirms that the only way in which to defeat and be permanently protected from the djinns is to embrace the Islamic faith.

Although the representation of the exorcism is accompanied by some of the most iconic signs and symbols of Islam, the appearance of the motif of the serpent demonstrates the author's adoption of Western Gothic motifs in an Islamic context. During the exorcism of Zühal, Arif says: 'The djinn came out

---

[47] Williams, *Art of Darkness*, p. 105. [48] Yıldırım, *Ecinni*, p. 136; my translation.
[49] Yıldırım, *Ecinni*, p. 230; my translation.

of Zühal's mouth like fog. It became a serpent on the floor and got away down a hole.'⁵⁰ Referring to the myth of Original Sin as it is described in the biblical Book of Genesis, Creed describes the serpent as a 'Christian symbol of woman's disobedience, unbridled sexual appetite and treachery'.⁵¹ While, in the Qur'an, the story of humankind's original transgression is told in a manner that is similar to that in the Bible, the verses do not explicitly state that Satan was disguised as a serpent. As Amira El-Zein in *Islam, Arabs, and Intelligent World of the Jinn* (2009) explains, the word 'serpent' was not originally included in the Quran: 'Qur'anic commentaries as well as *the Tales of the Prophets* invented a mythology of the serpent that is simply nonexistent in the Holy Book.'⁵² As El-Zein continues, popular commentary borrowed the serpent myth from 'ancient Near-Eastern beliefs, and mostly from oral Jewish accounts circulating in the Arabian Peninsula' during the spread of Islam in the region.⁵³ Moreover, according to the Quran, after Satan's interference, Adam and Eve were not cursed by God, but remained, instead, in a state of innocence and purity. In the context of *Ecinni*, this suggests that Zühal's evil transgressions are not pre-conditioned by an original sin. El-Zein also notes that djinns are frequently represented as being embodied as serpents in Islamic tradition.⁵⁴ The motif of the serpent in *Ecinni* thus refers to the djinn possession but evokes the same sexual connotations that Creed has identified in the biblical narrative, and, as a consequence, Zühal emerges as a figure of disobedience, treachery and unbridled sexual desire.

In the aftermath of the exorcism, when Deli Hafiz talks to Zühal about why this happened to her, Arif observes: 'He said to her that her faith was weak, and thus the djinns haunted her and also because of her desires and fancies as a beautiful girl.'⁵⁵ If the djinns possessed Zühal because of her sexual desire for Arif, the same desires are exorcised with the djinns in the form of the serpent. When Arif observes Zühal, who is listening to Deli Hafiz, he says that she had 'an exhausted, innocent and shy attitude'.⁵⁶ Arif's description of Zühal as innocent and shy only reinforces the fact that she is now free of her libidinous nature. Creed suggests that 'one of the major boundaries traversed' in possession narratives 'is that between innocence and corruption, purity and impurity'.⁵⁷ The djinn possession in *Ecinni* causes Zühal to mutate

---

⁵⁰ Yıldırım, *Ecinni*, p. 251; my translation. ⁵¹ Creed, *The Monstrous Feminine*, p. 33.
⁵² Amira El-Zein, *Islam, Arabs, and Intelligent World of the Jinn* (New York: Syracuse University Press, 2009), p. 99.
⁵³ Amira El-Zein, *Islam, Arabs, and Intelligent World of the Jinn*, p. 99.
⁵⁴ Amira El-Zein, *Islam, Arabs, and Intelligent World of the Jinn*, p. 99.
⁵⁵ Yıldırım, *Ecinni*, p. 251; my translation. ⁵⁶ Yıldırım, *Ecinni*, p. 251; my translation.
⁵⁷ Creed, *The Monstrous Feminine*, p. 32.

from innocence to corruption and from purity to impurity, transgressive transitions that also reveal her sexual desires as a young woman. Through the exorcism, Zühal as abject body is purified and made respectable or 'proper' for the conservative society in which she lives. Although, at the end of the novel, she commits suicide, leaving a note for Arif saying that, since she is now marked for life as *ecinni*, she does not deserve him, the exorcism of Zühal, together with the fact that her saviours are male characters, follows the pattern of traditional exorcism narratives. Zühal is victimised and becomes the monster and the damsel in distress interchangeably throughout the story, yet is eventually rescued by the Imam and Arif. In doing so, the Imam dispels and suppresses Zühal's sexuality and restores her to the crushing normality of everyday social existence.

The conservative ideological subtext of *Ecinni* has been developed further in such novels by Şafak Güçlü as *Lohusa: Ümmü Sübyan* (*Postpartum: The Mother of Infants*, 2014) and *Siccîn: Amel Defteri* (*Siccîn: The Book of Deeds*, 2015), and replicated in films including *Büyü* (*Dark Spells*, dir. Orhan Oğuz, 2004); *Semum* (dir. Hasan Karacadağ, 2008); *D@bbe: Bir Cin Vakası* (*D@bbe: A Djinn Accident*, dir. Hasan Karacadag, 2012); *Şeytan-ı Racim* (*The Cursed Satan*, dir. Arkın Aktaç, 2013); and *D@bbe: Cin Çarpması* (*D@bbe: Curse of the Jinn*, dir. Hasan Karacadag, 2013). In fact, according to Şimşek, out of sixteen djinn-themed films released between 2004 and 2015, twelve had female protagonists.[58] Ten of these women enjoyed modernised lifestyles and eight of the ten were not portrayed as religious people. In addition, six of these women had no children, rendering their characterisation relatively independent and thus incompatible with the traditional roles of women in a patriarchal society.[59] This brief analysis demonstrates that Islamic Gothic in Turkey is of a distinct type. As Williams points out, male Gothic 'focus[es] on female suffering, positioning the audience as voyeurs who, though sympathetic, may take pleasure in female victimisation'.[60] By actively appropriating the djinn as a tool of conservative propaganda, Islamic Gothic in Turkey, particularly in cinema, frequently feeds on the victimisation of women who are independent, modern and secular.

Nevertheless, such a predominance of conservative Turkish horror texts should not undermine the multi-layered approach that, as I argued earlier, is crucial for investigating the dichotomous nature of the ideological subtexts of

---

[58] Gizem Şimşek, *Türk Korku Sineması Kronolojisi 1914–2015* [The Chronology of Turkish Horror Cinema 1914–2015] (İstanbul: Pales Yayınları, 2017), p. 217.

[59] Şimşek, *Türk Korku Sineması Kronolojisi 1914–2015*, p. 217.

[60] Williams, *Art of Darkness*, p. 104.

Islamic Gothic in Turkey and elsewhere in the Middle East. Though limited, there are cinematic examples of the sub-genre that use the djinn figure in different ways, and which offer a counter-narrative to the conservative subtexts of Islamic Gothic. This is best exemplified in the films of the director Alper Mestçi, which usually follow male protagonists and offer a much more versatile interpretation of the djinn figure and its ideological import than what is figured in other Turkish films. His debut feature film *Musallat* (*Haunted*, 2004) is particularly noteworthy in this regard. The film follows a young man named Suat who leaves behind his family and young bride in the village and goes to work abroad in Berlin. Soon thereafter, he is troubled by nightmares and terrifying visions that are revealed to be hauntings of a djinn who is in love with his young bride. Once again, the rape motif is used as the bride dies giving birth to the djinn's baby and everyone, including the Imam who tries to help Suat, incurs the wrath of the djinn. The film differs from other examples, however, in that it victimises all characters, especially the male protagonist Suat; recitations from the Qur'an, moreover, do not restore the social normality that the djinn disrupts. In *Musallat*, Mestçi does not perpetuate the conservative conventions of Islamic Gothic and perhaps even offers a new perspective to the deep-seated anxieties of Turkish workers in Germany.

This is to say that the djinn figure in this film primarily functions as the manifestation of a migrant worker's experiences of being separated from his homeland and loved ones, and his sense of extreme cultural dislocation in an unfamiliar country. This is, indeed, a very familiar scenario for Turkish audiences. Since the 1960s, thousands of Turkish citizens have migrated to Germany and worked to send money back to their families at home. By juxtaposing the Turkish countryside with a Western metropolis such as Berlin, Mestçi in *Musallat* offers a different interpretation of a Gothic setting. Although the countryside figures in the film as traditional, superstitious and perhaps even barbaric – especially in the scene where women of the village stab the seemingly evil djinn baby in the heart – Berlin is also portrayed as a Gothic unknown that mainly serves to highlight Suat's depressive loneliness, his inexperience and the difficulties that he encounters in the process of social adjustment. Mestçi's choice to gothicise both cultural settings is therefore not undertaken out of the need to make ideological references to religious differences or to portray a Manichean struggle between Orthodox Islam and the secular West. Rather, it is to emphasise his protagonist's inner psychology and his anxieties as an exile, a migrant and an expatriate. This suggests an approach that does not work to justify and defend the status quo so much as to articulate cutting social critique – an approach that, as this chapter has argued, is rarely to be found in Islamic Gothic and horror texts in Turkey.

Conclusion

The revival of the Gothic mode in the age of globalisation has been the driving force of its various formulations in Islamic cultures. In this chapter, I have presented the emergence and development of Islamic Gothic in the Middle East, paying particular attention to Iran, Egypt and Turkey. Following a survey of early efforts to establish national Gothic traditions in the twentieth century, I have outlined the most prominent conventions and tropes of the sub-genre, such as the malevolent *djinn*, and explored the ways in which they have been used to develop a counter-narrative for both progressive and conservative politics. The parallels between the rise of Islamist ideology and Islamic Gothic in Turkey have been at the core of my arguments and they have shaped my investigation of literary and cinematic texts. By adhering to the zeitgeist of the country in the post-millennium, Islamic Gothic in Turkey has already exhausted the *djinn* metaphor, and its conservative implications have become predictable and often misogynistic. Female characters who subvert their usual portrayal as the victims of patriarchy and Islamic dogmas, who refuse the traditional gender roles that are dictated by the status quo and who emerge victorious in their fight against malevolent *djinns* have not yet been imagined in Islamic Gothic, neither in Turkey nor in the Middle East. And yet, they might be just what the sub-genre urgently needs for the Gothic mode to stimulate social change in the region.

3.20

Global Gothic 2: East Asian Gothic

DANIEL MARTIN

Defining East Asian Gothic

The critical category of 'Asian Horror' has drawn a considerable amount of attention from global audiences, evoking varied imagery from numerous national cinemas and literatures. Yet for all the success of Asian Horror – especially as a cinematic genre – it is a term that has been woefully ill-defined. Indeed, given that frightful films from Japan, Hong Kong, South Korea, Thailand, Mainland China and Vietnam reached international viewers in different ways and at different times, the notion of 'Asian Horror' encompasses so many films across decades of global media distribution that it holds little value as a meaningful collective category.

One of the persistent hurdles facing critics and academics attempting to define and redefine the boundaries of the horror genre in the context of East Asian cinema is the propensity to rely almost entirely on Western conceptions. The history and narrative morphology of the Hollywood and European horror film, and of the English-language horror novel, is an ongoing study, with many well-established rules and boundaries. The most prominent examples of 'horror' in Japan, South Korea and Hong Kong, however, pose challenges to these assumptions, largely due to different taste formations among audiences and a high degree of genre hybridity within the films themselves. The result is tonally diverse stories of death and murder, fear and abuse, supernatural rebirth and bloody revenge. Indeed, many 'horror' films from East Asia are simply not 'horrors' at all: they are romantic melodramas, martial arts comedies, police procedurals or psychological thrillers.

This is why 'Gothic' as a collective category becomes immensely more appropriate as a way to analyse these films and to begin to make observations about the stories, tones, themes and techniques that suggest some meaningful similarities in these otherwise distinct national cinemas. Though the meaning of the Gothic as a critical concept is itself widely contested and perpetually debated, the key arguments in Gothic studies cohere around one assumption: the Gothic is a tone, an atmosphere, a mode, a style. It is not as rigidly policed as a genre. The Gothic mode, then, becomes a more inclusive way to addend films (and other media narratives) from East Asia to the global canon of supernatural stories.

This chapter considers, broadly, the spooky and the supernatural in the cinemas of Japan, South Korea and Hong Kong, addressing the trends and themes of a historically and generically wide range of films in order to suggest ways in which presumptions about the fundamentals of Gothic may need to be reconfigured in the East Asian context. Though the focus of the chapter is largely on live-action films, acknowledgement will be made of important Gothic trends in literature, animation, comic books and video games. The discussion that follows explores several key facets of the East Asian Gothic mode: generic hybridity; the role of mythology, superstition and religion in crafting imaginative narratives; morality and audience sympathy; and, importantly, the historical moments at which these films first captured the attention of Western consumers and critics.

The central thread uniting the analysis of three distinct national cinemas concerns the narrative and thematic meaning of the figure of the ghost. How are local audiences expected and invited to respond to these avatars of the deceased? What do they reflect of contemporary society, and how do they comment on the past? The ghost in many of these films is not only an object of fear (indeed, it is frequently not an object of fear *at all*), but also, with varying frequency, a lover, or a hero, or a subject of profound pity and sadness. The following sections examine the evolving figure of the ghost across more than a century of cinema and storytelling in three key case studies: Japan, South Korea and Hong Kong.

Theorising an East Asian Gothic

In considering how a variety of narratives from East Asia could be understood in terms of Gothic theory, it is important to acknowledge the potential limitations of such an undertaking. In Katarzyna Ancuta's study of Gothic literature in Asia, she identifies the risk of 'linguistic colonization' in applying concepts derived from Western traditions to other cultures and contexts.[1]

---

[1] Katarzyna Ancuta, 'Asian Gothic', in David Punter (ed.), *A New Companion to the Gothic* (Chichester: Wiley-Blackwell, 2012), pp. 428–41.

Indeed, to understand how East Asian cinema exhibits Gothic characteristics also requires an acceptance of how these narratives reshape notions of Gothic traditions. Likewise, it becomes quickly apparent that there is simply no such thing as an 'Asian Gothic' mode; there are, rather, Asian Gothics, in the plural, since the collection of cultures is too diverse to constitute a homogenous category.[2]

Misha Kavka argues that Gothic cinema is, similarly, a meaningless category; while the horror film exists as a well-defined genre, the Gothic film refers instead to a wide range of films that often only faintly share certain characteristics.[3] This is certainly the case in the examples that will follow: the key paradigms of the Gothic mode in Japan, South Korea and Hong Kong vary and differ wildly not just from Western conceptions of the Gothic, but also from each other. Laura Hubner's valuable work on the connections between Gothic and fairy tales notes that Gothic is primarily defined by 'tone and atmosphere, generated by film aesthetics, style, mise-en-scène and narrative techniques', yet the East Asian Gothic mode features so much deviance that it necessitates a critical recalibration.[4]

An important aspect of this chapter will be to consider the ways in which East Asian Gothic narratives have reached Western audiences, and how the circumstances of distribution and marketing have profoundly affected reception. One of the most influential moments of the proliferation of East Asian Gothic cinema in the UK and United States occurred just after the turn of the century, thanks to a cynically brilliant branding campaign orchestrated by the British distributors, Tartan Films. Following the unexpectedly positive reception of Hideo Nakata's *Ring* (1998) on its release in UK cinemas in 2000, Tartan created a new sub-label, 'Asia Extreme', as a way of capitalising on a growing trend for violent and/or sexual films from Japan, Hong Kong and South Korea. The marketing of the Asia Extreme titles was designed to provoke controversy, and the dominant imagery of the label emphasised eroticism and violence in a manner that drew upon harmful Orientalist perceptions of Asia as excessive and indecent.[5] The Asia Extreme brand

---

[2] As Ancuta notes, given the vast multiculturalism of Asia, from its four billion inhabitants to its diasporas, any attempt at creating a unified category is 'asking for trouble'. See Ancuta, 'Asian Gothic', p. 428.
[3] Misha Kavka, 'The Gothic on Screen', in Jerrold E. Hogle (ed.), *The Cambridge Companion to Gothic Fiction* (Cambridge: Cambridge University Press, 2001), pp. 209–28.
[4] Laura Hubner, *Fairytale and Gothic Horror: Uncanny Transformations in Film* (London: Palgrave Macmillan, 2018), p. 3.
[5] For a more detailed discussion of the Asia Extreme phenomenon, see Daniel Martin, *Extreme Asia: The Rise of Cult Cinema from the Far East* (Edinburgh: Edinburgh University Press, 2015).

also proved influential in the way it reconceived genre. While early releases such as *Audition* (dir. Takashi Miike, Japan, 1999), *Dark Water* (dir. Hideo Nakata, Japan, 2002) and *A Tale of Two Sisters* (dir. Kim Jee-woon, South Korea, 2003) were clearly examples of the horror genre, many of the label's other high-profile films – *Bad Guy* (dir. Kim Ki-duk, South Korea, 2001), *A Snake of June* (dir. Shinya Tsukamoto, Japan, 2002), *Oldboy* (dir. Park Chan-wook, South Korea, 2003), *Battle Royale* (dir. Kinji Fukasaku, Japan, 2000), *Infernal Affairs* (dir. Andrew Lau and Alan Mak, Hong Kong, 2002) – fell outside this category.[6] By unifying such disparate films under the evocative banner of 'extreme' cinema, Tartan created a new canon of works that had a significant impact in the West – albeit with deeply problematic consequences, not least of which was the misrepresentation of how 'typical' these films were of their respective domestic cinemas. Eliding generic and national borders between films, the Asia Extreme brand inadvertently served to introduce (a portion of) the diversity of East Asian Gothic to Western audiences. Many of the films released this way are key examples of Gothic traditions in Korean, Hong Kong and Japanese cinema.

Indeed, while East Asian Gothic largely defies any attempt to establish general, shared characteristics, one point of affirming unity across these diverse East Asian and global Gothics can be found in what has been identified as a core theme, namely 'the uncanny return of something which has been expelled'.[7] From Japanese techno-Gothic revenge fantasies, Hong Kong's slapstick Gothic romance/kung-fu films, or South Korea's tear-jerking Gothic melodrama horror-tragedies, the notion of unforgettable and unforgivable crimes is core. History cannot be suppressed; those wronged will have their revenge.

---

[6] A note on language and naming conventions: the convention in many East Asian countries is to put the surname first, the given name second. However, as various filmmakers from Japan, Korea and Hong Kong have become, at different times, known in the West, differing conventions have emerged. This chapter places the given name first and family name second for all Japanese directors, as this is how many of them are best known to English-speaking audiences (e.g. Akira Kurosawa, Hayao Miyazaki). In the case of Korean names, possibly due to the relatively later arrival of Korean cinema in the West, many filmmakers became known with their name order preserved: Park is the surname; Chan-wook is the given name. This chapter therefore renders all Korean names in the surname-first order. In the case of Hong Kong, a further complication is that the vast majority of filmmakers have English as well as Chinese-language given names. All Hong Kong directors will be listed with their given name first and their surname second.

[7] Kavka, 'The Gothic on Screen', p. 211.

Japanese Gothic Cinema

While Gothic narratives in Japan long predate the rise of cinema, with a rich and vast folklore of ghosts (*yurei* and *onryō*) and monsters (*yokai*) expressed in oral traditions, literature and on stage, film has been the primary medium through which stories and images of the Japanese supernatural have reached global audiences. The Silver Lion Award given to *Ugetsu Monogatari* (dir. Kenji Mizoguchi, 1953) at the 1953 Venice Film Festival marked a watershed moment in the recognition of the Japanese Gothic; this tale of a potter who almost falls prey to a seductive ghost was widely admired, and was one of the first Japanese films to be commercially released in the USA. Colette Balmain notes that *Ugetsu Monogatari* instigated an 'Edo-Gothic' cycle of films in the domestic market: period tales of morality, love and desire that would prove dominant in Japan for most of the subsequent two decades.[8]

Yet while *Ugetsu Monogatari* featured supernatural events and a dangerous encounter with a ghost, it was understood in the West less as a horror film and more as a romantic drama, or even a humanist fable. It would not be until the release of the spectral anthology film *Kwaidan* (dir. Masaki Kobayashi) and its Special Jury Prize at the 1965 Cannes Film Festival that worldwide audiences encountered a 'pure' example of Japanese horror: a film of frightful spirits, designed to elicit fear and discomfort (Fig. 20.1). Perhaps the most interesting 'chapter' of the film, 'The Black Hair', expresses an important facet of the Japanese Gothic, and its recurring mythology around the encounter between humans and the undead. This segment, with long, silent sequences and very little dialogue, tells the story of an ambitious swordsman who abandons his wife in search of a more advantageous union. Regretting his callous decision, he apologetically returns, years later, to his first wife; after a tender reconciliation is revealed to be an illusion, the swordsman realises that his wife is actually long-dead, and is attacked by the remaining locks of her eponymous hair. 'The Black Hair' demonstrates that ghostly spirits in Japanese Gothic cinema are not always personified: immaterial curses or haunted places can cause just as much danger.

Kwaidan also draws attention to another important aspect of Japanese Gothic – and, arguably, much of East Asian Gothic, too: its multicultural influences. The difficulty in making definitive, sweeping proclamations about any one culture's Gothic mode comes in part from a lack of cultural purity in the films. *Kwaidan*, for example, was adapted from a hugely influential

---

[8] Colette Balmain, *Introduction to the Japanese Horror Film* (Edinburgh: Edinburgh University Press, 2008), p. 50.

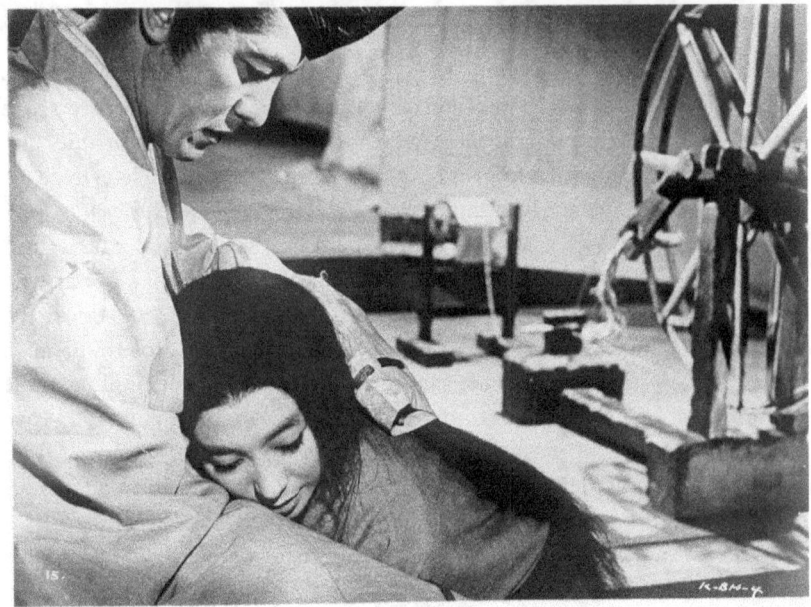

KWAIDAN in Eastmancolor
Toho International Cannes Film Festival Special Jury Prize Winner
Released by CONTINENTAL, a division of Walter Reade-Sterling, Inc.

Fig.20.1: Rentaro Mikuni is held by Michiyo Aratama in scene from the film *Kwaidan*, 1964. (Photo by Toho/Getty Images).

collection of short stories, *Kwaidan: Stories and Studies of Strange Things*, written by a Greek-Irish immigrant to Japan, Lafcadio Hearn, in 1904. Indeed, while Hearn's work is widely celebrated, it was the result of his obsessive pleasure in the unfamiliarity of Japan's ghost stories, a version of the country that was 'as much the offspring of his own imagination as it was reflective of a historical, geographical reality'.[9] The influence of foreign perspectives on Japan's own construction of its historical Gothic mythology is not the only manner of cultural appropriation at work. In fact, Japan's own multimedia Gothic productions often display significant affinity for Western traditions.[10] The extremely popular video game series *Resident Evil*

---

[9] Peter Bernard, 'Hearn, Lafcadio [Koizumi, Yakumo] [1850–1904]', in Salvador Murguía (ed.), *The Encyclopedia of Japanese Horror Films* (Lanham, Boulder, New York and London: Rowman and Littlefield, 2016), pp. 115–19.

[10] Jay McRoy, for instance, makes some persuasive arguments about the influence of Western cinema on Japanese directors such as Hideo Nakata and Takeshi Shimizu. See his *Nightmare Japan: Contemporary Japanese Horror Cinema* (Amsterdam and New York: Rodopi, 2008).

(1996–present) is one of Japan's most visible Gothic exports, yet the narrative is largely set in the USA and exhibits a nostalgic fondness for American cinema (most obviously George A. Romero's *Night of the Living Dead* series, 1968–2009) and a multitude of Americana. These 'survival horror' zombie games make inventive use of intrinsically non-Japanese Gothic spaces, from a cavernous midwestern mansion in the first game to an abandoned and infested police precinct in the second.

In addition to being multicultural in influence and origin, a significant proportion of Japanese Gothic cinema is multi-tonal, varying considerably in terms of genre and style. While the most common horror narratives of the 'Edo-Gothic' period featured vengeful ghosts and a grim fatalism – director Kaneto Shindo's *Onibaba* (1964) and *Kuroneko* (1968) are probably the best-known examples – many other Gothic films made before and since utilise the supernatural and the eerie in very different ways (Fig. 20.2). Japanese Gothic cinema, for instance, has an important erotic component: as Balmain notes, the 'erotic ghost story' is a 'sub-genre specific to Japan'. While Balmain's claim is not entirely accurate – Hong Kong has its own notorious tradition of semi-pornographic, or 'Category III', ghost films – the consistent production of erotic Gothic cinema does indicate the generic flexibility of the Japanese Gothic tradition. Likewise, Japanese films concerning ghosts, resurrection and the fragile barrier between the living and the dead are not necessarily frightful: benign, compassionate spectres have been the focus of such contemplative, quietly romantic films as *Yomigaeri* (dir. Akihiko Shiota, 2002) and *Journey to the Shore* (dir. Kiyoshi Kurosawa, 2015).

One of the earliest Gothic films produced in Japan is the short animation *Danemon Ban, The Monster Exterminator* (dir. Yoshitaro Kataoka, 1935). An action-comedy about a drunkard ghostbuster heroically defeating shapeshifting raccoons (*tanuki*), the film is nonetheless charged with genuine Gothic tension, especially while the protagonist is captured and shaved by mischievous magical creatures. Indeed, perhaps the most widely seen depiction of Japan's supernatural mythology of ghosts and goblins is Hayao Miyazaki's award-winning anime *Spirited Away* (2003), a warm family adventure film that nonetheless showcases a dizzying array of *yokai* in its Gothic, magical bathhouse.

For a Western audience, however, Japanese Gothic cinema is likely to be seen as a largely monolithic entity, consisting almost entirely of grim horror films about vengeful ghosts. The most influential and iconic Japanese horror is unquestionably Hideo Nakata's *Ring* (1998). The release of *Ring* in the UK was nothing short of sensational, the film attracting widespread critical

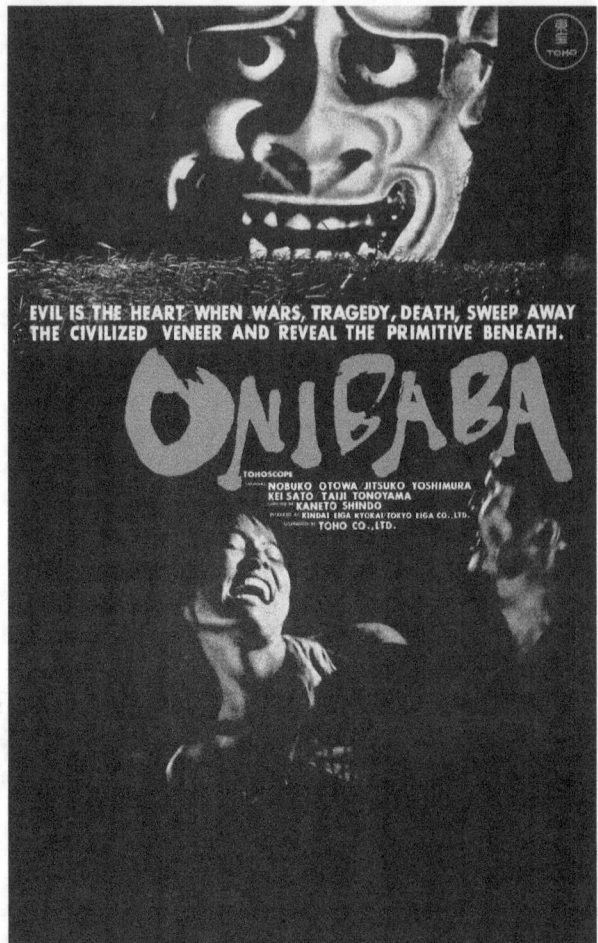

Fig.20.2: *Onibaba*, poster, US poster art, Jitsuko Yoshimura, 1964. (Photo by LMPC via Getty Images).

admiration and spurring a cycle of distribution for Asian cult and horror films in the West. The film generated sequels, prequels and remakes, and its malevolent female ghost, Sadako, rapidly became culturally iconic. *Ring* is perhaps the premier example of Japan's techno-Gothic cycle: the plot concerns a cursed videotape that serves to summon a vengeful ghost through television sets. The fusion of old-fashioned Gothic tropes (escapable curses and vengeful spirits) with new technology (particularly the notion of replicable media) was seen as particularly innovative, and the timing of *Ring*'s release in the UK, and its apparent place in an ongoing debate on the merits of Gothic horror, secured its historical significance.

The frightful ghost of *Ring*, Sadako, is an example of an *onryō* – a (typically female) spectre returning to the realm of the living to avenge a 'wrong' death, fulfilling what Ancuta calls a 'double role of victim and a vessel of evil'.[11] The central investigation that propels the narrative of *Ring* reveals that Sadako was a powerful psychic and the daughter of a disgraced prophet, assaulted and left to die at the bottom of a deep well. The film's protagonist assumes that her feelings of sympathy for Sadako's sad death, and the recovery of Sadako's remains, will appease the ghost; Sadako's vengeance, however, is unstoppable, and her victims are all entirely innocent of any specific wrongdoing against her. This is one key point at which the Japanese ghost deviates from her Korean and Chinese counterparts: Sadako seeks an indiscriminate vengeance, with a cruel desire to punish the living not by targeting individual wrongdoers, but by slaying anyone who encounters her curse. One of her potential victims, apparently fated to die by her will, is a small child. In precisely this way, then, Sadako is both victim and vessel of evil. The climax of *Ring* offers a bleak fatalism, implying that the curse of Sadako can only be avoided if it is passed on; her techno-haunting will spread like a virus, and can never be extinguished. Unlike the classical mode of Hollywood horror, in which heroes triumph and the monster is destroyed, Japanese Gothic narratives reach their peak or climax most often with an accommodation of evil and the restoration of balance.[12]

Ring can thus be understood as exemplary of traditions and tropes in Japanese Gothic storytelling. Yet *Ring* was also held up, on its initial release in the UK, as one of the most effective examples of a global Gothic style: the 'restrained tradition' of horror. *Ring* was offered to audiences at a time when the previously dominant Hollywood horror cycle of visually explicit postmodern slashers (exemplified by Wes Craven's *Scream*, 1996) was being supplanted by supposedly more 'sophisticated' American ghost stories such as *The Blair Witch Project* (dir. Daniel Myrick and Eduardo Sánchez, 1999) and *The Sixth Sense* (dir. M. Night Shyamalan, 1999). The critical vogue for these 'restrained' horrors meant that *Ring* found an immediately appreciative critical reception: it is a film without bloodshed or gore, relying instead on implied violence and carefully crafted jump-scares, in precisely the manner of Gothic cinema. Kavka has argued that if the audience is shown the object of

---

[11] Katarzyna Ancuta, 'Japanese Gothic', in William Hughes, David Punter and Andrew Smith (eds), *The Encyclopedia of The Gothic*, 2 vols (Chichester: Wiley-Blackwell, 2016), vol. 1, p. 371.
[12] Ancuta, 'Japanese Gothic', p. 372.

fear, it is a horror film; if the object of fear is hidden, it is Gothic.[13] *Ring* was therefore celebrated as a worthy addition to this supposedly prestigious canon of Gothic cinema, with critics praising the film, variously, for its 'subtle chills', as 'horror of a highly sophisticated nature' and as a work of 'true, unadulterated terror'.[14] Critics celebrated *Ring* for its serious, humourless tone, and compared the film to the literary works of the revered Gothic author M. R. James.[15] The British release of *Ring* therefore marked an important moment for East Asian Gothic: the acknowledgement of its place in the canon of global (if undeniably Western-dominated) literary and cinematic Gothic works.

The legacy of *Ring* was considerable: the film generated a sizable commercial franchise, encompassing video games, *manga* (comic books), and numerous sequels, prequels, TV series, remakes and spin-offs. The year 2016 saw the release in Japan of the eighth film, *Sadako vs. Kayako* (dir. Kōji Shiraishi), a crossover horror that pitted *Ring*'s enduring antagonist against the central ghost of the almost-as-popular *Ju-On* franchise, while the third in Hollywood's English-language remake series, *Rings* (dir. F. Javier Gutiérrez), was released in 2017.[16] Both series are set to continue.

The Japanese techno-Gothic cycle continued in films such as *Pulse* (dir. Kiyoshi Kurosawa, 2001), about ghosts invading the world of the living via the internet, and, as will be seen, the techno-Gothic mode spread to other Asian cinemas (perhaps most effectively in South Korean film). *Ring*'s director, Hideo Nakata, was responsible for another of the major Gothic hits of the post-*Ring* cycle: *Dark Water* (2002), a film that transforms the typical Japanese apartment complex into a deeply foreboding, haunted place, and which exemplifies Hubner's assertion that there is 'no happy ending in gothic' by depicting the protagonist effectively giving up her life and the chance to raise her beloved daughter in order to appease the tormented spirit of a dead child.[17]

---

[13] Kavka, 'The Gothic on Screen', p. 227.
[14] Anne Billson, 'Ring', *The Sunday Telegraph*, 20 August 2000 (Arts section), p. 8; Alan Jones, 'Ring', *Film Review*, September 2000, p. 32; Victoria Segal, 'The Fear Hunter', *The Times*, 12 August 2000 (Metro section), p. 24.
[15] For a more detailed discussion of the British critical reception of *Ring*, and the debates on horror and the Gothic that emerged among reviewers, see my article 'Japan's *Blair Witch*: Restraint, Maturity, and Generic Canons in the British Critical Reception of *Ring*', *Cinema Journal* 48:3 (May 2009): 35–51.
[16] The *Ju-On* franchise began with Takashi Shimizu's *Ju-On: The Grudge* (2002) and now includes three direct sequels, the aforementioned crossover spin-off, as well as two English-language Hollywood remakes.
[17] Hubner, *Fairytale and Gothic Horror*, p. 2.

Japanese Gothic film continues to attract international and domestic audiences and is only one facet of a multimedia Gothic enterprise that has existed in Japan for decades. The Japanese Gothic tradition, while multifaceted and frequently reimagined in creative ways, is nonetheless typically characterised by several key features: its vengeful, merciless, indiscriminately violent ghost; its willingness to incorporate facets of both modern and ancient life; and its tendency towards unsettling, unhappy narrative resolutions.

South Korean Gothic Cinema

As is the case with Japan, South Korea's Gothic traditions extend back throughout history, encompassing hundreds of years of mythology, arts and literature (indeed, the majority of this history predates the division of the country, and is therefore simply 'Korean' Gothic). South Korea's Gothic cinema likewise existed prior to the instigation of the horror genre in the country's film industry: films about ghosts and hauntings were made long before filmmakers began to adopt the visual language of horror and attempted to scare audiences. While *The Housemaid* (dir. Kim Ki-young, 1960) is widely regarded as the first South Korean horror film, there had been iconic films about righteous ghosts avenging their unfair deaths at least as early as the colonial-period silent film *The Story of Janghwa and Hongryeon* (dir. Kim Yeong-hwan, 1924).

The Story of Janghwa and Hongryeon exemplifies an important quality of Korea's depiction of ghosts. The film is based on a folk tale that has been adapted for film at least six times, most notably in Kim Jee-woon's radical reimagining, *A Tale of Two Sisters* (2003).[18] The basic story concerns two innocent girls, whose deaths are directly caused by the machinations of their wicked stepmother; the girls return as ghosts to compel a magistrate to expose the crime and punish the guilty. The 1924 film, then, while undeniably Gothic, was seen as a melodrama/legal justice fable rather than a horror, and its ghosts are vessels of virtue, in sharp contrast to the often indiscriminately vengeful *onryō* of the Japanese Gothic tradition. The depiction of ghosts as righteous avengers, carrying out morally just acts of

---

[18] See Robert Cagle, 'Diary of a Lost Girl: Victoriana, Intertextuality, and *A Tale of Two Sisters*', in Alison Peirse and Daniel Martin (eds), *Korean Horror Cinema* (Edinburgh: Edinburgh University Press, 2013), pp. 158–72; see also Wing-Fai Leung, 'From *A Tale of Two Sisters* to *the Uninvited*: A Tale of Two Texts', in Peirse and Martin (eds), *Korean Horror Cinema*, pp. 173–86.

warranted retribution, has continued to characterise much of South Korea's Gothic cinema.

South Korea's 'first' horror film, *The Housemaid*, is somewhat anomalous. Though universally admired by critics, and invariably cited as the first Korean horror film, *The Housemaid* deviates from the genre's usual patterns in several ways: its killer is far from righteous; moralities and sympathies are frequently unclear; and the central avenger is human rather than spectral. Telling the tale of an aspiring middle-class family who doom themselves by hiring a live-in domestic servant, *The Housemaid* charts the disastrous consequences of a husband's affair. The obsessed and resentful maid conducts masterful psychological warfare on the rest of the family, orchestrates the death of the young son and finally forces the object of her twisted affections into a double suicide. A bizarre coda – implying that all the infidelity, death and destruction that preceded it was merely a daydream – served to appease film regulators and fulfil audience expectations that, in a functioning Confucian society, evil cannot triumph.[19]

In terms of understanding the cultural specificity of South Korean Gothic cinema, the most instructive aspect of *The Housemaid* is its generic hybridity. The brilliance of the film's brooding tension is most often credited to the way in which the narrative combines one of Korean cinema's staples – romantic melodrama – with a new kind of Gothic atmosphere.[20] The *shinpa* genre was wildly popular during the 'Golden Age' of postwar cinema; derived from a theatrical tradition, *shinpa* films are exaggerated melodramas of love and loss that concern marital relations, family stability and societal barriers to love, and typically conclude with deeply sad 'tear-jerking' endings.[21] The grand innovation of *The Housemaid* was to make visible the troubling Gothic subtext of many of these films: stories of families destroyed by infidelity, of husbands and wives plotting against each other, turn the typically safe space of the family home into a threatening, tense environment. *The Housemaid* thus set a precedent for subsequent Gothic and horror films in South Korea, ensuring that melodrama and sadness – and not just fear – would be core components.

---

[19] Daniel Martin, 'South Korean Horror Cinema', in Harry M. Benshoff (ed.), *A Companion to the Horror Film* (Chichester: Wiley-Blackwell, 2014), pp. 424–5.

[20] Martin, 'South Korean Horror Cinema', p. 425.

[21] Darcy Paquet, '*Christmas in August* and Korean Melodrama', in Frances Gateward (ed.), *Seoul Searching: Culture and Identity in Contemporary Korean Cinema* (Albany, NY: State University of New York Press, 2007), pp. 37–54 (p. 44); Jinhee Choi, *The South Korean Film Renaissance: Local Hitmakers, Global Provocateurs* (Middletown, CT: Wesleyan University Press, 2010), p. 9.

The South Korean Gothic mode has often been preoccupied with Gothic spaces and the corruption of once-sacrosanct places into hives of danger and death. Lee Man-hee's masterful, Hitchcockian *The Devil's Stairway* (1964) is set almost entirely within a hospital, and successfully creates a deeply foreboding atmosphere, even a place of healing. *The Housemaid* inspired a slew of family-in-peril narratives, typically deploying an actual ghost as the primary object of fear: *A Devilish Homicide* (dir. Lee Yong-min, 1965), *A Public Cemetery under the Moon* (dir. Gwon Cheol-hwi, 1967) and *Suddenly a Dark Night* (dir. Ko Yeong-nam, 1981) are all concerned with threats to the family via a supernatural invasion of the home. The majority of these Gothic melodrama horror films feature a specific type of Korean ghost known as a *wonhon*. The *wonhon* is typically female, and has died an unfair, unjust death – often as a consequence of sexual assault or familial betrayal – but returns to exact a righteous revenge while serving, symbolically, to represent rebellion against patriarchal oppression.[22]

The family-focused Gothic horror of the domestic sphere was the dominant mode for decades. One of the most prominent Gothic thrillers of the 1990s, *Olgami* (dir. Kim Seong-hong, 1997), concerned the psychological warfare carried out by an obsessive mother against her son's new wife. Once again, the sanctity of the home was corrupted and fear was drawn from interpersonal family conflict. The central characters of the vast majority of South Korea's Gothic cinema had, for decades, been adults: couples on the verge of marriage, or parents raising children. Yet the 1990s saw a major shift in this pattern, as a new cycle emerged that centralised teenagers, and used Gothic motifs to turn the school, rather than the home, into a place of dread. *Whispering Corridors* (dir. Park Ki-hyung, 1998) was an unexpectedly scandalous – and popular – innovation, utilising the *wonhon* in an entirely new setting. The film literalises the intense miseries and pressures of the highly competitive high-school environment by depicting cruelly abusive teachers and a tragic, desperately sad ghost. The film's searing social critique caused prominent objections from the Korean Federation of Teachers' Associations, which only led to more interest from South Korea's teen audience.[23] The film's clear moral code – in which, again, the ghost is positioned as a force of justified violence – invited audiences to see the school's abusive teachers as

---

[22] Hyangjin Lee, 'Family, death and the *wonhon* in four films of the 1960s', in Peirse and Martin (eds), *Korean Horror Cinema*, pp. 23–34 (p. 33).

[23] Art Black, 'Coming of Age: The South Korean Horror Film', in Steven Jay Schneider (ed.), *Fear Without Frontiers: Horror Cinema Across the Globe* (Godalming: FAB Press, 2003), pp. 185–203 (p. 193).

the true embodiment of evil. Although the ghost herself is the source of considerable fear (for both the school's students, and, ideally, for the audience), she chooses her targets carefully, never hurting the innocents. The film's narrative structure ensures that sympathies are clear: before the teachers are brutally murdered, flashbacks (and present-day scenes) have revealed them to be both physically and psychologically abusive and sexually predatory. The reliance on flashback sequences is one of the core defining characteristics of contemporary South Korean horror: these films inevitably hinge on the revelation of a hidden crime, or a dark secret, that reconfigures audience sympathies and casts the violent pursuits of the central ghost in a different light. The protagonists of *Nightmare* (dir. Ahn Byung-ki, 2000), for example, appear initially to be innocent victims of a terrorising ghost until a flashback sequence late in the narrative reveals that they are all responsible, to some degree, for the murder of the now-vengeful *wonhon*. Indeed, the 'prolonged reverberances of the past within the present' are central not just to Korean horror, but are seen as a significant characteristic of broader traditions in the Gothic at large.[24]

In the classic mode, the hidden crimes that propelled the narrative were drawn from the repressed miseries of the family unit (the murder of a spouse, a sordid affair); the focus on adults meant that the incorporation of patterns of romantic melodrama were largely seamless. However, despite the broad shift in South Korean Gothic cinema – one triggered by *Whispering Corridors* – to teenaged characters, melodrama is still a core component. Though romance is featured far less often, the sentimentality and intense emotionality remain. Indeed, these films often foreground female protagonists in ways that the older cycle was unable to, especially through depictions of all-girl high schools; as Jinhee Choi notes, these horror films emphasise 'friendship, not kinship' as the crucial interpersonal dynamic.[25]

The fusion of Gothic and melodrama, then, is *the* persistent defining characteristic of South Korea's horror cinema, yet the tone of these films could pose challenges to traditional views of exactly how the Gothic is defined. Fred Botting's dismissal of Francis Ford Coppola's film *Bram Stoker's Dracula* (1992), which caused Botting to pronounce 'dead' the entire Gothic genre due to the way that the film supplanted horror with sentimentality, caused a great deal of debate within Gothic studies.[26] Yet while the sentimental tone and romantic content of melodrama can be seen as

[24] Hubner, *Fairytale and Gothic Horror*, p. 7.
[25] Choi, *The South Korean Film Renaissance*, p. 10.
[26] Fred Botting, *Gothic*, (London and New York: Routledge, 1996), p. 180.

incompatible with, if not antithetical to, 'true' Gothic traditions, such a view discounts the rich heritage of a country such as South Korea, in which the Gothic and melodrama are utterly inseparable. Choi has persuasively argued that South Korean horror is designed to evoke sadness as much (if not more than) fear.[27] The *wonhon* is not just someone to fear, but someone to pity. While the avenging ghost of Japanese Gothic was described as both the victim and the vessel of evil, the Korean Gothic emphasises a ghost who functions simultaneously as victim and hero, attracting a typically uncomplicated degree of audience sympathy.

Whispering Corridors initiated a trend that has continued to dominate, as heartbreaking stories of young people encountering wronged ghosts remains the norm. *Whispering Corridors* itself spawned numerous sequels, a real rarity in South Korea; the first of these, *Memento Mori* (dir. Kim Tae-yong and Min Kyu-dong, 1999), was especially important for its depictions of homosexual love in the context of a tragically haunted high school. *Memento Mori* has been widely analysed by critics and academics, and the film also falls within a growing global cycle of lesbian Gothic, identified by Kavka as films centring on a female protagonist as not just victim, but pro-active investigator (indeed, *Memento Mori*'s doomed central romance is a past event, uncovered by another girl in the course of the narrative).[28]

While the school has been a popular locale for South Korean Gothic cinema, local filmmakers have also incorporated aspects of the techno-Gothic, thus following Japan's grand success with *Ring*; indeed, there was even a Korean remake of *Ring*, Kim Dong-bin's 1999 film *The Ring Virus*. Recent examples of the techno-Gothic cycle include *Killer Toon* (dir. Kim Yong-gyun, 2013), about a serial killer inspired by an internet comic, but perhaps the best-known example, certainly for the international market, is Ahn Byung-ki's *Phone* (2002). Ahn's horror films were among the most popular of the 2000s, and he was, for a time, unusually committed to establishing himself as an *auteur* of Gothic horror in an industry that typically sees the genre as the exclusive province of first-time directors.[29] *Phone* took the techno-Gothic trappings of *Ring* – replacing the cursed videotape with a possessed cellphone – and used them in ways uniquely reflective of South Korea's horror traditions. The *wonhon* in *Phone* is perhaps the most exemplary

---

[27] Choi, *The South Korean Film Renaissance*, p. 137.
[28] Kavka, 'The Gothic on Screen', p. 219.
[29] Daniel Martin, 'Between the Local and the Global: "Asian Horror" in Ahn Byung-ki's *Phone* and *Bunshinsaba*', in Peirse and Martin (eds), *Korean Horror Cinema*, pp. 145–57 (p. 145).

instance of the tendency to depict ghosts as righteous and heroic: in one key scene, the likable protagonist, whose phone the ghost is haunting, is attacked by a hired killer as revenge for her crusading work as a news journalist. The ghost actually *intervenes* in the struggle, killing the attacker with supernatural power in order to protect an innocent life. This is a spirit with a moral code that is far removed from Sadako's child-murdering rage in *Ring*.

Yet for all the quintessential local sensibilities expressed in *Phone*, director Ahn has stalwartly refused to describe his films as examples of 'Korean' horror. Instead, Ahn insists that his work reflects a cultural mélange, incorporating influences from elsewhere in Asia and, especially, Hollywood; he thus categorises his own work, pointedly, as 'Asian Horror'.[30] While it is therefore important to consider the specificity of Gothic traditions in distinct countries within East Asia, it is equally important to acknowledge the shared sensibilities and influences between Japan, South Korea, Hong Kong and beyond.

Hong Kong Gothic Cinema

Hong Kong's Gothic cinema is uniquely characterised by its emphatic, frequently masterful blending of different genres and tones. While South Korea's Gothic is notable for seamlessly mixing the frightful and the melodramatic, Hong Kong's Gothic traditions express an even more elaborate fusion of dissonant styles. In essence, Hong Kong horror as a monotonal genre barely exists. Instead, the industry is famed for producing comedy-horrors, kung-fu-horrors, musical horrors and romance horrors. Frequently, these are combined more intricately, with the Gothic-martial-arts-comedy a common permutation.

Perhaps the best-known example of this particular generic blend, and one of the first Hong Kong Gothic films to find international distribution and significant cult appreciation, is *Mr. Vampire* (dir. Ricky Lau, 1985). The film is widely credited with initiating the popular 'hopping corpse' (*jiangshi*) subgenre: Gothic action-comedies about reanimated corpses terrorising small communities.[31] While the figure of the vampire is indelibly associated with Gothic film, literature and fashion in the West, Hong Kong's version of the creature is closer to what Hollywood cinema calls the zombie. The titular menace of *Mr. Vampire* is a barely animate corpse: due to the onset of rigor

---

[30] Martin, 'Between the Local and the Global', p. 145.
[31] John Charles, *The Hong Kong Filmography, 1977–1997* (Jefferson, NJ: McFarland, 2000), p. 212.

mortis, *jiangshi* have limited mobility, and thus 'hop' aggressively towards their prey; they leave their victims dead, with twin puncture wounds in the neck, but these are caused by thrusting fingernails, not piercing fangs; they can sense the location of their potential victims only by their breathing (if the heroes of such films hold their breath, they become effectively invisible to the predatory *jiangshi*). The inherent absurdity of the concept allows for the comedic element that is typical of such films; yet the deep-seated fear of the undead also gives the creature a genuinely frightening resonance for local audiences. There is a marked distinction, though, between how the vampiric/zombified monster is depicted in Western Gothic media and the figure's use in Hong Kong's popular culture.

Mr. Vampire deploys impressive martial arts throughout its action sequences. The central hero is not just a spiritual guide and expert on the supernatural, but also a master of kung fu. The protagonist's mastery of these diverse ancient skills and knowledge positions him as a repository of history, a personification of the past, giving the film one of its most potent themes: the clash of modernity and tradition in a rapidly transforming Hong Kong. The plot of *Mr. Vampire* hinges on the employment of Taoist Master Kau, regarded contemptuously as a bumpkin for his ignorance of tea-house etiquette by the same aristocratic family who hired him. His abilities are the salvation of the community, and the deep superstitions of his clients demonstrate the importance of the 'old ways' even to those who would embrace modernisation and Westernisation.

While the central threat of *Mr. Vampire* is its shambling *jiangshi*, an important subplot reflects another important aspect of Hong Kong's Gothic traditions. The film also includes a female ghost, predatory and seductive, who lures one of the younger trainee corpse-wranglers into a night of passion that binds the two of them together in a fatal curse. The heroic Master Kau must intervene to vanquish the ghost, but at the final moment of conflict, the genuine love between the ghost and her victim becomes clear: the young apprentice begs his teacher not to destroy the ghost, while the lovelorn spirit agrees to free her quarry and flee, so as not to cause him supernatural harm. This touching moment of melodrama is typical of an entire cycle of Hong Kong Gothic: romance horrors about the impossible love between humans (typically male) and ghosts (usually female). The extremely popular Gothic romance *A Chinese Ghost Story* (dir. Ching Siu-tung, 1987) represented the peak of this particular mode, and itself inspired numerous sequels and imitators.

The themes of prohibition and desire in the context of the 'forbidden' love between ghosts and humans are, according to Botting, a recurring trope of Gothic stories far beyond the confines of Hong Kong.[32] Yet the particular facets of Hong Kong's romantic ghost stories suggest a cultural specificity not found in other countries. While Japan's ghosts are usually merciless and malevolent, and South Korea's ghosts scrupulously moral, Hong Kong's ghosts – following a centuries-old literary tradition – are depicted far more ambivalently, neither completely harmless nor entirely an object of terror, offering their victims/lovers a mixture of infatuation and fear.[33] These tragedy-tinged spectral love stories are not, however, limited only to serious melodrama or chilling horror. Again, many broad comedies have been based on the subject. One such example, *My Cousin, the Ghost* (dir. Wu Ma, 1987), is an often-slapstick comedy of errors about a ghost who, unaware of his own death and supernatural status, is forced to deal with his foolish family and an amorous female spirit. One of the film's highlights is an indulgent, humorously self-aware and meta-textual moment of genuine affection between a human man and the ghost who loves him: as *Mr. Vampire* plays on a television set in the background, the couple tenderly waltz to the sounds of Ray Parker Jr's iconic *Ghostbusters* theme song. The central tension underpinning these untenable pairings revolves around questions of morality, mortality and selflessness: will the ghost doom the man she loves just to be with him?

Such Gothic romantic quandaries date back at least as far as Pu Songling's literary masterpiece *Strange Tales from a Chinese Studio*, a collection of short stories written in the seventeenth century that have profoundly shaped Hong Kong and China's Gothic popular culture. Intermingling history and mythology, Hong Kong's early Gothic cinema often drew on images and folklore from the past. Anthropomorphised animals are frequently invested with spiritual, fearful power, largely thanks to the potent legacy of the often-adapted sixteenth-century novel *Journey to the West*, about a heroic monkey warrior.[34] In the context of horror and the Gothic, the best known of these frightful animal folk stories is the legend of the White Snake, a fable about a pair of magical snakes – one white, one green – whose assumed identities as human sisters is complicated when the older of the two falls in love with

---

[32] Fred Botting, *Gothic*, 2nd edition (London and New York: Routledge, 2014), p. 9.
[33] John Minford, 'Introduction', in Pu Songling, *Strange Tales from a Chinese Studio* (London: Penguin, 2006), pp. xi–xxxi (p. xxii).
[34] Lianshan Chen, *Chinese Myths and Legends* (Cambridge: Cambridge University Press, 2011), p. 1.

a mortal man. The flexibility of the core elements of the story allow for numerous divergent interpretations: in some adaptations the snakes are highly sympathetic and the love is portrayed with a stirring, romantic tone; in other versions the snakes are monstrous, evil forces to be vanquished by heroic holders of spiritual power.[35] The tone of these films, likewise, can vary wildly, from children's fable or kitsch musical to earnest opera or erotic thriller.

While the 1980s is widely acknowledged as the 'peak' of Hong Kong cinema's horror genre, it was in the 1950s that films of the White Snake myth, and other narratives of ghostly romance, initially came to prominence and popularity. A cycle of often-overlooked Cantonese-language films of the decade used the figure of the female ghost – a *neoi gwei* – to tell didactic stories about the real-world horrors of arranged marriage, superstition, social values, poor living conditions and the relationship between the populace and colonial governance.[36] The potential for a Gothic cinema of ghosts and monsters to espouse positive moral values and comment on society in progressive ways – as, indeed, much of South Korea's own Gothic cinema did during its Golden Age – can be seen as an important evolution of the Gothic tradition. Botting has argued that Gothic literature, classically, was considered to be 'not good in moral, aesthetic or social terms' and even 'anti-social in content and function', yet Hong Kong's filmmakers have frequently used the Gothic as a tool to communicate meaningful moral ideas and ideals.[37]

These Gothic narratives of the 1950s are typically seen less as horror films and more in terms of melodrama, social realism or mythological adventure. For the majority of Hong Kong's own expert critics, a distinct horror genre emerged only in the 1980s, and even then, only in a highly fractured and hybridised form. With its pioneering fusion of martial arts, comedy and horror, Sammo Hung's *Encounters of the Spooky Kind* (1980) is credited with instigating the horror boom of the 1980s in Hong Kong. The central narrative sees a hapless martial artist contending with haunted locales, *jiangshi*, ghosts, witches, monkey-gods and a variety of ephemeral evil forces. Just as South Korea built its horror cinema on the foundation of its then most popular

---

[35] For a more detailed discussion of the White Snake myth in Hong Kong cinema, see Liang Luo, 'The White Snake in Hong Kong Horror Cinema: From Horrific Tales to Crowd Pleasers', in Gary Bettinson and Daniel Martin (eds), *Hong Kong Horror Cinema* (Edinburgh: Edinburgh University Press, 2018), pp. 34–51.

[36] Raymond Tsang, 'What Can a *Neoi Gwei* Teach Us? Adaptation as Reincarnation in Hong Kong Horror of the 1950s', in Bettinson and Martin (eds), *Hong Kong Horror Cinema*, pp. 19–33.

[37] Botting, *Gothic* (2nd edition), p. 2.

genre, melodrama, so too did Hong Kong establish its own horror genre by incorporating its most famed export and a guaranteed domestic crowd-pleaser: the kung-fu film. Virtually all of the Gothic cinema that followed was hybridised in some way, combining action, horror, comedy and tragedy. The introduction of the 'Category III' ratings bracket in 1988 led to a slew of horror-exploitation films replete with gore and sexual content, adding another component to Hong Kong's already diverse Gothic landscape.

Hong Kong's film historians and critics have often viewed the application of 'horror' as a generic category problematic in the context of domestic cinema. Stephen Teo has wryly noted that 'in the Hong Kong horror film, there really isn't any horror'.[38] Yu Cheng, meanwhile, decried emphatic generic hybridity as the chief indication of Hong Kong cinema's 'inability to establish a proper Horror genre'.[39] The difficulty experienced by critics and academics in defining a Hong Kong horror cinema suggests the value of viewing these films through the lens of the Gothic. Indeed, as Hubner has noted, the Gothic is 'pervasive' yet 'cannot be pinned down as a genre'.[40] Hong Kong's film industry is rich in challenging texts that defy simple, singular categorisation. Its Gothic cinema is consistently hyphenated: here, Gothic-comedy-kung-fu-romance-melodrama is the norm, not the exception. Perhaps the most common combination – one rarely acknowledged by Hong Kong's critics or filmmakers – is the fantasy-horror. Hong Kong's Gothic cinema draws from myth and legends that imagine the mortal and the magical side-by-side. Superstition is rarely baseless, and the appearance of supernatural beings that would suggest, to a Western critic, the applicability of the 'fantasy' label are often accepted as the genuine beliefs of a society that retains, however marginally, a deep spirituality.[41] In spite of its often-comedic framing, the Hong Kong Gothic thus resonates with significant power.

Conclusion: The Global and the Gothic in East Asia

The richness of Gothic traditions in East Asia is by no means limited to Japan, South Korea and Hong Kong. This chapter has only offered a brief survey of three national cinemas. There are thriving industries in other countries in East Asia that produce endlessly fascinating Gothic media. The cinema of

---

[38] Stephen Teo, 'The Tongue: A Study of Hong Kong Horror Movies', in Li Cheuk-to (ed.), *Phantoms of the Hong Kong Cinema* (Hong Kong: Urban Council, 1989), pp. 41–5.
[39] Yu Cheng, 'Under a Spell', in Cheuk-to (ed.), *Phantoms of the Hong Kong Cinema*, pp. 20–3.
[40] Hubner, *Fairytale and Gothic Horror*, p. 44.
[41] Bey Logan, *Hong Kong Action Cinema* (Woodstock: Overlook Press, 1996), p. 101.

Thailand, for example, has a storied history of horror film production and has been responsible for many of the most provocative Gothic narratives of recent years. Taiwan, Mainland China, Vietnam and Malaysia have all produced Gothic cinema that is eminently worthy of discussion and critical scrutiny.

An important aspect of any modern study of Gothic cinema is to acknowledge the globalising trend in popular culture and media production. No national cinema is culturally 'pure' and no Gothic tradition is immune to outside influence. Hollywood's Gothic and horror films and literature have undoubtedly been influenced by work that has emerged from East Asia over the past century. Indeed, collaborations have been set in place and inspiration has been exchanged on an international and inter-Asia basis for decades. *The Legend of the 7 Golden Vampires* (dir. Roy Ward Baker, 1974), for example, was a co-production between Britain's Hammer Studios and Hong Kong's Shaw Brothers Studios, combining martial arts (then enjoying its first crazed reception in the West) with Hammer's distinctly-styled Gothic sensibility. When South Korean filmmakers endeavoured to tell a Gothic story about a journey to an exotic locale, the result was *Muoi: The Legend of a Portrait* (dir. Kim Tae-kyeong, 2007), a film set almost entirely in Vietnam. The Gothic exists today, then, as something uniquely globalised yet, simultaneously, strikingly culturally specific. East Asian Gothic is far from a monolithic entity, yet its shared characteristics and global appeal attest to a universal desire to share stories of death and rebirth, justice and vengeance, triumph and dread.

3.21

Global Gothic 3: Gothic in Modern Scandinavia

YVONNE LEFFLER

Scandinavian Gothic in a Global Marketplace

Since the millennium, there has been a proliferation of Gothic narratives written, published and set in the Scandinavian countries. The Gothic mode has invaded all genres and media – crime fiction, children's and Young Adult fiction, literature and films, TV series and computer games. Many Scandinavian stories have also received global recognition by critics and audiences. John Ajvide Lindqvist's vampire novel *Let the Right One In* (*Låt den rätte komma in*, 2004), for example, was instantly a success both inside and outside Sweden and has been translated into many languages, including English. The novel was subsequently adapted into two films: a Swedish film directed by Tomas Alfredson in 2008, and an English-language remake, *Let Me In*, directed by the American director Matt Reeves and released in 2010. At the same time, the Danish filmmaker Lars von Trier launched *Anti-Christ* (2009) as a horror movie. The film attracted much attention, winning several awards and causing a heated debate about gender issues. Some years later, Sara Bergmark Elfgren and Mats Strandberg's Young Adult trilogy *Engelfors* (*Engelsforstrilogin*, 2011–13), as well as the Swedish film adaption of the first part, *The Circle* (2015), was an international success. In several interviews, the two writers confirm that they had been inspired by such international blockbusters as *Twin Peaks* and *Buffy the Vampire Slayer*.

All these works are instructive examples of the Gothic revival in modern Scandinavia. Most works are densely intertextual; Scandinavian Gothic writers and directors place themselves in a global Gothic tradition and take for granted that their audiences are genre-aware and familiar with not only anglophone Gothic but also other European traditions, as well as Asian horror fiction, especially Japanese films. Their stories frequently refer to canonised international works and display a playful attitude towards established genre norms. They also modify the genre in order to address topical contemporary political and social issues. One reason why Scandinavian Gothic has become so pervasive and popular in the last few decades is that it addresses and makes visible the political and ecological anxieties that haunt the Nordic countries and their welfare systems. In addition, they highlight how essential these anxieties are for the understanding of identities and ideologies in the region. On the one hand, these subjects make them highly relevant and topical to Scandinavian audiences; on the other, the same qualities, in combination with the Nordic atmosphere, attract international audiences. Today's writers and filmmakers often position their work within a recognised Nordic tradition, where the uncanny is associated with the landscape and notions of supernatural creatures of nature. As in earlier Scandinavian Gothic, the characters are depicted as victims of the surrounding landscape, the uncontrollable wilderness and its nightmarish past. However, even more distinctly so than in earlier stories, local folktales and myths are revived and used in modern Scandinavian Gothic narratives. Both creatures and magic from ancient popular belief and pagan traditions move into contemporary technological and urban society. This integration of Gothic elements and regional folklore in present-day fiction is particularly common in crossover literature and young-adult culture. It is also used in other hybrid genres, for example, in what could be called 'Gothic crime', where the criminal investigation is obstructed by supernatural activities that are connected with the local landscape.

In contemporary Scandinavian Gothic, it is possible to distinguish at least three distinct categories or ways of making use of Gothic elements and the specific Scandinavian setting. First, Gothic narratives are a vital part of today's flourishing crossover and young-adult narratives, in which the protagonists explore magic powers derived from popular belief and Scandinavian folktales. Second, many modern writers and filmmakers are exploring and developing a specific Scandinavian Gothic dating back to the mid-nineteenth century, where the Scandinavian landscape, the wilderness and its creatures play key roles as both antagonists and monsters. Third, Gothic elements and narrative strategies are progressively being integrated into other genres and discourses. In Scandinavia, some writers use Gothic elements to address current social anxieties in a narrative form that could be called 'Gothic realism'. In response to international blockbusters, some Scandinavian filmmakers have developed a certain kind of metafictional genre parody or satire, in which the Gothic qualities of certain Nordic circumstances and phenomena are exaggerated in a rib-tickling way. Another Gothic cross-genre is the

Gothic crime story, where the criminal investigation of a traditional detective story is complicated because of the interference of seemingly supernatural phenomena.

The Rise of Scandinavian Gothic

Given the region's predilection for realism, there was little scholarly interest in the rise of Gothic fiction in Scandinavia until very recently, from the 1980s onwards. However, an examination of the non-realist spectrum in Scandinavian literature and film reveals a prevailing Gothic tradition that dates at least as far back as the Romantic period, a literary strain that has now been identified and addressed by several Scandinavian scholars.[1] As I have demonstrated elsewhere, in the late eighteenth and the early nineteenth centuries, many of the well-known English, German and French Gothic novels were available to Scandinavian readers, and some of these were instantly translated into Swedish, Danish and Norwegian. Ann Radcliffe's *The Italian* (1797), Matthew Gregory Lewis's *The Monk* (1796) and François Guillaume Ducray-Duminil's *Victor, a Child of the Forest* (1796), for example, were widely read in Scandinavia around 1800. Some of the most popular Gothic novels were also adapted for the theatre. *The Italian*, for instance, was staged as *Eleonora Rosalba, or the Ruins in Paluzzi* in 1801–2, followed by *Victor, a Child of the Forest* at the same theatre, Arsenalen in Stockholm, in 1803–4.[2] Writers such as Ernst Theodor Amadeus Hoffmann, Eugène Sue and Edgar Allan Poe became popular later on. In particular, Hoffmann's works *The Devil's Elixirs* (*Die Elixiere des Teufels*, 1815) and *The Golden Pot* (*Der golden Topt*, 1814) influenced many Scandinavian writers. Although Scandinavian writers developed their own kind of Gothic fiction by locating their stories in local and regional social and geographical environments, they established themselves as unmistakably genre-aware by explicitly referring to internationally well-known Gothic works. Bernhard Ingemann's *The Sphinx* (*Sphinxen*, 1820), then, is a rewriting of Hoffmann's *The Golden Pot*,

---

[1] Mattias Fyhr, *Svensk skräcklitteratur 1: Bårtäcken över jordens likrum* (Lund: Ellerström, 2017); Kirstine Marie Kastbjerg, *Reading the Surface: The Danish Gothic of B. S. Ingemann, H. C. Andersen, Karen Blixen and Beyond* (PhD thesis; University of Washington, 2013); Sofia Wijkmark, *Hemsökelser: Gotiken i sex berättelser av Selma Lagerlöf* (Unpublished PhD thesis; Karlstad University, 2009); Henrik Johnsson, *Strindberg och skräcken. Skräckmotiv och identitetstematik i August Strindbergs författarskap* (Umeå: Bokförlaget H: ström, 2008); Yvonne Leffler, *I skräckens lustgård: Skräckromantik i svenska 1800–talsromaner* (Gothenburg: Skrifter utgivna av litteraturvetenskapliga institutionen vid Göteborgs universitet, 1991).

[2] Leffler, *I skräckens lustgård*, p. 41.

a labyrinthine tale about a young writer who increasingly confuses dreams and reality. Both Ingemann's *The Werewolf* (*Varulven*, 1834) and Victor Rydberg's serial *The Vampire* (*Wampyren*, 1848) are inspired by John Polidori's *The Vampyre* (1819).[3] While Rydberg rewrote and expanded upon Polidori's narrative, Ingemann transformed it into a story about a werewolf character and the devastating conflict between his bourgeois persona and his sexual drives, a motif also used by many later writers, including Tryggve Andersen in *Towards Night* (*Mot kvæld*, 1900).[4] Although there is no evident source text for Clas Livijn's fantastic tale 'A Fantasy of a Bad Conscience' ('Samwetets fantasi', 1821), it is one of the many Scandinavian narratives about a supernatural stalker in the tradition of Hoffmann's *The Devil's Elixirs*. In Livijn's story, a homecoming soldier finds himself followed by an axe-wielding grey man who can be interpreted as either an avenging ghost or an image of the soldier's bad conscience: his former girlfriend was executed for infanticide because he refused to help her when she became pregnant.

Hans Christian Andersen, as Kristine Marie Kjastberg demonstrates, repeatedly uses the motif of the double or doppelgänger. Although his Danish fairy tales and stories are more obviously influenced by Germanic folktales than easily recognisable Gothic originals, his story 'The Shadow' ('Skyggen', 1847) is a dreary tale of a devious doppelgänger that strongly recalls the Gothic tradition. Andersen's story illustrates the transmission of shadow to body, a process through which the shadow drains the original body of life.[5] Another version of a double is found in Andersen's 'The Red Shoes' ('De røde sko', 1845), a tale about losing control and the blurring of the distinction between clothing and body, the ego's willpower and bodily motion. Here, the accessory, the red shoes, ends up articulating and defining the captive subject and owner of the shoes, the young girl.

The motif of the overshadowing male double in combination with avenging ghosts is frequently used in August Strindberg's and Henrik Ibsen's works. As Henry Johnson has pointed out, many of Strindberg's stories

---

[3] For further details on how Polidori's story was expanded by Rydberg, see Yvonne Leffler, 'Vampyrmotivet och erotiken', in Birgitta Svensson and Birthe Sjöberg (eds), *Kulturhjälten. Viktor Rydbergs humanism* (Stockholm: Atlantis, 2009), pp. 155–68.

[4] For further details on Andersen's use of the motif of the werewolf, see Harald Bache-Wiig, 'Apokalypse nå! Tryggve Andersens Mot kvæld', in Torgeir Haugen (ed.), *Litterære skygger. Norsk fantastisk litteratur* (Oslo: Cappelen Akademisk Forlag, 1998), pp. 123–41 (pp. 128–33).

[5] The use of shadow and light in Andersen's 'The Shadow' has been explored by Kastbjerg, *Reading the Surface*, pp. 213–18.

concern the struggle for identity. In his tale *Tschandala* (1889), the male protagonist decides to kill another man, whom he suspects of evildoing, fearing that he himself is starting to lose his individual identity and what he calls their battle of minds. In *Ghost Sonata* (*Spöksonaten*, 1907), Strindberg combined the motif of the double with that of ghosts and the Nordic *fylgias*, mythological creatures that drain the living of their lifeblood. The drama gradually exposes a distorted version of reality in which the distinction between life and death is erased.[6] In Ibsen's play *Ghosts* (*Gengangare*, 1881), the Nordic motif of '*gengangare*', that is, a ghost returning to take revenge, is used as a metaphor for syphilis in order to highlight the hypocrisy of contemporary bourgeois society. In both Strindberg's and Ibsen's works, Gothic elements are regularly used to expose the problems and evils in their contemporary societies.

Many women writers also adjusted the Gothic mode to their particular aims and audiences. Here, the actions take place in a recognisably Scandinavian environment, often a real-life location, in which local history, myths and customs are of great importance to the plot. In *The House of the Devil* (*Hin Ondes hus*, 1853), a novella about a spooky house in Stockholm and its afflicted owner, Aurora Ljungstedt explicitly refers to Radcliffe's novels about haunted abodes.[7] In her story about a man and his evil double, 'Harold's Shadow' ('Harolds skugga', 1861), she alludes to Hoffmann's *The Devil's Elixirs* and anticipates Robert Louis Stevenson's *Strange Case of Dr Jekyll and Mr Hyde* (1886) in the way in which she transforms the motif of the double into a narrative about the civilised and primitive parts of a man's ego. Even more than Ljungstedt, the Swedish Nobel laureate Selma Lagerlöf developed Scandinavian Gothic into a place-focused genre, where the Nordic landscape plays an important role in the plot. *The Treasure* (*Herr Arnes penningar*, 1903), a novel that I have identified as the first Swedish thriller, is a combination of murder and ghost story, where the myth of werewolves, in combination with a punishing Arctic landscape, is used to enhance the Gothic atmosphere.[8] Sofia Wiljkmark's study of Lagerlöf has explored various aspects of the return of the past and the transgression of the boundaries between life and death, human self and monstrous beast, and fantasy and reality in such short stories as 'The Ancient Tomb' ('Stenkumlet', 1892) and 'Peace on Earth' ('Frid på

---

[6] The theme of identity in Strindberg's *Tschandala* and *Ghost Sonata* has been examined by Johnson, *Strindberg och skräcken*, pp. 141–7, 165–74.
[7] Leffler, *I skräckens lustgård*, p. 106.
[8] For a reading of *The Treasure* as a Gothic novel, see Leffler, *I skräckens lustgård*, pp. 153–66.

Jorden', 1917).[9] Thus, Lagerlöf recurrently used the Nordic wilderness and local folklore to depict the evil forces in nature and within human. Her Gothic style and rural settings, in turn, inspired other Scandinavian authors, including Ragnhild Jølsen. Jølsen's novel *Rikka Gan* (1904) is a narrative about opposing boundaries and a haunting past. As in many of Lagerlöf's works, Jølsen's story revolves around a conflict-ridden female protagonist who is bound to the site of her childhood, the mansion Gan. Jølsen elaborated upon, and twisted, the conventions of female Gothic into an eerie story about a woman who is in pursuit of identity but who is victimised by the history of her house and her family, and as Henning Howlid Wærp has argued, in that way Jølsen uses the Gothic mode to explore the female mind.[10]

A Scandinavian writer who first established herself as a Gothic writer in English was Karen Blixen, also known by her pseudonym Isak Dinesen. In *Seven Gothic Tales* (1934), 'The Supper at Elsinore' ('Et familieselskab i Helsingør') is an example of an uncanny ghost story set in Denmark. The detailed description of the town Helsingør and its history is integrated to heighten the suspense in this story of a merchant family. Incestuous undercurrents drive the plot and the actions of three siblings whom even death cannot part. In the end, the sisters – two old spinsters – summon their long-dead and executed brother in the siblings' former secret chamber in their old family home facing Hamlet's Kronborg in a wintery Helsingør. Their reunion is, as Kjastbjerg claims, both a return of the repressed and an atonement of the past and its implicit sins.[11] It is also, as in Lagerlöf's and Jølsen's stories, an eerie story about women's domestic confinement within physical and mental spaces, where the final family reunion – with explicit references to Shakespeare's *Hamlet* – even more clearly demonstrates the tyranny of the past.

Several early Scandinavian filmmakers sought to visualise the ambiguous imagery of popular Scandinavian beliefs. Benjamin Christensen's Swedish-Danish silent film *Häxan* (released in the US as *Witchcraft Through the Ages*, 1922) communicates prevalent ideas about witches, as well as facts about the witch trials that took place in the past. The ghostly visualisation of the ride of the witches inspired Walt Disney's illustration of Modest Mussorgsky's music

---

[9] For further details on the use of Gothic conventions in the short stories by Lagerlöf, see Wijkmark, *Hemsökelser*, 2009.

[10] H. Howlid Wærp, 'Utover enhver grense – Gotiske trek I Ragnhild Jølsens romancer', in Torgeir Haugen (ed.), *Litterære skygger. Norsk fantastisk litteratur* (Oslo: Cappelen Akademisk Forlag), pp. 101–21 (p. 110).

[11] For a reading of Gothic motifs in Blixen's story, see Kastbjerg, *Reading the Surface*, pp. 253–301.

Night on Bald Mountain (*Eine Nacht auf dem Kahlen Berge*) in his animated film *Fantasia* (1940). Victor Sjöström's Swedish-language film *The Phantom Carriage* (1921) is a *tour de force* that showcases the early technique of double exposure to illustrate the world of death and to highlight the Gothic qualities in Lagerlöf's 1912 novel, *The Soul Shall Bear Witness* (*Körkarlen*), on which the film was based. The first Scandinavian vampire film, Carl Theodor Dreyer's *Vampyr* (1931–2), explored at length in Chapter 1 of this volume, is structured as a journey to an isolated island, a settlement beyond time and space at the border of life and death, day and night.[12] The Gothic qualities of the Arctic setting in Finnish Lapland are explored in *The White Reindeer* (*Valkoinen peura*, 1952) by Erik Blomberg. The film expands on pre-Christian Sami mythology and shamanism in order to tell the story about a woman (Mirjame Kousmanen) whose visit to the local shaman turns her into a shapeshifting vampiric reindeer that attracts male herders with tragic results. In the film, the snow-clad Arctic landscape provides a sublime backdrop for an uncanny drama about sexual desire and female witchcraft. In Kåre Bergstrøm's Norwegian film *Lake of the Dead* (*De dødes tjern*, 1958), which is based on a novel by André Bjerke, the horrors are connected to a legend about a forest lake and an evil deed associated with the place. When six people arrive from Oslo to visit a friend, only to find him missing and his dog dead in the lake, they decide to stay to solve the mystery, but they soon find themselves exposed to the mysterious powers tied to the location, especially to the lake.

Even some feature films by the celebrated Swedish filmmaker Ingmar Bergman centre on Gothic and quasi-Gothic surrealist imagery, repetitive reflections and doppelgängers. The claustrophobic setting in the Swedish archipelago and the struggle for control and power between two women, a nurse (Bibi Andersson) and her traumatised silent patient (Liv Ullman), turn *Persona* (1966) into a psychological horror drama. The story explores the Jungian concept of persona and the themes of duality, insanity and vampirism in the depiction of the two women, where smoke and mirrors are used to make their faces double and dissolve in order to turn them into eerie doubles – or personas – of each other or of themselves. Even closer to the tradition of horror films is *Hour of the Wolf* (1968), which alludes to the characters in *Persona*. Bergman's film is about a painter (Max von Sydow) and his wife (Liv Ullman) on a small island, where he seeks to be cured from

---

[12] The Gothic focalisation technique in Dryer's *Vampyr* has been noted by Yvonne Leffler, *Horror as Pleasure: The Aesthetics of Horror Fiction* (Stockholm: Almqvist & Wiksell International, 2000), pp. 133–5. See also Chapter 1 in this volume for an extended reading of this film.

his insomnia but is frequently approached by weird people. What is real and what is his imagination is unclear, and when he is finally attacked by his pursuers or shadows, his wife is left alone in the woods. Just as in Dryer's and Blomberg's earlier film, Bergman's Gothic atmosphere in his early films revolves around the transgression of the individual's physical and psychological integrity that is achieved through the interplay between the characters and the settings.

Nature and Witchcraft in Scandinavian Crossover

As mentioned above, the Gothic tradition in Scandinavian literature and film around the millennium is densely intertextual. At the same time, however, it is possible to discern a specific Scandinavian version of Gothic narrative. The characteristics of an established Nordic tradition are particularly clear in today's crossover literature – that is, literature that is primarily intended for young adults. In this kind of fiction, the Gothic castle is replaced by the Nordic wilderness, and mythical creatures of nature and old folktales are accorded particular importance, while various kinds of shapeshifters, witches and concepts of magic are essential to the plot.

Contemporary Nordic crossover stories often relate how pubescent girls develop exceptional capabilities that then carry them into a magical world. As in old folktales and Andersen's fairy tales, the Gothic fantasy world of crossover fiction emphasises moral conflicts and explicates the life-choice that the protagonist must face in order to become an adult woman. The novels depict the girls' upbringing and transition to adulthood according to a traditional aesthetics of care, describing how the heroines must learn to pay attention to other living beings and live in harmony with nature. However, the stories also reassess the traditional female virtues, since it is precisely these female traits that are prerequisites for saving the world from evil and destruction.

Many crossover stories addressed to young girls emphasise the value of women's collective cooperation. In Mats Strandberg and Sara Bergmark Elfgren's best-selling Engelsfors Trilogy – *The Circle* (*Cirkeln*, 2011), *Fire* (*Eld*, 2012) and *The Key* (*Nyckeln*, 2013) – six teenage girls discover that they have developed supernatural abilities and thus have been chosen to battle against the evil demons that are taking over the woodlands surrounding the small village of Engelsfors. In Caroline L. Jensen's *Wolf Kindred* (*Vargsläkte*, 2011), Vera discovers that her grandmother and her friends are witches and that she has inherited her grandmother's ability to assume the shape of a wolf, or rather a werewolf, and thereby gain access to new and powerful forces of nature. As in many other witch novels for young readers, including Lene Kaaberbøl's *Wild Witch* (*Vildheks*) series (2010–), the good witches and shapeshifters in the Engelsfors Trilogy and in *Wolf Kindred* must learn to be responsible and compassionate women who are capable of cooperation and able to suspend their own interests for the benefit of others.

The hallmark of crossover literature is that the protagonists must learn to distinguish between good and evil and their respective attributes. In many examples, such as Kaaberbøl's *Wild Witch* series and Jensen's *Wolf Kindred*, there is an emphasis on the guidance of older women. On the one hand, this implies that the heroine is raised to adopt traditional female virtues, such as empathy, responsible cooperation and taking an interest in the welfare of other living beings. On the other hand, the stories describe an encouraging matriarchal world in which women are in charge and where women set the rules. These female coming-of-age novels thus advocate an anti-patriarchal power structure that is founded upon ancient Nordic traditions and a strong connection to nature and the regional landscape. This category of crossover literature proposes, with the support of Gothic elements and narrative strategies, a distinct counter-vision to the individualistic lifestyles that many young people are leading in the competitive urban societies of the new millennium.

The monstrous other is not always rooted in the wilderness and its alien creatures. Some female writers of Gothic stories situate the source of horror in modern Scandinavian family life, or even in the absence of established family relations. Today, writers such as Olga Ravn and Leonora Christina Skov, both of Denmark, are writing in a Gothic tradition. They join the tradition of their predecessors Selma Lagerlöf and Karen Blixen with guilt-ridden female protagonists possessing transgressive attributes and gender-political motives. Their female protagonists are fragmented self-images rooted in the absence of conventional nuclear families, family history and biological relations. Thus, it is not, as in many traditional Gothic narratives, a matter of women's bodies being threatened and assaulted so much as their psyches and their identities that are endangered and transformed. The female protagonists appear both with varying identities and in various shapes.

In *Celestine* (2015), Olga Ravn presents an internal psychological drama in the traditional Gothic setting of an ancient medieval castle. The female narrator and protagonist is possessed by a ghost named Celestine, one who, legend has it, was immured alive in the castle after refusing to marry the man that her father had chosen for her. By means of an unreliable narrative perspective, the narrator is gradually transformed into the ghost, thus replicating the destiny of Celestine. Here, being buried alive assumes a new significance, and the father's cruelty against Celestine is set against the emotional isolation experienced by the narrator as a little girl when her parents divorced and engaged in new relationships and families. The story about Celestine, and how it is linked to the narrator's family history and experience as a child, twists the perspective and makes the narrator appear more buried alive than the immured Celestine and her spectre themselves.

Leonora Christina Skov, too, modifies the familial and gender-based themes in her metafictional novel *Silhouette of a Sinner* (*Silhuet af en synder*, 2010), which consists of multiple timelines and several female protagonists. All the women in the text share a connection to Liljenholm Castle in Denmark as well as to its dysfunctional family. When the heiress of the castle arrives with her female partner, Agnes, a would-be author who intends to write a novel about the castle and its family, the writing project encompasses an investigation of not only the Castle of Liljenholm but also of the secrets surrounding Agnes's own family background. Stories within stories and unreliable narrators add to the mysteries connected to the castle and Agnes's origin. What starts as a plot variation of female Gothic romance turns out to be a complex negotiation of norms in which heterosexual gender norms and power relations are negotiated, and where the female narrator leaves behind the subordinated position of victimhood in search of information and identity. Her aim is not to win a husband but to discover her family roots and to construct an identity, and her antagonist is not a male oppressor but an older maternal figure attempting to protect her from painful information and, in the end, male oppression. In Skov's novel, the monster has been replaced with a helicopter mum, whose good intentions are the real danger to the gender-transgressive heroine in her search for truth and identity.

The ways in which Scandinavian writers place themselves in a global tradition of horror, while at the same time emphasising a particular Nordic tradition rooted in old folklore, is clearly demonstrated in Jenny Milewski's novel *Yuko* (2015). Although it explicitly refers to popular American horror stories, such as the slasher film series *Friday the 13th* and stories by Stephen King, the narrative revolves around the protagonists' familiarity with Nordic as opposed to Japanese popular belief and horror fiction. The setting is a Swedish university town where a dormitory is haunted by a diseased Japanese student. For a start, the protagonist's Swedish friends attempt to banish the stalking ghost with the help of Nordic exorcism, but they fail as the phantom acts not according to Nordic but to Japanese beliefs and horror conventions. The horror scenes are thus intensified by the misinterpretation of and discrepancy between two different traditions of horror and popular belief; Milewski both presumes and challenges her audience's knowledge of Gothic conventions as well as different traditions within the genre.

The Devious Wilderness

In Scandinavian folklore, untouched nature has long been the realm of supernatural powers and evil. The earliest Scandinavian writers immediately turned this concept of the Nordic wilderness into a Gothic trope. Selma Lagerlöf and other writers at the *fin de siècle* developed this tendency further. The wilderness as the aggressive other is even more predominant in modern and contemporary Gothic stories. Here, the protagonists are often modern city dwellers who, either due to coincidence, work or a holiday retreat, end up in an unfamiliar environment to which they are unable to adapt. The landscape as the unknown, as the fear-provoking other, is stressed as it is perceived from the visitor's viewpoint. Untamed nature becomes a devious space, not just a backdrop to what happens but a hostile antagonist. In films such as Michael Hjorth's *The Unknown* (*Det okända*, 2000), it becomes the ultimate monster. Hjorth's film is inspired by Myrick and Sández's *The Blair Witch Project* (1999), but in the Swedish version, the students are not exploring a local legend about a witch but the forest as such. In Hjorth's film, the force of nature acts as an external antagonist that fights the young researchers and prevents them from accomplishing their task, which is to investigate the effects of a forest fire. In some modern narratives, the landscape even forces the protagonists to act as its servants or slaves. In Andreas Marklund's novel *The Harvest Queen* (*Skördedrottningen*, 2007), for example, a young scholar and his girlfriend visit the northern region of Sweden to search for a missing friend, whom they believe to be the victim of a crime. On their way north, a snowstorm brings them to their friend's old farmhouse, where the Arctic climate keeps them imprisoned during the winter. During their stay, the male protagonist is gradually brought closer to the dark history of his ancestors, preparing him to become the next servant of the pagan death goddess, the 'Harvest Queen'.

Many contemporary Scandinavian narratives are structured as a journey from the ordinary everyday world of the city into a remote, hostile place in the wilderness, where the rules of life are different. In *The Unknown* and *The Harvest Queen*, the protagonists leave their quotidian routines in town to explore something unknown in northern Scandinavia, either as part of their work as scientists or as private detectives investigating the case of a missing friend. The encounter with untamed nature soon changes their assignment, and their exploration of the local environment becomes their main occupation. The landscape becomes the significant other, a mystery to be solved and an aggressive opponent to be fought. The protagonists' confrontations with wild nature place them in a state of mental dissolution, as individuals who are on the verge of collapse. After a time, no boundaries exist between the self and the environment, between man and nature nor between local history and present experiences. The border between the protagonists and the surrounding wilderness is gradually blurred as the protagonists start to act on behalf of the landscape, either by free will or as downcast slaves.

Accordingly, in many Scandinavian Gothic narratives, the setting, the powers of nature, and local ancient legends and myths play a major part. For example, in *The Harvest Queen*, the male protagonist is prey from the start because of his family's pagan past. The disappearance of his friend appears to be part of the plot to make him uncover his paternal grandfather's dark secret, as well as an alien and powerful reality beyond modern life, a world ruled by the merciless 'Harvest Queen'. The novel is an example in which the setting, the snow-covered landscape in northern Sweden, becomes a powerful character in its own right. Initially the landscape or its representative acts as an external threat, a hostile antagonist fighting the protagonists by using forces of nature. Later, wild nature starts to work as an internal enemy, actively invading the protagonist, using him or her as an instrument to fulfil its goal and thereby dissolving the distinction between outer and inner space, man and nature.

John Ajvide Lindqvist's novel *Harbour* (*Människohamn*, 2008) and Lars von Trier's film *Antichrist*, too, illustrate how an encounter with untamed nature leads to a breakdown of chronological time in a way that is typical of contemporary Scandinavian Gothic. The process starts with a child's death and a parent's traumatic experience. In *Harbour*, the male protagonist is haunted by the mysterious disappearance of his young daughter on a cold winter's day out on the frozen Baltic Sea. In *Antichrist*, the woman has a breakdown after her little boy falls to his death from an open window while she and her husband are making love. To recover from their loss, the parents of the boy retreat to their cottage in the woods. In both stories, the local landscape directs the characters' attention and actions and there is a fusion of landscape and character, and of the present time and the forgotten past. The landscape communicates by giving rise to hallucinations; it evokes repressed memories and makes the characters act as its instruments in bringing forth hidden crimes of the past. Although the horror in Ajvide Lindqvist's and Trier's stories centres on the recent past and the memories of traumatic events, its ultimate cause is, as in most Scandinavian Gothic, connected to what has occurred in the historical past. In *Harbour*, the father's search for his daughter calls forth repressed memories from his own childhood and youth; at the same time it unveils the secret of the island and an ancient pact between the inhabitants of the archipelago and the sea. In *Antichrist*, the parents' stay in the woods causes the father to experience strange hallucinations that are triggered by mythical beings in the landscape, while his wife manifests increasingly violent behaviour. In his visions, the father is confronted with uncomfortable images of his wife visiting the cottage alone – or together with their child – at the time when she was working on her thesis on witch trials in history. Thus, past, present and future gradually lose their chronological and historical order and tend towards an eternal present. What happens to the protagonists in *Harbour* and *Antichrist* appears to be integrated in a vibrating mental moment, one in which there is no distinct division between the actual environment and mental fantasy.

In addition to the bond between landscape and character in stories such as *Harbour* and *Anti-Christ*, there is a complex relationship between time and focalisation, between what is happening to the protagonists in the present time of narration and what happened in a certain place in the past. The protagonists are made to see and experience certain things connected to the Nordic topography and its local history. The landscape is always part of a barbaric state that subverts the modern world of science and the laws of time and space. When the protagonists surrender to their desires, they also give in to the power of the pagan past of the region. The past represents a threat to the protagonists, and Scandinavian writers and filmmakers often recall a prehistoric era, a period before Christianity was brought to Scandinavia. Although the protagonists' visit exposes dreadful events from just a few decades ago, as in Alexander L. Nordaas' film *Thale* (2012) or, to take a more recent example, Stefan Spjut's novel *Stallo* (2012), the horror in the stories dates back to a prehistoric era before human civilisation when nature ruled. When two crime-scene assistants in *Thale* are cleaning up a remote cottage in the Norwegian woods, they find an imprisoned female creature, Thale, who has been submitted to experiments by her captor, a scene which, as Johan Höglund argues, reminds viewers of colonial conquest and eugenic practices towards the native population.[13] However, Thale and

---

[13] Johan Höglund, 'Revenge of the Trolls: Norwegian (Post) Colonial Gothic, *Edda* 2 (2017): 115–29 (pp. 123–6).

her fellow forest creatures represent both another species and a pre-human stage in nature. The way in which she is depicted suggests to the audience that she belongs to the Nordic mythological 'hulder', a seductive female being with a tail and a hollowed-out back. In *Stallo*, when a child goes missing at the same time as certain wild animals start to act strangely, the daughter of a photographer, who once snapped a shot of what looks like a troll riding a bear, starts to believe her father actually took a picture of a troll, or what the local Sami people name 'stallo'. The female protagonist's investigation of the case discloses a hostile world of trolls and shapeshifters who are able to enslave human beings by taking over their minds, erasing their memories and human identity as they do so. In *Thale* and *Stallo*, the encounter with the creatures of nature results in the dissolution of categories, such as the mythic world of folktale and modern everyday life. It also subverts the notion of a reality consisting of a meaningful chain of cause, effect and teleological progress. The Nordic wilderness represents a cyclic, timeless and infinite state, a mental state in which chronology and spatial distinctions are dissolved.

Like other Gothic characters, the protagonists in Scandinavian stories give in to their repressed desires and are taken over by their dark sides, but unlike most other Gothic characters, their desires are bound to and activated by the landscape. When they lose control over their imagination and the ability to distinguish between reality and fantasy, there is a fusion between ego and landscape. However, the landscape should not be seen as a metaphor for a mood or the situation of the subject. It is not primarily there to enhance the atmosphere by causing storms and mists, but is rather of central importance to the plot. The landscape has a role of its own, interacting with the protagonists as an alien force or creature and directing their actions and perceptions. Its function is literally to transform the protagonists into savage uncivilised creatures, to prove that the human mind cannot be separated from the surrounding landscape – that the ego is a disordered wilderness.

Gothic Parody, Realism and Crime

The Gothic boom in Scandinavia at the millennium has brought about three distinct cross-genres, which could be called Gothic parody or satire, Gothic realism and Gothic crime. All three hybrid genres have resulted in best-selling fiction and blockbuster movies that have been well received outside Scandinavia and which have resulted in various imitations and remakes. The first internationally successful form of hybrid genre on the screen – the Gothic parody or satire – was Lars von Trier's satirical TV drama *The Kingdom* (*Riget*

I-II 1994–7), set in the neurosurgical ward of Copenhagen's main hospital, nicknamed 'riget', which means 'the realm' or 'the kingdom'. The series follows a number of characters, both staff and patients, as they encounter a succession of bizarre and supernatural phenomena. What happens in the ward leads the viewer progressively to see the hospital not as the realm of modern medicine but of death, especially as the happenings are accompanied by a chorus of dishwashers with Down's syndrome, who discuss the strange occurrences in the ward. Every episode begins with the same prologue that describes how the modern hospital was built on the site of the former bleaching ponds, a detail that seems to call forth the powers of an ancient spooky past. Although the hospital is a representation of modern technique, rational science and a well-organised workplace, the daily routines are troubled by a repressed past that enhances the satirical qualities. The success of the Danish miniseries resulted in an American remake, the serial called Stephen King's *Kingdom Hospital* (2004), which is located in a distinctly American setting, Lewiston, Maine, not a capital but a small town and on the site of a mill that manufactured military uniforms during the American Civil War.[14]

Several other Scandinavian parodies have won various international awards, including Anders Banke's vampire film *Frostbite* (*Frostbiten*, 2006), Roar Uthaug's ironic slasher film *Cold Prey* (*Fritt vilt*, 2006) and Tommy Wirkola's zombie parody *Dead Snow* (*Død snø*, 2009). As Gunnar Iversen argues, since 2000 the boom in horror films has blurred the distinction between art and genre cinema in a way that rethinks the genre itself.[15] Banke's film takes place in a small town north of the polar circle during midwinter, making the Nordic environment perfect for vampires as there is no daylight during the winter days. When some teenagers mistakenly hand out the geneticist Professor Becket's vampire pills at an end-of-term party, a hilarious parody of vampirism is displayed with wry references to previous vampire films. Similar parodic genre aesthetics are used in Uthaug's *Cold Prey* and Wirkola's *Dead Snow*. In both films, a group of young city people travel to the Norwegian mountains on a snowboard and ski vacation respectively, but in both cases, the intended retreat turns into a nightmarish battle. In *Cold Prey*, the snowboard tourists find themselves isolated at an empty hotel with

---

[14] On Nordic Gothic and transcultural adaptation, see Maria Holmgren Troy, 'Lost (and gained) in Translation: Nordic Gothic and Transcultural Adaptation', in Maria Holmgren Troy, Johan Höglund, Yvonne Leffler and Sofia Wijkmark (eds), *Nordic Gothic* (Manchester: Manchester University Press, 2020), pp. 147–68.

[15] Gunnar Iversen, 'Between Art and Genre: New Nordic Horror Cinema', in Mette Hjort and Ursula Lindqvist (eds), *A Companion to Nordic Cinema* (Oxford: Wiley-Blackwell, 2016) pp. 332–49.

a psychotic killer on the loose. In *Dead Snow*, the skiers are attacked by greedy Nazi zombies, who have been waiting for prey in the mountains since the German occupation of Norway during World War II. In all three films, the filmmakers Banke, Uthaug and Wirkola make the most of the snowbound Nordic environment to emphasise the extreme, barren surroundings in order to present an exaggerated version of a Gothic setting and plot.

A somewhat different metafictional horror film is André Øvredal's dark fantasy *Troll Hunter* (*Trolljegeren*, 2010). It is made in the form of a 'mockumentary' or 'found-footage' film about two students and their cameraman who set out to make a documentary about a suspected bear poacher but end up following him as a troll hunter as well as the only operative in the Troll Security Team, a top-secret branch of the Norwegian government. The depiction of the troll hunt, with ironic references to local folklore, highlights a topical subject, humankind's exploitation of natural resources and eradication of other species. Thus, Øvredal's film is an illustrative example of the ironic use of Gothic conventions to target not only the Gothic genre as such, but to make social and political points about urgent problems, such as the embattled ecosystem.

Øvredal's way of handling present-day issues in *Troll Hunter* leads over to the second cross-genre, which could be labelled 'Gothic realism' as it is a type of narrative characterised by a matter-of-fact inclusion of supernatural elements and creatures into a seemingly realistic and mundane contemporary world. Scandinavian Gothic realism of today – like magic realism in Latin American literature – could be read as stories of political and social subversion. In *Handling the Undead* (*Hanteringen av odöda*, 2005), John Ajvide Lindqvist includes Gothic elements to reveal poor conditions in contemporary Sweden and, as Sofia Wijkmark argues, the demise of the welfare state.[16] The novel revolves around the unexplained reanimation of thousands of recently deceased people and the conflicts that arise between local authorities and the relatives of the undead. The horrors are less created by the zombies than by the depiction of the relatives' grief and their reaction to death and their own mortality. Mats Strandberg also uses a combination of social realism and Gothic elements in his novels *Blood Cruise* (*Färjan*, 2015) and *The Nursing Home* (*Hemmet*, 2017). In *Blood Cruise*, two vampires, a mother and her uncontrollable son, board the ferry between Sweden and Finland. The routines of the staff and the passengers on board are challenged in a way that

---

[16] Sofia Wijkmark, 'Swedish Gothic and the Demise of the Welfare State', in Holmgren Troy, Höglund, Leffler and Wijkmark (eds), *Nordic Gothic*, pp. 47–64.

exposes the unsatisfactory state of things in the lives of the characters, as well as in contemporary society as such. The same political approach is applied in *The Nursing Home*, in which a formerly reticent woman's emotional problems and change of personality prompt her son to take her to a nursing home for demented patients. Her increasingly violent behaviour, in combination with certain supernatural happenings in the ward, makes her son and a nurse suspect that the old woman is possessed by an evil entity. Their investigation of her condition and use of exorcism turns the novel into a horror story, while at the same time exploring various stages of dementia and the customary ways of handling the patients.

In those cases in which films have been based on stories of Gothic realism, such as John Ajvide Lindqvist's transculturally successful vampire novel *Let the Right One In*, the subversive message has often been reduced or eliminated. Ajvide Lindqvist's novel depicts the unsatisfactory state of things in a suburb of Stockholm. The vampire motif is primarily used to reveal social problems in the modern welfare state, such as alienation, abuse, bullying and paedophilia. The portrayal of the boy Oscar, the vampire child Eli and the relationship between them challenges the established concepts of murder, homicide and killing. However, in Thomas Alfredson's Swedish-language film based on the novel, the social issues are relegated to the background, as is the urban setting; here, the exposure of sexual exploitation and paedophilia are played down in favour of the romance and friendship between Oskar and Eli. In the film, the horror scenes showing the attacks of the vampire and its assistant are more predominant than in the novel; they also take place in a visually elaborated Nordic setting, the snow-covered forest residues left within – or beyond – the suburb. Thus, Ajvide Lindqvist's exposure of the gloomy condition of the Swedish welfare state has been toned down for the depiction of two star-crossed young lovers and a visually attractive wintry setting.

The third example of a Scandinavian cross-genre could be called 'Gothic crime' since the stories start as ordinary realistic crime stories with a murder being committed and the initiation of the crime investigation. However, mystifying circumstances of a surreal or supernatural nature soon interfere with the investigation.[17] Johan Theorin's Öland Quartet – *Echoes from the Dead* (*Nattfåk*, 2007), *The Darkest Room* (*Skumtimmen*, 2008), *The Quarry* (*Blodläge*, 2010) and *The Voices Beyond* (*Rörgast*, 2015) – have been sold in more than

---

[17] Yvonne Leffler, 'Nordic Gothic Crime: Places and Spaces in Johan Theorin's Öland Quartet Series', in Holmgren Troy, Höglund, Leffler and Wijkmark (eds), *Nordic Gothic*, pp. 65–83.

twenty countries and are often categorised as Gothic thrillers rooted in the tradition of Nordic noir. The stories revolve around an amateur detective, an old retired sailor who spends his time in a private room in the old folks' home waiting for visits from his daughter and his brother's granddaughter, the investigating policewoman. In all four stories, the plotline of a modern crime investigation is combined with the depiction of a haunted place with a dark past on the Swedish island of Öland. For example, in *The Darkest Room*, a family moves to an old wooden house, Eel Point, on the coast close to a lighthouse. The couple's remote idyll is soon shattered when the wife is found drowned off the nearby rocks. As her husband struggles to take care of their children and keep his sanity in the wake of the tragedy, the house begins to exert a strange hold over him and the local legend about Eel Point seems to be true: that every Christmas the former but now dead inhabitants return. Moreover, in the last novel, *The Voices Beyond*, the dead seem to come alive when a teenage boy encounters and escapes what he believes to be a ship full of corpses except for a man carrying an axe. At the same time, an ex-pat soldier returns on his final deadly mission to defraud the boy's wealthy family. In both novels, the seemingly supernatural happenings are interconnected with the crimes committed, and with the double-narrative technique it is shown that the old detective both confronts his own past and finally solves the mystery, where the supernatural phenomena finally prove to be firmly grounded in the rational.

In addition to novels, several TV series have been produced in which a Gothic mystery is integrated into the plotline of a detective story. In 2015, two Swedish TV series were first broadcast, *Jordskott* (literal translation 'soil shoot'), directed by Henrik Björn and Anders Engström, and *Ängelby* (literal translation 'village of angels') by Johan Kindblom and Tomas Tivemark. In *Jordskott*, which was also broadcast in the UK in 2015, a female police detective returns to her hometown seven years after her daughter disappeared near the forest. Upon the detective's return, a boy is missing, and as she begins to look for similarities between the two cases, the police detective soon discovers that they are inextricably tangled with both local and mystical elements that want to save the forest from a local company that intends to exploit the land. *Ängelby*, broadcast in the UK in 2016, follows a mother of two, whose life is turned upside down and who seeks to start a new life in the village of Ängelby. As she drives to the village, she appears to hit and kill a local teenage ice-hockey star. However, when she reports the incident, the body has disappeared, and when she tries to settle in Ängelby, she realises that the disappearance of the boy's body is only the beginning of a series of weird and frightening events occurring in the neighbourhood. Unlike in Theorin's novels, the supernatural happenings in the two TV series are never given any natural explanation; instead, they are explored in a matter-of-fact way to prove the existence of phenomena that present-day people recognise from folktales and ancient myths. At the same time, the supernatural happenings can be interpreted as a punishing force that is targeted at ongoing wrongdoings and the exploitation of the environment, particularly the forest land outside the villages.

Hybridity, Folklore and Wilderness

In the twenty-first century, it is possible to discern three distinct categories of Scandinavian Gothic or ways of making use of Gothic conventions. The writers and filmmakers are remarkably genre-aware; they openly position their works in the established global tradition of Gothic, which in some cases results in playful metafictional references, genre parodies and satires. Many of them have also introduced and modified Gothic elements in other well-established genres, a practice that has given rise to hybridity and new cross-genres such as Gothic realism and Gothic crime. Moreover, during the last decades, a growing number of crossover and young-adult stories have appeared, in which supernatural beings and Gothic conventions are frequently explored, especially in stories addressing female audiences.

Whatever kind of Gothic works or media Scandinavian writers and filmmakers produce, they position themselves within a Scandinavian tradition of fiction and film. The dominant discourse of realism in Scandinavian culture and the repression of non-realistic modes since the mid-nineteenth century might explain the extensive development of Gothic cross-genres and the rise of Gothic realism, parodies and satires. The combination of social realism with Gothic elements in order to explore topical issues in contemporary society paved the way for the success of Ajvide Lindqvist's *Let the Right One In* and *Handling the Undead* in Sweden. To local critics, it demonstrated that Gothic conventions could be used for serious aims and to address contemporary anxieties. Parodic and satiric use of Gothic elements in order to highlight crucial topics in an amusing way has also become an established Scandinavian version of Gothic within the Scandinavian comedy tradition since von Trier's TV drama, *The Kingdom*.

The most distinct feature of Scandinavian Gothic, however, and one that has lasted from the early nineteenth century to the present day, is that the stories are located in a recognisable Scandinavian environment. The Gothic space is predominantly the Nordic wilderness, the vast dark fir forest, the snow-covered mountains or the Arctic coastline. Regional folklore, popular belief and ancient customs rooted in pagan times are frequently used to enhance the atmosphere. Whatever the sub-category of Scandinavian Gothic, there is a conspicuous and deep-rooted connection between the human characters and the surrounding landscape. Like most Gothic characters, the Scandinavian protagonists give in to their repressed desires, but their dark sides are clearly bound to and triggered by the Nordic wilderness, legendary creatures and the pagan past of the Scandinavian region. When the characters lose control over their senses and imagination, they are taken over by untamed nature. In some crossover stories, the female protagonist's bond to nature might, in the long run, be of benefit to her and her society, but in most other stories untamed nature plays a devious role. In many Gothic crime stories, as noted earlier, there is a complex relationship between time and focalisation, between what is happening in the present time of modern crime investigation and what once happened in the same place in the past. In some TV series, the encounter with the pagan forces of nature clearly results in a fusion of past and present, man and nature, myth and reality. Therefore, the investigation of the crime seldom reaches a satisfactory explanation. Instead, the protagonists in these and other stories are made to submit to the powers of nature that reside within them. As in most Scandinavian Gothic stories since the early nineteenth century, the ego and milieu seem to be united in an everlasting moment of chaos and horror. The human ego is not only attacked but is also invaded and eventually taken over by untamed nature and transported into an uncivilised prehistoric stage of myth and untamed Nordic nature.

3.22
Gothic in an Age of Environmental Crisis

SARA L. CROSBY

The Ghosts of Environmental Crisis

Throughout the summer of 2018, Europe broiled in unprecedented high temperatures that brought drought, crop failures, power shortages, wildfires, disease and death. Europe's paranormal investigators, however, had even more to worry about: apparently, the heatwave generated a 'major spike' in ghostly activity. Just as climatologists linked the soaring temperatures and the more mundane horrors that they produced to human-induced climate change, so too did distressed ghost hunters worry that global warming might be amplifying disruptive spectral behaviour and driving terrified residents from newly haunted houses. With tongue only somewhat in cheek, one commentator speculated that the intensified hauntings 'could be spirits coming back to do what they couldn't when they were alive – convince others that climate change is real and causing serious problems'.[1]

Whether one credits this report of environmental-activist ghosts or not, the story does draw attention to very 'real' and 'serious' problems. The 2018 IPCC report gives humanity only 12 years to reduce greenhouse gas emissions before we pass 1.5°C of warming and so slide from the merely disastrous into the catastrophic.[2] Earth is already in the midst of the sixth mass extinction, with humanity's pollution, habitat destruction and overconsumption impacting upon the planet like an asteroid strike or mass volcanic activity. Not only are we losing individual species at up to 10,000 times the

---

[1] 'Heatwave GHOSTS: Paranormal investigators report major summer spike in calls', *The Daily Star*, 6 August 2018 <www.dailystar.co.uk/news/weird-news/721496/UK-heatwave-weather-forecast-ghost-news-paranormal-investigators> (last accessed 19 January 2019); Paul Seaburn, 'Ghost Sightings Increase Tied to Climate Change', *Mysterious Universe*, 8 August 2018 <https://mysteriousuniverse.org/2018/08/ghost-sightings-increase-tied-to-climate-change/> (last accessed 19 January 2019).

[2] 'Summary for Policymakers of IPCC Special Report on Global Warming of 1.5°C approved by governments' <www.ipcc.ch/2018/10/08/summary-for-policymakers-of-ipcc-special-report-on-global-warming-of-1-5c-approved-by-governments/> (last accessed 19 January 2019).

natural rate, animal populations overall are crashing, with the World Wildlife Fund (or the World Wide Fund for Nature) estimating that we may have lost up to 70 per cent of the animals on the planet since 1970.[3] In perhaps the most cogent summation of the situation, the Global Footprint Network calculates that humanity is now consuming the natural resources of 1.7 Earths per year, meaning that we are no longer living on the interest but chewing into the capital that global ecosystems need in order to regenerate and sustain life on earth, including, of course, human life.[4]

To say that humanity is in an age of environmental crisis is an understatement, and yet we seem to have difficulty comprehending and facing that reality. Instead of shouting the emergency from the rooftops, the global culture industry has largely gone about its typical routine for decades, producing typical human dramas that engage with the crisis infrequently or superficially. This omission suggests a problem not just of politics but of representation and imagination too. Amitav Ghosh, for instance, has argued that mainstream art and literature practice 'modes of concealment that prevent ... people from recognizing their [ecological] plight'.[5] He points out that modern narrative forms perform this concealment by suppressing the nonhuman and reducing it from agent to a mere background for the play of human self-actualisation.

While such narcissistic 'concealment' might have functioned well enough in the age of fossil-fuel-driven, imperialist modernity, when global industrial capitalism could rely upon healthy ecosystems and construct human (colonial, white, male) identity from the conquest of seemingly infinite resources, this narrative mode founders and fails in an era of environmental limitation and threat. The first two decades of the twenty-first century have thus witnessed ecocritics' intensifying attempts to articulate alternatives to 'modes of concealment', which would convey a crucial new ecological awareness of the nonhuman. They have been framing this awareness in a variety of ways and calling it by various names, arguing that humanity must acquire an understanding of our 'living interconnections'; develop an 'eco-cosmopolitanism'; admit our 'transcorporeality'; recognise

---

[3] See 'Extinction Crisis', Center for Biological Diversity <www.biologicaldiversity.org/programs/biodiversity/elements_of_biodiversity/extinction_crisis/> (last accessed 12 February 2019); 'Living Planet Report', *WWF* <www.worldwildlife.org/pages/living-planet-report-2016> (last accessed 12 February 2019).

[4] 'Ecological Footprint', *Ecological Footprint Network* <www.footprintnetwork.org/our-work/ecological-footprint/> (last accessed 19 January 2019).

[5] Amitav Ghosh, *The Great Derangement: Climate Change and the Unthinkable* (Chicago: University of Chicago Press, 2016), p. 11.

'hyperobjects'; re-describe our 'dwelling places'; or acknowledge our 'uncanny intimacy' with the nonhuman.[6] In spite of these differing terminologies, the content of their messages has been remarkably consistent: human survival may depend upon overcoming the repression of nonhuman agency. We must instead pay vigorous attention to it and to our ecological relationship with it, including, especially, the revivified force of materials that humans have profoundly affected, such as global climate and our own waste.

Ecocritics, however, remain more perplexed about the best delivery mechanism for this message: what genres, styles and narratives can overcome our 'modes of concealment' and promote an ecological awareness conducive to survival? While there have been a plethora of suggestions: from 'slow' TV-like livestream feeds of an eagle nest, to avant-garde tonal music to 'cli-fi' (climate fiction) novels, one of the most intriguing suggestions involves the Gothic. Allan Lloyd Smith famously characterises the Gothic as a genre that unearths 'the repressed and denied, the buried secret that subverts and corrodes the present', and, in the first extensive scholarly exploration of the 'ecoGothic', Andrew Smith and William Hughes contend that the Gothic 'seems to be the form which is well placed to capture ... anxieties' about 'climate change and environmental damage' and to help produce 'environmental awareness' and draw attention to 'the political urgency of ecological issues'.[7]

Yet, while they do some of this consciousness-raising work, many of the usual ecohorror narratives – tales of wilderness horror, industrial extraction horror, animal horror and so on – still occur in settings at a far remove from their audiences' everyday lives. The kind of revelatory ecoGothic that Smith and Hughes describe (and that ecocritics wish for) would not only expose the

---

[6] Greta Gaard, 'Living Interconnections with Animals and Nature', in Greta Gaard (ed.), *Ecofeminism: Women, Animals, Nature* (Philadelphia, PA: Temple University Press, 1993), pp. 1–12 (p. 1); Ursula K. Heise, *Sense of Place and Sense of Planet: The Environmental Imagination of the Global* (Oxford: Oxford University Press, 2008), p. 61; Stacey Alaimo, *Bodily Natures: Science, Environment, and the Material Self* (Bloomington, IN: Indiana University Press, 2010), p. 2; Timothy Morton, *Hyperobjects: Philosophy and Ecology after the End of the World* (Minneapolis: University of Minnesota Press, 2013), p. 1; Bruno Latour, *Down to Earth: Politics in the New Climatic Regime*, trans. by Catherine Porter (London: Polity Press, 2018), p. 94; Ghosh, *Great Derangement*, p. 33. We should note that ecofeminist philosophers deserve a great deal of credit for originating much of this argument. Many of the men in the current crop of environmental thinkers fail to acknowledge this intellectual debt, with Simon Estok being a notable exception.

[7] Allan Lloyd Smith, *American Gothic Fiction: An Introduction* (London: Continuum, 2005), p. 1. Andrew Smith and William Hughes, 'Introduction', in Andrew Smith and William Hughes (eds), *EcoGothic* (Manchester: Manchester University Press, 2013), pp. 1–14 (p. 5). See also Dawn Keetley and Matthew Wynn Sivils (eds), *Ecogothic in Nineteenth-Century American Literature* (New York: Routledge, 2018).

agency of the nonhuman, but would also raise awareness of humanity's intimate relationship to it within the context of an ecological web of dependencies. Such a sense of intimacy and embeddedness is more easily evoked (and less easily avoided) in familiar, especially domestic, spaces. It requires a different kind of ecoGothic, one that takes us back home and hits us, like the heatwave ghosts, where we live: right in our haunted house.

Into the Bad *Oikos*

That the haunted house is becoming a key figure for understanding our current environmental crisis should not be terribly surprising. The Greek '*oikos*' translates roughly to 'house' or 'home' and gives us the prefix 'eco', signalling the rather perverse fact that 'house' or 'home' has long served as one of the most fundamental metaphors for conceptualising nonhuman nature and the human relationship to it. Unfortunately, as Simon Estok points out, that concept and that relationship have often been defined by 'ecophobia', which refers to 'the contempt and fear we feel for the agency of the natural environment', a hatred and horror of nature that enables its exploitation and destruction.[8] Ironically, this ecophobia-driven abuse has transformed nature from our old home – i.e. the pastoral, familiar, domesticated, Holocene nature of human civilisation – into a strange and terrifying house, a disturbed Anthropocene nature potentially inimical to the long-term continuance of human life, much less human civilisation.

As this transformation has slowly seeped into popular consciousness, so thinkers, from the blogger 'Darwinian Demon' to the philosopher Bruno Latour, have turned to the 'house' metaphor to conceptualise our new 'haunted' ecological reality. As Timothy Morton contends, 'Home, *oikos*, is unstable.' It has become 'a place of ... death-in-life and life-in-death, an undead place of ... ghosts ... demonic forces, and pollution'.[9] Humanity is left wandering through the rooms of a haunted house: a house 'of death-in-life and life-in-death', but also a house that has come suddenly alive in order to reveal the nonhuman or 'demonic agencies' that we failed to consider when nature was simply a quiescent background to the narrative of human

---

[8] Simon C. Estok, 'Theorizing in a Space of Ambivalent Openness: Ecocriticism and Ecophobia', *Interdisciplinary Studies in Literature and the Environment* 16 (Spring 2009): 203–25 (pp. 207–8). See also Simon C. Estok, *The Ecophobia Hypothesis* (New York: Routledge, 2018).

[9] Morton, *Hyperobjects*, pp. 117, 126.

drama. In a way, our planetary home has become what Stephen King famously called 'the Bad Place', at least of a rather particular kind.[10]

The traditional haunted house or Bad Place was most often simply inhabited by supernatural extensions of the human, but, with increasing frequency, such sites have instead come to be represented as invested with an organic nonhuman life of their own. In 1999, Dale Bailey noted this shift in contemporary haunted house tales towards 'a prosaic depiction of the supernatural in which the house itself is sentient and malign, independent of any ghosts which may be present (and very frequently none are)'.[11] I would argue that this change is less 'prosaic' and 'supernatural' and more ecological – at least in the significant line of haunted house ecoGothics that attribute the haunting agency to a nonhuman, organic, living house – to an ecosystem – rather than to a merely human or once-human presence. At the same time, however, these house-ecosystems also incorporate human agency as a necessary component and only achieve their sentience and malignity through an interaction with the human. As such, they encapsulate and illustrate the crisis-ridden, human-impacted ecosystems produced in the Anthropocene.

This kind of haunted house, a human-nonhuman crossover between a bad home and a bad nature, is a 'bad *oikos*'. The bad *oikos* confronts audiences with both nonhuman agency and the human entanglement with it and so demands that we extract ourselves from our 'modes of concealment'. It has thus become an important figure through which popular culture is working out humanity's new, troubled relationship with the ecosystems that support us. The remainder of this chapter will examine the bad *oikos*, exploring its origins in 1970s debates over ecofeminism and fossil fuels in texts such as Robert Marasco's *Burnt Offerings* (1973) and Anne Rivers Siddons's *The House Next Door* (1978), and then sketch its contemporary contours in a recent spate of texts from Darren Aronofsky's *mother!* (2017) through to Netflix's hit show *The Haunting of Hill House* (2018) to the surreal and weirdly popular YouTube animated series *Ghost House* (2018–). It will look more closely at the specific anxieties impelling these shiny new versions of the bad *oikos*, such as the dawning realisation that large-scale environmental degradation is a horrific act of child abuse and that this crisis is also responsible for inducing an intense new kind of identity-shifting transcorporeality. But first: where did the bad *oikos* come from, and what are 'the rules' that govern it?

---

[10] Stephen King, *Danse Macabre* (New York: Gallery Books, 1981), p. 278.
[11] Dale Bailey, *American Nightmares: The Haunted House Formula in American Popular Fiction* (Bowling Green, OH: Bowling Green State University Popular Press, 1999), pp. 5–6.

The Conditions of Sentience

The two foundational bad *oikos* texts are Edgar Allan Poe's 'The Fall of the House of Usher' (1839) and Shirley Jackson's *The Haunting of Hill House* (1959). Together, they establish the nonhuman agency and ecosystem structure of the bad *oikos*, while they also locate its origin in acts of interrelated ecophobia and misogyny. Jackson's Hill House is a 'live organism ... not sane', while the House of Usher's ecosystemic 'order of arrangement' of stones, fungi and tarn has produced 'conditions of sentience'.[12] However, both houses are only stung into malignant life by tyrannical men, who insist upon controlling and projecting themselves upon the environment and upon the women around them. Roderick Usher, for instance, awash in his own unacknowledged ecophobia and misogyny, tries to blame the estate and his sister for contaminating him with a diseased 'gloom', but the narrator ultimately unveils that particular 'concealment' by observing that in fact his friend's ego exudes the polluting 'radiation of gloom' upon the environment.[13] Similarly, Hugh Crain, the tycoon who built Hill House, drives it insane by designing the 'vile ... diseased' house in the same oppressively patriarchal spirit with which he constructed a 'foul, horrible' religious book meant to terrorise his daughters into obedience to God and to Crain, who stands in the place of God as 'author of thy being and guardian of thy virtue'.[14]

These 'rules' for the bad *oikos* – ecosystem organisation and disturbed nonhuman sentience provoked by ecophobia aligned with misogyny – would largely be repressed by most subsequent haunted house texts, even ones directly based on Poe or Jackson. For instance, the 1970s witnessed a popular eruption of haunted house Gothics inspired by Jackson's novel and its well-crafted 1963 film adaptation, Robert Wise's *The Haunting*, but most, including the *Hill House* adaptations, ran with the 'Hugh Crain' or 'men on the rampage' rather than the 'nonhuman organism on the rampage' trope and so compressed the nonhuman once again into the background for humans and their ghosts.[15] These included *Hell House* (book 1971, film 1973), Richard

---

[12] Shirley Jackson, *The Haunting of Hill House*, in Joyce Carol Oates (ed.), *Shirley Jackson: Novels and Stories* (New York: Library of America, 2010), pp. 241–417 (p. 243); Edgar Allan Poe, 'The Fall of the House of Usher', in Thomas Mabbott (ed.), *The Collected Works of Edgar Allan Poe: Tales and Sketches 1831–1842* (Cambridge, MA: Belknap Press, 1978), pp. 392–421 (p. 408).
[13] Poe, 'Fall of the House of Usher', p. 405.
[14] Jackson, *Haunting of Hill House*, pp. 264, 363–4.
[15] The phrase 'men on the rampage' as a description of a subset of the Gothic comes from Kate Ferguson Ellis, 'Can You Forgive Her? The Gothic Heroine and Her Critics', in David Punter (ed.), *A New Companion to the Gothic* (Oxford: Wiley-Blackwell, 2012), pp. 457–68 (p. 464).

Matheson's sensationalised gross-out revision of Jackson's *Hill House*; Jay Anson's 'based upon a true story' bestseller, *The Amityville Horror* (1977) and its seemingly unending movie franchise; Nobuhiko Obayashi's feverish *House* (1977); and, of course, Stephen King's *The Shining* (1978) and its luminous adaptation by Stanley Kubrick (1981). Even Stephen Spielberg got in on the horror with the wildly popular *Poltergeist* (1982–2015) series.

Yet, all of these texts returned to 'modes of concealment' by attributing the haunting to human agencies, even if these, in turn, were often traced back to 'nature-adjacent' indigenous peoples and their violated graves. During the 1970s, the nonhuman was for the most part left to splatter-fest 'nature strikes back' films that performed a Janus-faced ideology: amplification of ecophobia – Alfred Hitchcock's *The Birds* (1963), Steven Spielberg's *Jaws* (1975), William Girdler's *Grizzly* (1976), Irwin Allen's *The Swarm* (1978) – alternating with its critique – George McCowan's *Frogs* (1972), Michael Anderson's *Orca* (1977), John Frankenheimer's *Prophecy* (1979) and Walon Green's *The Hellstrom Chronicle* (1971).

There were two important exceptions to the erasure of the bad *oikos* during the 1970s: the two best-selling novels, Anne Rivers Siddons's *The House Next Door* (1978) and Robert Marasco's *Burnt Offerings* (1973), which was also adapted into a 1976 film directed by Dan Curtis and starring Karen Black and Bette Davis (Fig. 22.1). *Burnt Offerings*, in particular, with its suggestively theological title, has profoundly shaped the current resurgence of bad *oikos* narratives, which, as we will see in the next section, take on its vision for the bad *oikos* but attempt to soften or resist its overtly anti-environmentalist/anti-feminist politics.

The 1960s and 1970s, of course, witnessed the emergence of second-wave feminism and the modern environmental movement, and a notable subsection of these movements grappled with the theological underpinnings of environmental degradation. Thinkers such as Mary Daly, Lynn White, Jr, and even James Lovelock and Lynn Margulis with their 'Gaia hypothesis' named after an earth goddess were beginning to challenge the kind of patriarchal Christianity that actuated Hugh Crain and the ecophobia and misogyny that many saw curled in its centre. While White attributed the twentieth century's burgeoning ecological crises to Western religion's anthropocentrism, Daly and other ecofeminists pointed out that 'anthro' really did refer to 'man', and argued that the root of the oppression and exploitation of both women and nature lay in Western society's 'hierarchical dualisms', particularly the paired man/woman and society/nature, and the rejection of 'embodiment' and ecological 'embeddedness', which accompanied the

Fig.22.1: *Burnt Offerings*, poster, US poster, top from left: Oliver Reed, Karen Black, Burgess Meredith, Bette Davis, Eileen Heckart, 1976. (Photo by LMPC via Getty Images).

oppression of 'woman' and 'nature'.[16] Since, some theorists observed, a transcendent male god modelled and reinforced this structure, perhaps

[16] Mary Mellor, *Feminism and Ecology* (New York: New York University Press, 1997), pp. 68–9.

a more sustainable theological configuration would invoke an immanent female divinity. In Daly's words, '*God* represents the necrophilia of patriarchy, whereas *Goddess* affirms the life-loving be-ing of woman and nature.'[17] From this perspective, reaffirming a goddess/mother nature figure could help to restore the rights and authority that an ecophobic 'patriarchy' stole from both women and nature and so solve a quickly spiralling ecological degradation.

Marasco's *Burnt Offerings* bloomed out of, and ultimately contributed to, this ferment. However, the novel responded to the emergent feminist and environmentalist movements (and Poe and Jackson) by flipping their ecofeminist critiques on their heads and blaming the bad *oikos* and its horror on the environmentalists and feminists who love women and nature too much, instead of on the ecophobic patriarchs who degrade and exploit them. The few critics who have engaged with *Burnt Offerings*, both novel and film, tend to see its narrative – a family rents a too-good-to-be-true estate, which then preys upon them so it can repair itself – as a critique of 1970s empty materialism, embodied in the wife/mother Marian, with the house offering her false shows of 'consumption', 'investment', or 'middle-class domesticity'.[18] Such critical viewpoints are not exactly wrong. However, what the Allardyce house whispers to Marian is far more substantial than just the opportunity to play grand lady capitalist of the manor. It dangles a genuine ecofeminist lure: promising her the joy of environmental restoration and the glory of an earth mother-goddess – in other words, real ecological connection and, most intriguingly, real power.

The house can seduce Marian not because she is a materialist, but because she is an environmentalist materialist, for whom matter matters. For instance, when Marian first encounters the Allardyce home in its sick and decrepit state, she reacts with the heightened and embedded awareness of an environmentalist faced with a degraded ecosystem that she wants to heal: '"It kills me, such waste. Kills me!" She gave a low scream and hammered [her husband Ben's] chest with both fists.' Ben tries to temper her reaction, telling her to distance herself from the house and 'Stop taking it so personally', but, like a good environmentalist, she does take the 'waste' personally, reacting as

---

[17] Mary Daly, *Gyn/ecology: The Metaethics of Radical Feminism* (Boston, MA: Beacon Press, 1978, 1990), p. xlv.
[18] Bailey, *American Nightmares*, p. 72; Grady Hendrix, *Paperbacks from Hell: The Twisted History of 70s and 80s Horror Fiction* (Philadelphia, PA: Quirk Books, 2017), pp. 105–6; Dara Downey, 'Locating the Spectre in Dan Curtis's *Burnt Offerings*', in Murray Leeder (ed.), *Cinematic Ghosts: Haunting and Spectrality from Silent Cinema to the Digital Age* (London: Bloomsbury Academic, 2015), pp. 143–58 (p. 144).

if it impacts upon her own life, as, of course, environmental degradation does.[19]

Thus, Marian wants desperately to fix the house because its elements are not simply consumable 'things' to her, but rather living elements of an ecosystem in which she is becoming embedded. She loves the glowing plants, the gleaming woodwork, the golden chafing dishes and the dazzling old crystal not because she can reduce them to dollars, but rather because she adores them in their own breathing, living materiality as part of her own life:

> She walked slowly down the narrow passages, pulling the folds of her gown closer. Filling herself with the wonder of it all ... She stopped to touch the pattern of a leaf, to breathe in the fragrance, bending as if in homage to the sheer perfection of the flowers, of the life the house was offering her. It was alive, all around her it was alive, and how else had it come alive, but through her?[20]

This ecosystem – the house and its living things – is 'filling' her with life and becoming part of her living being.

Moreover, and perhaps even more importantly, as she scrubs and repairs and replants and as the house slowly heals, sloughing off old skin to reveal the new underneath, she realises that she is the almost goddess-like power behind it. It has 'come alive ... through her'. She spends hours in the sitting of room of the silent and unseen 'mother', Mrs Allardyce, listening to the house, feeling its strange hum, and as her awareness of the house grows and as she feels closer and closer to its 'mother', she begins to know 'the growing awareness of her power in the house, the enormity of the mystery enveloping her life'. The religious language of 'mystery' is purposeful. She is becoming 'mother' – the high priestess turned goddess of this ecosystem, its beating heart, worshipped by the Allardyces as 'our darling' without whom 'the whole thing would just come down ... and so would we ... so would we'.[21]

However, this awareness, this power, this urge to restore the damaged but still living ecosystem of the house – all things that would be seen as positive from the perspective of the emergent environmental and feminist movements – is shot through with 'uneasiness' and ultimately portrayed as vampiric, with Marasco setting up an irreconcilable opposition between sustaining female power and the environment and sustaining men and the family. Marian's first instinctive environmentalist reaction against the 'waste' inflicted upon the house involves her literally (if weakly) beating her

---

[19] Robert Marasco, *Burnt Offerings* (New York: Delacorte Press, 1973), p. 37.
[20] Marasco, *Burnt Offerings*, p. 214.   [21] Marasco, *Burnt Offerings*, pp. 57–8.

husband, and the narrative then draws a line immediately from there to her abandonment of her childcare duties, as she accuses Ben: 'I thought you were watching David.' The house, of course, injures David during this unmonitored interval. Then, as Marian grows closer to the bad *oikos* and its 'mother', she finds that 'her life might be slowly divorcing itself from' her husband's until she has 'no point of contact' and no 'genuine feeling' for Ben and David.[22] After engineering this betrayal, the house leeches the colour from Marian's hair, transforming her into the stereotyped witchy hag, and demands that her family become the 'burnt offerings' to 'our mother' so that their deaths may accompany Marian's final ascension to mother-goddess and union with the bad *oikos*. In this bad *oikos*, nature rejects its role as quiescent background and matter for use, and women refuse their roles as helpmeets and props to capitalism's nuclear family – things fervently to be wished for from an ecofeminist perspective. However, *Burnt Offerings* transforms them into a source of horror.

The bad *oikos* would not always be used to make such reactionary arguments, and the next major work in the tradition, Anne Rivers Siddons's *The House Next Door* (1978), would try to draw it back to its 'Usher' origins as a critique of ecophobic hubris, repurposed for the era of global warming. By 1978, the science of anthropogenic global warming was well established, and popular alarm over fossil fuels had begun stirring, layering itself over disturbing memories of the OPEC embargo's exposure of petroleum's instability and mixing with the outrage sparked by documentaries such as Barbara Kopple's 1977 Oscar-winning *Harlan County, U.S.A.*, which showed the world the horrific brutality that coal miners and their communities still endured. It was becoming more apparent that Western modernity rested upon what Stephanie LeMenager describes as 'a profoundly unsustainable and charismatic energy system'.[23] The unsustainability of fossil fuels involves not only anxieties over foreign control or 'peak oil' scarcity, but also about coal and oil's untenable, even apocalyptic, environmental cost both to 'sacrifice zones' (like Harlan County) on the front line of extraction's 'slow violence' and to the entire planet.[24] Their charisma, especially petroleum's,

---

[22] Marasco, *Burnt Offerings*, pp. 191, 231.
[23] Stephanie LeMenager, *Living Oil: Petroleum Culture in the American Century* (Oxford: Oxford University Press, 2016), p. 11. LeMenager is primarily concerned with oil, but in this instance her arguments can be extended to include coal.
[24] Rob Nixon, *Slow Violence and the Environmentalism of the Poor* (Cambridge, MA: Harvard University Press, 2011), p. 2.

helps silence such concerns, however, and stems from their association with a 'modern' aesthetic of incredible power and comfort.[25]

Siddons sets down her bad *oikos* in just such a privileged modern fossil-fuel bubble: an exclusive suburban neighbourhood, full of expensive but not flashy cars, where existence runs 'smoothly' for the comfortably wealthy who know how to enjoy lives of fine food and 'grace' in the 'shell' that cheap energy built for them.[26] However, Siddons creates a bad *oikos* that unearths the repressed horror supporting this world and metaphorically renders the double-sidedness of its energy system: its lure and its violence. Trouble begins in 'an oasis of wild, dark greenness', a wooded, be-creeked lot, the last wild space in the neighbourhood, which our protagonist, Colquitt Kennedy, considers a precious neighbourhood commons, in which she is personally embedded.[27] 'My mini-mountain', as she calls it, had seemed safe – too rocky and recalcitrant to develop – until a hotshot architect, Kim Dougherty, strip-mines a shiny new build out of its earth.[28] Colquitt terms the lot's destruction an apocalyptic 'the end', but, in spite of her pain, she has to admit that Kim's creation is as charming as he is. Gorgeous and seductive, it seems 'organic ... alive', as if it had grown, and yet it embodies the 'modern' – all air and angles and glass.[29]

Unfortunately, this beautiful home is really just another House of Usher, crafted out of an unsustainable ecophobia. Even in the drafting stage, the bad *oikos* signals a peculiar kinship with the ancient 'elemental' fossil fuels that undergird modernity: it appears drawn 'out of the pencilled earth like an elemental spirit that had lain, locked and yearning for the light, through endless depths of time, waiting to be released'.[30] And, like coal or petroleum, it is extracted by the most heroically hubristic, techno-extractive type of masculinity. Kim treats his 'oasis' with the same cold ego as an oil man or a mine owner. Instead of approaching the ecosystem with the embeddedness and adoration of Marian or Colquitt, he first evaluates it with a distant, almost hostile 'measuring, far-off look'.[31] He plans to dominate the terrain, and, as the 'Col' of the 2006 Lifetime Television movie adaptation (starring Lara Flynn Boyle) succinctly puts it, 'It feels like a violation.' Ultimately, the abusive extraction that he performs releases no benign 'elemental spirit', but

---

[25] The malignant sentience of oil has become a common theme for petro-themed horror fiction such as Reza Negarestani's infamous *Cyclonopedia* (2008).
[26] Anne Rivers Siddons, *The House Next Door* (New York: Pocket Books, 1978), p. 11.
[27] Siddons, *House Next Door*, p. 13. [28] Siddons, *House Next Door*, p. 17.
[29] Siddons, *House Next Door*, p. 36. [30] Siddons, *House Next Door*, p. 26.
[31] Siddons, *House Next Door*, p. 23.

a 'malign [nonhuman] intelligence' that works an insidious slow violence to destroy any animal, human or nonhuman, that comes within its ken.[32]

After witnessing the destruction that it wreaks upon their once-idyllic neighbourhood, Colquitt and her husband realise that their 'shell' is broken, and the novel holds out different potential solutions to the bad *oikos*, which echo the inchoate strategies deployed around global warming but which all fail to work. First, the Kennedys play environmentalist whistleblowers and go to the media with their 'haunted house' tale. Like anti-global warming activists, they are met with angry denial from corporate interests and their own community, all of whom are too deeply committed to the unsustainable system that has afforded them so much comfort. A deeply offended Kim then tries a different approach, one that doubles down on the techno-extractive ecophobic mindset: in an effort to salvage his own reputation, he purchases the house and pleads with his former friends, 'Let me fix things for you' – let me take over and tame the bad *oikos*.[33] Yet, repeating domination cannot repair the violation, and the Kennedys realise that Kim, not just the bad *oikos*, is cursed. They kill him and presumably burn the house (though the novel leaves their success ambiguous). They die in the attempt, but fruitlessly, because, as an epilogue reveals, Kim left behind more designs. The fossil-fuel-dependent structures of modernity are, literally, already written and cannot be killed.

This profoundly pessimistic ending was perhaps too nihilistic to satisfy permanently. The next generation of bad *oikos* texts would cast about for solutions and return obsessively to Kim's final claim: could the men who helped create the bad *oikos* indeed 'fix it'? Subsequent texts in this tradition try to answer this question largely by grappling again and again with *Burnt Offerings*, picking at the structural opposition that it created between men and mother/nature, as they finally face the most painful aspect of our contemporary environmental crisis: child abuse.

Dad Can Fix It

During the same ferociously hot summer that radicalised Europe's ghosts, 15-year-old Greta Thunberg began haunting the steps of Sweden's parliament, holding a sign in Swedish that, when translated, declared 'School Strike for the Climate' (Fig. 22.2) . Thousands of children in over 100 countries would eventually join her in massive demonstrations aimed at convincing adults to reverse the

---

[32] Siddons, *House Next Door*, p. 215. [33] Siddons, *House Next Door*, p. 348.

Fig.22.2: Swedish climate activist Greta Thunberg protests with her placard reading 'School strike for climate' as part of her Fridays for Future protest in front of the Swedish Parliament Riksdagen in Stockholm on 9 October, 2020. (Photo by Jonathan NACKSTRAND/AFP). (Photo by Jonathan Nackstrand/AFP via Getty Images).

ecological damage imperilling their lives. Later, when Thunberg spoke to world leaders gathered at the COP24 conference, she summed up the children's position in a statement that also exposed one of the most appalling aspects of ecological degradation: 'You say you love your children above all else, and yet you are stealing their future in front of their very eyes.'[34] The current environmental crisis, to put it simply, might be the most extensive and terrible act of child abuse ever committed.

This realisation has been slowly dawning upon humanity with intensifying horror, and the Gothic is helping to shepherd it into consciousness.[35] David

---

[34] John Sutter and Lawrence Davidson, 'Teen tells climate negotiators they aren't mature enough', *CNN* <www.cnn.com/2018/12/16/world/greta-thunberg-cop24/index.html> (last accessed 20 March 2019).

[35] Climate change is increasingly being framed and dealt with as an intergenerational crime. For instance, in 2015, the Children's Trust defined the crisis as a crime against children when it sued the US federal government and fossil-fuel industry for 'acts [which] discriminate against . . . young citizens, who will disproportionately experience the destabilized climate system in our country'. See *Juliana* v. *United States of America*, Case 6:15-cv-01517-TC, Document 7, page 8 <https://static1.squarespace.com/static/5 71d109b04426270152febe0/t/5742856e20c647f6636bd24f/1463977328000/YouthAmended ComplaintAgainstUS.pdf> (last accessed 20 January 2019).

Punter and Sherry Truffin have both noted how child abuse has started to take up more and more space in modern Gothic and horror narratives, and this is particularly true of the ecoGothic.[36] Climate disaster Gothics such as Benh Zeitlin's *Beasts of the Southern Wild* (2012), extractive industry Gothics, such as Larry Fessenden's oil field/global warming horror *The Last Winter* (2006) and Cody Duckworth's fracking tale *Harbinger* (2015), for instance, all start to frame ecological degradation as an attack on children, asking the same question that Siddons raised: can the people who caused it fix it? Can Dad fix it? The answer, in these texts at least, is a resounding 'No!', with adults, specifically male father figures, either incapable of saving their children or in denial and/or fully complicit in the abuse.

Recently, bad *oikos* texts have begun to tackle the same question: perhaps Dad can fix the environmental crisis? The answers so far have been decidedly mixed, but the most definitive and disturbing 'no' probably comes from Darren Aronofsky's 2017 art-horror film, *mother!*[37] Aronofsky claims that the film 'started with trying to figure out how to show how people treat our home ... how do I kinda take this frustration I'm having with how people are acting and how much we are taking and how little we're giving back'.[38] He does this by crafting a biblical allegory, which retells biblical history from genesis to apocalypse, but which is also an ecological allegory that revises *Burnt Offerings* by telling the story from the bad *oikos*/mother's perspective. In the words of the movie's 'mother' and star Jennifer Lawrence, 'It depicts the rape and torment of Mother Earth.' She goes on to note, in a stunning understatement, that 'It's a hard film to watch.'[39]

It is, indeed, a hard film to watch, primarily because Aronofsky applies Lynn White's and ecofeminists' insights about patriarchy and religion to *Burnt Offerings* to force us to stare at humanity's own ecophobia and how 'things' in the environment, the nonhuman background, might experience that behaviour, which ultimately bleeds over into monstrous child abuse. The usual way of forwarding civil rights through garnering sympathy for the

---

[36] David Punter, *The Literature of Terror, Volume Two: The Modern Gothic* (London: Longman, 1996), p. 178; Sherry R. Truffin, *Schoolhouse Gothic: Haunted Hallways and Predatory Pedagogues in Late Twentieth-Century American Literature* (Newcastle: Cambridge Scholars Publishing, 2008), pp. 7–8.

[37] *mother!* Dir. Darren Aronofsky. Paramount Pictures, Protozoa Pictures, 20th Century Fox. 2017.

[38] See <https://www.youtube.com/watch?v=uxaEwhJBK4k> (last accessed 25 February 2019).

[39] See <www.independent.ie/entertainment/movies/mother-explained-what-on-earth-is-that-yellow-potion-and-who-are-domhnall-and-brian-gleeson-36140827.html> (last accessed 25 February 2019).

oppressed is challenging when it comes to nonhumans such as soil, water, even animals. But the film nevertheless asks, 'How would an ecosystem feel?' and embodies the environment in the house and especially in 'mother', the beautiful, charismatic and vulnerable Lawrence. It insists on keeping the camera on her constantly, forcing us into sympathy with the tortured mother nature/bad *oikos* and making us watch for a full two hours as her sociopathic husband and his thoughtless worshippers destroy her piece by piece, eventually even ripping apart her child.

Lawrence's 'mother', like Marian, spends her time in a world of agential things: listening to the beating heart of her house, loving and monitoring and repairing ('I re-built this entire house, wall to wall'); but her husband, Him, a poet-God-creator played by Javier Bardem, continuously allows his fans, ever larger masses of destructive strangers, into the house to spill and smash and 'ruin ... everything'. In one exemplary scene, a funeral party ignores mother's pleas and destroys the kitchen, starting 'the flood', and as mother screams for them to get out, Him's only concern is that his worshippers continue to stroke his ego. He yells after them to come back because 'we'll fix it' – meaning mother will fix it – while he reacts to the horrific and senseless damage with typical ecophobic dismissal: 'Those are just things. They can be replaced.' Such casual contempt for nature chimes with Eve's (Michelle Pfeiffer) high-handed advice, namely that mother should concentrate on having children for Him and stop with her restoration work. Her drunken waving away the house with 'This ... this is all just ... setting' echoes the 'concealments' that reduce the nonhuman to 'just' quiescent things or a passive background to the human drama. Yet, even when mother does finally produce a child for Him, he insists on stealing the newborn and 'showing' him to the hordes, who promptly murder and, in the scene that provoked extreme reactions from the internet, eat him. This is child abuse in the most visceral way possible, a mob of adults ingesting a newborn, and it allegorises the vicious child-devouring abuse of ecological degradation.

In the end, when a ravaged mother finally transforms into the apocalyptic bad *oikos*, blowing up the house and destroying humanity and herself with it, Him cannot 'fix it'. Representing Mary Daly's 'necrophilia of patriarchy' and ecophobia, this God can only start over and destroy again in an endless loop of horror. He and modern human civilisation are doomed to this cycle because He/we cannot see mother/nature as having any real agency that is worth caring about. As Him sighs to a dying mother, 'I am I ... You? You were home.' He is a person. She was just setting. Within that binary dynamic that invests one term with agency and denies it to the other, the agent can only ever play a cosmic narcissist devouring every 'thing' and for whom, as Him tells mother, 'Nothing is ever enough.' The end of *mother!* is thus an absolute horror, leaving viewers stunned and furious and wondering what they have just watched. What they have watched, of course, is the ecophobic psychopathy driving the environmental crisis and its destruction of our own children.

Netflix's hit series, *The Haunting of Hill House*, has been an easier bad *oikos* for audiences to swallow.[40] It is far more hopeful that dad can fix everything and save the children – if he can sacrifice himself and his own ego. In fact, 'I can fix it' and variations on that plea are the single most-repeated phrases in the series. The narrative, very loosely based on Shirley Jackson with a strong infusion of Robert Marasco, follows a family, led by a now gentle and liberal Hugh Crain. The narrative hops back and forth from the past, when Hugh and his wife Olivia purchased Hill House and moved in with their five children, to the present misery of the five adult Crain children, scarred by Hill House and their mother's apparent suicide there.

The story crackles with anxiety about keeping children 'safe' in an environment that parents cannot control. Hugh and Olivia only bought Hill House because they were chasing a dream of creating a completely beneficent environment. They wanted to renovate and 'flip' Hill House, so they could 'sell it for a lot of money' that they could then use to build their 'forever house'. Olivia has designed that 'forever house' as an ideal ecosystem for children – a Holocene nature or a good *oikos* – with what she describes as a 'heart' and 'bones' and 'veins', a body that 'needs to breathe' so that 'it all works together to keep us safe and healthy inside'. Unfortunately, that drive to keep their children safe, to craft their own little lifeboat and cocoon them from 'the world' through the exploitation of the house that they do have, exposes the children to the bad *oikos* and all its trauma and death. It transforms Olivia from the good wife and mother, working on their good *oikos*, into the mad avatar of the bad *oikos*, who tries to poison her children so they can stay 'safe' in Hill House and avoid the horrific future that the house has shown her, and which this trauma helps to produce. As her ghost explains to Hugh, their good *oikos* was a fantasy, and the bad *oikos* 'is our forever house. It always was'.

On one level, that is absolutely true: there's no going back to pre-Anthropocene nature, no creating a new 'shell' or lifeboat, and the

---

[40] *The Haunting of Hill House*. Created by Mike Flanagan. FlanaganFilm, Amblin Television, Paramount Television, Netflix. Distributed by Netflix. 2018. First aired on 12 October 2018.

ecologically degraded bad *oikos* is our 'forever house' now. However, *The Haunting of Hill House* wants to have it both ways. It wants to acknowledge that truth but still construct a way out – both to contain/stay in the bad *oikos* and to flee it. Here, dad *can* fix it. For Olivia-ghost's claim that 'We're all safe now' in Hill House is patently false. Hugh needs to 'fix it' first, but this requires an approach that is different from the commodifying and controlling one that he had first used. Instead, he needs to stay in the house, maintain it. After all, as the grieving caretaker urges, '[t]his house, it's full of precious, precious things, and they don't all belong to you', including the ghosts of Olivia and the caretaker's child that Olivia poisoned, and so it must be maintained, not 'flipped' or destroyed. Still, the Crain children cannot stay in it and live, and so when, as adults, they are trapped and dying in the house, Hugh begs Olivia to release them: 'if you open that door right now, I will make you a promise that I will keep forever. Open that door. Please. Let me fix this.' She agrees and he commits suicide, sacrificing himself to her and the bad *oikos* and staying with them 'forever'.

It is a fantasy that we adults – 'Dad' – can just stay behind with our mad monstrous mother nature and fix the mess that our ecophobic commodification has made, letting the children go out into a hopeful world again. For that world that *The Haunting of Hill House* imagines looks rather like the same old one with all its old 'concealment' and patriarchal/ecophobic structures reinstituted in the children. For instance, before Hugh's sacrifice, his eldest son Steven is estranged from him, identifying with his mother so that he screams 'the wrong parent died', and refusing to manage his siblings properly or to reproduce and become a dad. After he sees what his father has done, he takes on the responsibility of keeping Hill House, albeit from a distance, and, acting as a gentle patriarch to his younger siblings, he decides to become a father. His last lines are a voiceover that twists the dark irony of Jackson's words into an affirmation: '"I am home", I thought and stopped in wonder at the thought. I am home. I am home.' Dad fixed it, and mother and environment are safely pacified and pushed back into the background so the happy human (white, male) story can once again unfold. This ending seems to reaffirm a comforting fantasy – much like another recent bad *oikos* text, Shudder's *Witch in the Window* (2018) – assuring us that Dad can fix it, if we are just willing to follow him back to some politically regressive paternalistic idyll. One sliver of ambiguity cuts in, however: The 'dead-eyed' look that Olivia gives her escaping children and us/the camera over Hugh's shoulder suggests that she and

Hill House may not be as willing to be 'fixed' and repressed as the narrative hopes.

Although only a moment, it is a powerful image that underlines the discomfiting nonhuman agency of the bad *oikos* that the series had explored throughout its run, the neat end notwithstanding. It thus points towards another strand of bad *oikos* narratives emerging out of youth culture. In these texts, the kids – or a kind of youth culture aimed at them – appear to be recognising that the way to live with the bad *oikos* and the environmental crisis that it signals is not to pretend that Dad can bring you back into a lost Holocene past of good *oikoi*, but rather to accept that the Anthropocene's bad *oikos* is already in your bones. It is part of you, changing you. You are the bad *oikos*.

It's Already (in) the House

One of the most disturbing scenes in *It*, Andy Muschietti's 2017 blockbuster reimagining of Stephen King's 1986 bestseller, is also the film's quietest. A long tracking shot flies us through the dark, filth-filled sewers where the child-eating It dwells and then, swiftly and smoothly with the sewage outflow, out into a sparkling riverine forest and then up above the glowing trees and down the river towards an iconic red barn in which one of our young protagonists is reluctantly preparing sheep for slaughter. The shot underlines the seamless physical and chemical osmosis between wild nature, human food/habitation/bodies, and human waste and so visually allegorises what Stacy Alaimo describes as 'trans-corporeality', in which a porous human corporeality 'is always intermeshed with the more-than-human world'.[41] The scene also points to a bile-inducing return of the repressed, the horrid return of our offal's nonhuman agency or 'vibrant matter' as Jane Bennett theorises it, which is ultimately distilled and allegorised in the abomination It.[42] Like the smorgasbord of exotic toxins that human industries produce, It also returns in all manner of forms and in surprisingly far-flung and intimate places – library, bathroom, garage, as well as in the town's haunted house, far from the sewers to which it was supposedly banished. Like our shit, It comes back though to torture the brains and bodies of our children as it insists that the supposedly passive nonhuman background will be noxious and agential foreground.

[41] Alaimo, *Bodily Natures*, p. 2.
[42] Jane Bennett, *Vibrant Matter: A Political Ecology of Things* (Durham, NC: Duke University Press, 2001), p. viii.

With this insight, the film aligns with an odd strand of ecoGothic texts that young people seem to be consuming and creating: not just narratives of children in peril but narratives about transcorporeal perils in a monstrous and unpredictable environment, which wonder, 'What if adults can't fix it?' Instead of reacting with hysterical terror to this possibility and what it signals – loss of control over nature/foreground/human identities/human bodies – many of these texts simply accept it, with a bit of a shrug and even a laugh. Thus, some of the newest bad *oikos* texts – from the young novelist Jac Jemc's sparkling *The Grip of It* (2017) to FilmCow's comic YouTube series, *Ghosthouse* (2018–) – centre on surreally passive characters who simply watch, baffled and perhaps a little irritated, as the house around them moves, thinks, acts and penetrates and changes them. Such weird matter-of-factness about what should horrify suspends their audiences between sardonic laughter and disgusted screams and models a pained acceptance.

This ironised acquiescence to ecological horror is a means of coping and it is understandable for the children who have no other choice, but, for responsible parties, one could argue that an emotional reaction that triggers constructive action – genuine fear – might serve us better. As Greta Thunberg told the elites gathered for the World Economic Forum in Davos, she demands just such a proper response:

> Adults keep saying: 'We owe it to the young people to give them hope.' But I don't want your hope. I don't want you to be hopeful. I want you to panic. I want you to feel the fear I feel every day. And then I want you to act. I want you to act as you would in a crisis. I want you to act as if our house is on fire. Because it is.'[43]

Hope or concealments may lace through even the most dystopian science fiction, but fear is the proper province of the Gothic.

In this chapter, I have attempted to shed some light on the multiple ways in which the Gothic's most essential trope, the haunted house, has been repurposed to reflect upon the contemporary environmental crisis. By reconceptualising the haunted house as an ecosystem and investing it with organic life and nonhuman agency, bad *oikos* narratives have gestured towards a way of overcoming 'modes of concealment' that Amitav Ghosh worries are cloaking ecological degradation from view and from action. At

---

[43] Greta Thunberg, 'Our house is on fire': Greta Thunberg, 16, urges leaders to act on climate', *The Guardian*, 25 January 2019 <www.theguardian.com/environment/2019/jan/25/our-house-is-on-fire-greta-thunberg16-urges-leaders-to-act-on-climate> (last accessed 20 March 2019).

the same time, the bad *oikos*'s necessary involvement of human agency – usually of the ecophobic kind – reflects the verities of the Anthropocene, when the human interconnection with the nonhuman has largely resulted in distortion and destruction of global ecosystems. Whether the solutions that various bad *oikos* texts imply – Dad fixes it, children accept it, and so on – induce any action or not remains to be seen.

The house of modern human civilisation, as Thunberg points out, is splitting and burning and crumbling, like the last horrific scenes in 'The Fall of the House of Usher', but unlike that story's narrator, we do not have the option of fleeing, and the ghosts that haunt our house are our own children. Articles on Thunberg and children's climate activism often frame their arguments along such lines as 'if politicians won't listen to scientists, maybe they'll listen to the children'. But, as the paranormal researcher cited at the beginning of this chapter suggested, maybe the Gothic has a role to play as well, and he asks, 'If the powers that be don't listen to scientists or experts, will they listen to ghosts?'[44]

---

[44] Seaburn, 'Ghost Sightings'.

3.23
Gothic and the Apocalyptic Imagination

SIMON MARSDEN

Imagining Apocalypse

Apocalypse, in its ancient biblical forms, is a genre concerned both with visions of the eternal and with social and political transformation. Written in contexts of national, political and religious crisis, apocalypse opens a vision of a future in which the injustices and reversals of the present will come to an end. Writers in the Jewish and early Christian traditions came to imagine this future in terms of a renewal of creation; the present, corrupted order of things would be replaced by a 'new heaven and earth' in which pain and suffering would come to an end and universal justice would be established. This new reality would be inaugurated by a divine action in which God would vindicate decisively the faithfulness of his people and pronounce judgement upon the worldly powers that opposed and persecuted them. In the early Christian churches, the restoration of creation was associated explicitly with the reversal of death itself. On the last day, St Paul writes, 'the Lord himself will come down from heaven, with a loud command, with the voice of the archangel and with the trumpet call of God, and the dead in Christ will rise first'.[1] The apocalypse would restore the world to something like its Edenic condition. Death and suffering would be abolished, the divided nations of humanity would live together in peace and the people would live in the unmediated presence of God.

Apocalyptic narratives told stories of a world that was to come, imagined in a series of fantastical images that frequently alluded to earlier apocalyptic texts. The apocalyptic visionary was allowed to see beyond the limited horizons of the present and to communicate to others – albeit in a heavily symbolic and frequently fantastical narrative mode – the future that they had glimpsed. Apocalypse, Kevin Mills argues, locates its narrator in 'an

---

[1] 1 Thessalonians 4: 16. For a fuller account of the emergence of early Christian belief in resurrection, see N. T. Wright, *The Resurrection of the Son of God* (London: SPCK, 2003).

indefinable cosmic embrasure from which he can look out on two worlds, seeing beyond the confines of time and space into the eternal'.[2] Biblical apocalypse opened an eternal perspective on present reversals and reaffirmed the ultimate faithfulness and justice of God. Early Christian apocalypses provided a vulnerable Christian minority with a vision of a future in which the faithful believers would be vindicated when Christ returned as judge of the living and the dead. History was orientated towards an ending that gave eternal significance to the present; the task of the believer was to live faithfully in the light of that ending.

As the sacred, ritually ordered experience of time was displaced in modernity by secular, chronological time, the belief that history was orientated towards a universal and meaningful end became increasingly difficult to sustain.[3] Enlightenment philosophy offered a new, secular eschatology of human progress that was predicated upon reason, science and the domination of nature. By the end of the nineteenth century, this narrative of progress had itself become increasingly unstable. Though older versions of theistic apocalyptic belief remained, the literatures of the nineteenth century showed a new tendency to imagine the end of the age not as the inauguration of a new world, but as a condition of waiting for a future that was endlessly deferred. Matthew Arnold's image of a present age 'wandering between two worlds, one dead / The other powerless to be born' incorporates the language of biblical apocalypse into a vision of an ending without renewal.[4] The end of the present order is followed neither by the new heaven and earth of Christian apocalypse nor by a new and better world built by human hands, as the Romantic radicals of the late eighteenth century had imagined.[5] The nineteenth century in England closed on images of a ruined future, whether in the entropic science-fiction dystopias of H. G. Wells or the bleak Romanticism of Thomas Hardy. In these imagined futures, there was no renewal of creation beyond the end of the present age, but only the gradual decline – or violent overthrow – of a complacent and corrupted world that seemed emptied of its former vitality.

---

[2] Kevin Mills, *Approaching Apocalypse: Unveiling Revelation in Victorian Writing* (Lewisburg, PA: Bucknell University Press, 2007), p. 164.
[3] Charles Taylor, *A Secular Age* (Cambridge, MA and London: Belknap Press, 2007), pp. 54–9.
[4] Matthew Arnold, 'Stanzas from the Grande Chartreuse', lines 85–6, in Matthew Arnold, *Selected Poems*, edited by Timothy Peltason (London: Penguin, 1994), p. 113.
[5] See Morton D. Paley, *Apocalypse and Millennium in English Romantic Poetry* (Oxford: Clarendon Press, 1999).

The pessimistic apocalyptic sensibility of the late nineteenth century yielded a new kind of literary visionary in Friedrich Nietzsche's madman, a prophetic figure who announces the death of God to a world of complacent, fashionable scepticism. Modern unbelievers, the madman declares, have never recognised the appalling implications of God's death; they speak confidently of faith as outmoded and obsolete, yet they continue to live as if the death of God had never occurred.[6] The madman describes a world shaken loose from its foundations and drifting endlessly through empty space. He is a prophetic visionary who gazes into an eternity emptied of God. Modernity has killed God, Nietzsche insists, yet modern humanity is not yet ready to confront the implications of its own deed. The coming future is one in which humanity must come to terms with the terrible silence that now surrounds it.[7]

Nietzsche's parable of the madman establishes an apocalyptic mode that would become a significant aspect of the Gothic imagination in the twentieth and twenty-first centuries. Like their biblical predecessors, apocalyptic writers of the early twentieth century attempted to imagine a new reality that might lie beyond the present age. For many, what they saw was a vision of horror. Once a literature of radical hope, apocalypse came to be reimagined as the violent overthrow of a world order already collapsing from within. If biblical apocalypse exemplifies what Frank Kermode has famously termed the 'sense of an ending', the apocalyptic horrors of the early twentieth century were predicated upon an ending without sense: a future that not only failed to reveal the fuller meaning of the present but seemed to deny even the possibility of such meaning.[8]

This pessimistic reconfiguration of the apocalyptic mode is integral to the Weird fiction that emerged as a significant subgenre of the Gothic in the twentieth century. The Weird apocalypse placed its visionaries at the interstices between the familiar order of the human world and the forces of chaos that threatened its overthrow. In these narratives, the apparent stability and order of human civilisation is exposed as a fragile illusion by the unveiling of the chaos by which it is surrounded. In William Hope Hodgson's *The House on the Borderland* (1908), a man identified only as the Recluse undergoes

---

[6] For a fuller account of the contexts and theological implications of the Nietzschean death of God, see Gavin Hyman, *A Short History of Atheism* (London: I. B. Tauris, 2010).

[7] Friedrich Nietzsche, *The Gay Science*, trans. by Thomas Common (New York: Barnes & Noble, 2008), aphorism 125.

[8] Frank Kermode, *The Sense of an Ending: Studies in the Theory of Fiction* (New York: Oxford University Press, 1967).

a visionary experience that echoes the nihilistic cosmic perspective of Nietzsche's madman. In the vision, the Recluse is carried deep into space, passing 'beyond the fixed stars, and ... into the huge blackness that waits beyond'.[9] Time is accelerated, and the Recluse witnesses a distant future in which the sun has cooled, recalling the similarly entropic far future in H. G. Wells's *The Time Machine* (1895). Unlike Wells's novel, however, Hodgson imagines a cosmos beyond human reason, inhabited by monstrous beings and structures that are incomprehensible to the Recluse. This realm of cosmic disorder threatens to escape the confines of the vision, intruding into and disrupting the Recluse's familiar world. At the close of his narrative, the Recluse, now returned to his house, hears sounds that suggest the final collapse of borders between the human world and the chaos beyond:

> Hush! I hear something, down – down in the cellars. It is a creaking sound. My God, it is the opening of the great, oak trap. What can be doing that? The scratching of my pen deafens me ... I must listen ... There are steps on the stairs; strange padding steps, that come up and nearer ... Jesus, be merciful to me, an old man. There is something fumbling at the door handle. O God, help me now! Jesus – The door is opening – slowly. Somethi –
> That is all.[10]

The Recluse's story is told via his journal, found by later travellers in the ruins of the house that, by the end of the novel, has apparently collapsed into the chasm that the Recluse believed to lie beneath it. This chasm is the source of the monstrous creatures that invade the house itself and which are also present in the Recluse's vision. The house occupies a liminal position between the apparent order of human civilisation and a realm of incomprehensible disorder: its collapse embodies the final overthrow of the Recluse's reason and intellectual control.

Hodgson's mode of Weird apocalypse subverts the essentially optimistic perspective of the apocalyptic tradition. As Lois Parkinson Zamora observes, 'Apocalyptic modes of apprehending reality appeal to us in our secular times because they rest on the desire that history possess structure and meaning, if only the structure and meaning we attribute to it in our literary forms and fictions.'[11] In Weird apocalypse, the sources of this apparent structure and meaning – history, culture, reason, science – are exposed as elaborate

---

[9] William Hope Hodgson, *The House on the Borderland and Other Novels* (London: Gollancz, 2002), p. 119.
[10] Hodgson, *The House on the Borderland and Other Novels*, p. 199.
[11] Lois Parkinson Zamora, *Writing the Apocalypse: Historical Vision in Contemporary U.S. and Latin American Fiction* (Cambridge: Cambridge University Press, 1989), p. 24.

and deceptive fictions. Such revelations of cosmic unreason are integral to the fiction of H. P. Lovecraft, in which human belief in an ordered and comprehensible universe is shattered by the discovery of a fuller reality that undermines even the possibility of rational order. In Lovecraft's stories, revelations of humanity's true situation invite madness and despair, as the narrator of 'The Call of Cthulhu' (1928) observes:

> The most merciful thing in the world, I think, is the inability of the human mind to correlate all its contents. We live on a placid island of ignorance in the midst of black seas of infinity, and it was not meant that we should voyage far. The sciences, each straining in its own direction, have hitherto harmed us little; but some day the piecing together of dissociated knowledge will open up such terrifying vistas of reality, and of our frightful position therein, that we shall either go mad from the revelation or flee from the deadly light into the peace and safety of a new dark age.[12]

Lovecraft's fiction develops the situation of metaphysical crisis depicted in Nietzsche's parable of the madman. In the Lovecraftian mythos, humanity has not simply failed to come to terms with the implications of the death of God, but, more trenchantly, is fundamentally incapable of doing so. The modern belief in an ordered, comprehensible reality is a necessary fiction that shields the human mind from a universe of infinite disorder. Lovecraft's version of the apocalyptic visionary occupies that figure's traditional location at the interstices between the present world and the infinite, but sees there visions of unnameable horror rather than redemption and recreation. 'For full three seconds I could glimpse that pandaemoniac sight', the narrator of 'He' (1926) recalls,

> and in those seconds I saw a vista which will ever afterward torment me in dreams. I saw the heavens verminous with strange flying things, and beneath them a hellish black city of giant stone terraces with impious pyramids flung savagely to the moon, and devil-lights burning from unnumbered windows.[13]

The story ends with the narrator 'gone home to the pure New England lanes up which fragrant sea-winds sweep at evening', a retreat to the ideological security of an American social order the horrifying collapse of which he has glimpsed.[14]

---

[12] H. P. Lovecraft, 'The Call of Cthulhu', in H. P. Lovecraft, *The Call of Cthulhu and Other Weird Stories*, edited by S. T. Joshi (London: Penguin, 1999), pp. 139–69 (p. 139).
[13] H. P. Lovecraft, 'He', in Lovecraft, *The Call of Cthulhu and Other Weird Stories*, pp. 119–29 (p. 126).
[14] Lovecraft, 'He', p. 129.

Cold War Catastrophe

If the Weird apocalypses of Hodgson and Lovecraft were philosophical descendants of Nietzschean nihilism, the first half of the twentieth century provided more material reasons for pessimistic visions of the future. As Lucie Armitt observes, twentieth-century Gothic is characterised by 'the manner in which the real-life horror of two world wars takes over from the imagined horrors of the supernatural and/or superstition'.[15] Images of catastrophe were no longer confined to fiction or film: in addition to the devastation caused by the wars themselves, the mid-twentieth century brought with it the West's discovery of the full horrors of the Holocaust and the new threat of nuclear warfare, the latter bound up also in Cold War paranoia and fears of Communist infiltration. Like the anxieties concerning anthropogenic climate change and environmental disaster that would become increasingly prevalent later in the century, these real-world events suggested the possibility that the end of the present age would arrive as catastrophe rather than renewal. End-of-the-world scenarios proliferated in mid-century popular culture, perhaps most obviously in science-fiction films such as *The Day the Earth Stood Still* (dir. Robert Wise, 1951), *When Worlds Collide* (dir. Rudolph Maté, 1951) and *The War of the Worlds* (dir. Byron Haskin, 1953). Where science fiction often ended with disaster averted, or at least survived, Richard Matheson's 1954 novel *I Am Legend* adopted a more pessimistic outlook. Set in the aftermath of a catastrophe that has already taken place, *I Am Legend* locates its protagonist, Robert Neville, as the only apparent survivor of an epidemic that has transformed humans into vampires. At the beginning of the novel, Neville lives alone in a house that is surrounded nightly by vampires who attempt to entice him out. He is a modern incarnation of Mary Shelley's 'last man', an obsolete remnant of the old world in a seemingly post-human America.

In *I Am Legend*, Marilyn Michaud argues, the 'theme of time as cyclical and corrosive is the organising mode of the text. As a figure of degeneration and tyranny, the vampire refutes the idea of progress, signalling instead the rise of power and corruption, and the inevitable movement towards decay'.[16] Neville's belief in his own 'last man' status is flawed: on his regular expeditions to destroy vampires as they sleep in the daytime, he has inadvertently killed still-living humans who have been infected with the germ but who are

---

[15] Lucie Armitt, *Twentieth-Century Gothic* (Cardiff: University of Wales Press, 2011), p. 2.
[16] Marilyn Michaud, *Republicanism and the American Gothic* (Cardiff: University of Wales Press, 2009), p. 70.

able to control its effects with drugs. The new society emerging in America is being built by these infected humans who regard Neville as a murderer and who execute him for his crimes against them. As Michaud argues, the novel's pessimistic ending represents a view of time as cyclical, with modern confidence in scientific and technological progress leading to new forms of self-destruction and the inevitable return of societal corruption.[17] Neville himself calls into question the ability of moral values to endure beyond the end of the society in which they took shape, denying their existence as anything other than shared social norms while also acknowledging their continued force as a habit of thought:

> Crossing your fingers, Neville? Knocking on wood?
> He ignored that, beginning to suspect his mind of harbouring an alien. Once he might have termed it conscience. Now it was only an annoyance. Morality, after all, had fallen with society. He was his own ethic.
> Makes a good excuse, doesn't it, Neville? Oh, shut up.[18]

The ambiguous status of morality in the post-apocalyptic world is revisited at the novel's conclusion. Facing his own execution, Neville momentarily sees himself through the eyes of the new society: 'To them he was some terrible scourge they had never seen, a scourge even worse than the disease they had come to live with. He was an invisible specter who had left for evidence of his existence the bloodless bodies of their loved ones.'[19] Neville has become to the new hybrid race what the vampires had been to him: a murderous threat that must be eliminated.

The post-apocalyptic landscape that Neville in *I am Legend* inhabits is the end-point of a society in terminal decline. The novel suggests that this collapse is both inevitable and cyclical; the vampire plague is the latest manifestation of a corruption that has recurred many times over in human history. 'It was the germ that was the villain', Neville concludes; 'The germ that hid behind obscuring veils of legend and superstition, spreading its scourge while people cringed before their own fears.'[20] The latest reappearance of the germ locates the collapse of modern American society within a longer history of progress and decline, while also registering historically specific concerns surrounding the Cold War, military technology, authoritarianism and materialism. As Bernice M. Murphy points out, 'The creatures that terrorise Neville in his boarded-up suburban home every night, like

---

[17] Michaud, *Republicanism and the American Gothic*, pp. 69–77.
[18] Richard Matheson, *I Am Legend* (London: Gollancz, 2001), p. 54.
[19] Matheson, *I Am Legend*, p. 160.   [20] Matheson, *I Am Legend*, p. 82.

[George] Romero's "Living Dead", are not alien "others"; they are fellow citizens, transformed, yet recognisable.'[21] A consumerist society consumes itself as ordinary Americans are infected by the germ and begin to feed on their neighbours.[22]

In the mid-twentieth century, Gothic versions of apocalypse were beginning to imagine bleak futures in which technologically advanced, capitalist societies became complicit in their own downfall. If the immediate cause of the end of the world as they knew it was often the emergence of such monstrous threats as Matheson's vampires, these narratives hinted that their Gothic monsters were creations or expressions of the corruption or instability already present within the society itself. As Michaud observes, 'In the Gothic imagination, culture or progress is often a movement towards decline and an open invitation to corruption and tyranny.'[23] In the second half of the twentieth century, Gothic apocalypse came increasingly to depict end-of-the-world scenarios in which this trajectory towards decline was played out at the level of national and/or global catastrophe. In these narratives, the failures of contemporary society not only play a part in causing disaster, but also persist beyond it as limitations on the capacity of survivors to rebuild the world after the end.

This theme of structural flaws that endure beyond the collapse of the structures themselves is central to George A. Romero's highly influential 1968 film *Night of the Living Dead*. In the film, a small group of human survivors take shelter in an isolated house as, without explanation, the dead begin to reanimate. The house functions as a microcosm of American society, drawing attention repeatedly to the ways in which the interactions between the survivors are shaped by race, gender and class. Ben (Duane Jones), the lone Black survivor, fends off a group of zombies, saving both his own life and that of Barbra (Judith O'Dea), who is in deep shock following the murder of her brother by one of the dead. When Ben discovers that two couples have been hiding in the cellar, he accuses them of ignoring Barbra's screams: 'you're telling us we got to risk our lives just because somebody might need help, huh?' objects Harry Cooper (Karl Hardman), a middle-aged white man whose shirt and tie

---

[21] Bernice M. Murphy, 'Horror Fiction from the Decline of Universal Horror to the Rise of the Psycho Killer', in Xavier Aldana Reyes (ed.), *Horror: A Literary History* (London: British Library, 2016), pp. 131–57 (p. 136).

[22] On the vampire as a metaphor of consumerism, see Rob Latham, *Consuming Youth: Vampires, Cyborgs, and the Culture of Consumption* (Chicago and London: University of Chicago Press, 2002).

[23] Michaud, *Republicanism and the American Gothic*, p. 76.

suggest a professional occupation.[24] As a financially comfortable, middle-class man who is entirely unwilling to risk himself for others, Harry represents a failed version of American individualism. It is Ben rather than Harry who risks his life in an attempt to obtain medicine for Harry's daughter, Karen, who has been bitten by a zombie. Harry's cowardice and selfishness are depicted as moral failures that weaken cooperation between the survivors and endanger the whole group. In a final irony, Harry dies in the cellar, killed and consumed by his own daughter – a final image, perhaps, of generational decline within an economically secure, but morally weak, white middle class.

If Harry's death suggests the corruption of an American ideal of individualism into moral and physical weakness, Ben's fate suggests that even the most resourceful and capable of individuals can still be victims of a degraded and inadequate state. When the authorities learn that the zombies can be killed by the destruction of their brains, groups of armed men, including police officers and civilians, begin to patrol the country in order to kill the walking dead with gunshots to the head. Ben, by now the only survivor left alive in the house, is shot dead by one of these groups, who mistake him for a zombie. The manner of Ben's death both recalls the assassination, earlier in the year, of Martin Luther King Jr and hints at wider resonances with the Civil Rights struggles of the decade. Earlier in the film, Harry's wife, Helen, learns that the house has a radio and insists that they should leave the cellar in order to use it: 'If the authorities know what's happening', she insists, 'they'll send people, tell us what to do.'[25] On one level, Ben's death at the hands of the very people who have been sent by the authorities suggests that Helen's confidence in the official response is misplaced. However, it also holds open the possibility that such confidence was always racially coded. Where the white, middle-class Coopers attempt to lock themselves in the cellar and wait for the 'authorities' to 'tell us what to do', Ben assumes throughout the film that he must take responsibility for his own survival. The film concludes with Ben shot dead on sight by a group of white men who make no attempt to confirm that he is a zombie before shooting, and who barely spare him a thought afterwards. The film's Black protagonist dies at the hands of an official response whose protection the white family takes for granted.

Though they employ familiar Gothic monsters in their visions of the end, the versions of apocalypse imagined by Matheson and Romero are identified

[24] *Night of the Living Dead.* Dir. George A. Romero. Image Ten, Continental Distributing. 1968. Dimension Extreme, 2008. DVD. 42:00.
[25] *Night of the Living Dead*, 51:00.

with science and nature rather than magic and the supernatural. The vampire plague in *I Am Legend* is created by a bacillus that is released in dust clouds caused by bombing. The aetiology of the reanimations in *Night of the Living Dead* is never identified conclusively, but at least one scientist associates it with radiation from a probe that has been destroyed in Earth's orbit. These seemingly supernatural or mythical versions of apocalypse, then, are rooted in the technological contexts of the Cold War: they allude to real-world military technologies, nuclear weaponry and the Space Race. They recall in secularised form the resurrection of the dead as it is imagined in New Testament eschatology, which becomes reanimation rather than rebirth, but the narratives invoke little sense of transcendence, even of the chaotic and nihilistic forms imagined by writers such as Hodgson and Lovecraft. In the decades that followed, however, Gothic apocalypse became more overt in its exploration of the genre's theological heritage, a tendency that has continued into the twenty-first century. As Andrew Tate has argued, prominent writers of contemporary apocalyptic fictions, 'consciously or otherwise, echo visionary ideas of biblical prophecy regarding the finite nature of human power'.[26] Indeed, one of the striking features of Gothic apocalypse since the late twentieth century is the extent to which the transcendent has returned as a central aspect of the post-apocalyptic world. The survivors of the contemporary Gothic catastrophe narrative frequently find themselves occupying a world in which God moves not only in mysterious ways but also, at times, in some disconcertingly obvious ones. If these narratives do not suggest a return to traditional forms of orthodox faith, they do perhaps hint that the philosophical as well as the economic and technological structures of modernity might be at risk of collapse.

Rationalism and Re-enchantment

This renewal of interest in theological aspects of the apocalyptic tradition reflects postmodernity's challenges to the coherence of modernity itself. If, as Graham Ward has argued, postmodernity is characterised by 'the re-evaluation of ambivalence, mystery, excess and aporia as they adhere to, are constituted by and disrupt the rational', Gothic apocalypse figures this cultural shift from modernity to postmodernity as the movement from the old world to the new.[27] One of the protagonists of Stephen King's *The Stand*

---

[26] Andrew Tate, *Apocalyptic Fiction* (London and New York: Bloomsbury, 2017), p. 19.
[27] Graham Ward, *Theology and Contemporary Critical Theory* (Basingstoke: Macmillan, 1996), p. 132.

(1978) makes this point overtly. 'Assume that the age of rationalism has passed', sociologist Glen Bateman tells his fellow survivors in post-apocalyptic America. After rationalism, he suggests, humanity would live in a re-enchanted world:

> 'Dark magic,' he said softly. 'A universe of marvels where water flows uphill and trolls live in the deepest woods and dragons live under the mountains. Bright wonders, white power. "Lazarus, come forth".' Water into wine. And ... and just maybe ... the casting out of devils.'[28]

King's apocalypse has secular origins: the human population of America is devastated by a superflu that has been created by the US military and released through accidental contamination. In the tradition of biblical apocalypse, however, this catastrophe is depicted not simply as an event within chronological time, but also as one that interrupts the regular flow of time and history. The passage of time in the old world is marked by the ticking of the grandfather clock in Frannie Goldsmith's family home: Frannie 'had been listening to its measured ticks and tocks all of her life'.[29] The apocalypse literally stops the clocks, including a town clock that, as Stu Redman observes, 'had not tolled since nine this morning'.[30] King revisits this image in his 1986 novel It, when the failure of the Derry town clock to chime the hour prompts one resident to fear that 'Suddenly all of those things – things he had spent his life working for – seemed in jeopardy.'[31] The failure of these clocks to mark the regular passage of time suggests that time itself, or the human experience thereof, has been disrupted. In The Stand, the survivors of the superflu must come to terms not only with the collapse of society as they have known it, but also with a shift in the nature of reality. Echoing the final battles between the assembled forces of heaven and hell in the book of Revelation, King's protagonists become participants in a struggle between Good and Evil, or God and Satan, represented by two opposing figures: the saintly Mother Abigail and the trickster-figure known as Randall Flagg. In the aftermath of the superflu, the survivors gather around one or the other of these figures, forming two communities that represent alternative versions of what the new world might be. As Glen Bateman tells his fellow community leaders in Mother Abigail's group, 'We're here under the fiat of powers we don't understand. For me, that means we may be beginning to accept – only

---

[28] Stephen King, The Stand (London: Hodder & Stoughton, 2011), p. 853.
[29] King, The Stand, p. 119. [30] King, The Stand, p. 308.
[31] Stephen King, It (London: Hodder & Stoughton, 2011), p. 1256.

subconsciously now, and with plenty of slips backward due to culture lag – a different definition of existence.'[32]

King's post-apocalyptic landscape, then, becomes the setting for a contest between two models of human being that become synonymous with the novel's two versions of community. The novel resists a simplistic moral binary in its division of the population: flawed people are drawn to both groups, and both groups achieve forms of community cohesion. The crucial difference lies in the organisation and structures of power within each community. Where Mother Abigail's Colorado town establishes democratic government, Flagg's Las Vegas is an authoritarian state; though framed in terms of theological metaphysics, the opposition between the two communities is rooted firmly in modern American history and politics. Mother Abigail's interpretation of Flagg's followers displays this blending of theological and political registers:

> He was a liar, and his father was the Father of Lies. He would be like a big neon sign to them, standing high to the sky, dazzling their sight with fizzing fireworks. They would not be apt to notice, these apprentice unshapers, that like a neon sign, he only made the same patterns over and over again.
> ...
> Some would make the deduction for themselves in time – his kingdom would never be one of peace. The sentry posts and barbed wire at the frontiers of his land would be there as much to keep the converts in as to keep the invader out.[33]

Though he is depicted overtly as Satanic, Flagg does not simply represent the return of an older religious or magical world that stands in opposition to the modern nation brought to an end by the superflu. Instead, the novel hints repeatedly that Flagg embodies multiple structural and ideological failures of modernity. Glen suggests that Flagg is 'the last magician of rational thought, gathering the tools of technology against us'.[34] Flagg's followers are ultimately destroyed by the nuclear weapons that he intends to use against the Colorado community, an end that both aligns him with one of modernity's most destructive technologies and identifies his commitment to that technology as fundamentally self-defeating. Flagg also represents the return of authoritarianism. Though his community is successful in many ways, its loyalty and strong work ethic are motivated at least in part by the threat of brutal punishments dealt out publicly to those suspected of failure or betrayal. Tom Cullen, sent to Las Vegas as a spy, recognises the missing

---

[32] King, *The Stand*, p. 852. [33] King, *The Stand*, p. 755. [34] King, *The Stand*, p. 853.

ingredient in Flagg's community: 'They were nice enough people and all, but there wasn't much love in them. Because they were too busy being afraid.'[35] The novel's various oppositions – God and Satan; Mother Abigail and Randall Flagg; Colorado and Las Vegas – serve to locate modern America's self-destruction in a wider cyclical history of moral and spiritual struggle between the creative, communal flourishing of free people and the destructiveness of authoritarian control and scientific hubris.

The End of History

Writers of Gothic apocalypse at the end of the twentieth century and the beginning of the twenty-first have retained much of their predecessors' scepticism towards narratives of progress. If the genre is no longer shaped by the specific concerns of the Cold War era, anxieties surrounding the possibility of nuclear destruction remain, provoked not only by nuclear accidents such as the explosions at Chernobyl in 1986 and Fukushima Daiichi in 2011, but also with renewed threats of domestic and international terrorism in the aftermath of the al-Qaeda attacks on the US in 2001.[36] The contemporary Gothic apocalypse offers a rejoinder to accounts of modern history as progress towards greater levels of global peace and prosperity, a view reflected in Francis Fukuyama's famous argument that the establishment of liberal democracy – and liberal capitalism as its economic counterpart – constituted the 'end of history':

> We can ... imagine future worlds that are significantly worse than what we know now, in which national, racial, or religious intolerance make a comeback, or in which we are overwhelmed by war or environmental collapse. But we cannot picture to ourselves a world that is *essentially* different from the present one, and at the same time better. Other, less reflective ages also thought of themselves as the best, but we arrive at this conclusion exhausted, as it were, from the pursuit of alternatives we felt *had* to be better than liberal democracy.[37]

For Fukuyama, the 'end of history' was the point at which no better model of society could be imagined. Improvements could be made to the functioning of the liberal society – the reduction of poverty, for example – and democracy itself could be undermined by the return of regressive and anti-democratic

---

[35] King, *The Stand*, p. 1167.
[36] Benjamin Percy's werewolf novel *Red Moon* (2013), for example, includes a nuclear attack on the US by a terrorist group based loosely on al-Qaeda.
[37] Francis Fukuyama, *The End of History and the Last Man* (London: Penguin, 1992), p. 46.

forces, but liberal democracy was incapable of replacement by a superior political and economic model.

In contrast, contemporary versions of Gothic apocalypse have frequently imagined versions of large-scale crisis that emerge from within the political and economic structures of liberalism (or neoliberalism) itself. Linnie Blake and Agnieszka Soltysik Monnet argue that 'as neoliberalism has come to dominate the ways we live, work, think, interact and introspect, harnessing the epistemological incertitude of the postmodern project in service of its aims, the gothic's ability to give voice to the occluded truths of our age has resulted in a global proliferation of gothic, and gothic-influenced, cultural artefacts' – a theme expanded on at more length in Blake's chapter in this volume.[38] Gothic narratives have explored the shadow side of liberalism as the 'end of history', not least by depicting liberal capitalism as the driver of environmental destruction and (particularly in the aftermath of the global financial crash of 2007–8) by imagining in exaggerated and monstrous forms the collapse of the modern economy. By no means all of these narratives are entirely pessimistic: many use the post-apocalyptic landscape as a site in which to explore alternative possibilities for society, and at least a few seem to hint that the end of the present political and economic order might be a kind of fortunate fall that opens up a space for new ways of being. If there is a common thread in these diverse narratives, however, it is the persistent suspicion that the liberal order in some way contains the seeds of its own collapse.

In this context, the fiction of the American horror writer Thomas Ligotti reads as a dark parody of the liberal end of history. Ligotti's stories often recall the prophetic nihilism of Lovecraft, but their visions of infinite disorder are grounded firmly in the neoliberal age. For Ligotti, even meaninglessness seems to have lost its meaning; revelation amounts to the discovery that 'existence consisted of nothing but the most outrageous nonsense, a nonsense that had nothing unique about it at all and that had nothing behind it or beyond it except more and more nonsense – a new order of nonsense, perhaps an utterly unknown nonsense, but all of it nonsense and nothing but nonsense'.[39] Where Lovecraft had imagined infinite chaos

---

[38] Linnie Blake and Agniezska Soltysik Monnet, 'Introduction: Neoliberal Gothic', in Linnie Blake and Agniezska Soltysik Monnet (eds), *Neoliberal Gothic: International Gothic in the Neoliberal Age* (Manchester: Manchester University Press, 2017), pp. 1–18 (p. 1).

[39] Thomas Ligotti, 'The Clown Puppet', in *Teatro Grottesco* (London: Virgin, 2008), pp. 53–64 (p. 63).

overthrowing the ordered, rational world of human experience, Ligotti depicts human subjects overwhelmed by their own pointlessness. Ligotti's characters are individuals trapped within the social and economic logic of neoliberalism: notionally free citizens, they become entirely compliant with the structures and systems that they inhabit. In 'The Town Manager' (2006), the residents of a town wait unquestioningly for the arrival of a new town manager each time the previous incumbent departs. One of the townspeople, aware of the increasing degeneracy of each new manager, chooses to leave, but finds only the endless repetition of the same system. 'I had fled that place in hopes of finding another that had been founded upon different principles and operated under a different order', he observes. 'But there was no such place, or none that I could find.'[40] Fukuyama's 'end of history' becomes a nightmare vision of stultifying sameness. In a final irony, the would-be escapee is recruited as the next town manager. The neoliberal order preserves itself by offering rewards of wealth and status to the few individuals who would rebel against it.

For the majority who do not rebel, the economic logic of neoliberalism ensures ever-greater levels of compliance. The narrator of 'Our Temporary Supervisor' (2006) is an employee in a factory, where the workers spend their days assembling metal components for purposes that are unclear even to them. When a new employee arrives and chooses to continue working through his lunch break, the other workers begin to emulate his behaviour, motivated by vague unease about the presence of a temporary supervisor and unwilling to be seen as underperforming in comparison to the newcomer. The stranger's performance, the narrator says, 'introduced the rest of us at the factory to a hitherto unknown level of virtuosity in the service of productivity'.[41] The workers voluntarily stop taking their breaks and no one objects as both the length of the working day and the speed of the work itself are gradually increased. Their lives are reduced to an endless routine of repetitive and dehumanising labour, but they choose to remain, unable to imagine or contemplate any kind of existence outside of the factory. The neoliberal order, Ligotti suggests, offers its subjects the notional status of free citizens while directing their choices towards participation within the system. The workers accept their own dehumanisation because they are more afraid of what might lie beyond their lives in the factory. As the narrator observes, 'Working at a furious pace, fitting together those small pieces of metal, helps keep our minds off such things.'[42]

---

[40] Thomas Ligotti, 'The Town Manager', in *Teatro Grottesco*, pp. 22–36 (p. 35).
[41] Thomas Ligotti, 'Our Temporary Supervisor', in *Teattro Grottesco*, pp. 99–118 (p. 112).
[42] Ligotti, 'Our Temporary Supervisor', p. 118.

Apocalyptic Returns

Anxieties surrounding the conditions of contemporary capitalism have been closely connected with the resurgence of the zombie in popular culture. Since the millennium, a series of high-profile – and often commercially successful – zombie apocalypse narratives have appeared, including Max Brooks's novel *World War Z* (2006) and its 2013 film adaptation (dir. Marc Forster); *I Am Legend* (dir. Francis Lawrence, 2007), a film that gives Matheson's novel a more optimistic conclusion; a remake of Romero's *Dawn of the Dead* (dir. Zack Snyder, 2004), along with director Edgar Wright's affectionate parody *Shaun of the Dead* (2004); Swedish novelist John Ajvide Lindqvist's *Handling the Undead* (2005; English translation 2009); and the long-running and highly popular television series *The Walking Dead* (2010–), based on the graphic novels of the same title by Robert Kirkman, Tony Moore and Charlie Adlard (2003–19). By no means all zombie apocalypse narratives are critical of contemporary economics or of consumerism – indeed, even those that do offer such critiques are themselves commercial products marketed and sold for 'consumption' by their audiences – but the genre does nonetheless often register unease both about the workings of the economy and the possibility of its collapse. In Brooks's *World War Z*, for example, at least one pharmaceutical executive sees the impending disaster as a business opportunity: 'A cure would make people buy it only if they thought they were infected. But a vaccine! That's preventative! People will keep taking that as long as they're afraid it's out there!'[43] Defending his decision to market ineffective preventatives to a panicking population, the executive insists upon the freedom of the consumer: 'you wanna blame someone', he insists, 'why not start with all the sheep who forked over their greenbacks without bothering to do a little responsible research. I never held a gun to their heads. They made the choice themselves'.[44] As his own testimony demonstrates, this argument is both technically true and misleading. The consumers of the useless vaccine were free citizens with the power of choice, but this freedom was always constrained by the manipulation of information by the government, the medical profession and the pharmaceutical industry, each of which colluded in maintaining the fiction that the vaccine was effective.

---

[43] Max Brooks, *World War Z: An Oral History of the Zombie War* (London: Duckworth, 2007), p. 55.
[44] Brooks, *World War Z*, p. 58.

Apocalypse, Kevin Mills reminds us, is 'a genre which grew out of disappointment'.[45] Apocalyptic narratives have always emerged from and responded to situations of crisis, threat and disillusionment with the present order of things. In this respect, the Gothic apocalypses of the twentieth and twenty-first centuries belong to an ancient literary tradition in which narratives of the end of the world, or of the world as we know it, are used to interrogate the faults of the present and, perhaps, to articulate the hope for something better. Implicitly or overtly, the orientation of Gothic narratives is frequently towards futures that subvert the redemptive hope of biblical eschatology. When the dead return in Gothic, they tend to do so not as the redeemed and resurrected bodies of Christian hope, but in the monstrous forms of zombies, vampires and spectres. In Gothic, John Sears observes, 'whatever returns is *never* Christ'.[46] Indeed, some recent Gothic fictions have made this subversion of Christian eschatology explicit. 'I can't profess to understand God's plan', says Hershel Greene in *The Walking Dead*, 'but Christ promised a resurrection of the dead. I just thought he had something a little different in mind.'[47] Ajvide Lindqvist's *Handling the Undead* explores the theological implications of the zombie at greater length, but its conclusions are ambiguous. The unexplained revival of the recently deceased in a Swedish town is received initially by many families as the miraculous return of their loved ones, but the returned dead prove to be diminished remnants of their living selves, preserving the physical form (often in states of decay) with little evidence of human consciousness or personality. The returned dead are not the violent monsters of more conventional zombie narratives, but neither are they obvious figures of redemptive hope. They are, rather, uncanny figures that call into question the relationship between identity and the body while interrogating the nature of mourning and the difficulty of letting go of the dead.

For all of their apparent pessimism about the future, however, contemporary Gothic apocalypses have explored tentative possibilities of hope that a better future might emerge from the ruins of the old world. Beyond its persistent interest in the difficulties of survival in the post-apocalyptic world and the frequent deaths of central characters, *The Walking Dead* has returned often to the question of how a form of society might be rebuilt. In a series that uses as its setting the crumbling remains of American cities and the rusting commodities of

[45] Mills, *Approaching Apocalypse*, p. 16.
[46] John Sears, *Stephen King's Gothic* (Cardiff: University of Wales Press, 2011), p. 16.
[47] 'Nebraska', *The Walking Dead*, season 2, episode 8.

capitalism, moments of renewal have often been based upon a return to the land, a direction also taken by the Gothic-inflected science-fiction series *Battlestar Galactica* (2004–9). Over the course of the series, *The Walking Dead* has examined multiple versions of community – some of them reflecting ultimately destructive models of authoritarian rule – and explored the question of how far the survivors might go in embracing violence as a necessary tool for survival without sacrificing their own humanity and their ability to rebuild a functioning community.

A more decisive vision of future hope is offered in Justin Cronin's *Passage* trilogy (2010–16), a post-apocalyptic vampire narrative that recuperates the genre's theological roots and which culminates in a landscape restored to an Edenic state of nature. As in King's *The Stand*, catastrophe is unleashed by a US military experiment gone wrong: a virus is released that transforms human beings into vampiric monsters ('virals') that rapidly destroy the population of North America and then the world. For Cronin, as for King, post-apocalyptic America becomes the site of a contest between two opposing figures, this time framed in terms derived from Augustinian theology. The ruler of the virals, known as Zero, is a figure of negation, an embodiment of the nothingness and undoing of creation that Augustine believed to be the essential nature of evil.[48] Zero's antagonist, Amy (a name derived from French and Latin terms meaning 'beloved'), is a messianic figure who seeks not to destroy the vampires, but to redeem them. The *Passage* trilogy sets the creative work of love in opposition to the destructive nothingness of evil and ends on a note of transformative hope as nature begins to restore itself. 'Here she would make her garden', the narrator concludes as Amy stands alone, the only remaining person on an American continent to which the descendants of the survivors will one day return; 'She would make her garden, and wait.'[49] Like *I Am Legend*, the *Passage* trilogy imagines a catastrophe that emerges through a combination of nature and modern military technology. Unlike Matheson's novel, however, Cronin's narrative closes on an image of a restored, Edenic landscape at the beginning of its repopulation by a human community that has remembered and attempted to learn from the disastrous errors of its predecessors. At a time of profound concern over the threat of anthropogenic climate change, it is a narrative that looks to new possibilities after the collapse of the world as we know it: a Gothic apocalypse that stakes its hope in the redeemability of human errors and offers glimpses of a world reborn in a future beyond the end.

---

[48] Charles T. Mathewes, *Evil and the Augustinian Tradition* (Cambridge: Cambridge University Press, 2001).

[49] Justin Cronin, *The City of Mirrors* (London: Orion, 2016), p. 553.

Select Bibliography and Filmography

All quoted printed sources, films and television programmes are referenced in full in the footnotes to the chapters in this volume. Rather than repeat that information here, this Select Bibliography lists only primary and secondary published works, films and series that are analysed in detail in the chapters, and for the most part excludes duplicate editions of the same text, internet sources as well as shorter reviews and articles.

Abbott, Stacey, 'Spectral Vampires: *Nosferatu* in the Light of New Technology', in Stefan Hantke (ed.), *Horror Film: Creating and Marketing Fear* (Jackson: University of Mississippi Press, 2004), pp. 3–20.

Abraham, Nicolas, 'Notes on the Phantom: A Complement to Freud's Metapsychology', trans. by Nicholas Rand, *Critical Inquiry* 13:2 (1987): 387–92.

Achebe, Chinua, 'An Image of Africa: Racism in Joseph Conrad's *Heart of Darkness*', in Helen Lauer and Kofi Anyidoho (eds), *Reclaiming the Human Sciences and Humanities through African Perspectives, Volume II* (Accra: Sub-Saharan publishers, 2012), pp. 929–40.

Adams, Tim, 'The Stephen King Interview, Uncut and Unpublished', *The Guardian*, 14 September 2000 <https://www.theguardian.com/books/2000/sep/14/stephenking.fiction> (last accessed 22 June 2019).

Agamben, Giorgio, *Homo Sacer: Sovereign Power and Bare Life*, trans. by Daniel Heller-Roazen (Stanford, CA: Stanford University Press, 1998).

Alaimo, Stacey, *Bodily Natures: Science, Environment, and the Material Self* (Bloomington, IN: Indiana University Press, 2010).

Aldana Reyes, Xavier, *Gothic Cinema* (London: Routledge, 2020).

Aldington, Richard, *Images of War* (London: Beaumont Press, 1919).

Alexander, Michelle, *The New Jim Crow: Mass Incarceration in the Age of Colorblindness* (New York: New Press, 2012).

al-Inss wa-l-jinn [Humans and Jinns]. Dir. Muhammed Radi. United Group. 1985.

American Horror Story. Created by Ryan Murphy and Brad Falchuk. FX Network, 20th Century Fox Television. 2011–. First aired in USA on 5 October 2011.

Anderson, Eric, Taylor Hagood and Daniel Cross Turner, 'Introduction', in Eric Anderson, Taylor Hagood, and Daniel Cross Turner (eds), *Undead Souths: The Gothic and Beyond in Southern Literature and Culture* (Baton Rouge: Louisiana State University Press, 2015), pp. 1–9.

Ancuta, Katarzyna, 'Asian Gothic', in David Punter (ed.), *A New Companion to the Gothic* (Chichester: Wiley-Blackwell, 2012), pp. 428–41.

Ancuta, Katarzyna, 'Japanese Gothic', in William Hughes, David Punter and Andrew Smith (eds), *The Encyclopedia of The Gothic*, 2 vols (Chichester: Wiley-Blackwell, 2016), vol. 1, p. 371.

Andeweg, Agnes and Sue Zlosnik, 'Introduction', in Agnes Andeweg and Sue Zlosnik (eds) *Gothic Kinship* (Manchester: Manchester University Press, 2013), pp. 1–11.

Anger, Kenneth, quoted in James Riley, *The Bad Trip: Dark Omens, New Worlds and the End of the Sixties* (London: Icon, 2019).

Anon., 'ARI Report 163', in *Gallup Looks at the Movies: Audience Research Reports 1940–1950* (Delaware: Scholarly Resources, 1979).

Anon., 'Winged Skulls and hot air balloons: The grave of Étienne-Gaspard Robert, pioneer of phantasmagoria', *Flickering Lamps* (3 July 2016) <https://flickeringlamps.com/2016/07/03/winged-skulls-and-hot-air-balloons-the-grave-of-etienne-gaspard-robert-pioneer-of-phantasmagoria/> (last accessed 30 August 2018).

Anon., *Trick or Treaty? Memes Flood in as UK Goes for Halloween Brexit With 'Zombie' PM* (2019) <https://sputniknews.com/viral/201904131074100523-halloween-brexit-theresa-may-zombie-government-memes/> (last accessed 15 April 2019).

Arata, Stephen D., 'The Occidental Tourist: *Dracula* and the Anxiety of Reverse Colonization', *Victorian Studies* 33:4 (1990): 621–45.

Armitt, Lucie, *Twentieth-Century Gothic* (Cardiff: University of Wales Press, 2011).

Arnold, Matthew, *Selected Poems*, edited by Timothy Peltason (London: Penguin, 1994).

Arslan, Savaş, *Cinema in Turkey: A New Critical History* (New York: Oxford University Press, 2011).

Ashcroft, Bill, Gareth Griffiths and Helen Tiffin, *The Empire Writes Back: Theory and Practice in Post-Colonial Literatures* (London and New York: Routledge, 1989).

Asylum: The Lost Footage. Dir. Dan T. Hall. Cyfuno Ventures, Vizmo Films, Gravitas Ventures. 2013.

Atasoy, Yıldız, *Turkey, Islamists and Democracy: Transition and Globalization in a Muslim State* (New York: I. B. Tauris, 2005).

Atwood, Margaret, *Alias Grace* (London: Virago Press, 2005).

Auerbach, Nina, *Our Vampires, Ourselves* (Chicago: University of Chicago Press, 1995).

Austen, Jane, *Northanger Abbey*, edited by John Davie (Oxford: Oxford University Press, 1971).

Bacevich, Andrew J., *American Empire: The Realities and Consequences of U.S. Diplomacy* (Cambridge, MA: Harvard University Press, 2002).

Bache-Wiig, Harald, 'Apokalypse nå! Tryggve Andersens Mot kvæld', in Torgeir Haugen (ed.), *Litterære skygger. Norsk fantastisk litteratur* (Oslo: Cappelen Akademisk Forlag, 1998), pp. 123–41.

Bailey, Dale, *American Nightmares: The Haunted House Formula in American Popular Fiction* (Bowling Green, OH: Bowling Green State University Popular Press, 1999).

Bainbridge, Simon, 'Lord Ruthven's Power: Polidori's "The Vampyre", Doubles and the Byronic Imagination', *The Byron Journal* 34:1 (2006): 21–34.

Bakhtin, Mikhail M., 'Forms of Time and of the Chronotope in the Novel: Notes Toward a Historical Poetics', in *The Dialogic Imagination: Four Essays by M. M. Bakhtin*, edited by

Michael Holquist, trans. by Caryl Emerson and Michael Holquist (Austin, TX: University of Texas Press, 1981), pp. 84–258.

Baldick, Chris, 'Introduction', in Chris Baldick (ed.), *The Oxford Book of Gothic Tales* (Oxford: Oxford University Press, 1992), pp. xi–xxiii.

Baldick, Chris and Robert Mighall, 'Gothic Criticism', in David Punter (ed.), *A New Companion to the Gothic* (Oxford: Wiley-Blackwell 2012), pp. 267–87.

Baldwin, Stanley, *This Torch of Freedom* (London: Hodder and Stoughton, 1935).

Balmain, Colette, *Introduction to the Japanese Horror Film* (Edinburgh: Edinburgh University Press, 2008).

Banks, Iain, *The Wasp Factory* (London: Macmillan, 1984).

Barnes, Djuna, *Nightwood* (London: Faber & Faber, 2001).

Battle: Los Angeles. Dir. Jonathan Liebesman. Columbia Pictures. 2011.

Bayer-Berenbaum, Linda, *The Gothic Imagination: Expansion in Gothic Literature and Art* (London and Toronto: Associated University Press, 1982).

Beard, Michael, *Hedayat's Blind Owl as a Western Novel* (New Jersey: Princeton University Press, 1990).

Beck, Richard, *We Believe the Children: A Moral Panic in the 1980s* (New York: Public Affairs, 2015).

Bennett, Jane, *Vibrant Matter: A Political Ecology of Things* (Durham, NC: Duke University Press, 2001), p. viii.

Berger, John, *Ways of Seeing* (London: BBC Books, 1972).

Bernard, Peter, 'Hearn, Lafcadio [Koizumi, Yakumo] [1850–1904]', in Salvador Murguía (ed.), *The Encyclopedia of Japanese Horror Films* (Lanham, Boulder, New York and London: Rowman and Littlefield, 2016), pp. 115–19.

Bhattacharyya, Harihar, 'Multiculturalism in Contemporary India', *International Journal on Multicultural Societies* 5:2 (2003): 148–61.

Bicakci, Tugce, 'The Origins of Turkish Gothic: The adaptations of Stoker's *Dracula* in Turkish Literature and Film', *Studies in Gothic Fiction* 4: 1/2 (2015): 57–69.

Biçakçi Syed, Tuğçe, 'Turkish B-Movie Gothic: Making the Undead Turkish', in Justin D. Edwards and Johan Höglund (eds), *B-Movie Gothic: International Perspectives* (Edinburgh: University of Edinburgh Press, 2018), pp. 139–53.

Birkenstein, Jeff, Anna Froula and Karen Randell (eds), *Reframing 9/11: Film, Popular Culture and the 'War on Terror'* (New York: Continuum, 2010).

Birkhead, Edith, *The Tale of Terror: A Study of the Gothic Romance*, Project Gutenberg, <https://www.gutenberg.org/ebooks/14154> (last accessed 30 December 2020).

Black, Art, 'Coming of Age: The South Korean Horror Film', in Steven Jay Schneider (ed.), *Fear Without Frontiers: Horror Cinema Across the Globe* (Godalming: FAB Press, 2003), pp. 185–203.

Blackmon, Douglas, *Slavery by Another Name: The Re-enslavement of Black Americans from the Civil War to World War II* (New York: Anchor Books, 2009).

Blake, Linnie, 'Vampires, Mad Scientists and the Unquiet Dead: Gothic Ubiquity in Post 9/11 Television', in Justin D. Edwards and Agnieszka Soltysik Monnet (eds), *The Gothic in Contemporary Literature and Popular Culture* (New York: Routledge, 2012), pp. 37–56.

Blake, Linnie, 'Trapped in the Hysterical Sublime: *Twin Peaks*, Postmodernism, and the Neoliberal Now', in Jeffrey Andrew Weinstock and Catherine Spooner (eds), *Return to*

Twin Peaks: New Approaches to Materiality, Theory, and Genre on Television (New York: Palgrave Macmillan, 2015), pp. 229–45.

Blake, Linnie, 'Catastrophic Events and Queer Northern Villages: Zombie Pharmacology in *In the Flesh*', in Linnie Blake and Agnieszka Soltysik Monnet (eds), *Neoliberal Gothic: International Gothic in the Neoliberal Age* (Manchester: Manchester University Press, 2016), pp. 104–21.

Blake, Linnie, 'Max Brooks's *World War Z* (2006) – Neoliberal Gothic', in Simon Bacon (ed.), *The Gothic: A Reader* (Oxford: Peter Lang, 2018), pp. 195–201.

Blake, Linnie, 'The Monster in the Living Room: Gothic Television of the Neoliberal Age', in David Punter (ed.), *The Edinburgh Companion to Gothic and the Arts* (Edinburgh: Edinburgh University Press, 2019), pp. 406–17.

Blake, Linnie, 'Neoliberal Gothic', in Maisha Wester and Xavier Aldana Reyes (eds), *Twenty-First-Century Gothic: An Edinburgh Companion* (Edinburgh: Edinburgh University Press, 2019), pp. 60–71.

Blake, Linnie, *The Wounds of Nations: Horror Cinema, Historical Trauma and National Identity* (Manchester: Manchester University Press, 2008).

Blake, Linnie and Agniezska Soltysik Monnet, 'Introduction: Neoliberal Gothic', in Linnie Blake and Agniezska Soltysik Monnet (eds), *Neoliberal Gothic: International Gothic in the Neoliberal Age* (Manchester: Manchester University Press, 2017), pp. 1–18.

Blake, Linnie and Agnieszka Soltysik Monnet (eds), *Neoliberal Gothic: International Gothic in the Neoliberal Age* (Manchester: Manchester University Press, 2017).

Blank, Trevor J. and Lynne S. McNeill (eds), *Slender Man Is Coming: Creepypasta and Contemporary Legends on the Internet* (Logan: Utah State University Press, 2018).

Bloch, Robert, *Psycho* (London: Corgi, 1959).

Bolens, Guillemette, *La Logique du Corps Articulaire: Les articulations du corps humain dans la littérature occidentale* (Rennes: Presses Universitaires de Rennes, 2000).

Boot, Max, 'The Case for American Empire: The most realistic response to Terrorism is for America to embrace its imperial role', *The Washington Examiner*, 15 October 2001 <https://www.washingtonexaminer.com/weekly-standard/the-case-for-american-empire> (last accessed 22 July 2020).

Borges, Jorge Luis, 'Borges and I', trans. by James E. Irby, in Jorge Luis Borges, *Labyrinths*, edited by Donald A. Yates and James E. Irby (Harmondsworth: Penguin, 1970), pp. 282–3.

Borschke, Margie, *This Is Not a Remix: Piracy, Authenticity and Popular Music* (New York: Bloomsbury, 2017).

Botting, Fred, 'Candygothic', in Fred Botting (ed.), *The Gothic* (Cambridge: D. S. Brewer, 2001), pp. 133–52.

Botting, Fred, 'Aftergothic: Consumption, Machines, and Black Holes', in Jerrold E. Hogle (ed.), *The Cambridge Companion to Gothic Fiction* (Cambridge: Cambridge University Press, 2002), pp. 277–300.

Botting, Fred, 'Future Horror (the Redundancy of Gothic)', *Gothic Studies* 1:2 (1999): 139–55.

Botting, Fred, *Gothic* (London and New York: Routledge, 1996).

Botting, Fred, *Gothic Romanced: Consumption, Gender and Technology in Contemporary Fictions* (London: Routledge, 2008).

Botting, Fred, *Gothic*, 2nd edition (London and New York: Routledge, 2014).

Botting, Fred, 'In Gothic Darkly: Heterotopia, History, Culture', in David Punter (ed.), *A New Companion to the Gothic* (Oxford: Blackwell, 2012), pp. 13–24.

Botting, Fred and Catherine Spooner (eds), *Monstrous Media/Spectral Subjects: Imaging Gothic from the Nineteenth Century to the Present* (Manchester: Manchester University Press, 2015).

Bowden, Mark, *Pitt Rivers: The Life and Archaeological Work of Lieutenant-General Augustus Henry Lane Fox Pitt Rivers* (Cambridge: Cambridge University Press, 1991).

Brantlinger, Patrick, *Imperial Gothic: Atavism and the Occult in the British Adventure Novel, 1880–1914* (Bloomington: Indiana University Press, 1985).

Brantlinger, Patrick, *Rule of Darkness: British Literature and Imperialism, 1830–1914* (Ithaca, NY and London: Cornell University Press, 1988).

Breton, André, 'English Romans Noirs and Surrealism', in Victor Sage (ed.), *The Gothick Novel* (Basingtoke: Macmillan, 1990), pp. 112–15.

Breton, André, 'From the First Manifesto of Surrealism', in Lawrence Rainey (ed.), *Modernism: An Anthology* (Oxford: Blackwell, 2005), pp. 718–41.

Briefel, Aviva and Sam J. Miller (eds), *Horror after 9/11* (Austin, TX: University of Texas Press, 2011).

Brink, André, *Devil's Valley* (London: Vintage, 2000).

Broderick, James F., *James Joyce: A Literary Companion* (Jefferson: McFarland & Co., 2018).

Brooks, Max, *World War Z: An Oral History of the Zombie War* (London: Duckworth, 2007).

Brown, Charles Brockden, *Edgar Huntly; or, Memoirs of a Sleep-Walker: With Related Texts* (Indianapolis: Hackett Publishing, 2006).

Brown, Simon, 'Censorship Under Siege: The BBFC in the Silent Era', in Edward Lambertini (ed.), *Behind the Scenes at the BBFC: Film Classification from the Silent Era to the Silver Screen* (London: BFI Publishing, 2012), pp. 3–14.

Brown, Wendy, 'American Nightmare: Neoliberalism, Neo-conservatism, and De-Democratization', *Political Theory* 34:6 (2006): 690–714.

Browning, John Edgar, 'Classical Hollywood Horror', in Harry Benshoff (ed.), *A Companion to the Horror Film* (Chichester: Wiley-Blackwell, 2014), pp. 225–36.

Bruhm, Steven, 'Contemporary Gothic: Why We Need It', in Jerrold E. Hogle (ed.), *The Cambridge Companion to Gothic Fiction* (Cambridge: Cambridge University Press, 2002), pp. 259–76.

Bryson, Norman, 'Todd Haynes's *Poison* and Queer Cinema', *InVisible Culture: An Electronic Journal for Visual Culture* 1: The Worlding of Cultural Studies (Winter 1998), para. 9 <www.rochester.edu/in_visible_culture/issue1/bryson/> (last accessed 15 December 2020).

Burnham, John, (ed.), *After Freud Left: A Century of Psychoanalysis in America* (Chicago: University of Chicago Press, 2012).

Burns, Hannah Piper and Evan Meaney, 'Glitches Be Crazy', in Nick Briz, Evan Meaney, Rosa Menkman, William Robertson, Jon Satrom and Jessica Westbrook (eds), *GLI.TC/H READER[ROR] 20111* (Unsorted Books, 2011), p. 74 <http://gli.tc/h/READERROR/GLITCH_READERROR_20111-v3BWs.pdf> (last accessed 1 September 2018).

Burroughs, William, *Naked Lunch* (London: Penguin, 2015).

Bush, George W., 'Remarks to the Community in South Bend, Indiana' September 5, 2002. *The American Presidency Project* <www.presidency.ucsb.edu/ws/index.php?pid=63576> (last accessed 22 July 2020).

Bush, George W., 'Remarks to the Troops at Ford Hood, Texas', 3 January 2003, *The American Presidency Project* <www.presidency.ucsb.edu/documents/remarks-military-personnel-fort-hood-texas> (last accessed 22 July 2020).

Bush, George W., 'Remarks in Halifax, Canada', *The American Presidency Project*, 1 December 2004 <www.presidency.ucsb.edu/ws/?pid=72844> (last accessed 20 July 2020).

Butler, Ivan, *Horror in the Cinema* (London: Zwemmer, 1967).

Butler, Judith, *Precarious Lives* (London: Verso, 2004).

Byron, Glennis (ed.), *Globalgothic* (Manchester: Manchester University Press, 2013).

Byron, 'Introduction', in Glennis Byron (ed.), *Globalgothic* (Manchester: Manchester University Press 2013), pp. 1–10.

Cagle, Robert, 'Diary of a Lost Girl: Victoriana, Intertextuality, and *A Tale of Two Sisters*', in Alison Peirse and Daniel Martin (eds), *Korean Horror Cinema* (Edinburgh: Edinburgh University Press, 2013), pp. 158–72.

Cameron, Allan, 'Facing the Glitch: Abstraction, Abjection and the Digital Image', in Martine Beugnet, Allan Cameron and Arild Fetveit (eds), *Indefinite Visions: Cinema and the Attractions of Uncertainty* (Edinburgh: Edinburgh University Press, 2017), pp. 334–52.

Cannell, Fenella, 'English Ancestors: The Moral Possibilities of Popular Genealogy', *Journal of the Royal Anthropological Institute* 17 (2011): 462–80.

Carey, Peter, *Jack Maggs* (London: Faber & Faber, 1997).

Çarkoğlu, Ali and Ersin Kalaycıoğlu, *The Rising Tide of Conservatism in Turkey* (New York: Palgrave Macmillan, 2009).

Carnivàle. Created by Daniel Knauf. 3 Arts Entertainment, Home Box Office (HBO). Distributed by HBO. 2003–2005. First aired in USA on 14 September 2003.

Carrell, Jennifer Lee, *The Speckled Monster: A Historical Tale of Battling Smallpox* (New York: Plume, 2004).

Carter, Angela, 'Afterword to *Fireworks*', in Angela Carter, *Burning Your Boats: Collected Short Stories* (London: Chatto and Windus, 1995), pp. 460–1.

Carter, Angela, *The Sadeian Woman* (London: Virago, 1979).

Carter, Angela, *The Magic Toyshop* (London: Virago, 1981).

Carter, Angela, *The Bloody Chamber and Other Stories* (Harmondsworth: Penguin, 1981).

Cascone, Kim, 'Residualism', in Caleb Kelly (ed.), *Sound* (Cambridge, MA: MIT Press, 2011), pp. 98–101.

Cash, W. J., *The Mind of the South* (New York: Vintage, 1961).

Castillo Street, Susan and Charles L. Crow, 'Introduction: Down at the Crossroads', in Susan Castillo Street and Charles L. Crow (eds), *The Palgrave Handbook to the Southern Gothic* (Basingstoke: Palgrave Macmillan, 2016), pp. 1–6.

Castle, Terry, *The Apparitional Lesbian: Female Homosexuality and Modern Culture* (New York: Columbia University Press, 1993).

Castle, William, *Step Right Up! I'm Going to Scare the Pants Off America* (New York: Putnam's Sons, 1976).

Chafe, William, *The Unfinished Journey: America Since World War Two* (New York: Oxford University Press, 1999).

Chariandy, David, *Soucouyant: A Novel of Forgetting* (Vancouver: Arsenal Pulp Press, 2007).

Charles, John, *The Hong Kong Filmography, 1977–1997* (Jefferson, NJ: McFarland, 2000).

Chen, Lianshan, *Chinese Myths and Legends* (Cambridge: Cambridge University Press, 2011).

Cheng, Yu, 'Under a Spell', in Li Cheuk-to (ed.), *Phantoms of the Hong Kong Cinema* (Hong Kong: Urban Council, 1989), pp. 20–3.

Childs, Peter, *Modernism* (London: Routledge, 2000).

Choi, Jinhee, *The South Korean Film Renaissance: Local Hitmakers, Global Provocateurs* (Middletown, CT: Wesleyan University Press, 2010).

Chomsky, Noam, *Hegemony or Survival: America's Quest for Global Dominance* (New York: Metropolitan Books, 2003).

Christie, Ian, 'The Visible and the Invisible: From "Tricks" to "Effects"', *Early Popular Visual Culture* 13:2 (2015): 106–12.

Chun, Wendy Hui Kyong, *Updating to Remain the Same: Habitual New Media* (Cambridge, MA: MIT Press, 2016).

Clarke, Susanna, *Jonathan Strange and Mr Norrell* (London: Bloomsbury, 2004).

Clery, E. J., 'The Genesis of "Gothic" Fiction', in Jerrold E. Hogle (ed.), *The Cambridge Companion to Gothic Fiction* (Cambridge, Cambridge University Press, 2002), pp. 21–40.

Corstorphine, Kevin, '"A Search for the Father-Image": Masculine Anxiety in Robert Bloch's 1950s Fiction', in Darryl Jones, Elizabeth McCarthy and Bernice M. Murphy (eds), *It Came from the 1950s: Popular Culture, Popular Anxieties* (Basingstoke: Palgrave Macmillan, 2011), pp. 158–75.

Cosslett, Tess, '"History from Below": Time-Slip Narratives and National Identity', *The Lion and the Unicorn* 26:2 (2002), 243–53.

Cottam, F. G., *The House of Lost Souls* (London: Hodder & Stoughton, 2007).

Creed, Barbara, *The Monstrous-Feminine: Film, Feminism, Psychoanalysis* (London: Routledge, 1993).

Cronin, Justin, *The City of Mirrors* (London: Orion, 2016).

Cronin, Justin, *The Passage* (New York: Ballantine Books, 2010).

Crow, Charles L., *American Gothic* (Cardiff: University of Wales Press, 2009).

Crow, Charles L., 'Southern American Gothic', in Jeffrey Andrew Weinstock (ed.), *The Cambridge Companion to American Gothic* (Cambridge: Cambridge University Press, 2017), pp. 141–55.

Crowley, Aleister, *Moonchild* (New York: Avon, 1971).

Cubitt, Sean, 'Temporalities of the Glitch: *Déjà Vu*', in Martine Beugnet, Allan Cameron and Arild Fetveit (eds), *Indefinite Visions: Cinema and the Attractions of Uncertainty* (Edinburgh: Edinburgh University Press, 2017), pp. 299–315.

Curtis Klause, Annette, *The Silver Kiss* (New York: Delacorte, 2001).

Dall'Asta, Monica, 'DEBATES: Thinking About Cinema: First Waves', in Michael Temple and Michael Witt (eds), *The French Cinema Book* (London: BFI Publishing, 2004), pp. 82–90.

Daly, Mary, *Gyn/ecology: The Metaethics of Radical Feminism* (Boston, MA: Beacon Press, 1978, 1990).

The Dark Tapes. Dir. Michael McQuown and Vincent J. Guastini. Thunder Road Incorporated. 2016. Epic Pictures Releasing, 2017. DVD.

Darvay, Daniel, *Haunting Modernity and the Gothic Presence in British Modernist Literature* (New York: Palgrave Macmillan, 2016).

Davis, Colin, *Haunted Subjects: Deconstruction, Psychoanalysis and the Return of the Dead* (Basingstoke: Palgrave Macmillan, 2007).

Davison, Graeme, *The Use and Abuse of Australian History* (Crows Nest, NSW: Allen and Unwin, 2000).

Dawson Varughese, E., *Reading New India: Post-Millennial Indian Fiction in English* (London: Bloomsbury, 2013).

Dax, Max, 'Interview with Thomas Ruff', in *Thomas Ruff*, Castello di Rivoli Museo d'Arte Contemporanea (Milan: Skira, 2009), pp. 70–5.

Dayan, Daniel and Elihu Katz, *Media Events: The Live Broadcasting of History* (Cambridge, MA: Harvard University Press, 1992).

Dean, Jodi, *Democracy and Other Neoliberal Fantasies: Communicative Capitalism and Left Politics* (Durham, NC and London: Duke University Press, 2009).

Derian, James Der, *Virtuous War: Mapping the Military–Industrial–Media–Entertainment Network* (Boulder, CO: Westview Press, 2001).

Devlin, Polly, 'London Revisited', British *Vogue*, 15 September 1968, pp. 152–3.

Didion, Joan, *The White Album* (London: Flamingo, 1993).

Dimen, Muriel, 'Politically Correct? Politically Incorrect?', in Carole S. Vance (ed.), *Pleasure and Danger: Exploring Female Sexuality* (London: Pandora, 1989), pp. 138–48.

Doane, Mary Ann, *The Desire to Desire: The Woman's Film of the 1940s* (Bloomington, IN: Indiana University Press, 1987).

Douglass, Paul, 'Byron's Life and His Biographers', in Drummond Bone (ed.), *The Cambridge Companion to Byron* (Cambridge: Cambridge University Press, 2004), pp. 7–26.

Dourish, Paul, 'Rematerializing the Platform: Emulation and the Digital-Material', in Sarah Pink, Elisenda Ardèvol and Dèbora Lanzeni (eds), *Digital Materialities: Design and Anthropology* (London: Bloomsbury Publishing, 2016), pp. 29–44.

Downey, Dara, 'Locating the Spectre in Dan Curtis's *Burnt Offerings*', in Murray Leeder (ed.), *Cinematic Ghosts: Haunting and Spectrality from Silent Cinema to the Digital Age* (London: Bloomsbury Academic, 2015), pp. 143–58.

Dracula AD 1972. Dir. Alan Gibson. Hammer Films, Columbia Warner Distributors. 1972.

Du Bois, W. E. B., *The Souls of Black Folk* (New York: Penguin Random House, 2018).

Dumas, Chris, 'Horror and Psychoanalysis: An Introductory Primer', in Harry M. Benshoff (ed.), *A Companion to the Horror Film* (Oxford: Wiley-Blackwell, 2017), pp. 21–37.

du Maurier, Daphne, *Rebecca* (London: Arrow Books, 1992).

Dunant, Sarah and Roy Porter, *The Age of Anxiety* (London: Virago, 1996).

Dworkin, Andrea, *Pornography: Men Possessing Women* (London: The Women's Press, 1981).

Edge, Thomas, '"Who Do You Think You Are?": Examining the African-American Experience in Slavery and Freedom through Family History Television', *The Journal of American Culture* 40:4 (2017): 341–54.

Edmundson, Mark, *Nightmare on Main Street: Angels, Sadomasochism, and the Culture of Gothic* (Cambridge, MA: Harvard University Press, 1997).

Edwards, Justin D., *Gothic Canada: Reading the Spectre of a National Literature* (Edmonton: University of Alberta Press, 2010).

Edwards, Justin D., 'Zombie Terrorism in an Age of Global Gothic', *Gothic Studies* 17:2 (November 2015): 12–25.

Ehrhart, W. D., *Passing Time: Memoir of a Vietnam Veteran Against the War* (Amherst, MA: University of Massachusetts Press, 1995).

Einhaus, Ann-Marie, *The Short Story and the First World War* (Cambridge: Cambridge University Press, 2013).

Eisner, Lotte H., *The Haunted Screen: Expressionism in the German Cinema and the Influence of Max Reinhardt*, trans. Roger Grieves (Berkeley and Los Angeles: University of California Press, 1977).

Eliot, T. S., *The Sacred Wood: Essays on Poetry and Criticism* (London: Methuen & Co Ltd, 1928).

Elliott, Kamilla, 'Gothic—Film—Parody', *Adaptation* 1:1 (2008): 24–43.

Elliott, Kamilla, *Portraiture and British Gothic Fiction: The Rise of Picture Identification, 1764–1835* (Baltimore, NJ: Johns Hopkins University Press, 2013).

Elliott, Will, *The Pilo Family Circus* (London: Quercus, 2007).

Ellis, Bill, 'The Highgate Cemetery Vampire Hunt: The Anglo-American Connection in Satanic Cult Lore', *Folklore* 104: 1/2 (1993): 13–39.

Ellis, Kate Ferguson, 'Can You Forgive Her? The Gothic Heroine and Her Critics', in David Punter (ed.), *A New Companion to the Gothic* (Oxford: Wiley-Blackwell, 2012), pp. 457–68.

Ellis, Kate Ferguson, *The Contested Castle: Gothic Novels and the Subversion of Domestic Ideology* (Urbana, IL: University of Illinois Press, 1989).

Ellis, Markman, *The History of Gothic Fiction* (Edinburgh: Edinburgh University Press, 2000).

El-Zein, Amira, *Islam, Arabs, and Intelligent World of the Jinn* (New York: Syracuse University Press, 2009).

Eppink, Jason, 'A Brief History of the GIF (so Far)', *Journal of Visual Culture* 13:3 (1 December 2014): 298–306.

Erb, Cynthia, *Tracking King Kong: A Hollywood Icon in World Culture* (Detroit, MI: Wayne State University Press, 1998).

Estok, Simon C., *The Ecophobia Hypothesis* (New York: Routledge, 2018).

Estok, Simon C., 'Theorizing in a Space of Ambivalent Openness: Ecocriticism and Ecophobia', *Interdisciplinary Studies in Literature and the Environment* 16 (Spring 2009): 203–25.

Faris, Wendy B., 'Scheherazade's Children: Magical Realism and Postmodern Fiction', in Lois Parkinson Zamora and Wendy B. Faris (eds), *Magical Realism: Theory, History, Community* (Durham, NC and London: Duke University Press, 1995), pp. 163–90.

Faulkner, William, *Requiem for a Nun* (London: Vintage, 1996).

Fergusson, Niall, *Colossus: The Price of America's Empire* (New York: Penguin, 2004).

Feuer, Jane, 'Genre Study and Television', in Robert C. Allen (ed.), *Channels of Discourse, Reassembled: Television and Contemporary Criticism*, 2nd edition (Chapel Hill and London: University of North Carolina Press, 1992), pp. 138–60.

Fiedler, Leslie A., *Love and Death in the American Novel* (New York: Criterion Books, 1960).

Fiedler, Leslie A., *Love and Death in the American Novel*, revised edition (Champaign, IL: Dalkey Archive Press, 1996).

Fink, Marty, 'AIDS Vampires: Reimagining Illness in Octavia Butler's "Fledgling"', *Science Fiction Studies* 37: 3 (November 2010): 416–32.

Fitzgerald, Lauren, 'Female Gothic and the Institutionalization of Gothic Studies', in Diana Wallace and Andrew Smith (eds), *The Female Gothic: New Directions* (Basingstoke: Palgrave Macmillan, 2009), pp. 13–25.

Flusser, Vilém, *The Shape of Things: A Philosophy of Design*, trans. by Anthony Matthews (London: Reaktion Books, 2012).

Forster, E. M., *Aspects of the Novel*, edited by O Stallybrass (Harmondsworth: Penguin, 2005).

Forster, E. M., *A Passage to India*, edited by Pankaj Mishra (Harmondsworth: Penguin 2005).

Fortier, Anne-Marie, *Multicultural Horizons: Diversity and the Limits of the Civil Nation* (London: Routledge, 2008).

Foster, Paul, 'Kingdom of Shadows: *Fin-de-siècle* Gothic and Early Cinema', in Fred Botting and Catherine Spooner (eds), *Monstrous Media / Spectral Subjects: Imaging Gothic from the Nineteenth Century to the Present* (Manchester: Manchester University Press, 2015), pp. 29–41.

Foucault, Michel, 'Of Other Spaces', trans. by Jay Miskowiec, *Diacritics* 16 (1986): 22–7.

Fowler, Alastair, *Kinds of Literature: An Introduction to the Theory of Genres and Modes* (Oxford: Oxford University Press, 1982).

Franklin, H. Bruce, *The Vietnam War and Other American Fantasies* (Amherst, MA: University of Massachusetts Press, 2000).

Frayling, Christopher, 'Foreword', in James Bell (ed.), *Gothic: The Dark Heart of Film* (London: BFI, 2013), pp. 5–7.

Frayling, Christopher, *Frankenstein: The First Two Hundred Years* (London: Reel Art Press, 2017).

Freud, Sigmund, 'The "Uncanny"', in Sigmund Freud, *Art and Literature*, Penguin Freud Library, Vol. 14, edited by Albert Dickson, trans. by James Strachey (Harmondsworth: Penguin, 1990), pp. 335–76.

Freud, Sigmund, *The Penguin Freud library*, edited by Angela Richards and Albert Dickson, trans. by James Strachey, 14 vols (London: Penguin Books Ltd, 1984).

Fried, Michael, *Why Photography Matters as Never Before* (New Haven, CT: Yale University Press, 2008).

Friedan, Betty, *The Feminine Mystique*, intro. by Lionel Shriver (Harmondsworth: Penguin, 2010).

Fukuyama, Francis, *The End of History and the Last Man* (London: Penguin, 1992).

Fyhr, Mattias, *Svensk skräcklitteratur 1: Bårtäcken över jordens likrum* (Lund: Ellerström, 2017).

Gaard, Greta, 'Living Interconnections with Animals and Nature', in Greta Gaard (ed.), *Ecofeminism: Women, Animals, Nature* (Philadelphia, PA: Temple University Press, 1993), pp. 1–12.

Gamer, Michael, *Romanticism and the Gothic: Genre, Reception, and Canon Formation* (Cambridge: Cambridge University Press, 2000).

Garner, Bianca, 'Sink Your Teeth Into This: Revisiting The Hunger (1983)', *Filmotomy: Dissecting Film from the Grit to the Stars*, 1 June 2018 <https://filmotomy.com/hunger-review-1983/> (last accessed 10 September 2020).

Gaskell, Jane, *The Shiny Narrow Grin* (London: Hodder and Stoughton, 1964).

Gaudier-Brzeska, Henri, 'Vortex Gaudier-Brzeska', in Mia Carter and Alan Friedman (eds), *Modernism and Literature: An Introduction and Reader* (Abingdon: Routledge, 2013), pp. 270–1.

Gelder, Ken, *Reading the Vampire* (London: Routledge, 1994).

Genovese, Eugene, *The Southern Tradition: The Achievements and Limitations of an American Conservatism* (Cambridge, MA: Harvard University Press, 1994).

Germaine Buckley, Chloé, *Twenty-First- Century Children's Gothic: From the Wanderer to the Nomadic Subject* (Edinburgh: Edinburgh University Press, 2018).

Ghosh, Amitav, *The Great Derangement: Climate Change and the Unthinkable* (Chicago: University of Chicago Press, 2016).

Gibbard Cook, Sarah, 'Feminists Differ in Second and Third Waves', *Women in Higher Education Banner*, 9 May 2014. Wiley Online Library <https://doi.org/10.1002/whe.10222> (last accessed 4 September 2018).

Gibbons, Luke, *Joyce's Ghosts: Ireland, Modernism and Memory* (Chicago: Chicago University Press, 2016).

Gibson, Andrew, *Towards a Postmodern Theory of Narrative* (Edinburgh: Edinburgh University Press, 1996).

Gilbert, Sandra M. and Susan Gubar, *The Madwoman in the Attic: The Woman Writer and the Nineteenth-Century Literary Imagination* (New Haven: Yale University Press, 1984).

Gittings, Christopher, '"Zero Patience": Genre, Difference, and Ideology: Singing and Dancing Queer Nation', *Cinema Journal* 41.1 (Autumn 2001): 28–39.

Glasgow, Ellen, 'Heroes and Monsters', in Julian Rowan Raper (ed.), *Ellen Glasgow's Reasonable Doubts: A Collection of Her Writings* (Baton Rouge: Louisiana State University Press, 1988), pp. 162–7.

Glover, David, 'The "Spectrality" Effect in Early Modernism', in Andrew Smith and Jeff Wallace (eds), *Gothic Modernisms* (Basingstoke: Palgrave Macmillan, 2001), pp. 29–42.

Go, Julian, *Patterns of Empire: The British and American Empires, 1688 to the Present* (Cambridge: Cambridge University Press, 2011).

Goddu, Teresa A., *Gothic America: Narrative, History, and Nation* (New York: Columbia University Press, 1997).

Göle, Nilüfer, *The Forbidden Modern: Civilisation and Veiling* (Ann Arbor, MI: University of Michigan Press, 1996).

Gomery, Douglas, 'The Economics of the Horror Film', in James B. Weaver III and Ron Tamborini (eds), *Horror Films: Current Research on Audience Preferences and Reactions* (New York: Routledge, 1996), pp. 49–62.

Gordon, Avery F., *Ghostly Matters: Haunting and the Sociological Imagination*, 2nd edition (Minneapolis: University of Minnesota Press, 2008).

Gorky, Maxim, 'Last Night I was in the Kingdom of Shadows', reprinted in Colin Harding and Simon Popple (eds), *In the Kingdom of Shadows: A Companion to Early Cinema* (London: Cygnus Arts, 1996), pp. 5–6.

Goyen, William, *The House of Breath* (Evanston, IL: Northwestern University Press, 1999).

Gray, Richard, 'Inside the Dark House: William Faulkner, *Absalom, Absalom!* And the Southern Gothic', in Susan Castillo Street and Charles L. Crow (eds), *The Palgrave Handbook to the Southern Gothic* (Basingstoke: Palgrave Macmillan, 2016), pp. 21–40.

Grieveson, Lee and Peter Krämer, 'Feature Films and Cinema Programmes', in Lee Grieveson and Peter Krämer (eds), *The Silent Cinema Reader* (London and New York: Routledge, 2004), pp. 187–95.

Grumberg, Karen, *Hebrew Gothic: History and the Poetics of Persecution* (Indiana: Indiana University Press, 2019).

Grunenberg, Christoph, 'Unsolved Mysteries: Gothic Tales from *Frankenstein* to the Hair-Eating Doll', in Christoph Grunenberg (ed.), *Gothic: Transmutations of Horror in Late Twentieth Century Art* (Cambridge, MA: MIT Press, 1997), pp. 213–158.

Guiley, Rosemary Ellen, *The Encyclopaedia of Demons and Demonology* (New York: Facts On File, Inc., 2009).

Gunkel, David J., *Of Remixology: Ethics and Aesthetics after Remix* (Cambridge, MA: MIT Press, 2016).

Gunning, Tom, 'The Cinema of Attractions: Early Cinema, its Spectator and the Avant-Garde', *Wide Angle* 8: 3/4 (1986): 63–70.

Gunning, Tom, 'Weaving a Narrative: Style and Economic Background in Griffith's Early Films', in Thomas Elsaesser (ed.), *Early Cinema: Space, Frame, Narrative* (London: BFI, 1990), pp. 336–47.

Gunning, Tom, 'Phantom Images and Modern Manifestations: Spirit Photography, Magic Theater, Trick Films, and Photography's Uncanny', in Murray Leeder (ed.), *Cinematic Ghosts: Haunting and Spectrality from Silent Cinema to the Digital Era* (New York, London, New Delhi, and Sydney: Bloomsbury, 2015), pp. 17–38.

Haefele-Thomas, Ardel, *Introduction to Transgender Studies* (New York: Harrington Park Press, 2019).

Hale, Nathan G. Jr, *The Rise and Crisis of Psychoanalysis in the United States: Freud and the Americans 1917–1985* (New York: Oxford University Press, 1995).

Han, Byung-Chul, *The Transparency Society*, trans. by Erik Butler (Stanford: Stanford University Press, 2015).

Hanks, Michele, *Haunted Heritage: The Cultural Politics of Ghost Tourism, Populism, and the Past* (London: Routledge, 2015).

Harrison, M. John, 'The Course of the Heart', in M. John Harrison, *Anima* (London: Gollancz, 2005), pp. 122–3.

Harrison, Sheri-Marie, 'New Black Gothic', *LA Review of Books*, 23 June 2018 <https://lareviewofbooks.org/article/new-black-gothic/#!> (last accessed 30 July 2018).

Hart, Michael and Antonio Negri, *Empire* (Cambridge, MA: Harvard University Press, 2000).

Harvey, David, *The New Imperialism* (Oxford: Oxford University Press, 2003).

Hasford, Gustav, *The Short-Timers* (Toronto and New York: Bantam Books, 1979).

Hasford, Gustav, 'Still Gagging on the Bitterness of Vietnam', *Los Angeles Times* (30 April 1980).

Haugen, Torgeir (ed.), *Litterære skygger. Norsk fantastisk litteratur* (Oslo: Cappelen Akademisk Forlag).

The Haunting of Hill House. Created by Mike Flanagan. FlanaganFilm, Amblin Television, Paramount Television, Netflix. Distributed by Netflix. 2018. First aired on 12 October 2018.

Hayles, N. Katherine, *Unthought: The Power of the Cognitive Nonconscious* (Chicago: University of Chicago Press, 2017).

H. D., 'From *A Tribute to Freud*', in Mia Carter and Alan Friedman (eds), *Modernism and Literature: An Introduction and Reader* (Abingdon: Routledge, 2013), pp. 555–8.

Healey, Emma, *Lesbian Sex Wars* (London: Virago, 1996).

Hearn, Marcus, *The Art of Hammer: Posters from the Archives of Hammer Films* (London: Titan Books 2010).

Heffernan, Kevin, *Ghouls, Gimmicks, and Gold: Horror Films and the American Movie Business, 1953–1968* (Durham, NC: Duke University Press, 2004).

Heilmann, Ann, and Mark Llewellyn, *The Victorians in the Twenty-First Century, 1999–2009* (Basingstoke: Palgrave Macmillan, 2010).

Heise, Ursula K., *Sense of Place and Sense of Planet: The Environmental Imagination of the Global* (Oxford: Oxford University Press, 2008).

Heller-Nicholas, Alexandra, 'The Only Word in the World is Mine: Remembering *Michelle Remembers*', in Keir-La Janisse and Paul Corpue (eds), *Satanic Panic: Pop-Cultural Paranoia in the 1980s* (Goldalming: FAB Press, 2016), pp. 19–32.

Heller, Joseph, *Catch 22* (New York: Dell, 1955).

Heller, Vivian, *Joyce, Decadence, and Emancipation* (Urbana, IL and Chicago: University of Illinois Press, 1995).

Hendrix, Grady, *Paperbacks from Hell: The Twisted History of 70s and 80s Horror Fiction* (Philadelphia, PA: Quirk Books, 2017).

Hervey, Benjamin, 'Contemporary Horror Cinema', in Catherine Spooner and Emma McEvoy (eds), *The Routledge Companion to Gothic* (London: Routledge, 2007), pp. 233–41.

Hewison, Robert, *The Heritage Industry: Britain in a Climate of Decline* (London: Methuen, 1987).

Higson, Andrew, *English Heritage, English Cinema: Costume Drama Since 1980* (Oxford: Oxford University Press, 2003).

Hoad, Neville, 'Miss HIV and Us: Beauty Queens Against the HIV/AIDS Pandemic', *CR: The New Centennial Review* 10:1 (Spring 2010): 9–28.

Hodgson, William Hope, *The House on the Borderland and Other Novels* (London: Gollancz, 2002).

Hogle, Jerrold E., 'The Ghost of the Counterfeit in the Genesis of the Gothic', in Allan Lloyd Smith and Victor Sage (eds), *Gothick Origins and Innovations* (Amsterdam: Rodopi, 1994), pp. 23–33.

Hogle, Jerrold E., 'Introduction: The Gothic in Western Culture', in Jerrold E. Hogle (ed.) *The Cambridge Companion to Gothic Fiction* (Cambridge: Cambridge University Press, 2002) pp. 1–20.

Hogle, Jerrold E., 'History, Trauma and the Gothic in Contemporary Western Fictions', in Glennis Byron and Dale Townshend (eds), *The Gothic World* (Abingdon and New York: Routledge, 2014), pp. 72–81.

Höglund, Johan, *Imperial Gothic: Popular Culture, Empire, Violence* (New York: Routledge, 2014).

Höglund, Johan, 'Gothic Haunting Empire', in Maria Holmgren Troy and Elisabeth Wennö (eds), *Memory, Haunting, Discourse* (Karlstad: Karlstad University Press, 2005), pp. 243–54.

Höglund, Johan, 'Parables for the Paranoid: Affect and the War Gothic' *Continuum: Journal of Media and Cultural Studies* 27:3 (2013): 397–407.

Höglund, Johan, 'Revenge of the Trolls: Norwegian (Post) Colonial Gothic', *Edda* 2 (2017), 115–29.

Holden, Philip, 'The "Postcolonial Gothic": Absent Histories, Present Contexts', *Textual Practice* 23:3 (2009): 353–72.

Holdsworth, Amy, *Television, Memory and Nostalgia* (London: Palgrave Macmillan, 2011).

Holt, Victoria, *Mistress of Mellyn* (London: Harper, 2006).
Horner, Avril, '"A Detour of Filthiness": French Fiction and Djuna Barnes's *Nightwood*', in Avril Horner (ed.), *European Gothic: A Spirited Exchange, 1760–1960* (Manchester: Manchester University Press, 2002), pp. 230–51.
Horner, Avril and Sue Zlosnik, 'Strolling in the Dark: Gothic Flânerie in Djuna Barnes's *Nightwood*', in Andrew Smith and Jeff Wallace (eds), *Gothic Modernisms* (Basingstoke: Palgrave, 2001), pp. 78–94.
Hoskins, W. G., *The Making of the English Landscape*, new edition (Harmondsworth, Penguin, 1985).
Howlid Wærp, H., 'Utover enhver grense – Gotiske trek I Ragnhild Jølsens romancer', in Torgeir Haugen (ed.), *Litterære skygger. Norsk fantastisk litteratur* (Oslo: Cappelen Akademisk Forlag, 1998), pp. 101–21.
Hoy, Meredith, *From Point to Pixel: A Genealogy of Digital Aesthetics* (Hanover, NH: Dartmouth College Press, 2017).
Hubner, Laura, *Fairytale and Gothic Horror: Uncanny Transformations in Film* (London: Palgrave Macmillan, 2018).
Hutchings, Peter, *The Horror Film* (London: Longman, 2004).
Hutchings, Peter, 'Monster Legacies: Memory, Technology and Horror History', in Lincoln Geraghty and Mark Jancovich (eds), *The Shifting Definitions of Genre: Essays on Labeling Films, Television Shows and Media* (Jefferson, IN: McFarland, 2007), pp. 216–28.
Hutchings, Peter, 'Tearing your Soul Apart: Horror's New Monsters', in Victor Sage and Allan Lloyd Smith (eds), *Modern Gothic: A Reader* (Manchester: Manchester University Press, 1996), pp. 89–103.
Hyman, Gavin, *A Short History of Atheism* (London: I. B. Tauris, 2010).
Hynes, Samuel, *The Soldier's Tale: Bearing Witness to a Modern War* (New York: Penguin Books, 1997).
I'll Take My Stand: The South and the Agrarian Tradition, by Twelve Southerners (New York: Harper & Row, 1962).
Incense for the Damned. Dir. Robert Hartford-Davis. Lucinda Films/Titan International Productions, Titan Films Distribution Ltd. 1970.
Inglis, David and Mary Holmes, 'Highland and Other Haunts – Ghosts in Scottish Tourism', *Annals of Tourism Research* 30:1 (2003): 50–63.
Iversen, Gunnar, 'Between Art and Genre: New Nordic Horror Cinema', in Mette Hjort and Ursula Lindqvist (eds), *A Companion to Nordic Cinema* (Oxford: Wiley-Blackwell, 2016) pp. 332–49.
Jackson, Shirley, *The Bird's Nest* (London: Michael Joseph, 1955).
Jackson, Shirley, *We Have Always Lived in the Castle* (New York: Viking, 1962).
Jackson, Shirley, *The Haunting of Hill House*, in Joyce Carol Oates (ed.), *Shirley Jackson: Novels and Stories* (New York: Library of America, 2010), pp. 241–417.
Jacobs, Jason, *The Intimate Screen: Early British Television Drama* (Oxford: Oxford University Press, 2000).
James, M. R., *The Complete Ghost Stories of M. R. James* (London: Penguin, 1984).
Jameson, Fredric, 'Periodizing the 60s', *Social Text* 9:10 (1984): 178–209.
Jameson, Fredric, *Postmodernism, or, The Cultural Logic of Late Capitalism* (London: Verso, 1991).

Jancovich, Mark, '"Bluebeard's Wives": Horror, Quality and the Paranoid Woman's Film in the 1940s', *Irish Journal of Gothic and Horror Studies* 12 (2013) <https://irishgothichorror.files.wordpress.com/2018/03/bluebeards-wives.pdf> (last accessed 3 April 2019).

Jancovich, Mark, 'Beyond Hammer: The First Run Market and the Prestige Horror Film in the early 1960s', *Palgrave Communications* 3 (2017) <www.nature.com/articles/palcomms201728> (last accessed 3 April 2019).

Jancovich, Mark, 'Shadows and Bogeymen: Horror, Stylization and the Critical Reception of Orson Welles During the 1940s', *Participations: A Journal of Audience and Reception Studies* 6: 1 (May 2009): 25–51.

Jancovich, Mark, '"The English Master of Movie Melodrama": Hitchcock, Horror and the Women's Film', *Film International* 9:3 (2011): 51–67.

Jancovich, Mark, 'Ingrid Bergman', in Elizabeth McCarthy and Bernice M. Murphy (eds), *Lost Souls of Horror and the Gothic* (Jefferson, NC: McFarland, 2016), pp. 34–7.

Jancovich, Mark, '"Where it Belongs": Television Horror, Domesticity, and *Alfred Hitchcock Presents*', in Kimberly Jackson and Linda Belau (eds), *Horror in the Age of Consumption* (New York: Routledge, 2017), pp. 29–44.

Jancovich, Mark, *Horror: The Film Reader* (London: Routledge, 2002).

Jenkins, Henry, *Convergence Culture: Where Old and New Media Collide* (New York: New York University Press, 2006).

Johansen, Emily, 'The Neoliberal Gothic: *Gone Girl*, *Broken Harbor*, and the Terror of Everyday Life', *Contemporary Literature* 57:1 (Spring 2016): 30–55.

Johnson, Chambers, *The Sorrows of Empire: Militarism, Secrecy, and the End of the Republic* (New York: Metropolitan Books, 2004).

Johnsson, Henrik, *Strindberg och skräcken. Skräckmotiv och identitetstematik i August Strindbergs författarskap* (Umeå: Bokförlaget H: ström, 2008).

Jolley, Elizabeth, *The Well* (London: Penguin Books, 1986).

Jones, David J., *Gothic Machine: Textualities, Pre-cinematic Media and Film in Popular Visual Culture, 1670–1910* (Cardiff: University of Wales Press, 2011).

Jones, James, *The Thin Red Line* (New York: Dell, 1962).

Jowett, Lorna and Stacey Abbott, *TV Horror: Investigating the Dark Side of the Small Screen* (London: I. B. Tauris, 2013).

Joyce, James, *Dubliners*, edited by Terence Brown (Harmondsworth: Penguin, 2000).

Kamal Jha, Raj, *Fireproof* (London: Picador, 2007).

Kaplan, Amy and Donald E. Pease (eds), *Cultures of United States Imperialism* (Durham, NC: Duke University Press, 1993).

Kastbjerg, Kirstine Marie, *Reading the Surface: The Danish Gothic of B. S. Ingemann, H. C. Andersen, Karen Blixen and Beyond* (Unpublished PhD thesis; University of Washington, 2013).

Kavka, Misha, 'The Gothic on Screen', in Jerrold E. Hogle (ed.), *The Cambridge Companion to Gothic Fiction* (Cambridge: Cambridge University Press, 2001), pp. 209–28.

Keetley, Dawn, 'Introduction: Six Theses on Plant Horror; or, Why Are Plants Horrifying?', in Dawn Keetley and Angela Tenga (eds), *Plant Horror: Approaches to the Monstrous Vegetal in Fiction and Film* (Basingstoke: Palgrave Macmillan, 2016).

Keetley, Dawn and Matthew Wynn Sivils (eds), *Ecogothic in Nineteenth-Century American Literature* (New York: Routledge, 2018).

Kermode, Frank, *The Sense of an Ending: Studies in the Theory of Fiction* (New York: Oxford University Press, 1967).

Kilgour, Maggie, 'Dr Frankenstein Meets Dr Freud', in Robert K. Martin and Eric Savoy (eds), *American Gothic: New Interventions in a National Narrative* (Iowa City: University of Iowa Press, 1998), pp. 40–54.

King, Richard A., *A Southern Renaissance: The Cultural Awakening of the American South, 1930–1955* (New York: Oxford University Press, 1980).

King, Stephen, *Danse Macabre* (London: Warner, 1991).

King, Stephen, *It* (London: Hodder & Stoughton, 2011).

King, *The Stand* (London: Hodder & Stoughton, 2011).

Kivisto, Peter, 'We Really Are All Multiculturalists Now', *The Sociological Quarterly* 53 (2012): 1–24.

Klein, Naomi, *No Is Not Enough: Resisting Trump's Shock Politics and Winning the World We Need* (London: Penguin, 2018).

Knock Knock 2. Dir. Chris Sheng. Red Baron Films, Indican Pictures. 2011. Lionsgate Home Entertainment, 2012. DVD.

Kortenaar, Neil, 'Multiculturalism and Globalization', in Coral Ann Howells and Eva-Marie Kröller (eds), *The Cambridge Companion to Canadian Literature* (Cambridge: Cambridge University Press, 2004), pp. 556–80.

Kracauer, Siegfried, 'Hollywood's Terror Films: Do They Reflect an American State of Mind?', *New German Critique* 89 (2003): 105–11.

Kymlicka, Will, *Multicultural Odysseys: Navigating the New International Politics of Diversity* (Oxford: Oxford University Press, 2009).

Lammers, Tim, 'Interview: Ransom Riggs thrilled to enter "Peculiar" world of Tim Burton', *DirectConversations.com*, 2 September 2016 <https://directconversations.com/2016/09/02/interview-ransom-riggs-thrilled-enter-peculiar-world-tim-burton/> (last accessed 27 April 2019).

Land of the Dead. Dir. George A. Romero. Universal Pictures. 2005.

Laskawy, Michael and Todd Haynes, 'Poison at the Box Office: AN INTERVIEW WITH TODD HAYNES, *Cinéast* 18:3 (1991): 38–9.

Latham, Rob, *Consuming Youth: Vampires, Cyborgs, and the Culture of Consumption* (Chicago and London: University of Chicago Press, 2002).

Latour, Bruno, *Down to Earth: Politics in the New Climatic Regime*, trans. By Catherine Porter (London: Polity Press, 2018).

Lawrence, D. H., *Women in Love*, edited by David Farmer, Lindeth Vasey and John Worthen (Cambridge: Cambridge University Press, 1987).

Ledwon, Lenora, '*Twin Peaks* and the Television Gothic', *Literature/Film Quarterly* 21:4 (1993): 260–70.

Lee, Hyangjin, 'Family, Death and the *Wonhon* in Four Films of the 1960s', in Alison Peirse and Daniel Martin (eds), *Korean Horror Cinema* (Edinburgh: Edinburgh University Press, 2013), pp. 23–34.

Leeder, Murray, 'Introduction', in Murray Leeder (ed.), *Cinematic Ghosts: Haunting and Spectrality from Silent Cinema to the Digital Era* (New York, London, New Delhi and Sydney: Bloomsbury, 2015), pp. 1–14.

Leeder, Murray, *Horror Film: A Critical Introduction* (New York: Bloomsbury, 2018).

Leffler, Yvonne, 'Vampyrmotivet och erotiken', in Birgitta Svensson and Birthe Sjöberg (eds), *Kulturhjälten. Viktor Rydbergs humanism* (Stockholm: Atlantis, 2009), pp. 155–68.

Leffler, Yvonne, *I skräckens lustgård: Skräckromantik i svenska 1800–talsromaner* (Gothenburg: Skrifter utgivna av litteraturvetenskapliga institutionen vid Göteborgs universitet, 1991).

Leffler, Yvonne, *Horror as Pleasure: The Aesthetics of Horror Fiction* (Stockholm: Almqvist & Wiksell International, 2000).

The Legend of the Witches. Dir. Malcolm Leigh Border Film Productions/Negus Fancey, Border Film Productions. 1970.

LeMenager, Stephanie, *Living Oil: Petroleum Culture in the American Century* (Oxford: Oxford University Press, 2016).

Lenoir, Tim and Luke Caldwell, *The Military-Entertainment Complex* (Cambridge, MA: Harvard University Press, 2018).

Lentin, Alana and Gavan Titley, *The Crises of Multiculturalism: Racism in a Neoliberal Age* (London: Zed Books, 2011).

Lessig, Lawrence, *Remix: Marking Art and Commerce Thrive in the Hybrid Economy* (London: Penguin, 2008).

Leung, Wing-Fai, 'From *A Tale of Two Sisters* to the *Uninvited*: A Tale of Two Texts', in Alison Peirse and Daniel Martin (eds), *Korean Horror Cinema* (Edinburgh: Edinburgh University Press, 2013), pp. 173–86.

Lévi, Éliphas, *The History of Magic*, trans. by A. E. Waite (London: Rider & Company, 1913).

Lévy, Maurice, 'FAQ: What is Gothic?', *Anglophonia* 15 (2004): 23–37.

Levinas, Emmanuel, *Alterity and Transcendence*, trans. by M. B. Smith (New York: Columbia University Press, 1999).

Lewis, Wyndham, 'Vortices and Notes: Futurism, Magic and Life', *BLAST* 1 (1914): 132–5.

Lewis, Wyndham, *Tarr*, edited by Scott W. Klein (Oxford: Oxford University Press, 2010).

Liénard-Yeterian, Marie and Agnieszka Soltysik Monnet, 'The Gothic in an Age of Terror(ism)', *Gothic Studies* 17:2 (November 2015): 1–9.

Ligotti, Thomas, *Teatro Grottesco* (London: Virgin, 2008).

Lively, Penelope, *The Whispering Knights* (London: Pan Books, 1973).

Lloyd, Christopher, 'Southern Gothic', in Joel Faflak and Jason Haslam (eds), *American Gothic Culture: An Edinburgh Companion* (Edinburgh: Edinburgh University Press, 2016), pp. 79–91.

Lloyd Smith, Allan, 'Postmodernism/Gothicism', in Victor Sage and Allan Lloyd Smith (eds), *Modern Gothic: A Reader* (Manchester: Manchester University Press, 1995), pp. 6–19.

Lloyd Smith, Allan, *American Gothic Fiction: An Introduction* (London: Continuum, 2005).

Löfflmann, Georg, 'Hollywood, the Pentagon, and the Cinematic Production of National Security', *Critical Studies on Security* 1:3 (2013): 280–94.

Logan, Bey, *Hong Kong Action Cinema* (Woodstock: Overlook Press, 1996).

Loomba, Ania, Savir Kaul, Matti Bunzl, Antoinette Burton and Jed Esty, 'Beyond What? An Introduction', in Ania Loomba, Savir Kaul, Matti Bunzl, Antoinette Burton and Jed Esty (eds), *Postcolonial Studies and Beyond* (Durham, NC: Duke University Press, 2005), pp. 1–38.

Lorde, Audre, 'The Transformation of Silence into Language and Action', in Audre Lorde, *Sister Outsider* (Freedom: The Crossing Press, 1984), pp. 40–4.

Lovecraft, H. P., *The Case of Charles Dexter Ward* (London: Victor Gollancz, 1951).

Lovecraft, H. P., *The Call of Cthulhu and Other Weird Stories*, edited by S. T. Joshi (London: Penguin, 1999).

Lowenthal, David, *The Past Is a Foreign Country* (Cambridge: Cambridge University Press, 1985).

Lowenthal, David, *The Heritage Crusade and the Spoils of History* (Cambridge: Cambridge University Press, 1997).

Löwy, Michael, 'The Current of Critical Irrealism: "A moonlit enchanted night"', in Matthew Beaumont (ed.), *Adventures in Realism* (Oxford: Blackwell, 2007), pp. 193–206.

Luckhurst, Roger, 'The Contemporary London Gothic and the Limits of the Spectral Turn', *Textual Practice* 16.3 (2010): 527–46.

Luckhurst, Roger, 'Gothic Colonies, 1850–1920', in Glennis Byron and Dale Townshend (eds), *The Gothic World* (Abingdon and New York: Routledge, 2014), pp. 62–71.

Luo, Liang, 'The White Snake in Hong Kong Horror Cinema: From Horrific Tales to Crowd Pleasers', in Gary Bettinson and Daniel Martin (eds), *Hong Kong Horror Cinema* (Edinburgh: Edinburgh University Press, 2018), pp. 34–51.

MacCabe, Colin, *Performance* (London: BFI/Bloomsbury, 2020).

Maguire, Ryan, 'The Ghost in the MP3', *Proceedings: International Computer Music Association (ICMC) and Sound and Music Computing (SMC)*, Athens, Greece, 14–20 September 2014, pp. 243–7 (p. 244) <http://ryanmaguiremusic.com/media_files/pdf/TheGhostICMC.pdf> (last accessed 26 August 2018).

Malchow, H. L., *Gothic Images of Race in Nineteenth-Century Britain* (Stanford: Stanford University Press, 1996).

Malin, Irving, *New American Gothic* (Carbondale, IL: Southern Illinois University Press, 1962).

Mandal, Anthony, 'Gothic 2.0: Remixing Revenants in the Transmedia Age', in Lorna Piatti-Farnell and Donna Lee Brien (eds) *New Directions in 21st-Century Gothic: The Gothic Compass* (London: Routledge, 2015), pp. 84–100.

Mannoni, Laurent, *The Great Art of Light and Shadow: Archaeology of the Cinema* (Exeter: Exeter University Press, 2000).

Manon, Hugh S. and Daniel Temkin, 'Notes on Glitch', *World Picture* 6 (2011) <www.worldpicturejournal.com/WP_6/Manon.html> (last accessed 19 August 2018).

Marasco, Robert, *Burnt Offerings* (New York: Delacorte Press, 1973).

March, William, *The Bad Seed* (New York: HarperCollins, 1997).

Martin, Daniel, 'Between the Local and the Global: "Asian Horror" in Ahn Byung-ki's *Phone* and *Bunshinsaba*', in Alison Peirse and Daniel Martin (eds), *Korean Horror Cinema* (Edinburgh: Edinburgh University Press, 2013), pp. 145–57.

Martin, Daniel, *Extreme Asia: The Rise of Cult Cinema from the Far East* (Edinburgh: Edinburgh University Press, 2015).

Martin, Daniel, 'Japan's *Blair Witch*: Restraint, Maturity, and Generic Canons in the British Critical Reception of *Ring*', *Cinema Journal* 48: 3 (May 2009): 35–51.

Martin, Daniel, 'South Korean Horror Cinema', in Harry M. Benshoff (ed.), *A Companion to the Horror Film* (Chichester: Wiley-Blackwell, 2014), pp. 424–5.

Martin, Sara, 'Gothic Scholars Don't Wear Black: Gothic Studies and Gothic Subcultures', *Gothic Studies* 4.1 (2002): 28–43.

Marx, Karl, *Capital: A Critique of Political Economy*, Volume 1, trans. by Ben Fowkes (Harmondsworth: Penguin, 1976).

Matheson, Richard, *I Am Legend* (London: Gollancz, 2001).

Mathewes, Charles T., *Evil and the Augustinian Tradition* (Cambridge: Cambridge University Press, 2001).

McCarthy, Anna, 'Visual pleasure and GIFs', in Pepita Hesselberth and Maria Poulaki (eds), *Compact Cinematics: The Moving Image in the Age of Bit-Sized Media* (New York: Bloomsbury, 2017).

McCullers, Carson, 'The Flowering Dream: Notes on Writing', in *Carson McCullers: Stories, Plays and Other Writings* (New York: Library of America, 2017), pp. 510–17.

McEvoy, Emma, *Gothic Tourism* (Basingstoke: Palgrave Macmillan, 2016).

McGrath, Patrick, 'Transgression and Decay', in Christoph Grunenberg (ed.), *Gothic: Transmutations of Horror in Late Twentieth Century Art* (Cambridge, MA: MIT Press, 1997), pp. 159–60.

McGrath, Patrick and Bradford Morrow, 'Introduction', in Patrick McGrath and Bradford Morrow (eds), *The New Gothic* (London: Picador, 1993), pp. xi–xiv.

McLuhan, Herbert Marshall, 'The Southern Quality', *The Sewanee Review* 55:3 (1947): 357–83.

McNally, David, *Monsters of the Market: Zombies, Vampires and Global Capitalism* (Chicago, IL: Haymarket Books, 2012).

McNeillie, Andrew (ed.), *Collected Essays of Virginia Woolf*, 6 vols (New York: Harcourt, 1988).

McRoy, Jay, *Nightmare Japan: Contemporary Japanese Horror Cinema* (Amsterdam and New York: Rodopi, 2008).

Mehl, Dieter and Christa Jansohn, 'General Editors' Preface', in D. H. Lawrence, *The Woman Who Rode Away and Other Stories*, edited by Dieter Mehl and Christa Jansohn (Cambridge: Cambridge University Press, 2001), pp. xxi–xxii.

Mellor, Mary, *Feminism and Ecology* (New York: New York University Press, 1997).

Mencken, H. L., 'The Sahara of the Bozart', in Huntington Cairn (ed.), *The American Scene: A Reader* (New York: Knopf, 1977), pp. 157–68.

Menkman, Rosa, *The Glitch Moment(um)* (Amsterdam: Colophon, 2011).

Mernissi, Fatima, *Beyond the Veil: Male-Female Dynamics in Muslim Society* (London: Al Saqi Books, 1985).

Me Too Movement at <https://metoomvmt.org/> (last accessed 4 August 2020).

Michaud, Marilyn, *Republicanism and the American Gothic* (Cardiff: University of Wales Press, 2009).

Mighall, Robert, 'Vampires and Victorians: Count Dracula and the Return of the Repressive Hypothesis', in Gary Day (ed.), *Varieties of Victorianism: The Uses of a Past* (London: Palgrave Macmillan, 1998), pp. 236–49.

Mignolo, Walter, *The Darker Side of Western Modernity: Global Futures, Decolonial Options* (Durham, NC: Duke University Press, 2011).

Miles, Robert, *Gothic Writing, 1750–1820: A Genealogy*, 2nd edition (Manchester: Manchester University Press, 2002).

Mills, Kevin, *Approaching Apocalypse: Unveiling Revelation in Victorian Writing* (Lewisburg, PA: Bucknell University Press, 2007).

Miltner, Kate M. and Tim Highfield, 'Never Gonna GIF You Up: Analyzing the Cultural Significance of the Animated GIF', *Social Media + Society* 3:3 (2017): 1–11.

Mincheva, Dilyana, '*Sense8* and the Praxis of Utopia', *Cinephile* 12:1 (Spring 2018): 32–9.

Minford, John, 'Introduction', in Pu Songling, *Strange Tales from a Chinese Studio* (London: Penguin, 2006), pp. xi–xxxi.

Modleski, Tanya, *Loving with a Vengeance: Mass-Produced Fantasies for Women* (New York: Routledge, 1990).

Moers, Ellen, *Literary Women: The Great Writers* (New York: Doubleday, 1976).

Moers, Ellen, *Literary Women* (London: The Women's Press, 1978).

Morgan, Robin, 'Introduction: The Women's Revolution', in Robin Morgan (ed.), *Sisterhood is Powerful: An Anthology of Writings from the Women's Liberation Movement* (New York: Random House, 1970), pp. xiii–xli.

Morrison, Toni, *Beloved* (London: Picador, 1987).

Morrison, Toni, *Playing in the Dark: Whiteness and the Literary Imagination* (Cambridge, MA: Harvard University Press, 1992).

Morrot, Gil, Frédéric Brochet and Denis Dubourdieu, 'The Color of Odors', *Brain and Language* 79 (2001): 309–20.

Morton, Timothy, *Hyperobjects: Philosophy and Ecology after the End of the World* (Minneapolis: University of Minnesota Press, 2013).

Moss, Zoe, 'It Hurts to Be Alive and Obsolete: The Ageing Woman', in Robin Morgan (ed.), *Sisterhood is Powerful: An Anthology of Writings from the Women's Liberation Movement* (New York: Random House, 1970), pp. 170–5.

mother! Dir. Darren Aronofsky. Paramount Pictures, Protozoa Pictures, 20th Century Fox. 2017.

Mullan, Bob, *R. D. Laing: Creative Destroyer* (London: Cassell, 1997).

Mulvey, Laura, 'Visual Pleasure and Narrative Cinema', in Laura Mulvey, *Visual and Other Pleasures* (Basingstoke: Macmillan, 1989), pp. 14–26.

Mulvey, Laura, 'Afterthoughts on "Visual Pleasure and Narrative Cinema" Inspired by King Vidor's *Duel in the Sun* (1946)', in *Visual and Other Pleasures* (Basingstoke: Macmillan, 1989), pp. 29–38.

Mulvey, Laura, *Death at 24x a Second: Stillness and the Moving Image* (London: Reaktion, 2006).

Mulvey-Roberts, Marie, *Gothic Immortals: The Fiction of the Brotherhood of the Rosy Cross* (Abingdon: Routledge, 1990).

Murphy, Bernice M., 'Horror Fiction from the Decline of Universal Horror to the Rise of the Psycho Killer', in Xavier Aldana Reyes (ed.), *Horror: A Literary History* (London: British Library, 2016), pp. 131–57.

Murphy, Bernice M., *The Rural Gothic in American Popular Culture: Backwoods Terror and Horror in the Wilderness* (Basingstoke: Palgrave Macmillan, 2013).

Musser, Charles, *Before the Nickelodeon: Edwin S. Porter and the Edison Manufacturing Company* (Berkeley, CA: University of California Press, 1991).

Naremore, James, 'A Season in Hell or the Snows of Yesteryear', in Raymond Borde and Etienne Chaumeton (eds), *A Panorama of American Film Noir* (San Francisco: City Lights, 2002), pp. vii–xxi.

Navas, Eduardo, *Remix: The Bond of Repetition and Representation* (2009) <http://remixtheory.net/?p=361> (last accessed 16 November 2014).

Nead, Lynda, *The Haunted Gallery: Painting, Photography, Film, c1900* (London: Yale University Press, 2007).

Nevins, Jess, *Heroes and Monsters: The Unofficial Companion to The League of Extraordinary Gentlemen* (Austin, TX: MonkeyBrain, 2003).

Newman, Michael Z., 'GIFs: The Attainable Text', *Film Criticism* 40:1 (2016), no pag.

Ng Hock Soon, Andrew, 'Adorno, Foucault, and Said: Toward a Multicultural Gothic Aesthetic', *Concentric: Literary and Cultural Studies* 33 (2007): 177–98.

Nietzsche, Friedrich, *The Gay Science*, trans. by Thomas Common (New York: Barnes & Noble, 2008).

Ní Fhlainn, Sorcha, *Postmodern Vampires: Film, Fiction, and Popular Culture* (London: Palgrave Macmillan, 2019).

Night of the Living Dead. Dir. G. A. Romero. Image Ten, Continental Distributing. 1968. Dimension Extreme, 2008. DVD.

Nixon, Nicola, 'When Hollywood Sucks, or, Hungry Girls, Lost Boys, and Vampirism in the Age of Reagan', in Joan Gordon and Veronica Hollinger (eds), *Blood Read: The Vampire as Metaphor in Contemporary Culture* (Philadelphia: University of Pennsylvania Press, 1997), pp. 115–28.

Nixon, Rob, *Slow Violence and the Environmentalism of the Poor* (Cambridge, MA: Harvard University Press, 2011).

Nolan, Emer, *James Joyce and Nationalism* (London: Routledge, 1995).

Oakley, Ann, *The Sociology of Housework* (Oxford: Basil Blackwell, 1974).

O'Connor, Flannery, 'Some aspects of the Grotesque in Southern Fiction', in Sally and Robert Fitzgerald (eds), *Mystery and Manners* (London: Faber and Faber, 1972), pp. 36–50.

O'Day, Marc, '"Mutability is having a field day: The Sixties Aura of Angela Carter's Bristol Trilogy', in Lorna Sage (ed.), *Flesh and the Mirror: Essays on the Art of Angela Carter* (London: Virago, 1994), pp. 24–59.

O'Flynn, Paul, 'Production and Reproduction in *Frankenstein*', *Literature and History* 9:2 (1983): 194–213.

Olivier, Marc, 'Glitch Gothic', in Murray Leeder (ed.), *Cinematic Ghosts: Haunting and Spectrality from Silent Cinema to the Digital Era* (London: Bloomsbury Academic, 2015), pp. 253–70.

Olson, Christopher J. and Carrie Lynn D. Reinhard, *Possessed Women, Haunted States: Cultural Tensions in Exorcism Cinema* (London: Lexington Books, 2017).

'Our History 1884–1945', *The National Trust* <www.nationaltrust.org.uk/lists/our-history-1884-1945> (last accessed 1 February 2019).

Özkaracalar, Kaya, 'İslami korku filmlerinin ideolojik/siyasi topoğrafyası'[The Ideological/Political Topography of Islamic Horror Films], *İleri Haber*, 13 February 2016 <http://ilerihaber.org/yazar/islami-korku-filmlerinin-ideolojiksiyasi-topografyasi-50243.html> (last accessed 26 November 2020).

Paley, Morton D., *Apocalypse and Millennium in English Romantic Poetry* (Oxford: Clarendon Press, 1999).

Palmer, Paulina, 'From "Coded Mannequin" to Bird Woman: Angela Carter's Magic Flight', in Sue Roe (ed.), *Women Reading Women's Writing* (Brighton: Harvester, 1987), pp. 179–201.

Paquet, Darcy, 'Christmas in August and Korean Melodrama', in Frances Gateward (ed.), *Seoul Searching: Culture and Identity in Contemporary Korean Cinema* (Albany, NY: State University of New York Press, 2007), pp. 37–54.

Parikka, Jussi, *What Is Media Archaeology?* (Cambridge: Polity Press, 2012).

Parry, Benita, 'Materiality and Mystification in *A Passage to India*', *Novel: A Forum on Fiction* 31:2 (1998): 174–94.

Patterson, James, *Grand Expectations: The United States, 1945–1974* (New York: Oxford University Press, 1996).

Pearson, Roberta E. and William Uricchio, 'How Many Times Shall Caesar Bleed in Sport?: Shakespeare and the Cultural Debate about Moving Pictures', in Lee Grieveson and Peter Krämer (eds), *The Silent Cinema Reader* (London: Routledge, 2004), pp. 155–68.

Peirse, Alison, *After Dracula: The 1930s Horror Film* (London and New York: I. B. Tauris, 2013).

Pepys, Samuel, *Eyewitness Accounts: London's Great Plague* (Gloucestershire: Amberly Press, 2014).

Performance. Dir. Donald Cammell and Nicholas Roeg. Goodtimes Enterprises, Warner Brothers. 1970.

Phillips, Kendall, *A Place of Darkness: The Rhetoric of Horror in Early American Cinema* (Austin, TX: University of Texas Press, 2018).

Pirie, David, *A Heritage of Horror: The English Gothic Cinema, 1946–1972* (London: Avon, 1973).

Pirie, David, *The Vampire Cinema* (London: Quarto, 1977).

Pirie, David, *A New Heritage of Horror: The English Gothic Cinema* (London: I. B. Tauris, 2008).

Poe, Edgar Allan, 'The Fall of the House of Usher', in Thomas Mabbott (ed.), *The Collected Works of Edgar Allan Poe: Tales and Sketches 1831–1842* (Cambridge, MA: Belknap Press, 1978), pp. 392–421.

Poison. Dir. Tod Haynes. Bronze Eye Productions, Zeitgeist Films. 1991. Zeitgeist Films, 2011. DVD.

Potter, Rachel, *Modernist Literature* (Edinburgh: Edinburgh University Press, 2012).

Pound, Ezra, *Gaudier-Brzeska: A Memoir* (London: John Lane, 1916).

Power, Jennifer, *Movement, Knowledge, Emotion: Gay Activism and HIV/AIDS in Australia* (Canberra: Australian National University Press, 2011).

Praz, Mario, *The Romantic Agony* (London: Fontana Library, 1960).

Punter, David, 'Hungry Ghosts and Foreign Bodies', in Andrew Smith and Jeff Wallace (eds), *Gothic Modernisms* (Basingstoke: Palgrave, 2001), pp. 11–28.

Punter, *The Literature of Terror: A History of Gothic Fictions from 1765 to the Present Day*, 2 vols (London: Longman, 1996).

Punter, David, *The Literature of Terror, Volume One: The Gothic Tradition* (London: Longman, 1996)

Punter, David, *The Literature of Terror, Volume Two: The Modern Gothic* (London: Longman, 1996).

Punter, David, *Postcolonial Imaginings: Fictions of a New World Order* (Edinburgh: Edinburgh University Press, 2000).

Punter, David, *The Gothic Condition: Terror, History and the Psyche* (Cardiff: University of Wales Press, 2016).

Quéma, Anne, 'The Gothic and the Fantastic in the Age of Digital Reproduction', *English Studies in Canada* 30:4 (2007): 81–119.

Raven, Simon, *Doctors Wear Scarlet* (Kelly Bray, Cornwall: House of Stratus, 2001).
Recker, Laurel, 'Zombie Palimpsests: Translating US Occupation in White Zombie', *M/m* vol. 3, cycle 3 (August 20, 2018) <https://modernismmodernity.org/forums/posts/zombie-palimpsests> (last accessed 23 June 2020).
Reed, Ishmael, *Flight to Canada* (New York: Random House, 1976).
Rhodes, Gary D., *Tod Browning's Dracula* (Sheffield: Tomahawk Press, 2014).
Rhys, Jean, *Wide Sargasso Sea*, edited by Angela Smith (London: Penguin Books, 2000).
Rich, B. Ruby, *New Queer Cinema: The Director's Cut* (Durham, NC and London: Duke University Press, 2013).
Rice, Anne, *Interview With the Vampire* (London: Sphere, 2008).
Rieder, John, *Colonialism and the Emergence of Science Fiction* (Middletown, CA: Wesleyan University Press, 2008).
Rigby, Jonathan, *English Gothic: A Century of Horror Cinema*, 2nd edition (London: Reynolds and Hearn Ltd, 2002).
Rigby, Jonathan, *American Gothic: Sixty Years of Horror Cinema* (London: Reynolds and Hearn Ltd, 2007).
Riggs, Ransom, *Miss Peregrine's Home for Peculiar Children* (Philadelphia: Quirk Books, 2011).
Riggs, Ransom, *Talking Pictures: Images and Messages Rescued from the Past* (New York: IT Books, 2012).
Riquelme, John Paul, 'Modernist Gothic', in Jerrold E. Hogle (ed.) *The Cambridge Companion to the Modern Gothic* (Cambridge, Cambridge University Press, 2014), pp. 20–35.
Robb, David L., *Operation Hollywood: How the Pentagon Shapes and Censors the Movies* (New York: Prometheus Books, 2004).
Roberts, Les, 'Mortality after the 2003 Invasion of Iraq: A Cross-Sectional Cluster Sample Survey', *The Lancet* 368 (12 October 2006): 1421–8.
Robins, Anna Gruetzner, '"Manet and the Post-Impressionists": A Checklist of Exhibits', *The Burlington Magazine* 152 (December 2010), 782–93.
The Rocky Horror Picture Show. Dir. Jim Sharman. Michael White Productions, 20th Century Fox. 1975.
Roy, Arundhati, *Listening to Grasshoppers: Field Notes on Democracy* (London: Hamish Hamilton, 2009).
Rubin, Louis D. Jnr, *The Faraway Country: Writers of the Modern South* (Seattle: University of Washington Press, 1963).
Rudd, Alison, *Postcolonial Gothic Fictions from the Caribbean, Canada, Australia, and New Zealand* (Cardiff: University of Wales Press, 2010).
Rudkin, David, *Penda's Fen* (London: Davis Poynter Ltd, 1975).
Rudkin, David, *Vampyr* (London: BFI Publishing, 2005).
Rudolph, Lloyd I. and Susanne Hoeber Rudolph, 'Living with Multiculturalism: Universalism and Particularism in an Indian Historical Context', in Richard A. Shweder, Martha Minow and Hazel Rose Markus (eds), *Engaging Cultural Differences: The Multicultural Challenge in Liberal Democracies* (New York: Russell Sage Foundation, 2002), pp. 43–62.
Russ, Joanna, 'Somebody's Trying to Kill Me and I Think It's My Husband: The Modern Gothic', *The Journal of Popular Culture* 6:4 (1973): 666–91.

Russo, Maria, 'Ransom Riggs Is Inspired by Vintage Snapshots', *The New York Times*, 19 October 2018 <www.nytimes.com/2013/12/31/books/ransom-riggs-is-inspired-by-vintage-snapshots.html> (last accessed 28 April 2019).

Saadawi, Ahmed, *Frankenstein in Baghdad*, trans. by Jonathan Wright (London: Oneworld, 2018).

Sadleir, Michael, 'The Northanger Novels', *The Edinburgh Review* 246:501 (1927): 91–106.

Sage, Victor (ed.), *The Gothick Novel: A Casebook* (Basingstoke: Macmillan, 1990).

Sage, Victor and Allan Lloyd Smith, 'Introduction', in Victor Sage and Allan Lloyd Smith (eds), *Modern Gothic: A Reader* (Manchester: Manchester University Press, 1995), pp. 1–5.

Şahintürk, Zeynep, 'Djinn in the Machine: Technology and Islam in Turkish Horror Film', in Linnie Blake and Xavier Aldana Reyes (eds), *Digital Horror: Haunted Technologies, Network Panic and the Found Footage Phenomenon* (London and New York: I. B. Tauris, 2016), pp. 95–106.

Said, Edward W., *Culture and Imperialism* (London: Chatto & Windus Ltd., 1993).

Samuels, Raphael, 'Politics', in Graham Fairclough, Rodney Harrison, John H. Jameson Jnr and John Schofield (eds), *The Heritage Reader* (Abingdon: Routledge, 2008), pp. 274–94.

Scharf, Natasha, *The Art of Gothic: Music + Fashion + Alt Culture* (London: Omnibus Press, 2014).

Schauer, Bradley, *Escape Velocity: American Science Fiction Film, 1950–1982* (Middletown, CT: Wesleyan University Press, 2017).

Schneier, Bruce, *Data and Goliath: The Hidden Battles to Collect Your Data and Control Your World* (New York: W. W. Norton & Company, 2015).

Schopp, Andrew and Matthew B. Hill, *The War on Terror and American Popular Culture* (Madison, NJ: Fairleigh Dickinson University Press, 2009).

Schwartz, Joseph, *Cassandra's Daughter: A History of Psychoanalysis in Europe and America* (London: Penguin, 1999).

Scofield, Martin (ed.), *Ghost Stories of Henry James* (Hertfordshire: Wordsworth Editions Limited, 2001).

Sconce, Jeffrey, *Haunted Media: Electronic Presence from Telegraphy to Television* (Durham, NC: Duke University Press, 2000).

Scovell, Adam, *Folk Horror: Hours Dreadful and Things Strange* (Leighton Buzzard: Auteur Publishing, 2017).

Scull, Andrew, *Madness in Civilisation: A Cultural History of Insanity from the Bible to Freud, From the Madhouse to Modern Medicine* (London: Thames and Hudson, 2015).

Sears, John, *Stephen King's Gothic* (Cardiff: University of Wales Press, 2011).

Sengers, Gerda, *Women and Demons: Cultic Healing in Islamic Egypt* (Leiden and Boston: Brill, 2003).

Sense8. Dir. Lana Wachowsky, Lilly Lachowsky, James McTeigue, Tom Tykwer and Dan Glass. Anarchos Productions, Georgeville Television, Javelin Productions, Motion Picture Capital, Studio JMS, Unpronounceable Productions. Distributed by Netflix. 2015–2018. First aired in US on 5 June 2015.

Service, Robert, *The Best of Robert Service* (London: A & C Black, 2000).

Sexton, Anne, 'Rapunzel', in Anne Sexton, *Transformations* (Boston: Houghton Mifflin, 1971), pp. 35–42.

Shafik, Viola, 'Egypt: A Cinema Without Horror', in Steven Jay Schneider and Tony Williams (eds), *Horror International* (Detroit: Wayne State University Press, 2005), pp. 273–89.

Shapiro, Stephen, 'Transvaal, Transylvania: Dracula's World-System and Gothic Periodicity', *Gothic Studies* 10.1 (2008): 29–47.

Shaw, Valerie, *The Short Story: A Critical Introduction* (Abingdon: Routledge, 1983).

Shelley, Mary, *Frankenstein: The 1818 Text*, edited by Marilyn Butler (Oxford: Oxford University Press, 2008).

Showalter, Elaine, *The Female Malady: Women, Madness and English Culture, 1830–1980* (London: Virago, 1985).

Siddons, Anne Rivers, *The House Next Door* (New York: Pocket Books, 1978).

Siegel, Joel, *Val Lewton: The Reality of Terror* (London: Secker and Warburg, 1972).

Silver, Sean, 'The Politics of Gothic Historiography, 1660–1800', in Glennis Byron and Dale Townshend (eds), *The Gothic World* (Abingdon and New York: Routledge, 2014), pp. 3–14.

Şimşek, Gizem, *Sinemada Korku ve Din: 2000 Sonrası Amerikan ve Türk Filmlerinde Cin Unsurunun Çözümlenmesi [Horror and Religion in Cinema: The Analysis of the Djinn Figure in post-2000 American and Turkish Horror Films]* (İstanbul: Pales Yayınları, 2016).

Şimşek, Gizem, *Türk Korku Sineması Kronolojisi 1914–2015 [The Chronology of Turkish Horror Cinema 1914–2015]* (İstanbul: Pales Yayınları, 2017).

Sinclair, Iain, 'Who Cares for the Caretaker?', in Iain Sinclair and Rachel Lichtenstein, *Rodinsky's Room* (London: Granta, 2000), pp. 131–51.

Sinclair, May, 'The Villa Désirée', in Cynthia Asquith (ed.), *The Ghost Book* (London: Pan Books Ltd, 1970), pp. 9–21.

Sinclair, May, *Uncanny Stories* (Hertfordshire: Wordsworth Editions Ltd, 2006).

Sinha, Indra, *Animal's People* (London and New York: Simon & Schuster, 2007).

Skal, David J., *Hollywood Gothic: The Tangled Web of Dracula from Novel to Stage to Screen* (New York and London: W.W. Norton & Company, 1990).

Skal, David J., *The Monster Show: A Cultural History of Horror* (New York: Norton, 1993).

Skal, David J., *The Monster Show: A Cultural History of Horror* (London: Plexus, 1994).

Skura, Meredith Ann, *The Literary Use of the Psychoanalytic Process* (New Haven, CT: Yale University Press, 1981).

Slater, Lauren, *The Drugs that Changed Our Minds: The History of Psychiatry in Ten Treatments* (London: Simon and Schuster, 2018).

Slotkin, Richard, *Regeneration through Violence: The Mythology of the American Frontier 1600–1860* (Norman, OK: University of Oklahoma Press, 2000).

Smith, Andrew, *The Ghost Story, 1840–1920: A Cultural History* (Manchester: Manchester University Press, 2010).

Smith, Andrew, *Gothic Literature*, 2nd edition (Edinburgh: Edinburgh University Press, 2013).

Smith, Andrew, 'Vampirism, Masculinity and Degeneracy: D. H. Lawrence's Modernist Gothic', in Andrew Smith and Jeff Wallace (eds), *Gothic Modernisms* (Basingstoke: Palgrave Macmillan, 2001), pp. 150–66.

Smith, Andrew and William Hughes, 'Introduction', in Andrew Smith and William Hughes (eds), *Empire and the Gothic: The Politics of Genre* (Basingstoke: Palgrave Macmillan, 2003), pp. 1–12.

Smith, Andrew and William Hughes, 'Introduction', in Andrew Smith and William Hughes (eds), *EcoGothic* (Manchester: Manchester University Press, 2013), pp. 1–14.

Smith, Michelle and Lawrence Pazder, *Michelle Remembers* (London: Michael Joseph, 1981).

Soltysik Monnet, Agnieszka and Steffen Hantke, 'Ghosts from the Battlefield: A Short Historical Introduction to the War Gothic', in Agnieszka Soltysik Monnet and Steffen Hantke (eds), *War Gothic in Literature and Culture*, (New York: Routledge, 2016), pp. xi–xxv.

Sonvilla-Weiss, Stefan, 'Introduction: Mashups, Remix Practices and the Recombination of Existing Digital Content', in Stefan Sonvilla-Weiss (ed.), *Mashup Cultures* (Wien: Springer, 2010), pp. 8–23.

Southey, Robert, Preface to *A Vision of Judgement*, quoted in Fred Parker, 'Between Satan and Mephistopheles: Byron and the Devil', *The Cambridge Quarterly* 35:1 (2006): 1–29.

Spadoni, Robert, *Uncanny Bodies: The Coming of Sound Film and the Origins of the Horror Genre* (Berkeley, CA: University of California Press, 2007).

Spencer, Jane, 'Afterword: Feminist Waves', in Stacy Gillis, Gillian Howie and Rebecca Munford (eds), *Third Wave Feminism: A Critical Exploration* (Basingstoke: Palgrave Macmillan, 2007), pp. 298–303.

Spooner, Catherine, 'Gothic in the Twentieth Century', in Catherine Spooner and Emma McEvoy (eds), *The Routledge Companion to Gothic* (London: Routledge, 2007), pp. 38–48.

Spooner, Catherine, 'Twenty-First-Century Gothic', in Dale Townshend (ed.), *Terror and Wonder: The Gothic Imagination* (London: The British Library, 2014), pp. 180–205.

Spooner, Catherine, '"Clothes are our weapons": Dandyism, Fashion and Subcultural Style in Angela Carter's fiction of the 1960s', in Marie Mulvey-Roberts (ed.), *The Arts of Angela Carter* (Manchester: Manchester University Press, 2019), pp. 166–82.

Spooner, Catherine, *Fashioning Gothic Bodies* (Manchester: Manchester University Press, 2004).

Spooner, Catherine, *Contemporary Gothic* (London: Reaktion Books, 2006).

Steenberg, Lindsay, *Forensic Science in Contemporary Culture: Gender, Crime and Science* (London: Routledge, 2012).

Sterne, Jonathan, *MP3: The Meaning of a Format* (Durham, NC: Duke University Press, 2012).

Stobie, Cheryl, 'Sisters and Spirits: The Postcolonial Gothic in Angelina N. Sithebe's *Holy Hill*', *Current Writing: Text and Reception in Southern Africa* 20:2 (2008): 26–43

Stoker, Bram, *Dracula*, edited by Roger Luckhurst (Oxford: Oxford University Press, 2011).

Stryker, Susan, *Transgender History: The Roots of Today's Revolution*, revised edition (New York: Seal Press, 2017).

Sugars, Cynthia, *Canadian Gothic: Literature, History, and the Spectre of Self-Invention* (Cardiff: University of Wales Press, 2014).

Sullivan, Jack, *The Penguin Encyclopaedia of Horror and the Supernatural* (New York: Viking, 1986).

Sullivan, Walter, *A Requiem for the Renascence: The State of Fiction in the Modern South* (Athens, GA: University of Georgia Press, 1976).

Summers, Montague, *The Gothic Quest: A History of the Gothic Novel* (London: Fortune Press, 1938).

Tan, Sandi, *The Black Isle* (New York: Grand Central Publishing, 2012).
Tate, Andrew, *Apocalyptic Fiction* (London and New York: Bloomsbury, 2017).
Taylor, Charles, 'You Can't Always Get What You Want: On Stephen King', *The Nation*, December 21, 2011 <www.thenation.com/article/you-cant-always-get-what-you-want-stephen-king/> (last accessed 22 July 2020).
Taylor, Charles, *A Secular Age* (Cambridge, MA and London: Belknap Press, 2007).
Teo, Stephen, 'The Tongue: A Study of Hong Kong Horror Movies', in Li Cheuk-to (ed.), *Phantoms of the Hong Kong Cinema* (Hong Kong: Urban Council, 1989), pp. 41–5.
Thieme, John, *Postcolonial Con-Texts: Writing Back to the Canon* (London and New York: Continuum, 2001).
Thomassen, Lasse, *British Multiculturalism and the Politics of Representation* (Edinburgh: Edinburgh University Press, 2017).
Thunberg, Greta, 'Our house is on fire': Greta Thunberg, 16, urges leaders to act on climate', *The Guardian*, 25 January 2019 <www.theguardian.com/environment/2019/jan/25/our-house-is-on-fire-greta-thunberg16-urges-leaders-to-act-on-climate> (last accessed 20 March 2019).
Thurley, Simon, *Men from the Ministry: How Britain Saved its Heritage* (New Haven and London: Yale University Press, 2013).
'Timeline of Conservation Catalysts and Legislation', *Historic England* <https://historicengland.org.uk/whats-new/features/conservation-listing-timeline/> (last accessed 1 February 2019).
Tinniswood, Adrian, *The Long Weekend: Life in the English Country House Between the Wars* (London: Jonathan Cape, 2016).
Townshend, Dale, 'Terror and Wonder: The Gothic Imagination', in Dale Townshend (ed.), *Terror and Wonder: The Gothic Imagination* (London: The British Library, 2014), pp. 10–37.
Tourgée, Albion W., 'The South as a Field for Fiction', in Mark Elliott and John David Smith (eds), *Undaunted Radical: The Selected Writings and Speeches of Albion Tourgée* (Baton Rouge: Louisiana State University Press, 2010), pp. 203–11.
Troy, Maria Holmgren, Johan Höglund, Yvonne Leffler and Sofia Wijkmark (eds), *Nordic Gothic* (Manchester: Manchester University Press, 2020).
Truffin, Sherry R., *Schoolhouse Gothic: Haunted Hallways and Predatory Pedagogues in Late Twentieth-Century American Literature* (Newcastle: Cambridge Scholars Publishing, 2008).
Tsang, Raymond, 'What Can a *Neoi Gwei* Teach Us? Adaptation as Reincarnation in Hong Kong Horror of the 1950s', in Gary Bettinson and Daniel Martin (eds), *Hong Kong Horror Cinema* (Edinburgh: Edinburgh University Press, 2018), pp. 19–33.
Twitchell, James, *Dreadful Pleasures: An Anatomy of Modern Horror* (New York: Oxford University Press, 1985).
Uğur, Veli, *1980 Sonrası Türkiye'de Popüler Roman* [*Popular Fiction in Turkey After 1980*] (İstanbul: Koç Üniversitesi Yayınları, 2013).
Uhlin, Graig, 'Playing in the Gif(t) Economy', *Games and Culture* 9:6 (2014): 517–27.
Uttley, Alison, *A Traveller in Time* (London: Jane Nissen Books, 2007).
Vampyr. Dir. Carl Theodor Dreyer. Tobis Filmkunst, Vereinigte Star-Film GmbH, Conti-Film. 1932. Eureka, 2008. DVD.
Vance, Carole S., 'More Danger, More Pleasure: A Decade After the Barnard Sexuality Conference', in Carole S. Vance (ed.), *Pleasure and Danger: Exploring Female Sexuality* (London: Pandora, 1989), pp. xvi–xxxix.

Varma, Devendra P., *The Gothic Flame* (London: Arthur Barker Ltd, 1957).

Victor, Jeffery S., *Satanic Panic: The Creation of a Contemporary Legend* (Chicago: Open Court, 1993).

Voigts, Eckart, 'Memes and Recombinant Appropriation', in Thomas Leitch (ed.), *The Oxford Handbook of Adaptation Studies* (Oxford: Oxford University Press, 2017), pp. 285–302.

Waldman, Diane, '"At Last I Can Tell It to Someone!": Female Point of View and Subjectivity in the Gothic Romance film of the 1940s', *Cinema Journal* 23:2 (1984): 29–40.

Walker, Rebecca, *To Be Real* (New York: Anchor, 1995).

Wallace, Diana, 'Uncanny Stories: The Ghost Story as Female Gothic', *Gothic Studies* 6:1 (2004): 57–68.

Ward, Graham, *Theology and Contemporary Critical Theory* (Basingstoke: Macmillan, 1996).

Ward, Jesmyn, *Sing, Unburied, Sing* (London: Bloomsbury, 2018).

Wark, McKenzie, 'Securing Security', *Kritikos: An International and Interdisciplinary Journal of Postmodern Cultural Sound, Text and Image* 2 (2005) <http://intertheory.org/security.htm> (last accessed 22 July 2020).

Warwick, Alexandra, 'Feeling Gothicky?', *Gothic Studies* 9:1 (2007): 5–15.

Wasson, Sara, *Urban Gothic of the Second World War: Dark London* (Basingstoke: Palgrave Macmillan, 2010).

Waters, Sarah, *Fingersmith* (London: Virago, 2002).

Waters, Sarah, *The Little Stranger* (London, Virago, 2009).

Waugh, Evelyn, *Brideshead Revisited: The Sacred and Profane Memories of Charles Ryder* (London: Eyre Methuen, 1978).

Waugh, Patricia, *Harvest of the Sixties: English Literature and its Background 1960 to 1990* (Oxford: Oxford University Press, 1995).

Weinstock, Jeffrey A. (2013), 'Invisible Monsters: Vision, Horror, and Contemporary Culture', in Asa Simon Mittman and Peter J. Dendle (eds), *The Ashgate Research Companion to Monsters and the Monstrous* (Farnham: Ashgate, 2013). pp. 275–89.

Wells, H. G., *The War of the Worlds* (London: Everyman, 1996).

Wells, Rachel, 'Digital Scale: Enlargement and Intelligibility in Thomas Ruff's *JPEG* Series', in Alexandra Moschovi, Carol McKay and Arabella Plouviez (eds), *The Versatile Image: Photography, Digital Technologies and the Internet* (Leuven: Leuven University Press, 2013), pp. 205–21.

Westengard, Laura, *Gothic Queer Culture: Marginalized Communities and the Ghosts of Insidious Trauma* (Lincoln, NE: University of Nebraska Press, 2019).

Wheatley, Dennis, *The Devil Rides Out* (London: Bloomsbury, 1934).

Wheatley, Helen, *Gothic Television* (Manchester: Manchester University Press, 2006).

Wijkmark, Sofia, *Hemsökelser: Gotiken i sex berättelser av Selma Lagerlöf* (Unpublished PhD thesis; Karlstad University, 2009).

Williams, Anne, *Art of Darkness: A Poetics of Gothic* (Chicago: University of Chicago Press, 1995).

Williams, Tennessee, *A House Not Meant to Stand*, edited by Thomas Keith (New York: New Direction, 2008).

Williams, Tony, *Hearths of Darkness: The Family in the American Horror Film* (Jackson, MS: University Press of Mississippi, 2014).

Williams, William Appleman, 'The Frontier Thesis and American Foreign Policy', *Pacific Historical Review* 24:4 (1955): 379–95.
Wilt, Judith, 'The Ghost and the Omnibus: The Gothic Virginia Woolf', in Andrew Smith and Jeff Wallace (eds), *Gothic Modernisms* (Basingstoke: Palgrave Macmillan, 2001), pp. 62–77.
Wisker, Gina, 'Crossing Liminal Spaces: Teaching the Postcolonial Gothic', *Pedagogy* 7:3 (Fall 2007): 401–25.
Wisker, Gina, *Contemporary Women's Gothic Fiction: Carnival, Hauntings and Vampire Kisses* (Basingstoke: Palgrave Macmillan, 2016).
Withers, Matt, 'Get a Brexit-themed look for Halloween with these masks', *The New European*, 23 October 2018 <www.theneweuropean.co.uk/top-stories/dress-as-the-monsters-of-brexit-this-halloween-1-5747550> (last accessed 15 April 2019).
Wood, Robin, 'An Introduction to the American Horror Film', in Robin Wood and Richard Lippe (eds), *American Nightmare: Essays on the Horror Film* (Toronto: Festival of Festivals, 1979), pp. 7–28.
Wood, Robin, *Hollywood from Vietnam to Reagan* (New York: University of Columbia Press, 1986).
Woolf, Leonard, 'Foreword', in Leonard Woolf (ed.), *A Haunted House* (London: The Hogarth Press, 1944), pp. 7–8.
Woolf, Virginia, *A Haunted House*, edited by Leonard Woolf (London: The Hogarth Press, 1944).
Woolf, Virginia, *Collected Essays*, 3 vols (London: The Hogarth Press, 1966).
WReC (Warwick Research Collective), *Combined and Uneven Development: Towards a New Theory of World-Literature* (Liverpool: Liverpool University Press, 2015).
Wright, Angela, *Mary Shelley* (Cardiff: University of Wales Press, 2018).
Wright, Julia M., 'American Gothic Television', in Joel Faflak and Jason Haslam (eds), *American Gothic Culture: An Edinburgh Companion* (Edinburgh: Edinburgh University Press, 2016), pp. 129–44.
Wright, Julia M., *Men With Stakes: Masculinity and the Gothic in US Television* (Manchester: Manchester University Press, 2016).
Wright, N. T., *The Resurrection of the Son of God* (London: SPCK, 2003).
Wright, Patrick, *On Living in an Old Country: The National Past in Contemporary Britain* (London and New York: Verso, 1985).
Yaeger, Patricia, *Dirt and Desire: Reconstructing Southern Women's Writing, 1930–1990* (Chicago: University of Chicago Press, 2000).
Yıldırım, Orhan, *Ecinni: Aykırı Dünyayla İlişkiler [Djinni: Relations with the Other World]* (İstanbul: IQ Yayıncılık, 2003).
Zamora, Lois Parkinson, *Writing the Apocalypse: Historical Vision in Contemporary U.S. and Latin American Fiction* (Cambridge: Cambridge University Press, 1989).
Zarcone, Thierry, 'Shamanism in Turkey: Bards, Masters of the Djinns and Healers', in Thierry Zircon and Angela Hobart (eds), *Shamanism and Islam: Sufism, Healing Rituals and Spirits in the Muslim World.* (London; New York: I. B. Taurus, 2013), pp. 169–201.
Zarzycka, Agata, 'The Gothicization of World War II as a Source of Cultural Self-Reflection in *Miss Peregrine's Home for Peculiar Children* and *Hollow City*', in Steffen Hantke and Agnieszka Soltysik Monnet (eds), *War Gothic in Literature and Culture* (London: Routledge, 2016), pp. 229–44.

Zero Patience. Dir. John Greyson. Zero Patience Productions and Téléfilm Canada, Cineplex Odeon Films. 1993.

Žižek, Slavoj, 'Multiculturalism, or, the Cultural Logic of Multinational Capitalism', *New Left Review* 225 (1997): 28–51.

Žižek, Slavoj, *Welcome to the Desert of the Real* (London: Verso, 2002).

Index

Abbott, Stacey, 3, 25–6, 29
Abraham, Nicolas, 254
Absalom, Absalom (Faulkner), 65, 69
aesthetics, Modernist Gothic and, 44–9, 50
African American writers. *See also specific writers*
   Southern Gothic literature and, after World War II, 74–6
Age of Anxiety, 369–70
   Imperial Gothic and, 370
Agee, James, 76
Agrarians, as regional group, 71–2
Agrippa, Cornelius, 160
Ahn Byung-ki, 417–18
AIDS narratives, Queer Gothic and, 264–82
   contagion and, 265–6, 268–9, 278–9
   guilt and innocence and, of affected individuals, 265
   homophobia influenced by, 265–6
   LGBTQ+ identity and, 265–6
   medical timeline of AIDS discovery, 264–5
   medication development, 275, 279–80
   moral judgement of affected individuals, 265
   from 1981 to 1991, 266–75
      The Hunger, 266–71
      Poison, 266, 271–5
   from 1993 to 2018, 275–82
      Sense8, 266, 275, 279–82
      Zero Patience, 266, 275–9
   physical deterioration and, 265–6
   politics and, 275
Ainsworth, William Harrison, 10
Alaimo, Stacy, 462
Aldington, Richard, 48
Alfred Hitchcock Presents (television), 96
Alias Grace (Atwood), 124
All the King's Men (Warren), 73
alternative history genre, 174–7

Alt-Right movement, 299–301
American Horror Story: Cult (television), 299–300
American Psycho (film), 294
Amirpour, Ana Lily, 383, 385
The Anatomist (Bridie), 224
Ancuta, Katarzyna, 404–5
And the Band Played On (Shilts), 275–6
Andersen, Hans Christian, 37–8, 427
Andersen, Tryggve, 427
Anderson, Eric, 68
Andeweg, Agnes, 233
Anger, Kenneth, 215
Anil's Ghost (Ondaatje), 356
Animal's People (Sinha), 133–4
Antichrist (film), 435–6
anti-psychiatry movement, 191
Anvari, Babak, 383, 385
apocalyptic Gothic
   Cold War catastrophe, 470–4
   as end of history, 477–9
   future in, optimism about, 480–2
   rationalism in, 474–7
   re-enchantment in, 474–7
   religious history of, 465–6
   theoretical approach to, 465–9
   Weird fiction, 467–70
   zombies in, 480
      consumerism symbolism and, 480–1
apparitions and ghosts, 50–8
   AIDS and, 274–9, 280–1
   digital culture and, 331–5, 338–9
   environmental crisis and, 444–7
   in found footage horror, 327
   in ghost stories, 50–1, 54–8
   in *The Haunting of Hill House*, 460–1
   in Hong Kong Gothic, 419–21
   in Japanese Gothic, 405, 407–13
   in phantasmagoria, 29–30

apparitions and ghosts (cont.)
  in photography, 315–16
  in Scandinavian Gothic, 427–8, 432–3
  in South Korean Gothic, 405, 413–18
  on television, 224, 230, 233
Arata, Stephen D., 46
Armitt, Lucie, 6, 470
Arnold, Matthew, 466
Aronofsky, Darren, 458–60
Arvonen, Helen, 244
As I Lay Dying (Faulkner), 64–5, 75–6, 351
Ashcroft, Bill, 120, 365
Asia Extreme, 405–6
Aspects of the Novel (Forster, E. M.), 47, 54
Asquith, Cynthia, 50, 56
Atwill, Lionel, 87–8
Atwood, Margaret, 124
Auden, W. H., 151
Auerbach, Nina, 257
Austen, Jane, 17, 19, 131, 303
avant-garde movement, 44–5, 58–9

Bacevich, Andrew J., 371
The Bad Seed (March, W.), 188–9
Badreaux, Jean, 26–7
Bailey, Dale, 448
Bainbridge, Simon, 204–5, 218
Baker, Roy Ward, 263
Baldick, Chris, 8–9, 214, 317, 321–2, 351
The Ballad of the Sad Café (McCullers), 62
Ballard, J. G., 11
Banke, Anders, 438
Banks, Iain, 11, 161–2, 168, 170–1
Bảo Ninh, 115
Barker, Will, 34
Barnes, Djuna, 11, 43, 59
Barrymore, John, 83
Battlefield Gothic, 100–1, 107–8, 111–12
Baudelaire, Charles, 49
Bayer-Berenbaum, Linda, 37
Beaumont, Charles, 187
Beck, Richard, 195–6
The Beetle (Marsh), 366, 377
Bell, Vanessa, 45
Bellamy, Ralph, 98
Beloved (Morrison), 75, 77, 254–8
  cryptonomy in, 255
  rape themes in, 256
  sexuality in, 256–7
  vampire imagery in, 255–6
Benson, E. F., 11
Bentley, Thomas, 34
Bergman, Ingmar, 430–1

Bergstrøm, Kåre, 430
Besant, Annie, 160
The Best Years of Our Lives (film), 109–10
Bhabha, Homi K., 365
Bhattacharyya, Harihar, 360
Bibby, Michael, 13
Bierce, Ambrose, 99–100, 109, 116
The Bird's Nest (Jackson), 189, 190
Birkhead, Edith, 2–3, 50
birth myth, *Frankenstein* as, 6
bisexual vampires, 262–4
Bjerké, Andre, 430
Black Boy (Wright, R.), 74–5
The Black Cap (Asquith), 56
Black writers. *See* African American writers
Blackwood, Algernon, 11, 224
Blade (film), 295–6
The Blair Witch Project (film), 326–7
Blake, Linnie, 375, 478
Blake, William, 293–4
Blatty, William Peter, 192
Blavatsky, Helena, 160
The Blind Owl (Hedayat), 386–7
Blixen, Karen, 429, 432
Bloch, Robert, 180–1, 186–7
Blomberg, Erik, 430
The Bloody Chamber (Carter), 253, 258
Bluebeard narrative
  female Gothic and
    in *The Magic Toyshop*, 252
    in popular romance texts, 245
    in Hollywood Gothic films, 92–3
Bogart, Humphrey, 110
Bogeymen of Brexit, 319–22
Bolens, Guillemette, 100
Boot, Max, 371
Booth, Walter R., 30
border anxiety, Imperial Gothic and, 381–2
Borges, Jorge Luis, 217–18
Borschke, Margie, 307
Botting, Fred, 8, 13–14, 27, 102, 308, 325, 421
  on death of Gothic, 20, 353–4, 416–17
  on Gothic as heterotopia, 359–60
Bowen, Elizabeth, 50, 56, 106
Bowie, David, 269
Boyd, William, 151
Braddon, Mary Elizabeth, 268
Bram Stoker's Dracula (film), 20, 39, 416–17
Brantlinger, Patrick, 101, 119, 366–7
Breton, André, 4–5, 43–4
  avant-garde movement and, 58–9
  Surrealism and, 59
  unconscious and, 58–9

514

Brideshead Revisited (Waugh), 143, 144
Bridie, James, 224
Brill, Dunja, 13
Brink, André, 123–4, 129–30. See also *Devil's Valley*
Brite, Poppy Z., 211–12
Brodber, Erna, 132–3
Brogan, Kathleen, 67
Brontë, Charlotte, 6, 125, 244
Brooks, Max, 290–2, 480
Brown, Charles Brockden, 354, 367–8
Brown, Dan, 160
Brown, Simon, 3
Brown, Wendy, 286
Browning, Tod, 24–5, 30–1, 80–1, 83–4, 286
Bruhm, Steven, 185–6, 198
Bruno, Giordano, 160
Bryson, Norman, 273–4
Buber, Martin, 120
Bulwer-Lytton, Edward, 160
Buñuel, Luis, 58–9
Burnham, John, 181–2, 194
Burns, Hannah Piper, 330
Burnt Offerings (novel) (Marasco), 448, 450, 452–4
Burroughs, Edgar Rice, 368
Burroughs, William, 213–14
Burton, Tim, 314–15
Bush, George W., 286, 370, 375
Butler, Ivan, 80
Butler, Judith, 100–1
Byron (Marchand), 205–6
Byron, George Gordon, Lord, 161–2, 205–8, 213, 218–19
Byron, Glennis, 14–15, 16, 385–6
Byronic hero, 205–10, 213, 218–19, 220
vampires and, 204–5, 208–9, 210–12

Cabell, James Branch, 70
The Cabinet of Dr Caligari (film), 45
Cadwalladr, Carole, 290
Caldwell, Erskine, 63, 73
Caldwell, Luke, 379
'The Call of Cthulhu' (Lovecraft), 469
Cammell, Donald, 215–18
Canada, multiculturalism in, 346–50
under Multiculturalism Act of 1988, 346
vocabulary of monstrosity in, 348–9
Cannell, Fenella, 236
cannibalism, within remix culture, 308
Capote, Truman, 78, 184
Carey, Peter, 123–4, 130–2
Çarkoğlu, Ali, 392

Carmilla (Le Fanu), 268, 302–3
Carnivàle (television), 285–9
Carrell, Jennifer Lee, 265
Carter, Angela, 11–12, 200, 201–2, 244
The Bloody Chamber, 253, 258
Heroes and Villains, 201–2
The Magic Toyshop, 249–53
Bluebeard narrative in, 252
rape themes in, 251–2
The Sadeian Woman, 258
'The Snow Child', 253–4
Cartier, Rudolph, 225
Cascone, Kim, 333–4
The Case of Charles Dexter Ward (Lovecraft), 161–2, 164–5
Cash, W. J., 71
Cassavetes, John, 98
Castle, William, 81, 97, 98
The Castle of Otranto (Walpole), 10, 99, 141
Castricano, Jodey, 9–10
Cat People (film), 90–1
Catch-22 (Heller), 110–11
Chaney, Lon, 82–3, 87
Chaney, Lon, Jr, 98
Chariandy, David, 346–50
charms and spells, in occult, 170–1
Chesnutt, Charles, 70
Un Chien Andalou (film), 58–9
Child of God (McCarthy, C.), 76–7
Childs, Peter, 58
Chomsky, Noam, 300, 371
Christie, Ian, 30
Chun, Wendy, 309
La chute de la maison Usher (*The Fall of the House of Usher*) (film), 40–1
cinema. See silent cinema and film
City of Mirrors (Cronin), 298–9
Civil War, in US, 109
Clarke, Susanna, 161–2, 174–5
Clery, E. J., 2–3
Clive, Colin, 84–5
Clock Without Hands (McCullers), 62
Clouzot, Henri-Georges, 81, 96
Clover, Carol, 6, 186
Cock, Gerald, 232–3
Cocozza, Paula, 316–17
Coeur Fidèle (film), 40
The Coherence of Gothic Conventions (Sedgwick), 8–9
Cold War
in apocalyptic Gothic, 470–4
as propaganda, 94–5
War Gothic and, 108–9

Cold War catastrophe, 470–4
Coleridge, Samuel Taylor, 164
Collins, Wilkie, 120–1, 387
Columbella (Whitney), 244
communal violence, from multiculturalism, 355–9
Communism, Surrealism and, 5
Condon, Richard, 109
Conrad, Joseph, 11, 17, 45, 49, 128–9
Conroy, Gretta, 53–4
consumerism, zombies and, 480–1
contagion, 21, 342
  AIDS and, 265–6, 268–9, 278–9
  colonialism and, 47–8
  zombies and, 276
Contemporary Gothic (Spooner), 14, 304
convergence culture, 305–9
  commodification of, 306–8
  copyright in, 306–8
  monstrosity in, 305
  ownership rights in, 306–8
  technological advances and, 306
Cook, Sarah Gibbard, 245–6
Cooper, Susan, 151
Coover, Robert, 11–12
Coppola, Francis Ford, 20, 39, 416–17
copyright, in convergence culture, 306–8
Corelli, Marie, 11, 34–6, 160
Corman, Roger, 214
Corstorphine, Kevin, 180
Cosmic Regionalism, 184
Cosslett, Tess, 149
Cottam, F. G., 161–2
counterculture, Gothic elements in
  contemporary presentations of, 211–12, 218–20
  Easy Rider as iconic expression of, 199–200
  Performance, 215–18
  psychedelia and, 213–15, 220
  in rock music, 220
  theoretical approach to, 199–202
  in UK, 199–200
  vampires and, 202–12
    Byronic hero as, 205–6, 208–9, 210–12
    in films, 210–12
    Hammer Studios, 202–5
    The Vampyre and, 204–5, 218
country house crisis, 143–6
  in *Brideshead Revisited*, 143, 144
  Country Life, 143, 157–8
  definition and scope of, 143–4
  National Trust Act of 1937, 143–4
  in *Rebecca*, 144–6

Country Life (magazine), 143, 157–8
The Course of the Heart (Harrison, M. J.), 161–2, 172–4
Creed, Barbara, 6, 186, 187, 397, 399
'The Cremation of Sam McGee' (Service), 122–3
The Crimes of Love (Marquis de Sade), 201
Cronin, Justin, 21, 298–9, 482
Crow, Charles L., 68, 184–5
Crowley, Aleister, 161–4, 212
cryptonomy (trans-generational haunting), 254, 255
Cubitt, Sean, 330
cultural Jim Crow, 75–6
cultural memory, in Southern Gothic literature, in US, 68–9
Curry, Tim, 263–4
The Curse of the Crimson Altar (film), 214–15
Curtis, Dan, 226–7
Curtiz, Michael, 87–8
Cybergothic, 325

Dali, Salvador, 58–9
Dall'Asta, Monica, 38
Daly, Mary, 450–2
Danse Macabre (King), 183
The Dark is Rising (Cooper), 151
Dark Shadows (television), 209, 227
The Dark Shore (Howatch), 244
Dark Waters (film), 412
Darwin, Charles, 58
Davenport-Hines, Richard, 13–14
Davis, Colin, 330
Dawley, J. Searle, 34–6
Day of the Dead (film), 105
Dayan, Daniel, 232–3
de la Mare, Walter, 50
Dead Lovers are Faithful Lovers (Newman, F.), 75–6
Dean, Jodi, 300
A Death in the Family (Goyen), 76
Deathdream (film), 113–14
decolonial theory, 278–9, 365–6, 368–9
decolonisation, postcolonial Gothic and, 118
del Toro, Guillermo, 296–7
Delamotte, Eugenia C., 6
Deneuve, Catherine, 267–70
Der Derian, James, 379
Derrida, Jacques, 9, 55
Derviş, Suat, 386
desire, 253–4, 420–1
The Devil Rides Out (film), 214–15
The Devil Rides Out (novel) (Wheatley, D.), 161–2, 166–7

Devil's Valley (Brink), 123–4, 129–30
Devlin, Polly, 199–200
Les Diaboliques (film), 81, 96
Diary of a Drug Fiend (Crowley), 162
Dickens, Charles, 10, 34–5
　Great Expectations, 130–1
　Oliver Twist, 238
　The Pickwick Papers, 28
Didion, Joan, 200
Dinesen, Isak. See Blixen, Karen
disaster Gothics, 458
disease. See contagion, AIDS narratives
The Divided Self (Laing), 191
djinns, 384, 388–9, 393–4, 400–1
　Ecinni: Aykırı Dünyayla İlişkiler (Yıldırım),
　al-Inss wa-l-jinn (film), 388–90, 394
Doane, Mary Ann, 92–3
Doctors Wear Scarlet (Raven), 207–8
Doherty, Francis Michael, 206
doppelgänger. See double or doppelgänger
Dorsey, Sean, 281
double or doppelgänger, 57, 148, 149–50, 216–17, 247, 315–16
　in Scandinavian Gothic, 427–8
Douglas, Robert, 265
Douglass, Paul, 206
Dourish, Paul, 325–6
Doyle, Arthur Conan, 11, 161, 368
Dr Jekyll and Mr Hyde (film) (1931), 84, 86–7
Dr Jekyll and Mr Hyde (novel) (Stevenson), 274, 293, 302–3, 428
Dracula (film) (1931), 24–5, 30–1, 80–1, 82–5
　mysticism themes in, 84
　reviews of, 83
Dracula (film) (US: Horror of Dracula) (film) (1958), 202–3
Dracula (novel) (Stoker), 28–9, 49, 165, 268
　contemporary adaptations of, 202–3, 210–12, 302–3
　Imperial Gothic in, 366, 368
Dracula AD 1972 (film), 210–12
Dream of a Rarebit Fiend (Porter, E. S.), 37–8
Dreyer, Carl Theodor, 22–5, 430. See also Vampyr
Du Bois, W. E. B., 75
du Maurier, Daphne, 140, 143, 145, 225
Dubliners (Joyce), 49, 51–4
Ducray-Duminil, François Guillaume, 426
Dugas, Gaëtan, 275–6
Dumas, Chris, 186
Dunant, Sarah, 370
Dunn, J. Allan, 368

Duong Thu Huong, 115
Dupont, E. A., 39

East Asian Gothic. See also Hong Kong Gothic Cinema; Japanese Gothic Cinema; South Korean Gothic Cinema
　Asia Extreme, 405–6
　definition of, 403–4
　international collaborations in, 423
　theoretical approach to, 404–6
　methodology in, 406
Easy Rider (film), 199–200
Ecinni: Aykırı Dünyayla İlişkiler (Djinni: Relations with the Other World) (novel) (Yıldırım), 394–9
ecocriticism, 446
ecofeminism, 458–9
Ecogothic, 8
economic injustice, as theme, in Southern Gothic literature, 67
Edgar Huntly (Brown, C. B.), 367–8
Edge, Thomas, 235
Edison, Thomas, 34–6
Edmundson, Mark, 13–14
Edo-Gothic period, in Japan, 409
Edwards, Justin D., 14–15, 134, 378
egalitarianism, remix culture and, 307
Egypt, Islamic Gothic in, 390
Einstein, Albert, 58
Elfgren, Sara Bergmark, 424, 431–2
Eliot, George, 17, 135
Eliot, T. S., 53–4, 57, 60
Elliott, Kamilla, 310, 322
Elliott, Will, 118–19
Ellis, Bret Easton, 12, 294
Ellis, Kate Ferguson, 6
Ellis, Markman, 3–4, 309–10
Ellison, Ralph, 74–5
Encounters of the Spooky Mind (film), 421–2
environmental crisis Gothic. See also specific works
　disaster Gothics, 458
　ecocriticism and, 446
　ecofeminism and, 458–9
　ghost stories and, 444–7
　haunted houses
　　in films, 449–50, 451
　　nonhuman sentience in, 449–56
　oikos and, 448–56
　second-wave feminism themes and, 450–2

environmental crisis Gothic (cont.)
  transcorporeality and, 462–4
  humanity and, 445
  as intergenerational crime, 457
  oikos and, 447–56
    haunted houses and, 448–56
    transcorporeality and, 462–4
  parental agency in, 458–62
    for fathers, 460–2
    for mothers, 458–60
Epstein, Jean, 40–1
era of attractions, early cinema as, 31
Erb, Cynthia, 87
Evans, Robert, 98
evolutionary theory, psychoanalysis and, 181
The Exorcist (Blatty), 192, 193–4

Facebook, postdigital Gothic and, 337–41
The Fall (del Toro and Hogan), 296–7
false magicians, 162–3
Fantasmagorie (Robert), 4–5
Farage, Nigel, 319–20
Farrow, Mia, 98
Faulkner, William, 61–2, 64–5, 75–6, 184
  Absalom, Absalom, 65, 69
  As I Lay Dying, 64–5, 351
  Requiem for a Nun, 66
  Sanctuary, 64–5
  The Sound and the Fury, 65, 71–2
female gaze, 247–8
female Gothic
  Beloved, 75, 254–8
  Bluebeard narrative and
    in *The Magic Toyshop*, 252
    in popular romance texts, 245
  cryptonomy and, 254
    in *Beloved*, 255
  desire and, 253–4
  libertine sexuality in, for women, 258–60
    in *Fingersmith*, 259–60
    in *The Magic Toyshop*, 258–9
    pornography and, 258–60
  The Magic Toyshop, 249–53, 258–9
  Mistress of Mellyn, 244, 246–9
  Modern Gothics
    popular romance and, 244–6
    Russ on, 244–5
    Super-Male trope in, 244–5
  older women in, 253–4
    in *Fingersmith*, 259–60
  popular romance and, 242–6
    Bluebeard narrative in, 245

  as Modern Gothics, scope of works in, 244–6
  Rebecca and, 242–3
  Super-Male trope, 244–5, 254
  theoretical approach to, 242–6
  the uncanny in, 246
The Feminine Mystique (Friedan), 242–3, 244
feminism. *See also* female Gothic
  contemporary, 261
  ecofeminism, 458–9
  Friedan and, 242–3
  Rebecca and, 242–3
  second-wave, 6
    in environmental crisis Gothic, 450–2
    Gaia hypothesis, 450–2
    in haunted house stories, 450–2
    origins of, 244
    in Southern Gothic literature, after World War II, 75–6
  third-wave, 245–6
Fergusson, Niall, 371
Fiedler, Leslie A., 5, 11, 63, 75, 200–1, 205, 367
Filkins, Dexter, 117
film. *See* Hollywood Gothic; silent cinema and film
film noir, 94, 110
Fincher, David, 294–5
Fireproof (Jha), 356, 360–3
Fitzgerald, Lauren, 243
Fleenor, Juliann E., 6
Les Fleurs du mal (Baudelaire), 49
Flusser, Vilém, 325
folk horror, 150–5, 170, 218, 220, 264
folklore, in Scandinavian Gothic, 442–3
forever war, 117
The Forever War (Haldeman), 117
Forster, E. M., 46–9, 54
Forster, Paul, 28–9
Fortier, Anne-Marie, 355–6
Fowler, Alistair, 7
Frankenstein (film) (1910), 34–6
Frankenstein (film) (1931), 24–5, 30–1, 84–6
Frankenstein (novel) (Shelley, M.), 6, 17, 25–6, 133–4, 161, 229
  contemporary adaptations of, 302–3
  Satanic references in, 213
Frankenstein in Baghdad (Saadawi), 356–9
Frayling, Christopher, 3, 34–6
Freaks (film), 286
Freemasonry, 160
French and Indian War, 99
French Symbolism, 44
Freud, Sigmund, 3–4, 56, 63, 324

American psychoanalysis influenced by, 181–2, 196
Oedipus Complex, 180–1
postdigital Gothic and, 324–5
On the Interpretation of Dreams, 3–4
on 'The Uncanny', 3–4, 246
unconscious and, 58
'Freudian Fiction' (Woolf), 57–8
Friedan, Betty, 242–3, 244
From a Buick 6 (King), 373–4
frontier Gothic, in US, 367–8
Fry, Roger, 43
Fukuyama, Francis, 477–8
Full Metal Jacket (film), 114–15
Fuller, Roy, 106

Gaia hypothesis, 450–2
Gaines, Ernest J., 78
Gamer, Michael, 7–8
Gance, Abel, 114
Gardner, Gerald, 212
Garner, Alan, 151
Gaskell, Jane, 208–9
Gatiss, Mark, 151
Gaudier-Brzeska, Henri, 48
Gauguin, Paul, 44
Gay, William, 76–7
Gelder, Ken, 14, 206
gender. *See also* female Gothic; feminism; women
 magic and, differences in, 174
Genet, Jean, 271–2, 273
Genovese, Eugene, 78
German Expressionist cinema, 83
Get Out (film), 354–5
Ghosh, Amitav, 445, 463–4
ghost sounds, MP3s and, 334–5
ghost stories. *See* apparitions and ghosts
Ghost Stories of an Antiquary (James, M. R.), 141
ghosts. *See* apparitions and ghosts
Ghoul (television), 229
Gibbons, Luke, 54
Gibson, Andrew, 305
Gibson, William, 11–12
GIFs. *See* Graphic Interchange Formats
Giger, H. R., 316
Gilbert, Sandra M., 6, 252–3
Gillis, Greg, 307
Girard, René, 63
A Girl Walks Home Alone at Night (film), 383, 385
Gittings, Christopher, 275–6, 277
Glasgow, Ellen, 63, 70, 72
glitch Gothic, 326–31

 in found footage horror films, 326–31
 analogue media in, 329
 The Blair Witch Project, 326–7
 editing in, 329
 in film trailers, 328
 ghost stories and, 330–1
 as replacement for music score, 329–30
 as structural bookends, 328
 materiality in, 331
 Unfriended: Dark Web, 338–41
Globalgothic (Byron), 14–15
globalisation of Gothic. *See specific topics*
Go, Julian, 371
Goddu, Teresa A., 67
God's Little Acre (Caldwell, E.), 63
Godwin, William, 160
Göle, Nilüfer, 396–7
'The Good Lady Ducayne' (Braddon), 268
Goodlad, Lauren M. E., 13
Gordon, Avery F., 276, 277, 280, 282
Gordon, Caroline, 73
Gorky, Maxim, 3
 on silent cinema, 25–7
Goth: Identity, Style, and Subculture (Hodkinson), 13
Goth music and subculture
 Byronic hero and, 220
 development of, 12–14
 Gothic Studies compared to, 13
 in *The Hunger*, 267
 in United Kingdom, 12–14
Gothic (Botting), 13–14, 20, 27, 102, 416, 421
Gothic (film), 218–19
The Gothic, Postcolonialism, and Otherness (Khair), 125
Gothic America (Goddu), 67
The Gothic Flame (Varma), 5, 11
The Gothic Quest (Summers), 4–5
Gothic Studies, 6–10
 decoupling from concept of genre, 7–8
 establishment of, 6
 as formal discipline, 7
 Goth subculture compared to, 13
 identity politics and, 6–7
 institutionalisation of, through expansion of scholarship, 16–17
 on school syllabus, 16–17
 second-wave feminism and, 6
 'spectral turn', 9–10
Gothic Television (Wheatley, H.), 222
Gothic: Transmutations of Horror in Late-twentieth-century Art (Grunenberg), 13–14, 17–18

Gothicisation of history, 221–2
Gove, Michael, 15
Goyen, William, 76
Graham, Patrick, 229
Grand Guignol, in Gothic television, 230–1
Grange, Amanda, 257
Grange, Jean-Christophé, 240
Graphic Interchange Formats (GIFs), 313–19
   commercialisation of, 314–15
   image appropriation and
      recontextualisation in, 319
   institutionalisation of, 314–15
   repetition and, 315–17
Great Expectations (Dickens), 130–1
The Great God Pan (Machen), 162
The Great Tradition (Leavis), 17
Green, Henry, 106
Greene, Graham, 106
Greyson, John, 266, 275–9
Griffiths, Gareth, 120
Griswold, Samuel, 235
Grunenberg, Christoph, 13–14, 17–18
Gubar, Susan, 6, 252–3
Güçlü, Şafak, 400
Gunkel, David, 308
Gunning, Tom, 29, 31

Haefele-Thomas, Ardel, 6, 21
Haggar, Walter, 34
Haggard, H. Rider, 366
Haggard, Piers, 151
Hagood, Taylor, 68
Haiti, US occupation of, *White Zombie* and, 103–4
Haldeman, Joe, 117
Hale, Nathan G., 181–2, 184
Halperin, Victor, 88, 103–4
Hammer Studios films, 80–2, 97, 202–5, 210–12
Han, Byung-Chul, 120, 128
Handling the Undead (Lindqvist), 358, 442, 480, 481
Hangsaman (Jackson), 189–90
Hanks, Michele, 137
Hannibal (Harris, T.), 294
Harbour (Lindqvist), 435–6
Hardt, Michael, 368–9
Hardy, Thomas, 466
Harris, Joel Chandler, 70
Harris, Thomas, 198, 293–4
Harrison, Joan, 96
Harrison, M. John, 161–2, 172–4
Harrison, Sheri-Marie, 353
The Harvest Queen (film), 434–5

Harvey, David, 371
Hasford, Gustav, 114–15
The Haunted Castle (film), 38–9
The Haunted Curiosity Shop (film), 30
Haunted Heritage (Hanks), 137
'A Haunted House' (Woolf), 60
haunted houses, in relation to environmental crisis
   in films, 449–50, 451
   nonhuman sentience in, 449–56
   oikos and, 448–56
   second-wave feminist themes and, 450–2
   transcorporeality and, 462–4
haunting
   aesthetics of, 50
   AIDS narratives and, 282
   in criticism, 9–10
   cryptonomy and, 254
   glitch Gothic and, 330, 331, 333
The Haunting of Hill House (Jackson), 189
The Haunting of Hill House (television), 230, 460–2
Hawks, Howard, 85–6
Hawthorne, Nathaniel, 354
Hayles, Katherine, 323–4
Haynes, Todd, 266–7, 271–5
Hearn, Lafcadio, 407–8
The Heart is a Lonely Hunter (McCullers), 62
Heart of Darkness (Conrad), 45, 49, 128–9
Hedayat, Sadegh, 386–7
Heller, Joseph, 110–11
Heller-Nicholas, Alexandra, 195
Hepworth, Cecil, 34
heritage cinema, 138–9
The Heritage Industry (Hewison), 138
heritage movement, in UK. *See also specific works*
   contemporary revision of, 155–8
   country house crisis, 143–6
      in *Brideshead Revisited*, 143, 144
      Country Life, 143, 157–8
      definition and scope of, 143–4
      National Trust Act of 1937, 143–4
      in *Rebecca*, 144–6
   expansion of, 155–8
   folk horror and, 150–5
      as concept, development of, 151
   as heritage romance, 147–50
   landscape history and, 150–5
   National Trust and, 147–8
      National Trust Act of 1937, 143–4
   neo-heritage, 140
   objects in, 140–3

in works of James, M. R., 140–3
theoretical approach to, 137–40
  changes in, 139–40
  scope of, 137–8
Hermetic Corpus, 160
Heroes and Villains (Carter), 201–2
Herr, Michael, 114–15
Hervey, Benjamin, 32
Hewison, Robert, 138
high Modernism, 49
Highfield, Tim, 314–15
Higson, Andrew, 138–9
Hitchcock, Alfred, 89, 91, 96, 119
Hjorth, Michael, 434–5
Hoberman, J., 272
Hodgson, William Hope, 467–8
Hodkinson, Paul, 13
Hoffman, E. T. A., 3–4, 426
Hogan, Chuck, 296–7
Hogg, James, 10
Hogle, Jerrold E., 235, 327–8, 373
Höglund, Johan, 101
Holden, Philip, 135–6
Holdsworth, Amy, 236
Hollywood Gothic, in films. *See also specific films*
  film noir and, 94
  German Expressionist cinema as influence on, 83
  monsters in, 93–8
  psychological horror, 93–8
  range of productions for, 82
    increase in, 83, 87–8
  realism in, 88–93
  respectability as goal of, 88–93
  RKO Studio, 87
  science fiction cycle in, 81, 93–8
    Cold War propaganda in, 94–5
    genres in, 94
    literary roots of, 94
    women in, 95
  serial killer narratives, 294–5
  theoretical approach to, 80–2
  Universal Studios films, 80–8
  Vampyr as influence on, 24–5
  Vietnam War in, 113–14
  war veterans in, 109–10
  women in, 91–3
    Bluebeard narrative, 92–3
    paranoid woman theme, 91–2
    in science fiction genre, 95
Holmes, Mary, 137
Holt, Victoria, 205, 244, 246–9, 251
Hong Kong Gothic Cinema, 418–22

desire themes in, 420–1
Encounters of the Spooky Mind, 421–2
ghost romances in, 421
Mr Vampire, 418–19
My Cousin, the Ghost, 420
Horner, Avril, 59
horror. *See* folk horror; psychological horror
Horror and Religion in Cinema (Şimşek), 393
Hoskins, W. G., 140, 150–1
The House in Paris (Bowen), 56
The House Next Door (Siddons), 448, 454, 455–6
A House Not Meant to Stand (Williams), 65
The House of Arden (Nesbit), 148
The House of Breath (Goyen), 76
House of Dracula (film), 202–5
The House of Lost Souls (Cottam), 161–2, 175–7
The House on the Borderland (Hodgson), 467–8
Howatch, Susan, 244
Howells, William Dean, 185
Hubner, Laura, 405
Hughes, William, 121, 365–6, 446
Hulme, T. E., 178
Hung, Sammo, 421–2
The Hunger (film), 266–71
The Hunger (novel) (Strieber), 266–7
The Hunger and Other Stories (Beaumont), 187
Hunter, Meredith, 199–200
Huntington, Samuel P., 369–70
Hurston, Zora Neale, 74–5
Hutchings, Peter, 32, 81–2, 89
Hynes, Samuel, 108

I Am Gabriella! (Maybury), 244
I Am Legend (Matheson), 21, 187–8, 470–2
Ibsen, Henrik, 427–8
identity politics. *See also* feminism; LGBTQ+ identity
  Gothic Studies and, 6–7
'If the Dead Knew' (Sinclair), 56, 57
IGA. *See* International Gothic Association
I'll Take my Stand (Genovese), 78, 79
'Illuminati', 160
Images of War (Aldington), 48
immortality, as personal quest, 173
Imperial Gothic, 101. *See also specific topics; specific works*
  Age of Anxiety and, 370
  alien invasion themes in, 378–81
    military entertainment complex and, 379
    US Department of Defense and, film funding and support by, 379–81
  anti-Enlightenment and, 366
  border anxiety and, 381–2

Imperial Gothic (cont.)
  in postcolonial era, 365–6, 368–73
  reverse colonisation narratives and, 377
  theoretical approach to, 364–8
    decolonial theory and, 365–6, 368–9
  in US
    development of, 367
    frontier Gothic, 367–8
    after World War II, 369–70
    xenophobia and, 368
  Vietnam War and, 111–12
  War on Terror and, in U.S., 364–5, 373–81
    Bush and, 370, 375
    fatalities during, 376
    in literature, 372–3
    11 September attacks and, 370–1
    zombies in, 377–8
imperialism, Modernist Gothic and, 44–9
imprisonment, racial neoliberalism and, 351–5
In a Lonely Place (film), 110
In Cold Blood (Capote), 78
In the Flesh (television), 292–3
In the Lake of the Woods (O'Brien), 114
Incense for the Damned (film), 210
Inequality for All (film), 290
Ingemann, Bernhard, 426–7
Inglis, David, 137
al-Inss wa-l-jinn (Humans and Jinns) (film), 388–90, 394
International Gothic Association (IGA), 16–17
International Monetary Fund, 283
Interview with the Vampire (Rice), 211, 255–6
Invisible Man (Ellison), 74–5
Islam, Arabs, and Intelligent World of the Jinn (El-Zein), 399
Islamic Gothic. *See also* Turkey
  in Egypt, 390
  in Middle East, 385–90
    djinns and, 388–9
    Gothic novels in, 387
    Western tropes in, 387–9
  theoretical approach to, 383–90
IT (King, S.), 198, 475
The Italian (Radcliffe), 426
Iversen, Gunnar, 438

Jack Maggs (Carey), 123–4, 130–2
Jackson, Shirley, 168, 354
  The Bird's Nest, 189, 190
  Hangsaman, 189–90
  The Haunting of Hill House, 38–9, 189
  psychoanalysis themes in, 189–91

We Have Always Lived in the Castle, 161–2, 168–9, 189, 190–1
Jacobs, Robert D., 73
Jacobs, W. W., 224
Jacob's Ladder (film), 115–16
Jagger, Mick, 215–19
James, Henry, 17, 45, 49, 50
James, M. R., 50, 140, 141, 142
  heritage objects in works of, 140–3
James, William, 55–6
Jameson, Fredric, 199–200
Jancovich, Mark, 3
Jane Eyre (Brontë), 6, 125, 244
Japanese Gothic Cinema, 407–13
  Dark Water, 412
  Edo-Gothic period, 409
  Kwaidan, 407–8
  multicultural influences in, 407–8
  Onibaba, 409, 410
  Ring, 405, 409–12
  Ugetsu Monogatari, 407
Jenkins, Henry, 306
Jensen, Caroline L., 431–2
Jha, Raj Kamal, 356, 360–3
Johnson, Boris, 319–20
Johnson, Chambers, 371
Johnston, Derek, 3
Jolley, Elizabeth, 123–4
Jølsen, Ragnhild, 428–9
Jonathan Strange and Mr Norrell (Clarke), 161–2, 174–5, 178
Jones, David J., 3
Jones, James, 110–11
Joseph, M. K., 206
The Joss (Marsh), 120–1
Journey's End (Sherriff), 84–5
Joyce, James, 46–7, 49, 51–4, 55–6
jpeg (photographic series) (Ruff), 335–7
jpegs, postdigital Gothic and, 335–7
Jubilee (Walker, M.), 78
Jul, Christen, 23
Julian, Rupert, 36–7

Kaaberbøl, Lene, 431–2
Kalaycıoğlu, Ersin, 392
Karloff, Boris, 85, 87
Katz, Elihu, 232–3
Kavan, Anna, 106
Kavka, Misha, 405
Keefe, Andy, 292–3
Keetley, Dawn, 145–6
Kennedy, John F., 112
Khair, Tabish, 125

Kilgour, Maggie, 185–6
Kim Jee-woon, 413
Kinds of Literature (Fowler), 7
King, Richard, 73–4
King, Stephen, 183, 197–8, 354, 373–4, 448–474–477
The Kingdom (television), 437–8
Kipling, Rudyard, 132, 148
Kjastberg, Kristine Marie, 427
Knauf, Daniel, 285–9
Kopple, Barbara, 454
Korean War, 108–9
Kortenaar, Neil Ken, 347–8
Kracauer, Siegfried, 92, 93
Kramer, Larry, 271
Kristeva, Julia, 63, 397
Kubrick, Stanley, 114–15
Kwaidan (film), 407–8
Kymlicka, Will, 349

Lagerlöf, Selma, 432, 434
Laing, R. D., 191, 201
Lancet, 376
landscape history, 150–5
Land of the Dead (film), 289–90
The Last Man (Shelley, M.), 21, 265
Latour, Bruno, 447
Laughton, Charles, 87
LaVey, Anton, 212
Lawrence, D. H., 46
Le Fanu, Joseph Sheridan, 49, 50, 268, 302–3, 387
The League of Extraordinary Gentlemen (film), 374
Leary, Timothy, 201–2
The Least of all Evils (Arvonen), 244
Leavis, F. R., 17
Ledwon, Lenora, 221
Lee, Christopher, 202–5
Lee, Harper, 78
Lee, Spike, 235
Leeder, Murray, 25–6
The Legend of the Witches (film), 212–13
LeMenager, Stephanie, 454–5
Leni, Paul, 38
Lenoir, Tim, 379
Lentin, Alana, 343–4, 350
lesbian vampires, 257, 262–4
Lessig, Lawrence, 307, 314
Let the Right One In (Lindqvist), 424, 440, 442
Lévi, Éliphas, 161
Levin, Ira, 192–3, 199–200
Levinas, Emmanuel, 120
Lévy, Maurice, 324
Lewis, Matthew Gregory, 2–3, 59, 161

The Monk, 43–4, 58–9, 161–2, 372–3, 398, 426
Lewis, Wyndham, 43–4, 60
Lewton, Val, 90–1
LGBTQ+ identity, Queer Gothic and. *See also specific films*
 AIDS and, 264–82
 contagion and, 265–6, 268–70, 278–9
 decriminalisation of, 262–3
 lesbian and bisexual vampires, 257, 262–4
 liberation movement and, 262–4
The Life of Charles Peace, 34
Ligotti, Thomas, 478–9
Lindqvist, John Ajvide, 358, 424, 435–6, 439, 440, 442
Literary Women (Moers), 6, 243
The Literature of Terror (Punter), 7, 11–12, 372
The Little Match Seller (film), 37–8
Little Sister Death (Gay), 76–7
The Little Stranger (Waters), 140, 155–8
Lively, Penelope, 140, 151–3
Livjin, Clas, 427
Ljungstedt, Aurora, 428
Lloyd, Christopher, 68
Lloyd Smith, Allan, 1, 13–14, 201
Löfflmann, Georg, 379–80
Lombard, Carole, 88
London, Jack, 368
London Blitz, in War Gothic, 105–6
Look Homeward Angel (Wolfe), 71–2
Loomba, Ania, 370
Lorde, Audre, 259–60
Lorre, Peter, 88
The Lost World (Doyle), 368
Love Among the Ruins (Percy), 77–8
Love and Death in the American Novel (Fiedler), 5, 63, 200–1, 205, 367
Lovecraft, H. P., 161–2, 184, 468–9
Lovelock, James, 450–2
Lowenthal, David, 138
Löwy, Michael, 345
Lucifer Rising (film), 215
Luckhurst, Roger, 9, 382
Lugosi, Bela, 84, 87–8, 103, 202
Lytle, Andrew, 66

Machen, Arthur, 162
The Madwoman in the Attic (Gilbert and Gubar), 6, 252–3
magic, in Gothic contexts
 in alternative history genre, 174–7
 The Case of Charles Dexter Ward, 161–2, 164–5
 contemporary approaches to, 178
 The Course of the Heart, 161–2, 172–4

magic, in Gothic contexts (cont.)
    definition of, 159–60
    The Devil Rides Out, 161–2, 166–7
    false magicians, 162–3
    'female witchcraft' and, 174
    Freemasonry and, 160
    gender differences in, 174
    in Gothic Horror, 172–4
    Hermetic Corpus, 160
    history of, in West, 160
    The House of Lost Souls, 161–2, 175–7
    'Illuminati' and, 160
    immortality and, as personal quest, 173
    Jonathan Strange and Mr Norrell, 161–2, 174–5
    magical associations, 160–1
    'male magic', 174
    Moonchild, 161–3
    occult themes and, 160–1, 166–7, 175–7
        charms and spells, 170–1
        supernatural and, 166
    rites and rituals, 161–3
        repetition as, 172–3
    Rosicrucianism and, 160
    Society for Psychical Research and, 167
    spilt religion and, 178
    theoretical approach to, 159–62
    The Wasp Factory, 161–2, 168, 170–1
    We Have Always Lived in the Castle, 161–2, 168–9
The Magic Toyshop (Carter), 249–53
    Bluebeard narrative in, 252
    female sexuality in, 258–9
    rape themes in, 251–2
magical associations, 160–1
magical realism, 118–19, 128, 129–34
Magnus, Albertus, 160
Maguire, Ryan, 334–5
Magus, Simon, 160
Mailer, Norman, 110–11
Major, John, 342
The Making of the English Landscape (Hoskins), 140, 150–1
Malchow, H. L., 120–1
Malin, Irving, 185
Mamdani, Mahmood, 355–6
Mamoulian, Rouben, 84
The Man Who Laughs (film), 83
The Manchurian Candidate (Condon), 109
Mandal, Anthony, 304–5
Mandela, Nelson, 130
Mannoni, Laurent, 27
Manon, Hugh S., 327
Mansfield Park (Austen), 131

Manson, Charles, 199–200
Marasco, Robert, 448, 450, 452–4
March, Frederic, 84
March, William, 188–9
Marchand, Leslie A., 205–6
Mareuil, Simone, 58–9
Margulis, Lynn, 450–2
marital betrayal, 192–3
Marklund, Andreas, 434–5
Marsh, Richard, 34–6, 120–1, 366, 377
Martin, Sara, 13
Marx, Karl, 58, 284
mashups, in remix culture, 303
materiality, in glitch Gothic, 331
Matheson, Richard, 21, 187–8, 470–2
Matisse, Henri, 44
Maturin, Charles, 2–3, 49, 160, 164
    Melmoth the Wanderer, 10, 161–2, 327
        Satanic references in, 213
May, Theresa, 319
May Sinclair Society, 55
Maybury, Anne, 244
McCabe, Colin, 218
McCarthy, Anna, 317
McCarthy, Cormac, 76–7, 78
McCullers, Carson, 11, 61, 77, 184
    The Ballad of the Sad Café, 62
    Clock Without Hands, 62
    The Heart is a Lonely Hunter, 62
    A Member of the Wedding, 62
    Reflections in Golden Eye, 62
McGrath, Patrick, 12, 17–18
McLuhan, Marshal, 73
McNally, David, 305
Meaney, Evan, 330
The Meaning of Witchcraft (Gardner), 212
media. *See* new media; *specific topics*
Melmoth the Wanderer (Maturin), 10, 161–2, 213, 327
Melville, Herman, 128–9
A Member of the Wedding (McCullers), 62
Memento Mori (film), 417
Men from the Ministry (Thurley), 147
Mencken, H. L., 70, 71
Mendelssohn, Felix, 57
Menkman, Rosa, 327
Mernissi, Fatima, 397
Mestçi, Alper, 401–2
Meyer, Stephenie, 15–16, 208, 211–12, 284
Michaud, Marilyn, 470–1, 472
Michelle Remembers (Pazder and Smith, M.), 194–5, 196–7
Midnight's Children (Rushdie), 133–4

Index

Mighall, Robert, 8–9, 203
Mignolo, Walter, 365, 368–9
Miles, Robert, 6–8
military entertainment complex, 379
Mills, Kevin, 465–6, 481
Miltner, Kate M., 314–15
Milton, John, 212–13
Mincheva, Dilyana, 279–80
The Ministry of Fear (Greene), 106
Miracle of the Rose (Genet), 273
Miss Peregrine's Peculiar Children novels (Riggs), 311–13
Mistress of Mellyn (Holt), 244, 246–9
  female gaze in, 247–8
  Rebecca (novel) as literary influence on, 246–7
Mitchell, Dominic, 292–3
Moby-Dick (Melville), 128–9
Modern Gothics
  popular romance and, 244–6
  Russ on, 244–5
  Super-Male trope in, 244–5
Modernist Gothic
  aesthetics and, 44–9
    in Forster works, 46–9
    of haunting, 50
    in Woolf works, 45
  apparitions and ghosts in, 50–8
    in ghost stories, 50–1, 54–8
  avant-garde and, 44–5
  classical modes in, 49
  early development of, 43
  French Symbolism as influence on, 44
  ghost stories, 50–1
    by women writers, 54–8
  high Modernism and, 49, 60
  imperialism and, 44–9
  primitivism and, 45–6
  Romanticism and, as response to, 43–4, 49
  in short stories, 51–4
    in Joyce works, 51–4
  theoretical approach to, 43–4
  unconscious in, 58–60
    Breton and, 58–9
    Freudian influences on, 58
  Victorian Gothic and, 43
  war as theme in, 44–9
Modleski, Tanya, 244–5
Moers, Ellen, 6, 243
Monbiot, George, 299
The Monk (Lewis, M. G.), 43–4, 58–9, 161–2, 372–3, 398, 426
The Monkey's Paw (Jacobs, W. W.), 224

monsters, in Hollywood Gothic films, 93–8
Moonchild (Crowley), 161–3
Moore, Alan, 374
Morgan, Robin, 247
Morrison, Toni, 76–7, 244
  Beloved, 75, 254–8
  Paradise, 75
  Playing in the Dark, 77
  Song of Solomon, 75
Morrow, Bradford, 12
Morton, Timothy, 447
Mother! (film), 458–60
The Moviegoer (Percy), 66
MP3s, as compression method, 331–5
  digital process for, 333–4
  ghost sounds lost to, 334–5
Mr Darcy, Vampire (Grange, A.), 257
Mr Vampire (film), 418–19
Mrs Dalloway (Woolf), 52
Mukherjee, Neel, 135
multiculturalism
  in Canada, 346–50
    under Multiculturalism Act of 1988, 346
    vocabulary of monstrosity in, 348–9
  communal violence as result of, 355–9
    Frankenstein in Baghdad, 356–9
  critique of, 363
  as discourse, in UK
    construction of, 343
    racism and, 343–4
    theoretical approach to, 342–6
  Fireproof, 360–3
  Get Out, 354
  as heterotopia, 359–63
  in Japanese Gothic Cinema, 407–8
  racial neoliberalism and, in US, 350–5
    in films, 354–5
    imprisonment and prison system, 351–5
    in novels, 351–4
  Sing, Unburied, Sing, 351–4
  Soucouyant, 346–50
Multiculturalism Act of 1988, Canada, 346
Mulvey, Laura, 318
Mulvey-Roberts, Marie, 160
Murnau, F. W., 38–9
  The Haunted Castle (film), 38–9
  Nosferatu (film), 21, 39
  Phantom (film), 39
Murphy, Bernice M., 395, 471–2
Musallat (film), 401–2
My Cousin, the Ghost (film), 420
Myal (Brodber), 132–3
The Mysterious Mother (Walpole), 109

Nakata, Hideo, 405, 409–12
The Naked and the Dead (Mailer), 110–11
Naked Lunch (Burroughs, W.), 213–14
Naremore, James, 91
narrativisation of Gothic, through silent film, 29–31, 33–6
  respectability as result of, 33
National Trust, in UK, 147–8
  National Trust Act of 1937, 143–4
Native Son (Wright, R.), 74–5
nature themes, in Scandinavian Gothic, 431–4
  wilderness, 434–7, 442–3
Nead, Lynda, 27, 29
Negri, Antonio, 368–9
neo-heritage, 140
neoliberal Gothic. *See also* racial neoliberalism
  Alt-Right movement and, 299–301
    Donald Trump and, 299–300
    in television, 299–300
  American Dream and, criticism of, 285–9
    in *Carnivàle*, 285–9
  in popular culture, 284
  serial killers in, 293–5
    in films, 294–5
  theoretical approach to, 283–4
  vampires, 295–9
    in films, 295–6
    in literature, 298–9
    in television, 296–8
  zombies, 289–93
    in literature, 290–2
    rise of capitalism and, 289
    in Romero films, 289–90
    in television, 292–3
Neoliberal Gothic (Monnet and Blake, L.), 375
Nesbit, E., 148
The New European, 320
The New Gothic (McGrath and Morrow), 12
new media, remix culture and, 309–13
  photographs and, 310–13
  recycling of content in, 309
New Southern Studies, 61
Newman, Frances, 75–6
Newman, Michael Z., 314
Ng, Andrew Hock Soon, 14–15, 344
Ní Fhlainn, Sorcha, 266–7
Nickelodeons, 33–4
Nickerson, Natalie, 107–8
Nietzsche, Friedrich, 323, 467–90
The Night Eternal (del Toro and Hogan), 296–7
Night of the Living Dead (film), 105, 199–200, 472–4

Nightingale at Noon (Summerton), 244
Nightmare on Main Street (Edmundson), 13–14
Nightwood (Barnes), 43, 59
Nixon, Nicola, 268
Nordaas, Alexander, 436–7
Norrington, Stephen, 295–6, 374
Northanger Abbey (Austen), 19
Nosferatu (film), 21, 39
Novel Without a Name (Duong Thu Huong), 115
Nyby, Christian, 94–5

Oakley, Ann, 245
Oates, Joyce Carol, 11–12
Obama, Barack, 351
objects, in heritage movement, 140–3
  in works of James, M. R., 140–3
O'Brien, Tim, 114–15
occult themes, 160–1, 166–7, 175–7
  charms and spells, 170–1
  supernatural and, 166
'An Occurrence at Owl Creek Bridge' (Bierce), 116
O'Connor, Flannery, 61–2, 64, 73, 184
O'Day, Marc, 220
Oddie, Bill, 235
Oedipus Complex, 180–1
oikos, 447–56. *See also* haunted houses; *specific films*
  haunted houses and, 448–56
  transcorporeality and, 462–4
Olgami (film), 415
Oliver, John, 338
Olivier, Marc, 3
Olson, Christopher, 390
On Living in an Old Country (Wright, P.), 138
On the Interpretation of Dreams (Freud), 3–4
Ondaatje, Michael, 356
O'Neill, Kevin, 374
Onibaba (film), 409, 410
Onions, Oliver, 50
The Orchard Keeper (McCarthy, C.), 76–7
Orientalism (Said), 365
Our Vampires, Ourselves (Auerbach), 257
Outer Dark (McCarthy, C.), 76–7
Øvredal, André, 439
The Owl Service (Garner), 151
ownership rights, in convergence culture, 306–8
Özkaracalar, Kaya, 392–3

Palmer, Paulina, 6, 250
Paracelsus, 160

Paradise (Morrison), 75
Paradise Lost (Milton), 212–13
paranoid woman, as theme, in Hollywood Gothic films, 91–2
parent–child relationships
   environmental crisis and, 458–62
      for fathers, 460–2
      for mothers, 458–60
   psychoanalysis of, 180–91
      Oedipus Complex, 180–1
      Pathological Mommy trope, 196–7
Parikka, Jussi, 325–6
Parker, Fred, 213
The Passage (Cronin), 21, 298–9, 482
A Passage to India (Forster, E. M.), 47–8
The Past Is a Foreign Country (Lowenthal), 138
Pathological Mommy trope, 196–7
patriarchy, in Turkey, 395–6
PATRIOT Act, US (2001), 297
Paul, Robert, 30
Pazder, Lawrence, 194–5, 196–7
Peake, Mervyn, 106
Pearson, Roberta E., 33–4
Peele, Jordan, 354–5
Peirse, Alison, 24–5
Pelissier, Anthony, 231–2
Penda's Fen (Rudkin), 140, 151, 153–5
Penny Cinemas, 33–4
Pentagon Papers, 112–13
Pepys, Samuel, 265
Percy, Walker, 66, 77–8
Performance (film), 215–18
The Peril of the Pacific (Dunn), 368
Persona (film), 430–1
Phantasmagoria, 27–8
Phantom (film), 39
The Phantom of the Opera (film), 36–7, 39, 82, 83
Philip, Marlene NourbeSe, 347–8
Phillips, Kendall, 24–5, 30–2
Phillips, Trevor, 343
photographs, in remix culture, 310–13
Picasso, Pablo, 46
The Pickwick Papers (Dickens), 28
The Picture of Dorian Gray (Wilde), 49, 302–3
Pilgrimage (Richardson), 55–6
The Pilo Family Circus (Elliott, W.), 118–19
Pirie, David, 80
Plath, Sylvia, 11
Playing in the Dark (Morrison), 77
Poe, Edgar Allan, 21, 34–6, 50, 64, 265, 426
Poison (film), 266, 271–5
   Genet and, 271–2

   sociocultural context for, 271
Polanski, Roman, 98
Polidori, John William, 204–5, 206, 218, 219
The Popular Novel in England 1770–1800 (Tompkins), 2–3
popular romance stories, 242–6
   Bluebeard narrative in, 245
   as Modern Gothics, scope of works in, 244–6
pornography, in female Gothic, 258–60
Porter, Edwin S., 37–8
Porter, Katherine Ann, 73
Porter, Ray, 370
A Portrait of the Artist as a Young Man (Joyce), 55–6
postcolonial Gothic. *See also specific works*
   ahistoricity and, 135–6
   decolonisation and, 118
   Devil's Valley, 123–4, 129–30
   opposition and, 133–6
   realism and, 135
   the scream as element of, 119–22
      academic approaches to, 120–2
      the self and, 120, 128–9
   theoretical approach to, 118–19
   Wide Sargasso Sea, 120, 123–9
postdigital Gothic. *See also* glitch Gothic
   cognitive assemblages and, 323–4
   Cybergothic, 325
   Facebook and, 337–41
   in films, 338–41
   Freud and, 324–5
   jpegs and, 335–7
   MP3s, as compression method, 331–5
      digital process for, 333–4
      ghost sounds lost to, 334–5
   theoretical approach to, 323–6
postmodernism, 202
   neoliberalism and, 285
post-traumatic stress disorder (PTSD), 99–100, 113, 114–15
Pound, Ezra, 48, 55–6
Power, Jennifer, 265
Praz, Mario, 2–3, 11, 205
Pride and Prejudice and Zombies (Grahame-Smith), 303, 306
Priestley, J. B., 231
Primitivism, 45–6
The Principles of Psychology (James, W.), 55–6
prison system, racial neoliberalism and, 351–5
Proust, Marcel, 135
psychedelia, 213–15, 220
Psycho (Bloch), 180–1, 186–7

Psycho (film), 119
psychoanalysis. *See also* Freud, Sigmund, the uncanny
  in American popular Gothic
    anti-psychiatry movement, 191
    child abuse and, 195–6
    Cosmic Regionalism in, 184
    European influences on, 183–4
    evolutionary theory and, 181
    expansion of, 182–3
    of female agency, as disruptive threat, 193–4
    Freudian influences on, 181–2, 196
    Golden Age of Popularisation, 181–2
    in Gothic critical frameworks, 3–4
    in Jackson works, 189–91
    marital betrayal and, 192–3
    Michelle Remembers and, 194–5, 196–7
    in New American Gothic, 184–5
    Oedipus Complex, 180–1
    parent–child relationships and, 180–91
    Pathological Mommy trope, 196–7
    repression as concept in, 196
    satanic horror and, 192–8
    Satanic Ritual Abuse panic, 194–6, 197
    theoretical approach to, 180–91
    in works of King, S., 197–8
  Gothic criticism and, 2, 3–5, 10
  Modernism and, 58
psychological horror
  Alfred Hitchcock Presents, 96
  in Hollywood Gothic films, 93–8
  Scandinavian Gothic and, 430–1
  on television, 96
psychological trauma, in War Gothic, 99–100
  post-traumatic stress disorder and, 113, 114–15
PTSD. *See* post-traumatic stress disorder
Puck of Pook's Hill (Kipling), 148
Punter, David, 1, 7, 16, 20–1, 213–14, 323–4, 457–8

Queer Gothic, 8. *See also* AIDS narratives
  LGBTQ+ identity
    decriminalisation of, 262–3
    liberation movement and, 262–4
  The Rocky Horror Picture Show, 263–4
  vampires in
    bisexual, 262–4
    lesbian, 257, 262–4
    queer sexuality and, 268–9
Quéma, Anne, 316
The Quest of the Silver Fleece (Du Bois), 75

Quijano, Anibal, 365, 368–9

Rabaté, Jean-Michel, 9–10
racial injustice, as theme, in Southern Gothic literature, 67
racial neoliberalism, in US, 350–5
  in films, 354–5
  imprisonment and prison system, 351–5
  in novels, 351–4
racial purity myths, 130
racism
  multiculturalism and, in UK, 343–4
  purity myths and, 130
  in Southern Renaissance, in literature, 79
Radcliffe, Ann, 2–3, 161, 323, 426
  The Italian, 426
  'On the Supernatural in Poetry', 372
  The Romance of the Forest, 141, 327
Radi, Muhammed, 388–90
Railo, Eino, 2–3
Rains, Claude, 98
Ransom, John Crowe, 71
rape, as literary theme
  in *Beloved*, 256
  in *The Magic Toyshop*, 251–2
'Rapunzel' (Sexton), 254
rationalism, in apocalyptic Gothic, 474–7
Raven, Simon, 207–8
The Raven (film), 34–6
Ravn, Olga, 432–3
Read, Herbert, 4
Reading the Vampire (Gelder), 206
Reagan, Ronald, 283
realism. *See also* magical realism
  in Hollywood Gothic films, 88–93
  postcolonial Gothic and, 135
  in Scandinavian Gothic, 437–42
Rebecca (du Maurier), 140, 143
  country house crisis themes in, 144–6
  female Gothic and, 242–3
  Mistress of Mellyn influenced by, 246–7
  television adaptation of, 225
Rebecca (film), 89
Red Dragon (Harris, T.), 293–4
Redding, Arthur, 6
Reed, Ishmael, 64
re-enchantment, in apocalyptic Gothic, 474–7
Rees-Mogg, Jacob, 319–20
Reflections in Golden Eye (McCullers), 62
regional identity, Southern Gothic literature influenced by, 69–74
  Agrarians group, 71–2
  artistic themes in, 69–70

Southern culture and, 71–2
Reich, Robert, 290
Reinhard, Carrie Lynn, 390
Rekulak, Jason, 311
Remix (Lessig), 307
remix culture
  appropriation and juxtaposition of Gothic themes, 303–4
  Bogeymen of Brexit, 319–22
  cannibalism within, 308
  convergence culture and, 305–9
    commodification of, 306–8
    copyright in, 306–8
    monstrosity in, 305
    ownership rights in, 306–8
    technological advances and, 306
  Dracula (novel) and, 302–3
  egalitarianism as element of, 307
  Frankenstein (novel) and, 302–3
  Graphic Interchange Formats (GIFs), 313–19
    commercialisation of, 314–15
    image appropriation and recontextualisation in, 319
    institutionalisation of, 314–15
    repetition and, 315–17
  mashups and, 303
  new media and, 309–13
    photographs, 310–13
    recycling of content and, 309
  origins of term, 307
repetition
  Graphic Interchange Formats and, 315–17
  in magic rites and rituals, 172–3
repression
  as psychoanalytic concept, 196
  in Southern Gothic literature, 66–7
Requiem for a Nun (Faulkner), 66
A Requiem for the Renascence (Sullivan), 77
respectability
  in Hollywood Gothic films, 88–93
  through silent film, 33–6
  through narrativisation, 33
The Return of Count Yorga (film), 210–11
reverse colonisation narratives, 377
revivals. *See* remix culture
Rhodes, Gary, 24–5
Rhys, Jean, 120, 123–9, 135–6, 161–2
Rice, Anne, 11–12, 211–12, 255–6
Rich, B. Ruby, 272
Richardson, Dorothy, 55–6
Ridley, Arnold, 231–2
Rieder, John, 368
Rigby, Jonathan, 25, 31–2

Riggs, Ransom, 310–13, 314
Ring (film), 405, 409–12
rites and rituals, in magic, 161–3
  repetition as, 172–3
Robert, Étienne-Gaspard, 4–5, 27–8
rock music, influence of Gothic on, 12–14, 220
The Rocky Horror Picture Show (film), 263–4
Roeg, Nicholas, 215–18
RKO Studio, Hollywood Gothic films and, 87
Roll Jordan Roll (Genovese), 78
The Rolling Stones, 216, 218–19. *See also* Jagger, Mick
Roman noirs, 4
The Romance of the Forest (Radcliffe), 141, 327
The Romantic Agony (Praz), 2–3, 205
Romanticism, 5, 43–4, 49
Romero, George, 105, 199–200, 472–4
Roosevelt, Franklin D., 285–6
Rosemary's Baby (Levin), 192, 199–200
Rosicrucianism, 160
Rossellini, Roberto, 93
Rousseau, Jean-Jacques, 332
Rubin, Louis D., 73, 77, 79
Rudd, Alison, 134–5
Rudkin, David, 140, 151, 153–5
Ruff, Thomas, 335–7
Rule of Darkness (Brantlinger), 366–7
Rumsfeld, Donald, 289–90
Rushdie, Salman, 120, 133–4
Russ, Joanna, 242, 244–5
Russell, Ken, 218–19
Rydberg, Victor, 426–7

Saadawi, Ahmed, 356–9
The Sadeian Woman (Carter), 258
Sadleir, Michael, 2–3, 4
Sage, Victor, 1, 13–14
Şahintürk, Zeynep, 393
Said, Edward W., 47, 131, 365
Sanctuary (Faulkner), 64–5
'The Sandman' (Hoffman), 3–4
Satan, 192–8
  child abuse and Satanism, 195–6
  in counterculture, 212–18
    Performance, 215–18
    psychedelia and, 213–15, 220
  in *Frankenstein* (novel), 213
  Melmoth the Wanderer, 213
  Satanic Ritual Abuse panic, 194–6, 197
  in Turkish film, 389, 401
Scandinavia, Gothic in
  crime themes in, 437–42
  double identity in, 427–8

Scandinavia, Gothic in (cont.)
  female writers and, 428–9
  in films, 429–30
    psychological horror genre, 430–1
    surrealist themes in, 430–1
  in global marketplace, 424–6
  international literature in, dissemination of, 426
  nature themes in, 431–4
    wilderness, 434–7, 442–3
  parody in, 437–42
  popular belief systems in, 429–30
    folklore and, 442–3
  realism in, 437–42
  revival of, 424–5
  rise of, 426–31
  television in
    crime themes, 437–42
    parody in, 437–8
  witchcraft themes in, 431–4
Scarborough, Dorothy, 50, 51
Schauer, Bradley, 95–6
Schneier, Bruce, 338
Schwartz, Joseph, 181
science fiction, in Hollywood Gothic films, 81, 93–8
  Cold War propaganda in, 94–5
  genres in, 94
  literary roots of, 94
  women in, 95
Sconce, Jeffrey, 325
Scott, Jane M., 175
Scott, Tony, 266–7, 269
Scott, Walter, 70
the scream, in postcolonial Gothic, 119–22
  the self and, 120, 128–9
Scull, Andrew, 182, 183–4
Se7en (film), 294–5
Sears, John, 481
second-wave feminism
  in environmental crisis Gothic, 450–2
    Gaia hypothesis, 450–2
    Gothic Studies and, 6
  in haunted house stories, 450–2
Sedgwick, Eve Kosofsky, 8–9
Self, Will, 11–12
Sense8 (television), 266, 275, 279–82
serial killers, in neoliberal Gothic, 293–5
Service, Robert, 122–3
Seurat, Georges, 44
Seven Years' War, 99
Sexton, Anne, 244, 254

sexuality. *See also* Queer Gothic
  in *Beloved*, 256–7
    rape themes, 256
  in female Gothic, libertine sexuality and, 258–60
  in *Fingersmith*, 259–60
  in *The Magic Toyshop*, 258–9
  pornography and, 258–60
  in *The Magic Toyshop*, 258–9
  vampires and, role in female sexual awakening, 257
Şeytan (film), 389–90
Shakespeare, William, 34–5, 52
The Shape of Things (Flusser), 325
Sharman, Jim, 263–4
Shaw, Valerie, 51
She (Haggard, H. R.), 366
Shelley, Mary, 2–3, 21, 84–5, 160, 265
  Frankenstein (novel), 6, 17, 25–6, 133–4, 161, 170, 213, 218, 228–9, 247, 264, 302–3
  The Last Man, 21, 265, 470
Shelley, Percy Bysshe, 160
Sherriff, R. C., 84–5
Shilts, Randy, 275–6
The Shining (King, S.), 198
shinpa genre, 414
The Shiny Narrow Grin (Gaskell), 208–9
short stories, Modernist Gothic in, 51–4
The Short-Timers (Hasford), 114–15
The Shrinking Man (Matheson), 187–8
Siddons, Anne Rivers, 448, 450, 454, 455–6
Siegel, Carole, 13
The Silence of the Lambs (Harris, T.), 198, 294
silent cinema and film. *See also specific films*
  adaptations and, 33–6
    of Dickens works, 34–5
    of Shakespeare works, 34–5
  cinematic experimentation in, 36–41
    of mental states, 37–8
    of subjective experience, 38–9
  early cinema, 25–33
    as era of attractions, 31
    literary influences on, 28–9
    Phantasmagoria as influence on, 27–8
    scholarship on, 29
    trick effects in, 30
  German Expressionist cinema, 83
  Gorky on, 25–7
  narrativisation of Gothic through, 29–31, 33–6
  respectability as result of, 33
  Nickelodeons, 33–4

Penny Cinemas, in UK, 33–4
respectability of, 33–6
  through narrative integration, 33
supernatural and photographic and,
    synergy between, 27–8
technological advances in, 36–41
  colour as, 36–7
  in UK, 34–5
    Penny Cinemas in, 33–4
Silver, Sean, 310
Şimşek, Gizem, 393, 400
Sinclair, May, 50, 54–7
Sing, Unburied, Sing (Ward, J.), 351–4
Sinha, Indra, 133–4
Sithebe, Angelina N., 132–3
Skal, David J., 24–5
Skov, Leonora Christina, 432, 433
Skura, Meredith, 255–6
Slater, Lauren, 183
slavery. See also Southern Gothic literature
  postcolonial Gothic and, 125–6
Slender Man, 341
Smith, Andrew, 44, 46, 121, 365–6, 446
Smith, Michelle, 194–5, 196–7
'The Snow Child' (Carter), 253–4
Society for Psychical Research, 167
Soltysik Monnet, Agnieszka, 375, 478
Song of Solomon (Morrison), 75
Sonvilla-Weiss, Stefan, 308
The Sorrow of War (Bảo Ninh), 115
Soucouyant (Chariandy), 346–50
The Souls of Black Folk (Du Bois), 75
The Sound and the Fury (Faulkner), 65, 71–2
South Korean Gothic Cinema, 413–18
  in domestic spaces, 415–16
  The Housemaid, 413–15
  Memento Mori, 417
  Olgami, 415
  Phone, 417–18
  shinpa genre, 414
  The Story of Janghwa and Hongryeon, 413–14
  Whispering Corridors, 415–16, 417
Southern Gothic literature, in US, from
    1919 to 1962. See also specific writers
  contemporary, 73
  cultural memory in, 68–9
  economic injustice themes in, 67
  in New Southern Studies, 61
  Poe and, 64
  racial injustice themes in, 67
  regional identity as influence in, 69–74
    Agrarians group, 71–2
    artistic themes influenced by, 69–70

Southern culture and, 71–2
  repression in, 66–7
  social formations as theme in, 63–4
  Southern Renaissance, 61–2
    critical response to, 77–9
    racial exclusivity in, 79
    after World War II, 74
  theoretical approach to, 61–9
    criticism in, 64
  after World War II, 74–9
    Black writers and, 74–6
    cultural Jim Crow and, 75–6
    feminist writers and, 75–6
    Southern Renaissance after, 74
Southern Renaissance, 61–2
  critical response to, 77–9
  racial exclusivity in, 79
  after World War II, 74
Southern Vampire Mysteries (Harris, C.), 297–8
Southey, Robert, 213
Spadoni, Robert, 84
Specters of Marx (Derrida), 9, 55
Spencer, Richard, 79
spilt religion, 178
Spinoza, Baruch, 166–7
Spivak, Gayatri Chakravorty, 365
Spooner, Catherine, 13, 14, 32, 304, 317, 326, 332,
    372, 385–6
The Stand (King, S.), 474–7
Steenberg, Lindsay, 237, 240
The Stepford Wives (Levin), 192–3
Sterne, Jonathan, 332–3
Stevenson, Robert Louis, 28, 34–6, 274,
    302–3, 428
Stir of Echoes (Matheson), 187–8
Stobie, Cheryl, 132–3
Stoker, Bram, 265
  Dracula, 28–9, 49, 165, 268, 302–3, 366
The Story of the Amulet (Nesbit), 148
Straczynski, J. Michael, 266, 275. See also Sense8
The Strain (del Toro and Hogan), 296–7
The Strain (television), 296–7
Strandberg, Mats, 424, 431–2, 439–40
Street, Susan Castillo, 68
Strieber, Whitley, 266–7
Strindberg, August, 427–8
Styron, William, 63, 77
Sue, Eugène, 426
Sugars, Cynthia, 348
Sullivan, Walter, 77
Summers, Montague, 4–5
Summerton, Margaret, 244
Super-Male trope, 244–5, 254

supernatural
  in Gothic television, 231–2
  occult themes and, 166
  in silent film, 27–8
The Supernatural in Modern English Fiction (Scarborough), 50, 51
Surrealism
  Breton and, 59
  Communism and, 5
  in Gothic critical frameworks, 4–5
  Roman noirs and, 4
  in Scandinavian Gothic, 430–1
Surrealism (Read), 4
Suttree (McCarthy, C.), 76–7
Symbolism. *See* French Symbolism

The Tale of Terror (Birkhead), 2–3, 50
Talking Picture (Riggs), 310–11
Tate, Allen, 71, 73
Tate, Andrew, 474
Tate, Sharon, 199–200
Tawfik, Ahmad Khaled, 383
Taylor, Charles, 374
technology. *See also* glitch Gothic; postdigital Gothic; science fiction; *specific topics*
  Gothic television and, 232
  in War Gothic, 117
television, Gothic elements in. *See also specific topics*
  The Addams Family, 224–5
  Alfred Hitchcock Presents, 96
  Alt-Right movement, 299–300
  in contemporary era, 228–31
    cable and streaming services, 228–30
    serialisation in, return to, 230
    supernatural themes, 231–2
    technology in, 232
  cultural influences on, from other media, 224–5
  Dark Shadows, 209, 227
  definition of, 222–3
  era of availability and, 226–8
  Era of Scarcity and, 225–6
  as essence of medium, 231–3
  Ghoul, 229
  Gothic mode, 234–40
    historical television and, 234–6
    literary adaptations in, 238–9
    talk show genre and, 236
    television dramas and, 237–8, 239–40
    true crime and crime dramas and, 237
  Gothicisation of history, 221–2
  Grand Guignol aspects, 230–1
  history of, 223–31
  neoliberal Gothic and
    Alt-Right movement, 299–300
    vampires and, 296–8
    zombies in, 292–3
  in ongoing series, 226–8, 237–8
    return to serialisation, 230
  in UK, 227–8
  in US, 209, 227, 230
  Rebecca, television adaptation of, 225
  in Scandinavia
    crime themes, 437–42
    parody in, 437–8
  Sense8, 266, 275, 279–82
  theoretical approach to, 221–2
  in UK, 223–4, 232–3
    serialisation in, 227–8, 230
  in US, serialisation in, 227, 230
  vampires, 209
Temkin, Daniel, 327
Teo, Stephen, 422
Terror and Wonder: The Gothic Imagination (exhibition), 18–20
Thale (film), 436–7
The Thanatos Syndrome (Percy), 66
Thatcher, Margaret, 283
Theorin, Johan, 440–1
The Thin Red Line (Jones, J.), 110–11
The Thing from Another World, 94–5
The Things They Carried (O'Brien), 114–15
The Third Life of Grange Copeland (Walker, A.), 78
Thomassen, Lasse, 345
Thunberg, Greta, 456–7, 463
Thurley, Simon, 147
Tiffin, Hellen, 120
Titley, Gavan, 343–4, 350
To Kill a Mockingbird (Lee, H.), 78
To the Lighthouse (Woolf), 45
Tobacco Road (Caldwell, E.), 63
Tompkins, J. M. S., 2–3
'Tom's Diner', 331–2, 334–5
Toomer, Jean, 74–5
Torok, Maria, 254
Totem and Taboo (Freud), 56
Tourgée, Albion W., 69–70
Townshend, Dale, 2–3, 19
transcorporeality, 462–4
Transformations (Sexton), 254
trans-generational haunting. *See* cryptonomy
trauma, 109–10, 171, 172–3, 222
  AIDS and, 280–2
  in childhood, 186–7, 188–9, 190, 196–7, 198

cinematography and, 40
colonialism and, 47–8
detective drama and, 246
in Gothic criticism, 10
in Modernist Gothic, 49
neoliberalism and, 291–2
9/11 and, 373–4
postcolonialism and, 348
post-traumatic stress disorder (PTSD), 99–100, 113–15
shell shock and, 54
slavery and, 255
in Southern Gothic, 66–7, 68
war and, 182, 239–40
A Traveller in Time (Uttley), 140, 148–50, 151–2
Trevelyan, Charles, 147
The Trip (film), 214
Troll Hunter (film), 439
True Blood (television), 297–8
Trueblood, Paul Graham, 206
Truffin, Sherry, 457–8
Trump, Donald, 299–300
Turkey, Islamic Gothic in, 383–5
  demonology themes, 384–5
  djinns, 384, 388–9, 393–4, 400–1
  global popularity of, 385
  in horror films, 384–5, 386, 391–402
  national identity as influence on, 392–3
  patriarchy in, 395–6
  political ideology as influence on, 391
The Turn of the Screw (James, H.), 45, 49
Turner, Daniel Cross, 68
Twain, Mark, 70
The Twelve (Cronin), 298–9
Twilight (Meyer), 15–16, 208, 211–12, 284

US. *See* United States
Ugetsu Monogatari (film), 407
UK. *See* United Kingdom
Ulysses (Joyce), 49
'The Uncanny' (Freud), 3–4, 246
the uncanny
  in digital media, 325–6, 327
  double, 217
  in female Gothic, 246
  media, 232, 315–16, 325–6
  in Scandinavian Gothic, 425
  in silent cinema, 23–4, 25, 26–7, 29
  technological uncanny, 36, 40–1
Uncle Silas (Le Fanu), 387
Uncle Tom's Children (Wright, R.), 74–5
unconscious, in Modernist Gothic, 58–60

Breton and, 58–9
Freudian influences on, 58
Undead Souths, 68
Under the Moons of Mars (Burroughs, E. R.), 368
Under the Shadow (film), 383, 385
Unfriended (film), 338–9
Unfriended: Dark Web (film), 338–41
United Kingdom (UK). *See also* heritage movement; multiculturalism; television
  counterculture in, Gothic elements in, 199–200
  London Blitz, 105–6
  multiculturalism in, as discourse, 343
  racism and, 343–4
  theoretical approach to, 342–6
  National Trust Act of 1937, 143–4
  National Trust in, 143–4, 147–8
  silent film in, 34–5
  Penny Cinemas, 33–4
  War Gothic in, 105–6
United States (US). *See also* Hollywood Gothic; psychoanalysis; Southern Gothic literature; television; *specific topics*
  Civil War, 109
  Department of Defense and, film funding and support by, 379–81
  Imperial Gothic in
    development of, 367
    frontier Gothic, 367–8
    after World War II, 369–70
    xenophobia and, 368
  occupation of Haiti, 102–4
  PATRIOT Act, 297
  racial neoliberalism in, 350–5
    in films, 354–5
    imprisonment and prison system, 351–5
    in novels, 351–4
  Universal Studios films, Hollywood Gothic and, 80–8
The Unknown (film), 434–5
Uricchio, William, 33–4
Uthaug, Roar, 438
Uttley, Alison, 140, 148–50, 151–2

vampires. *See also specific films*
  in *Beloved*, 255–6
  in counterculture, 202–12
  Byronic hero and, 205–6, 208–9, 210–12
  in films, 210–12
  The Vampyre and, 204–5, 218

533

vampires (cont.)
  neoliberal Gothic and, 295–9
    in films, 295–6
    in literature, 298–9
    in television, 296–8
  in Queer Gothic
    bisexual vampires, 262–4
    lesbian vampires, 257, 262–4
    queer sexuality and, 268–9
  sexuality and
    female sexual awakening, 257
    queer, 268–9
Vampyr (film), 22–5, 430
  as adaptation of literary work, 22
  audience response to, 24
  cinematography in, 23–4
  Hollywood Gothic genre influenced by, 24–5
  as hybrid of sound and silent film, 23
  mise-en-scène for, 22
The Vampyre (Polidori), 204–5, 206–7, 218–19
Van Elferen, Isabella, 13
van Gogh, Vincent, 44
van Helmont, Jan Baptist, 166–7
Vance, Carole, 261
Varieté (film), 39
Varma, Devendra P., 5, 11
Varughese, Emma Dawson, 344–5
Vega, Suzanne, 331–2, 334–5
Veidt, Conrad, 83
The Velvet Horn (Lytle), 66
Verhoff, Hans Paul, 271
Victor, Jeffrey S., 196
Victorian Gothic, 28, 43. See also *specific texts*
Victorian Hauntings (Wolfreys), 9
Vietnam War, 101–2, 111–16
  Battlefield Gothic and, 111–12
  in films, 113–14
  Full Metal Jacket, 114–15
  Imperial Gothic and, 111–12
  Jacob's Ladder, 115–16
  in novels, 114–15
  Pentagon Papers and, 112–13
Villa Diodati, 218–19
violence. See communal violence
vodou, as sign of otherness, 127
Vogue (magazine), 199–200
von Trier, Lars, 424, 435–6

Wachowski, Lana, 266, 275. See also *Sense8*
Wachowski, Lilly, 266, 275. See also *Sense8*
Wahbi, Yusuf, 387
Waite, A. E., 159

Waldman, Diane, 92–3
Walker, Alice, 78, 249–50
Walker, Margaret, 78
Walker, Rebecca, 249–50
The Walking Dead (television), 481–2
Wallace, Diana, 54
Wallace, Jeff, 44
Walpole, Horace
  The Castle of Otranto, 10, 99, 141
  The Mysterious Mother, 109
War Gothic. See also World War II; *specific wars*
  Battlefield Gothic and, 100–1
    Pacific theatre and, 107–8
    Vietnam War and, 111–12
  Cold War themes in, 108–9
  dehumanisation of enemies in, 117
  film noir and, 110
  forever war and, 117
  Gulf War, 102
  Imperial Gothic and, 101
    Vietnam War and, 111–12
  Korean War, 108–9
  London Blitz and, 105–6
  in Modernist Gothic works, 44–9
  psychological trauma in, 99–100
  post-traumatic stress disorder and, 113, 114–15
  technology in, 117
  theoretical approach to, 99–102
  time range for, from 1930 to 1991, 101–2
  US Civil War, 109
  Vietnam War, 101–2, 111–16
    Battlefield Gothic and, 111–12
    in fiction novels, 114–15
    in films, 113–14
    Imperial Gothic and, 111–12
    Pentagon Papers and, 112–13
  war veterans in, 109–11
    in films, 109–10
    in novels, 110–11
  zombies in, 102–5
    in films, 103–4
    in Romero films, 105
    as soldiers, 104–5
    US occupation of Haiti, 102–4
The War of the Worlds (Wells), 368, 378–81
War on Terror, 364–5, 373–81
  Bush and, 370, 375
  fatalities during, 376
  in literature, 372–3
  11 September attacks and, 370–1
  zombies in, 377–8

war veterans, in War Gothic, 109–11
  in films, 109–10
  in novels, 110–11
Ward, Graham, 474
Ward, Jesmyn, 351–4
Wark, McKenzie, 380
'A Warning to the Curious' (James, M. R.), 142
Warren, Robert Penn, 71, 73
Warwick, Alexandra, 9
The Wasp Factory (Banks), 161–2, 168, 170–1
Wasson, Sara, 105–6
The Waste Land (Eliot, T. S.), 57
Waters, Sarah, 140, 155–7, 244
Waugh, Evelyn, 143
We Have Always Lived in the Castle (Jackson), 161–2, 168–9, 189, 190–1
Weinstock, Jeffrey A., 305
Weir, Kevin J., 315–17, 318
Weird fiction, 467–70
Welcome to the Desert of the Real (Žižek), 370
The Well (Jolley), 123–4
Welles, Orson, 91
Wells, H. G., 11, 28, 86, 87, 368, 466
Welty, Eudora, 73, 78
Westengard, Laura, 266, 280–1, 282
Whale, James, 24–5, 30–1, 84–5
Wharton, Edith, 50
Wheatley, Dennis, 161–2, 166–7
Wheatley, Helen, 222
The Whispering Knights (Lively), 140, 151–3
White, Lynn, Jr, 450–2, 458–9
The White Album (Didion), 200
White Zombie (film), 103–4
Whitney, Phyllis A., 244
Who Do You Think You Are? (television), 234–6
Wide Sargasso Sea (Rhys), 120, 123–9, 135–6, 161–2
  slavery in, 125–6
  vodou as sign of otherness in, 127
Wiene, Robert, 45
Wild Hunt of Hagworthy (Lively), 151
Wilde, Oscar, 28, 34–6, 49, 274, 302–3
Wiljkmark, Sofia, 428–9
Williams, Anne, 245, 396
Williams, Tennessee, 61–2, 63, 65
Wilt, Judith, 43
Wirkola, Tommy, 438
Wisker, Gina, 121–2, 256, 257
witchcraft, 162, 172
  repeal of Witchcraft Act (UK), 212
  in Scandinavian Gothic, 431–4
  Wicca, 212–13

witch hunts, 164–5
  among women, 174
Witchcraft Today (Gardner), 212
Wolfe, Thomas, 71–2
The Wolfman (film), 89–90
Wolfreys, Julian, 9
The Woman in White (Collins), 387
women. *See also* feminism; *specific topics*
  agency of, as disruptive threat, in psychoanalysis, 193–4
  in female Gothic, older women and, 253–4, 259–60
  ghost stories by, 54–8
  in Hollywood Gothic films, 91–3
    Bluebeard narrative, 92–3
    paranoid woman theme, 91–2
  in science fiction genre, 95
  in Scandinavian Gothic, 428–9
  vampires and, role in sexual awakening, 257
  witchcraft and, 174
Women in Love (Lawrence), 46
Wood, Robin, 186, 390
Woodward, C. Vann, 73
Woolf, Virginia, 43, 45, 52, 57–8, 60
  aesthetics and, 45
Woolrich, Cornell, 92
World Bank, 283
World Trade Organization, 283
World War II
  Imperial Gothic after, in US, 369–70
  Southern Gothic literature after, 74–9
    Black writers and, 74–6
    cultural Jim Crow and, 75–6
    feminist writers and, 75–6
    Southern Renaissance after, 74
  War Gothic and
    London Blitz and, 105–6
    Pacific Theatre and, 107–9
World War Z (Brooks), 290–2, 378, 480
Wray, Fay, 87–8
Wright, Angela, 265
Wright, Julia M., 222–3
Wright, Patrick, 138
Wright, Richard, 74–5
Wyler, William, 109–10

Yaeger, Patricia, 67
Yıldırım, Orhan, 394–9
You Can't Go Home Again (Wolfe), 72
Yu Cheng, 422

Zamora, Lois Parkinson, 468–9
El-Zein, Amira, 399
Zero Patience (film), 266, 275–9
Žižek, Slavoj, 349, 370
Zlosnik, Sue, 233
zombies. *See also specific films*
  in apocalyptic Gothic, 480
    consumerism symbolism and, 480–1
  in neoliberal Gothic, 289–93
    in literature, 290–2
    rise of capitalism and, 289
    in Romero films, 289–90
    in television, 292–3
  in Romero films, 105
    neoliberal Gothic and, 289–90
  in War Gothic, 102–5
    in films, 103–4
    in Romero films, 105
    as soldiers, 104–5
    US occupation of Haiti, 102–4
  in War on Terror, 377–8
Zuckerberg, Mark, 337

For EU product safety concerns, contact us at Calle de José Abascal, 56–1°,
28003 Madrid, Spain or eugpsr@cambridge.org.

www.ingramcontent.com/pod-product-compliance
Lightning Source LLC
LaVergne TN
LVHW021650060526
838200LV00050B/2283